AN INTRODUCTION
TO CONTEMPORARY
INTERNATIONAL LAW

LUNG-CHU CHEN

AN INTRODUCTION
TO CONTEMPORARY
INTERNATIONAL LAW

A POLICY-ORIENTED PERSPECTIVE

SECOND EDITION

YALE UNIVERSITY PRESS

NEW HAVEN AND LONDON

Published with assistance from the Kingsley Trust Association Publication Fund established by the Scroll and Key Society of Yale College.

Designed by Nancy Ovedovitz and set in Times Roman and The Sans type by Keystone Typesetting, Inc., Orwigsburg, Pennsylvania. Printed in the United States of America by Vail-Ballou Press, Binghamton, New York.

Library of Congress Cataloging-in-Publication Data
Chen, Lung-chu, 1935–
An introduction to contemporary international law : a policy-oriented perspective / Lung-chu Chen. — 2nd ed.
p.   cm.
Includes bibliographical references and index.
ISBN 0–300–08454 — 4 (cloth : alk. paper). — ISBN 0–300–08477–3 (paper : alk. paper)
1. International law.   I. Title.
KZ3110 .C48 2000
341 — dc21   00-036815

A catalogue record for this book is available from the British Library.

The paper in this book meets the guidelines for permanence and durability of the Committee on Production Guidelines for Book Longevity of the Council on Library Resources.

10 9 8 7 6 5 4 3 2 1

In Affectionate Memory of
Myres S. McDougal (1906–1998)
and
Harold D. Lasswell (1902–1978)
Proponents of an International Law of Human Dignity

CONTENTS

PREFACE TO THE SECOND EDITION

International law is a continuing process of authoritative decision by which members of the world community identify, clarify, and secure their common interests. These common interests consist of minimum world order and optimum world order. *Minimum world order* refers to the minimization of unauthorized coercion and violence — in other words, the maintenance of international peace and security. *Optimum world order* refers to the widest possible shaping and sharing of values, for example, respect, power, enlightenment, well-being, wealth, skill, affection, and rectitude, popularly expressed in terms of human rights, self-determination and self-governance, education and global communication, health and environmental protection, trade and development, transfer of technology, human solidarity and diversity, and social justice.

The end of the Cold War did not put international law out of business. On the contrary, although the threat of a nuclear holocaust might have been reduced for the time being, the need for maintaining minimum world order and for securing optimum world order has become ever more pressing.

As humankind ushers in a new millennium and a new century of knowledge and power, the degree of global interdependence has deepened, and the amazing frequency of transnational interactions continues to accelerate. The global village is real in fact and in perception. "Globalization" has become a catch word of the new era. As an ongoing process of authoritative decision, international law is as dynamic as ever and constitutes a distinct part of the globalizing process. Taking one another into account, all actors — nongovernmental as well as governmental — have intensified their transnational interactions, generating ever-increasing and interpenetrating transnational effects.

Since the publication of the first edition in 1989, there have been many changes in the world, and so many significant events have happened in the field of international law. Just to name a few: the fall of the Berlin Wall and the end of the Cold War; the disintegration of the Soviet Union and the formation of the Commonwealth of Independent States; the breakup of Yugoslavia and the conflicts in the Balkans; the establishment of the International Criminal Tribunals for the former Yugoslavia and for Rwanda; the transition from the apartheid government to a nonracial democracy in South Africa; the Rio Earth Summit and the adoption of Agenda 21, a comprehensive plan for global action in all areas of sustainable development; the entering into force of the U.N. Convention on the Law of the Sea, and the concomitant establishment of the International Seabed Authority and of the International Tribunal for the Law of the Sea; the establishment of the World Trade Organization to replace the GATT as the only international body overseeing international trade; the creation of the office of United Nations High Commissioner for Human Rights and the operation of the U.N. Convention on the Rights of the Child; the adoption of the Rome Statute of the International Criminal Court; and U.N. and U.S. responses to the Iraqi invasion of Kuwait and the continuing struggle with Iraq over enforcing the U.N. cease-fire resolutions.

All these and other developments are reflected in this edition. In updating and preparing the second edition, I benefited a great deal from the comments and suggestions received from many people who have used the first edition of the book and from the assistance and support rendered by many. My deep appreciation to all of them.

The inspiration of my mentors — Myres S. McDougal and Harold D. Lasswell — was as present for this edition as for the original edition. The recent passing of Professor McDougal meant the loss of a great mentor, counselor, and friend to me. It also meant the loss of one of the great international legal scholars of all time, but his legacy to humankind will live forever. Both Mac and Harold will be dearly missed.

W. Michael Reisman was wonderful and helpful in many ways. Jordan J. Paust was thorough in reviewing an early draft of the entire revised manuscript and was generous in offering numerous and invaluable suggestions and comments.

Throughout the years my students at New York Law School have been, in a practical sense, participants in the ongoing enterprise and have offered many helpful suggestions. I especially wish to thank Maria-Alana Recine and Stephanie McQueen for outstanding research assistance. Thanks also go to Ken Ayers, Susan Hennigan, Celena Mayo, and Cliff Scott for their assistance.

At New York Law School I am indebted to Dean Harry H. Wellington and Associate Dean Ellen Ryerson for their strong and continued support, including summer research grants. Professor Joyce Saltalmachia and her library staff were consistent and efficient in rendering professional service; Reference Librarian Marta Kiszely, my faculty library liaison, was ever cheerful, diligent, and efficient in meeting a flow of requests for assistance.

At Yale Law School, I am grateful to Dean Anthony T. Kronman for encouragement and support. At Yale University Press, Jane Zanichkowsky was excellent in her role as copy editor.

In Taiwan, I wish to thank Law Professor Chao-Yuan Huang of Taiwan University and Dr. Yann-huei Song of Academia Sinica for their invaluable suggestions and assistance. At the New Century Foundation, my thanks go to En Wei Lin, Hsueh Chin Chen, Su Mei Chiu, and Chien Shou Lu for their assistance.

For this edition, as for the first, the affection, patience, and support of Judy and our family were a constant source of comfort and strength.

PREFACE TO THE FIRST EDITION

International law is perhaps the most dynamic area of law today and one of the most important, as global interdependence deepens and the transnational movement of people, ideas, goods, and services continues to grow. It is an ongoing process of decision through which the members of the world community identify, clarify, and secure their common interests — both minimum world order (in the sense of minimizing unauthorized coercion and violence) and optimum world order (in the sense of fostering the widest possible shaping and sharing of all values). In this process, nation-states have played and continue to play the dominant role. But nonstate participants — international governmental organizations and nongovernmental organizations and associations — are playing increasingly significant roles. The individual, in particular, acting both alone and as a group representative, is the ultimate participant, performing all the functions relevant to making and applying law.

As one who is identified with the policy-oriented approach developed by Myres S. McDougal and Harold D. Lasswell and their associates (dubbed by some the New Haven School), I have sought as author to bring the essence and insights of the approach to bear on major international legal problems in the rapidly changing context of the earth-space arena.

Unlike conventional works in international law, this book is organized and structured in terms of the process of decision by reference to participants (nation-states, international governmental organizations, nongovernmental organizations and associations, and the individual), perspectives (minimum world order and optimum world order), arenas of decision (establishment and access), bases of power (authority and effective control over people, resources, institutions, and events), strategies (diplomatic, ideological, economic, and military), outcomes, and effects.

As humankind grapples with a host of transnational problems — armed conflicts and the control of armaments, trade and investment, the use and control of the sea and outer space, global environment, illicit drug trafficking, transnational flows of information, technology transfer, human rights, refugees, religious warfare, and so on — it becomes evident that international law is too important to be left to international lawyers and decision makers alone. Individual citizens must rise to the challenge of contemporary international law in the search for a world public order of human dignity. They must:

- Think globally to meet the ever-present challenge of global interdependence and interdetermination.
- Think temporally not only about the present generation but about posterity.
- Think contextually to relate decision making to all community levels and all value sectors of social interaction.
- Think and act creatively in the common interest, mobilizing all available problem-solving skills and resources in the pursuit of both minimum and optimum order.

I hope that not only students of international law but other citizens concerned with law and world affairs will find this book helpful. As an introductory treatise, it seeks to be comprehensive in scope yet selective in emphasis; and the notes are kept to an absolute minimum.

My debts to Professors McDougal and Lasswell, long proponents of an international law of human dignity, are enormous and apparent — the book is dedicated to them. As a member of the New Haven School, I have drawn freely on prior collaborative work with them (especially *Human Rights and World Public Order,* published by Yale University Press in 1980) and also, in the words of McDougal, "on a great variety of past contributions, jointly planned, discussed, and written by members of a large group who regard their work as common property." I am most grateful to Mac, who, with his characteristic generosity, has read the entire manuscript and made many valuable criticisms and suggestions.

I am also deeply grateful to Professors Richard A. Falk of Princeton University, Rosalyn Higgins of the London School of Economics and Political Science, and Jordan J. Paust of the University of Houston Law Center for having read the entire manuscript and offered numerous valuable criticisms and suggestions for improvement. My thanks also go to Professor Gunther F. Handl of Wayne State University Law School and Siegfried Wiessner of St. Thomas University School of Law for helpful comments and suggestions in connection with chapters 27 and 11, respectively.

Thanks are also due my students at New York Law School, especially my outstanding research assistants Raymund Johansen and Gary Gross. The assistance of Frances Civardi, Carmen Giordano, Sylvia Ospina, Christopher Portelli, and Erik Strangeways at an earlier stage is also gratefully acknowledged.

Esther J. Chen, the fourteen-year-old in-house word processing expert of my family, has been indispensable throughout the preparation of various drafts and the final manuscript. Words are inadequate to express professional appreciation and parental pride.

At New York Law School I am indebted to Dean James F. Simon and Associate Dean Randolph N. Jonakait for strong and consistent support (financial and other). Professor Joyce Saltalamachia and her library staff were instrumental in maintaining a flow of books and other documentation. My appreciation for support and encouragement also goes to colleagues E. Donald Shapiro, B. James George, Jr., Arnold H. Graham, Jane P. Helm, Gerald Korngold, and Edward B. Samuels.

I thank the Dana Fund for International and Comparative Legal Studies for a summer research grant at an early stage of this project, for which I especially thank Professor Richard W. Edwards, Jr., of the University of Toledo College of Law. A grant from the Ernst C. Stiefel Fund, for which I wish to thank Dr. Ernst Stiefel, was helpful in seeing the book through the press.

At Yale Law School I am grateful to Deans Guido Calabresi and Harry H. Wellington for continued support. Professor Morris L. Cohen and his library staff were immensely helpful.

The officers of the Yale University Press have been generous in encouragement and support. I owe a special debt of gratitude to Marian N. Ash and John G. Ryden. Laura J. Dooley was perceptive, understanding, and skillful in her role as manuscript editor.

Finally, I wish to thank my parents, parents-in-law, and extended family for all their encouragement and support. My wife, Judy, and children, Ellie, Harold, and Esther, cheerfully bore the brunt of my absorption in this work and lovingly endured the pressure. Without their affection, patience, and support this book would never have been completed.

PART ONE

DELIMITATION OF THE TASK

1

International Law in a Policy-Oriented Perspective

International law is perhaps the most dynamic area of law today and one of the most important, although particular aspects of international law may appear to be quite stable. It is made through international agreements (multilateral and bilateral) and through customary behavior and expectations. Compared to national legal systems, international law is decentralized; yet without international law, a basic stability in world order would not be possible.

International law is developing at an ever greater pace as the world community becomes increasingly interdependent, owing in part to the growing movement of people, ideas, goods, and services across national boundaries. This area of law has become recognizably much broader than law governing the relationships between governments, although such law has regulated individuals and groups in the past. Individual human beings, the ultimate participants in any legal process, interact with increasing frequency and intensity across nation-state lines in a host of group forms. But nation-states have historically played, and continue to play, a predominant role as actors at the international level. International governmental organizations, proliferating rapidly in recent years and manifesting varying degrees of comprehensiveness and specialization, also participate in all decision functions and help to shape attitudes and behavior. Nongovernmental associations and organizations of all kinds, such as multinational corporations and human rights organizations, are increasingly transnational in membership, goals, areas of activity, and impacts.

International law and national law sometimes conflict, and it is international law that should prevail. States (and the individuals who compose the state) are held to international standards. This is the essence of the supremacy of international law so indispensable to maintaining world order. For hundreds of years the relations between international and national law have been intimate and interpenetrating, and those relations continue to grow and become more evident.

Every citizen of the world should have some basic understanding of international law, whatever his or her station or profession may be. In the contemporary world of increasingly complex interdependencies, almost all social problems are transnational in nature, requiring a global or regional solution: armed conflicts and control of armaments; civil strifes; energy crises; trade, investment, and capital flows; exploration of ocean resources and the use of outer space; environmental problems (for example, radioactive fallout, acid rain, air and marine pollution); control of epidemics and of illicit traffic in narcotics; flows of information and data technology transfer; deprivations of human rights (apartheid, discrimination, genocide, and so on); religious warfare and strifes; flows and resettlements of refugees; and reunions of families broken by oppression, conflicts, or disasters — just to name a few. One cannot deal with local and national problems effectively without adequate orientation to the global context. Particular legal problems must be approached in light of the whole.

International law, like all law, is a continuing process through which the common interests of the members of the world community are clarified and secured. It seeks to attain a minimum order, in the sense of minimizing unauthorized coercion, and to achieve an optimum order, in the sense of the widest possible shaping and sharing of all values (respect, power, enlightenment, well-being, wealth, skill, affection, and rectitude). The ultimate goal should be the establishment of a world community of human dignity. Toward this goal, education in the broadest sense is crucial. We cannot be content with the status quo. We must think about new ways to build a better world.

As global interdependencies deepen, what happens in one country increasingly affects others, and communities must take one another into account when making choices and decisions. International law brings a distinct and vital dimension to citizenship education. Citizens of the world must be taught to think globally, to think contextually, and to think creatively for the common interest.

MYTHS AND REALITIES ABOUT INTERNATIONAL LAW

In spite of the profound importance of international law, misconceptions abound. Sometimes it is not taken seriously. Those who do this exhibit a range of perceptions about international law:

- There is no international law as such, because the world community is a jungle where naked power counts.

- International law is not really law but a form of international morality or political doctrine.
- International law is a sham, a political facade used to justify the expediency of national policy; international law provides a convenient justification or pretext for certain conduct of states.
- International law is made to be broken at will when the vital interests of a sovereign state are involved.
- International law is weak, without centralized institutions of lawmaking and law enforcement (that is, there is no world legislature, no world police or jails).
- International law is for specialists and is irrelevant to ordinary people.

International law undeniably has not always functioned as effectively and perfectly as desired, but this may also be said of national laws. No social process is free from the law violator. The difference is a matter of degree. Gross violations of international law do occur — and often with seeming impunity. But on the whole, compliance with norms of international law is a cardinal fact of the contemporary life in our world community of interdetermination and reciprocity. International law does matter. Otherwise, nation-state officials would not take pains to justify the "lawfulness" of their conduct by recourse to norms of international law.

For instance, after Korean Airlines Flight 007 was shot down by the Soviet Union in September 1983, killing all 269 people on board, the Soviet government, although it gave evasive, inconsistent accounts, did not flatly assert: "Yes, we shot down the airplane and violated international law. So what?" On the contrary, it sought to justify the lawfulness of its action by asserting that the Korean airliner had intruded into Soviet airspace and was engaged in a spy mission, even though it was leaving Soviet territory. A nation-state does not lightly dismiss the relevance of international law.

Or take the Iranian hostage seizure case. This episode, which involved the seizure of American diplomats and the takeover of the American embassy in Tehran in 1979 and related efforts to secure the hostages' release, raised a staggering range of international legal issues, including the following.

Does international law really matter, and does it even exist? Does it matter whether the activities involved are lawful?

Who makes international law, and who applies it? Who decides whether activities are lawful? Who reviews such decisions, and how — the United Nations (Security Council or General Assembly), or the International Court of Justice? The United States government, the Iranian government, other governments? The press? International law experts? Nongovernmental organizations and associations, or concerned citizens of the world?

One might inquire as to the criteria used to determine whether the activities involved are lawful. For example, what international legal norms were violated — the protection of diplomatic immunity? The inviolability of legation? Norms governing state responsibility? Norms proscribing hate-mongering propaganda? Others?

The issue is raised of just who in Iran was responsible — the militant students who initiated the act of seizure or the Iranian government? At what point? What are relevant prescriptions of state responsibility by international law? Could the Khomeini regime justify its action in terms of revolutionary change within Iran? It could be asked whether revolutionary change absolves the new government from international obligations vis-à-vis other states. And, how compelling are claims that this action was precipitated by the long history of U.S. intervention in the internal affairs of Iran and by the refusal of the United States to extradite the shah and to return his assets to the Iranian government?

There were other issues as well, such as the measures in response taken by President Carter: freezing all Iranian assets in American banks, cutting off oil imports from Iran, and collectively deporting Iranian students unlawfully present in the United States. And further, whether the United States acted lawfully in admitting the shah for medical treatment; whether the United States was obligated to extradite the shah to the Khomeini government; and whether the United States was obligated to return the shah's U.S. assets to the Iranian government. What legal issues were raised when Panama and Egypt granted the shah asylum?

In addition, there was the role of negotiation in freeing the American hostages. For example, what was the role of third-party mediation in the process of dispute settlement? What role did world public opinion play? Was the abortive military attempt to rescue the hostages by the United States lawful, or did it violate the territorial integrity of Iran? Was it an act of permissible self-defense, an evacuation mission, or humanitarian intervention? What part did the United Nations play? How about the international banking community, and others?

One might also ask how the case was brought before the International Court of Justice. Did both parties appear before the court? Did the court have jurisdiction over the case? Did world opinion influence any of these events? One might also ask what the proceedings were before the court, what issues the court addressed, and what its decisions were. And, how the contending parties reacted to these decisions.

Was the agreement of settlement achieved through Algeria's mediation valid, or was the agreement made under duress? Could the Reagan administration have lawfully repudiated the agreement, and if so, on what grounds? To what extent would the terms of such an agreement be honored both externally and internally?

Then there is the question of the nature of this agreement within the framework of the U.S. constitutional system. Does this agreement violate the mandate of the U.S. Constitution? What is the nature of this agreement? Is it a presidential agreement, a form of executive agreement? Is it equivalent to a treaty? What internal and external effects does it have? What role can and should U.S. courts play?

What relevance do acts of state and issues of sovereign immunity have, especially if relevant acts do themselves violate international law?

Finally, we might ask what this case tells us about the utility of international law (direct or indirect) and its limitations. For example, what about the question of sanctions (enforcement) in international law?

This array of legal questions underscores how prominently and pervasively international law figures in the entire episode. The Iranian hostage case offers an excellent example through which many of the major aspects of international law can be explored and studied.

More recently, the violent war that erupted in the former Yugoslavia in August 1990 raised a host of legal questions, notably: What is the status of the law of war and the law of neutrality under contemporary international law? How relevant and effective is the policy of prohibiting use of force proclaimed by the U.N. Charter? What is the law governing self-defense? At what point does a civil war — in this case caused by the breakup of a state — become an international conflict? What are the laws governing intervention? Who are the "aggressors" and who the "defenders," and who decides? Would it have been permissible for a nonbelligerent state to arm the Bosnian Muslims, clearly the weakest party and in the eyes of many the "defenders"? What is the relationship between the belligerent parties — that is, were Bosnia-Herzegovina, Croatia, and Slovenia merely renegade republics that needed to be brought back into line, as asserted by a Serbia desperate to maintain and expand its authority over a unified Yugoslav state? Or were they states legitimately asserting their rights to self-determination and independence? What is the relevance of international humanitarian law governing armed conflicts? What response would be permissible for nonbelligerent states individually and collectively, particularly in the face of mounting evidence of "ethnic cleansing" and other atrocities? The role that the international community and individual states play in bringing an end to hostility is yet another question. How effective was the United Nations in this regard?

In the aftermath of the Cold War and in response to conflicts such as those in the former Yugoslavia, Iraq, and Rwanda, the Security Council in the past ten years has taken an increasingly active role in global peacekeeping and peacemaking, raising even further questions for international law. How relevant and effective is the policy of prohibiting the use of force proclaimed by Article 2(4) of the U.N. Charter? Should U.N. member states provide the council with increased peacekeeping or peacemaking powers? Should a standby peacekeeping fund be established, or should national troops be earmarked for call-up by the council? Should the Security Council have a small, multinational force on standby, ready for dispatch to hot spots? What about joint training exercises between designated national forces? And what if the Security Council had been unable to pass a resolution authorizing military action against Iraq?

Aside from such dramatic cases as KAL 007, the Iranian hostage case, and the war in the former Yugoslavia, the issue of lawfulness arises in many other contexts. Recent examples include:

- the claims concerning U.S. involvement in mining operations near Nicaraguan harbors
- the claims by Iran against the use of chemical weapons by Iraq
- the claims by Israel to destroy the nuclear reactor of Iraq
- the claims by Israel to retaliate against Lebanon for Palestinian incursions
- the claims by the United Kingdom to use force in response to the forcible seizure of the Falkland Islands by Argentina
- the claims by the United States to assist the government in El Salvador and the contras in Nicaragua
- the claims of refugees from the armed conflicts in Central America to protection in various nation-states
- the claims by various states to expropriate the property of foreign nationals and corporations
- the claims by the United States to extend the application of its antitrust law beyond its borders
- the claims by France to conduct nuclear tests in the area of its Pacific isles
- the claims by Russia to intervene forcibly in Chechnya
- the claims by the United States to restore democracy in Panama and Haiti
- the claims by the United States to provide humanitarian relief in Somalia
- the claims by NATO powers to engage in humanitarian interventions in Bosnia and in Kosovo
- the claims by Indonesia to use force to suppress the East Timorese demands for independence
- the claims by China to use force to annex Taiwan in the name of reunification
- the claims by the Security Council to freeze Iraqi assets held in other countries in order to provide for war reparations to victims of Iraqi aggression

These claims and activities raise the issue of lawfulness. But who decides whether they are lawful? And how is lawfulness determined? Does it really matter whether certain activities are lawful? If unlawful, so what? What can be done to the violator, and by whom?

These and similar questions not only reaffirm the relevance of international law in world affairs but also point to the limitations inherent in the contemporary international legal system.

Unlike domestic legal systems, the international legal system is essentially decentralized; effective power is centered on territorial communities known as nation-states. Many power centers exist, not just one. No centralized institutions have sufficient authority and resources to make, apply, and enforce law globally and to adjudicate disputes. We do have the United Nations, but the United Nations is far from being a world government. The U.N. General Assembly is not a world parliament that makes law and imposes taxes on member states. The secretary-general is not the chief executive of a world government. The United Nations is not somehow distinct from member states but belongs to all of its members, with all the advantages, problems, and, most importantly, responsibilities of ownership. Only the member states have the power to undertake the task of renewing the framework of global cooperation to shape a new world order.

Unfortunately, this new world order has of late been characterized by vicious internal conflicts, unleashed in large measure by the collapse of communism and the end of the Cold War. Nationalistic and ethnic tensions have become the predominant element in conflicts around the globe. The relaxation of authoritarian regimes and the destructive effects of civil conflicts have strained fragile state structures, leading, in cases such as Somalia, Rwanda, and Bosnia, to the dissolution of states into regions controlled by competing factions, to widespread violence, and to human rights abuses.

The most powerful office in the world, in popular perception, is the presidency of the United States, and yet the United States will not, and cannot, be a "world policeman." The International Court of Justice, although commonly known as the World Court, lacks the authority of compulsory jurisdiction. Because its jurisdiction is contingent on the consent of states, few international disputes come before the court for adjudication. Its light caseload stands in stark contrast to the heavy caseload of the U.S. Supreme Court.

When an unlawful act is alleged, a counterclaim usually follows. Who is right and who wrong? Who decides? In the general absence of a centralized authoritative decision maker, it falls on individual nation-states, through their officials, to decide, although all of us are involved as reviewers and ultimate participants in shaping attitudes and behavior: your claims against mine, and my characterizations against yours. Here nation-state officials perform what is known as the "double function": they act simultaneously as claimants and as judges. They engage in "auto-interpretation" — they are judges of their own acts, they interpret the legal implications of their own conduct. The cumulative effect of such individual assertions and characterizations often leads to a sense of confusion, uncertainty, and frustration. Law, after all, is on whose side? Why are disputing states unwilling to submit their disputes to a third-party decision maker?

The contemporary international legal system is still state-centered and places an inordinate emphasis on "national sovereignty" and "equality of states." Effective power is still overwhelmingly concentrated in individual states, though obviously some states wield far greater power than others, and even some private groups wield more effective power, control more wealth, and enjoy more respect in the community than some nation-states. Thus, even after a determination is made about the unlawfulness of certain conduct, effective sanctions in the form of centralized command and the federal marshal, familiar in a domestic legal order, are generally not forthcoming. International law is especially fragile in its inability to impose effective sanctions against gross violations of international law. How did the world community respond to the Soviet invasion of Afghanistan and to its military operations in that country? What remedies were available in the case of KAL 007? How long did it take to obtain the release of the American diplomats seized in Iran? How was it done? What accounts for the apparent failures of the world community to prevent large-scale human suffering in Cambodia, the former Yugoslavia, Somalia, Rwanda? Confronted with dramatic cases of this kind — gross violations made with seeming impunity — concerned citizens naturally wonder where international law is and how good it is, and this explains a lot about some of the popular myths regarding international law in a crisis.

It is worth noting that several sanctioning measures are available, though not in the form of centralized sanctions. In a decentralized legal order, securing compliance with authoritative norms depends largely on reciprocity, retaliation, and relevant expectations. If you scratch my back, I will scratch yours. If you twist my arm, I will twist yours. If you claim a continental shelf along your coastal lines, we will do the same. If you claim a two-hundred-mile fishery zone, we will do the same — we might even claim five hundred miles. In the final analysis, the real policing and stabilizing power comes from the shared perception of common interest. This is the keystone of international law, as in all forms of law. When effective elites and officials realize that they have more to gain through cooperation than through arbitrary claims that provoke excessive counterclaims and even anarchy, they learn, sooner or later, how to act with self-restraint.

International law may have its weaknesses and limitations, but it makes an important contribution to world order. International law, like all law, is a continuing process of authoritative decision through which the common interest of the members of the world community is identified, clarified, and protected.

INADEQUACIES OF TRADITIONAL APPROACHES TO INTERNATIONAL LAW

The difficulties and limitations inherent in a state-centered, decentralized system are compounded and exacerbated by the inadequacies associated with traditional approaches to international law.

International law has its origins in the natural law school and has been influenced in varying degrees by all major schools of jurisprudence. The past influence of the positivist (analytical) school lingers, despite recent signs of growing receptivity to new, more pragmatic theories. The late nineteenth- and early twentieth-century approaches to international law, as dominated by the positivist school, were rule-oriented, conceiving international law as a body of rules — indeed, often unrealistically as rules merely between states.

The rule-oriented approaches tend to view international law dogmatically as a static body of auto-operational rules — rules that are given and self-contained and operate automatically. The judicial task is said to be to discover and enforce, in particular cases, extant "correct rules." Logical derivation is the intellectual task stressed: when behavior can be sustained by statements logically derived from existing rules, it is regarded as "legal" or "lawful." In this perspective, international law operates automatically within its autonomous realm of self-contained rules, with its own internal logical mechanism.

Such rule-oriented approaches to international law have several inadequacies: (1) failure to grasp the notions of decision (choice) in the legal process; (2) insufficient attention to the goals (policies) for which rules are devised and to value consequences of particular applications of rules; (3) failure to relate rules to the dynamic context of interaction involving the international and domestic social processes and to the ongoing process of decision making; (4) failure to grasp the normative ambiguity involved in rules; (5) failure to come to grips with the generality and complementarity involved in rules; and (6) failure to develop and employ adequate intellectual skills in problem solving.

The underlying assumption of the rule-oriented approaches is that law is "rules" and nothing more. But law *is* more. The nature of the judicial task is not confined to impartial discovery and application of supposedly neutral rules, and no application of a rule can be neutral in terms of social consequences. International law is a continuing process of authoritative decision and cannot be adequately described by mere reference to the derivations from past decisions that are termed rules. Rules are not self-applicatory and do not change by themselves.

Rules are made and applied by human beings. The task of applying law is not merely to discover correct rules but to make choices, to make decisions.

Making choices (decisions) inevitably involves policy considerations (what are the policy purposes for which certain rules are developed and maintained?) and involves considerations of alternatives (what are alternative value consequences of making one choice or another?). This the rule-oriented approaches are unwilling to acknowledge openly. In the guise of impartial discovery of correct, neutral rules, rule-oriented observers refuse to concede that applying rules involves choice and instead dismiss policy considerations and alternative thinking as beyond the realm of law. But whether they acknowledge it or not, rule-orienters cannot escape the necessity and burden of choice in their purported impartial search for correct rules in concrete cases. They may disguise the element of choice, but they cannot escape it. Decisions (choices) cannot be made by neutral decision makers (neutral human beings) neutrally applying neutral rules that are neutrally derived. Rules simply do not decide cases: people decide, and rules may provide only minimal guidance in decision making.

Indeed, rules are not autonomous absolutes and do not exist in a vacuum. Divorced from policy and context, rules are skeletons without body and soul. Rules cannot make much sense without reference to policy or the purposes for which they are created and maintained. Rules cannot be meaningfully understood without reference to the context of interaction that gives rise to legal controversies and to the ongoing process of decision making in which rules are made and remade, applied and reapplied, by human decision makers in response to changing demands and expectations under an ever-changing context of conditions. The dynamism of the law in real life cannot be grasped by mere reference to law in the abstract. Law in the social process is dynamic and based on what real human beings think and do. The fact that the relatively peaceful dissolution of the Soviet Empire caught most international legal scholars completely by surprise indicates the extent to which rule-oriented approaches fail to anticipate the element of human, dynamic choice in response to changing conditions and perceptions of value consequences.

Traditional approaches to international law, with their obsession with inherited rules, also fail to grasp the normative ambiguity involved in their reference to rules. Rules are perceived as given, rigid, self-contained, and automatic in application. Their doctrinal concepts purport to refer simultaneously to the events that precipitate decision, to the factors that affect decision, and to the outcomes of decision. A simple statement that "this is law" ("this is the rule") may be loaded with ambiguity: it may refer to patterns of past decision, to probable future decision, or to a preferred future decision. This approach fails to distinguish past decision from probable future decision and from preference for future decision. It even confuses statements of past trends in decision with scientific inquiry concerning factors affecting decision.

Rules not only have normative ambiguity but are commonly phrased in general and abstract ways and manifest complementarity — rules travel as pairs of complementary opposites, for example, domestic jurisdiction versus international concern, aggression versus self-defense, impermissible coercion versus permissible coercion, or the conclusions "murder" versus "self-defense." When a legal claim is matched by a counterclaim, it is certain that the application of relevant rules is neither clear nor autonomous but requires interpretation and selection. Rigid rules cannot be relied on automatically to resolve a controversy without consideration of context and function. Consider whether a particular form of violence leading to the death of a human being is "murder" or "self-defense" in a domestic context. The two conclusions, tied to black-letter rules (that is, one cannot "murder" but one can kill in "self-defense"), are easy to identify, but they are not self-applying.

Creative thinking about new solutions is impaired by the overemphasis on past decision by the rule-oriented approaches. Inherent in their preoccupation with past decision is the assumption, conscious or unconscious, that what has been done in the past will, and should, be repeated in the future. Under this assumption, a study of a set of self-contained or given rules in terms of syntax and logic is considered sufficient. This ignores the changing contexts in which new problems arise and particular decisions are made. This completely fails to take into account the dynamic character of the legal process — especially the international legal process. It fails to mobilize relevant intellectual skills to solve ever-emerging problems.

THE POLICY-ORIENTED APPROACH OF THE NEW HAVEN SCHOOL

In an effort to remedy the inadequacies inherent in the traditional approaches, Myres S. McDougal and Harold D. Lasswell (and many associates) have developed a policy-oriented approach. This approach, occasionally called a configurative or policy science approach, has been dubbed the approach of the New Haven School.

Building on the insights of American legal realism, the New Haven School has moved beyond the basic insights and horizon of legal realism. It seeks not only to demolish the traditional approaches of rigid rule orientation, unrealistic as they often are, but also to provide a constructive jurisprudence of problem solving.

Recognizing that law is a continuing process of authoritative decision for clarifying and securing the common interest of community members, the policy-oriented approach stresses that law serves not only as a limit on effective power but also as a creative instrument in promoting both order and other values. Inherited rules are to be interpreted and applied not as autonomous absolutes but in light of the fundamental community policies they are intended to serve in contemporary contexts

To grasp the dynamics of international law in the contemporary global context, the policy-oriented approach identifies international law as an ongoing process of authoritative decision in which many decision makers continually formulate and reformulate policy. These decision makers formulate policies projecting desired consequences into living contexts as well as respond to words describing what prior decision makers have done in earlier contexts. Its design is not merely to offer a dynamic concept of what is meant by international law but also to detail the role of decision processes at all community levels and to mobilize and integrate appropriate intellectual skills to maximize the utility of international law. It is a theory *about* international law rather than a theory *of* international law. It projects and relates international law to the living context of the contemporary world rather than to the inner or unreal world of autonomous rules and logical exercises. Function and context, goals and expectations, trends, conditions, projections, and alternatives are properly within its domain of concern and inquiry.

In sum, this policy-oriented approach is contextual, problem-solving, and multimethod in nature. It is contextual in the sense of viewing the role of law in society dynamically, by relating it to relevant social, community, and decisional variables. It is problem-solving in the sense of recognizing the intrinsic function of law as an instrument of policy for promoting a preferred social order and in the sense of providing an effective tool to optimize the function of law. It is multimethod in the sense of seeking to mobilize and integrate relevant intellectual skills to facilitate effective problem solving toward the establishment of a more peaceful, abundant, and just world — a world community of human dignity.

The broad outlines of this policy-oriented approach include: (1) the establishment of an observational standpoint; (2) the formulation of problems; (3) the delimitation of the focus of inquiry; (4) the explicit postulation of public order goals; and (5) the performance of intellectual tasks.

1. *The establishment of the observational standpoint.* In approaching international legal problems on a global scale, it is essential to make manifest the standpoint of the observer. An observer's standpoint needs to be kept as distinct as humanly possible from the process under scrutiny so that appropriate criteria for appraisal can be developed.

The appropriate observational standpoint, as stressed by the New Haven School, is that of citizens of the world community who are identified with the future of humankind as a whole rather than with the primacy of any particular group. This standpoint is especially vital in international law — operating as it does in a generally decentralized legal system without centralized institutions of lawmaking and application, in which nation-states in general serve simultaneously as claimants and decision makers — if the common interests are to be clarified, identified, and secured. The responsibility of the scholar who is concerned with enlightenment as well as of the decision maker who is concerned for all the consequences of his or her decisions through time is to ascertain and specify the common interests of all peoples in their transnational interaction — in all their interpenetrating communities, both territorial and functional. It is imperative that both the scholarly inquirer and the established decision maker acquire an observational standpoint that is as free as possible from parochial interests and cultural biases, which will enable them to ascertain and clarify for the active participants in the different communities common interests that these participants are otherwise unable to perceive. The clarity and fidelity with which this standpoint is maintained affects every other feature of inquiry: how problems are defined, what goals are postulated, and what intellectual skills are employed.

2. *The formulation of problems.* Recognizing the important bearing of the formulation of problems on the outcome of inquiry, the New Haven School has developed an economical and comprehensive way of categorizing problems to ease study through time and across community boundaries. It seeks formulations that are acceptable as matters of taste to different cultures but that can also be made to transcend differences in culture, community, and time so as to foster comparisons in goals, trends, and conditions. It stresses that particular problems are most effectively and economically formulated in terms of disparities between demanded values and their achievement in community processes.

It seeks to make problems operational and manageable by adopting a set of value categories borrowed from ethical philosophers and other normative specialists: respect, power, enlightenment, well-being, wealth, skill, affection, and rectitude. Values are preferred events — what people cherish. And these eight values can be defined succinctly:

Respect: Freedom of choice, equality, and recognition
Power: Making and influencing community decisions
Enlightenment: Gathering, processing, and disseminating information and knowledge
Well-being: Safety, health, and comfort
Wealth: Production, distribution, and consumption of goods and services; control of resources

Skill: Acquisition and exercise of capabilities in vocations, professions, and the
   arts
Affection: Intimacy, friendship, loyalty, positive sentiments
Rectitude: Participation in forming and applying norms of responsible conduct

The aggregate of all these values may be described as *security*.

This set of values is supplemented by a set of institutional practices taken
from cultural anthropologists: participation, perspectives, situations, base values, strategies, and outcomes. Through these operational indices, value categories can be made comprehensive and inquiry can be made as detailed as required. Problems in authoritative decision, as integral components of effective
power processes, are generally described in terms of decision makers, basic
policies, structures of authority, bases of power, strategies, and decision outcomes. Such an explicit and economic categorization aids the performance of
relevant intellectual tasks. It facilitates a detailed clarification of basic community policies in relation to particular problems and allows one to analyze past
trends in decision in terms of their approximation to preferred policies, to
identify the important factors affecting decisions and outcomes, to assess the
probable costs and benefits of the different options in decision to common
interests, and to develop better alternatives to implement preferred community
policies.

3. *The delimitation of the focus of inquiry.* In delimiting the focus of inquiry,
the policy-oriented approach seeks to be both comprehensive and selective. It
establishes a focus on authoritative decisions in their context, placing dual
emphasis on the conception of law to be deployed and the larger context to be
studied.

The New Haven School characterizes law not as rules only but as a continual
process of authoritative decision by which people identify, clarify, and secure
common interests. It is concerned with decision that embodies both perspectives and operations. It is concerned with what people do as well as what people
say and expect. It is especially concerned with authoritative decision — that is,
decision in which elements of authority and control are properly balanced. Authority refers to the normative expectations of relevant social actors — expectations of community members about who is to make what decisions, in what
structures, by what procedures, and in accordance with what goals and criteria.
Control refers to effective participation in the choices that are put into community practice. The key to a viable conception of law is to incorporate both
authority and control so that legal scholarship will not drift into the fantasy
lands of naked power or semantic law. In the absence of decision characterized
by authority, international law is an expression of naked power. When control

does not accompany decision, international law or at least decisional outcome may become mere illusion and mockery.

The processes of authoritative decision within any community must be related to the larger social process that envelops such decision making. In international law, the New Haven School orients itself to the most comprehensive context of the earth-space arena, as punctuated by global interdependence, in which people interact.

Viewed comprehensively, humanity today presents the fact of a global community, wholly comparable to the internal communities of lesser territorial groupings, in the sense of interdetermination and interdependence in the shaping and sharing of all values. Vital within this larger community process is an ongoing process of effective power, also global in its reach, in which decisions are taken and enforced by severe deprivations or high indulgences, regardless of the wishes of any particular participant. Operating within this globally effective power process is a comprehensive process of authoritative decision in which a continual flow of decisions are made by those who are expected to make them, in accord with criteria expected by community members, in established structures of authority, by those with enough bases of power to secure necessary control, and by authorized procedures.

The comprehensive process of authoritative decision consists of two distinct, though interrelated, kinds of decisions: *constitutive decisions,* which establish and maintain the ongoing process of authoritative decision, and *public order decisions,* which emanate from the constitutive process to regulate all other community value processes. In other words, "constitutive process" refers to those decisions that identify and characterize authoritative decision makers, identify and project basic community policies, establish appropriate structures of authority, allocate bases of power for sanctioning purposes, authorize procedures for making different kinds of decisions, and perform all the various decision functions (intelligence, promotion, prescription, invocation, application, termination, and appraisal) essential to maintain and administer general community policy. In brief, these seven decision functions may be defined as follows:

Intelligence: Gathering, processing, and disseminating information essential to decision making

Promotion: Advocacy of general policies and the urging of proposals

Prescription: Projecting authoritative community policies about the shaping and sharing of values

Invocation: Provisional characterization of events in terms of community prescriptions

Application: Final characterization and execution of prescriptions in concrete
    situations
Termination: Ending a prescription or arrangement within the scope of a pre-
    scription
Appraisal: Evaluating performance in decision process in terms of community
    goals

"Public order" decisions refer to those decisions, emerging as outcomes of the
established constitutive process, that shape and maintain the protected features
of the community's value processes. Both processes of effective power and of
authoritative decision must be studied closely if the dynamics of international
law are to be grasped.

In an interdependent world, the degree of effectiveness of international law
does not depend merely on the social and decision processes within any single
territorial community. It depends also on the operation of such processes within
a whole hierarchy of interpenetrating communities — from local or national to
regional and global. It requires a firm grasp of the dynamic interplay between
transnational and national processes of decision and their reciprocal impacts.

4. *The explicit postulation of public order goals.* In any process of authoritative decision, policy choices and consequences are inescapable, whether one
cares to admit it or not. The insistent question for every decision maker or other
evaluator is to what basic policy goals he or she, as a representative of the larger
community of humanity and of its various component communities, will ascribe as the primary postulates of public order for inspiring and fashioning
particular choices.

The New Haven School confronts this question squarely by articulating and
appraising policy considerations openly and explicitly in terms of the common
interest. The comprehensive set of public order goals it recommends for postulation, clarification, and implementation are those which today are commonly
characterized as the basic values of human dignity or of a free society. This is
not an idiosyncratic or arbitrary choice but the product of many heritages.

The contemporary image of people as capable of respecting themselves and
others and of constructively participating in shaping and sharing all human
dignity values is the culmination of many trends in thought. These trends are
secular as well as religious; their origins extend far back into antiquity and
come down through the centuries with vast cultural and geographical reach.
The postulate of human dignity can no longer be regarded as the eccentric
doctrine of lonely philosophers and peculiar sects. This postulate, in the sense
of demands for the greater production and wider sharing of all values and a
preference for persuasion over coercion, has been incorporated, with varying

completion and precision into a great cluster of global and regional prescriptions, both conventional and customary, and into the constitutional and legislative codes of many national communities.

The emphasis is on the postulation and clarification of public order goals rather than their derivation by the exercise of logical, syntactic skill. It contributes precious little to rational decision to engage in the syntactic exercises in infinite regress. Peoples subscribing to different styles in derivation have long demonstrated that they can cooperate to promote the values of human dignity regardless of the faiths or creeds they employ for justification. The shared demands for human dignity values can be given effective expression through different institutional practices and cultural adaptations.

The recommended postulation of basic goal values differs from a mere exercise in faith. The New Haven School does not expect to acquire new knowledge by postulation alone. Acquisition of new knowledge requires the systematic and disciplined exercise of all relevant intellectual skills.

5. *The performance of intellectual tasks.* The intellectual tasks essential to rational decision and effective inquiry extend beyond exercises in logical derivation and restrictive conceptions of science to a whole series of distinct, yet interrelated, activities. These tasks include:

a. The clarification of goals. This involves detailed specifications of postulated goals, whatever the level of abstraction of their initial formulation, to be disciplined by empirical observation and analysis in particular social contexts.

b. The description of past trends in decision. This historical task emphasizes not anecdotal treatment of isolated tidbits of doctrine and practice but systematic inquiry in terms of degrees of approximation to clarified goals and policies for constitutive process and public order.

c. The analysis of factors affecting decision. Trends in past decision are useful to project probable future developments and invent alternatives only if the factors affecting those decisions are identifiable. The scientific task employed here is concerned especially with the interplay of the multiple factors affecting prior decision, the complex of predispositional and environmental factors, not with dogmatic determinations of causality.

d. The projection of future trends. Problem solving is oriented toward the future, and the policy-oriented approach seeks to anticipate the future as much as humanly possible. The futuristic task seeks to anticipate and project expectations about the future as an aid to problem solving. The method is not one of dogmatic prophecy of inevitability but one of developmental constructs, embracing a spectrum of futures, from the most to the least desirable in terms of human dignity values, to be tested in the light of all available knowledge and information.

e. The invention and evaluation of policy alternatives. The policy-oriented approach explicitly encourages the cultivation of creativity and the invention of new alternatives in policy, norms, institutional structures, and procedures for the optimal realization of preferred goals. Particular alternatives are to be evaluated in terms of gains and losses in relation to all clarified goals and to be disciplined by the available knowledge concerning trends, conditioning factors, and future probabilities. All the other intellectual tasks will be synthesized and brought to bear on the search for integrated solutions with promise of optimum gains and minimum costs.

These intellectual tasks are distinct yet interrelated. Each affects and is affected by the others. It is crucial that all of these tasks be performed systematically and contextually in relation to specific problems.

The foregoing are the basic features associated with the New Haven School of international law. As system builders, its proponents have developed a comprehensive framework for inquiry that embraces a complex set of terms, concepts, maps, values, institutions, functions, processes, and intellectual skills that are part and parcel of the whole system. To a newcomer the whole apparatus, at first glance, might appear too awesome, novel, radical, complex, and intimidating. Understandably, reactions vary — from outright hostility and calculated indifference to loyal defense, support, and recommended emphases. Common criticisms are that the system's metalanguage is hard to understand; that its approach is open-ended and susceptible to subjective manipulation; that it generates more uncertainty about law than it provides general and stable guidance for conduct; that the entire approach is too complex, cumbersome, and demanding to apply; and that it provides merely a wordy way of stating the obvious.

This is no place to indulge in detailed rebuttal of these criticisms, a job that has already been done well by others elsewhere.[1] Suffice it to say that although McDougal-Lasswell writings[2] are not bedtime readings or for the hurried reader, they are regarded as among those rare intellectual commodities certain to yield generous returns to those able and willing to invest time in them. Dynamic, complex realities of transnational interaction cannot be reduced to simple, rigid formulas. International law in action cannot be insulated from the dynamics of international politics and relations. Profound insights require laborious efforts to absorb. In awarding the Certificate of Merit to McDougal and his associates in 1962, the American Society of International Law characterized their work as "one of the most significant contributions of our time to international law . . . marked by boldness of imagination, originality and depth of insight, and scrupulous adherence to a comprehensive conceptual framework."[3] Looking back at the international law literature of the past four decades, one cannot help but marvel at how significant and far-reaching the McDougal-Lasswell contributions have been — there has not been total adoption and incorporation, to be sure, but, in the favorite lexicon of Lasswell, diffusion through partial restriction and incorporation.

A comprehensive exposition of international law in the grand fashion of the New Haven School would indeed take many volumes, as witness those volumes that have been published to date.[4] As an introduction to orient the reader to international law generally, such is beyond the scope of the present task. In dealing with various aspects and problems of international law, however, the essence of the special concerns of policy-oriented jurisprudence will be, it is hoped, significantly reflected.

To examine the contemporary global constitutive process of authoritative decision, with special emphasis on the role played by, and the protections afforded, nation-states, I propose to explore in succession each of the basic features of the process: participants, perspectives, arenas, bases of power, strategies, outcomes, and effects.

PART TWO

PARTICIPANTS

In recent decades, participation in the global constitutive process of authoritative decision has been greatly democratized. All participants — conveniently categorized as nation-states, international governmental organizations, nongovernmental organizations and associations (including political parties, pressure groups, and private associations), and individual human beings — now openly or recognizably play important roles and perform numerous functions. The role of nation-states has been, and continues to be, predominant at the international level. International governmental organizations, now recognized as appropriate "subjects" of international law, participate in all functions. Political parties, though often receiving no formal recognition, exert effective influence on many authoritative decisions. Pressure groups actively seek to promote and influence decision making. Multiplying hosts of private associations, dedicated to values other than power, are increasingly transnational in membership, goals, organizational structure, spheres of activity, and influence. Individuals, acting both alone and as representatives of groups, have ample opportunity to participate in all the activities that comprise the making, invocation, application, and termination of law. Indeed, individuals are the ultimate participants in the international legal process and in each organization or association mentioned above. Such a realistic role has been recognized at various times but appears to be increasingly evident in the latter part of the twentieth century.

2

Nation-States

Since the rise of the nation-state system in the seventeenth century, nation-states have played, and continue to play, a predominant role in the global processes of decision. With their control of unique territorial bases, nation-states remain the overwhelmingly dominant participants in the world arena, although each is not equally dominant and some participants wield more effective power, wealth, and other values. The officials of nation-states are still by far the most important participants in the performance of all decision functions at the international level. They make and apply, or participate in making and applying, all aspects of international law.

The term *nation-state,* though not altogether satisfactory, has gained wide acceptance. In common usage, it refers to a territorially organized community that achieves, or makes claim to, the highest degree of effective power and authority in the global power process. It is distinct from "nation" in the anthropological sense. Nation-states, enjoying the greatest degrees of freedom in decision, as traditionally expressed in degrees of "independence" and "sovereignty," are in contrast to lesser entities, including protectorates, mandated territories, trust territories, non-self-governing territories, and associated states, which are neither fully independent nor sovereign. The component unit of a federation, often known as a state, is distinguishable from the nation-state. In popular usage, the nation-state is variously referred to as nation, state, country, or body politic. The relevant context will help clarify what is meant when equivalent terms are used.

What criteria, then, distinguish nation-states from nonstate entities? In other words, how does one identify a nation-state? The traditional prescription is expressed in the Montevideo Convention on Rights and Duties of States of 1933: "The State as a person of international law should possess the following qualifications: (a) a permanent population; (b) a defined territory; (c) government; and (d) capacity to enter into relations with other States." This formulation, with slight refinements and nuances here and there, has been widely accepted in theory. In practice, some unusual situations may present considerable difficulty in relation to each condition. A permanent population, together with a defined territory, is meant to signify a reasonably stable territorial community. The frontiers of a nation-state need not be fully settled and defined. International law generally does not require a nation-state to adopt a particular form of government but expects its government to be authoritative, effective, and capable of conducting international relations with other nation-states.

The nation-state formed as a response to demands for better protection and security for the individual in the chaos of declining feudalism. Since then, the nation-state has been the major framework within which demands for shaping and sharing values (power, wealth, respect, enlightenment, and so on) are expressed and fulfilled. Because nation-states represent both the symbol and the fact of accumulated value assets, individuals have sought many of their values through close identification with the nation-state of which they are members. When the degree of transnational interdependence was relatively low, this emphasis on the nation-state as a principal instrument of value shaping and sharing and decision making was easily understandable.

Our epoch is marked by nationalism — yet it is also marked by global interdependence. Though the nation-state, with its inherited perspectives and institutions, continues to command the primary loyalty of peoples about the globe, the functional imperative of transnational cooperation has become more evident and pressing. The past role of the nation-state cannot be taken for granted without a critical reappraisal in light of the changing demands, expectations, and conditions of the present. Indeed, many have begun to argue that we may be living in an age of transition in which the nation-state may well have come to outlive its usefulness. Adjusting the role of the nation-state to the functional needs of global interdependence is vital.

In the contemporary world scene, nation-states of varying sizes and strengths — superpowers, major powers, intermediate powers, and small states — coexist. They differ widely in population, territory, resources, science-based technology, defense capabilities, institutions, and projected public order systems. Nominal equality in law is one thing, and the actual discrepancy in effective power is something else.

In recent decades the number of nation-states has multiplied greatly, thanks to the disintegration of empires and the transformation of ex-colonies into independent states. This is most vividly reflected in the relatively recent and dramatic expansion of membership in the United Nations, from the original 51 in 1945 to 188 in 1999.

The proliferation of new nation-states has brought a considerable measure of democratization to the global processes of decision making. With the massive increase of non-European states, the contemporary international legal system has moved from a Eurocentric, Christian order toward one of universal participation. Virtually all the territorial communities — with all the richness of their diverse religious and cultural heritages — in the different continents are represented. Guided by the fundamental principles of sovereign equality and one state–one vote, all nation-states, large and small, new and old, have become active participants in the global process of decision making. Most recently, with the addition of newly independent Soviet bloc countries to the community of independent states, the Cold War has had to make way for new global perspectives in economics, peace and security, and the sharing of information and cooperation between states. It is a relative democracy in action on a global scale, giving effective expression to the aspirations and interests of the peoples around the world, although the one-state, one-vote formula does not fully represent the world's people, resources, institutions, and so forth.

New states located throughout Asia and Africa, together with Latin American countries, have imparted a distinctive character to participation in the world arena. As a group, they have been loosely and variously labeled as newly independent, developing, underdeveloped, nonaligned, Afro-Asian, and third world countries. Although these nations are far from homogeneous in terms of history, geography, economic development, and political orientation, they do share certain perspectives toward the global process of decision making and some special concerns because of their past experiences with the colonial powers and their present preoccupation with nation building and modernization.

The predominance of European states in the nineteenth century, during which many rules of international law were developed, has not unnaturally aroused suspicion and reservations among newly independent states. Many new states ask whether they can reasonably be expected to abide by those rules that they had played little or no part in formulating and that were the product of what they regard as an alien civilization. In the words of Oliver J. Lissitzyn: "International law is a heritage of the Christian West. In the age of expansion of Europe it was largely imposed on the rest of the World. More often this was a matter of Western self-interest rather than a matter of Christian morality. . . . Can a body of principles and precedents exclusively Western in origin be successfully transmuted into a world law which is freely accepted by nations of widely different historical backgrounds?"[1]

Although no wholesale rejection of international law has been seriously voiced, the new nation-states have challenged the authority of inherited customary rules in several key sectors. Their challenge is particularly vehement in the following areas:

1. Customary law of state responsibility for injury to aliens. The problem of state responsibility arising from injury to aliens, as will be discussed in later chapters, vividly exemplifies the cleavage between the new states and the old Western states. In the perspectives of the new states, customary law in this area is colored by the unequal relationship between great powers and small powers, and for too long "state responsibility" was a frequent excuse for coercion against the weaker states.

Controversy has centered especially on customary rules governing nationalization and expropriation. The newly independent states generally find themselves in the position of debtor upon their birth into the family of nations. Resentful of past subordination and deprivations and determined to achieve the goal of national development, they challenge the customary law of providing "prompt, adequate, and just compensation" for expropriated foreign property within their borders. They often feel, because of past colonial exploitation, that they should receive, rather than pay, compensation for nationalization measures to further the public purpose of national development.

2. State succession. The rapid proliferation of new states has raised serious problems in the field of state succession: whether a new state is bound by some or all of the international legal obligations incurred by its predecessor. Can it simply pick and choose, beyond the right to participate in the ongoing process of law formation? As I will treat in Chapter 28, divergent views have been in contention, ranging from universal succession through selective succession to outright rejection based on a clean-slate theory.

3. Unequal treaties. The dilemmas of state succession are especially acute in relation to treaties. The concept of unequal treaties has been developed and invoked to repudiate all those international agreements that are found to unduly burden new states. Though the concept remains highly controversial, unequal treaties generally refer to treaties having the character of inequality (unequal in bargaining power, in relative benefits and burdens, and so on) or the element of coercive imposition.

4. Compulsory third-party decision making. Nation-states as a whole are notorious for being unwilling to submit to compulsory third-party decision, which allegedly might compromise their "sovereignty." The general distrust of the inherited norms of international law has made the new states even more reluctant to have their hands tied. Hence, their initial disposition was to avoid running the risks of third-party adjudication according to a traditional law that

they feel generally favors powerful creditor states and to keep their options open.

Because of their discontent with rules inherited from the past, these nations generally favor revision so that specific norms can be formulated or reformulated, with all deliberation and explicitness, in light of new demands and expectations and contemporary conditions. This is exemplified by the final implementation of the United Nations Convention on the Law of the Sea, a comprehensive treaty adopted in 1982 after some ten years of intense negotiation by more than 150 delegations and implemented in 1994 after another twelve years of negotiations over provisions disputed between newer nation-states and the developed powers.

In addition to the law of the sea, the insistent demands of the new states to change and reform international law have been propagated in connection with a New International Economic Order and a New World Information and Communication Order. These demands for new orders, comprehensive in scope, have extended far beyond the sectors of wealth and enlightenment. In a profound sense, they represent enormous attempts to reshape the entire global process of decision making — both authoritative decision and effective power. They are highly controversial but cannot be ignored.

In the drive to codify and reform international law in general and to establish new orders in particular, these new nations have mustered impressive voting strength. Known as the Group of Seventy-Seven within the framework of U.N. bloc politics (though the number now exceeds 130), the third world countries command a two-thirds majority in the parliamentary arena of the United Nations (the General Assembly) or its equivalent forum (for example, a specially convened conference) to pass one resolution after another. Their numerical unity is especially apparent in response to issues perceived as part of the North-South confrontation. This automatic overwhelming majority has led to a mounting tension between numerical strength and effective power. In a real world where the effective power process is constantly operating, genuine support of community members must be measured in terms of effective power as well as numerical strength. The conjunction of numerical strength and effective power is crucial. Democracy and responsibility go hand in hand. Without effective power, sheer numerical strength is hollow. Without popular support, effective power can be sheer arrogance.

The agonizing process in which claims and counterclaims — at times exaggerated, radical, and even absurd — are pressed reflects how international law evolves in response to the changing demands and expectations of the active participants.

As eloquently articulated by B. V. A. Roling, the emergence of the new states in the contemporary world arena strikingly resembles the rise to power of the working classes in the national communities of the West.[2] With democratization, the previously deprived and submerged groups were able to demand greater participation in the processes of authoritative decision and effective power and in other value sectors. Their demands for legal protection of organized labor first seemed radical and dangerous but eventually gained acceptance by the dominant and opposing elements, thanks to a process that sought the common interest by accommodating competing demands. Where the common interest in orderly change and reform fails to take hold, where all-or-nothing attitudes persist in polarizing struggling classes, the outcome can be violent upheaval.

This historic lesson from national development is no less cogent for humanity and the world community as a whole. International law, like all law, is far from static. It is a continuing process of identifying, clarifying, and securing the common interest in response to the changing demands and expectations of all participants (not merely nation-states) in the decision processes under constant change.

The key is common interest — the common interest of all participants from both short-term and long-term perspectives. The search for the common interest is a continuous and laborious process. There is no room for one-sided nonnegotiable demands that disregard the common interest. It is obvious that the demands of the new states for change and reform need to be, and are, tempered by their keen perception that international law serves the interests of all participants, especially the weaker ones that require special protection. It is equally apparent that in a world of growing interdependence, the security and prosperity of the few cannot endure in a sea of miseries.

Today all nation-states share a common destiny of survival on spaceship earth. In common parlance, "We are all in this together." Nation-states, like living organisms, are born, grow, mature, decline, and eventually die. The developing life cycle brings challenges and opportunities. The changing role of nation-states will be promising as nation-states seize new opportunities to communicate and collaborate in the face of formidable new challenges in an age of transition.

THE PRINCIPLE OF SELF-DETERMINATION

The driving force behind the rapid and vast proliferation of new states after World War II is the principle of self-determination. This precept has been asserted with increasing vigor and frequency in recent decades, and the number of peoples involved in claims to self-determination has greatly expanded.

The demand for self-determination is an important dimension of the demand for freedom in our world. It is the demand of human beings to form groups and to identify with groups that can best promote their pursuit of values in both individual and aggregate terms.

The new era of self-determination can be symbolized by the contrasting fates of Biafra and Bangladesh — the former failed to achieve secession from Nigeria; but the latter achieved secession from Pakistan. As former colonial peoples and territories substantially disappear, attention to claims of self-determination has shifted from colonial to noncolonial contexts. Despite some contemporary doubts as to the viability of some new nation-states, it is undeniable that self-determination played a leading role in accelerating the emancipation of millions of people from colonial shackles. It was the driving force behind postwar decolonization.

The demands of humanity to secure an optimum freedom and wide sharing of power have been made under a variety of legalistic labels and contexts. Self-determination may be invoked singly or in combination with other labels, such as sovereignty, independence, and nonintervention.

Comprehensively formulated, claims to self-determination can be divided into two basic categories:

1. Claims involving establishment of a new state — that is, claims by a group within an established state to form a new state from part of the preexisting state
2. Claims not involving establishment of a new state, notably:
   a. Claims of a state to be free of external coercion and interference
   b. Claims of a state to control its own natural resources (that is, economic self-determination)
   c. Claims of a people to overthrow their effective rulers and establish a new, authoritative government in the whole of a state (that is, the right of revolution)
   d. Claims of a group within a state to enjoy autonomy
   e. Claims of a group to enjoy such special protections as language rights, religious rights, and land rights

The present focus relates primarily to the first category — namely, claims of a group within an established state to form a new state from part of an existing state and hence to establish and maintain its own internal decision processes and external relations.

The modern principle of self-determination originated in the sixteenth century when nation-states first emerged. It was deeply rooted in the contemporary concept of nationality. The principle of national self-determination crystallized at the end of World War I under the strong championship of President Woodrow Wilson. In his words, "No peace can last, or ought to last, which does not recognize and accept the principle that governments derive all their just powers from the consent of the governed, and that no right anywhere exists to hand people about from sovereignty to sovereignty as if they were property."[3]

Because of its universal appeal rooted in the concept of human dignity and human rights and linked to the maintenance of world order, self-determination was enshrined in the Charter of the United Nations, as sustained by the systems of international trusteeship and non-self-governing territories. A major purpose of the United Nations, according to Article 1(2) of the charter, is to "achieve friendly relations among nations based on respect for the principle of equal rights and self-determination of peoples, and to take other appropriate measures to strengthen universal peace."

Both the International Covenant on Civil and Political Rights and the International Covenant on Economic, Social, and Cultural Rights accord a prominent place to the principle of self-determination. In identical words, both covenants proclaim in their first article that "[a]ll peoples have the right of self-determination. By virtue of that right they freely determine their political status and freely pursue their economic, social and cultural development." This principle has been affirmed and reaffirmed by the landmark Declaration on the Granting of Independence to Colonial Countries and Peoples (1960),[4] the Declaration on Principles of International Law Concerning Friendly Relations and Co-operation Among States in Accordance with the Charter of the United Nations (1970),[5] and many other United Nations resolutions, such as the proclaiming of the International Decade for the Eradication of Colonialism (1990–2000). The impressive record of the United Nations in facilitating independence of former trust territories and non-self-governing territories is common knowledge. The application of self-determination in the colonial context has done much to change today's world map and to affect the world constitutive process of authoritative decision.

Without going into detail, the United Nations practice in the colonial context can be highlighted in terms of "who gets self-determination, when, and how." First, let us look at the question of who is eligible for self-determination. The charter stipulates "self-determination of peoples," not states, and hence leaves the door wide open to arguments over who is entitled to self-determination — who constitutes a proper self-determining "unit." In ascertaining the basic unit of "nation" or "peoples" to exercise self-determination, the sociological, geographical, historical, psychological, and political factors of a social context have been recognized as relevant in U.N. practice. Thus, reference is generally made to the distinct features of population concerned in terms of race, language, religion, or cultural heritage. It is also considered pertinent to discuss whether territory is involved and whether the territory is identifiable or sufficiently contiguous to constitute one geographical unit. The wishes of the peo- ple — their demands, expectations, and identifications — are commonly con- ceded to have great weight.

After a provisional identification of who is entitled to self-determination, decision makers face the problem of when and under what conditions self- determination is to be realized. In terms of timing, whereas most member states favor self-determination for all dependent peoples without undue delay, they generally agree that cases differ too much from one another to warrant the adoption of blanket timing. Nevertheless, the overall pace of decolonization is breathtaking.

The plebiscite has become a useful device to determine political self- determination. The key standard of authority of any government recognized by international law is that based on the "will of the people" (as enunciated in Article 21[3] of the Universal Declaration of Human Rights), a will best ex- pressed in free and genuine elections, but a will that is a dynamic process in which individuals freely participate. The importance of effective and impartial international supervision of every phase of the plebiscite process has been clearly demonstrated as in the case of East Timor in August 1999. Persuasion is obviously a desirable alternative to violence and coercion. But international law also acknowledges (or bows to the reality) that on occasion armed struggle may be the last resort open to a people oppressed under systematic subjugation. During apartheid in South Africa, for example, some resolutions of the General Assembly recognized the propriety of self-determination assistance to those who sought to overthrow the government, and were instrumental in producing the radical reforms in that country that led to the abolition of apartheid and South Africa's readmittance to the U.N. fold in 1994.

In terms of outcomes, although self-determination is commonly equated with independence, it is not necessarily so. Arrangements other than independence, when freely chosen by the people concerned, are also acceptable. Viewed in terms of United Nations practice and the context of world politics, self- determination ranges from considerable self-government inside an existing state, through an autonomous status within an established state, to complete independence. The fundamental requirement inherent in the concept of self- determination is a process or procedure, not a preset outcome. Whether the choice in a particular case is independence or otherwise is less important than whether it is genuinely and freely made by the people concerned. If the freedom of choice of the people is sustained, the policy objective of self-determination is fulfilled, although self-determination is actually a continual process. The deci- sions of the United Nations manifest the flexibility that is realistically adapted to the contextual complexities of world affairs.

Viewing United Nations practice as a whole, it appears that the world community has as much interest as the people directly concerned in seeing that solutions to self-determination problems will benefit everyone. Hence, in dealing with a claim to self-determination, the United Nations is concerned with: (1) the prospect of the territory or people concerned becoming a viable state; (2) the present stage of advancement toward self-government; and (3) the effect of granting or refusing the exercise of self-determination in terms of regional and international peace, the effectuation of authoritative governmental processes and human rights, and impacts on all regional and global value processes. It is considered essential that the people directly concerned have a reasonable prospect of becoming a viable entity — politically, economically, and so on — in this increasingly interdependent world.

The accelerating pace of decolonization in the post–World War II era brought about the radical multiplication of many more smaller units — now called ministates — and compounded by the breakup of the Soviet Union into a multitude of republics has resulted in much international concern about the viability of the existing ministates and the desirability of adding potential ministates. Although no formula has been worked out to determine how small is too small for the purposes of self-determination, the point that a new entity should be capable of developing itself as a viable entity and capable of acting responsibly in the external arena is widely appreciated. It is increasingly recognized that the very existence and function of a new entity have value consequences far beyond its own borders. An increased awareness of the relation of respect for human rights to optimum world order may lead to new perspectives on the role of the nation-state entity as a vehicle for the attainment of human dignity.

Will the experience gained from the past five decades be relevant for the future? Will the experience gained from the accelerated independence of former trust territories and non-self-governing territories be relevant for the future? Will self-determination be relevant to the case of secession? Yes, indeed! This is so even though national elites understandably have approached the subject with great caution and skepticism. Self-determination is an ongoing process for people to forge and express their shared identity and destiny under ever-changing conditions in the collective pursuit of power, respect, and other values.

So long as social process moves on, human beings will continue to search for individual and group identities in an attempt to associate or dissociate with certain groups. Self-determination is not a one-shot affair. The attainment of independence from dependency does not foreclose human aspirations to search for appropriate group identification and affiliation in the defense and fulfillment of all important values.

Until the birth of Bangladesh as an independent state in 1971, it was generally assumed that in the contemporary world self-determination did not include the right of secession in the sense of a group breaking off from an established nation-state. The success of Bangladesh has significantly changed people's expectations. Indeed, change is a cardinal principle in human affairs. Change occurs to groups as well as individuals. It is critical that demands for change in value fulfillment through group identification, association, and expression in the name of self-determination are effected to serve the common interest of the world community. The recent experiences of the former Yugoslavia and the former Soviet Union emphasize the need for careful scrutiny of each claim to determine whether its fulfillment would promote security and foster human dignity values.

Though the basic community policy of self-determination has been affirmed and reaffirmed, a key problem remains: how to make its application relevant in particular instances to facilitate optimum achievement of the common interests — both minimum public order (in the sense of minimizing unauthorized coercion) and optimum public order (in the sense of the widest possible shaping and sharing of all values). It is a pressing challenge.

In a decentralized world in which the effective power of state participants is patently discrepant, decision in support of or in rejection of particular claims for self-determination will remain essentially decentralized, in the absence of effective collective decisions. Hence, it is essential that appropriate criteria be articulated and formulated to guide rational decision making, unilateral or otherwise. Any serious review of a demand for self-determination from general community perspectives requires a careful contextual scrutiny, a systematic and rigorous appraisal of many features of the situation. Whether to support a claim must depend on the answers to many questions about each feature of the context, with the significance of any one feature being dependent on the total configuration.

The test we recommend to determine whether to grant or reject a demand for self-determination is not whether a given situation is colonial or noncolonial but whether granting or rejecting the demands of a group would move the situation closer to goal values of human dignity, considering in particular the aggregate value consequences for the group directly concerned and the larger communities affected. Self-determination should be viewed in the context of interdetermination. In other words, the basic question is whether separation or unification would best promote security and facilitate effective shaping and sharing of power and of all the other values for most people. A proper balance between freedom of choice and the viability of communities must be maintained.

It is essential to examine alternative consequences of either granting or rejecting claims for separation or unity. Specific consideration should be given to the following: (1) the degree to which the demanding group can form a viable entity, in terms of both its internal processes and its capacity to function responsibly in its relations with other entities; (2) the probable consequences of independence (separation) for the remaining people in the entity of which it has been a part; and (3) the consequences of demanded independence (separation) or unity (unification) for the aggregate pattern of value shaping and sharing for the peoples of the surrounding communities and for the world at large. All these probable consequences must be ascertained and tested in a given context by a careful analysis of the factors involved: participants, perspectives, situations, base values, strategies, outcomes, and effects.

Some of the more important points about relevant features may be briefly indicated:

In terms of perspectives, it is critical to ascertain the intensity of demands in a population, observing the degree and intensity of support on the part of the elite and the rank and file, respectively. Identifications are crucial, especially the intensity and inclusivity of identification with a territorial community and the range and degree of identification with regional and global communities. Hence, it is vital to ascertain: (1) the degree to which the elite and the rank and file of the aspiring group identify with an existing or projected territorial community; (2) the extent to which members of the aspiring group associate themselves with all members of an existing or projected territorial community; (3) the degree to which members of the aspiring group identify with a class or ethnic or political or linguistic group; (4) the degree of territorial inclusivity; and (5) the range and degree of identification with regional and global communities and the degree of conformity to regional and global public policies. Another component is the matter-of-fact expectations about the past, present, and future entertained by the different participants. It is important to explore in which direction and to what extent alternative courses of action will affect these expectations.

In terms of participation, attention should be directed to observe how a particular group that makes a demand for separation fits in with the territorial and functional groups in the contemporary world and to compare what changes in participation are being sought by demanders and by those who oppose the demand.

It is important to ask: Do the people concerned actively participate in making the demand? What choices were available to these people in the past? What choices would be open to them in the future? Would granting the demand lead to significant value shaping and better distribution of values? Would participation in the relevant value processes be effectively widened?

Regarding situations, one must compare the present and proposed structures of authority, both functional and territorial, and ascertain the degree of sharing of a common destiny in reference to the larger community. One must also note the length of time over which previous factors have been integrated and consider alternative time intervals for future integration and consolidation, crisis circumstances, and so forth.

With regard to base values, consideration should be given to consequences of accepting or denying a particular demand in terms of values. What are the present distributions of values of different groups? What changes are demanded in terms of authority and controlling values? What are the available alternatives and the probable consequences for people, territory, institutions, and resources?

In terms of viability of a political community, inquiry can be directed in terms of consideration for security, power, wealth, and other values. The most important of all the features are the outcomes in terms of the impact on different values expected to attend each option for the aspiring group, the old entity to which the aspiring group belongs, and the larger surrounding communities, including the global community. Hence, the critical test in considering a claim to self-determination is to evaluate the aggregate value consequences for all those communities, potential as well as existing, in honoring or rejecting the claim and to honor the option that will promote the largest net aggregate of common interest by fully estimating the relative costs and benefits of the different options for each of those communities.

In making this recommendation, I do not mean to oversimplify or underestimate the enormous complexity and difficulty attending many of the seemingly intractable controversies about self-determination. Notice, for example, the claims for self-determination made by the following peoples: The Palestinians, Lebanese, and Kurds; the Koreans, Taiwanese (Formosans), Tibetans, East Timorese, and Tamil people in Sri Lanka; the Serbs, Croats, Slovenians, and Bosnian Muslims in the former Yugoslavia; the Albanians in Kosovo; the Chechens in Russia, Armenians, and the Germans of Romania; the Catalans and Basques of Spain, the Scots, the Welsh, the Catholics of Northern Ireland, and the French Canadians of Quebec; the Ibos, Somalis, and the non-Muslim peoples in southern Sudan; and various indigenous groups. (For many years, indigenous groups have been existing on lands over which they have little or no control and have suffered various deprivations, including conquest, actual and cultural genocide, forced expulsion from their land and dwellings, and compulsory taking of their natural resources. The demands inherent in their claims for self-determination range from the classic sense of establishing a new state to a high degree of autonomy within the existing state to special protection of land rights, cultural rights, religious rights, and so on.)

Although the trend of past decisions indicates that the United Nations, in dealing with issues relating to self-determination, often stresses the basic distinction between colonial and noncolonial issues, this distinction need not be conclusive, particularly when colonialism is narrowly understood to be the domination by whites of non-whites. The essence of self-determination is human dignity, human rights, and authority of the people. Underlying the concept of human dignity is the insistent demand of the individual to form groups freely and to identify with groups that can best promote and maximize the pursuit of values in both individual and aggregate terms. The formation and reformation of groups are ongoing.

Legal doctrines operate in pairs of complementarity, herein exemplified by the interplay between self-determination and territorial integrity. Is the seeming conflict between territorial integrity and self-determination irreconcilable? And how about territorial integrity: for whom or what purpose and with what social consequences?

It has become increasingly apparent that absolute adherence to territorial integrity is no virtue — rather, it is self-defeating — when the people who demand freedom are subject to systematic deprivations on a vast scale. The principle of territorial integrity must not serve as a shield for tyrants, dictators, or totalitarian rulers; it must not become a screen behind which human deprivations are justified, condoned, and perpetuated. Today the world is too interdependent, humanity is living too closely together, to permit the doctrines of domestic jurisdiction or territorial integrity to become an instrument of oppression, politicide, and deprivation. Moreover, new perspectives on human rights have opened the possibility that artificial political entities based on territorial integrity alone may someday have to be replaced by institutions more realistically reflecting human dignity values.

Empires rise and fall; nation-states and territorial boundaries come and go. But the demands of humanity for freedom and human dignity will remain strong.

An ongoing process in the search of the self in relation to others, self-determination is profoundly associated with the essence of human dignity. When decisions regarding self-determination are rationally and adequately made, they will greatly contribute to the common interest of humankind in achieving both minimum and optimum order.

THE THEORY AND PRACTICE OF RECOGNITION

The application of the principle of self-determination has led to the establishment of many new states in recent decades. But when does a territorial community come into formal existence as a nation-state, as a full member of the world community? Does it come about automatically when a territorial group meets the widely accepted conditions of statehood: control over a group of people, control over a defined or definable territory, and a government capable of interacting with other entities and assuming international responsibility? If so, who decides whether a group has met such traditional conditions of statehood, and who reviews those decisions? If not, what else will be required? Does a new body politic come into being as a result of self-proclamation and effective control or as a consequence of recognition by other existing entities? This raises the issue of recognition in international law.

Recognition in international law is a highly confusing topic both in theory and in practice. The term *recognition* itself gives ambiguous reference simultaneously to both facts and legal consequences. Is de facto recognition different from de jure recognition? Is recognition, with its inherited ambiguity and confusion, merely a ritual, or does it possess considerable significance? What impact should human rights, the precept of authority, and self-determination have on the process of recognition?

In an interdependent world of constant change, recognition problems persist. In the most comprehensive sense, recognition choices are made in response to the dynamics of change in the social process. Within a nation-state such changes may relate to patterns of participation; patterns of demands, expectations, and identification; aggregate situations in time, space, institutions, and crises; authority and control patterns; the overall distribution of value assets; strategies and procedures for the employment of value assets; and the aggregate outcomes in the shaping and sharing of all values. Such changes, though internal, inevitably generate effects external to the group concerned, thanks to the interactive nature of the global system—a system of growing interdetermination and interdependence in which participants act and react by taking one another into account.

Recognition problems that particularly vex international and national decision makers arise in a number of contexts, notably the emergence of new states, changes of government or retention of effective power through extraconstitutional means, territorial changes resulting from use of force, and the rivalry (belligerency or insurgency) in a civil strife. The post–Cold War era has been characterized by violent civil wars that have led to the creation of a number of new states. The particular need for recognition arises when the birth of a new nation-state or the seizure of power by a new government of an existing state is an extraordinary political event. In the case of recognizing an entity as a new state, what is extraordinary usually involves a revolutionary separation from another state. Though every new state holds out for recognition, the process of recognition is routine if the new entity results from peaceful separation from an existing state, as is the case with most of the new states under decolonization.

In the case of recognition of a new government, if the transfer of power from one government to another results from the ordinary and authoritative constitutive process, the question of recognition poses no difficulty. Only when the change of government is extraconstitutional, such as by a revolution, a coup d'état, martial law, or a radical departure from the prescribed line of succession, is a decision called for as to whether the new or newly changed regime should be recognized as authoritative. The great majority of recognition problems involve recognition of regimes as the governments of already recognized states without affecting the continuity of legal identity of the states.

Our principal concern here is with the emergence of a new state — that is, the question of recognizing the state. In this sense, recognition refers to the authoritative decision by one nation-state to signify its willingness to accept another territorial community as a nation-state, as a full participant, for a wide range of purposes, in the global processes of authoritative decision. The question of recognizing a particular government will be dealt with insofar as it relates to this question.

A wide consensus exists among international lawyers that the minimum conditions of statehood requisite to recognition consist of territory, people, political institutions, and the capacity to fulfill international obligations. They disagree, however, on the modalities for applying these criteria to concrete cases, as manifested in the basic difference in their perspectives regarding the nature of recognition. Much ink has been spilled over the question of whether recognition is declaratory or constitutive in nature. The declaratory theory holds that recognition merely declares, and is automatic upon, the "objective" existence of the conditions of statehood. The constitutive theory maintains that the presence of objective conditions of statehood is itself insufficient to endow formal statehood on a new entity — formal recognition by other existing states is essential to making a new entity a full member of the community of nations. The declaratory-constitutive controversy relates primarily to recognition of states and only incidentally to recognition of governments.

The practice of recognition lies somewhere in between the two theories. The declaratory theory, in its search for objective pronouncement of factual existence, cannot escape the element of subjective appreciation in determining whether a particular territorial community has demonstrated all the required conditions. Of the requisite conditions of statehood, determining whether there exists a government capable of responsible interaction with other territorial communities is particularly challenging. Nothing is automatic or objective about making such a determination. By contrast, constitutive theorists and practitioners cannot really operate in a vacuum without regard for relevant legal precepts and for factual situations concerning people, territory, and institutions.

Closely related to recognition of states is the recognition of government. This question becomes acute when an extraconstitutional change in government takes place without affecting the continuity of legal identity of the established state. If a governmental change results from ordinary constitutional procedures, recognition by others is automatic and implicit, through such communications as messages of felicitation. But when a governmental change results from extraconstitutional means, the questions of authority and recognition take on special significance: Is the claiming government to be recognized as the government representative of the state it purports to represent? Do other states (governments) have the duty to extend recognition to such a claiming government? Under what conditions? Does such recognition signify approval of the recognized government and its practices? Or does it simply acknowledge effective control by the claiming government in the state involved? The tenor of the questions thus raised, though somewhat akin to the constitutive-declaratory controversy, is distinct.

Again, practice varies widely, and the practice and the theory are far from congruent. Decision makers have made use of recognition in various ways, depending largely on the context of political conditions and their perception of the national interest involved in a change of government. Take, for instance, the practice of the United States. Early in its history, recognition was tied to standards of authority and democratic values. Throughout most of the nineteenth century, it was a general U.S. policy to accord recognition to stable governments without attempting to confer approval. But the recognition policy became more complex as various administrations introduced different policy considerations, including popular support, free elections, ability and willingness to honor international obligations, sound political orientation, positive attitude toward foreign investment, and proper treatment of U.S. citizens. The United States has employed recognition as a deliberate instrument to support antimonarchical governments under George Washington, to foster economic expansion under Theodore Roosevelt, to promote constitutional democracy under Woodrow Wilson, to check the spread of communism under Dwight D. Eisenhower, and to encourage the growth of market economies and democracy in the newly independent states of the former Soviet Union. The net effects are to create the impression that recognition signifies approval of a government and its practices, whereas nonrecognition means disapproval and causes considerable confusion regarding the legal implications of recognition and considerable practical difficulties. In recent years the United States has sought to separate the element of approval or disapproval from an act of recognition and has approached the problem of recognizing a government in terms of willingness to establish diplomatic relations to facilitate direct mutual interaction. What impact does such a policy have on self-determination? Is it likely that human dignity, the precept of authority found in the Universal Declaration of Human Rights, and other human rights can be realistically and rationally served by ignoring legal policies at stake and the details of context?

In theory and in practice, a distinction is often made between de jure and de facto recognition. Generally speaking, when a government is recognized as de facto, its effective control is recognized; if a government is deemed de jure, recognition is extended to the permanency of its effective control and formal authority. Though de facto recognition is often regarded as a prelude to de jure recognition, the distinction is often blurred. Furthermore, the modality of recognition may be either express or implied (for instance, through conclusion of a bilateral treaty of a general nature).

In an interactive world, the value consequences of bestowing or withholding recognition are far from trivial. In the words of Kaplan and Katzenbach, "Recognition of a new government normally results in increased prestige and stability at home; access to state funds on deposit in other states; access to private and governmental loans because of legal ability to pledge the state's credit; diplomatic and consular status for its agents in the recognizing entity; access to foreign courts and immunity from foreign process; establishment of normal trade relations; a capacity to request assistance from the recognizing government in the form of financial assistance, supplies, and even military aid; respect in other states for its laws and decrees; and benefits of existing treaty arrangements. The absence of formal recognition has the effect of suspending most or all of these rights insofar as the non-recognizing state controls them. They may be accorded to another claimant, or they may simply be suspended."[6]

Hence, controversy arises as to the permissibility of premature recognition or deliberate nonrecognition. During a civil strife, premature recognition bestowed on the rebellious group can be used as a means of influencing the outcome of the strife. Customarily, as long as the duly constituted government or mother state commands effective control of the substantial part of territory and exercises its authority, it is presumed to represent the state. Unless there are indications beyond reasonable doubt that the rebellious group has effective control over a substantial part of the territory with reasonable expectations of stability and permanency, and the parent state or duly constituted government has discontinued effective efforts to reestablish its control and authority over the lost territory, other nation-states are obligated to refrain from recognizing the new regime. Premature recognition of a rebellious group as either a new state or a new government is traditionally frowned on as impermissible "intervention." The real difficulty, given the highly decentralized nature of recognition, is to determine the appropriate timing for recognition of a new regime as effected unilaterally by individual states.

In 1903, when Panama seceded from Colombia, the United States lost no time in recognizing Panama as an independent state, with a view to preventing Colombia from reasserting its authority and control over the rebellious territory. Though the United States government justified its action by citing security interests in the Caribbean and inclusive interests for the construction of the Panama Canal, this has frequently been cited as a classic example of premature recognition. In modern times, premature recognition is increasingly justified in terms of support for self-determination or for "wars of national liberation." Some commentators have suggested that the premature recognition of the breakaway Yugoslav republics in large part precipitated the war in the former Yugoslavia.

Deliberate nonrecognition, like premature recognition, can have a devastating effect on a target regime. If a state or a government meets those criteria that are commonly accepted by international law, are other nation-states obligated to recognize this state or government? Or is recognition of a state or government a matter of discretion, to be granted or withheld as a state sees fit? The impact of withholding recognition is particularly keen when preponderant differences in bases of power exist between the recognizing and the target state or government. As indicated, recognition by a powerful nation-state usually carries with it not only increased access to the international arena of authority but also advancement of external position. Conversely, a denial of recognition can deprive and adversely affect the relative influence of the target regime in international affairs. At times the protracted refusal of recognition by a powerful state may even adversely affect the internal position of the target regime. A major purpose of the U.S. refusal to recognize the People's Republic of China in the 1950s and 1960s was to isolate it and hasten its passing from the international scene.

In real life, however, the significance and consequences flowing from complex acts of recognition do not lend themselves to neat explanation by pure theory. Take, for instance, the notable case of the People's Republic of China and the Republic of China.

The People's Republic of China (PRC) is variously known as China, mainland China, and Communist China. The Republic of China (ROC) is variously known as Taiwan, Formosa, and Nationalist China. Both before and after the ROC was replaced by the PRC in the United Nations in 1971 — and both before and after relations between the United States and China were "normalized" and Taiwan was "derecognized" in 1979 — a number of knotty legal questions persisted: Are there two successor states — Communist China and Nationalist China — as a result of the Chinese civil war of 1949? If so, which is new, which is old, and which represents the authentic state of China? By what criteria would one determine this authenticity? If there is only "one China" and "Taiwan is part of China," as claimed by the ruling elites in Beijing, what are the respective statuses of the PRC and the ROC? Does the PRC represent a state or only a government? Does the ROC represent a state or only a government? Do the PRC and the ROC each fulfill the traditional requirements of statehood? What are the legal effects of the normalization of U.S.-China relations and the derecognition of Taiwan? What is the international legal status of Taiwan? Who owns Taiwan? Since its formation in 1949, the PRC has never extended its effective control over Taiwan; what, then, is the basis of its legal claim over Taiwan? Which of the following labels most aptly describes the current situation: "one China," "one China, two governments," "one China — but not now," "two Chinas," or "one China, one Taiwan"? Will the future of Taiwan be determined by peaceful "reunification" with "the motherland" (mainland China), through negotiation by "the Chinese on both sides of the Taiwan Straits," through forcible "liberation" by China, or by all twenty-two million inhabitants of Taiwan as a right of self-determination? Answers to these questions will not be easy, even for experts in this area. Without going into detail, a few observations are in order.

The continuing controversies about "one China," "one China — but not now," "two Chinas," and "one China, one Taiwan" stem from the basic uncertainty of Taiwan's status in international law after World War II. Although the rival regimes of Nationalist China and Communist China both have claimed, for different reasons and motivations, that there is only one China and that Taiwan is an integral part of China, such major powers as the United States, the United Kingdom, France, Canada, and Australia have long taken the position — especially before each recognized the PRC — that the legal status of Taiwan remained undetermined. In their views, Taiwan — a Japanese colony from 1895 to 1945 and, technically, a territory under Allied military occupation entrusted to Generalissimo Chiang Kai-shek from 1945 to 1951 — was formally detached from Japan in 1951 but has not since been attached to any state. Though Japan's renunciation of its "right, title and claim" over Taiwan was made unmistakably clear in the 1951 peace treaty with Japan, the beneficiary of the renunciation was not specified. The shared expectation was that the legal status of Taiwan, though temporarily left undetermined because of current exigencies, would be decided in the future in light of the purposes and principles of the United Nations Charter. Because of this long-held position, these former Allied powers (except the United Kingdom, which extended recognition to the PRC shortly after its birth in 1949) simply "took note of," or "acknowledged," rather than "recognized," China's position that Taiwan was part of China when they established diplomatic relations with the PRC in the 1970s. The words were chosen with all deliberateness and care and help explain the constant controversy about who owns Taiwan and the continuing, insistent demands on the part of the Taiwanese people for self-determination.

Before the PRC gained a seat in the United Nations, the question of Chinese participation came before the United Nations year after year, generating the bitter debate over whether the question was one of "credentials," "representation," or "admission" of a new member state. When the United Nations acted to seat the PRC on October 25, 1971, the General Assembly voted to "restore all its rights to the People's Republic of China and to recognize the representatives of its Government as the only legitimate representatives of China to the United Nations, and to expel forthwith the representatives of Chiang Kai-shek from the place which they unlawfully occupy at the United Nations and in all the organizations related to it."[7] Overnight, the ROC, which had gained respectable recognition as "the only legitimate government of China" within the United Nations and elsewhere for two decades, by more states than the PRC, suddenly found itself an international outcast. The trend toward formal recognition of the PRC thus accelerated in the 1970s, culminating in the recognition of the PRC as the sole legitimate government of China by an overwhelming majority of the representatives of the world's nations.

The dramatic change of U.S. policy toward China and Taiwan is in line with this overall trend. Before President Richard M. Nixon's journey to China in February 1972, the United States recognized the ROC as the only legitimate government of China, supported it in the form of a mutual defense treaty, and adopted the policy of nonrecognition of the PRC to "hasten the passing of the Communist regime on mainland China."[8] After Nixon's journey and until the end of 1978, the United States and the PRC developed their economic and cultural ties and maintained "unofficial relations" through the establishment of "liaison offices" in each other's capitals while the official relations between the ROC and the United States continued. On January 1, 1979, the United States and the People's Republic of China agreed to "recognize each other and to establish diplomatic relations": the United States "recognizes" the government of the PRC as "the sole legal Government of China" and "acknowledges the Chinese position that there is but one China and Taiwan is part of China"; meanwhile, "the people of the United States will maintain cultural, commercial, and other unofficial relations with the people of Taiwan."[9] With this aboutface, the liaison offices located in Washington, D.C., and Beijing were elevated to embassies, whereas the "unofficial relations" between the United States and

Taiwan were carried forward through new institutions in lieu of old-fashioned embassies — the American Institute on Taiwan and the Coordinating Council for North American Affairs, both staffed by foreign service officers on loan. To fill the security gap created by President Jimmy Carter's termination of the mutual defense treaty with Taiwan, the U.S. Congress in April 1979 adopted the Taiwan Relations Act, declaring, among other things, that "peace and stability" in the "Western Pacific area" are "matters of international concern," that "the United States decision to establish diplomatic relations" with the PRC "rests upon the expectation that the future of Taiwan will be determined by peaceful means," that "any effort to determine the future of Taiwan by other than peaceful means" will constitute "a threat to the peace and security of the Western Pacific area" and be "of grave concern to the United States," and that "the preservation and enhancement of the human rights of all the people on Taiwan are hereby reaffirmed as objectives of the United States."[10] The act stipulates: "The absence of diplomatic relations or recognition shall not affect the application of the laws of the United States with respect to Taiwan. . . . Whenever the laws of the United States refer or relate to foreign countries, states, governments, or similar entities, such terms shall include and such laws shall apply to Taiwan."[11] The Taiwan Relations Act specifies further that treaty relations (at the time of derecognition of Taiwan, fifty-nine international agreements were in force between the United States and Taiwan, excluding the mutual defense treaty) remain essentially unchanged, as do Taiwan's standing to sue and be sued, the choice of law rules, rights and obligations, and ownership of property.

After derecognition, what is Taiwan? Do recognition of the PRC and derecognition of the ROC involve recognition of state or recognition of government? De jure or de facto recognition? What has taken place and what changes have occurred? Although the United States may be constrained from calling Taiwan a government or a state, it continues, for all practical purposes, to treat Taiwan as a de facto government or state with virtually all the attributes characteristic of such entities. Judged by the long-established requirements of statehood, both China and Taiwan — existing as separate states for five decades — fulfill such requirements.

But since the ruling Kuomintang (Nationalist) regime in the past persisted in professing that the ROC represents China and that Taiwan is only part of China (in order to perpetuate and legitimize its authoritarian power structure in Taiwan), it was suggested that "claiming statehood" be added as the fifth requirement of statehood.[12] On July 9, 1999, Taiwan's president, Lee Teng-hui, responded to this claim unequivocally. He stated that the relationship between Taiwan and China is a "special state-to-state relationship." He proclaimed clearly the fact and will of Taiwan as a state, thereby satisfying fully the suggested fifth requirement.

Today, the relationship of the entities across the Taiwan strait is, indeed, a state-to-state relationship. The key question is "effective control" over Taiwan. Militant rhetoric of claim does not constitute a form of effective control. For more than five decades since the founding of the PRC in October 1949, it has not governed or extended effective control over Taiwan for a single day. Taiwan has indeed existed as a country independent of the PRC. Thanks to the common efforts of the Taiwanese people, Taiwan has evolved as a sovereign, independent state. This is a great success story of self-determination. The principle of self-determination is a fundamental principle of international law having the character of jus cogens under the Charter of the United Nations.

When the international legal status of a territory is in dispute, a U.N.-sponsored plebiscite by all its inhabitants would be an ideal means of peaceful resolution. A plebiscite is not the only way of achieving self-determination, however. All the inhabitants of a disputed territory, through a joint effort, can develop their distinct political, economic, social, and cultural system. That is effective self-determination — self-determination in action. As stated above, both international covenants on human rights accord the principle of self-determination a prominent place, stating that "all peoples have the right of self-determination. By virtue of that right they freely determine their political status, and freely pursue their economic, social and cultural development."

After Japan renounced all its sovereignty, rights, and claims over Taiwan (including the Penghu) in 1952 according to the terms of the San Francisco Peace Treaty with Japan, neither the Republic of China nor the PRC was the designated beneficiary of Japan's renunciation. (The Peace Treaty, concluded in 1951, became operative in 1952.) Taiwan's sovereignty belongs to neither the ROC nor the PRC but rests with all the inhabitants of Taiwan. This is the very essence of "popular sovereignty" in the contemporary epoch. The transfer of a territory is not a matter of property transaction; transfer affects the survival, human rights, and welfare of all a territory's inhabitants. Decade after decade, endowed with their inherent sovereignty, the people of Taiwan have worked together day in and day out to control their own political status and to develop their distinct economic, social, and cultural system. Their remarkable achievements in these spheres are testimony to their effective self-determination. Taiwan fulfills all the conditions of statehood under international law.

Taiwan is Taiwan, and China is China and there are stark contrasts between these two separate states. Taiwan's history has been marked by indigenous patterns of political, economic, social, and cultural development stretching back for centuries. Taiwan, in recent years, has undergone a transition to democracy from authoritarian rule under perpetual martial law, holding its first democratic presidential election in 1996 despite Beijing's unlawful attempts to intimidate voters. The Taiwanese people today enjoy human rights and freedoms, as well as a remarkable level of economic growth. China, in contrast, continues to be under the dictatorship of the Chinese Communist Party. It has fallen back upon authoritarian practices to silence political dissent, routinely denying its citizens human rights and freedoms that are taken for granted in Taiwan.

That Taiwan has existed as an independent, sovereign state is a reality. There is no need for Taiwan to make a formal declaration of independence in the manner of the American Declaration of Independence. Yet the continued use of "Republic of China" as the official title of Taiwan has caused a great deal of confusion, both internally and externally. How to make Taiwan a "normal" state both in name and in fact is a continuing concern of the people of Taiwan. As it should be: self-determination is a continuing process of decision and nation-building.

"Recognition" and "derecognition," "official" and "unofficial" relations, de jure or de facto, PRC and ROC, and what have you — it would be quite a nightmare to attempt to dissect this complex picture neatly in terms of a pure theory of recognition. Complex realities, as confounded by conflicting dogmas, do not lend themselves to neat theory. In the long run pragmatism prevails, and old rhetoric continues to flourish. To paraphrase Justice Oliver Wendell Holmes, Jr., the practice of recognition is more a matter of life experience than of pure logic.

The confusion in the theory and practice of recognition stems in no small measure from the highly decentralized and discretionary nature of recognition. Individual, unilateral action, rather than collective action, prevails.

To minimize confusion in the field, international lawyers have made a variety of suggestions: eliminate the practice of recognition; take "politics" out of recognition decisions; define the duty of recognition; prohibit premature recognition; distinguish de jure from de facto recognition, or simply obliterate the distinction; distinguish recognition from establishment of diplomatic relations; limit recognition problems to recognition of states and deal with governmental change in terms of willingness to establish diplomatic relations; substitute collective recognition for individual recognition; focus on the question of "representation" of an entity in transnational arenas of authority instead of the question of recognition of states and governments, and so on. In addition to the traditional criteria for statehood, the U.S. secretary of state, heralding a new policy on the recognition of states in response to the dissolution of Yugoslavia, has indicated as relevant five principles. Recognition is to be granted in accordance with a new state's adherence to the following:

1. Determination of the future of the country peacefully and democratically
2. Respect for all existing borders, both internal and external, with change only through peaceful and consensual means
3. Support for democracy and the rule of law, emphasizing the key role of elections in the democratic process
4. Safeguarding of human rights, based on full respect for the individual and including equal treatment of minorities
5. Respect for international law and obligations, especially adherence to the Helsinki Final Act and the Charter of Paris[13]

The European Community has affirmed that its member states will grant recognition to new states under guidelines resembling those set forth by the secretary of state.[14]

Though the frustrations and considerations behind these thoughtful suggestions are well taken, the problem of recognition, in its varied forms and contexts, is unlikely to disappear, given the continuation of a decentralized and dynamic international system of nation-states. The real-life problems cannot be waved away. The important point is to realize what is at stake in a recognition decision and to seek to enhance the degree of rationality in making recognition decisions — individually and collectively — by taking seriously the legal policies and common interests involved, with specific reference to the demands, expectations, and interests of the aspiring group or community, neighboring communities, and regional and world public order.

3

International Governmental Organizations

International governmental organizations, created by nation-states to promote common purposes through agreement among themselves, serve a dual function in the global constitutive process: they act as distinctive participants in decision making and provide necessary structures of authority for other participants. Because of the increasing complexity and interdependence evident in international relations, such organizations have proliferated even more rapidly than nation-states in recent years, and they manifest varying degrees of comprehensiveness and specialization. They engage in or facilitate the collective performance of many decision functions. They may be concerned generally with all values or specialized to particular values, and they may be global, regional, or local in geographic reach.

Nation-states, to enhance cooperation, have moved from ad hoc, occasional conferences toward establishing permanent, continuous structures of cooperation. Understandably, such cooperative enterprises began on a limited scale with respect to particular subject matters. Many of the organizations that came into being in the nineteenth century, such as the various European river commissions, the International Telegraph Union (1864), and the Universal Postal Union (1874), addressed specific areas of concern. A comprehensive, multipurpose organization, the League of Nations, came into being following World War I. The International Labor Organization was also created during the same period. The league, which continued to be centrally focused on Europe, was less than universal and fell far short of achieving its goals of maintaining world minimum order.

The United Nations, which celebrated its fiftieth anniversary in 1995, has built on the experience of the league and is the most comprehensive general-purpose organization in the world. As the keystone of the contemporary system

of international governmental organizations, it provides the backbone structures of authority for the global constitutive process in order to secure both
minimum and optimum world order. Since its creation, the United Nations has
undergone significant constitutive development, including greatly expanded
membership and activities. The General Assembly has become a worldwide
forum for expressing the intense aspirations for change demanded by both
developed and developing states and has greatly expanded its base of authority.
Similarly, the Security Council has been transformed, through broad conceptions of minimum order, into an agency for the more general application of
policies, and has taken on a greatly expanded role with preventive diplomacy
and increasingly multifunctional operations. The Economic and Social Council, with its expanding concern for economic, social, cultural, and humanitarian
affairs, is carrying forward its formidable work toward creating conditions for
optimum fulfillment of values about the globe. The Trusteeship Council, having
completed its historic mission concerning trust territories, now meets as and
where occasion may require. The International Court of Justice, another major
organ of the United Nations, plays an important judicial role and has experienced an increasingly busy caseload, although it is hampered by a lack of
compulsory jurisdiction. The Secretariat of the United Nations, headed by the
secretary-general, is the permanent executive arm, providing a corps of international civil servants. Revitalization and restructuring of the United Nations
intergovernmental machinery, with, for example, the creation of a deputy
secretary-general, promises to create more dynamic and effective relations
among the major intergovernmental organs and is a crucial component of the
reform process currently under way at the United Nations.

The United Nations is fortified by a network of international governmental
organizations that specialize in particular values or subjects. These functional
organizations play specialized roles in the world arena. Notable examples in-
clude the United Nations Educational, Scientific, and Cultural Organization
(UNESCO); the World Health Organization (WHO); the Food and Agriculture
Organization (FAO); the United Nations International Children's Emergency
Fund (UNICEF); the International Labor Organization (ILO), mentioned above;
the International Bank for Reconstruction and Development (World Bank); the
International Monetary Fund (IMF); the International Telecommunication
Union (ITU); and the Universal Postal Union (UPU).

The cooperation of nation-states occurs not only at the global level but at the
regional level. Interdependence requires that cooperation of nation-states be carried forward at all community levels. The U.N. Charter envisages and encourages the development of regional organizations so that collaborative arrangements can be made to fit particular needs of specific regions. These regional

organizations, dealing with defense, trade, human rights, dispute settlement, and other matters, are highly diverse; and in the post–Cold War era, multilateral regional organizations have been playing an unprecedented role in many fields, forming part of the tension between what have been called the new regionalism and the new globalism.[1] Most operate independently without formal ties to the central organization — the United Nations. Notable among the regional organizations of general scope are the Organization of American States (OAS), the Organization of African Unity (OAU), the complex of European Community organizations, the League of Arab States, the Association of Southeast Asian Nations (ASEAN), and the Commonwealth of Independent States (CIS), made up of former Soviet bloc countries. Each projects a program of broad concern and seeks to employ local initiatives, resources, and potentials to pursue regional cooperation for established goals. The North Atlantic Treaty Organization (NATO) and the now defunct Warsaw Treaty Organization (Warsaw Pact), two rival alliance-type products of the Cold War, once symbolized the postwar East-West conflict, but the collapse of the Soviet Union and subsequent dissolution of the Warsaw Pact have altered the balance of power in Europe. NATO has been transformed into a peacekeeping alliance aimed at combating regional instability and based on mutual cooperation with non-NATO countries, including those of the former Soviet bloc, some of which have even joined NATO. The newly formed Euro-Atlantic Partnership Council allows the former Soviet nuclear power Ukraine to consult with NATO in times of regional crisis, creating a new security council that spans the European continent.[2]

The development of the European Community is particularly noteworthy. Beginning with the European Coal and Steel Community (formed by France, West Germany, Italy, Belgium, the Netherlands, and Luxembourg) and later joined by the European Economic Community and the European Atomic Energy Community, the European Union has come a long way. The community institutions manifest certain distinct features — often characterized as "supranational" — notably the important authority in policy making and execution conferred on commissioners to act on behalf of the community independently of their governments, and the competence of community organs to deal directly with individuals and business enterprises within member states. Although reliance on member governments continues to be heavy, the European Union continues to set timetables for European integration and monetary union, and expanded membership is contemplated as well for the twenty-first century.

Although today it is taken for granted that international governmental organizations, forming an expanding global network, are appropriate "subjects" of international law, this recognition did not come about without a legal battle. For a long time it was widely held that nation-states — and only nation-states —

were the exclusive subjects of international law. The question of the legal status of the League of Nations, though widely discussed, was never judicially determined. The issue of the United Nations's international legal personality was faced squarely by the International Court of Justice in 1949 in the landmark case *Reparations for Injuries Suffered in the Service of the United Nations*.[3] After Count Bernadotte of Wisborg, the United Nations mediator in Palestine, was murdered in 1948, the United Nations, while considering whether to bring a claim against Israel (then not yet a member of the United Nations) for its failure to prevent or punish the murderers, was confronted with the question of whether it was legally competent to file such a claim. The General Assembly directed the following question to the court for an advisory opinion:

> In the event of an agent of the United Nations in the performance of his duties suffering injury in circumstances involving the responsibility of a State, has the United Nations, as an Organization, the capacity to bring an international claim against the responsible *de jure* or *de facto* government with a view to obtaining the reparation due in respect of the damage caused (a) to the United Nations or (b) to the victim or to persons entitled through him?[4]

To answer that question, the court considered it necessary to examine first whether the United Nations possesses an international personality. In words ringing and comprehensive, the court stated:

> The subjects of law in any legal system are not necessarily identical in their nature or in the extent of their rights, and their nature depends upon the needs of the community. Throughout its history, the development of international law has been influenced by the requirements of international life, and the progressive increase in the collective activities of States has already given rise to instances of action upon the international plane by certain entities which are not States. This development culminated in the establishment in June 1945 of an international organization whose purposes and principles are specified in the Charter of the United Nations. But to achieve these ends the attribution of international personality is indispensable.[5]

The court then proceeded to note the wide range of U.N. functions, those it actually performed as well as those authorized by its charter. Stressing that such functions could be explained only in terms of the international personality of the United Nations, the court stated that

> the Organization was intended to exercise and enjoy, and is in fact exercising and enjoying, functions and rights which can only be explained on the basis of the possession of a large measure of international personality and the capacity to operate upon an international plane. It is at present the supreme type of international organization, and it could not carry out the intentions of its founders if it was devoid of international personality. It must be acknowledged that its Members, by

entrusting certain functions to it, with the attendant duties and responsibilities, have clothed it with the competence required to enable those functions to be effectively discharged.

Accordingly, the Court has come to the conclusion that the Organization is an international person.[6]

What does it mean for the United Nations to possess an international personality? It means, in the words of the court, "that it is a subject of international law and capable of possessing international rights and duties, and that it has capacity to maintain its rights by bringing international claims."[7] These international claims can be brought against a nonmember as well as a member of the United Nations.

In this unprecedented opinion, the court also sounded a cautionary note, stating that to say the United Nations is an international person "is not the same thing as saying that it is a State, which it certainly is not, or that its legal personality and rights and duties are the same as those of a State. Still less is it the same thing as saying that it is a 'super-State,' whatever that expression may mean."[8]

With this bold stroke the court made it perfectly clear that states are not the only subjects of international law. Many other international governmental organizations, like the United Nations, with their own objectives, structures, and functions in the world arena, similarly possess international personality and are subjects of international law.

Membership in international governmental organizations is generally open only to nation-states, with further restrictions as may be imposed by the constitutive agreement involved. Membership in the United Nations, for example, is stipulated in Article 4 of the charter:

1. Membership in the United Nations is open to all other peace-loving states which accept the obligations contained in the present Charter and, in the judgments of the Organization, are able and willing to carry out these obligations.
2. The admission of any such state to membership in the United Nations will be effected by a decision of the General Assembly upon the recommendation of the Security Council.

As expounded by International Court of Justice in two of its advisory opinions, a member cannot predicate its consent to the admission of a state on conditions not specified in Article 4(1), and a recommendation for admission by the Security Council must precede a General Assembly decision.[9] This means that admission of a new member is subject to veto by a permanent member of the Security Council.

Obviously, for most international governmental organizations, the most important base of power is formal authority granted by member states to the organization. The formal authority thus granted varies widely from organization to organization in terms of area of concern, the degree of decision-making authority, the scope of people to be affected, and the applicable constitutive instrument. Particular grants of legal capacity and of certain privileges and immunities are especially noteworthy because of their importance in affording proper access and protection and in securing the independent and effective performance of official duties. Such grants again differ from organization to organization and are communicated through constitutive instruments, agreements between organizations and member states, or national legislation.

Article 104 of the United Nations Charter states: "The Organization shall enjoy in the territory of each of its Members such legal capacity as may be necessary for the exercise of its functions and the fulfilment of its purposes." And Article 105 stipulates in part:

1. The Organization shall enjoy in the territory of each of its Members such privileges and immunities as are necessary for the fulfilment of its purpose.
2. Representatives of the Members of the United Nations and officials of the Organization shall similarly enjoy such privileges and immunities as are necessary for the independent exercise of their functions in connection with the Organization.

Note the emphasis on functional necessity as the basis for and extent of privileges and immunities. These privileges and immunities, though often compared to the immunities and privileges customarily enjoyed by national diplomats, are more limited in scope and nature. Understandably, nation-state elites are reluctant to accord the functionaries of international governmental organizations more privileges and immunities than necessary. The Convention on the Privileges and Immunities of the United Nations (1946) reiterates that the United Nations has juridical personality and spells out its legal capacity to contract, to acquire and dispose of property, and to sue.

International governmental organizations increasingly perform many of the functions traditionally discharged through bilateral diplomacy. They also perform many innovative functions generated partly by global interdependence and partly by the wide-ranging goals projected by the world community.

For many organizations the intelligence function is not only an activity but a raison d'etre. In fact, the initial stimulus to form international organizations stemmed from the recognition that, in certain specialized or technical areas, sharing information and knowledge among nations was essential to the growth of the field. Organizations whose formation was motivated by such considerations include the Universal Postal Union and the International Telegraph Union. Information gathering and dissemination is today the principal focus of some international organizations, such as the International Meteorological Organization (IMO). For other organizations it forms an essential part of their prime mission, as exemplified by reports prepared for the U.N. Security Council, which are instrumental in the council's efforts to maintain international peace and security.

The promotion of goals and policies thought to be desirable is a highly visible function of international governmental organizations. The numerous resolutions passed by the U.N. General Assembly, though generally hortatory in nature, have had a clear influence on the conduct of nations. Designating a particular time to study and act on an issue, such as the International Year of the Child, exemplifies another aspect of the promoting function.

The expansion of the prescribing function by international governmental organizations, though not without controversy, has been remarkable. The preeminent role of the General Assembly, as discussed in chapter 22, has been especially striking. Although few have questioned that organizations can prescribe for their own members through internal decision processes, the competence of organizations to conclude agreements with states or other entities has been disputed, a problem reminiscent largely of the lingering myth that states are the only proper subjects of international law. In practice, however, international governmental organizations do enter into various agreements—for example, agreements conferring privileges and immunities on the organization. A keen observer of the work of the U.N. specialized agencies has noted the emerging trends as follows: "While the obsession with the paramount nature of sovereignty still reigns supreme in power politics, the law of Specialized Agencies, in so far as it follows in the wake of scientific and technical progress, has tended to intensify methods of functional co-operation and promote a measure of world integration."[10] This cooperation and integration have been advanced by the acceptance of the doctrine of implied powers expressly granted in their constitutive documents but also those implied from the documents and those developed in practice.

The prescribing function, at least as practiced by the United nations, can extend to nonmember nations. Article 2(6) of the U.N. Charter provides: "The Organization shall ensure that States which are not Members of the United Nations act in accordance with these Principles so far as may be necessary for the maintenance of international peace and security." This deviation from the general principle that only the parties to a treaty are bound by it rests on the special character of the United Nations as the paramount organization endowed with the task of maintaining international peace and security and characterized by virtual universality in membership.

The invoking and applying functions, like the prescribing function, have expanded in scope despite perceived encroachments on "national sovereignty." The sanctions attempted by the United Nations against the old apartheid regime of South Africa on the Namibia question and then more generally with respect to domestic apartheid provide a notable example. Clearly the prescribing function would be an empty exercise if the prescriptions could not be invoked and applied. The expansion in the area of human rights enforcement is a particularly remarkable development. Although some structures, such as the European Commission of Human Rights and the European Court of Human Rights, both of which began operating in the 1950s, have been in place for some time, others are of more recent vintage, such as the adoption of an individual petition system by the United Nations for redress of violations of the International Covenant on Civil and Political Rights. International tribunals for the former Yugoslavia and Rwanda have been established by the U.N. Security Council to prosecute grave violations of the 1949 Geneva Convention and international humanitarian law.[11] The ultimate sanction — expulsion — presents a highly delicate problem, because expelling a state from an international governmental organization for violating its obligations may remove that member from pressures that could lead to fulfillment of those obligations.

The terminating function may operate by various mechanisms. The agreements concluded by international governmental organizations, like those concluded by states, may provide for denunciation or other means of withdrawal from the agreement. Such agreements may also be for a limited period and may expire of their own force if not renewed. The organizations may, by exercise of their internal processes, suspend or expel a noncomplying member. Suspension has generally been used only for nonpayment of dues. Expulsion is rarely used and, as mentioned above, may be counterproductive.

Finally, international governmental organizations are continually appraising their roles and performance and refining their approach. The important role of international governmental organizations as participants in the international legal process has greatly expanded in the past few decades and will likely continue to expand for the foreseeable future. Specialized organizations will become ever more important as scientific, technological, and cultural interdependence increases. The United Nations, given its broad mission of maintaining international peace and security, as well as advancing the welfare of all peoples, continued at its fiftieth anniversary to retain its position as a paramount participant in international law.

The sustained growth of international governmental organizations reflects not merely the increasing vigor of transnational interactions but also the shared perception of participants that many of their preferred values can be obtained only through or in conjunction with collaborative transnational action. In dealing with problems of transnational magnitude and impact, such organizations dilute the importance of historic, somewhat arbitrary and unnatural, national boundaries. They may gradually provide alternatives to the overweening power of nation-state officials and may help open the internal activities of nation-states to external observation. They begin to constitute, in a manner of speaking, an organized conscience of the world and to bring a world public opinion to bear on world affairs. Additionally, the international civil servants who staff such organizations increasingly develop loyalties to the organizations themselves and seek, in various ways, to fortify their viability as instruments of inclusive goals.

Though the proliferation of international governmental organizations has been impressive, the aggregate contribution of such organizations to global decision making has been less so. The resources, independent of state control, made available to such organizations have been far from adequate. The structures of the organizations remain somewhat primitive, lacking proper regional or functional balance. Their technical procedures are largely unsystematized and uneconomical. Too often particular national elites still view such organizations as instruments of their own national policy rather than as instruments to clarify and protect genuine common interests. In theory, international governmental officials (international civil servants) are required to perform their functions independently of outside influence, including that of their home state. But in practice such independence is often compromised. A careful balance among member states is maintained in staffing international governmental organizations; and, under a reward system having to do with the support of the home state, an international official often feels compelled to maintain ties with his home state, giving rise to the problem of multiple or split loyalties.

When the United Nations marked its fortieth anniversary in 1985, contemporary popular perceptions, as summarized by Ambassador Tommy Koh (formerly permanent representative to the U.N. from Singapore), characterized the United Nations as an organization that, though still alive after forty, had failed to maintain world peace and security.[12] The U.N. was perceived as "drowning in a sea of paperwork and suffocating under an avalanche of paper," as an organization of double standards, with the General Assembly seen "less and less as a forum which expresses the decent opinion of mankind."[13] These popular perceptions, though at the time painfully true to a considerable extent, must be contrasted to the United Nations' achievements at fifty.

At its fiftieth anniversary in 1995, massive institutional reform was under way in response to widespread criticism; yet the United Nations since then has enjoyed a dramatic resurgence in popularity. Today the United Nations is seen by many as an institution which, at this stage in history, "provides the most realistic opportunity for developing reasonable rules" in the area of humanitarian intervention and the achievement of a just world order.[14] With the demise of the bipolar world hopes have reemerged for a new world order where the dictates of ideological competition may give way to greater political, social, and economic cooperation. The new world order envisioned is to be built on the twin pillars of international law and international institutions; and a renewed, resurgent United Nations, a dramatic reduction in nuclear and conventional weapons, and an increase in the number of new democracies are presenting new opportunities for enhancing global cooperation.[15]

A widespread lament has always been that the United Nations has fallen far short of the shared expectations of its founders. It has failed, by and large, in its role as preserver of minimum world order. Though World War III has not come to pass thus far, nuclear terror, previously maintained under a precarious system of superpower deterrence, continues as nuclear weapons and technology fall into the hands of unstable, fragmented states. Armed conflicts of lesser magnitudes, many stemming from long-suppressed ethnic, religious, and cultural differences that have emerged with the thawing of the Cold War, and the continuation of oppressive regimes have sustained and heightened expectations of violence. According to varying estimates, sizable interstate armed force was used about two hundred times in the four decades following World War II. Since 1989, there have been nearly one hundred armed conflicts in the world, all but five of which were internal. The helplessness and frustration people have felt in dealing with governmental and private terrorism have generated a pervasive sense of international anarchy and personal insecurity.

The original plan of establishing a standing United Nations force has never come into being. The unity of the major powers in the maintenance of world order, as contemplated by the framers of the U.N. Charter, long proved illusory as the veto power accorded the five permanent members of the Security Council became a tool of obstruction rather than one of big-power cooperation. But the collapse of the Soviet Union, with Russia assuming the former Soviet seat on the Security Council, seemed to have freed the council to intervene in disputes around the globe for a time, and the council was able to become increasingly interventionist in the handling of regional conflicts. Given the fluidity of the post–Cold War order, however, nothing can be taken for granted. The invocation of the inviolability of "national sovereignty" is by no means a thing of the past.[16] Nevertheless, the expansion of peacekeeping missions around the world has transformed the U.N.'s role in global security.

The enhanced authority of the General Assembly to cope with crises of peace and security in the event of the paralysis of the Security Council, as authorized by the Uniting for Peace Resolution, has proved less than effective.[17] The incongruity between voting numbers and effective power, as exacerbated by bloc interests and politics, is such that many of the assembly's numerous resolutions simply cannot, and do not, command serious attention and effective support. (The total contribution of half its members amounts to less than 2 percent of its budget.) The raw, reflexive display of automatic numerical majority, without adequate consideration of the merits of each resolution, has often resulted in double standards and has done much to alienate "the minority" whose effective support (and financial support) really counts. The democratic principle of "one state, one vote," when divorced from the realities of population, wealth, power, and respect and from the principle of responsibility, becomes hollow and self-defeating. For many years, bypassing, rather than turning to, the United Nations in times of crisis was the norm, in contrast to the last decade.

Other shortcomings of the United Nations already alluded to or to be added include the festering issue of split loyalties among international officials and civil servants; an overblown and inefficient bureaucracy; the tendency of the organization to be a paper mill, long on rhetoric and short on action; and the tendency to be "an octopus walking in every direction at once."[18]

And after marking its fiftieth anniversary in 1995, the United Nations has continued to come under criticism. Some, believing it is supposed to be an international superforce, have imagined the United Nations "to be like the Great Oz, a lot of sound and fury but nothing behind the show."[19] In the post–Cold War world, there is a sense that the United Nations is overstretched, in search of missions, and without clear priorities.[20]

Much can be criticized in terms of both the past record and the current shape of the United Nations. But would the world community be better off without it? Definitely not! Its achievements, given the constraints of reality, have been substantial and significant. In the area of maintaining minimum world order, the United Nations has taken on an increasingly important role. The last fifty years have seen an evolution of U.N. peacekeeping, peacemaking, and peacebuilding in what has come to be known as preventive diplomacy. Since 1945, forty-three United Nations peacekeeping operations have been instrumental in preventing the escalation of armed conflicts, terminating hostilities, preventing the recurrence of fighting, and facilitating conflict resolution in areas such as

India and Pakistan, Central America, the Middle East, Haiti, Africa, and, since the breakup of the former Soviet Union, in Eastern and Central Europe. For example, U.N. peacekeepers facilitated the withdrawal of Soviet troops from the Baltics. Between 1988 and 1997 alone thirty peacekeeping forces were created, and there are currently seventeen peacekeeping operations under way in places such as Cyprus, Bosnia-Herzegovina, Georgia, Liberia, southern Lebanon, the Golan Heights, and Tajikistan. In 1988, U.N. peacekeeping forces were awarded the Nobel Peace Prize. As of 1999, there were seventeen peace-keeping operations around the world.

In addition, the United Nations, in pursuit of peaceful resolution of conflicts, continues to undertake various peacemaking efforts, not only in the Security Council and the General Assembly but through the good offices of the secretary-general and his special representatives. Such efforts are currently directed to areas of protracted conflict, including the Middle East, Cyprus, Kampuchea, Iran and Iraq (the Persian Gulf), Afghanistan, central Africa, and Central America. Thanks to the U.N.-mediated Agreement on Afghanistan, signed in Geneva in April 1988, the phased withdrawal of Soviet troops from Afghanistan was completed by February 15, 1989, as scheduled. The eight-year Iran-Iraq war was ended in 1991, with a cease-fire and withdrawal of all troops to internationally recognized boundaries called for by the Security Council. In the Persian Gulf crisis of 1990–1991, the basis for international action in the form of economic sanctions and military action against Iraq lay in Security Council resolutions, rather than in unilateral action. In 1995 the United Nations Protection Force (UNPROFOR) deployed in Bosnia-Herzegovina for aid distribution and the protection of "safe areas" formally transferred power to international NATO-commanded forces who would oversee implementation of the Dayton peace accord, after four years of U.N. supervision in which NATO's first shots ever were fired.

In spite of slow and halting progress, the United Nations has persisted in its original effort toward the elimination and control of weapons of mass destruction and the peaceful use of nuclear energy. With the end of the cold war, slowing the escalation of deadly weaponry has come within reach, with unilateral moratoriums reached on nuclear testing by the United States and the Russian Federation. As of 1995, there were at least fourteen major global and regional arms control and disarmament treaties in place, controlling or prohibiting the production, storage, and use of conventional, nuclear, biological, and chemical weapons. A U.N. task force on arms reduction has found that the "peace dividend" from the end of the Cold War included, by 1995, a decline in global military spending by almost one-quarter since 1987.

Its vital role in the acceleration of decolonization and emancipation is historic. At the end of World War II, more than 750 million people lived in colonial and other dependent territories. Today, all eleven trust territories have either become independent states or have voluntarily chosen to associate with a state. The non-self-governing territories under the jurisdiction of the Special Committee of 24 on Decolonization dwindled to seventeen territories as of 1999.

The United Nations has been the driving force behind the contemporary global human rights movement (see chapter 12). From the development of a global bill of human rights and a host of ancillary instruments to the crusade against apartheid and racial discrimination, the United Nations has been indispensable. It has afforded special protection and assistance to millions and millions of refugees and to countless children around the world. The recent creation of the post of United Nations High Commissioner for Human Rights, as well as current reform proposals for a cabinet-level position dedicated exclusively to human rights matters, promises that the United Nations will continue to provide human beings with relief, refuge, and development far into the twenty-first century.

Its work in the codification and development of international law ranges from the law of treaties and the law of diplomatic relations to the law of the sea and the law of outer space and includes important documentations of customary prescription and clarification of U.N. Charter obligations.

Finally, in its pursuit of optimum world order, the United Nations has also dealt, and at times more effectively, with manifold problems relating to economic, social, humanitarian, and cultural development: trade, monetary systems, environment, population, agriculture and food, hunger, disease, poverty, industry, science and technology, transnational corporations, social development, financial assistance, education, communications and transportation, technical cooperation, and emergency relief.

Accordingly, despite "unfulfilled dreams," the United Nations has filled and continues to fill a vital role in facilitating transnational cooperation. As former secretary-general Javier Pérez de Cuéllar once pointed out, without "the safety net" that the United Nations provides, "the world would certainly be a much more dangerous and disorderly place."[21] And to echo a popular sentiment: If the United nations did not exist today, humankind would have to invent something like it. The dreams of the founders were visionary and inspiring. It is up to each succeeding generation to experience and express contemporary dreams in light of the legacy, a legacy which, fortunately for humankind, has reached century's end and the horizon of the new century. As the Independent Working Group on the Future of the United Nations stated in 1993, the United Nations did not come through its first fifty years unscathed; and "like any good vessel, it needs refitting, weak timbers replaced, compasses reset."[22] The United Nations can only be as effective as its members make it. Fortunately, today those members have an opportunity, made available by sweeping technological, social, and political change, to face the twenty-first century with a new spirit of global cooperation and commitment to the common interest of humankind.

4

Nongovernmental Organizations and Associations

As the world constitutive process of authoritative decision becomes increasingly democratized, the role of nongovernmental groups in transnational interactions has continued to grow enormously. In this chapter nongovernmental groups include, but go beyond, those associated with NGOs, nongovernmental organizations known within the circles of the United Nations and other international governmental organizations. Nongovernmental actors can be conveniently divided into two categories: political parties and nongovernmental organizations and associations (including pressure groups and private associations). Political parties, though often not formally recognized, exert effective influence on many transnational decisions. Pressure groups, which attempt to influence both formal and effective decisions, are increasingly transnational in operation and reach. Multiplying hosts of private associations primarily concerned with values other than power manifest their growing transnational character in membership, objective, structure, activity, and impact.

POLITICAL PARTIES

Political parties are organized groups that present comprehensive programs of policy and seek to place their candidates in government positions through election or otherwise. They play an important part in global processes of effective power and affect the performance of many functions in authoritative decisions.

Political parties make their strongest impact in the organization and management of particular nation-states. Party representatives gain access to the public organs of the nation-state through election, appointment, and integration into executive, legislative, judicial, and administrative institutions at all levels of government. The same person may be a key actor both within a political party and within a state's structures of authority. In addition, political parties often provide unofficial channels for policies to be initiated and communicated.

The way any particular state is shaped by political parties naturally has its external impact. Modern techniques of mass communication and transportation enable political parties to become highly organized, to centralize their command, to coordinate national and international operations, and to participate effectively in power processes, both in and out of government and within and beyond the boundaries of any nation-state. Although international governmental organizations may make no formal provision for access by political parties as such, representatives of parties do gain access through other identifications, especially those of the state. In the transnational parliamentary arenas, such as the Consultative Assembly of the Council of Europe, the participants, being parliamentarians conditioned by domestic party politics, often find themselves torn by the clashes between transnational party groupings and loyalties and national identifications.

Some political parties deliberately seek transnational effects and play roles in intelligence, recommending, prescribing, invoking, and appraising functions, having significant effects on the formulation and application of global policies. In recent decades, four major transnational political party movements — the Communist, Socialist, Christian Democratic, and Liberal internationals — have operated with varying degrees of effectiveness. These transnationals differ significantly in projected goals and platforms, formal structures and official staffs, internal factions, available resources, strategies employed, and overall influence as measured by affiliated groups and external relations.

The greatest threat to shared power in global decision making posed by political parties is that they may degenerate into "political orders," which are characterized by monopoly of power and the claim of exclusive legality. The Communist Internationale once typified such a transnational political order. After the Comintern and Cominform were dismantled in 1943 and the mid-1950s, respectively, the International Department of the Communist Party of the Soviet Union was often regarded as their successor embodiment, until the collapse of the Soviet system left Communism largely discredited across the globe. A lesser threat is that political parties may be so parochial and nationalistic as to have little identification with the range of humanity.

NONGOVERNMENTAL ORGANIZATIONS AND ASSOCIATIONS

A salient trend in contemporary global politics and relations is the phenomenal growth of nongovernmental organizations (NGOs), as contrasted with international governmental organizations (IGOs). Since its creation in 1907, the Union of International Associations at Brussels has maintained a central registry and information service for all international organizations, nongovernmental as well as governmental. Its *Yearbook of International Organizations, 1999/2000* lists a grand total of 50,373 organizations of all types, of which 43,958 (87 percent) are nongovernmental and 6,415 (13 percent) are governmental.[1] The numbers of nongovernmental organizations in the broadest sense are staggering, and the days when NGOs adopted a low profile are gone. The activity of NGOs has become an essential dimension of all levels of public life around the world.

Nongovernmental organizations differ greatly in membership, size, objective, structure, geographical reach, available resources, strategy, and overall effectiveness. They are increasingly transnational in each of these features and play a growing role in transnational decision making, affecting various value sectors. Today NGOs are assuming functions that previously had been considered the responsibility of states, for example, the provision of public services such as education and health; in this process, NGOs have become a larger source of development and relief assistance than even the United Nations.[2] The values pursued by nongovernmental organizations and associations extend to each of the basic values: power, respect, enlightenment, well-being, wealth, skill, affection, and rectitude.

Those that relate to power are exemplified by various groups devoted to peace, disarmament, and national liberation movements. The status of national liberation movements, aimed at establishing authority and control over particular territory, has been controversial under international law. African liberation movements have been accorded observer status and occasionally full membership in many intergovernmental organizations. Pursuant to U.N. resolutions, they have participated in U.N. bodies in the specialized agencies and in international conferences under the aegis of the United Nations. One such movement, the African National Congress, now heads the South African government, brought to power by democratic elections. The Palestine Liberation Organization (PLO), in particular, has achieved a high international profile, achieving special observer status in the United Nations, ties to regional organizations, and recognition by many states, including Israel. In 1994 the PLO assumed authority over the West Bank when Palestinian self-rule was established in portions of the occupied territories by the Oslo peace agreement.

Those that relate to wealth, as exemplified by the International Chamber of Commerce, trade associations, and multinational corporations, establish and maintain a global economy, affecting the production and distribution of goods and services everywhere. Those that relate to enlightenment, as exemplified by the International Press Institute and the International Law Association, gather, process, and disseminate information transnationally. Those that relate to well-being, as exemplified by environmental groups and the International Red Cross, seek to enhance health, safety, and comfort transnationally. Those that relate to skill, as exemplified by labor unions and various professional associations, attempt to maintain professional ties and collaboration transnationally. Those that relate to affection, as based on ethnic, religious, linguistic, kinship, and other ties, seek to establish and maintain congenial relationships, group identifications, and collaboration transnationally.

Those that relate to rectitude, as symbolized by the Roman Catholic Church, the World Council of Churches, the World Jewish Congress, the World Muslim Conference, and other religious organizations, formulate and communicate norms of responsible conduct transnationally. The Roman Catholic Church continues to be the religious organization with the highest degree of cohesion, leadership, and hierarchy. Unique in its internal and external relations, the Vatican maintains a diplomatic corps and possesses a recognized competence to make international agreements, although the legal status of the church remains controversial in the literature. The leader of the church is a recognized international figure who performs important decision functions in the world arena. The incumbent leader, Pope John Paul II, through his numerous pilgrimages to many lands, has become the most traveled, most talkative, and most televised pope in history.

The organizations concerned with respect include human rights organizations, dedicated to the defense and fulfillment of human rights, and honorific societies (for example, the Nobel Foundation) that recognize and bestow honor for preeminent contributions to the common interest. Human rights organizations have proliferated so much that a "human rights industry" has emerged. Among the important human rights organizations are Amnesty International, the International Commission of Jurists, the International League for Human Rights, and the Anti-Slavery Society for the Protection of Human Rights (formerly known as the Anti-Slavery Society). Amnesty International, a winner of the Nobel Peace Prize, seeks to protect both prisoners of conscience and all other prisoners from torture and execution. The International Commission of Jurists is dedicated to fostering the understanding and observance of the rule of law and the legal protection of human rights throughout the world. The International League of Human Rights, one of the oldest human rights NGOs, is concerned with all human rights, taking as its platform the Universal Declaration of Human Rights. The Anti-Slavery Society has long been in the forefront of campaigns to eradicate slavery and slavery-like practices from the earth.

Organizations that seek particular power objectives are sometimes known as pressure groups, whereas those dedicated primarily to shaping and sharing values other than power are referred to as private associations. Pressure groups, unlike political parties, do not present comprehensive political programs and candidates for elective office. The difference between pressure groups and private associations is often a matter of emphasis or degree, because even private associations often seek power outcomes in the sense of influencing decision making (both national and transnational) in areas of special concern.

The influence of pressure groups and private associations on decision making has grown tremendously in recent years. Such organizations circulate the globe and employ all media of communication in pursuit of their power purposes or other values. They can operate with minimal regard for national boundaries, and the communications revolution affords them practically unlimited geographic reach. Many such organizations have acquired consultative status or comparable relations with the United Nations (notably with the Economic and Social Council) or other international governmental organizations (ILO, UNESCO, WHO, FAO, and so on). Indeed, with the phenomenal growth of the NGO sector over the past twenty years, an understanding today of United Nations politics would be incomplete without making an appraisal of the impact of NGOs, responsible for far-reaching changes to the U.N. system. Questions concerning their role in U.N. politics are assuming new importance and complexity.

The importance of nongovernmental organizations is formally recognized by the United Nations Charter. Article 71 of the charter stipulates: "The Economic and Social Council may make suitable arrangements for consultation with nongovernmental organizations which are concerned with matters within its competence. Such arrangements may be made with international organizations and, where appropriate, with national organizations after consultation with the Member of the United Nations concerned." Effective power thus obtains a formal voice in the processes of authoritative decision, enabling nongovernmental organizations to use their expertise to serve the common interest.

The Economic and Social Council has created three categories of consultative status for NGOs. Category I organizations are concerned with most of the activities of the council and have demonstrated capabilities to make marked and sustained contributions toward U.N. objectives. They are closely involved with the economic and social life of the peoples of the areas they represent, and their broad membership represents major segments of population in many countries. Category II organizations are more limited, having special concern and competence in areas of activity covered by the council. The third category, officially designated Roster, refers to other organizations that lack general or special consultative status but, in the views of the council or the U.N. secretary-general, are capable of making occasional contributions to the work of the council or its subsidiary bodies or other U.N. bodies within their competence. The ECOSOC has established an open-ended working group to review the arrangements under which it consults with NGOs. In the near future, the structure of the United Nations may be modified so that ECOSOC is divided into two, an Economic Council and a Social Council, each to function on a daily basis much as the Security Council does today, and each to continue working closely with the NGOs.

The NGOs may send representatives to sit as observers and to speak at public meetings of the Economic and Social Council and its subsidiary bodies. They may submit memorandums concerning the work of the council and its subsidiary bodies and have such memorandums circulated as U.N. documents. They may also consult with the United Nations Secretariat on matters of mutual concern. Category I organizations may even submit proposals for the council's agenda. In 1997 NGOs working on behalf of the environment as well as women's and other human rights groups addressed, for the first time in U.N. history, a special session of the General Assembly on implementation of Agenda 21, the blueprint for sustainable development agreed upon at the 1992 UNCED conference in Rio de Janeiro, popularly known as "Earth Summit."

The nongovernmental organizations and associations exert influence on the whole range of decision functions (intelligence, promoting, prescribing, invoking, applying, terminating, and appraising). They can take stands that state officials are unable or unwilling to take, and they often represent minority interests threatened by the state. They can campaign intensely for their purposes unhampered by overall policy considerations. Some NGOs such as Amnesty International are able to successfully employ a dual strategy, working directly with the U.N. system while maintaining an independence that allows public criticism of U.N. shortcomings and failures.[3]

In terms of the intelligence function, nongovernmental organizations provide a vast global network for gathering, processing, and disseminating information on a wide range of subjects covering every value sector. This is the core function of many. They not only supplement information from governmental sources but often obtain data unavailable from governmental sources. They provide important information concerning the conditions of human rights, political participation, literacy and communications, global environment, health, hunger, or disasters, economic development, developing science and technology, population and family planning, religious conflicts, and so on. In exposing governmental deprivations of human rights, nongovernmental organizations have played a vital role. They have represented their constituencies so well in exposing injustices that in some countries they function as the "ersatz opposition" and have become themselves a target of government repression.[4] Regular reports by Amnesty International on the status of torture in various countries have been instrumental in curbing governmental abuses in the treatment of prisoners of conscience. Information concerning slavery and slavery-like practices, as furnished by the Anti-Slavery Society, has kept alive humanity's continuing campaign to eradicate such practices of human indignity. The global watch to protect and maintain a livable human environment depends in no small measure on the vigilant efforts of various environmental groups.

It is no secret that most nongovernmental organizations and associations are specialized in making recommendations and advocating policy alternatives, including intense efforts toward securing enactment of prescriptions. Thanks to modern means of communication and transportation, NGOs have developed a vast network of contacts around the globe. Aside from access to governmental officials on a personal or small-group basis, they rely increasingly on the media of mass communication, appealing directly to the world's people. By mobilizing world public opinion they have achieved notable successes in such fields as human rights, environmental protection, economic development, peace movement, and armament control.

Although the formal prescribing function is generally within the domain of governmental officials, NGOs have occasionally played a direct role in the prescribing process, going well beyond that of promotion. The role played by the International Committee of the Red Cross (ICRC) in adopting the protocols additional to the Geneva Conventions (1949) is well known in international legal circles. The two additional protocols, enhancing the protection of victims of international armed conflicts (Protocol I) and of noninternational armed conflicts (Protocol II), were adopted at the Diplomatic Conference on the Reaffirmation and Development of International Humanitarian Law Applicable in Armed Conflicts. The ICRC was the driving force in the preparatory work leading to the adoption of the two additional protocols, in response to the changing needs of the world community. Before the diplomatic conference, the ICRC organized several consultative meetings of experts to study the 1949 Geneva Conventions, making and scrutinizing proposals until the additional protocols could be drafted for adoption at the diplomatic convention.

Less well known is the special role played by the Carnegie Endowment for International Peace in securing the adoption of the Protocol Relating to the Status of Refugees (1967), which expands the scope of the applicability of the Convention Relating to the Status of Refugees (1951) and enlarges the function of the Office of United Nations High Commissioner for Refugees. By removing the temporal restriction — refugees "as a result of events occurring before 1 January 1951," as in the convention of 1951 — the protocol extends the substantive protection of the convention from refugees caused primarily by World War II and by the incipient cold war, as originally contemplated, to refugees world-wide who had otherwise been left unprotected. The Carnegie Endowment, approached by the U.N. High Commissioner for Refugees, sponsored a meeting of legal experts (both scholars and governmental officials) to recommend alternatives for liberalizing the convention of 1951 in order to deal with the growing worldwide problem of refugees in the 1960s.[5] That colloquium's recommendation that the dateline of 1951 be removed by means of a protocol to the existing convention led in December 1966 to the U.N. General Assembly's adoption of the protocol, which entered into force on October 4, 1967. The protocol of 1967 is often called the Bellagio Protocol. More recently, NGOs played a significant role in drafting the Convention on the Rights of the Child and have assumed key functions in its implementation and monitoring.

The invoking function normally involves provisional characterization of certain conduct or events in terms of conformity with or deviation from existing community prescriptions. In the U.N. General Assembly, although formal invocation in the sense of placing a matter on the provisional agenda is restricted to member states, an NGO may do so indirectly by finding an acquiescent member delegation. Provisional characterization of a particular conduct or event as a deviation from community prescription often precedes the formal process of authoritative application. Access to such formal decisional arenas is still limited, but nongovernmental organizations are increasingly playing an important role in international litigation. Most of the major transnational structures for the implementation of human rights (for example, U.N. Human Rights Commission, the European Commission on Human Rights, and the Inter-American Commission on Human Rights) permit NGOs to be petitioners directly or to represent individual victims (see chapters 7 and 23). Not to be ignored, however, is the role of nongovernmental organizations in informal invocation, which does not take the form of a particular legal complaint addressed to a particular tribunal. Nongovernmental organizations often find informal invocation highly useful in curbing governmental abuses or lawlessness to publicize specific violations of international norms by particular governments, especially in such fields as human rights and environmental protection.

In terms of application, some nongovernmental organizations play an extremely important role in securing compliance with certain prescribed norms. The International Committee of the Red Cross, a major component of the International Red Cross, for example, plays a unique role in international humanitarian law. As an independent humanitarian institution, the ICRC serves as a neutral intermediary in cases of armed conflicts and disturbances. It is entrusted with the task of protecting and assisting the victims of wars both international and internal under the Geneva Conventions and Protocols for the protection of war victims.

In the field of transnational air transport, the International Federation of Airline Pilots' Association (IFALPA), which consists of national associations of pilots in about fifty countries, plays an important role in combating aerial hijacking. It has contributed to effective application of the antihijacking prescriptions through boycotting all air traffic to states unwilling to take effective antihijacking measures. It has also played a part in the safety regulations for transnational air transport developed and maintained by the International Civil Aviation Organization (ICAO). When ICAO reduced the permissible distance between airborne planes from 120 to 90 miles, IFALPA protested and threatened to strike, and the rule was rescinded.

The terminating function, in putting an end to the authority of existing prescriptions, is the other side of the same coin. Any new prescription involves modifying or terminating existing expectations of authority. Nongovernmental actors thus play as important a role in termination as in prescription. Given accelerating change in our time and the characteristic inertia of governmental officials and bureaucrats, initiatives to modify or terminate outmoded prescriptions often come from nongovernmental organizations and associations.

The appraising function, which is designed to assess successes and failures in terms of projected goals and policies, is highly democratic and open to all participants. Nongovernmental organizations can play an especially important role in this function, since official actors tend to be immersed in their own pressing business, moving from crisis to crisis or simply from daily routine to daily routine. The functioning of world constitutive process and the overall quality of world public order can be greatly improved by mobilizing the creativity, expertise, skills, and resources of nongovernmental organizations and associations that specialize in various fields.

Multinational corporations play an increasingly important role in contemporary transnational interactions. Because they are profit-oriented, multinational corporations are commonly treated as distinct from NGOs in general. Multinational corporations are corporations and associations that operate transnationally in finance, transportation, communication, mining, fishing, agriculture, manufacturing, wholesaling, retailing, and other areas of economic life. They apply modern technologies to activities ranging from production and marketing to finance and management. Multinational corporations have grown in number, size, activities, and importance thanks to technological developments, new management techniques, and transnational networks of communication and transportation. Because they operate across many state boundaries, they serve as a global vehicle to transfer and disseminate capital, skill, and technology. Transnational trade policy is largely formulated, directly or indirectly, by participants in international wealth processes. The larger transnational corporations negotiate directly with nation-state representatives in a new form of diplomacy: agreements with these corporate giants may surpass treaties between states in terms of values affected and the prescribing effect engendered. They have contributed greatly to the internationalization of production, finance, and ownership and to the growing integration of national economies into a world economy. According to UNCTAD, today the world economy is more integrated than at any other time in history, and multinationals and foreign direct investment are leading the globalization of trade and finance that is now reshaping business and labor markets around the world.[6]

Because they may possess more resources than most nation-states, multinational corporations have sometimes been seen as threats to nation-states. Their impact on the shaping and sharing of values, both actual and potential, has provoked increasing alarm. Profit-oriented by nature, multinational corporations have come to be perceived variously as exploiters of the labor and physical resources of the developing countries, environmental polluters, manipulators of currencies and commodities, tax dodgers, users of corrupt business practices, supporters of reactionary regimes, corrupters of the democratic process, and instruments of their national governments. They have recently gained particular notoriety due to the exposure of the widespread business practice of bribery — corrupting and conspiring with power elites to the detriment of democratic values and the masses of the population. A growing body of evidence shows that the globalization of free markets currently in favor among most governments is producing devastating results in some parts of the world, ranging from community social collapse to increasing gaps between rich and poor as two-thirds of the world's people are marginalized by globalization trends.[7]

Though they are labeled multinational, transnational, or international, multinational corporations owe their creation to national laws. Their success in operation, however, depends greatly on the transnational recognition of such national laws. Typically, a multinational corporation is incorporated under the domestic law of a nation-state, acquiring nationality of the state of incorporation. Yet as their operations expand in geographical reach and in magnitude of impact and grow in complexity, it has become increasingly apparent that conflicting national laws are inadequate to deal with manifold problems having to do with multinational corporations. Some commentators have expressed the belief that in the post–Cold War era, multinational corporations are more powerful actors than governments, and that they even behave imperially.[8] Thus, although multinational corporations have become effective actors in the global processes of wealth, power, skill, and enlightenment, they have also become the target of special concern and international regulation. The United Nations has become a center for such undertaking.

In 1972 the Economic and Social Council called together a group of eminent experts to study the role and impact of transnational corporations and to recommend measures toward international accountability, and as a follow-up in 1974 two permanent bodies were established to deal with the problems of multinational corporations. After reorganization only one body, the U.N. Commission on Transnational Corporations, remains, now called the Commission on International Investment and Transnational Corporations. The locus of U.N. activities concerning international investment has shifted to the Department of Economic and Social Development in the Secretariat. (The commission was retained largely because developing countries, wary of the influence of multinationals, insisted on continuing U.N. oversight.) The commission has given special attention to ways to halt corrupt practices involving multinational corporations, making it a top priority to develop a code of conduct for the activities of transnational corporations. This was an arduous task that finally collapsed under ECOSOC auspices but still continues in interstate discussions in bilateral, regional, and plurilateral settings. Whereas some states have undertaken exclusive, unilateral programs of investment liberalization, others have demonstrated a greater readiness to join in more inclusive, plurilateral agreements about the rules of the foreign investment game.[9]

The role of multinational corporations has persisted as an issue in many fora, both inside and outside the United Nations. For example, during the apartheid regime, the role of American-based multinational corporations in South Africa sparked considerable debate and other forms of provocation in many arenas. The United States responded with various governmental attempts at limiting the apparent widespread criticism of American investments there. Many American companies asserted that their presence in South Africa would help promote change and weaken the effects of apartheid by employing workers from all socioeconomic and racial groups within the country in accordance with the Sullivan principles of promoting equality (see chapter 18).

It is certain that disinvestment in apartheid South Africa by foreign companies resulted in a major outflow of capital, and today the new democratic South African government appeals for long-term foreign investment in its economy as South Africa struggles with the issues of privatization in rebuilding its economy and rejoining the community of nations. It cannot be overemphasized that in a global economy of ever-increasing interdependence, the common interest would require that a code of conduct and related measures not contain provisions so inimical to the interests of transnational enterprises as to cause their general withdrawal from the developing countries.

Private associations, whether concerned with wealth or with other values, characteristically seek and attain effects on transnational decision making. Their efforts bear directly both on the constitutive process, in the making and application of law, and on all the features of effective power and public order that sustain the constitutive process. The wealth, enlightenment, skill, well-being, and so on that they control afford them important bases in effective power. By furnishing many of the structures of interaction through which global society is established and maintained, they affect the production and distribution of all public order values, with consequent effects on the quality and direction of the constitutive process. The danger from private associations, like that from pressure groups, is that they may use their resources in ways incompatible with genuine, long-term common interest because of their preoccupation with one value or a narrow range of values and their limited identifications. Some are interested in long-term effects, but others seem interested in maximizing short-term outcomes for their own interest.

5

The Individual

Individual human beings, acting through all the group and institutional forms already mentioned, communicate and collaborate continuously in every phase of effective and authoritative decision as well as in the shaping and sharing of all values. Individuals may act in the name of, or as representatives of, organizations and associations, or they may act simply in their own right as individuals. Whatever their multiple identifications, individuals are the ultimate actors in all social processes. In addition to their common roles in effective power, individuals increasingly are achieving recognized roles in the processes of authoritative decision and review.

One of the dominant historical myths in international law (especially in the latter nineteenth and early twentieth centuries) had been that states, not individuals or their other associations (or even nations), are the only appropriate "subjects" of international law. Under this exaggerated and unrealistic expectation of the nation-state as the exclusive subject of international law, as buttressed by the inordinate emphasis on positivism and state sovereignty, there had been a tremendous reluctance to recognize other participants in world social process as active subjects of international law. Even international governmental organizations were once denied acceptance as subjects of international law; their role was obscured and their legal personality questioned. The role of nongovernmental participants — political parties, pressure groups, and private associations — was regarded as a matter of sociology rather than law. Individuals often were regarded as objects, not subjects, of international law. As "objects" of international law, individuals were for all practical purposes treated in the same breath as territory, resources, treaties, and so on.

Under the positivist doctrine of subject-object dichotomy, the individual was not deemed the bearer of rights or duties in international law. Under such a myth, an individual enjoys benefits and bears burdens under international law *not directly* but only indirectly, as bestowed by the nation-state. Any direct contact between the individual and international law is viewed as an exception, an aberration. An individual has no direct access to transnational tribunals for remedies and can secure transnational protection only through a nation-state protector. Thus Emmeric de Vattel's famous dictum that an injury to an individual is an injury to the state of which he or she is a member. This fiction is closely linked to the concept and requirement of nationality and makes the security and fulfillment of the individual dependent on the willingness of the state to protect him or her (see chapter 12). Only the state of nationality is permitted to espouse claims of deprived individuals at the international level against other states. Because a state's competence to protect its nationals is regarded as independent of the interests of the individual concerned, the state has the discretion to decide whether to espouse claims on behalf of its nationals.

The positivist-oriented notion that states are the only proper subjects of international law is belied by all the contemporary facts about participation in the global processes of effective power and authoritative decision as well as the existence of private rights and duties. This notion, unknown to international law's founding fathers and deriving from certain parochial misconceptions of the late nineteenth century, lingers because it may expediently serve the power purposes of state elites, especially those who govern without authority. One significant factor in contemporary effective power is that many state elites will not tolerate their nationals complaining to other state elites or the larger community of humankind about the deprivations within their particular communities.

However clever the Vattelian fiction might have been, the fact remains that the individual is the ultimate beneficiary even of the remedy of diplomatic protection. State responsibility is incurred for failure to comply with the international standard for the treatment of aliens. The international standard protecting aliens (meaning potentially all human beings) and state responsibility for injuries to aliens constitute a vital part of customary international law, not an exception or aberration. The proscriptions of piracy, war crimes, breaches of neutrality, violence against ambassadors, and the slave trade, for example, were clearly directed to the individual. Even before the era of the United Nations, individuals were permitted a certain degree of access to transnational arenas of authority, such as the right of petition under the Mandates system (established by the League of Nations to administer the former colonial territories of Germany and Turkey toward the ultimate goal of self-government), the Central American Court, and the regime for the protection of minorities. Additionally, in many domestic settings, individuals had access to domestic courts and other decisional fora for presentation of claims based on international law, especially in the United States.

A major development after World War II was of course the trials of Nazi war criminals. The Charter of the International Military Tribunal at Nuremberg held individual persons responsible for crimes against peace, war crimes, and crimes against humanity. At the IMTs at Nuremberg and Tokyo and in subsequent proceedings, thousands of individuals were tried and convicted, and many were executed. These trials clearly imposed direct personal responsibility on individuals and dismissed the defenses of superior orders and of obedience to state law. "Crimes against international law," in the words of the International Tribunal, "are committed by men, not by abstract entities, and only by punishing individuals who commit such crimes can the provisions of international law be enforced." [1]

As international law expanded its concern from abstract entities of nations and states to real-life human beings, it ushered in a new era of human rights, underscoring the central place of human beings in transnational interaction and the fundamental dignity and worth of all human beings. The atrocities of the Third Reich not only led to the Nuremberg trials but also brought home the vivid message that human rights and peace are indivisible. Massive deprivations of human rights, if unchecked, would not only devastate individuals and groups concerned but would also threaten international peace and security. Thus, the U.N. Charter recognized the precept of human dignity, enunciated the protection of human rights as a major goal of the organization, and recognized human rights obligations for member states. The Security Council today has continued to use its authority under the charter to protect the rights of individuals, creating special international tribunals to bring rights violators to trial for war crimes, genocide, and crimes against humanity.

Thanks to the contemporary human rights movement, a global bill of human rights (see chapter 12) has emerged and is developing. The changes from the positivist orientation of the late nineteenth and early twentieth centuries have been noteworthy. Human rights are no longer matters of domestic jurisdiction but are of international concern. Global concern for human welfare has extended from alien rights in particular to human rights in general. International law has expanded its scope of concern for the protection of all human beings — protecting them against mistreatment not only by foreign governments but also by their own governments. The international law of human rights protects all human beings, regardless of nationality.

The intense demands of the peoples of the world for all human dignity values have been incorporated into the corpus of international human rights law. Through the adoption of the Universal Declaration of Human Rights in 1948, the entry into force of the International Covenant on Civil and Political Rights and its first optional protocol and of the International Covenant on Economic, Social, and Cultural Rights in 1976, and the workings of customary law, a comprehensive global bill of human rights is developing. This global bill of rights, which originated with the U.N. Charter and has been sustained by a multiplying host of specific human rights conventions (both global and regional), additional protocols, authoritative decisions, and expressions, represents a tremendous collective effort. It is assuming the attributes of customary international law, and several more specific rights have already obtained such a status. The human rights prescriptions, expressing the widely shared and intensely held demands and expectations of humankind, are made extremely difficult to modify or terminate.

Transnational structures of authority and procedures for application have been established and maintained to supplement long-standing domestic procedures and to secure greater compliance with the high legal standards set forth in the global bill of human rights. More important, individuals and private groups are given increased, though still limited, access to arenas of transnational authority to bring complaints about human rights deprivations against even their own governments. The capacity of individuals and private groups to invoke human rights prescriptions before appropriate transnational decision makers is so enhanced that the subject-object theory cannot explain or wish it away. Indeed, a state-centered international law is being transformed into an international law of homocentricity.

The subject-object dichotomy would appear highly superficial and confusing; even its proponents have tremendous difficulty in agreeing to what is meant by a "subject" of law. The intellectual confusion and unreality of the subject-object theory stem largely from its positivist roots of rule orientation, conceiving international law as a body of rigid, autonomous rules capable of automatic problem-solving without human choice. The inadequacies associated with the rule-oriented approach were pointed out in chapter 1. Students of international law must emancipate themselves from the trap of the subject-object dichotomy.

Viewed comprehensively and realistically, international law is a continuing process of decision and review aimed at identifying, clarifying, and securing the common interest of the members of the world community. It is a process in which various participants (actors) play various roles in making and applying international law and the related decision functions, granting the continuing dominance of nation-states in the whole process. The meaningful inquiry concerns not what persons are technically subjects and objects for a body of static rules but who actually participates in the global process of decision making and who performs what functions.

In playing varying roles in this process, different participants — states, non-state actors, and individuals — make different claims for protection. Understandably, nation-states are interested in making such claims as comprehensive and continuous control over territory, resources, international agreements, and employment of other instruments of policy; yet individuals are particularly concerned with access to particular territorial communities and with protection and enjoyment of various human rights. Although nation-states continue to play the most prominent role in the prescribing (and terminating) and applying functions, individuals and private groups play important roles in regard to other decision functions: intelligence, promotion, invocation, and appraisal. Further, as noted above, individuals (whether in the name of the state, as private groups, or on their own) are realistically the ultimate participants.

The decision functions in which individuals as individuals have long played a significant part transnationally include the intelligence, promoting, and appraising functions. Under the concept of "custom" that creates law through widely congruent patterns of people's behavior and other communications, individuals and their private associations have always participated in the prescribing function. To invoke the authoritative application of transnational prescriptions, individuals have had and continue to have access to national courts; they are increasingly afforded access to transnational arenas of authority, notably in the field of human rights protection.

Although the dominant role of the nation-state at the international level remains a contemporary reality, it is worth noting that the "omnipotent" nation-state is but one of many structures or processes that individuals develop to protect and fulfill their interests. The nation-state is a human institution that does not realistically exist apart from individuals who enjoy the sharing of values or who are relatively oppressed. Nothing inherent in international law would preclude individuals or nonstate entities from playing recognizably greater roles in the global process of decision making. In fact, they play such roles whether they or we perceive such a fact and whether such a role is merely one of deference.

Originally designed to shield individuals from the tyranny, exploitation, and anarchy of feudalism, the nation-state has generally been assumed to be the structure most appropriate for achieving a more fulfilling life for all. Like all other human institutions, when the nation-state fails to serve such common interest, its traditional role is subject to critical scrutiny in the light of other competing institutions. In the face of both the ever-growing pressures of global interdependencies that defy artificial and arbitrary national boundaries and the growing perception of these interdependencies, the contemporary state system can be expected to be under increasingly severe challenge.

The alternatives in world constitutive process of authoritative decision open to individuals who aspire toward a world community of human dignity need not be misconceived. The choice open to humankind is not one of simple dichotomy: either a world controlled solely by sovereign nation-states or a world government that supplants all existing nation-states. Our world is one of pluralism and diversity, a global arena in which various participants — groups (territorial and functional, governmental and nongovernmental) and individuals — constantly interact under changing conditions. All group participants — nation-states, international governmental organizations, political parties, pressure groups, and private associations — are forms of associations through which individuals cooperate to fulfill their demands. In the final analysis, these group forms are highly malleable instruments created and maintained by people to clarify and secure their common interest. They offer an almost infinite spectrum of potentiality for arranging and rearranging functional and geographic structures and practices toward this end.

PART THREE

PERSPECTIVES

6

Minimum Order and Optimum Order

The perspectives of the effective elites of the world, which infuse the global processes of authoritative and controlling decision, can be described in terms of demands, identifications, and expectations and the contending systems of public order projected.

The basic policy objectives for which the effective elites of the world maintain the global constitutive process of authoritative decision are to promote the common interests of all peoples and to reject all claims of special interest. In the most comprehensive sense, the function of law in any community is to maintain a uniformity in decision in clarifying and securing common interest and to minimize decisions that are made without regard to the consequences for others. The common interests that are sought to be protected fall into two broad categories: inclusive interests and exclusive interests. By *inclusive interests* is meant demands and expectations about activities that have a high degree of collective impact, having important consequences across community lines on a transnational or global scale. By *exclusive interests* is meant demands and expectations about activities whose effect extends primarily to the peoples of a single territorial community.

From a global perspective, the inclusive interests of the peoples of the world include, first, maintaining minimum order in the sense of minimizing unauthorized violence and other coercion. The provisions of the United Nations Charter vividly reflect the aspirations and general expectations of the peoples of the world regarding this fundamental interest. It is the one interest indispensable to any community governed by law. Arbitrary decision by coercion is inimical to our very concept of law as uniformity of decision in accord with community expectation. Beyond minimum order, however, the peoples of the world have more extensive interests in what may be called optimum order, in the sense of the greatest production and widest distribution of all demanded values that can be attained with available resources.

The establishment of the United Nations ushered in a new era, projecting eloquently the fundamental goals — minimum order and optimum order — for the general community of humankind. The United Nations, like its predecessor, the League of Nations, seeks to maintain world minimum public order (peace and security) as a primary goal. From the Westphalian concept that tolerated and condoned the use of force as an instrument of change, through the Hague Conferences, the League of Nations, and the Kellogg-Briand Pact, there developed an ever more insistent demand for outlawing the use of force save for purposes of self-preservation and collective enforcement action. This demand was crystallized and incorporated in the U.N. Charter. The charter provisions, including Article 2(4) and other ancillary provisions, have contributed immensely to the clarification, if not consistent implementation, of this most intense demand for minimum order. It is widely recognized today that the most important purpose for which the global constitutive process of authoritative decision is established and maintained is that of achieving a basic public order both by minimizing unauthorized coercion and by protecting the expectations created by agreement and customary behavior. This reflects a shared perception that only when minimum public order is secured can optimum public order (in the sense of the greatest production and widest possible sharing of all values) be seriously pursued and attained.

But there is a corresponding recognition that, in a world community of growing interdependence, minimum order cannot be securely established and maintained without the supporting conditions of a viable optimum order, enabling a greater production and wider distribution of all values under conditions of security. Minimum and optimum order constantly interact: they affect and reinforce each other.

Again, the goal of optimum order has found eloquent expression in authoritative prescription, reflecting the rising common demands of the peoples of the world for a greater production and a wider sharing of all basic values: respect, power, enlightenment, well-being, wealth, skill, affection, and rectitude. These rising common demands for enhancement of the quality of life in every value sector are the demands for human rights in the most comprehensive and dynamic sense.

Beginning with the U.N. Charter, extending through the Universal Declaration of Human Rights, to the international covenants on human rights and a host of more specialized conventions and ancillary expressions about human rights, a growing body of prescriptions makes comprehensive and detailed reference to the same basic values embodied in the bills of rights of the more mature nation-states and expressed in other forms for centuries past. The U.N. Charter, in its preamble, reaffirms "faith in fundamental human rights, in the dignity and worth of the human person, in the equal rights of men and women" and pledges to "promote social progress and better standards of life in larger freedom" and to "employ international machinery for the promotion of the economic and social advancement of all peoples." Proclaiming the protection of human rights as a major goal, the charter, in Article 55, emphasizes that "universal respect for, and observance of, human rights and fundamental freedoms" is indispensable to "the creation of conditions of stability and well-being which are necessary for peaceful and friendly relations among states." The Universal Declaration of Human Rights, regarded at its adoption in 1948 merely as "a common standard of achievement" without authoritative effect, has become widely accepted as a customary international law binding on all nation-states and also as an authoritative standard for interpreting human rights guaranteed under the U.N. Charter. The International Covenant on Civil and Political Rights (and its optional protocols) and the International Covenant on Economic, Social, and Cultural Rights, providing further treaty-based protections, have been in effect since 1976. Together these three are widely regarded as an international bill of human rights. The demands for human dignity values, as prescribed in this international bill of human rights, find further specifications in the host of specialized human rights conventions and other ancillary expressions that seek to protect a particular category of individuals, deal with a particular value, or apply to a particular region.

Viewed from the historical evolution of international law, this twentieth-century movement for the transnational protection of human rights is remarkable, although the domestic protection of human rights has had a long, rich history that has too often gone unnoticed by international scholars. Centered on national elites, international law was long preoccupied with the interrelations of states as entities. When human rights problems were conceded to fall within the legal domain, they were often treated as matters of "domestic jurisdiction" of particular states. It was commonly assumed in the late nineteenth and early twentieth centuries that how a state treated its own nationals was beyond the realm of international law, precluding interference by other states.

The identifications of the effective elites that establish and maintain the global constitutive process, like those of the general population, remain multiple and ambivalent, manifesting tendencies toward both expansion and contraction. In a world in which social process is characterized by increasing perceptions of comprehensive interdependencies as well as rising demands for self-determination and autonomy among different groups, it can be expected that the identifications of effective and authoritative decision makers will waver between a rational concern for all humanity and less constructive parochial concerns. The best promise of the future is that a deepening understanding of the conditions of both minimum order and optimum order will facilitate a better balance between inclusive and exclusive identifications and interests.

One manifestation of the trend toward inclusive identification is the increasing reference to the term *mankind* in legal instruments (*humankind* would be more up-to-date). Examples abound: the U.N. Charter refers in its preamble to wars as the "scourge of mankind"; the Nuclear Nonproliferation Treaty admonishes the "devastation that would be visited upon all mankind by a nuclear war"; the Antarctic Treaty seeks to protect the "interests of science and mankind"; the Outer Space Treaty declares outer space to be the "province of mankind" and astronauts to be the "envoys of mankind." The concept of the "common heritage of mankind," as made popular by Ambassador Arvid Pardo of Malta, spotlights this growing inclusive identification with humanity. This concept has been expressed in the U.N. Convention on the Law of the Sea and in the Moon Treaty, respectively making the ocean floor and its resources beyond the limits of national jurisdiction and the natural resources of the moon and other celestial bodies the "common heritage of mankind."

The expectations of peoples that affect constitutive process would appear, under the universalizing influence of science and technology, to include an increasingly common and realistic map of world social process. Expectations have often been unrealistic in the past, when modes of communication were few, education was poor, and interchanges across national boundaries were rare. Whatever the facts of interdependence, they were not always perceived realistically. Thanks to increasing communication and literacy and wider use of science and technology, peoples everywhere are acquiring far more comprehensive, realistic maps of the world. Expectations about manifold events in world affairs are on the whole becoming more contextual and rational. Although expectations of violence and of continuing deprivations and nonfulfillments in a world of real and perceived scarcity are still widely shared, there is a growing recognition of the conditions of interdependence under which individuals and groups can fulfill their demands for values.

The end of the Cold War and the transformation of the international system have brought radical changes in conceptions of national authority.[1] International human rights programs have supplanted the older absolute notions. The increasing perception by peoples of a global interdependence has greatly contributed to fostering a more realistic recognition that a paramount goal of global constitutive process must be that of protecting the common interests of peoples while rejecting all claims of special interest.

The contemporary world is still marked by division. Though the East-West ideological confrontation has come to an end, it has been eclipsed by North-South economic division, as the developed and developing worlds differ on a growing number of issues, especially regarding the global economy and the global environment. Basic ideological differences in political, social, and economic systems once led to manifested differences in the types of public order systems demanded and projected, both domestically and transnationally, but these demands are changing, and even converging, in the post–Cold War, post-Communism world, as peoples around the globe seek the market economy and as the number of democracies increases.[2] Universality remains yet a vision, however. Division and interdependence have persisted as realities that cannot be ignored.

In their classic article "The Identification and Appraisal of Diverse Systems of Public Order," McDougal and Lasswell point out that there is at present no comprehensive universal legal order with a consensus about goals on the global scale.[3] The world is characterized by "diverse systems of public order," and thus to speak of "universal international law" is to indulge in make-believe. Many who wish to see such a universal international legal order speak as though it were already a reality. In so doing, they draw attention away from "the vital issues on which the diverse systems of public order that now dominate the world scene are *not* united." A major detrimental result of indulging in "make-believe universalism" is that it tends to undercut the norms of international law that do enjoy a general consensus and are generally effective in bringing about a degree of world public order. It is more appropriate in today's world "to speak of international *laws* or multinational law, than of international law."[4] McDougal and Lasswell conclude by stressing that only by keeping these vital divisions out in the open can progress be made toward a more comprehensive legal order.

Until the collapse of the Soviet Union, two rival views of international law posed an enormous challenge to humankind, in search of the common interest in the earth-space arena of the nuclear age. While the Western perspective stressed both customary law and treaty law, the communist (socialist) perspective emphasized the law of agreement (tacit or express).

The Western perspective, with long customary roots, is basically the outgrowth of three centuries of relations among the major Western European nations. Although the principle of *pacta sunt servanda* in the realm of international agreements has been called the heart of international law, custom has brought about the lion's share of law governing international relations in the West. It has been noted that in recent decades international law has been drifting more and more toward a treaty basis; yet customary law remains vigorous in governing transnational interactions, and the realistic process of treaty law functions in a manner not unlike the dynamic process of customary law, based as they are on patterns of expectation and behavior through time.

In contrast, the communist (socialist) perspective, as led by the now-defunct Soviet Union, adopted a nineteenth-century positivist orientation that minimized the significance of customary international law, emphasizing instead the value of international agreements. In 1917, the Soviet Union entered the "world stage" perceiving itself as a radically new phenomenon and refusing to accept customary international law as binding. It reasoned that customary law had arisen in the precommunist era and represented a public order of which the USSR was not a part. The Soviet Union showed a tendency to choose from among principles of customary law, and even in the realm of treaty law played fast and loose with traditional law by asserting that the cardinal principle of *pacta sunt servanda* was qualified by an exception for "unequal treaties."

Above all, the Soviet Union advocated the principles of peaceful coexistence as the paramount guide of contemporary international law, at least with respect to international law between so-called socialist and nonsocialist states. Discounting variations in different versions of formulation, the core principles of peaceful coexistence (among socialist and nonsocialist states), as originally enunciated, were five: mutual respect for sovereignty and territorial integrity; mutual nonaggression; nonintervention in internal affairs; equality and mutual benefits; and peaceful coexistence.[5] The principles of peaceful coexistence, originating in the Panch Shila principles, adopted by China and India in 1954, found various expressions in Soviet foreign policy statements and legal writings.

The West was hesitant to accept these principles at face value. A major cause of Western distrust of peaceful coexistence was the original communist doctrine of the inevitability of war between the communist and capitalist worlds and the doctrine of wars of national liberation. Although this inevitability theory had to be revised in light of the nuclear threat of mutual annihilation, its theme of continuing class struggle remained unabated. Most important, the Soviet government did not appear to practice what it preached, as witnessed in its treatment of the Balkan states, especially its military suppression of the internal changes in Hungary and in (former) Czechoslovakia. Its standard answer was that the principles of peaceful coexistence were applicable only to the relations between communist and capitalist states, and did not extend to the "fraternal" relations between socialist states.

Such a double standard was of course incompatible with the goal of securing a world public order of human dignity. Furthermore, on close examination, none of the first four core principles of peaceful coexistence were really new as international norms; all had been incorporated earlier in the U.N. Charter. Only the fifth, proclaiming "peaceful coexistence" as a guiding principle of international law, was new.

The Cold War between East and West, in terms of lives affected, wealth consumed, geographical reach, and long-term environmental consequences, was one of the greatest conflicts of human history.[6] Marked by continuing high expectations of violence and continuous mobilization for war by two military antagonists whose alliances incorporated a large part of the globe, the Cold War involved more human beings than any other conflict. It "deformed" traditional international law, as the long effort to restrict unilateral action, the "hallmark of civilized political arrangements," was impeded by the veto power of the superpower security system.[7] At the height of the Cold War, two worlds existed on the planet, between which trade and other human contact were drastically reduced; in many ways, there were two systems of international law and two systems of world public order, and few thought it would ever end.[8]

But end it did. On the heels of a 1980s revival of the Cold War, a rapid succession of largely peaceful revolutions spread across Eastern Europe and across to Russia. The Soviet Union dissolved and its empire collapsed. The international system was transformed, as the Warsaw Pact disintegrated and the Brezhnev Doctrine was discarded. The norms governing superpower conflict and the underpinnings of the international system were completely changed.

The comparatively peaceful collapse of the Soviet Empire was a virtually unprecedented event in world history. Contrary to expectations of rule-oriented and neo-realist theories, the fall of the Soviet bloc· was not the result of war, different alliance patterns, or the emergence of another superpower, nor even the outcome of a sudden gap in military capabilities.[9] One important factor was the fact that at that time, the strongest powers in the international system were, or aspired to be, liberal democracies.[10] Externally, a nonthreatening West and its support for Mikhail Gorbachev's reforms, accompanied by invitations to join multilateral institutions and by offers of large-scale financial aid for economic reform, helped transition along, encouraging reformers, swaying hard-liners, and heightening expectations. Internally, after decades of efforts by opposition groups, a "civil society" was created under which human values of existence and initiative independent of the Communist state could develop.[11] Direct contacts and learning between opposition groups began to flourish and spread, first through Polish society and then across Eastern Europe and Russia. Economic

modernization, increased communications across boundaries, and an improvement in optimum order created a better-educated constituency with new values
and expectations, and new demands for institutional and constitutive changes.

Soviet elites began to think inclusively, demonstrating that the Soviet government was no longer willing to use the Eastern European countries as a means
to the Communist Party's ends. Realist theories cannot explain why the Soviets
did not instead become more aggressive in response to instability at home and
throughout the bloc states, nor why the capitalist West did not behave oppor-
tunistically in response to the weakening empire.[12]

Under perestroika, glasnost, and "the new thinking" in Soviet foreign policy,
the Soviet state moved to join the "community of nations" and "the common
European home," embracing multilateralism. Significantly, for Mikhail Gorbachev the community of nations was not simply the sum of states recognized
in accordance with international law, but a collection of states participating in
the multilateral institutions of the postwar era.[13]

The end of the Cold War may mean the lessening of one particular pattern of
violence, but it does not necessarily mean the beginning of peace.[14] The Soviet
Union is belatedly undergoing decolonization, and the result so far has been
increasing instability. Other conflicts around the globe, which were not merely
phenomena of the Cold War but existed in their own right, continue to diminish
both minimum and optimum world order, and these areas may become more
prone to North-South division as their former strategic value decreases. The
revolutionary appeal of socialism may have subsided, but there is no shortage
of ideologies to take its place for which people are willing to resort to violence;
Islamic fundamentalism, for example, is fast spreading across the globe. Finally, the capitalist West is "hardly impervious" to stress and instability; environmental degradation and rapid economic transformation threaten many
human values around the planet.[15] It is not entirely clear that globalization is the
way to achieve optimum values and the sharing of all human values. In an
increasingly interdependent world the West, despite victory for its free-market
ideology, cannot ignore processes that may disrupt hopes for the new international order.

The international political system is at the threshold of a time of hope, but the
need for international law will now be more urgent than during the Cold War.[16]
A new world order has emerged, made up of multilateral institutions that have
provided mechanisms for consensus and cooperation in relations among and
between the industrial democracies, as well as between the industrial democracies and the former Eastern bloc states.[17] This new, cooperative pattern of
relations may have to coexist with the historic, conflict-prone pattern that continues to mark relations among other former Communist states and among

many lesser developed countries, as well as between all those states and the developed Western world.[18] Thus, the challenge to international lawyers in the post–Cold War era must be to clarify the inclusive, common interests of a world community that is ever-changing. International lawyers may continue to draw on historic policies — bearing in mind, of course, that the constitutive and institutional arrangements that were once devised to achieve those policies may no longer be pertinent or effective.[19]

PART FOUR

ARENAS

7

Establishment of and Access to Arenas of Authority

The structure of authority and other situations in which the participants in the international legal system interact have shown both a remarkable expansion and a modest movement toward organized, inclusive form. A major contribution of the United Nations and other intergovernmental organizations is to provide a range of diplomatic, parliamentary-diplomatic, parliamentary, adjudicative, and executive arenas in which all the effective participants in the world power process can interact. This development has been fortified by a comparable interactive network established by burgeoning nongovernmental organizations primarily concerned with values other than power. Consequently, the interactions of the decision makers whose choices in sum shape global policy have become more timely and continuous — less episodic and more responsive to crisis.

Similarly, though certain official arenas remain closed to some effective participants, there has been a general trend toward openness in arenas and a parallel movement toward making appearance compulsory for participants whose choices affect community policy. Both openness and compulsoriness are necessitated by growing interdependence in effective power.

ESTABLISHMENT

The institutional structures, in which both official and unofficial interactions occur and which manifest varying degrees of organization, may be depicted in terms of five distinctive patterns of interaction.

1. *Diplomatic:* The diplomatic arena, characterized by interelite communications, has a long tradition. From foreign office to foreign office various matters concerning international law are handled. From recognition of a state or a

government to the establishment of formal diplomatic relations, the necessity of ensuring the sanctity of diplomatic missions and premises, the inviolability of diplomatic personnel, and the confidentiality of diplomatic communications have long been sustained. Absent formal diplomatic relations, contacts are maintained in unorganized arenas.

2. *Parliamentary-Diplomatic:* Occasional conferences dealing with a broad range of international law concerns have grown in frequency and importance. The comprehensive, protracted Third United Nations Conference on the Law of the Sea (UNCLOS III, 1973–82) is the most important recent development. Other important conferences include the Vienna Conference on the Law of Treaties (1969), the Diplomatic Conference on the Reaffirmation and Development of International Humanitarian Law Applicable in Armed Conflicts (Geneva, 1974–77), the U.N. Conference on the Human Environment (Stockholm, 1972), the World Food Conference (Rome, 1974), the U.N. Decade for Women Conference (Nairobi, 1985), the United Nations Conference on Environment and Development, or Earth Summit (Rio de Janeiro, 1992), the International Conference on Population and Development (Cairo, 1994), the World Summit for Social Development (Copenhagen, 1995), the World Conference on Human Rights (Vienna, 1993), and the World Conference on Women (Beijing 1995). These conferences, touching on various value sectors and subjects on a global scale, contribute in many ways to the making and application of international law. They have greatly facilitated the performance of such important functions as intelligence (gathering and exchange of information and knowledge) and planning, appraisal (evaluating past and existing inadequacies), promotion (suggesting concrete proposals and advocating future courses of action), and prescription (adopting new international agreements). Although they may exude "more rhetoric than action," they are vital to generating and crystallizing expectations of the members of the world community in the manifold concerns of international law.

3. *Parliamentary:* Guided more or less by doctrines of majority rule and of equality in representation, parliamentary arenas are, as compared to the two previous arenas, characterized by a higher level of organization and continuity. On the global level, the foremost parliamentary arena is of course the U.N. General Assembly, as assisted by a host of subsidiary entities. Next come the Security Council, the Economic and Social Council (and its functional commissions), and the Trusteeship Council.

The emergence of institutions having the characteristics of parliamentary bodies is not confined to the United Nations. It extends to specialized agencies and regional organizations. Note, for example, the International Labor Conference of the International Labor Organization (ILO, characterized by the tripartite system of representation), the General Conference of the United Nations Educational, Scientific, and Cultural Organization (UNESCO), the World Health Assembly of the World Health Organization (WHO), the Board of Governors of the International Monetary Fund (IMF, characterized by the principle of one state, one governor, wielding unequal votes based on a system of quotas), the Board of Governors of the World Bank, the Consultative Assembly of the Council of Europe, the General Assembly of the Organization of American States (OAS), the General Council of the League of Arab States, the Assembly of Heads of State and Government of the Organization of African Unity (OAU), and the Council of Heads of State and the Council of Heads of Government of the Commonwealth of Independent States (CIS). These arenas provide forums for discussing virtually any problem relating to international law and affairs.

4. *Adjudicative:* Adjudicative arenas, characterized by third-party decision as well as by distinctive procedures and criteria of decision, include tribunals of all degrees of organization. Typical examples are the International Court of Justice, the Court of Justice and the Court of First Instance of the European Communities, the European Court of Human Rights, the Inter-American Court of Human Rights, and numerous arbitral tribunals. The International Criminal Court is the latest addition to the world adjudicative arena, although the spirit of cooperation has been tempered by disagreement over its jurisdiction. On the national level, recourse is increasingly made to judicial tribunals for matters regarding transnational law.

5. *Executive:* Executive arenas include the international secretariats of both official and nonofficial participants and the executive arenas of nation-states. Among notable official international secretariats are the U.N. Secretariat, the International Labor Office of ILO, and the secretariats of UNESCO, WHO, FAO, and so on. The office of the secretary-general of the United Nations, given its comprehensive global responsibilities, is especially important.

In terms of geographical range, institutional structures may be universal, general, plurilateral, regional, or bilateral. The scope of participation may extend to the entire earth-space arena or to small groups of actors.

All these types of arena have historically exhibited many, not always compatible, trends: from unorganized interactions to organized structures of decision; from loose association to a high degree of institutionalization; from the elementary diplomatic and parliamentary-diplomatic arenas to the more complex parliamentary, adjudicative, and executive arenas; from ad hoc to permanent and continuous structures of authority; and from imbalance in geographic and functional structures toward balanced development of both territorial (national, regional, and global) and functional organizations.

The structuring of arenas per se does not guarantee the content and quality of international law. Nevertheless, the more pluralistic the structures, the greater the likelihood that different interests will be protected. As a wide range of structures of authority becomes available, different participants with varying bases of power may take advantage of opportunities to enhance the protection accorded many individuals and groups.

In a state-centered world, the global arena is still characterized by an absence of centralized institutions specialized to the decision functions relevant to international law. In terms of geographical diffusion, modest movement has been made toward appropriate regionalism, as exemplified by the European Union, the OAS, the OAU, the CIS, the League of Arab States, and the Association of Southeast Asian Nations (ASEAN). This movement falls far short of appropriate and effective regionalism necessitated by global interdependencies. Wide gaps continue to exist between the structures of the global community and those of national communities.

ACCESS

The established transnational arenas of authority are generally open to nation-states; many remain closed to individuals and private groups. Most notably, nonstate claimants still lack access to the International Court of Justice. Article 34(1) of the statute of the court stipulates that "only States may be parties in cases before the Court." Thus, in contentious proceedings, access is denied not only to private groups and individuals but also to international governmental organizations.

Some international governmental organizations, however, are able to request advisory opinions on certain general questions. Article 96(1) of the U.N. Charter authorizes the General Assembly and the Security Council to request "the International Court of Justice to give an advisory opinion on any legal question." Article 96(2) enables other organs of the United Nations and specialized agencies to seek, with the approval of the General Assembly, advisory opinions of the court "on legal questions arising within the scope of their activities." Neither states nor individuals can make such requests.

Generally speaking, the individual still depends largely on a protecting state for access to other transnational arenas. Unless the individual's state of nationality is willing to espouse his or her claim, he or she may get little succor (see chapter 12). But individuals have always enjoyed access to municipal and national courts under varied conditions. Access by individuals and groups of persons to transnational arenas of authority has appeared recently to be increasing.

The right of individual petition was firmly established to facilitate the process of decolonization; individuals and groups in colonial territories have been accorded ample access to the Trusteeship Council, the Committee of Twenty-Four on Decolonization, the Council of Namibia, and so on. A significant regional development relates to the Court of Justice of the European Communities, which was created to serve the projected objectives of the European Economic Community, the European Coal and Steel Community, and the European Atomic Energy Community. In addition to member states of the communities, individuals, firms, and institutions of the communities are given access to the court under prescribed conditions.

The most notable development in affording individuals and private groups access to transnational arenas of authority for the protection of their own rights is in the field of human rights. The trend toward greater access for the individual may be noted especially in relation to developments within the U.N. Commission on Human Rights, the optional protocols to the International Covenant on Civil and Political Rights, the International Convention on the Elimination of All Forms of Racial Discrimination, the European Convention on Human Rights, and the Inter-American Commission on Human Rights.

The fundamental significance of this trend is underscored by A. H. Robertson:

> The real party in interest, if a violation occurs, is the individual whose rights have been denied; and the violation will in all probability have been the act of the authorities of his own government. Under the classic concept of international law the individual has no *locus standi,* on the theory that his rights will be championed by his government. But how can his government be his champion, when it is *ex hypothesi* the offender? What is necessary therefore, is to give the individual a right of appeal to an international organ which is competent to call the offending party to account.[1]

The trend toward the right of individual petition within the United Nations began with the trusteeship system. The U.N. Charter provides in Article 87(b) that the General Assembly and the Trusteeship Council may "accept petitions and examine them in consultation with the administering authority." The council prescribed detailed provisions for dealing with petitions by its rules of procedure. With the acceleration of the decolonization process, the right of individual petition was extended from the trust territories to non-self-governing territories. The Committee of Twenty-Four on Decolonization, the Special Committee on the Policies of Apartheid of the Government of the Republic of South Africa, and the Council of Namibia have all played important roles in receiving and acting on individual petitions.

The access of individuals and private groups to the Commission of Human Rights has had a more tortured path. When the commission commenced its work in 1947, it declared itself without authority to deal with specific complaints about human rights. The Economic and Social Council quickly confirmed this self-denying policy. For the next two decades, the many thousands of complaints to the United Nations, made annually by individuals and groups, were practically ignored, unless such complaints related to a colony or to South Africa. The ritualistic response of the United Nations was simply to forward the "communication" to the government concerned.

As the world community became increasingly apprehensive about apartheid, racial discrimination, and other gross human rights deprivations, repeated attempts were made to modify this self-denying rule so as to augment "the capacity of the United Nations to put a stop to violations of human rights *wherever they may occur.*"[2]

The upshot of these successive efforts was the adoption in 1970 by the Economic and Social Council of the famous Resolution 1503, establishing procedures for the Commission and the Sub-Commission on Prevention of Discrimination and Protection of Minorities to deal with "communications relating to violations of human rights and fundamental freedoms" and authorizing the subcommission to adopt rules on the admissibility of communications.[3] Under these procedures a working group of the subcommission is authorized to make the initial examination of all communications concerning human rights, and of replies by governments, received by the United Nations, and to decide which communications are to be referred to the full subcommission. Admissible communications may originate "from a person or group of persons" who are "victims" of "a consistent pattern of gross and reliably attested violations of human rights and fundamental freedoms," from "any person or group of persons who have direct and reliable knowledge of those violations, or nongovernmental organizations acting in good faith . . . and having direct and reliable knowledge of such violations."[4] On receipt of the communications brought by the working group, the subcommission decides whether to refer to the Commission on Human Rights particular situations "which appear to reveal a consistent pattern of gross and reliably attested violations of human rights and fundamental freedoms within the terms of reference of the Sub-Commission."[5]

It is the responsibility of the Commission on Human Rights to review the situations referred to it by the subcommission and to decide whether a situation calls for a thorough study by the commission or an investigation by an ad hoc committee to be appointed by the commission. Such an investigation is contingent on "the express consent of the state concerned" and "constant cooperation" with that state. The commission decides, on completion of the study or the investigation, whether to make recommendations to the Economic and Social Council.

Although this access to the commission by individuals and private groups is indirect and limited, it is vital. The commission is for all practical purposes the only official forum potentially open to all the individuals of the world for bringing complaints about human rights violations and not confined to particular individuals and groups identified through the jurisdiction of a particular ratifying state to a particular convention.

Under the International Covenant on Civil and Political Rights, the right of individual petition is stipulated not by the covenant itself but by the optional protocol to the covenant. Any contracting state to the covenant, in becoming a party to the optional protocol, recognizes the competence of the Human Rights Committee "to receive and consider communications from individuals, subject to its jurisdiction who claim to be victims of a violation by that State Party of any of the rights set forth in the Covenant" (Article 1). A substantial body of case law is now based on this right.

Under the International Convention on the Elimination of All Forms of Racial Discrimination, the Committee on the Elimination of Racial Discrimination is empowered to deal with complaints filed by one state party against another and with petitions by individuals under the conditions prescribed in Article 14. Unlike the state-to-state complaint procedure, the procedure of individual petitions is made subject to the option of state parties to the convention. "A State Party," under Article 14(1), "may at any time declare that it recognizes the competence of the Committee to receive and consider communications from individuals or groups of individuals within its jurisdiction claiming to be victims of a violation by that State Party of any of the rights set forth in this Convention." The same provision, however, adds that "no communication shall be received by the Committee if it concerns a State Party which has not made such a declaration." The competence of the committee regarding individual petitions is, further, operative "only when at least ten States Parties" have made the requisite declarations of acceptance, a condition that was finally fulfilled in 1982, thirteen years after the convention entered into force.

The most successful story is the system of individual petitions developed under the European Convention on Human Rights. Under Article 25 of the convention, individuals may bring complaints before the European Commission on Human Rights — even against their own governments. Concerned that not all governments were ready for such a radical innovation in international law, the European convention made the right of individual petition optional. Any "person, non-governmental organization or group of individuals claiming to be the victim of a violation by one of the High Contracting Parties of the rights set forth in the Convention" may file petitions to the secretary-general of the Council of Europe. Complaints may be brought regardless of nationality or domicile of the petitioner, provided that the petitioner was within the jurisdictional domain of the respondent government when the alleged violation occurred.

Access to the European Court of Human rights has been accorded only to states parties to the convention and to the European Commission on Human Rights, not to individuals or private groups. But this has not entirely precluded the individual applicant (who is, after all, the interested party) from having his views presented before the court. Although the individual could not require the case to go to the court, he became a full party once the commission brought the case. There would thus be three parties before the court: the defendant government, the plaintiff (the individual), and the commission. Reform of the convention system, arising from new circumstances in Europe such as the fall of the Berlin Wall and increased workload due to an increase in membership, has resulted in the streamlining of convention machinery, however. Protocol No. 11 will replace the two-tiered control system of the commission and the court with a single European Court of Human Rights. The individual will then have direct access to an international court to complain about violations of human rights protected by the convention.

The Inter-American Commission on Human Rights did not enjoy authority to act on individual petitions when it came into operation in 1960. In 1965 the commission was empowered to consider individual petitions complaining of violations of certain rights contained in the American Declaration of Rights and Duties of Man of 1948. Thanks to a protocol amending the Charter of the Organization of American States, adopted in Buenos Aires in 1967 and coming into effect in 1970, the commission has been elevated in status from "an autonomous entity" to a principal organ of the OAS, and its authority in handling individual petitions and discharging other functions has been greatly fortified.

Turning to national arenas, individuals have always enjoyed, under various prescribed conditions, access to national and municipal courts. A matter of special importance in international law has to do with access by foreign states or governments to domestic courts. The key to such access is "recognition" by the forum state. Generally speaking, only a recognized state or government may bring a lawsuit as plaintiff in the domestic courts of the recognizing state. Unrecognized states or governments cannot bring lawsuits before the courts of the state refusing recognition. Thus, for example, the Soviet government was consistently denied access to both federal and state courts in the United States before it received U.S. recognition.

COMPULSORY THIRD-PARTY DECISION MAKING

Closely related to the question of access by complainants is that of bringing recalcitrant respondent states into contentious proceedings. Generally speaking, there is still no way to compel or ensure the attendance of defendant states before transnational tribunals.

Suits brought before the International Court of Justice depend largely on the consent of the state being charged. The court's jurisdiction to try contentious cases is based on the consent, either express or implied, of the state parties. Consent may be given ad hoc by a special agreement between the parties concerned or by prior agreement. About a quarter of the cases before the court came through such special agreements. Prior consent takes two forms: by an international agreement conferring jurisdiction on the court, and by a general declaration accepting the "compulsory" jurisdiction of the court. Some 265 international agreements involving more than sixty states have conferred jurisdiction on the court regarding the interpretation and application of these agreements, which cover subjects ranging from commerce, navigation, and fisheries to consular relations. The Iranian hostage case, for example, was brought to the court by invoking several treaties dealing with diplomatic and consular relations.[6]

The optional acceptance of "compulsory jurisdiction" of the court is based on Article 36(2) of the Statute of the International Court of Justice. This provision, commonly known as the "optional clause," reads as follows:

> The states parties to the present Statute may at any time declare that they recognize as compulsory *ipso facto* and without special agreement, in relation to any other state accepting the same obligation, the jurisdiction of the Court in all legal disputes concerning:
> a. the interpretation of a treaty;
> b. any question of international law;
> c. the existence of any fact which, if established, would constitute a breach of an international obligation;
> d. the nature or extent of the reparation to be made unconditionally or on condition of reciprocity on the part of several or certain states, or for a certain time.

As of 1994, only 58 of 187 eligible states had accepted the court's compulsory jurisdiction under this optional clause. The percentage today of the accepting states in relation to the total membership of the court is much lower than during the era of the Permanent Court of International Justice (in 1940, 32 of 52 states). Of the five permanent members of the Security Council, only the United States and the United Kingdom had accepted it. Neither the Soviet Union nor any other state of the Soviet bloc ever accepted the court's compulsory jurisdiction; the Russian Federation, successor state to the former USSR, has not accepted compulsory jurisdiction either, although some former bloc states have.

For states that have accepted compulsory jurisdiction of the court, reservations attached to their acceptances are so many as to greatly diminish the scope of compulsory jurisdiction. The so-called Connolly Reservation exemplifies such limitation. In subscribing to the optional clause in 1946, the United States made a reservation to exclude from the court's compulsory jurisdiction "disputes with regard to matters which are essentially within the domestic jurisdiction of the United States of America *as determined by the United States of America*" (emphasis added).[7] When a state continues to act as the judge of whether a particular matter falls within its domestic jurisdiction, it becomes obvious that what the right hand grants is, by one and the same stroke, taken away by the left hand. This bad example has been followed by many other countries. In the same vein, the United Kingdom, in its adherence to the optional clause, retains the competence to reject the court's jurisdiction in any dispute at any time before a case is actually filed.[8]

The difficulty caused by reservations is further exacerbated by the fact that the optional clause operates on the basis of reciprocity: each state accepts compulsory jurisdiction vis-à-vis another state only to the extent that the obligations undertaken in their respective declarations mutually correspond. Consequently, the court can acquire compulsory jurisdiction over a particular dispute only when both plaintiff and defendant states made declarations that bring that dispute within the court's domain.

In November 1984 the court was uncharacteristically bold in asserting its jurisdictional authority, over the strong objections of the United States, to hear a case brought by Nicaragua against the United States, *Case Concerning Military and Paramilitary Activities in and against Nicaragua*.[9] The court's decision on the issue of jurisdiction followed its prior issuance of provisional measures in May 1984, ordering the United States to cease any attempts to blockade or mine Nicaraguan ports and to refrain from threatening the territorial integrity and political independence of Nicaragua by any military or paramilitary activities.[10] The United States claimed that the court lacked jurisdiction partly on the ground that Nicaragua had never validly accepted the court's compulsory jurisdiction because it had failed to deposit the requisite ratification of the Protocol of Signature of the Statute of the Permanent Court of International Justice (the predecessor of the incumbent court), which contained the optional clause of compulsory jurisdiction. The court rejected this claim, finding that Nicaragua's 1929 declaration — as distinguished from "ratification" — accepting the compulsory jurisdiction of the permanent court unconditionally was "valid from the moment it was received" and remained so "at the moment when Nicaragua became a party to the Statute of the new Court."[11] The court stressed the "constant acquiescence" on the part of Nicaragua, noting especially that for nearly forty years international organizations authorized to handle "such declarations" had consistently included Nicaragua in the lists of states accepting the compulsory jurisdiction of the court.[12] The court stated that when Nicaragua, as an original member participating in the San Francisco Conference, signed and ratified the U.N. Charter, thereby accepting the statute of the new court, it consented to transfer its 1929 declaration (which was valid for an unlimited period) to the International Court of Justice.

Another ground of U.S. opposition to the court's jurisdiction related to the principle of reciprocity involving temporal factors. When the United States subscribed to the optional clause in 1946, it stated that "this declaration shall remain in force for a period of five years and thereafter until the expiration of six months after notice may be given to terminate this declaration."[13] On April 6, 1984 — three days before Nicaragua formally filed suit against the United States in the court — the United States sought to modify its 1946 declarations by stating that

> The aforesaid [1946] declarations shall not apply to disputes with any Central American state arising out of or related to events in Central America, any of which disputes shall be settled in such a manner as the parties to them may agree. Notwithstanding the terms of the aforesaid declaration, this proviso shall take effect immediately and shall remain in force for two years.[14]

The court was thus faced with the question whether the United States was free to disregard the six months' notice requirement contained in its 1946 declaration before a competent state had filed a claim. The United States contended that it was free to do so because Nicaragua was not similarly bound by such a temporal restriction in its 1929 declaration and was able to withdraw without six months' notice. The United States and Nicaragua obviously were not, in the view of the United States, "accepting the same obligation," as stipulated in Article 36(2) of the court statute. The court again rejected the U.S. contention, declaring that "reciprocity cannot be invoked in order to excuse departure from the terms of a State's own declaration, whatever its scope, limitations or conditions."[15] The court stated that the principle of reciprocity applies only to the scope and substance of commitments, not to the formal conditions of their duration.

Additionally, the court based its jurisdiction in part on the dispute settlement clause embodied in the 1956 Treaty of Friendship, Commerce, and Navigation between the United States and Nicaragua despite that treaty's exception for national security. The court also rejected the U.S. contention that the case was inadmissible or nonjusticiable because it involved issues of national security and self-defense and that matters of peace and security fall within the domain of the Security Council and are unsuitable for adjudication by the court.

In protest of the court's November 1984 decision on jurisdiction, the United States, on January 18, 1985, formally withdrew from "the proceedings initiated by Nicaragua in the International Court of Justice."[16] It reiterated that the proceedings "are a misuse of the Court for political purposes" and that "the Court lacks jurisdiction and competence over such a case."[17] Characterizing the court's decision as "a marked departure from its past, cautious approach to jurisdictional questions,"[18] the United States stressed that the decision "is erroneous as a matter of law and is based on a misreading and distortion of the evidence and precedent."[19] On October 7, 1985, the United States took a further step by terminating its acceptance of the compulsory jurisdiction of the court. It was a severe blow to the prospects of compulsory third-party decision making. Yet, despite withdrawing its acceptance of the court's compulsory jurisdiction the United States has subsequently been a party to several cases before the court.[20]

On a more encouraging note, its fiftieth anniversary saw the International Court of Justice at a time when it was busier than ever. In 1991–1992, the court had the largest number of cases in its history.[21] In 1999, the International Court of Justice was busy reviewing several important cases, including the aerial incident of August 10, 1999 — *Pakistan v. India;* the armed activities in the territory of the Congo; and the legality of the use of force in Kosovo — *Yugoslavia v. Belgium, Yugoslavia v. Canada, Yugoslavia v. France, Yugoslavia v. Germany, Yugoslavia v. Italy, Yugoslavia v. Netherlands, Yugoslavia v. Portugal, Yugoslavia v. UK, Yugoslavia v. United States,* and *Yugoslavia v. Spain.* Moreover, there has been a modest increase in the number of declarations of acceptance of compulsory jurisdiction under "the optional clause" of Article 36(2).[22] In addition, the United Nations has set up a special fund to assist developing states in litigating before the International Court of Justice.

Furthermore, a number of human rights conventions do confer jurisdiction on the International Court of Justice over disputes concerning interpretation and application of such conventions. The list includes the Convention on the Prevention and Punishment of the Crime of Genocide, 1948 (Article 9); the Supplementary Convention on the Abolition of Slavery, the Slave Trade, and Institutions and Practices Similar to Slavery, 1956 (Article 10); the Convention on the Political Rights of Women, 1953 (Article 9); the Convention Relating to the Status of Refugees, 1951 (Article 38); and the Convention on the Reduction of Statelessness, 1961 (Article 14). Typically, the relevant provision reads as follows: "Any dispute which may arise between any two or more Contracting

States concerning the interpretation or application of this Convention, which is not settled by negotiation, shall at the request of any one of the parties to the dispute be referred to the International Court of Justice for decision, unless they agree to another mode of settlement."

The settlement of disputes by ad hoc arbitral tribunals depends as much on state consent as on judicial settlement. Occasionally, states may even refuse to participate in arbitral proceedings to which they have given prior consent. Though arbitration was highly popular in medieval times as a means of settling international disputes, its use greatly diminished with the rise of the modern state system, which overemphasized the sovereign quality of states. Thanks largely to the series of Jay Treaties concluded by the United States with Great Britain and other nations and to the Alabama Arbitration (1871) between the United States and Great Britain, arbitration was revived as a method of third-party decision in the nineteenth century. This revival culminated in the establishment of the Permanent Court of Arbitration under the Hague Convention for the Pacific Settlement of International Disputes, concluded in 1899, amended in 1907, and still in effect. The name Permanent Court, however, appears to be a misnomer. The entity consists of little more than a permanent panel from which arbitrators can be chosen, and the court itself must be constituted from case to case on an ad hoc basis. There is no machinery whatsoever for compulsory jurisdiction; few states are willing to make unequivocal prior commitment to arbitrate potential disputes.

An apt example of how even a prior commitment to compulsory arbitration may be frustrated is the case of *Interpretation of Peace Treaties with Bulgaria, Hungary, and Romania* (1950).[23] The peace treaties, concluded by the Allies with Bulgaria, Hungary, and Romania, coming into effect in September 1947, contained certain provisions for observance of human rights. They also provided, on the insistence of the Soviet Union, that disputes arising under the treaties be referred to arbitral tribunals ("conciliation commissions") rather than to the International Court of Justice. In 1949 the United States and the United Kingdom brought complaints before the U.N. General Assembly, accusing the governments of Bulgaria, Hungary, and Romania of having violated the human rights obligations of the peace treaties. Having duly followed and exhausted the treaty procedure for the settlement of the disputes, the United States and the United Kingdom requested in August 1949 that Bulgaria, Hungary, and Romania join in forming the conciliation commissions contemplated in the treaties. But Bulgaria, Hungary, and Romania refused to appoint an arbitrator on their behalf and hence were able to frustrate the arbitration of these disputes. The International Court of Justice, responding to a request of the U.N. General

Assembly, declared in this advisory opinion that, unless and until both parties to the dispute had appointed their arbitrators, the secretary-general of the United Nations was not empowered to appoint a third arbitrator.

Fortunately, in recognition of the vital importance of compulsory third-party decision for settling disputes in a decentralized world, a slow trend has continued toward the establishment of such decision.

After the United Nations came into being, the International Law Commission undertook the first major effort to formulate a comprehensive draft convention on arbitral procedure. At its first session in 1949, the commission selected arbitral procedure regarding international disputes as one of the topics for codification. Convinced that every phase of arbitral procedure should reflect some degree of compulsoriness, the commission prepared a draft convention and presented it to the General Assembly in 1953. According to the draft, an undertaking to arbitrate would entail the consequence of empowering the International Court of Justice to decide the arbitrability of the dispute, thereby preventing one of the parties from evading arbitration by claiming the dispute to be outside the scope of the agreement. The court would further be authorized to maintain the immutability of the tribunal, once constituted, even if one of the parties should choose to withdraw its arbitrator.

The draft was unfavorably reviewed by the General Assembly, which especially criticized the "quasi-compulsory jurisdictional procedure" and the commission's proposal for concluding a convention on arbitral procedure. In 1955 the assembly decided to return the draft to the commission for further consideration, in light of the comments of governments and the discussion in its Sixth Committee. In 1957 the commission, instead of undertaking a thorough revision of the draft, decided to keep the substance of the draft intact and to submit it to the General Assembly as a set of draft articles that could serve as model rules for states in particular arbitrations. "[No] longer presented in the form of a potential general treaty of arbitration,"[24] the Model Rules on Arbitral Procedure prepared by the commission were submitted to the General Assembly in 1958. The assembly voted to bring these model rules to "the attention of Member States for their consideration and use, in such cases and to such extent as they consider appropriate, in drawing up treaties of arbitration or *compromis*."[25]

Another significant attempt toward establishing compulsory third-party decision occurred at the U.N. Conference on the Law of the Sea in 1958. In addition to the four conventions (dealing with the territorial sea and the contiguous zone, the high seas, fisheries, and the continental shelf), the conference adopted an optional protocol of signature concerning the compulsory settlement of disputes (entering into force on September 30, 1962). The optional protocol, forerunner to the present compulsory third-party dispute resolution system, which entered into force with the 1982 Convention on the Law of the Sea, provided for the compulsory jurisdiction of the International Court of Justice regarding "disputes arising out of the interpretation or application of any Convention on the Law of the Sea" (except that on fisheries). Any party to the optional protocol could bring a dispute before the court, or, if the parties so chose, submit the dispute to conciliation or arbitration.

The movement toward compulsory third-party decision received reinforcement in the Vienna Convention on Diplomatic Relations of 1961 and the Vienna Convention on Consular Relations of 1963. There was an optional protocol concerning the compulsory settlement of disputes in relation to each of the two conventions. Article 1 of each of the optional protocols, in identical words, stipulates: "Disputes arising out of the interpretation or application of the Convention shall lie within the compulsory jurisdiction of the International Court of Justice and may accordingly be brought before the Court by an application made by any party to the dispute being a party to the present Protocol."

The next important development came with the Vienna Convention on the Law of Treaties of 1969. The shared concern for compulsory third-party decision finds expression in Article 66 of the convention and the annex to the convention, which were adopted after painstaking efforts. According to Article 66, any party to a dispute arising under the *jus cogens* articles of the convention may submit the dispute to the International Court of Justice for adjudication when the procedures in Article 33 of the U.N. Charter have failed to reach a solution within twelve months, provided the parties have made no agreement to refer the dispute to arbitration. A party to a dispute concerning "the application or the interpretation of any of the other articles in Part V" of the convention may set in motion certain conciliation procedures embodied in the annex to the convention through a request to the secretary-general of the United Nations.

In the same vein, there has been a gradual movement toward compulsory third-party decision in matters relating to human rights. Unlike the right of individual petition that is provided for on an optional basis under the existing human rights conventions (global and regional), the state-to-state complaint system is made compulsory under both the International Convention on the Elimination of All Forms of Racial Discrimination and the European Convention on Human Rights. The convention on the elimination of racial discrimination stipulates in Article 11(1) that "if a State Party considers that another State Party is not giving effect to the provisions of this Convention, it may bring the matter to the attention of the Committee [on the Elimination of Racial Discrimination]. The Committee shall then transmit the communication to the State Party concerned." The detailed procedures for dealing with such a state-to-state complaint are specified in the remainder of Article 11, and in Articles 12 and

13. Similarly, the European Convention on Human Rights provides for a compulsory state-to-state system in Article 24: "Any High Contracting Party may refer to the Commission, through the Secretary General of the Council of Europe, any alleged breach of the provisions of the Convention by another High Contracting Party." (Unhappily, the American Convention on Human Rights makes it optional.) In a decentralized world in which reciprocity operates, states are understandably reluctant to resort to such complaint procedures against other states for human rights violations, as attested by the experiences under these two conventions. Nevertheless, the availability of these compulsory state-to-state complaint procedures does contribute significantly to the international protection of human rights, thanks to the abiding impact of prevention and deterrence.

The most recent and important development in this area relates to the regime of dispute settlements under the U.N. Convention on the Law of the Sea of 1982, which finally became a reality when the convention went into force in 1994. This convention, recognizing the imperative of compulsory third-party decision making, contains elaborate provisions for the settlement of disputes, stipulated in more than two dozen articles and several annexes. Such imperative is particularly compelling for this comprehensive and complex treaty. Thanks to the protracted and strenuous efforts to accommodate competing demands and interests on a wide range of issues, and despite the compromise between competing demands that resulted in the supplementary agreement and subsequent ratification of the convention, the 1982 treaty still contains some formulas of generality and deliberate ambiguities bound to generate a continuing flow of controversy in its interpretation and application.

The regime for settling disputes under the convention is characterized by simplicity, flexibility, and complexity, containing elements of both choice and compulsoriness. The convention mandates that contracting parties settle by peaceful means their disputes relating to the convention's interpretation and application. It enunciates an overriding policy of honoring freedom of choice of contracting parties, respecting above all the mode of dispute settlement agreed on between the parties involved. The parties to a dispute can by agreement select any method of dispute settlement they wish. Disputing parties can not only bypass the procedures set forth in the convention by prior agreement and use some other mode of dispute settlement (bilateral, regional, or general) but also can agree *at any time* to settle their dispute by a different method even after they have submitted themselves to a procedure provided for in the convention. When they cannot agree on the means of settlement, they are obligated to submit most types of dispute to a compulsory procedure entailing decisions binding on all parties concerned. Here again flexibility prevails. Instead of providing a unitary system of dispute settlement, the convention offers states a number of options: a special International Tribunal for the Law of the Sea, to be established under the convention, the International Court of Justice, an international arbitral tribunal, or a special technical arbitral tribunal. Certain types of dispute are placed under the conciliation procedure, a procedure whose outcome is not binding on the parties. The provisions for exceptions to the compulsory judicial settlement or arbitration, embodied notably in Articles 297, 298, and 186–191 of the convention, are where the real complexities lie. In a nutshell, the three major exceptions relate to (1) disputes relating to the exercise by a coastal state of its sovereign rights or jurisdiction in the Exclusive Economic Zone; (2) disputes concerning sea boundary delimitation, military or law enforcement activities, or disputes brought before the Security Council of the United Nations; and (3) disputes relating to seabed mining.

These new forums for dispute resolution will benefit both general international law and the law of the sea. Their availability may encourage their use and thus add to the body of jurisprudence overall in international law.[26]

Another remarkable development is the active and impressive role played by the Iran–United States Claims Tribunal established under the Declaration of Algeria of 1981, which deals with private claims of U.S. nationals against Iran and of Iranian nationals against the United States.[27] A more recent development is the establishment by the Security Council of a claims tribunal to control seized Iraqi assets and handle claims for war reparations by victims of the Iraqi invasion of Kuwait, with private claims ranging from physical injury and loss of life to the cost of putting out oil fires set by Iraqi forces.[28]

PART FIVE

Bases of Power

The aggregate bases of power of nation-states are not a static quantum but are in constant flux. They represent an ongoing community process in which the decision makers of nation-states manage resources and people through a variety of institutional practices and arrangements to pursue their goals in the world arena. Though dynamic in nature, these bases of power can be conveniently described in terms of resources, people, and authority. To participate in the global power process, nation-state elites seek to control resources and people and to exert authority in decision making.

Nation-states claim and employ many resources, including not only land masses but also rivers, oceans, airspace, outer space, ships, aircraft, and so forth. These resources exhibit varying degrees of exclusivity and shareability. Though some, notably land masses and closely proximate waters and air space, permit only some shared use and competence, others, such as international rivers, the oceans, airspace over the oceans, and outer space, are highly shareable. Claims by nation-states to these resources differ in comprehensiveness of authority and in scope and duration of control.

People are important assets for nation-states, but people differ from other bases of power in that they are rational beings with inherent dignity — the ultimate actors in any social interaction or decision. Although elites seek to control people, people demand protection and fulfillment; they demand human rights in a comprehensive and dynamic sense. A human rights dimension is present in every social interaction and in every authoritative decision.

Authority is an important source of power. Authority builds on authority. Its essence is the freedom to make decisions, the freedom to create and maintain institutions and practices. In the contemporary world, allocation of authority to nation-states is effected both vertically and horizontally: vertically between the general community and the nation-states, and horizontally between and among nation-states in relation to particular events.

8

Control over Territory

The contemporary state system, building on a key notion that a nation-state occupies a definite part of the surface of the earth, embodies territorial organization with a high degree of exclusivity. Unlike other resources, land masses are generally perceived to tolerate, only in the most modest degree, shared use by states and shared competence in administration of such use.

Under the traditional notion of "territorial sovereignty," a nation-state normally exercises, subject to the limitations imposed by international law, the competence to prescribe and apply law to persons, things, and events within its territorial domain to the exclusion of other states. In principle, the boundaries of a state's territory define the reach of its authority based on territoriality.

Territorial authority ("territorial sovereignty") of a state extends to all rivers and lakes within its territory and to its internal waters and territorial sea. The state's authority over such waters is as plenary as the authority it exercises over land masses. Territorial sovereignty extends further to the airspace superjacent to its territory and to the airspace above all waters of its territorial reach.

National control over territory historically bears a striking resemblance to private ownership of land. Early international law relied heavily on the Roman law of property in developing principles to govern the acquisition of territory.

The customary international law governing the acquisition of territory developed when the European powers were the dominant participants in the world arena. Acquiring territory was part of the "empire-building" processes of the competing colonial powers. In acquiring vast overseas territories, resources, and markets, the rival powers proudly proclaimed themselves to be carrying the "white man's burden" on a "civilizing mission" around the world.

These empires, sharing the heritage of Christianity and a strong sense of national unity, acquired substantial military strength, due to the dynamic growth

of science, technology, and industry. Immediate targets of expansion were uninhabited regions or regions inhabited by "savages or semi-civilized peoples."
Areas suitable for migration, such as the land masses of North and South
America, Australia, New Zealand, and parts of Africa, were occupied through
full settlement. The next target was Asia. In the populous areas of Asia, European migration for permanent settlement was not especially important. The
paramount pursuits were physical resources and markets, linked in various
ways to expansion in religion, culture, education, health, and other sectors. In
one form or another, weak territorial communities of the Asian continent became the prey of European colonial powers. The next major targets were the
remaining areas of the African continent, which, though not fully suitable for
permanent settlement, were valuable as a resource base and as a potential
market. The polar areas and rather isolated islands, finally, though practically
uninhabitable or with scarce resources, were sought primarily for their potential
significance in modern strategy.

In the course of expansion all instruments of policy, especially military
force, were mobilized. Among the colonial powers there were early settlers and
latecomers, and relative power positions fluctuated in the world balancing of
power. Within loose restrictions the use of military force, even to acquire
territory, was permitted as an instrument of change. The damaging repercus-
sions of the use of force were, understandably, not as far-reaching as in today's
world, given the low interdependence and rudimentary technology of weaponry
at that time. Further, the concept of the survival of the fittest was at its height in
both international and domestic arenas in the nineteenth century. Since the
expansionist powers identified their role as a civilizing mission, concern for the
aspirations of the local inhabitants of a newly acquired territory received little
weight in developing customary international law regarding the acquisition of
territory. The overriding concern of the decision makers, the major powers at
that stage of history, was how, in a power-balancing world, to stabilize community expectations in favor of consolidating the fruits of expansion.

As they eventually developed, the modalities of acquiring territory under
traditional international law have been generally classified into five categories:
accretion, occupation, prescription, conquest (or subjugation), and cession.

Accretion results from natural (slow) or artificial land formations. It presents
little problem. In contrast, avulsion — the sudden, unnatural shift in boundary
matters — does not change ownership.

Occupation applies only to "unappropriated territory" — that is, *terra nullius*. Occupation has a private law analogy. According to Roman law property
not owned by any person (*res nullius*) *is* subject to appropriation by occupation,
which required both the intent to assert ownership (*animus*) and manifestation

of physical control (*factum*). By analogy this private law rule was extended to cover the acquisition by a state of title over uninhabited territory. During the era of colonial expansion, a vital question was whether this principle could apply to territory inhabited by relatively uncivilized native tribes.

Prescription is technically defined as "the acquisition of sovereignty over a territory through continuous and undisturbed exercise of sovereignty over it during such a period as is necessary to create under the influence of historical development the general conviction that the present condition of things is in conformity with international order."[1] Thus conceived, the definition of this technical term differs significantly from that of the prescribing function referred to elsewhere in this book. Jennings sums up the distinction between occupation and prescription in these words:

> Occupation can only apply to territory that is *res nullius;* it is in all cases lawful in origin, and the mere passage of time has no place in it, provided only that the apprehension of the territorial sovereignty be effective. Prescription, on the other hand, is a portmanteau concept that comprehends both a possession of which the origin is unclear or disputed, and an adverse possession which is in origin demonstrably unlawful. For prescription, therefore, the possession must be long continued, undisturbed, and it must be unambiguously attributable to a claim to act as sovereign. It depends as much on the quiescence of the former sovereignty as on the consolidation through time of the new.[2]

One element common to all acquisition of territories is "effective control," irrespective of modalities. This has been clearly demonstrated by such famous cases as the *Island of Palmas* case (United States v. Netherlands, 1928),[3] *Sovereignty over Clipperton Island* (France v. Mexico, 1931),[4] and the *Legal Status of Eastern Greenland* (Denmark v. Norway, 1933).[5] Claims based on discovery, or symbolic acts, are generally insufficient to acquire title. Unlike bare discovery, in the sense of first sighting, claims based on symbolic or ceremonial acts of possession (such as flag raising or making a proclamation) have been given considerably greater weight in practice. In practically every territorial dispute, the contesting states have generally sought to establish, by proof of symbolic acts of possession, the earliest possible connection with the disputed area. Though claims based on such symbolic acts were once regarded as sufficient to establish title, the necessity of limiting such claims soon became apparent with their proliferation. Hence, the recognition of claims based on discovery and symbolic acts of possession was transformed into the requirement of actual occupation or possession. In other words, effective control is required, despite the abundance of the literature debating what constitutes effective control. The kind of effective control historically required to acquire title to the larger land masses of the earth involves not only some single act of assertion of naked power but a continuous and comprehensive process in use and enjoyment. This process has been observed to require

> an identifiable participant taking effective control of the resource, as effectiveness may be determined by the varying characteristics of the resource and context, giving notice to the world through appropriate ceremonials or otherwise of its intent to acquire, asserting authority over the resource in its management as a continuing base of power, and employing the resource in strategies appropriate to its characteristics in the production of values.[6]

Evidently, the underlying policy consideration is to maximize resource use, because an effective occupant is in the best position to exploit resources fully.

The profound changes since World War II are vividly reflected in the flow of decisions dealing with former colonies. Because of the tremendous proliferation of new nation-states, the older European powers no longer take the initiatives that lead to territorial change. Instead, the ex-colonies-turned-new-states have become the dynamic participants in redrawing the map of the world. The chief objective in acquiring territory is no longer proclaimed to be a "civilizing mission" or part of building empires. New objectives enter the political process and stimulate new justifications for permissible alterations of territory. Foremost among these innovations is an intense demand that the boundaries of bodies politic conform to popular aspirations so as to protect human rights and enhance world public order.

The bases of power among nation-states continue to show patent discrepancies. The patterns of disputes over territory, however, have changed markedly. In the colonial era the dominant controversies were either between great powers and small powers or among great powers. High expectations of violence accompanied these confrontations; lesser powers formerly were quickly policed by a major power or their cause escalated into conflict between great powers. Then, during the Cold War, territorial clashes between small powers generated a threatening climate, punctuated by overt acts of violence. Today, in the post–Cold War era, the greatest threat to public order and human rights is the proliferation of ethnic-based violence, as ethnic hatreds long suppressed or ignored have unleashed "centrifugal forces," pulling states apart from Africa to Europe to South and Central Asia.[7]

The territorial problems that have arisen from the demise of colonial empires, the fall of the Soviet Union, and the emergence of new states are far too different and complex to be met adequately by the customary rules of the past. As unappropriated land masses on the planet have vanished, the traditional law originally designed to deal with territorial changes involving such land masses has lost relevance. (It may, however, experience a resurgence in an age of astropolitics, although the 1967 Space Treaty prohibits nation-state acquisition of ownership of celestial bodies.) Furthermore, constitutive changes in the international order, relating to human rights, have led to the recognition that self-determination is no longer limited to decolonization but includes internal and relative self-determination as well. New norms in international law are needed to account for these changes.[8]

Though all instruments of policy continue to be employed by claimant states to support territorial claims, the use of military force as a means of change, particularly of territorial change, is explicitly prohibited by the Charter of the United Nations. Before the establishment of the United Nations, the use of military force to acquire territories or other valued assets was not regarded as impermissible — even in the form of large-scale "war." The "subjugation" (or "conquest") of a territory and its people as a result of armed attack was an acceptable mode of affecting transfers of a territory from one nation-state to another. Though the Covenant of the League of Nations made "resort to war" unlawful under certain circumstances, it fell short of outlawing "war" altogether. In the nineteenth and early twentieth centuries, there was, understandably, less common interest in restraining violence. The prevailing policy then sought to localize coercion by giving community approval to quick settlement of disputes through superior strength.

Because territorial expansion and acquisition often disrupted world public order, there were, even during that period, some initiatives to deny the fruits of expansion to aggressors through collective nonrecognition. The Stimson doctrine, named after Secretary of State Henry L. Stimson under President Herbert Hoover for his advocacy of refusing to recognize as legally valid any changes resulting from Japan's seizure of Manchuria in 1931 in violation of treaty obligations, typified this line of effort. The traditional international law regarding conquest, however, has been most profoundly affected by the new expectations incorporated in the U.N. Charter. The charter projects both a negative policy of minimizing the deliberate use of coercion as a means of value change and a positive policy of promoting the shaping and sharing of values by persuasion. In its negative formulation, the principle seeks to ban any unilateral use of coercion by one state against another as an instrument of value change. Article 2(4) of the charter states, "All Members shall refrain in their international relations from the threat or use of force against the territorial integrity or political independence of any state, or in any other manner inconsistent with the Purposes of the United Nations." In its positive formulation, it seeks to foster the stability in the expectation of freedom from unauthorized coercion that is indispensable to the optimum production and distribution of values. Article

2(3) stipulates, "All Members shall settle their international disputes by peaceful means in such a manner that international peace and security, and justice, are not endangered." Taking the charter as a whole, it would appear that the threat or use of force is generally prohibited except for self-defense and community police action. Although a minority dissents, it is increasingly conceded that contemporary international law has no place for the acquisition of territory through conquest or subjugation.

It has been asserted that the acquisition of territory resulting from self-defense against an aggressor state is still permissible, since self-defense remains permissible. That argument, however, misconceives the scope of self-defense. Under contemporary international law, self-defense (see chapter 19) is regarded as permissible insofar as it is necessary and proportionate to repel aggression. As soon as aggression is repelled, the state acting in self-defense must cease its defensive operations lest it become an aggressor. It is not necessary to acquire title over the aggressor's territory in order to exert the "necessary and proportionate" degree of self-defense required to repel aggression. To draw a fine distinction between the acquisition of territory by permissible coercion and by impermissible coercion would most assuredly open a Pandora's box, highly destructive of the fundamental policy of maintaining world public order. A clear and ever-present danger is posed by licensing "acquisition by permissible coercion" in this decentralized world, where the maintenance of minimum public order depends so heavily on the reciprocity and mutual restraint of nation-states in their interaction. In this vein, the Declaration of Principles of International Law concerning Friendly Relations and Cooperation among States in accordance with the Charter of the United Nations (1970) provides that "the territory of a State shall not be the object of acquisition by another State resulting from the threat or use of force. No territorial acquisition resulting from the threat or use of force shall be recognized as legal."[9] This provision has been interpreted to mean that no acquisition of territory is permitted by the use of force, even if it is a lawful exercise of self-defense in accord with the U.N. Charter. The Security Council's denunciation under Resolution 242 of Israel's occupation of territory taken during the 1967 war is a reflection of this community policy.[10]

Cession involves the transfer of territory by treaty from one nation-state to another; its counterpart in private law is transfer of property in land. Traditionally, there have been two types of cession: noncoercive and coercive. Cession made free from coercion, as in the U.S. purchase of Alaska, leaves little ground for objection if the necessary internal processes of decision conform to appropriate standards. But cessions resulting from coercion require a critical reappraisal in the light of contemporary community policies. Since the U.N.

Charter makes it impermissible to acquire territory by conquest, a cession designed to formalize the fruit of unlawful coercion evidently cannot be accepted. But note the operation of intertemporal law — that is, this fundamental change in community policy cannot be applied retroactively to the acquisition of territory by conquest or coercive cession in the past; otherwise, established usages would suddenly dissolve, and the world order would become ever more insecure.

The world community today faces a number of territorial problems either inadequately settled or left unsettled after World War II. Affecting cession after a large-scale armed conflict via a peace treaty is a time-honored practice. A peace treaty is commonly regarded as an authoritative expression of the shared expectations of both victorious and defeated powers following the formal termination of a state of "hostility." Even when conquest was fully permissible, traditional international law deferred to peace treaties as superseding provisional arrangements made during hostilities. The underlying policy consideration is profound. Expectations expressed amid hostility are generally dictated by military expediency and necessity for victory. Other relevant policy considerations tend to disappear or to receive scant attention. The commitments made under the emergency conditions of wartime offer, at best, a precarious foundation for future order; they are most likely to lead to the disruption of public order sooner or later. Hence the imperative and practice of a cooling-off period for noncoercive negotiation after hostilities cease. Only in an atmosphere of relative nonviolence and nonemergency can both sides be expected to consider all the relevant interests at stake in shaping a more durable policy. This explains the importance attached to the role of the "peace treaty" under traditional international law. A primary function of such an instrument is to ascertain unequivocally the shared expectations of the parties, especially the defeated powers, concerning any change of territory. Territorial clauses are particularly well drafted in order to prevent subsequent claims of ambiguity; any transfer of territory is prescribed in no uncertain terms.

The establishment of the United Nations has not altered the significance of peace treaties as an authoritative expression of the shared policy of both victorious and defeated states at the close of hostilities. But its charter does inject a new community policy into the situation involving territorial changes: the principle of self-determination. Even in the nineteenth century, efforts were made to mitigate deprivations imposed on inhabitants in cases of cession by mandating a plebiscite, which enabled the populations most concerned to express their preferences and make their choices. Several treaties concluded during that period stipulated that cession could not take effect without the genuine consent of the inhabitants, as expressed through a plebiscite. President Wilson's

championing of the principle of self-determination did reecho grandly throughout the globe but achieved limited success in the territorial settlements after
World War I. It was in the establishment of the United Nations that a great
multilateral treaty proclaimed the principle of self-determination to be a fundamental policy of the world community. The practice of the United Nations to
date has made it clear that respect for the genuine aspirations of the people
concerned is the ultimate guide for effecting territorial change. The principle of
self-determination, as elaborated in chapter 2, assumes particular significance
in the context of territorial transfer.

This principle was most eloquently reaffirmed in the famous opinion on *Western Sahara* rendered by the International Court of Justice in 1975.[11] Western Sahara, administered as Spanish Sahara until 1976, borders Morocco, Mauritania,
and Algeria. Although Spain expressed its willingness to decolonize the territory in accord with the relevant U.N. resolutions calling for self-determination,
Morocco and Mauritania pressed their respective territorial claims to the territory. In December 1974 the U.N. General Assembly requested the International
Court of Justice to render an advisory opinion on the following two questions:

1. Was Western Sahara . . . at the time of colonization by Spain a territory
   belonging to no one (*terra nullius*)?
   If the answer to this question is in the negative,
2. What were the legal ties between this territory and the Kingdom of Morocco
   and the Mauritanian entity?[12]

In its opinion of October 16, 1975, the court answered the first question in the
negative. In response to the second question, the court found that certain legal
ties existed between the territory and Morocco and the Mauritanian entity but
that these were not ties of "territorial sovereignty." The court concluded that it
"has not found legal ties of such a nature as might affect the application of
resolution 1514 (XV) in the decolonization of Western Sahara and, in particular, of the principle of self-determination through the free and genuine expression of the will of the peoples of the Territory."[13] Since the court opinion the
following have occurred: the purported division ("annexation"), in defiance of
the court opinion, of Western Sahara upon Spain's withdrawal from the territory
in February 1976; the proclamation of the establishment of the Sahara Arab
Democratic Republic (SADR) by the POLISARIO Front on February 28, 1976;
the subsequent Moroccan occupation of the Mauritanian zone in 1979; recognition of the POLISARIO Front as the legitimate representative of the Saharan
people by the U.N. General Assembly on November 21, 1979; admission of
SADR as the fifty-first member of the Organization of African Unity (OAU)
on February 22, 1982, despite Morocco's strong opposition; Morocco's with-

drawal from the OAU on November 12, 1984, in protest over the seating of the POLISARIO delegation; and the continuing desert war between Moroccan forces and POLISARIO Front guerrillas. Despite a cease-fire declared in 1991, and the presence of U.N. peacekeeping forces to implement a referendum on self-determination, the Western Sahara issue remains at an impasse. This simply confirms the contemporary importance of respecting the paramount principle of self-determination in the case of territorial transfer.

Many of the important points made in this chapter — especially the prohibition of the use of force in the acquisition of territory — were vividly illustrated by the dispute between Argentina and the United Kingdom over the Falkland Islands. On April 2, 1982, the armed forces of Argentina invaded the Falkland Islands of the South Atlantic over the sovereignty of these islands (called *Islas Malvinas* by the Argentinians), inhabited by fewer than two thousand people. Their title had been disputed intermittently by Argentina since 1833, when the British seized and occupied the islands. During seventeen years of negotiations preceding the invasion, the United Kingdom and Argentina had failed to resolve the dispute. The Argentine forces overran a small British garrison and quickly captured the islands. One day later, April 3, the U.N. Security Council adopted Resolution 502, which determined the existence of "a breach of the peace," demanded "an immediate cessation of hostilities" and "an immediate withdrawal of all Argentine forces from the Falkland Islands," and called on Argentina and the United Kingdom to seek a diplomatic solution to the dispute.[14] Following failed mediation by the United States and the U.N. secretary-general, the United Kingdom succeeded in retaking the islands by force of arms as a matter of self-defense. Argentina surrendered on June 14, and the seventy-four-day war came to an end. On November 4, 1982, the General Assembly passed a resolution urging the United Kingdom and Argentina to negotiate their dispute over title to the Falkland Islands.[15]

In support of their respective claims for title to the islands, both Argentina and the United Kingdom have invoked such traditional modalities for the acquisition of territory as discovery, occupation, and prescription and have raised the issue of self-determination, but they have emphasized different sets of relevant facts and temporal features. Argentina has stressed its succession to Spain's early title to the islands upon its independence from Spain in 1816 and the factor of contiguity. The United Kingdom has insisted that its title to the Falkland Islands has long been perfected and hence cannot be disturbed by mere protest or claim to contiguity, because the United Kingdom has exercised effective, unbroken, open, and peaceful control and administration over the islands since 1833, aside from the fact that all the inhabitants there today are British and wish to remain under British rule.

As the matter stands, a negotiated solution appears remote. So does an authoritative determination by an international tribunal. But the Falkland Islands conflict has underscored the utmost importance of a fundamental community policy governing territorial disputes under contemporary international law — non-use of force.

In any event, today it is keenly perceived that much more than acreage is involved in changing the status of a territory; human beings simply cannot be disposed of as if they were sand and rocks. In the celebrated dictum of Judge Hardy C. Dillard in *Western Sahara,* "It is for the people to determine the destiny of the territory and not the territory the destiny of the people." When a territorial transfer occurs, it involves more than territory in the abstract — indeed, the entire community process of authority and control over people, resources, and institutions is at stake. Changes extend to the external as well as the internal process of a given domain. If territorial changes are to occasion the least peril to world public order, any settlement must be in accord with two interdependent policies: minimization of unauthorized coercion and self-determination. Any territorial change imposed against these basic community policies carries the seeds of its own destruction and resembles a time bomb that threatens world security.

In addition to the rules governing title to territory, international law has developed a distinct and extensive body of principles dealing with the delimitation of boundaries. Although state boundaries are usually established by treaty or custom in general terms, the precise delimitation of a particular boundary can encounter enormous difficulties. Delimitation problems not only arise between new states with ill-defined boundary lines but may also involve particular areas for delimitation within states having long-standing uncontested boundaries. A preferred state practice is to form commissions, which are mandated to implement the guidelines agreed on by the parties involved in a particular boundary dispute. Several important decisions of the International Court of Justice have shed light in this area.

9

Control and Use of the Sea

Any realistic consideration of the international law of the sea must begin with the peculiarities of the social process by which the seas are exploited and enjoyed. This process has many salient features. The sea, well known for its spatial-extension resources, can accommodate manifold needs for navigation and transit. Unlike the land masses, the sea is a relatively shareable resource; it is vast and its expanses are great. Its known resources comprise both renewable, flow resources and nonrenewable, stock resources. Tremendous numbers of people have the technologies to exploit these resources. Many objectives can be satisfied from using and exploiting the seas, notably transportation, communication, the production of food, and the exploitation of minerals. The use of the oceans may affect every value people cherish, and scientific knowledge and developing technologies may yet disclose new uses. The strategy employed may be cooperative and noncompetitive: what one gets, others may also get. The cooperative use and enjoyment of the oceans in the past three centuries has resulted in a tremendous production of goods and services for distribution to all humankind.

It has been traditionally assumed that the ocean space and its resources were inexhaustible; hence each participant has been accorded a high degree of freedom on the high seas to engage in accepted activities without undue interference.

Contemporary realities have rendered this earlier assumption invalid, with the growing realization that the extent to which the resources of the sea can be exploited is limited. Certain species of fish have been overexploited. Problems of economic recoverability greatly affect the availability of nonliving resources from the sea. Rapid increases in offshore petroleum drilling activities and in the volume of traffic at sea make risk of collision at sea of pressing concern in coastal zone management. Problems of marine pollution associated with oil and waste disposal, moreover, require attention in the community effort to protect the ocean ecosystem. International straits assume new strategic significance in an age of astropolitics.

Broadly conceived, three types of claims on the sea can be identified. The first are claims to access — the use and enjoyment of the ocean. The second are claims to competence (jurisdiction) in making and applying law regarding activities on the oceans. The third are claims to resources.

These three types of claims may be made with regard to any of the waters of the globe — to areas technically described as internal waters, the territorial sea, and the contiguous zone. More recently, they are made with regard to the continental shelf and the exclusive economic zone. They are, of course, always made in relation to the high seas.

Some caution is in order in using the terms *internal waters, territorial sea, contiguous zone, continental shelf, exclusive economic zone,* and *high seas.* These technical terms, normative-ambiguous, refer both to facts and to legal consequences and purport both to describe and to state preferences. At this point it is better to keep clear their factual reference in terms of the geographical distribution of these types of claims to global waters. Too often the labels are used merely to express justifications behind different decisions or choices among competing claims.

BASIC COMMUNITY POLICY

The paramount function of the international law of the sea is to protect and secure the common interests, inclusive and exclusive, of the peoples of the world and to reject all claims of special interest. Consisting of a flow of decisions that emanate from the larger constitutive processes of the world community, it is designed to establish an ordered, economic, effective way for the peoples of the world most fully to exploit the entire oceans in their common interest.

The common interests to be protected fall into two broad categories: inclusive and exclusive. By *inclusive interests* is meant demands and expectations about activities that have a degree of collective impact, generating significant transnational or global consequences. By *exclusive interests* is meant demands and expectations about activities whose impact extends primarily to the peoples of a territorial community. The common interests are secured through the proper harmonization of both inclusive and exclusive interests.

Perceived comprehensively, the inclusive interests of the peoples of the world include maintaining minimum order, in the sense of minimizing un-authorized coercion and violence, and pursuing optimum order, in the sense of the greatest production and widest distribution of all demanded values that are attainable with available resources. For centuries the public order of the oceans has sought to achieve both minimum order and optimum order. Keeping the oceans of the world open for the shared use of all those having the necessary capacities and skills has contributed mightily to the greater aggregate produc-tion and distribution of goods and services to benefit all humankind.

An exclusive interest, as an essential component of the common interest, refers to interests regarding which community members have a shared concern because of the distinct impacts of the activities involved, though not exactly in the same manner and degree. For instance, an important interest of every state of the world is to protect the community processes on its land masses from dangers and threats from the oceans. Hence, every state has an interest in the waters proximate to it, which will permit it to preserve the security and integrity of its community processes and to pursue the greatest productivity and fairness in distribution. No two states of the world, however, have the same interest in proximate waters. Canada and Mexico, respectively, have different interests in the waters immediately off their coasts from those the United States has in the waters off its coasts. Given the length of its coastlines, the United States has the most extensive interests of this kind; many other states, meanwhile, have com-parable interests, though in different degrees. Because of this comparability in interest it has long been perceived to be in the common interest of all states that every state be accorded some degree of control over proximate waters.

By a *special interest* is meant a claim that is destructive in its impact on others and bears no rational relation to a genuine exclusive interest that can be shared with others. For example, the extravagant claims for two-hundred-mile territorial seas by some countries (such as Chile, Peru, and Ecuador) are claims of special interest, made without regard for their impact on others and with destructive consequences for the total production and distribution of goods and services. Such claims cannot be made with promises of reciprocity and do not represent genuine exclusive interests. Should other states follow suit and make comparable claims, the common interest would disintegrate completely, with countries losing out in the end.

Special interests are by definition inimical to common interests. When states depart from the yardstick of common interest, the only alternative is naked power. If a state makes a claim that it cannot make with a promise of reciprocity to other states, it invites coercive response and violent retaliation. What is meant, then, by special interests are those interests that are asserted against the community without regard to their impact. A major purpose for which the global constitutive process is maintained is to reject claims of special interest and to secure a public order based on common interest.

For every state of the world, exclusive interests increase the closer one is to shore, and the farther one moves from the shore, the more inclusive interests predominate. It would appear, in light of several centuries of successful cooperative enjoyment of the oceans, that a strong presumption is given in favor of the inclusive interest. Where many people are able and willing to engage in production, where the resource is highly shareable, and where the utmost production can be achieved by sharing, a presumption exists in favor of sharing. This does not mean that exclusive interests should be disregarded. What is required for rational decision is a way of accommodating the exclusive interests of the coastal states in proximate waters with the inclusive interests of all states in the utmost enjoyment of all waters in the light of differences in context.

The perception of what constitutes inclusive interest and exclusive interest has evolved over time, reflecting the changing demands and expectations of the peoples of the world under ever changing conditions, especially the advancement in science-based technology. The task of attaining the common interest by harmonizing both inclusive and exclusive interests and by rejecting special interests is a complex and dynamic process. The tension inherent in this delicate task has been manifested in the trends in decision and development.

TRENDS IN DECISION

Since 1609, when Hugo Grotius propounded the doctrine of the freedom of the seas, the bulk of the international law of the sea has developed through custom. This body of customary law sustained a public order of the ocean for more than three centuries. Customary law, as policed by reciprocity, retaliation, and self-restraint, gives some assurance of rationality and stability.

Historically, as underscored by the early debate between Grotius and John Selden — open sea versus closed sea — tension between the freedom of the seas for inclusive use and the appropriation of the seas for exclusive use has been perennial. The regime of the territorial sea represented exclusive use and that of the high seas, inclusive use. Within the narrow confine of territorial seas, inclusive use for the general community was circumscribed to accommodate the exclusive interest of the coastal state: though noncoastal states enjoyed the right of innocent passage, they had no right to its resources. In contrast, beyond the territorial sea was the regime of the high seas, providing inclusive use to all states, allowing them to navigate freely and to use its resources.

The international law of the sea is not a mere static body of rules but a whole decision-making process. It is a process of uninterrupted interaction, of continuous demand and response, in which the decision makers of particular nation-states unilaterally put forward diverse claims to use the world's seas, and other decision makers, both national and transnational, respond by either accepting or rejecting them. This process, grounded in the practices and sanctioning expectations of nation-state officials, is always changing and developing, as the demands and expectations of peoples are modified by the exigencies of new interests and technology and by other evolving conditions in the world arena.

Although the customary law of the sea offered considerable rationality and stability for more than three hundred years, the slow evolutionary process tended to fall behind the changing pace of the world. During the era of the League of Nations, attempts toward codification made at the Hague conference in 1930 were without success.

After the creation of the United Nations, the first major undertaking for codification was the First United Nations Law of the Sea Conference in 1958, in which more than eighty states participated. Four conventions were adopted, dealing, respectively, with the territorial sea and the contiguous zone, the high seas, the continental shelf, and fishing and conservation of the living resources of the high seas. With the exception of the convention on the continental shelf, the other three conventions reflected essentially the long-acknowledged customary law.

The failure to agree on the breadth of the territorial sea at the Second United Nations Conference on the Law of the Sea in 1960 was a significant omen — the collapse of an old order of the sea and an accelerating search for a new order to govern the use, exploitation, and enjoyment of the oceans.

The advance of technology has led not only to new uses of the ocean, especially the exploitation of oil and gas on the continental shelf and the future mining of polymetallic nodules in the deep seabed and ocean floor, but also to intensified demands for access to the ocean resources. The rush by coastal states to grab the resources of the seas through extravagant claims for the expansion of maritime zones, the growing concern about overfishing and marine pollution, and the insistent demands of the newly independent states have become highly pronounced. The imperative search for the common interest in a world of complex interdependencies and of proliferating nation-states of diverse backgrounds, amid conflicting national claims and the rapid development of science-based technologies, has most recently inspired and led to a sustained, collective effort to formulate a comprehensive convention on the law of the sea.

The Third United Nations Conference on the Law of the Sea (UNCLOS III) was an ambitious, comprehensive undertaking. It dealt not just with particular problems but with the entire spectrum of issues in the contemporary law of the sea. The convening of UNCLOS III was traceable to the Sea Bed Committee, established in 1967 by the General Assembly to consider the question of the deep seabed lying beyond the limits of national jurisdiction; the impetus came from Arvid Pardo, then Malta's ambassador to the United Nations, who first called world attention to the immense resources of the seabed and ocean floor beyond the limits of national jurisdiction and proposed that such resources be kept as the "common heritage of mankind."[1] From its first organizational session in December 1973 to the adoption of the final act in December 1982 (with 149 delegations participating), UNCLOS III took eleven formal sessions, holding altogether some ninety-four weeks of meetings. The conference proceeded by a consensus approach without formal vote-taking, seeking to accommodate, in dealing with a wide range of issues, competing and conflicting demands and interests of participants — notably, between the major maritime powers and the coastal states; between coastal states and landlocked and geographically disadvantaged states; between food supply through optimum yield and conservation of living resources; between coastal fishing and distant-water fishing; between states with broad continental shelves and states with narrow continental shelves; between developed and developing nations; between exploitation of mineral resources and environmental concerns; and between marine research and national security.

When the U.N. Convention on the Law of the Sea came up for formal adoption on April 30, 1982, the vote was recorded at the request of the United States. The convention was adopted 130 to 4, with 17 abstentions. The convention contains 320 articles and nine annexes. Its seventeen parts deal with the following: (1) use of terms and scope (Article 1); (2) territorial sea and contiguous zone (Articles 2–33); (3) straits used for international navigation (Articles 34–45); (4) archipelagic states (Articles 46–54); (5) exclusive economic zone (Articles 55–75); (6) continental shelf (Articles 76–85); (7) high seas (Articles 86–120); (8) regime of islands (Article 121); (9) enclosed or semi-enclosed seas (Articles 122–23); (10) right of access of landlocked states to and from the sea and freedom of transit (Articles 124–32); (11) the Area (Articles 133–91); (12) protection and preservation of the marine environment (Articles 192–237); (13) marine scientific research (Articles 238–65); (14) development and transfer of marine technology (Articles 266–78); (15) settlement of disputes (Articles 279–99); (16) general provisions (Articles 300–304); and (17) final provisions (Articles 305–20).

The nine annexes are (1) highly migratory species; (2) Commission on the Limits of the Continental Shelf (containing 9 articles); (3) basic conditions of prospecting, exploration, and exploitation (22 articles); (4) statute of the enterprise (13 articles); (5) conciliation (14 articles); (6) statute of the International Tribunal for the Law of the Sea (41 articles), (7) arbitration (13 articles); (8) special arbitration (5 articles); and (9) participation by international organizations (4 articles).

Part XI of the 1982 Convention originally called for a highly interventionist administration of deep seabed resources, reflecting the demands of a then socialist-leaning third world to an extent unacceptable to "pioneer investors" and to the United States (particularly under the Reagan administration) and other developed nations. Because of strong objections by these parties to Part XI, ratification of UNCLOS III was held up for ten years. However, in response to significant political and economic changes as well as an approaching ratification deadline, consultations begun in 1990 brought all nations around to form the agreement, a compromise that allowed the entire Convention to come into effect in 1994. The new Law of the Sea Treaty (and the accompanying agreement) builds on the prevailing practice of participating states, reflects the evolution of international law in response to the changing globe, and charts a new course in some areas, notably in its ratification procedures and its compulsory third-party dispute settlement system. Many nations, including the United States, generally regard the 1982 Convention as the authoritative expression of existing international law.

It is possible only to spotlight key areas of concern and interest:

Internal Waters

Internal waters refers to the waters on the landward side of the baseline by which the territorial sea is measured, including lakes, rivers, canals, ports, bays, and historic bays. International law authorizes states to make law for their internal waters — to regulate the use of these waters and to decide who can come in, who has to keep out, and what they can do while they are in there.

A coastal state has complete authority over its internal waters, because internal waters adjoin the land territory of a state. This authority is nearly as comprehensive as sovereignty over the land masses.

A state has complete authority to control access of vessels, both private and governmental, to internal waters. In this zone of waters, no right of innocent passage for foreign vessels exists. Under customary international law, foreign ships do not enjoy a general right of access to a state's ports. The Convention and Statute on the International Regime of Maritime Ports of 1923 enunciated the policy of freedom of access to ports by foreign merchant ships on the basis of reciprocity. Although it has not been widely ratified, such access is generally and widely effected through bilateral treaties on the condition of reciprocity.

Once foreign ships enter ports or other internal waters, they are subject to the territorial sovereignty of the coastal state. The coastal state may prescribe and apply its laws against foreign ships and those on board, with such exceptions as operations of sovereign and diplomatic immunities, matters of the captain's discipline over the crew, and matters of "internal economy" of foreign ships. Every foreign ship (including warships) in internal waters must comply with the laws governing navigation, health, safety, and port administration of the coastal state.

Each state has complete authority over the resources of its internal waters, which are generally reserved for exclusive national exploitation.

The Territorial Sea

The *territorial sea,* also known as territorial waters, marginal sea, and the maritime belt, refers to the belt of sea adjoining the coast over which a coastal state asserts sovereign authority. The sovereignty of the coastal state extends to the airspace over the territorial sea and its seabed and subsoil. The territorial sea is measured seaward from the baselines delimiting internal waters.

Before UNCLOS III, wide disagreement existed about the most basic of sea law issues, the breadth of the territorial sea. The three-mile territorial sea, which originated in the cannon-shot rule, was strongly challenged in the 1960s and the 1970s. In the early 1980s, of the 137 independent coastal states, only a small minority (24) followed the three-mile rule; a few claimed six miles, the overwhelming majority (79) claimed twelve miles, and 26 states claimed a territorial sea of more than twelve miles (some reaching as far as two hundred miles). The first U.N. conference in 1958 failed to agree on the width of the territorial waters, and the second U.N. conference in 1960 failed by one vote to adopt the proposal to extend the territorial sea to six miles. The Law of the Sea Convention settles this long-contested issue, providing, in Article 3, that the outer limits of the territorial sea are not to exceed twelve nautical miles from the baseline.

The normal baseline from which the width of the territorial sea is measured is the low-water mark. But because of peculiar geographical configurations or other considerations, some states have departed from this practice by drawing straight baselines across bays and areas of the coast indented by fjords and islands. This delimitation method was approved by the International Court of Justice in 1951 in the Anglo-Norwegian *Fisheries* case.[2] The court held that the Norwegian scheme of baseline delimitation, employing a series of straight lines of varying lengths to link a number of points most of which were not on the mainland, was permissible in international law. This method, incorporated in the Geneva Convention on the Territorial Sea (1958), is reaffirmed by the Law of the Sea Convention in Article 7.

The territorial sea is functionally regarded as the seaward extension of a coastal state's territory over which is exercised sovereignty, limited only by the corresponding exercise of the right of other states to "innocent passage." This right affords ships of all states the right to navigate through the territorial sea, for the purpose of traversing it without entering internal waters, or of proceeding to or from internal waters, provided the passage is innocent. Passage is innocent if it does not prejudice the peace, good order, or security of the coastal state. The new convention, in Article 19(2), specifies a list of acts that are "prejudicial to the peace, good order or security of the coastal state" in order to secure greater stability and to minimize potential conflicts of arbitrary unilateral determinations and retaliations. It also prohibits discrimination based on the flag or destination of a ship.

The right of innocent passage is applicable to all ships, including warships; the new convention deliberately does not distinguish between merchant ships and warships. The right of innocent passage, however, does not extend to aircraft or submerged submarines. Aircraft are not permitted to pass over territorial waters without the coastal state's consent, and submarines must navigate on the surface and show their flags (Article 20).

International Straits

With the expansion of the territorial sea from three to twelve miles, the high seas corridors of some 116 straits used for international navigation, whose widths are between six and twenty-four miles, would be lost (for example, the Straits of Gibraltar, Hormuz, and Malacca). What would then happen to the long-established freedom of navigation on the high seas waters of international straits, a freedom clearly affirmed by the International Court of Justice in the *Corfu Channel* case of 1949?[3]

From the outset of UNCLOS III, the major maritime powers were acutely concerned with this problem. They predicated their acceptance of a twelve-mile territorial sea on a guarantee of unimpeded passage, for warships as well as merchant ships, through the straits thus affected.

In response, the new convention creates a regime of transit passage, applicable to straits "used for international navigation between one part of the high seas or an exclusive economic zone and another part of the high seas or an exclusive economic zone" (Article 37). It is designed to secure the common interest by providing freedom of navigation through, over, and under these straits, as well as safeguarding the safety and environmental interests of straits states. It seeks to redress a deficiency of the pre–UNCLOS III law that failed to make a meaningful distinction between passage through the territorial sea and transit of straits.

The right of transit passage is to be distinguished from the right of innocent passage: the former applies to straits used for international navigation, whereas the latter applies to passage through all other territorial seas not located within such straits. Transit passage involves freedom of navigation and overflight for the sole purpose of continuous and expeditious transit of the strait. Transit passage extends to aircraft and embraces the right of submerged transit by submarines through such straits. In addition, states bordering straits are not permitted to hamper or suspend transit passage.

Archipelagos

A number of states (such as Indonesia, the Philippines, and Fiji) whose territories consist of groups of islands lying near one another, have made claims to have the waters between their islands recognized as internal waters so as to achieve national unity, integrity, and security. The potential impact on the freedom of navigation is enormous.

The new convention endows archipelagic states with sovereign authority over all waters within the archipelagos but, in Article 53, subjects such authority to a right of "archipelagic sea lanes passage" through archipelagic waters. This right, similar to transit passage, extends to all aircraft and ships, including submerged submarines. The convention prescribes specific guidelines for delimiting archipelagic sea zones.

Archipelagic states retain sovereignty over airspace above their waters and to the seabed below and may designate sealanes and air routes for the purpose of transit passage. These courses should follow the normal traditional passage routes to afford foreign ships and aircraft an unobstructed right of passage. Archipelagic sealane passage is thus essentially equivalent to the right of transit passage through straits.

The Contiguous Zone

Beyond the territorial sea, all coastal states are accorded under Article 33 of the new convention a contiguous zone, an area not extending more than twenty-four nautical miles (formerly twelve miles) from the baselines from which the territorial sea is measured. In this belt, a coastal state may exercise its authority to prevent or punish violations of its regulations concerning customs, immigration, and fiscal and sanitary matters committed or intended to be committed within its territory or territorial sea.

When the coastal state has good reason to believe that a ship has violated its laws and regulations, it may pursuant to Article 111 undertake "hot pursuit" of a foreign ship in order to apprehend it. The chase must be commenced when the foreign ship is in the pursuing state's territorial sea or contiguous zone and must cease when the pursued ship enters the territorial sea of its own state or of a third state. A coastal state's exercise of criminal jurisdiction on board a foreign ship is proper only when such ship is passing through the territorial sea and is limited to prosecution for acts that would have deleterious effects in the coastal state's territory.

The Exclusive Economic Zone

One of the most radical and far-reaching transformations in the law of the sea under the new convention is the new authority given to coastal states over an enormous ocean area, designated as the exclusive economic zone. The exclusive economic zone is a belt of ocean two hundred nautical miles wide in which coastal states have sovereign rights to explore and exploit natural resources of the superjacent waters and seabed. This zone, constituting about one-third of the world's oceans, is especially rich in fisheries resources. It is estimated that about 99 percent of the total world catch of ocean fish comes from seas within exclusive economic zones.

The Convention on Fishing and Conservation of Living Resources of the High Seas of 1958 recognized the particular interest a coastal state has in maintaining the productivity of the living resources in any area of the high sea adjacent to its territorial sea. Many states simply went ahead to claim a two-hundred-mile territorial sea to protect fisheries.

The trend toward a two-hundred-mile exclusive economic zone began with the claims for exclusive fishery areas off their shores by Latin American states and was fortified by whaling industries eager to protect their rights of access.

The nature of the exclusive economic zone has been disputed. Many maritime nations, including the United States, regard it as essentially part of the high seas that is subject to special economic rights for the coastal states. Some others regard it as a further extension of the territorial sea within which foreign states may exercise certain high seas rights.

In the exclusive economic zone, coastal states enjoy sovereign rights not for comprehensive purposes but for particular purposes, especially the management of natural resources. All other states of the world community may share in the use of and access to these zones. Coastal states, under Article 56 of the new convention, have sovereign rights regarding natural resources and certain economic activities and enjoy certain types of authority over scientific research and environmental protection. A state's sovereign rights to explore, exploit, conserve, and manage extend not only to all living resources in the zone but also to nonliving resources of the seabed, its subsoil, and superjacent waters and other related activities (such as the production of energy from the water, currents, and winds).

All other states enjoy, under Article 58, essentially high seas freedoms — namely, freedom of navigation and overflight in the zone and freedom to lay submarine cables and pipelines. They may also engage in a variety of permissible uses relating to these freedoms, including certain naval operations, weather monitoring, recreational swimming, and so on.

Landlocked and geographically disadvantaged states (especially those in the region) are accorded the right to participate in exploiting part of the zone's fisheries when the coastal state cannot harvest them all itself (Articles 69 and 70).

The convention stresses the importance of reciprocity between coastal states and all other states. Although the coastal state must give due regard to the rights and duties of other states in relation to the zone, all other states must regard the rights and duties of the coastal state and comply with its laws.

The Continental Shelf

Geographically speaking, the continental shelf constitutes the area of the seabed that is the natural prolongation of the coastal land out beneath the sea to the point where the seabed begins its precipitous descent into the ocean abyss. The areas of continental shelves contain virtually all of the oceans' known nonliving organic resources, including oil and gas.

Contemporary international law on the continental shelf is said to have begun with President Truman's proclamation of 1945 claiming the natural resources of the subsoil and seabed of the continental shelf adjacent to the United States. This act was quickly emulated by the United States's regional neighbors (Mexico, Argentina, and so on) and other countries.

By the convening of the First United Nations Conference on the Law of the Sea in 1958, the question of the continental shelf had become a major subject of common concern, leading to the conclusion of the Convention on the Continental Shelf. The convention, in Article 1, recognized the sovereign rights of coastal states to explore the continental shelf and to exploit its natural resources, extending "to a depth of 200 meters or, beyond that limit, to where the depth of the superjacent waters admits of the exploitation of the natural resources." The second of the two criteria — known as the exploitability test — was less than precise and soon became a major source of controversy because of the changing technology of resource exploitation.

In the protracted process of negotiation under UNCLOS III, the task of defining the continental shelf was enormous, because the competing interests of the coastal states with extensive continental shelves, the two superpowers, the Arab states (none of which has a continental shelf exceeding two hundred miles), and the landlocked and geographically disadvantaged states were to be given balanced and judicious considerations. A complex formula of delimiting the continental shelf was thus adopted.

Under the complex formula of Article 76 of the new convention, the continental shelf of the coastal state extends to the edge of the continental margin, where the seabed drops off into the deep ocean, or to a distance of 200 miles where the continental margin does not extend that far. When the outer edge of the continental margin extends beyond 200 miles from the coastal state's baselines, the limit of the continental shelf shall lie where the thickness of sedimentary rocks is at least 1 percent of the shortest distance from such point to the nearest point on the continental slope, as long as this distance is no more than 60 miles from the continental slope. In no case shall the limit of the shelf lie more than 350 miles from the coastal state's baselines or more than 100 miles beyond the 2,500-meter depth line (isobath), whichever is greater. Thus, in effect, the continental shelf has four possible outer limits: 200 nautical miles; the outer edge of the continental margin; 350 nautical miles; and 100 miles from the 2,500-meter isobath.

The coastal state has sole sovereign rights to the natural resources of its continental shelf. But this does not affect the status of the waters above it. The two are legally independent. The rights of the coastal state must not, therefore, in their exercise, cause any "unjustifiable interference" with any rights of other states that may inhere in these superjacent waters. The status of a seabed area as continental shelf likewise does not affect the rights of other states to lay submarine cables or pipelines across it.

The new convention imposes three new duties on the coastal state in reference to its continental shelf: (1) the state must set up environmental standards as to resource exploitation on its entire continental shelf; (2) the state must pay a percentage of all revenue derived from exploitation of the shelf, beyond a two-hundred-mile distance, into a special international fund for the benefit of developing countries; and (3) the coastal state may not prohibit marine scientific research on the shelf beyond a two-hundred-mile distance outside specified development areas.

States with opposite or adjacent shorelines must decide on a boundary between their continental shelves in accordance with Article 83. The overriding guidance is to reach an "equitable solution." One interesting example of such a delimitation is set forth in the *Gulf of Maine Case,* decided by the International Court of Justice under its chambers procedure in October 1984.[4] In drawing a single maritime boundary dividing both the continental shelves and the exclusive fisheries zones of Canada and the United States in the Georges Bank area, centering around the Gulf of Maine, the court interestingly steered clear of all sociological or scientific arguments and instead based its decision on more clearly apparent geographical factors.

High Seas

Under the Convention on the High Seas of 1958, the high seas comprise all oceans not included in internal waters and the territorial sea. With the inclusion of the exclusive economic zone, the new convention does not define the high seas but simply applies its provisions on the high seas to all parts of the seas beyond the exclusive economic zones. The convention also makes most of the provisions on the high seas applicable within the exclusive economic zone insofar as they are not incompatible with the prescriptions governing the exclusive economic zone.

The high seas are open to all states, coastal and landlocked, and all enjoy their freedoms. These include (1) freedom of navigation; (2) freedom of overflight; (3) freedom to lay submarine cables and pipelines; (4) freedom to construct artificial islands and other installations; (5) freedom of fishing; and (6) freedom of scientific research.

On the high seas, every state has the competence to sail ships flying its flag. Ships on the high seas are required, as a matter of common interest, to comply with regulations governing the safety of navigation, the protection of life at sea, and the minimization of marine pollution, as primarily prescribed by the flag state.

Both warships and state-owned or state-operated ships enjoy complete immunity from jurisdiction of any state other than the flag state while on the high seas.

Unless otherwise permitted by treaty, passage of a foreign vessel on the high seas may be interfered with only in certain circumstances. Any state's warship may seize a pirate ship on the high seas. A pirate ship is defined as one used by private individuals for private acts of violence or depredation against another ship, its passengers, or their property while outside the jurisdictional domain of any state.

On the high seas, any state's warship may also board a ship suspected of engaging in the slave trade or one that is a "stateless vessel." Under the new convention it is also permissible under certain circumstances for a state's ship to board a foreign ship that is engaged in unauthorized broadcasting on the high seas.

International Seabed Area

A novel development in the new convention is the inclusion of a comprehensive legal regime to explore and exploit the bottom of the deep ocean in areas beyond the continental shelf of any state. The Area, as the international seabed area has come to be known, comprises the seabed and subsoil beyond the limits of national jurisdiction. For a time interest centered on potential riches in polymetallic nodules, which contain manganese, nickel, copper, and cobalt and lie on or just below the surface of the deep seabeds, with the greatest concentration in the Pacific Ocean near Hawaii.

In making the mineral resources of the Area a "common heritage of mankind," the convention does not permit any state to claim, exercise sovereign authority over, or appropriate any part of the deep seabed or its resources. Instead, the convention creates an International Seabed Authority (the Authority, ISA) to govern the regime of the deep seabed with the Enterprise as its operating arm and adopts a "parallel system" of exploration and exploitation. The Enterprise has the responsibility to carry out activities in the Area directly and also to transport, process, and market minerals recovered from the Area.

The Authority, having the standard structure of an international governmental organization, consists of an assembly, a council, and a secretariat. The assembly, composed of all states parties to the convention, is the supreme organ of the Authority, responsible for prescribing general policies. Matters of substance are decided by a two-thirds majority.

The council, consisting of thirty-six members, is endowed with the important authority to prescribe mining regulations and procedures, restrictive environmental orders, and so on. The formula for representation on the council, as a result of intense struggle and negotiations, is complex, seeking to accommodate the demands of the important producers of certain minerals with those of the most important consumers and to balance the needs of various communities in terms of technology and actual production.

The Agreement

The 1982 Convention took nearly twelve years to ratify, owing to the developed nations' perception that ISA provisions and representation on the council did not correspond to their interest and investment in deep seabed mining operations. However, the fall of the Soviet Union, a new spirit of international cooperation following the end of the Cold War, a strong shift toward market-oriented economies, and a weakened Group of Seventy-Seven all contributed to the ability of all participants to come to an agreement revising Part XI.[5] In addition, the feasibility of getting the acclaimed nodules had receded well into the twenty-first century, while many developing nations were now, for all practical purposes, "developed" nations more appreciative of neoliberal economic theories.

The ISA's power to impose production limitations was eliminated, and the

Enterprise was streamlined, some of its advantages over private mining companies taken away. In addition, objectionable provisions requiring large fees from miners ($1 million a year), transfer of technology, and the sharing of surplus wealth with less developed nations (including groups such as the PLO) were completely eliminated. The agreement ensures that market approaches will dominate, with industrialized countries guaranteed an influence commensurate with their interests and investments. The United States is guaranteed a seat on the council, and future amendments cannot be adopted over U.S. objections.

Thus, key provisions to redistribute global wealth — in decision-making, production limitation, and finance and amendment procedures — were revised in the 1994 agreement to reflect a preference for emphasizing interests, not merely numbers, in international decision-making.

Article 4 (2) of the 1994 Agreement states that "no state or entity may establish its consent to be bound by the Agreement unless it has previously established or establishes at the same time its consent to be bound by the Convention." The agreement is to be applied as a single document with the 1982 convention. All future ratifications or accessions to the convention would imply consent to the agreement, and no state may consent to the agreement without consent to the convention. This linkage is essential, because in reality Part XI was not the most important subject under negotiation at UNCLOS III. The deep seabed negotiations concerned a use that had not yet taken place, whereas other parts of UNCLOS III address contemporary activities with direct benefits for the international community. With this linkage, widespread adherence to the entire convention will protect many important interests in the oceans.

The procedures devised for ratification of the agreement were quite flexible, allowing, for example, consent either directly or by implication and allowing provisional application under certain conditions. (The Seabed Council granted provisional membership to the United States until November 1998.) This flexibility, in contrast to formalistic procedures from the nineteenth century, is due to the increased role in international law played today by international institutions and multipartite diplomacy since the time of the League of Nations.

Rather than formulated rules found only in precedent and archives, the law of the sea was formed by a multiplicity of participants and agreements in a new, dynamic process of patient negotiation, quiet consultation, and public debate.[6] Hailed as "the Constitution of the Oceans," it is a comprehensive legal system under the auspices of the United Nations, reflecting vast advances in the making of international law in this century.

Dispute Settlement System of the 1982 Convention

The 1982 Convention (Part XV, Articles 279–299) establishes the dispute settlement system regarding the interpretation and application of its provisions. Its approach was designed to encourage all participants to accept compulsory and binding dispute settlement, and it reflects the growing trend in international law for the acceptability of such third-party dispute resolution.

Parties are encouraged to settle disputes by the means of their mutual choice, including negotiation and conciliation. If these fail the compulsory binding dispute settlement system becomes operative. All participants, upon signing, ratifying, or acceding to the convention, are allowed to choose one or more of three forums: (1) the Tribunal for the Law of the Sea; (2) the International Court of Justice; and (3) arbitration. Disputes involving marine fisheries, the marine environment, and marine scientific research and navigation are assigned a fourth forum. Disputes regarding deep seabed mining are referred to a special chamber of the tribunal. Where disputing parties have not preferred the same forum or have chosen none at all, then arbitration becomes the compulsory mechanism. If the disputing parties prefer the same forum, that forum has jurisdiction beginning upon the unilateral application of either disputant.

Part XV, the world's first compulsory dispute settlement system, is designed to encourage all participants to accept compulsory, binding settlement of disputes as a key part of the 1982 convention. Because it provides a variety of options, the convention encourages the peaceful settlement of disputes, which is, after all the most important objective of international law.[7]

To recapitulate the substantive law of the sea in terms of functional claims rather than maritime zones:

1. *Claims for access (navigation, passage):* A state has complete authority to control access of vessels to internal waters; there is no right of innocent passage for foreign vessels. Within the territorial sea, all states enjoy the right of innocent passage. The right of transit passage applies to international straits. The archipelagic sea lanes passage, a functional equivalent of transit passage, applies to archipelagic waters. The freedom of navigation and overflight applies to exclusive economic zones as well as the high seas.

2. *Jurisdictional authority (competence to make and apply law):* Within internal waters and the territorial sea, the coastal state has exclusive competence to make and apply law to any activities occurring therein. Within the contiguous zone, the coastal state may assert a competence to make and apply law in control of activities relating to customs, fiscal, immigration, and sanitary matters. On the high seas, each state makes and applies law to its own ships, and no state can apply its unilateral competence to the ships of other states except

for violations of certain norms of international law, absent other agreements between individual states.

3. *Resources:* The control of resources within internal waters and the territorial sea is in the hands of the coastal state. The coastal state's control of the resources of its continental shelf is exclusive in that the non-use of all or part of them does not give any other state the right to exploit them. In contrast, the coastal state's control of the resources within its exclusive economic zone is qualified, and shared, by the right of other states to harvest surplus resources under prescribed conditions. The living resources of the high seas are open to all. But the mineral resources in the deep seabed area are internationalized under the rubric of "the common heritage of mankind."

APPRAISAL

The Law of the Sea Convention represents an unprecedented, comprehensive effort to deal with the manifold problems relating to the contemporary use, enjoyment, and exploitation of the oceans. When the UNCLOS III Conference met in Caracas, Venezuela, in 1974, the United States sent the largest delegation by far of any nation to the opening session. But eight years later, when the convention was adopted and opened for signature on December 10, 1982, in Montego Bay, Jamaica, the United States was not among the 119 nations that signed the convention at the grand ceremony.

Owing largely to its opposition to the deep seabed mining provisions, the United States refused to sign the convention and, further, refused to participate as an observer at the preparatory commission, which engaged in drafting regulations to govern deep seabed mining. The basic position of the United States was that the bulk of the convention reflected customary international law upon which the United States would continue to rely regarding matters concerning the law of the sea. In 1983, President Reagan proclaimed the establishment of an Exclusive Economic Zone in which the United States would exercise sovereign rights over living and nonliving resources within two hundred nautical miles of its coast — reflecting in essence the relevant prescriptions embodied in the convention. Reagan also took the occasion to declare the readiness of the United States to "exercise and assert its navigation and overflight rights and freedoms on a worldwide basis in a manner that is consistent with the balance of interests reflected in the Convention."[8]

Fortunately, the 1994 agreement, embodying changes in Part XI and assuring the United States and other industrialized states a voice commensurate with their interests, brought the United States into the convention. With seabed mining sites established by exploration already conducted by U.S. companies affirmed, and with a seat on the council guaranteed, the United States is expected to ratify the convention. The implications of ratification by the United States are great. But even with the coming into force of the 1982 convention, many questions remain. Will the law of the sea sustain the stability of expectations necessary to deal with a range of matters, including the rights of warships to pass through international straits, the allocation of fishing resources among competing states and the conservation and management of fishing stocks, the exploration of oil and gas on the continental shelves close to land, the mining of the mineral resources in the deep seabed, and the protection of the ocean environment in fragile coastal zones? What portions of the convention reflect customary law, and what portions represent new codification? Now that the convention is in effect, what will be the relations in the realm of the ocean between the nonratifying states and the ratifying states? In sum, what will be the world public order of the oceans?

So far, all participants have been able to adapt and compromise in a world transformed by deep social, political, and economic changes such as the end of the Cold War; recognition of our ecosystem's fragility, exhaustibility and need for protection; and great advances in technology, such as deep sea mining. The one criterion that should guide all decisions is of course to secure the common interest of all humankind and reject special interests asserted by any state.

10

Control and Use of Other Resources

In the preceding two chapters, we have largely examined claims by states to acquire territory and resources for their exclusive use. We now turn to certain resources that, except airspace over national territorial domain, are not subject to exclusive appropriation by states. These resources, which permit a high degree of shared use by appropriate accommodation, are shareable resources, also known as strategic resources. The common interest in achieving the optimum production of goods and services to benefit all humankind depends on shared use and an inclusive competence in defense of such use.

Among the important shareable resources are international rivers, airspace (over the oceans), outer space, the polar regions, and the global environment. We examine them in succession.

INTERNATIONAL RIVERS

International rivers, lying in part within the borders of two or more states or forming the boundary between two or more states, affect, geographically and economically, the territories of two or more states. Contiguous rivers serve as state boundaries, and successive rivers traverse two or more states.

International rivers offer multiple uses—navigational and nonnavigational. The interest in navigation has long historical roots. Before the modern industrial era, the flow of water in most international rivers met the needs of all participants, and the unilateral diversion of water, if it occurred at all, caused few hardships for different riparian communities. The coming of the industrial age, with the proliferation of large urban centers and highly developed irrigation and other technologies, has radically changed that: the flow of water in many rivers has appeared insufficient to meet the requirements of all claimants, especially in the absence of appropriate river basin development and management. Increasingly, communities make claims to use the waters for irrigation, hydroelectricity generation, industrial uses, domestic consumption for drinking and sanitation purposes, "municipal use" for whole communities, fishing, and recreational use. States that share watercourse systems are hypersensitive to any diversion of waters, pollution by fertilizers and pesticides, or other interference with enjoyment. The pattern of claim and counterclaim and the factors affecting decision about particular river systems have thus become much more complex.

How to accommodate competing claims for multiple uses of riparian states within one international river system? Although navigational use was once considered paramount, this need not be so. The traditional concern for freedom of navigation has been increasingly overshadowed by growing demands for equitable use. Indeed, navigational use needs to be accommodated with competing demands for other uses.

Inherent in the demands and potential for multiple use of international rivers are certain unities or interdependencies within particular drainage basins. Because of a physical unity or interdependence, activities carried out upstream may affect downstream uses, and vice versa. Hydroelectric power generation, for example, may divert a significant quantity of water from an international river at the expense of downstream users. Irrigation by an upper riparian state may substantially diminish the amount of water available to downstream users and may pollute an international river with fertilizers and pesticides. Pollution and heavy consumption by industrial users may curtail water available for domestic and recreational use. In contrast, the unilateral appropriation of water for irrigation by an upstream state may be frustrated by the threat by the downstream state to close the river for navigational purposes. A lower riparian state may refuse to receive a natural flow of water by erecting a dam for hydroelectric power purposes and cause that water to flood valuable land in a neighboring state.

In sum, the very unities or interdependencies within any particular drainage basin make international rivers an important shareable resource suitable for inclusive competence and shared enjoyment. It requires comprehensive, integrated regional planning to achieve the common interest in the optimum production and equitable distribution of values for all participants.

Because of divergent configurations of factors and different participants involved in differing international river systems, this overriding policy of shareability has found expression neither in general customary law nor in general multilateral treaties. Instead, it has been expressed in a large number of specific agreements entered into by only the riparian states. Notable among such treaty arrangements are those relating to the Danube, the Rhine, the Oder, the Elbe, and the Columbia.

In terms of navigation, there appears to be no customary right concerning freedom of navigation in international waterways, despite a contrary assertion going back to Hugo Grotius. The efforts to establish such freedom through treaty, beginning with the Treaty of Paris of 1814 and the Congress of Vienna of 1815, led to the conclusion of the Barcelona Convention on the Regime of Navigable Waterways of International Concern of 1921. Under the Barcelona Convention the contracting states mutually agree that their vessels shall navigate freely on defined navigable waterways of international concern, and riparian states are authorized to regulate navigation and take police and customs measures in a nondiscriminatory manner. The Barcelona Convention, however, is of more theoretical than practical importance because of the small number of ratifications. The practical enjoyment of freedom of navigation in international rivers, in Europe and in other continents, depends in large part on specific treaty arrangements (for which international river commissions were thus established) for particular river systems.

Turning to nonnavigational uses, two principles governing inclusive use appear to be emerging: a riparian state may not act unilaterally so as to harm the interests of other riparians, and the priority of uses of waters should be guided by the test of reasonableness, despite the divergences of variables involved in different river systems.

Riparian states generally have equal rights to use an international river, so that the waters and their benefits are equitably apportioned, taking into account such factors as prior use practices, historic rights, beneficial (nonwasteful) use, and relative need. Transnational decisions in the area reflect the concern to accommodate the respective interests of riparian states. The needs of upper and lower riparian states, for instance, are typically regulated with the requirement of advance notice and consultation regarding particular uses. Some problems may arise without such procedures in large-scale irrigation cases, as where waters are drastically diverted to benefit one state only or where waters flowing to the lower riparian are contaminated. One prominent example is an incident concerning the U.S. use of the Colorado River for irrigation, which caused a great increase in the salinity of the river. Tremendous areas of Mexican farming land were devastated when contaminated waters reached them.

In order to protect these rights to equitable use, states have widely accepted the Helsinki Rules on the Uses of the Waters of International Rivers.[1] Adopted in 1966 by the International Law Association, the rules are regarded as reflecting then-existing international law. The Helsinki Rules provide in Article 4 that "each basin State is entitled, within its territory, to a reasonable and equitable share in the beneficial uses of waters of an international drainage basin." A "reasonable and equitable share" is to be determined in the light of all the relevant factors in a particular context. Such factors, as illustrated in Article 5(2) of the rules, include the geography of the basin, the hydrology of the basin, the climate affecting the basin, past practice in using the waters of the basin, the relative economic and social needs and population dependencies of each basin state, the comparative costs of alternative uses available, and so on. Such a contextual approach is essential in the pragmatic search for the common interests of all participants.

The International Law Commission began to include the nonnavigational uses of international watercourses in its agenda of work in 1973, and the U.N. General Assembly adopted the Convention on the Law of the Non-navigational Uses of International Watercourses in May 1997. Whereas the Helsinki Rules employed the concept of an "international drainage basin," in the sense of "a geographical area extending over two or more States determined by the watershed limits of the system of waters, including surface and underground waters, flowing into a common terminus,"[2] the International Law Commission has employed a more comprehensive term, *international watercourse*. This distinct shift extends the concern of the commission not only to international river basins but to all other transnational waterways, including lakes, canals, dams, reservoirs, and other surface and subsurface waters. Article 5(2) of the convention provides that "watercourse States shall participate in the use, development and protection of an international watercourse in an equitable and reasonable manner. Such participation includes both the right to utilize the watercourse and the duty to cooperate in the protection and development thereof, as provided in the present Convention." In addition, each system state is entitled to "a reasonable and equitable participation" (within its territory) in this shared resource.[3] It has been noted that the choice of the word *participation* suggests the concomitant duty of states to contribute constructively to the management and conservation of watercourse systems. The pledge to independently and jointly preserve the ecosystems of international watercourses, embodied in Article 20, reflects a commitment to sustainable development and inclusive behavior. The convention employs a dispute settlement system providing for a series of stages beginning with consultation and negotiation and moving to impartial fact-finding, mediation, conciliation, and arbitration or judicial settlement.

AIRSPACE

The advent of aircraft at the turn of the twentieth century raised new problems in international law: who has authority to control access to the superjacent airspace of nation-states and of the high seas and to regulate aviation activities by aircraft, both commercial and military?

Territorial communities have important interests in activities in the airspace superjacent to their territories. The most important interests include the security of the state's territorial base, enhancement of wealth through transportation of people, goods, and mail by air, and safety for persons and property on land. The security of a state may be threatened from the superjacent airspace in many ways: aerial intelligence and observation, unauthorized penetration into airspace, parachuting agents into territory, dropping supplies to agents and local insurgents, disseminating propaganda material hostile to the subjacent state, and so on.

Because of these critical factors, states have shown a remarkable uniformity in claiming comprehensive, exclusive authority over territorial airspace. By this claim they seek to control access to and use of the airspace above their land masses and territorial waters and to prescribe and apply authority over all activities taking place within such airspace. Any theoretical desirability for inclusive, shared use of the domain of airspace is simply overwhelmed by the general preoccupation with national security in a divided world marked by continued expectations of violence.

International law, through both customary practice and explicit agreement, has accorded nation-states a high degree of exclusive authority, at once comprehensive and continuing, over the airspace above their territories. Every state enjoys "complete and exclusive sovereignty" over the airspace above its territory, including its territorial sea.

The view in support of extending the historic doctrine of "freedom of navigation" to airspace, as advanced in the early days of air flight, was quickly relegated to oblivion when World War I vividly demonstrated the monstrous threats posed by aerial warfare and activities.

The overriding policy of airspace sovereignty found expression in the Paris Convention on the Regulation of Aerial Navigation of 1919 and in subsequent multilateral treaties. It is unequivocally reaffirmed in the Chicago Convention on International Civil Aviation of 1944, commonly regarded as the Constitution of Air Law. Article 1 of the Chicago Convention states: "The contracting States recognize that every State has complete and exclusive sovereignty over the airspace above its territory."

Airspace is now commonly accepted as an appurtenance of the subjacent territory. Under the comprehensive, continuing, exclusive authority thus established, access to such airspace depends on the explicit permission of the subjacent state, at its pure discretion.

Efforts to secure through a multilateral treaty some measure of shared access to territorial airspace for regular international air services have been less than successful. Though high hopes were expressed at the Chicago conference in 1944, participants on the whole insisted too heavily on exclusive control to concede any inclusive use of territorial airspace. The Chicago Convention itself failed to incorporate any of what came to be known as the "five freedoms." Instead, two supplementary agreements were formulated: the International Air Transit Agreement and the International Air Transport Agreement. The former contains the first two freedoms:

1. The privilege of free passage without landing;
2. The privilege of flying across with noncommercial, technical landing only (for instance, refueling, repairs, emergencies).

The latter contains the other three freedoms:

3. The privilege of commercial discharge from the home state of the aircraft or airline;
4. The privilege of commercial embarkation to the home state of the aircraft or airline;
5. The privilege of conveying passengers, cargo, and mail between any two contracting States.

The first two, also known as transit rights, are widely accepted. The latter three, also known as traffic rights, which relate to commercial conveyance of passengers, cargo, and mail, have not gained much acceptance. The fifth freedom in particular has become the focal point of bargaining among states in the exchange of traffic rights.

Whatever concessions to the inclusive use of territorial airspace of states that have been granted have resulted largely from bilateral agreement. In practice, an extensive network of thousands of such agreements covers every state of the world. The trend has been accentuated by the proliferation of newly independent states. This reflects the need for states to participate in the flow of world air commerce in an interdependent world of growing mobility and the jealous promotion of national wealth processes, including special protection of domestic aviation industry. It is of course also a matter of prestige.

In spite of the many treaty exceptions to the principle of exclusivity in territorial airspace, nation-states have shown readiness to prevent or repel, by force if necessary, any unauthorized intrusions into their aerial domain. On occasion, certain states have gone so far, in defense of the inviolability of their aerial domain, to use brute force in reacting to the intrusions by an unarmed civilian aircraft either in distress or unintentionally off course. The incident of Korean Air Lines 007, involving the shooting down of a strayed South Korean civilian aircraft over Soviet airspace in September 1983, is a notable example.

The exclusive authority of states extends only to the airspace above state territory, including the territorial waters. Beyond its territorial domain, no state has comprehensive, continuing authority over airspace; that is, the airspace over the high seas is a domain for inclusive use. States are permitted to exercise, as regards ships on the water, an occasional, limited exclusive competence for particular purposes in airspace over the high seas.

OUTER SPACE

The launching of Sputnik I in 1957 ushered in the space age. Two fundamental concepts that have affected humankind — space and time — have thus undergone radical changes, moving from an earth-oriented concept of space and distance to one that encompasses the galaxies. Distance, and the time required to traverse it, have likewise been altered. No longer is space an immense void, gazed at by humans from their earthly environment; it is now part of their experience, a place to walk or float untethered, to cover miles in seconds. Thanks to these spectacular developments, humankind today is capable of leaving the earth and exploring and using outer space. Space law has emerged as a distinct branch of international law.

Though a vast frontier has opened up for exploration and use, the people conducting activities in space are the same people who have been acting on earth. The relevant actors, group and individual, pursue the precise objectives they have sought on earth: power, wealth, enlightenment, skill, and so on. Space is potentially a great shareable resource for humankind: it provides new vistas and challenges. The possibilities to produce greater goods and services through new modes of communication, transportation, and weather control and through newly discovered resources are enormous. At the same time, access to space has endowed humankind a new capability to destroy itself. As space activities generate great collective impact on all peoples of the world, the interdependencies in the shaping and sharing of values that have characterized the earth arena of our time can only intensify with the accelerating conquest of space.

Many important issues of international space law have engaged the attention of experts, scholars, and decision makers. The issues, both existing and potential, relate to access and competence in the domain of space; maintaining both minimum order and optimum order in space; the nationality of spacecraft; jurisdiction over space activities and spacecraft; the enjoyment and acquisition of resources; the establishment of enterprisory activities; and interactions with advanced forms of non-earth life. This inventory of major specific issues suggests the relevance of human experience on earth to the emerging legal problems in space.

An impressive corps of space law has developed within a remarkably short time, thanks to the heritage of customary law and the codification efforts of international governmental organizations, notably the United Nations and the International Telecommunication Union. The United Nations Committee on the Peaceful Uses of Outer Space (UNCOPUOS), created in 1959, has figured prominently in this endeavor. Thanks to its draftsmanship, five major international agreements concerning space have come into being:

1. Treaty on Principles Governing the Activities of States in the Exploration and Use of Outer Space, Including the Moon and Other Celestial Bodies, 1967 (hereafter Outer Space Treaty of 1967) (effective October 10, 1967);
2. Agreement on the Rescue of Astronauts, the Return of Astronauts, and the Return of Objects Launched into Outer Space, 1968 (effective December 3, 1968);
3. Convention on International Liability for Damage Caused by Space Objects, 1972 (effective October 9, 1973);
4. Convention on Registration of Objects Launched into Outer Space, 1975 (effective September 15, 1976); and
5. Agreement Governing the Activities of States on the Moon and Other Celestial Bodies, 1979 (hereafter Moon Agreement).

The boundless and inexhaustible vastness of space makes it highly suitable for shared use by multiple participants at a minimum cost in mutual interference. The cumulative experience of humankind in the productive shaping and sharing of values through the inclusive enjoyment of the oceans, the airspace above the oceans, international rivers, and the polar regions clearly points to the high desirability of comparable inclusive use of space — opening up the vast domain of space to free and equal access of all peoples who can attain the necessary capabilities.

Fortunately, the United Nations enunciated this policy early on. In its famous Resolution 1721 on International Cooperation in the Peaceful Use of Outer Space, the General Assembly in 1961 proclaimed the following guiding principles:

1. International law, including the Charter of the United Nations, applies to outer space and celestial bodies;
2. Outer space and celestial bodies are free for exploration and use by all

States in conformity with international law and are not subject to national appropriation.[4]

It was clear from the outset that outer space would not be subject to the same restrictions as airspace — where each state has exclusive sovereignty over its airspace.

This policy has been reaffirmed by the Outer Space Treaty of 1967, sometimes dubbed the Magna Carta of space law. Article 1 states in part:

> The exploration and use of outer space, including the moon and other celestial bodies, shall be carried out for the benefit and in the interests of all countries, irrespective of their degree of economic or scientific development, and shall be the province of all mankind. Outer space, including the moon and other celestial bodies, shall be free for exploration and use by all States without discrimination of any kind, on a basis of equality and in accordance with international law, and there shall be free access to all areas of celestial bodies.

Article 2 bans national appropriation: "Outer space, including the moon and other celestial bodies, is not subject to national appropriation by claim of sovereignty, by means of use or occupation, or by any other means." Other provisions deal with other aspects relating to space activities.

A comparable regime of freedoms and obligations was set forth in the Moon Agreement of 1979. Included in these freedoms are those for scientific investigation, exploration, and use without discrimination and for establishment of manned and unmanned stations. Article 11 makes the moon and its natural resources "the common heritage of mankind" and forbids national appropriation of any portion of the moon. The Moon Agreement is the first treaty to effectuate the concept of the "common heritage of mankind." Going beyond the vague notion of the "province of mankind," it mandates that an international regime be established to govern the exploitation of the natural resources of the moon and other celestial bodies as soon as such exploitation is about to become feasible.

From the inception of the space age, one persistent question has been the upward extent of sovereign authority of territorial communities. A state enjoys "complete and exclusive" sovereignty in the airspace above its territory, and, theoretically, outer space begins where airspace ends. But, where does airspace end? In other words, where and how to demarcate the line between airspace and outer space? The issue defies an easy solution.

Three major contending approaches exist: the "spacial" (geographical), the functional, and the pragmatic. The spacial approach favors an agreement on an easily determinable boundary at a certain altitude above sea level (say, 70 or 100–110 kilometers). The functional approach, rejecting any arbitrary boundary, focuses on the nature of space activities and asserts that airspace cannot exceed the lowest point at which free orbit of satellites may efficiently occur. The pragmatic approach maintains that a delimitation between airspace and outer space would serve no practical purpose and could unwittingly stifle future space activities and the growth of space law.

The delimitation issue, though regarded as academic by some, was dramatized in 1976 when eight equatorial countries joined in issuing the Bogota Declaration to claim sovereignty over segments of the geostationary orbit lying above their national territories. The geostationary orbit, essential for many broadcasting activities, is that position directly above the equator in which a satellite orbits with the same rotation and speed as the earth's. In asserting exclusive authority over what is deemed to be a finite resource in a unique part of space, the declaration states that "the geostationary synchronous orbit is a physical fact linked to the reality of our planet and its existence depends exclusively on its relation to gravitational phenomena generated by the earth, and that is why it must not be considered part of outer space."[5] This view clearly contradicts the widely shared expectation that the geostationary orbit is a shared resource not subject to national appropriation.

Though the demarcation issue remains an open question, space activities have moved forward and have been expanding. It has become part of customary law that artificial satellites orbiting the earth operate in the domain of outer space, beyond the territorial sovereignty of the underlying state. And a state does enjoy complete and exclusive authority over its space vehicles, laboratories, or stations in free space.

The claim for exclusive authority and control over geostationary orbit, though unacceptable to the world community at large, is another manifestation of the general demand of the developing nations for transfers of technology and sharing of resources, moving from the earth to the space arena. As space activities expand, new problems arise. The increasing commercialization of space has led to problems ranging from "space debris" pollution to the possibility of advertising from outer space. The problems relating to the space shuttle and to the "star wars" proposal have engaged particular attention.

The overall success of the space shuttle has opened the door for developing a routine distinct transportation system and for establishing large colonies in space. A highly versatile aerospace vehicle, the space shuttle ascends into space with the aid of rockets and returns to earth landing on a runway much like a conventional aircraft. Unlike traditional expendable launch vehicles, the space shuttle is practically reusable and is capable of placing satellites in orbit much more economically than could expendable launch vehicles. The advent of the space shuttle raises the question whether the space shuttle is to be regarded as "aircraft" or "spacecraft" and whether, during its ascent and descent, its flights should be regulated by conventional air law and related traffic regulations or governed by the treaties relating to outer space activities.

The question of minimum order in space — peaceful use of outer space — has been a matter of continuing concern since the dawn of the space age. Although the overriding goal of "peaceful use" has been affirmed and reaffirmed, views have diverged about what is meant by peaceful use, especially when the military instrument is somehow involved. The issue was sharpened thanks to President Reagan's proposal for research in the Strategic Defense Initiative, popularly known as star wars. Research on antisatellite weapons and lasers continues to consume staggering amounts of resources, and the proliferation of spy satellites, many of them commercial, threatens to unleash an arms race in space, plaguing hopes for space's peaceful and nonmilitary use.

From man orbiting the earth, walking in space, and setting foot on the moon, to the advent of a reusable winged space shuttle and probes sent to Mars, humankind has indeed come a long way, in less than four decades, in its continuing effort to conquer space. But the concern for peace in space is in the final analysis earthbound. Minimum order in space and minimum order on earth are inseparable.

POLAR REGIONS

Because of their location and climate, the polar regions — the Arctic and the Antarctic — present unique problems in international law. As knowledge concerning the polar regions has increased and the technology necessary to exploit them has developed, legal problems have likewise increased.

The Arctic and Antarctic regions are commonly conceived of as more or less similar in nature. This is true only to a limited extent. Whereas the Arctic consists of an ocean nearly surrounded by land and covered by shifting masses of ice, the Antarctic is a vast ice-covered continent encircled by a frozen sea. The Antarctic is appreciably colder and more prone to intense storms than the Arctic. In terms of human habitation, the Antarctic is also more remote. Both regions are rich in living resources; the extent of mineral resources is yet to be determined.

Territorial claims over the polar regions involve complex issues, due largely to their extreme and uninhabitable conditions. In general, the norms governing the acquisition of territory by states, especially the requirements of effective occupation, have been relaxed in the polar regions because of these characteristics.

In the Arctic, despite the lack of any truly effective occupation, the claims of surrounding states have now achieved the level of a legal status quo. Territorial sovereignty in the Arctic is no longer questioned, though the legal bases for the various territorial claims of the five Arctic powers — Russia, Denmark, Norway, Canada, and the United States — are not identical. The validity of these claims extends only to the various Arctic islands and their attendant territorial seas, not to the Arctic Ocean proper.

The Soviet Union, however, claimed that several extensive Arctic seas on its coast constituted so-called historic seas and as such Soviet internal waters, and Russia in its place continues to assert the same. Claims to sovereignty over the Arctic Ocean have been advanced in terms of the "sector theory." The sector theory involves delimiting Arctic claims according to boundaries created by the extension of the longitudinal meridians from the existing boundary between states northward to the North Pole. It is designed, in part, to ensure sovereignty over islands within the sector, whether or not discovered. As such, it would dispense with the minimal requirement to establish valid claims to new territory under customary international law. The Soviet Union was the most strident supporter of the sector theory. To a lesser degree Canada has also relied on it for claims of Arctic sovereignty. Both the United States and Norway have expressly rejected its validity.

United States sovereignty in the Arctic extends to Alaska and certain specified adjacent islands under a treaty of transfer with Russia of 1867. Canadian sovereignty over the Arctic archipelago to its north, though once claimed under the sector theory, is definitely achieved by various expeditions. Denmark's sovereignty over all of Greenland was recognized in 1933 by the Permanent Court of International Justice in the famous case of *Legal Status of Eastern Greenland*.[6] Norwegian sovereignty over Spitsbergen and Bear Islands was recognized in the Treaty of Paris in 1920. Under the terms of the treaty, however, mining rights are reserved to the forty other parties to the agreement. Besides Norway, only the Soviet Union, today the Russian Federation, has taken advantage of these rights. Although the Soviet Union insisted that its sovereignty over the islands to its north is satisfied under the sector theory, its long-undisputed possession and control of these islands was said to give it title beyond doubt. Russia continues to enjoy this status.

Another unsettled issue is the Soviet, now Russian, claim to sovereignty over the Northeast Passage. This route passes through several large seas that indent the northern coast of the former Soviet Union. The Russians consider these seas "historic" and, as such, internal waters in which no right of innocent passage by foreign ships exists. In opposition to the Russian position, it has been argued that the term *historic seas* is unknown under international law and that "historic bays" are inconceivable without headlands between which a baseline can be drawn. As to the contention that passage through these waters requires the assistance of Russian icebreakers, the counterargument is simply that a nation using the passage could supply its own icebreakers. (In any event, such reasoning is at least inapplicable to air navigation.) If this route were to become an internationally used passage, then the straits between the Russian mainland and its islands should also be opened to foreign use as transit straits under the Convention on the Territorial Sea and Contiguous Zone of 1958.

The situation concerning claims of territorial sovereignty in the Antarctic is not as well settled as in the Arctic. A principal reason has been the lack of any generally agreed-on criteria by which valid claims can be established. Thus, while one nation will proclaim an area to be its sovereign territory, another nation, based on the same facts, will deny that claim. In one region, three nations have simultaneously claimed sovereignty.

Thus far seven states have made claims to portions of Antarctica: United Kingdom (1908); New Zealand (1923); France (1924); Australia (1933); Norway (1939); Chile (1940); and Argentina (1942). These claims consist of pie-shaped sections that extend, except in one instance, from latitude 60° south to the South Pole. The British sector extends further north to include the Falkland Island Dependencies.

Two legal bases are set forth for the territorial claims in Antarctica. The Northern Hemisphere claimants have invoked discovery, whereas the Southern Hemisphere claimants have relied on the theory of contiguity (similar to the sector theory), under which Antarctic territory within the same approximate meridians of latitude as the claiming state are held subject to sovereignty.

The United States, though having made no claims of sovereignty in Antarctica, has expressly reserved the right to put forth such a claim in the future. In the meantime, neither the United States nor Russia recognizes any claims of sovereignty on the continent.

Interest in the Antarctic was heightened by the commemoration of the International Geophysical Year (IGY), 1957–58. The IGY began a period of cooperative scientific investigation precipitating the building of numerous Antarctic state research bases. This development, coupled with attempts to assert exclusive control, posed a threat of cold war and militarization; hence, interested states were prompted to enter into the Antarctic Treaty of 1959. The treaty was concluded by all seven claimant states, United States, the Soviet Union (now Russia), and other states with substantial Antarctic interests (Belgium, Japan, and South Africa). The treaty represents an important step in international cooperation.

The primary objectives of the treaty are twofold: the peaceful use of Antarctica and the promotion of free scientific investigation and cooperation. The application of the treaty is limited to the area south of 60° south latitude. Article

1(1) stipulates that military measures are prohibited, including "the establishment of military bases and fortifications, the carrying out of military maneuvers as well as the testing of any weapons." The driving force behind the original signing of the treaty was the interest in guaranteeing that state activities in the region would not affect existing claims to territorial sovereignty. Article 6 incorporates this guarantee, freezing all claims of territorial rights in the continent and precluding new territorial claims during the life of the treaty. The treaty also seeks to control the actions of nonsignatories as far as they relate to the Antarctic. The treaty does not attempt to keep nonsignatories out of Antarctic affairs but encourages the participation of all states in Antarctic research carried out in conformity with the treaty provisions.

The treaty creates a mechanism to work out future disputes regarding such issues as resource exploitation, which is not specifically addressed otherwise. Article 9 provides that the original contracting parties or those that conduct substantial scientific research shall participate in periodic consultative meetings to consider and recommend "measures in furtherance of the principles and objectives of the Treaty." Whereas the United States, in keeping with its policy of nonrecognition of Antarctic claims, would allow free access, claimant states would deny such access to their claimed sectors. Hence, management of the system has an administrative problem.

Though the treaty is open to accession by other states, only those judged to have undertaken "substantial scientific research activities" are to become "consultative parties" and to participate in managing the system. As of 1997, fourteen states had joined the original twelve as voting, consultative parties, in addition to sixteen nonvoting, nonconsultative parties.

When the treaty was concluded the primary focus was on scientific investigation and cooperation. With recent reports of Antarctica's resource potential, both living and mineral, world attention has increasingly shifted to exploring and exploiting the potential mineral resources of Antarctica. Several developing nations, led by Malaysia, have charged that the treaty is unfair and demanded that the United Nations declare the resources of Antarctica a "common heritage of mankind" and establish a committee on Antarctica; some treaty powers feared that any revision might jeopardize the treaty. In 1991, however, the Protocol on Environmental Protection to the Antarctic Treaty was finally signed in Madrid, banning mineral and oil exploration outright in the continent for at least fifty years. The protocol, setting forth a comprehensive, legally binding system of environmental regulations for wildlife protection, waste disposal, marine pollution, and continued monitoring of Antarctica, reaffirms the status of Antarctica as an area reserved for peaceful purposes.

Although there was for some time disagreement over whether Antarctica should be governed by the present treaty or by the United Nations, the General Assembly has been able to reach consensus on "the question of Antarctica," recognizing the treaty and its associated instruments "as furthering the purposes and principles of the U.N. Charter."[7] Agencies of the United Nations are regularly invited to participate as expert organizations in Antarctica Treaty meetings.

THE GLOBAL ENVIRONMENT

In talking about the global environment, there is a tendency to associate it narrowly with the questions of pollution of all kinds — water, air, river, marine, industrial, oil spill, waste, and so on. The questions of pollution have undoubtedly done much to sensitize the environmental concern of our time. But pollution does not exhaust the range of problems concerning the global environment.

In a comprehensive sense, the global environment relates to the entire earth-space arena. All of the respective resources discussed above are but components of the larger global environment. The plants, *Homo sapiens* and other animals, and microorganisms that inhabit the planet are united with one another and with their nonliving surroundings by a network of complex and interdependent components, both natural and cultural, which constitute a planetary ecosystem. But, in the opinions of many competent experts, this delicate ecological unity is in grave jeopardy. In the words of McDougal and Schneider,

> It is the more specific ecological unities or interdependences — physical, engineering, and utilization — of this comprehensive ecosystem which make our whole earth-space environment a single shareable, and necessarily shared resource. What is true about the shareability of the oceans, the atmosphere, the airspace and the enfolding outer space, and the land masses when considered separately, is no less true of the indivisible whole which they comprise.[8]

State activities having potentially harmful transnational effects are wide ranging and include exploitation of resources, uses of international rivers, nuclear testing, weather modification, industrial waste disposal, oil transport, and exploration of the oceans and outer space. The devastating potential of nuclear weapons testing has been widely recognized. Efforts to change weather by cloud seeding or diversion of hurricanes or tornadoes may have devastating consequences for other communities. Concentrated industrial activities may cause acid rain, increased acidity levels in precipitation (sulfur dioxide), which can harm structures, as well as crops, fish, and other organisms across national boundaries. The failure by both developed and developing countries to reduce emissions of "greenhouses" gases such as carbon dioxide may lead to global warming and devastating climactic change on Earth. Nuclear accidents, such as the 1984 explosion at the Chernobyl atomic power plant near Kiev, can result in increased levels of deadly radiation around the globe. (Eleven days after Chernobyl, increased levels of radiation were detected as far away as Japan.)

Pollution knows no boundary. In keeping the earth-space arena a healthy, livable environment for future as well as present generations, it crucial that a high degree of inclusivity be maintained in dealing with manifold problems associated with the global environment.

Historically, serious transnational pollution problems were tackled by invoking and applying international law relating to the responsibility of states, territorial sovereignty, and the freedom of the sea. A customary expectation is that states are obliged not to use or permit the use of their territories so as to cause substantial transnational environmental harm. Three transnational decisions — the *Corfu Channel Case*,[9] the *Trail Smelter Case*,[10] and the *Lake Lanoux Case*[11] — have been especially influential in this regard.

In *Corfu Channel*, Albania's knowing failure to warn a British warship passing through its territorial waters of the existence of a mine field in those waters obliged Albania to compensate Britain for injury to its ship and crew. The International Court of Justice held that a state has an "obligation not to allow knowingly its territory to be used for acts contrary to the rights of other States."[12] In the *Trail Smelter* arbitration, it was ruled that a privately owned Canadian smelter that emitted sulfur dioxide fumes causing substantial damage to privately owned farmland in the state of Washington should be subject to strict emission controls to prevent future damage. Like *Corfu Channel*, this decision signifies that a state may not act to permit serious transnational injury. This has obvious implication for activities generating transfrontier pollution. In the *Lake Lanoux* arbitration, Spain disputed France's right to divert waters from the lake (which is situated in France but empties into a stream that crosses into Spain) in order to generate hydroelectric power. The tribunal decided in favor of France because the activity was determined not to adversely affect Spain — there would be no diminution in water quality or harm to agriculture or other human needs.

The contemporary environmental concern entered a new era with the convening in 1972 of the United Nations Conference on the Human Environment in Stockholm. The conference adopted the Declaration on the Human Environment,[13] commonly known as the Stockholm Declaration, calling on "the Governments and peoples to exert common efforts for the preservation and improvement of the human environment, for the benefit of all the people and for their posterity," and an action plan spotlighting a global monitoring system. The declaration contains a set of principles that deal with the protection of the natural environment, the preservation and protection of flora and fauna, the use of renewable resources, restrictions on the discharge of toxic substances, the prevention of marine pollution, and the relation between environmental protection and economic development. A key provision seeks to accommodate the sovereign right of states to exclusive enjoyment of their resources with the need for environmental protection.

Two decades after Stockholm, in the largest gathering of its kind in human history, world leaders met at Rio de Janeiro to cooperate in meeting common environmental challenges in what became familiarly known as the "Earth Summit," the United Nations Conference on Environment and Development (UNCED, 1992). Several important documents were approved, including a United Nations Framework Convention on Climate Change. Most important, as part of the Rio Declaration an agreement was signed on a comprehensive plan of action. Called "Agenda 21," that plan serves as a blueprint for fighting pollution and poverty, advancing toward better use of world resources into the twenty-first century and charting a new course of global partnership for sustainable development.[14]

A key topic at Rio was the debate over "sustainable development." The relation between economic growth and environmental degradation has become an increasingly contentious issue: as many poorer countries focus on economic growth to meet needs of growing populations, they are concerned that the industrialized North will use environmental considerations to curb growth in developing countries, in a sort of "green" colonialism consigning those countries to permanent economic inequality.[15] Environmentalists, on the other hand, fear that in the pursuit of growth developing countries will not sufficiently recognize the severity of threats to the global environment. So it has been, unfortunately, that political disputes, economic disparities, and an overemphasis on exclusive interests have hampered progress and dampened the spirit of Rio. Environmental trends have not improved; atmospheric concentration of greenhouse gases continues to grow, species are being extinguished at an unprecedented rate, and deforestation continues.

The shared concern for a healthy environment was amply manifested by the acute concern for marine pollution in the course of negotiating and formulating the United Nations Convention on the Law of the Sea. Several marine environmental disasters beginning in the 1960s, especially the 1967 *Torrey Canyon* disaster, underscored the urgent need to preserve and protect the marine environment and its creatures. Unfortunately, the *Torrey Canyon* has since been overshadowed by oil spills such as the *Exxon Valdez* disaster, which spewed nearly eleven million gallons of oil onto the Alaskan coast in 1994, causing severe damage and suffering to birdlife, sea mammals, and fisheries.

The new convention contains a rather elaborate chapter (Part XII, Articles 192–237) designed to protect and preserve the marine environment. Article

192 stipulates the general obligation of states to protect and preserve the marine environment. To fulfill this obligation, states are required under Article 194 to take, individually or jointly, all measures "necessary to prevent, reduce and control pollution of the marine environment from any source," using "the best practicable means at their disposal and in accordance with their capabilities." The convention identifies the sources of marine pollution: land-based sources; pollution due to seabed activities within national jurisdiction; pollution due to seabed activities outside national jurisdiction; marine dumping; pollution from ships; and pollution from and through the atmosphere.

Several of these provisions constitute entirely new prescriptions. In the area of land-based pollution, no new international law is created by convention, and each state is left to control such sources within its national jurisdiction. Some of the provisions dealing with pollution due to seabed activity within national jurisdiction are new law. No problem should arise as to pollution resulting from the exploitation of the deep seabed, since all such activities will be carried out under the supervision of the International Seabed Authority in accordance with international standards. Pollution from ships is a major issue, since it is by this means that pollution moves most easily from one jurisdiction to another or to the high seas. The newly created "port state jurisdiction" is a particularly innovative feature (see Articles 218–20). A compromise was struck between the coastal states, which supported the competence to adopt supplementary legislation concerning pollution control in the exclusive economic zone, and the flag state bloc, which opposed such proposals. According to the compromise formula, (1) states should accept the universal jurisdiction of port states to punish discharge violations of international rules and standards; (2) ships are to be bound only by the national laws and regulations of the flag state and by the applicable international rules and standards; (3) coastal states will have, within their exclusive economic zones, the right to enforce international rules and standards applicable to foreign ships. This balance allows coastal states to protect their interests while preventing unilateral actions by them and ensures uniformity of regulations applicable to all ships.

11

Control of People: Nationality and Movement

People are the most important element of statehood; without people, territory, resources, and institutions are meaningless. The viability of a territorial community depends on people sufficient in numbers, capabilities, skills, and loyalties.

Nation-state elites naturally seek to exert comprehensive and continuing control of people to protect and consolidate their value positions within the state and to control state power. The basic way they do this, in the contemporary world of the nation-state system, is through nationality. Bearing in mind all the normative ambiguities associated with the concept of nationality, nationality is a tie, a link, the membership, to a nation-state. Through it state elites acquire, exercise, and terminate control over people. Nationality determines who the members of a national political community are and is employed by state elites to assert continuing control over certain people for comprehensive and manifold purposes.

A related device is to regulate the movement of people across state lines. This is the question of who is to be admitted (for what purposes, why, and how long) and excluded by states and who is allowed to stay and who is to be expelled (deported) or extradited. In an age of nation-states, state boundaries represent boundaries of movement. By controlling transnational movement of people, state elites control who may gain and maintain physical access to territorial communities and resources. Physical access is of course the key to full participation and enjoyment in the value processes of a territorial community.

Nationality is relevant not only in the context of movement across borders but in a variety of legally regulated human endeavors: political rights and duties, diplomatic protection, access to resources, conflicts over states' competencies to prescribe and apply law, and so on, as will be discussed further in chapters 12 and 14.

In seeking to control people in terms of both membership and movement, state elites are dealing with human beings. Human beings, unlike nonhuman resources, are not mere objects of manipulation by power elites. They pledge allegiance and obey commands, but they also demand protection and fulfillment.

Thus, although state elites characteristically claim a comprehensive and continuing competence to control and regulate people by conferring and withdrawing nationality and transnational movement, individual human beings have become increasingly assertive in demanding human rights protection concerning nationality and freedom of movement, both internally and transnationally. They demand the freedom to acquire and change membership affiliation with a political community; they demand the freedom to enter, to stay in, and to leave a particular territorial community to maximize pursuit of different values.

Inherent in the question of membership affiliation and movement of people are two distinct dimensions: power and human rights. The tension between the two is clear. How then can the clashing demands be harmonized to serve the interest of all?

THE CLARIFICATION OF GENERAL COMMUNITY POLICY

In the face of the increasing assertiveness of the individual in the name of human dignity and human rights, nation-state elites generally strive to maintain and exercise their traditional competence to control and regulate the national membership and flow of people, in addition to controlling the flow of capital, goods, and services. The primary concern of state elites is, all too commonly, to control people in relation to resources as base of national power. The underlying question is thus how to harmonize the individual's freedom of affiliation and movement with the need of the nation-state to regulate and control people because of its security, development, quality of life, capacity to absorb newcomers, or other considerations, with due regard to the value consequences beyond the claimants immediately involved.

The established decision makers of the international community historically have honored, in varying degrees, two complementary policies in allocating competence over peoples. The first, greatly favored when expectations of large-scale violence are low, promotes human rights and encourages freedom in the movement of people and easy changes in group membership, much the same as it fosters the free flow of goods, services, capital, and ideas. The other, gaining prominence under conditions of continuing expectations of imminent violence, puts a premium on the interests of states to consolidate their bases of power through rigorous controls over people, including restrictions on change of national membership and on freedom of transnational movement.

From a long-term perspective, the first policy would progress toward a non-segregated world of human dignity in which people, resources, and ideas can move freely to achieve optimum shaping and sharing of all values and in which the present disparities in the distribution of people in relation to the earth's resources could eventually be redressed equitably around the globe. Its support for the general freedom of group membership and movement would foster the utmost freedom for the individual in choosing a place to live, work, and enjoy.

Yet policies, like legal doctrines, operate in pairs of complementarity. From a short-term perspective, given the present structure of the world arena, states do share some interests that may in varying contexts require limiting this preferred policy of the utmost individual freedom. Despite contemporary technological developments, people remain an important base of power for each territorial community in the world. Both the security, in the minimum sense of freedom from external violence and coercion, and the quality of society, in terms of the greater production and wider sharing of all values, that a community can achieve depend intimately on the numbers and characteristics of its members. Furthermore, territorial communities share important interests in maintaining harmonious relationships among themselves and in avoiding situations of potential conflict in their claims to ascribe national membership and to regulate the flow of people. Different communities have a common interest in a certain economy in expending resources in their practices to allocate members and provide regulation and protection in transnational processes of authoritative decision.

The cardinal task in search of the common interest is thus that of achieving an accommodation in particular instances between the complementary policies reflected in the demands of states and the demands of individuals, an accommodation that will, in the long run, best promote the largest net, aggregate achievement of human dignity values. The strong presumption for freedom of movement needs to be balanced by other genuine public order considerations — the maintenance of security, health, food, livelihood, development, morals, and so on for the particular community, taking into account also the impact on neighboring states, the regional community, and the world community.

TRENDS IN DECISION AND CONDITIONING FACTORS

Regarding trends in decision, we shall deal first with the claims relating to control of community members via nationality and then with the claims relating to control of movement of people. The overall trends in decision were shaped in the past by the paramount interests of state elites in the control of people as important bases of power and are increasingly influenced by human rights considerations. The interplay of the power dimension and the human rights dimension is discernable.

Control of Community Membership via Nationality

We shall deal in sequence with (1) conferment of nationality; (2) withdrawal of nationality, voluntary and involuntary; (3) statelessness; and (4) multiple nationality.

Conferment of Nationality

Nation-states enjoy a high degree of discretion in conferring nationality under international law. The limitations on this discretionary competence remain far from clear. The Hague Convention on Nationality of 1930 contains, not without ambivalence, both a grant of competence and a limitation. Articles 1 and 2 state that it is "for each State to determine under its own law who are its nationals" and that any question "whether a person possesses the nationality of a particular State shall be determined in accordance with the laws of that State." But the nationality law of each state "shall be recognized by other States in so far as it is consistent with international conventions, international custom, and principles of law generally recognized with regard to nationality." The convention fails to specify the criteria of conferment that are recognized or required by international law.

Thus, criteria for limiting states' competence to confer nationality are to be inferred from customary expectations and practice. For conferment of nationality at birth, states have commonly employed either one or both of two principles: *jus sanguinis* (conferment of nationality by blood relation) and *jus soli* (conferment of nationality based on place of birth). The principle of jus sanguinis, at least as old as Roman law, is favored by the civil law countries. The principle of jus soli, an outgrowth of the feudal system, is preferred by the common law countries. The general trend is toward a mixed system, employing both principles in varying combinations. The uniformity in exclusive reliance on these two principles has been such that some commentators consider it a customary rule that no other grounds are permissible.

As a reflection of the traditional power concern of state elites, these two principles of conferment of nationality at birth disregard human volition. An individual cannot choose his or her parents or place of birth. The bulk of humankind have their nationality thrust upon them, with little effective prospect of change.

Concerning grounds subsequent to birth, states have sought to confer nationality on the basis of consent or a variety of factors, including marriage, recognition by affiliation, legitimation, adoption, paternity, residence or domicile, land ownership, and holding a public post.

Conferment of nationality on the basis of consent is in keeping with a policy of human dignity. The essence of naturalization is to foster a person's voluntary choice of a particular nationality.

In contrast, imposing nationality on individuals against their will, individually or collectively, is incompatible with the generally accepted principles of international law. Compulsory naturalization on such bases as land ownership or residence is impermissible. In the nineteenth century, for example, when certain Latin American countries (such as Mexico and Peru) undertook to impose nationality on aliens who owned real property in the country, such a practice of "expropriating" people was vigorously protested by other states and declared inimical to international law by international tribunals.

Similarly, compulsory naturalization simply on the ground of residence is impermissible. In 1889, for example, the Provisional Government of Brazil proclaimed that all aliens residing in Brazil on November 15, 1889, would automatically become Brazilian nationals unless they should express a contrary intention before appropriate Brazilian officials within six months. This decree provoked severe condemnation and protests of nonrecognition by other states, including France, Great Britain, Italy, Portugal, Spain, and the United States. Another notorious example is the mass imposition of German nationality on nationals of German ethnicity of the territories occupied by Nazi Germany during World War II.

Consent to naturalization need not be explicit but may be inferred. Thus, in conferring nationality on such grounds as marriage, adoption, legitimation, and recognition by affiliation, decision makers commonly infer or assume an element of volition on the part of the individual concerned or those representing him or her.

The effect of marriage on nationality differs widely in national laws. Thanks to the influence of two competing principles — the traditional principle for the unity of the family and the new principle honoring the freedom of a married woman to choose her own nationality — national laws exhibit three basic patterns: (1) the nationality of the wife follows automatically that of the husband; (2) marriage to a man of a different nationality affects the nationality of the wife, but provisions are made to minimize the wife's statelessness or double nationality; and (3) the woman has the right to choose her own nationality, and marriage will not affect her nationality.

From a human rights perspective, marriage should have no automatic effect on the nationality of either spouse. In marrying a national, an alien woman does not necessarily signify her intention to identify with the state of which her husband is a national or to sever her ties with the state of her nationality. As the demand for the equality of the sexes intensifies, the trend is toward the principle honoring the freedom of choice of nationality for a married woman. The Convention on the Nationality of Married Women of 1957 emphatically affirms this trend in Article 1: "Each Contracting State agrees that neither the celebration nor the dissolution of marriage between one of its nationals and an alien, nor the change of nationality by the husband during marriage, shall automatically affect the nationality of the wife."

With regard to minor children, the considerations of family unity sustain the general practice that the child follows the father's nationality in the case of legitimation and adoption and that minor children are included in the naturalization process of their parents. Because the element of volition on the part of minors is absent, it has increasingly been urged that minors be accorded the option to resume their original nationality on attainment of adulthood.

Compulsory naturalization has tended to occur in the case of territorial transfer. In the past, when one state ceded a territory to another, the ceding state was generally considered competent to transfer the allegiance of the inhabitants, and the acquiring state was expected to confer its nationality on those inhabitants. These harsh results are often mitigated by human rights considerations, however. Sometimes a plebiscite is conducted to ascertain whether a transfer of territory accords with the wishes of the majority of its inhabitants. Frequently, as stipulated in many treaties of cession or of peace, state practice offers individual inhabitants of the ceded territory an option on nationality, including retaining their original nationality.

In contrast to compulsory naturalization, state elites seek to control membership in a territorial community by denying naturalization to people who actively seek it. A long-established doctrine states that naturalization is a privilege within the discretion of the state, not a right of the applicant.

States differ widely in the scope and severity of limitations attached to voluntary naturalization. Limitations placed on the applicant may relate to residence, age, race, moral character, political belief, health, wealth, and skill. When these preconditions are coupled with onerous administrative requirements, applicants are often effectively denied naturalization.

The requirement of residence, as the most important index of a person's factual attachment to a territorial community, is a common precondition for naturalization. Fulfilling the residence requirement depends on access to territory, with appropriate immigrant status. Yet, such access is itself subject to difficult and often arbitrary conditions. Residence requirements, moreover, vary from state to state in terms of the necessity of physical presence and the length of stay and range from two to ten years. (In special cases, such as sports celebrities needed for the Olympics, top scholars, or scientists, the required length of stay could be eliminated.)

Some states require that an applicant for naturalization be of good moral character at the time of filing a petition. The United States insists that the applicant demonstrate good moral character throughout the requisite probationary period of residence. The requirement of good moral character, elusive and highly susceptible to arbitrary application, has been the major source of litigation concerning naturalization in the United States. The requirement of good moral character was introduced back in 1790, but the term received no statutory definition until 1952. In that year Congress sought to clarify the law by enumerating specific grounds that would preclude a finding of good moral character, including adultery, polygamy, prostitution, drunkenness, and gambling. The good moral character test nevertheless remains a source of uncertainty and inhibition for persons seeking naturalization; both the Immigration and Naturalization Service and the courts continue to exert wide discretion in its application. The arbitrary and inconsistent application of the requirement is evidenced by the decisions concerning the sexual behavior of unmarried aliens and the suitability of homosexuals for citizenship. The courts, moreover, are permitted to find in their discretion that, although an applicant for naturalization has committed none of the statutorily proscribed acts, he or she is for "other reasons" a person not of good moral character.

It appears that conferment of nationality at birth is far from an individual act of volition. Although consent receives greater emphasis in connection with conferment of nationality after birth, involuntary naturalization is not a thing of the past, and efforts toward voluntary acquisition of nationality often fail. The power concern of state elites tends to overshadow the concern for individual human rights.

Withdrawal of Nationality

Nationality may be withdrawn or lost at the initiative of the individual or of the state conferring nationality, with or without the consent of the individual. An individual who takes the initiative to terminate his or her nationality is engaged in voluntary expatriation. The withdrawal of nationality based on the genuine consent of the individual does not cause alarm. The real difficulty is to draw the fine line between genuine consent and involuntary withdrawal. We treat in sequence the three traditional categories: (1) voluntary expatriation; (2) withdrawal upon consent, genuine or constructive; and (3) involuntary withdrawal.

Voluntary expatriation. The right to change one's nationality is gaining recognition as a fundamental human right. Such a right affords individuals opportunity to escape the bondage of the effective elites of any community. Voluntary expatriation — the right to renounce nationality — is at the heart of the right to change it. Just as access to a territorial community is crucial to any realistic right to acquire nationality, so is the right of egress to any effective right of voluntary expatriation.

State practice in this area appears to be quite restrictive and harsh toward the individual. Many states still do not recognize the right of unconditional voluntary withdrawal of nationality. Where the right receives nominal recognition, the conditions commonly imposed are so many and onerous as to practically vitiate the right. State elites are understandably reluctant to yield their control over people as important bases of power.

Notable among the barriers to voluntary expatriation are the following:

1. Fulfillment of exacting procedures is required for renunciation of nationality. A United States national, when in a foreign country, for example, is required to make a statement of renunciation before a U.S. diplomatic or consular officer in the form prescribed by the secretary of state, although this serves the purpose of assuring requisite intent.
2. A person is not allowed to expatriate him- or herself while in the territory of the expatriating state. Foreign naturalization often results in the automatic loss of initial nationality, and expatriation is expected to occur abroad. Obviously, an effective right of voluntary expatriation depends on an effective right of emigration.
3. A person is barred from expatriating him- or herself while the expatriating state is at war. For instance, Great Britain and many other Commonwealth nations prohibit expatriation in a "foreign" (non-Commonwealth) state in time of war to prevent nationals from evading military service. Naturalization in an enemy state may be regarded as an act of treason, a political offense against the state.
4. Expatriation may be contingent on the grant of official permission by the expatriating state. Most states will not grant such permission unless and until the individual has fulfilled certain obligations, especially military service and tax payments. The "conditional expatriation" under the former Soviet Union and its fraternal states was particularly harsh and inimical to human dignity because the required conditions were not publicly disclosed.
5. Voluntary expatriation is commonly contingent on acquisition of another nationality. The purported purpose is to minimize statelessness.

It would appear that state elites show little disposition of loosening control of people as bases of power, although there is increasing community support of the individual's right to voluntary expatriation. Both the Universal Declaration

of Human Rights and the American Convention on Human Rights provide that
no one shall be "arbitrarily" denied the right to change his or her nationality.

Withdrawal upon genuine or constructive consent. In contrast to the withdrawal of nationality based on the genuine consent of the individual, states may,
in the interest of promoting harmonious relations with other countries, withdraw nationality on the basis of the "voluntary" performance of particular acts.
The inquiry then becomes: Are the potentially severe consequences for individuals justified by a sufficient common interest in the avoidance of conflict among
nations?

Nation-states have traditionally imposed the loss of nationality as the consequence of particular acts, ranging from the most explicit form of voluntary
renunciation of nationality to instances in which consent is either absent, con-
trived, or fictitious. Acts evidencing consent may include execution of formal
instruments of renunciation, deliberate acquisition of the nationality of another
state, taking an oath of allegiance to another state, protracted residence abroad,
military service in foreign armed forces, voting in foreign political elections,
employment by foreign governments, marrying an alien man, and the naturalization of parents by another government.

Regarding some of these acts, the withdrawal of nationality occurs under
conditions that clearly approximate genuine consent. Transnational recognition
of withdrawal in such circumstances may indeed be necessary to afford effective protection to the expatriate. This applies to executing formal instruments of
renunciation, deliberately acquiring the nationality of another state, and taking
an oath of allegiance to another state. Executing a formal instrument of renunciation is explicitly designed for voluntary expatriation. The element of voluntari-
ness is present in the case of foreign naturalization that is based on deliberate
choice rather than compulsion. An individual's oath or other formal declaration
of allegiance to a foreign state implies that he or she is dividing allegiance
between that foreign state and the state of nationality; the individual concerned
is thus placed in the position where his or her services might be claimed by more
than one state, rendering it virtually impossible for the state of nationality to
provide him or her protection vis-à-vis that foreign state. Many states make
military service in a foreign country a ground for withdrawal of nationality
under the assumption that such service is incompatible with loyalty to the state
of nationality. Voting in a foreign political election as a ground for loss of
nationality may be unique to the United States. It is reasoned that participation
in the public affairs of another country implies such a political attachment to the
foreign country as to be incompatible with continued allegiance to the United
States. The constitutionality of this particular imposition was first sustained in

Perez v. Brownell (1958)[1] and later rejected in *Afroyim v. Rusk* (1967)[2] by the U.S. Supreme Court, with attention to human rights precepts.

Nationality is sometimes withdrawn if a national has resided abroad continuously over an extended period, normally ranging from two to ten years. This reflects policy considerations inherent in the requirement of a genuine link as the basis of nationality. Although this policy is generally directed to naturalized nationals, it is extended to nationals by birth in some countries.

The effect of marriage on a wife's nationality varies in national laws. Just as a woman may automatically or by certain action acquire the nationality of her foreign husband on marriage, so may she automatically or by certain action lose her original nationality by marrying an alien. Historically, under the twin doctrines of family unity and of implied consent, a woman automatically lost her original nationality and acquired her husband's on marrying a foreign national in most states. The recent trend is distinctly moving away from the fiction of implied consent and toward the equality of the sexes — marriage to a foreign national will entail no automatic loss or acquisition of nationality for the wife.

With respect to minor children, nationality laws are again far from uniform. In converse to the acquisition of nationality, a minor's nationality may be withdrawn upon the foreign naturalization of the father or widowed mother. This practice, though promoting the unity of family allegiance, does not reflect genuine consent on the minor's part. Hence, the trend is moving toward retaining the minor's nationality after the foreign naturalization of his or her parents, even if this means possessing multiple nationality. However, if the minor must automatically lose his or her original nationality upon the foreign naturalization of the parents, it is increasingly urged that the minor be given an option to choose his or her nationality upon reaching majority.

Withdrawal without consent as punishment. Assertions are sometimes made that the state has the unlimited competence to withdraw nationality. In practice states act only on certain relatively restricted grounds. Questions have been raised about the permissibility of such withdrawal. Within the United States it is urged with increasing vigor that the withdrawal of nationality as a sanction for misconduct having no bearing on the common interest in the management of people may constitute cruel and unusual punishment in violation of the Constitution. An analogous inquiry would be applicable in the realm of international law.

States may currently seek to impose loss of nationality as a sanction in response to crimes against the state, including evasion of military service or desertion from the armed forces in time of war; hostile political affiliations and activities; and possession of certain racial, ethnic, or religious characteristics.

States often impose loss of nationality for conviction of crimes regarded as serious attacks on the state. The range of such conduct typically includes treason, desertion from the armed forces, and evasion of military service. The Soviet Union at an early date employed the sanction of denationalization and expulsion against individuals convicted of being "enemies of the toiling masses."

In the United States, the question whether deprivation of nationality is a permissible sanction for desertion or evasion of military service has been litigated. In *Trop v. Dulles* (1958)[3] the U.S. Supreme Court declared that denationalization because of a court-martial conviction for desertion in time of war was "cruel and unusual punishment" in violation of the Eighth Amendment to the Constitution. Characterizing denationalization as "the total destruction of the individual's status in organized society," the court emphasized that "it is a form of punishment more primitive than torture, for it destroys for the individual the political existence that was centuries in the development."[4] Similarly, the Court, in *Kennedy v. Mendoza-Martinez* (1963),[5] declared unconstitutional a statute purporting to denationalize individuals who left or remained outside the United States to evade military service, again on the ground that such measures constituted cruel and unusual punishment.

Denationalization for hostile political affiliations and activities is peculiar to the twentieth century. Although the ancient world was not unfamiliar with banishment for certain hostile political activities and affiliations, deprivation of nationality for such conduct was rare before World War I. After that war denationalization was frequently resorted to as a sanction against "disloyalty or disaffection, acts prejudicial to the State or its interests, collaboration with the enemy," or "advocacy of subversive activities."[6]

Perhaps the most pervasive denationalization measures of this kind occurred in Russia in the wake of the Bolshevik Revolution. In 1921 the Bolshevik government issued a decree that in substance provided that all persons who remained outside the confines of Russia and who had either been absent for four years without official permission or had served in hostile foreign armies or participated in counterrevolutionary organizations would be deprived of Russian citizenship. These denationalization measures were aimed at Russian nationals who had opposed the Bolshevik regime; the upshot was an unprecedented mass denationalization of some two million people, ushering in a tragic era of political refugees.

Other states, including Italy, Turkey, and Germany, subsequently employed denationalization widely and expanded its sanctioning power to cover various types of undesirable conduct. Following World War II, for instance, several Eastern European nations mandated that any national who committed "any act prejudicial to the national and state interests" would be denationalized.[7] Similarly, the United States, during the Cold War, enacted the Expatriation Act of 1954, which purported to denationalize persons who advocated the overthrow of the government under the doctrines of the Communist Party.

The final category in which denationalization has occurred — racial, ethnic, religious, or other related grounds — is particularly notorious because of its association with the Nazi and fascist atrocities. In 1933 the newly ascendant Nazi regime used the artifice of denationalization to help institute and secure its policy of "racial purity." In that year Hitler's government denaturalized thousands of naturalized citizens (primarily Jews) and in 1941 denationalized all German Jews residing abroad. Confiscation of property accompanied deprivation of nationality. A mass exodus of Jews followed these anti-Semitic measures. Denationalization was applied both to persons who had emigrated from Germany during the Third Reich and to Jews of German nationality who had never set foot in Germany. The Jewish wives and children of all such nonresident Germans were also denationalized. Several satellite states of the Axis undertook similar measures against Jews.

After World War II, in reaction to the Holocaust, Czechoslovakia imposed losses of nationality en masse on persons of the German and Hungarian "races." Poland and Yugoslavia similarly denationalized persons of the German "race."

In spite of past assertions by such distinguished authors as Manley Hudson and Paul Weis that international law sets no limit on the competence of states to deprive individuals of nationality, general community expectations today would appear to be moving toward curtailing such allegedly "unlimited" competence. The views of Hudson and Weis, reminiscent of the traditional emphasis on the elite control of people as a basis of national power, may reflect the expectations of the past, but they do not represent community expectations of the present and the probable future.

International law has historically established restraints on this competence: a state cannot deprive individual persons of nationality and then expel them to other states. And as the contemporary global concern for human rights intensifies, additional restraints on such competence are evolving. The fundamental community policy of minimizing statelessness has had general and growing support. The peremptory norm (jus cogens) of nondiscrimination, outlawing differentiations based on such invidious grounds as race, sex, and religion, will make unlawful many types of denationalization. Indeed the whole network of more fundamental policies for the protection of human rights, as incorporated in the United Nations Charter, the Universal Declaration of Human Rights, the International Covenants on Human Rights, and other human rights instruments,

global and regional, may be properly construed to prohibit use of denationalization as a form of human indignity and of "cruel, inhuman and degrading
treatment or punishment,"[8] much in the same manner as the interpretation by
the U.S. Supreme Court.

Statelessness

The status of statelessness — a person without formal membership in any body
politic — entails a dramatic deprivation of the power and other values of an
individual. Just as nationality is the "right to have rights" within the state, so
nationality is the right to have protection in rights by a state on the transnational
level. Treated as an international outcast, an "unprotected person," the stateless
person may be subjected to severe and all-encompassing deprivations, far beyond those common to aliens. He or she has little or no access to authoritative
decision, on either national or international levels. The stateless person has no
state to protect him or her and lacks even the freedom of movement to find a
state that will protect him or her. In a world based on nation-states, statelessness
means "the loss of a community willing and able to guarantee any rights
whatsoever."[9]

The powerlessness of the stateless person is most pronounced in the limitation on freedom of movement — to enter, to stay in, and to leave a particular
territorial community. Because of widespread rigorous requirements for travel
documents, notably a valid passport and an entry visa, a stateless person, lacking necessary documents, usually encounters great difficulty in locating a state
willing to receive him or her. Unable to enter the territory of a state lawfully, the
individual is often compelled to do so clandestinely. Such illegal entry keeps
haunting the stateless person.

The important causes of statelessness derive from the formulation and application of the nationality laws of states without adequate regard to human
rights. The diversity of nationality laws, as exacerbated by the inherited myth of
viewing nationality regulation as a matter of domestic jurisdiction, has created
many gaps in the conferment of nationality both at and after birth.

Statelessness at birth generally arises from the inadequacy and diversity of
nationality laws, which usually employ the principles of jus soli and jus sanguinis, but not always jus soli and varying forms of jus sanguinis. A notable
example is a child born in a jus sanguinis country of parents of a strict jus soli
country. Statelessness subsequent to birth arises when a person loses nationality
or nationalities without acquiring another.

In a succession of efforts since World War I, the international community has
sought to eliminate or to reduce statelessness and to improve the position and
treatment of stateless persons through mitigation of attendant hardships. During

the era of the League of Nations, the landmark development was the Hague Conference for the Codification of International Law of 1930, which adopted the Convention on Certain Questions Relating to the Conflict of Nationality Laws and the Protocol Relating to a Certain Case of Statelessness. The renewed efforts after the creation of the United Nations have been represented in general human rights protection and specific conventions relating to stateless persons.

To minimize statelessness at birth, the fundamental policy is that a person is presumed to have acquired the nationality of the state of birthplace where no other nationality is acquired at birth. This policy has found authoritative expression in both general and specific formulation of various conventions. The Universal Declaration of Human Rights provides most generally, in Article 15(1), that "everyone has the right to nationality." The International Covenant on Civil and Political Rights, though lacking a nationality provision applicable to everyone, stipulates in Article 24(3) that "every child has the right to acquire a nationality." Article 20(2) of the American Convention on Human Rights is most to the point: "Every person has the right to the nationality of the state in whose territory he was born if he does not have the right to any other nationality." The Convention on the Reduction of Statelessness of 1961 deals more specifically with contingencies of statelessness. It requires, for example, a contracting state to grant its nationality to a person born in its territory who would otherwise be stateless. And a foundling present in the territory of a contracting state is presumed to have been born within the territory and of parents possessing the nationality of that state. Birth on a ship or in an aircraft will be deemed as having occurred in the territory of the state whose flag the ship flies or in the territory of the state in which the aircraft is registered.

To minimize statelessness subsequent to birth, a parallel policy is to make loss of nationality contingent upon acquiring another nationality. This policy has been reflected in prescriptions governing the consequences of voluntary renunciation of nationality. The Hague Convention provides, in Article 7, for example, that an expatriation permit issued by a state "shall not entail loss of the nationality of the State which issues it unless the person to whom it is issued possesses another nationality or, unless and until he acquires another nationality." Similarly, Article 7 of the Convention on the Reduction of Statelessness reads in part: "If the law of a Contracting State entails loss or renunciation of nationality, such renunciation shall not result in loss of nationality unless the person concerned possesses or acquires another nationality."

The policy of minimizing statelessness, however, may on occasion operate to tie a person involuntarily to a political community with which he or she has lost all sense of identification and loyalty and from which he or she cannot expect genuine protection. To obviate such an outcome, the Convention on the

Reduction of Statelessness underscores that implementation of the policy of minimizing statelessness should neither interfere with the freedom of movement, including ingress and egress, nor with the right of asylum, as projected in the Universal Declaration of Human Rights.

To make "the right to a nationality" meaningful, the liberalization of states' requirements for naturalization is crucial. Facilitation of naturalization by removing burdensome requirements is widely perceived as the key to reducing existing statelessness. But states are notoriously reluctant, for various real or imagined reasons, to undertake the necessary humanitarian measures. A modest step forward is reflected in Article 32 of the Convention Relating to the Status of Stateless Persons of 1954: "The Contracting State shall as far as possible facilitate the assimilation and naturalization of stateless persons. They shall in particular make every effort to expedite naturalization proceedings and to reduce as far as possible the charges and costs of such proceedings." A comparable provision is found in Article 34 of the Convention Relating to the Status of Refugees.

The general policy of making loss of one nationality contingent upon acquisition of another applies to situations in which withdrawal of nationality is based on the individual's consent, real or constructive. Consent is normally inferred from a wide range of acts, including deliberate acquisition of the nationality of another state, pledging an oath of allegiance to another state, protracted residence abroad, marriage to an alien man, naturalization of parents by another government, legitimation, and adoption.

Thus the Convention on the Reduction of Statelessness provides, in Article 7(2), that a national seeking "naturalization in a foreign country shall not lose his nationality unless he acquires or has been accorded assurance of acquiring the nationality of that foreign country." And, with limited exceptions, a national shall not be made stateless because of "departure, residence abroad, failure to register or on any similar ground." Concerning the effect of marriage on the nationality of women, the trend has moved not only away from the woman's automatic loss of her nationality on marriage to an alien but toward the equality of the sexes. Thus the Convention on the Nationality of Married Women of 1957 declares, in Article 1, that "neither the celebration nor the dissolution of marriage between one of its nationals and an alien, nor the change of nationality by the husband during marriage, shall automatically affect the nationality of the wife." It adds in Article 2 that "neither the voluntary acquisition of the nationality of another State nor the renunciation of its nationality by one of its nationals shall prevent the retention of its nationality by the wife of such national."

Efforts to mitigate or improve the treatment of stateless persons, contrasted with efforts to minimize statelessness, are commonly considered in conjunction with the treatment of refugees. Technically speaking, the concept of statelessness (having no nationality) and the concept of being a refugee (fleeing one's country in fear) differ. Just as refugees may or may not be stateless, so stateless persons may or may not be refugees. Refugees who have a nationality, nominally, may not be any better off than stateless persons in terms of governmental protection. Refugees who have a nominal nationality but enjoy no protection from their home government are known as de facto stateless refugees, as distinguished from de jure stateless refugees. The majority of refugees in the contemporary world belong to the de facto stateless category. Such refugees and stateless persons share one fate — they are left unprotected. This intimate, though not identical, relationship between stateless persons and refugees finds concrete expression in the substantially identical provisions of two parallel conventions: the Convention Relating to the Status of Stateless Persons of 1954, and the Convention Relating to the Status of Refugees of 1951, and its protocol.

Patterned after the Refugee Convention of 1951, the Convention Relating to the Status of Stateless Persons adopts five broad, somewhat overlapping categories of treatment to be accorded stateless persons: (1) general protection (re: rights granted apart from the convention, access to courts, administrative assistance, identity papers, travel documents, nonexpulsion, naturalization, nondiscrimination, transfer of assets, and personal status); (2) national treatment (re: access to courts, elementary education, rationing, artistic rights and industrial property, public relief, labor legislation and social security, and religion); (3) favorable alien treatment (re: right of nonpolitical association, nonelementary education, housing, movable and immovable property, wage-earning employment, self-employment, and liberal professions); (4) treatment accorded to nationals of the country of habitual residence (re: access to courts, artistic rights, and industrial property); and (5) alien treatment (re: general provision and freedom of movement).

Multiple Nationality

Individuals with multiple nationality, in contrast with stateless persons, are claimed by more than one state and may sometimes enjoy the advantages of greater protection in terms of multiple protecting states and permanent physical access to more than one state. They may, however, find themselves subjected to greater responsibilities and burdens. They may be in multiple jeopardy in terms of military service, taxation, and subjection to jurisdiction.

Multiple nationality, like statelessness, results from the diversity of state laws in conferring and withdrawing nationality. Dual nationality, occurring at birth, is most commonly the product of the simultaneous application of the principles of jus soli and jus sanguinis. A person becomes a dual national, for example, when born in a jus soli country of parents with the nationality of a jus sanguinis country. Multiple nationality occurs after birth when a person acquires another nationality through application or such events as marriage and adoption without losing his or her original nationality.

International efforts to regulate multiple nationality, as with statelessness, have been twofold: minimizing the occurrence of multiple nationality and ameliorating the deprivations imposed on people of multiple nationality.

The Hague Conference for the Codification of International Law of 1930 remains the most important effort to deal with the problem. Theoretically, multiple nationality at birth could be eliminated by an outright universal adoption of a single principle for conferment. Such an approach, however, was found unacceptable as intruding on sovereign legislative power. Attention centered on minimizing the number of cases of multiple nationality.

Although the desire for minimizing dual nationality found unanimous expression in the final act of the conference, adopted solutions to the question of multiple nationality were limited in scope. The Hague Convention, in Article 6, provides:

> Without prejudice to the liberty of a State to accord wider rights to renounce its nationality, a person possessing two nationalities acquired without any voluntary act on his part may renounce one of them with the authorization of the State whose nationality he desires to surrender.
>
> The authorization may not be refused in the case of a person who has his habitual and principal residence abroad, if the conditions laid down in the law of the State whose nationality he desires to surrender are satisfied.

The most profound hardships imposed on persons of multiple nationality are those that result from the traditional restrictive doctrine of protection, as expressed in Article 4 of the Hague Convention: "A State may not afford diplomatic protection to one of its nationals against the State whose nationality such person also possesses." An international tribunal will thus ordinarily decline jurisdiction where the claimant is alleged to be a national of both the claimant state and the respondent state.

The harsh effects of this doctrine have been ameliorated by applying the principle of effective nationality, also known as active or dominant nationality. The Hague Convention provides that under the doctrine of effective nationality an individual is ascribed the nationality of either the country in which he or she is habitually and principally resident or that of the country to which, under the circumstances, he or she appears to be most closely connected.

The International Court of Justice eloquently expounded the principle of effective nationality in the *Nottebohm* case (1955),[10] notwithstanding the unfortunate outcome based on the inappropriate application of the genuine link theory in the absence of a multiple nationality issue. The court, building on the analogy of dual nationality, stated:

> International arbitrators have decided in the same way numerous cases of dual nationality, where the question arose with regard to the exercise of protection. They have given their preference to the real and effective nationality, that which accorded with the facts, that based on stronger factual ties between the person concerned and one of the States whose nationality is involved. Different factors are taken into consideration, and their importance will vary from one case to the next: the habitual residence of the individual concerned is an important factor, but there are other factors such as the center of his interests, his family ties, his participation in public life, attachment shown by him for a given country and inculcated in his children, etc.[11]

Similarly, the Italian — United States Conciliation Commission, in the *Merge* case (1955), stated:

> The principle, based on the sovereign equality of States, which excludes diplomatic protection in the case of dual nationality, must yield before the principle of effective nationality whenever such nationality is that of the claiming State. But it must not yield when such predominance is not proved, because the first of these two principles is generally recognized and may constitute a criterion of practical application for the elimination of any possible uncertainty.[12]

The most dramatic deprivation for a person of multiple nationality relates to the burdens of military service. Intense demands for military service appear to be the principal source of friction between states in their competing claims to control individuals having multiple nationality. Thus the 1930 Hague Conference adopted the Protocol Relating to Military Obligations in Certain Cases of Double Nationality. Under Article 1 of the protocol, a person having multiple nationality "who habitually resides in one of the countries whose nationality he possesses, and who is in fact most closely connected with that country, shall be exempt from all military obligations in the other country or countries." Elaborate provisions governing military obligations are found in the European Convention on Reduction of Cases of Multiple Nationality and Military Obligations in Cases of Multiple Nationality of 1963.

Control of Movement of People

We deal in sequence with the following: (1) state competence to admit, to exclude, and to expel versus individual demands to enter, to stay, and to leave; (2) asylum; and (3) extradition.

State Competence to Admit, to Exclude, and to Expel Versus
Individual Demands to Enter, to Stay, and to Leave

In earlier times, when national boundaries were relatively open, transnational interaction was less frequent, and means of transportation and communication were relatively underdeveloped, freedom of transnational movement was a minor question. Furthermore, as international law was regarded as concerned "exclusively" with nation-states, it was often indifferent to the fate of the individual. The whole problem of movement for people was approached not from the perspective of protecting individual human rights but from the paramount consideration of protecting and consolidating the bases of power of states, control over people being a principal source of power bases. Hence customary international law recognized the exclusive competence of the nation-state to control and regulate people for entry into, sojourn within, and departure from, its territory, a manifestation of what was said to be "sovereignty" of the state.

The growing contemporary concern for the protection of human beings, as symbolized by global and regional human rights programs, is challenging the traditional exclusive competence of the nation-state to regiment people and to regulate their movement. As state power is deemphasized, people's power is stressed. Concern for the right to enter, to stay, and to leave is an expression of the increasing general concern for the protection and fulfillment of human rights. Specific new prescriptions have developed in regard to the freedom of transnational movement.

The Universal Declaration of Human Rights, in Article 13, proclaims:

1. Everyone has the right to freedom of movement and residence within the borders of each State.
2. Everyone has the right to leave any country, including his own, and to return to his country.

Comparable freedom of movement is provided in Articles 12 and 13 of the International Covenant on Civil and Political Rights, with greater detail. Article 12 reads:

1. Everyone lawfully within the territory of a State shall, within that territory, have the right to liberty of movement and freedom to choose his residence.
2. Everyone shall be free to leave any country, including his own.
3. The above-mentioned rights shall not be subject to any restrictions except those which are provided by law, are necessary to protect national security, public order (*ordre public*), public health or morals or the rights and freedoms of others, and are consistent with the other rights recognized in the present Covenant.
4. No one shall be arbitrarily deprived of the right to enter his own country.

Article 13 deals with the expulsion of aliens:

Any alien lawfully in the territory of a State Party to the present Covenant may be expelled therefrom only in pursuance of a decision reached in accordance with law and shall, except where compelling reasons of national security otherwise require, be allowed to submit the reasons against his expulsion and to have his case reviewed by, and be represented for the purpose before, the competent authority or a person or persons especially designated by the competent authority.

These provisions, although phrased in general terms, unequivocally affirm community expectations about the right to enter (return) for nationals, the right to leave for both nationals and nonnationals, and the right to stay (including not only freedom of internal movement and residence but also freedom from arbitrary expulsion). Comparable prescriptions in the regional human rights conventions, European and American, have reinforced these expectations.

Under customary international law it is generally accepted that a nation-state is competent to limit the admission of aliens to its territory, for either temporary or permanent purposes. The authority of a state to regulate matters of immigration is deemed plenary and "inalienable." The actual exercise of this competence is restrained by treaty, domestic laws, comity, and the practical need of intercourse with people of other communities. This continues to be the prevailing practice today, as evidenced by the omission of any stipulation of the right of access of nonnationals to a territorial community in any of the human rights conventions mentioned above. The prime exception is to allow long-term residents (nonnationals) to return to the land of domicile, which is sometimes justified on the theory of "acquired rights." But it is equally well established that nationals shall not be denied the right of entry into their own country, as seen in customary international law and recent human rights prescriptions.

The general right of nationals to return to their own country is hampered and frustrated by various practical limitations and pretexts:

1. Claimants are subjected to onerous burdens in proving their nationality;
2. Some nation-states use decrees of denationalization to deny the right of entry of their own nationals;
3. Cumbersome requirements for obtaining passports or reentry permits are made applicable to nationals;
4. Excessive fees for return are imposed;
5. Certain people are classified as a special category of nationals whose right to entry is curtailed;
6. Persecution or the threat of persecution is used to prevent or deter refugees from returning to their land of origin.

In the matter of sojourn, the focus is commonly on aliens. An alien resident — lawfully admitted — does enjoy a measure of protection against arbitrary expulsion. In exercising its authority to control people, a state may in general deport (expel) an alien for violating its laws and, under special circumstances, order the alien expelled on reasonable grounds of public policy, provided due process requirements are met. But a government is not permitted to engage in the collective expulsion of a group of people for discriminatory reasons. President Idi Amin Dada's mass expulsions of some forty thousand Asians of Indian origin from Uganda in 1972 was clearly a gross violation of international law. In January 1983 Nigeria ordered approximately two million foreign workers to be expelled and deported; about half of those were Ghanaian nationals. Ghana's prompt reception of its returning nationals averted an international crisis. Germany in recent years has come under criticism for its proposed expulsion of ethnic Gypsies.

The right to leave a territorial community in theory applies to nationals as well as aliens. But in practice this right is greatly constrained in many communities, especially for nationals, because of rigorous requirements of travel documents (passport or its equivalents) and other practical barriers. The right to leave, or the right to travel, may be for temporary purposes or for permanent emigration. Temporary or otherwise, the right to leave is contingent on obtaining a passport or its equivalent. The passport serves not only as a certificate of identity but as some sort of guarantee of "returnability" — the receiving state is assured that the passport holder can return to another country.

Some governments refuse to issue passports on grounds of national interest (security, foreign relations, brain drain, and so on) or on various spurious, arbitrary grounds; some offer no explanation. Sometimes strings are attached, such as area restrictions, keeping certain countries off limit. Other barriers to the exercise of the right to leave include (1) requiring renunciation of nationality as a condition to leave the country; (2) suspiciously viewing the exercising of the right to leave as a crime; (3) imposing exorbitant fees or exit taxes; (4) making reprisals, sanctions, and harassments against an applicant and family. The question of emigration of Soviet Jews attracted particular attention in the 1970s.

Asylum
Asylum, in contemporary international law usage, has become a term of art, referring to admission of a special category of aliens — refugees — people who flee their land of origin because they genuinely fear persecution for political, racial, or religious reasons. This fear of persecution distinguishes refugees from ordinary immigrants.

The twentieth century has been called the century of homeless people. To-gether with stateless persons, refugees are unprotected people. Increasingly the world community is witnessing a new type of people "in orbit," not astronauts but "refugees in orbit." A typical refugee in orbit wanders from country to country in quest of some one country that will let him or her in to stay. During the protracted period of quest, the refugee is shuffled from airplane to airplane and confined in airports. Compelled to leave the country of residence and lacking proper identity and travel documents, many people cannot disembark legally anywhere. In earlier times one could always jump ship. But today, under the closed national boundary system policed by more sophisticated entry and exit control, such unfortunate persons are condemned to a nightmarish cycle of enforced airplane journeys and periods of practical imprisonment in airport waiting rooms. In addition to refugees in orbit, the plight of "boat people," cast adrift and at the mercy of predators, and undocumented Haitian and Central American refugees have also dramatized the plight of refugees in our time.

Continuous transnational effort has been made, beginning under the League of Nations and extending through the United Nations system under the aegis of the Office of the United Nations High Commissioner for Refugees, to improve the status and treatment of those who flee their country in fear of persecution because of political, religious, or other reasons. The Convention Relating to the International Status of Refugees of 1933 and the Convention Relating to the Status of Refugees of 1951—whose scope of application has been greatly expanded by the adoption of the Protocol Relating to the Status of Refugees in 1967—contain elaborate provisions for the treatment of refugees. But they have sidestepped the prior question of whether refugees are to be accorded a right of asylum under international law. The reluctance to confront the issue of asylum reflects significant deference to the sensitivity of state elites in relation to political dissenters and other refugees.

The first important attempt to remedy this basic inadequacy in prescription came in 1948 with the adoption of the Universal Declaration Human Rights. Article 14 of the declaration provides that "everyone has the right to seek and to enjoy in other countries asylum from persecution." Though the critical word-ing, "enjoy" instead of "be granted," is not as strong as it should be, this prescription does signify a deep community concern to transform the matter of asylum from the domain of "state discretion" to that of international humani-tarian concern. Regrettably, the International Covenant on Civil and Political Rights fails to include a comparable, much less a stronger, provision.

This deficiency has been partially remedied by the adoption of the Declara-tion on Territorial Asylum by the U.N. General Assembly in December 1967, in clear recognition of the growing importance of according asylum to the politically or otherwise persecuted.[13] This declaration, in Article 1(1), provides that "asylum granted by a State, in the exercise of its sovereignty, to persons entitled to invoke article 14 of the Universal Declaration of Human Rights, including persons struggling against colonialism, shall be respected by all other States." The declaration emphasizes that an act of asylum is not an unfriendly act toward other states but a humanitarian act. An individual thus protected shall not be, in the words of Article 3(1), "subjected to measures such as rejection at the frontier or, if he has already entered the territory in which he seeks asylum, expulsion or compulsory return to any State where he may be subjected to persecution." The follow-up effort to give the declaration more body and substance in the form of a convention, though slow and protracted, is expected to be completed in due course.

No rejection at the frontier, no expulsion or compulsory return to a state — these are the essential ingredients of what has come to be known the principle of *non-refoulement,* a principle related to the responsibility of the state not to become an accomplice in foreseeable deprivations of human rights. This principle has become well established in international law. According to the convention of 1951 and the Protocol Relating to the Status of Refugees of 1967 and other related instruments, refugees shall not be returned against their will to the land of origin where they are in danger of persecution on political, racial, religious, or other grounds. Meanwhile, efforts have been made to establish the right of voluntary repatriation for refugees, as symbolized by Article 5 of the OAU Convention Governing the Specific Aspects of Refugee Problems in Africa of 1969. This article reads in part as follows:

1. The essentially voluntary character of repatriation shall be respected in all cases and no refugee shall be repatriated against his will.
2. The country of asylum, in collaboration with the country of origin, shall make adequate arrangements for the safe return of refugees who request repatriation.
3. The country of origin, on receiving back refugees, shall facilitate their resettlement and grant them the full rights and privileges of nationals of the country, and subject them to the same obligations.
4. Refugees who voluntarily return to their country shall in no way be penalized for having left it for any of the reasons giving rise to refugee situations.

Extradition

Extradition involves the formal surrender by one state to another, at the latter's request, of an individual reasonably accused or convicted of a crime. A newer form involves the rendering of an accused to an international criminal tribunal.

The alleged offense has ordinarily been committed within the territory of the requesting state or aboard a ship or aircraft flying its flag, and the alleged offender has taken refuge within the territory of the surrendering state. Requests for extradition are generally handled through the diplomatic channel.

Extradition and asylum are closely related, inasmuch as refusal of extradition may in effect constitute the granting of asylum and extradition the denial of asylum. But they are neither identical nor merely two sides of the same coin. The institutional practices of extradition and asylum have developed side by side, with distinct purposes and functions. Extradition is designed to secure criminal justice and to minimize crime by denying criminal fugitives a safe haven and by having them brought to justice through orderly procedures of transnational cooperation. Asylum, by contrast, is peculiarly humanitarian, designed to provide a safe haven for individuals fleeing their land of origin to escape political, religious, or racial persecution. (In practice, asylum may be extended to alleged criminal offenders, especially political offenders who have not engaged in acts of international crime.)

Increasing mobility of people across national borders means that it also becomes easier for criminal fugitives to move from country to country. Transnational cooperation is required to facilitate crime detection and criminal justice. Such cooperation may take various forms: police cooperation is one, extradition another.

In our contemporary world where nation-states remain jealous of their "territorial sovereignty," state boundaries are, legally at least, barriers to transnational judicial cooperation. Customary international law does not mandate such cooperation. International law does not require states to extradite criminals in the absence of treaty arrangements. The United States will not formally extradite without a treaty but will receive individuals without a relevant treaty.

As a matter of practical necessity and common interest, nation-states have established an extensive network of extradition treaties (both bilateral and multilateral), as supplemented by national laws, to secure judicial cooperation on the basis of reciprocity. These treaties are mostly bilateral, but the number of multilateral treaties, such as various regional conventions on extradition in Latin America and the European Convention on Extradition of 1957, is growing.

Although provisions for extradition vary from treaty to treaty, they exhibit certain common features: (1) the principle of dual or double criminality, also known as the principle of double extraditability; (2) the principle of speciality or specificity of crimes; (3) the principle of nonextradition of nationals; and (4) the principle of nonextradition of political offenders.

Under the principle of double criminality, an act is extraditable only when it constitutes a crime according to the laws of both the requesting state and the requested state or, of course, international law. The treaty may enumerate extraditable offenses or may refer to extraditable offenses generally as any acts that, under the laws of both parties, are criminal offenses and punishable by a certain minimum penalty. Rooted in the considerations of reciprocity, it is designed to ensure that a person will not suffer punishment for offenses not recognized as criminal by the requested state. How to determine whether the requirement of dual criminality is met — by the name of crimes listed or by substantive facts, the facts adduced in support of the request for extradition — can sometimes be a taxing question.

In this connection, is the requesting state required to present evidence of guilt before the requested state as a precondition for granting a request for extradition? As a general practice, the United States and the United Kingdom consider it essential to make out a prima facie case of guilt against an alleged fugitive criminal. Many other countries consider it sufficient when the warrant has been duly issued, and identity established, and the procedural and substantive stipulations of the extradition treaty are met.

Under the principle of speciality, the extradited person may be tried in the requesting state only for the offenses for which extradition was granted. Normally, the consent of the extraditing state can be obtained post hoc by waiver.

According to the principle of nonextradition of nationals, a state is under no obligation to extradite an alleged criminal who is one of its own nationals. This is traditionally justified on the grounds that a person should not be withdrawn from his or her natural judge and that a state owes to its nationals the protection of its laws. In general, civil law countries seek to exempt nationals in bilateral treaties, whereas common law countries do not. The United States, for example, will surrender its own nationals, unless the relevant treaty provides otherwise, and does not consider exemption of nationals to be customary.

The principle of nonextradition of political offenders, though well known, is fairly recent in origin. In ancient times and in the Middle Ages, extradition arrangements were designed primarily to secure the surrender of political offenders, rather than common criminals, as a means of wiping out political enemies. The trend to limit the surrender of political offenders gained influence in the wake of the French Revolution. In the turbulent arena for brute power struggle, where winners take all and losers not only lose power but may well become targets of persecution or liquidation, such a humanitarian exception is vital, especially for power elites, present and potential.

This notable exception for crimes of a political character, though laudable in theory, has sometimes generated considerable difficulty in application. How to determine what constitutes political offenses? By the motive, act, character, or effect involved? Theories diverge, although there are two basic types: (1) the pure political offense (for example, crimes against the state such as subversion or espionage) and (2) the mixed or relative political offense. The problem is exacerbated when the elements of a common crime and a political offense are intertwined (that is, in the case of a so-called relative political offense) — an act of killing, for example, that fits the schedule of such extraditable offenses as murder but was committed with a political motive or to flee political or other persecution. In spite of the vast literature in this area, political motive seems essential although a workable test is yet to be formulated.

It has been clearly established that certain acts are per se excluded from the purview of political offenses. These include such violations of international law as war crimes, genocide and other crimes against humanity, hijacking, and other impermissible terrorist acts, which are especially abhorrent and widely condemned.

Terrorism in all its forms has aroused worldwide concern in our time. In 1985, the United Nations resolutely condemned as criminal all forms of terrorism, and in 1990 the International Law Commission adopted an article expressly condemning such conduct in the framework of a Draft Code Against the Peace and Security of Mankind (Article 16, International Terrorism). There has been a deepening, shared perception that terrorism threatens all members of the world community: the taking of hostages, for whatever reasons, violates fundamental human rights and is no more justifiable in a struggle for national liberation than it is in international warfare. Nevertheless, some forms of terroristic tactics may be permissible (for example, between combatants in an armed conflict). The common interest, or "enlightened self-interest," in conventional wisdom requires transnational cooperation to combat transnational terrorism. International efforts continue to be directed against aircraft hijacking and sabotage, hostage taking, and bombing attacks against random civilians.

One effective way to deal with offenders of acts of terrorism — hijacking, kidnapping, and so on — is to deny them refuge. Refusal of asylum, via extradition in particular, is crucial in efforts to combat transnational terrorism. This policy is incorporated in important conventions designed to combat terrorism: (1) the Hague Convention for the Suppression of Unlawful Seizure of Aircraft, 1970; (2) the Montreal Convention for the Suppression of Unlawful Acts Against the Safety of Civil Aviation, 1971; (3) the Convention on the Prevention and Punishment Crimes Against Internationally Protected Persons, including Diplomatic Agents, 1973; and (4) the International Convention Against the Taking of Hostages, 1979. Common to these antiterrorist conventions is the requirement that states "extradite or submit to prosecution" persons reasonably

accused of the proscribed offenses. A contracting state enjoys universal jurisdiction by treaty over an offender, and the plea of political reasons is greatly
curtailed under these conventions.

APPRAISAL

Under the interplay of the power dimension and the human rights dimension,
the present state of practice governing nationality and transnational movement
for the individual leaves much to be desired, despite considerable progress
toward humanitarianism. The traditional state competence to control and regulate territorial membership of people and their movement and activities is
matched, and challenged, by intensifying demands for freedom in membership
affiliation and in transnational movement.

Central to the contemporary state system is the concept of nationality. The
question of nationality is closely linked to the freedom of transnational movement. The degree to which the right to enter, to stay, and to leave a territorial
community is protected depends largely on whether a person is a national, an
alien, or a refugee. The traditional emphasis on "sovereign rights" in the conferment and withdrawal of nationality and in exclusion and expulsion, if left unchecked, would not only threaten the human rights of the individual but jeopardize friendly relations among states and even world minimum public order.

Nationality is a concept created in the past to foster a minimum organization
of the world under past conditions. The reference and function of the concept
cannot and must not remain static. It must be dynamic and responsive to the
demands, expectations, and identifications of peoples under changing conditions of the global and national constitutive processes.

As human beings seek greater protection and fulfillment of all values, through
ever-growing transnational interactions and movement, in an interdependent
world of universalizing science and technology, nationality must be made to
serve the development and happiness of human beings. Nationality must not be
used to perpetuate human bondage by anchoring people, against their will, in a
particular territorial community or alternatively casting them adrift when it is
withdrawn. The time has come to make the international law of nationality and
transnational movement defend and fulfill the rights of the individual. When
freedom of membership affiliation and freedom of movement become a reality,
when people are free to identify and change community membership and to
choose the place to live, work, and enjoy, we may bid farewell to "the century of
homeless people" and help usher in a new era of human dignity.

12

Protection of People: From Alien Rights to Human Rights

Even under positivist theory when the nation-state was regarded as the only subject of international law and the question of human rights was addressed domestically, it was recognized that customary law developed to protect aliens who still owed allegiance to the state of their nationality despite physical presence in the host country. Aliens in the host community are "nationals abroad" from the perspective of the state of their nationality.

The basic idea was that people are important bases of power for a nation-state. Statehood, in the long tradition of international law, consists of three essential elements: territory, people, and institutions.

The practice of proper treatment of aliens began on a reciprocal basis and quickly spread because of the common interest involved: if you respect and protect our nationals abroad, we will respect and protect your nationals within our borders. Such reciprocal deference benefits not only individuals but also the friendly relations of states. Every human being is a potential alien.

THE REMEDY OF DIPLOMATIC PROTECTION

Customary law for the protection of aliens is well developed. Though the host state where aliens reside regards them as aliens, the state of their origin (nationality) simply regards them as nationals abroad. The host state sees it as a question of treatment of aliens. The state of nationality sees it as a question of protecting nationals abroad. These are two sides of the same coin. Since nationals abroad are regarded as important assets for the state of nationality, any deprivations imposed on nationals abroad are considered an offense against the state of nationality.

The diplomatic instrument historically has played an important part in protecting nationals abroad. This diplomatic remedy, commonly known as "diplomatic protection," developed in response to state responsibility incurred for failing to conform to the international standard for the treatment of aliens and was greatly colored by the state-centered perspective of the nineteenth century. Though long established, this remedy is often cumbersome in application.

Under the lingering myth that the individual is an inappropriate subject of international law, the individual in principle must turn to the state of nationality for protection against external entities when the domestic remedies of the depriving state are of no avail. This remedy requires the nationality link and permits the state of nationality, and only the state of nationality, to protect injured persons, to espouse their claims against other states.

Influenced by Emmeric de Vattel's theory that an injury to a national abroad is an injury to the state of nationality, traditional international law regards a state's competence to protect its nationals as independent of the individual's interest. The state thus enjoys discretion whether to espouse claims on behalf of its nationals at the international level. Because of their overriding concern for national interests of all sorts (such as minimizing friction with a friendly nation), state elites tend to give short shrift to individual deprivees, placing them largely at the mercy of state officials.

Under the requirement of the continuity of nationality, an individual claimant must possess the nationality of the espousing state from the instant of deprivation, through the presentation of the claim, and normally until final settlement. An individual claimant who loses or changes nationality after having sustained a deprivation may find him- or herself unable to secure remedy. Although the state of nationality at the time of deprivation is precluded from espousing the claim because the individual is no longer its national, the new state of nationality is disqualified because the individual was not its national at the time of deprivation. Such technical limitation has led arbitral tribunals to reject innumerable claims.

The concept of nationality itself may sometimes be questioned or distorted so as to deny protection to individual persons. As discussed in chapter 11, states enjoy a broad competence in conferring nationality on individuals and commonly defer to one another's conferments. But individuals occasionally find themselves devoid of a protecting state and denied of a hearing on the merits of their claims because ambiguous and spurious conceptions of nationality are invoked or tests over and beyond any customary conception are imposed. Several famous cases, such as *Nottebohm*,[1] *Flegenheimer*,[2] and *Barcelona Traction*[3] dramatically illustrate such miscarriages of justice.

In *Nottebohm*, Friedrich Nottebohm, born a German national in 1881, moved to Guatemala in 1905 to reside and do business there, without ever applying for

Guatemalan citizenship. He lived there until 1943, when he was arrested and sent to the United States for internment as an enemy alien. In between these dates, Nottebohm had made trips from Guatemala to Liechtenstein to visit his brother and to Germany. In October 1939 he went to Liechtenstein and was granted naturalization on an exemption from the three-year residence requirements. He took an oath of allegiance to Liechtenstein and consequently forfeited his German nationality under the nationality law of Liechtenstein. He returned to Guatemala early in 1940 and registered his change in nationality in the Guatemala Register of Aliens.

Following his release from prison in the United States in 1946, he applied for readmission to Guatemala but was rejected; hence, he took up residence in Liechtenstein. In the meantime, the Guatemalan government, having classified him as an enemy alien, expropriated his extensive properties without compensation.

Liechtenstein thus brought an action against Guatemala in the International Court of Justice, charging that Guatemala had violated international law "in arresting, detaining, expelling and refusing to readmit Mr. Nottebohm and in seizing and retaining his property."[4] Guatemala contended that Liechtenstein's claim on behalf of Nottebohm was inadmissible in light of the nature and circumstances of his naturalization.

In denying Liechtenstein's competence to protect Nottebohm and declaring the case inadmissible, the court relied on a "genuine link" theory of "real and effective nationality."[5] Under this theory certain "factual ties" or "genuine connections" between the naturalized person and the naturalizing state must exist. These ties might include habitual residence, center of interests, family ties, participation in public life, or other attachments. Since such genuine connection was found missing here, the court concluded that Guatemala was not obligated to recognize Nottebohm's naturalization.

The application of the genuine link theory, borrowed from the very different context of dual nationality problems, deprives an individual of a hearing on the merits and the protection by a state willing to espouse his or her claim in the transnational arena. The net effect is an immense loss of protection of individual human rights.

In *Flegenheimer,* one Albert Flegenheimer, on the basis of his U.S. citizenship, claimed that he was protected against prior property seizures by the government of Italy under the terms of the Treaty of Peace with Italy of 1947. The property seizures took place during World War II. Flegenheimer's father had been a naturalized U.S. citizen who in 1874 had returned to his native land, Germany (Kingdom of Wurttemberg). Flegenheimer was born there in 1890, but since his father was of U.S. citizenship, the United States recognized his

U.S. citizenship in 1942, after Flegenheimer had fled to Canada to escape Nazi persecution. Flegenheimer was granted a U.S. passport in 1946 and a certificate of nationality in 1952.

A claim brought on Flegenheimer's behalf by the United States was rejected by the Italian-American Conciliation Commission. According to the terms of the relevant treaty provision, only "United Nations nationals" could be parties to such claims.

In concluding that Flegenheimer was not a U.S. national, the commission substituted its own criterion for that of the conferring state. The commission even took upon itself the act of looking to a treaty of 1868 between the United States and Wurttemberg, even though the United States obviously considered Flegenheimer a full American citizen.

This case has been criticized as a usurpation of the claimant state's right to appraise the facts on which it has based its decision to confer nationality. The result, as in *Nottebohm,* is that the claimant is denied a forum in which to present international claims and have them judged on their merits.

A somewhat different situation existed in *Barcelona Traction.* Instead of denial of a nation's right to represent an individual to whom it has granted citizenship, in this case the state that could have "successfully" brought a claim on behalf of the injured party, a corporation, declined to do so.

The case involved a corporation formed in Canada to supply the city of Barcelona, Spain, with lighting and electricity. In 1948 Spain declared the corporation bankrupt and seized its assets. For reasons not made public, Canada refused to follow through on an international claim against Spain. Belgium, a large number of whose nationals owned stock in the Barcelona Traction Company, thus filed suit with the International Court of Justice. As part of its opposition to jurisdiction, Spain claimed that Belgium lacked standing to bring a claim on behalf of shareholders in a foreign corporation. The court accepted this contention, and again the case was dismissed without judgment on its merits.

The court reasoned that, although the shareholders really suffered the financial harm resulting from Spain's actions against Barcelona Traction, so long as the corporation survived as a legal entity and was not dismantled only it was capable of raising claims based on misdeeds against it. Since this could be accomplished only through Canadian intervention, and since Canada had sole discretion to decide whether such a claim should be pressed, its decision was final and the shareholders lacked international recourse.

In the contemporary world, diplomatic remedies to protect individuals are further subject to limitations inherent in decentralized lawmaking and application. Dominated by considerations of reciprocity and effective power, a state's decision to act as a protector does not guarantee that the individual national will receive effective protection. Vacillation, trade-offs, and compromises among state elites are not uncommon.

STANDARD FOR THE TREATMENT OF ALIENS

Closely linked to the question of diplomatic protection is when a particular state responsibility occurs for failing to treat aliens properly. In other words, what is the commonly accepted standard for the treatment of aliens?

In ancient times the alien was commonly looked on as an enemy, outside one's "tribe," and hence was treated as an outlaw; parochial community expectations kept him powerless and unprotected. As the Roman Empire expanded, aliens were gradually accorded protection under the *jus gentium,* a law made applicable to foreigners as well as citizens, as distinguished from the *jus civile,* which applied exclusively to Roman citizens. The earlier harsh treatment of aliens was, theoretically at least, further ameliorated with the spread of Christian and other religious ideas of the unity of mankind. In the feudal period of the early Middle Ages in Europe, international commerce was sufficiently localized so that the few persons living abroad for commercial purposes had only minimal property rights. With the expansion of international commerce and the development of more powerful centralized governments, the rights of aliens increased correspondingly.

With the coming of the modern nation-state system, a more humanitarian attitude toward aliens began to develop. The founding fathers of contemporary international law asserted that all persons, alien or other, were entitled to certain natural rights, or inalienable rights of mankind. Francisco de Vitoria was among the first to emphasize fair treatment of aliens and subjugated people. Taking for granted the right of free access to territorial communities, Grotius stressed the idea that as far as possible states must accord the alien a status equal to that of its nationals. It was Vattel, however, who first expounded a coherent and influential doctrine for the protection of aliens. Writing more than a century after Grotius, as mercantilism was becoming modern capitalism and as a vast European expansion overseas was beginning, Vattel created the theoretical basis for much subsequent decision. Viewing the state as an entity composed of the sovereign and his citizens, Vattel stressed that the state had a right to protect its citizens, wherever they might be. An injury to an individual alien was asserted to be an injury to the state of nationality.

Ever since Vattel, and following the spread of the industrialization and of European culture throughout the world, a unique customary international law for the special protection of aliens has developed. This body of law is constituted by decisions from foreign office to foreign office, as well as by decisions of international and national tribunals (often in terms of the "denial of justice"); it is fortified by the opinions of publicists and a vast network of relatively uniform treaties of "friendship, commerce, and navigation." The competence of states to protect their members from injuries abroad in this relatively unorganized world serves in many contexts to protect the interest of a state in an important base of power (its nationals) as well as the basic human rights of the alien individual.

Within the broad, historic development of this law, two standards about the responsibility of states, both of which purport to include a norm prohibiting discrimination against aliens, have competed for general community acceptance. One is described as the doctrine of "national treatment," or "equality of treatment," and provides that aliens should receive equal, and only equal, treatment with nationals. The second is described as a "minimum international standard" and specifies that, however poorly a state may treat its nationals, certain minimums in humane treatment cannot be violated in relation to aliens. A review of the flow of decision and communication in the development of the customary law about aliens, especially the recent, more general prescriptions about human rights, indicates that the second of these standards has become the widely shared community expectation.

Because it is generally assumed that states may differentiate between nationals and aliens in a manner that reasonably reflects the varying obligations and loyalties of the two groups, states reciprocally honor the lawfulness of a variety of such differentiations: in, for instance, permissible access to territory, participation in government, and ownership or control of important natural resources. But it is almost universally accepted that with respect to aliens' participation in many important social processes, states may discriminate only when such discrimination is substantially related to differential obligations and loyalties, not merely on the basis of national origin.

The principle of "national treatment," whereby a state will autonomously invoke its own subjective interpretation of the required standard of treatment, would effectively leave aliens at the mercy of their host state. In a world in which many states are tyrannical, totalitarian, or otherwise oppressive, such an outcome is not desired and cannot be accepted. States ought not to be permitted to escape accountability for violating the rights of aliens vis-à-vis the artifice of the "national treatment" principle.

The doctrine of a "minimum international standard," in sharp contradiction to the doctrine of "national treatment," insists that a state cannot escape responsibility for the inhumane treatment of aliens by alleging that it treats its own nationals inhumanely. This widespread, long-accepted doctrine prescribes a minimum common standard in relation to many important sectors in the social process that states must observe in treating aliens, irrespective of how they treat their own nationals: the established standards of justice and civilization, recognized as part of universal international law. The standard in this century was refined through a synthesis of a series of decisions, including those from international conferences, the Permanent Court of International Justice, various domestic and international or regional tribunals, and treaties, especially those concerning friendship, navigation, and commerce.

The minimum international standard for treatment of aliens, like all prescriptions that must be related to the many features of differing contexts, is necessarily abstract. The distinction between lawful differentiation of the status between nationals and aliens on a reasonable basis and arbitrary and unlawful discrimination against the alien must depend not only on the values that are primarily at stake but also on varying features of the institutional practices by which such values are sought and shaped. The minimum international standard has, despite this fundamental difficulty (shared by most important prescriptions), been frequently and widely applied to protect aliens in many value and institutional contexts. The protection typically extends to the alien's legal capacity and access to domestic courts; respect for the alien's physical safety and religious freedom; equity of commercial treatment as to other aliens, especially in regard to property expropriation; and respect for the alien's substantive and procedural legal rights, including the right to adequate remedy.

THE CONTEMPORARY GLOBAL HUMAN RIGHTS MOVEMENT

In the latter part of the nineteenth century focus was placed primarily on a particular category of human beings — aliens — because of the elite concern to control its people. In a sense, everybody is a potential alien and may thus enjoy the special protection of international law at some time. Concurrent with this peculiar protection, however, was the interrelated notion that how a state treats its nationals is its own business. Hence the irony that aliens sometimes enjoyed more protection than nationals, at least at the international level.

How to resolve this irony? Take away customary protection accorded to aliens? No. That would be a step back toward a public order of human indignity.

The lessons of World War II, more particularly the atrocities of the Third Reich, brought home that large-scale deprivations of human rights not only decimate individuals or groups but endanger peace and security. Hence the U.N. Charter underscored the close link between human rights and peace and security, the intimate interplay between minimum world order and optimum world order. The promotion and protection of human rights was made a prime objective of the United Nations, along with those of maintaining peace and security and promoting self-determination.

This new perception inspired the contemporary human rights movement. The point is not to take away the customary protection accorded nationals abroad (only when abroad) or to ignore the corpus of human rights that developed in the eighteenth century and found greater protection domestically, but to upgrade the standard of protection for all human beings — nationals or non-nationals. It has increasingly become apparent that nation-states (or those who control them) are often the most significant deprivers of human rights. Human beings — even those tied to a particular territorial community through the link of nationality — must not be treated merely as resources or objects to be manipulated by state elites. They are individual human beings entitled to human dignity and as such must be accorded decent protection and treatment. Hence the growing demands for human rights for every human being.

The atrocities of the Nazis also brought home that individual decision makers must not be allowed to hide behind the abstract entity of the state to escape personal responsibility. Crimes and atrocities against humanity must not escape persecution merely because perpetrators were acting in the name of the state. The trials of war criminals at Nuremburg and Tokyo imposed direct responsibility on individuals and dismissed the defense of superior orders, acts of state, and related claims to immunity.

This signified the clear and universal recognition that the individual is the ultimate actor — the ultimate beneficiary and the ultimate victim — in any social interaction and decision making, national or transnational. Such recognitions provide the driving force behind the contemporary global human rights movement, although they do not lack precedence, especially in the eighteenth century.

The contemporary global human rights movement is heir to other great historic movements for human dignity, freedom, and equality. It expresses the enduring elements in most of the world's great religions and philosophies. It builds on the findings of modern science about the close link between respect for human dignity and all other values, between human rights and peace.

AN EMERGING GLOBAL BILL OF HUMAN RIGHTS

The peoples of the world, whatever their differences in cultural traditions and institutional practices, today demand most intensely all the basic rights conveniently summarized in terms of the greater production and wider sharing of values of human dignity. This heightening intensity in demand and expectation is observable in every feature of the global process of effective power. This intensity can be seen in the official and nonofficial participants making the demands, the spectrum of values demanded, the global reach of these demands, enormous resources and manpower committed, all modalities of communication employed, and the range of functions and activities undertaken.

This intensity of demand for the better effectuation of human rights infuses every constituent community, national and regional, of the larger global community. The history of the establishment of bills of rights within many of the more mature nation-states (as, for example, within the United Kingdom, the United States, and France) is well known. Most newly independent states have clearly expressed comparable aspirations by incorporating, or making reference to, the provisions of the Universal Declaration of Human Rights in their formal constitutions. And regional communities have established or sought to establish on a broader geographic basis effective bills of rights in light of their peculiar cultural attitudes and institutional practices.

In a comparable fashion, a comprehensive global bill of human rights has emerged and is developing. A bill of rights, as an expression of widely shared and intensely demanded values, is sometimes given a variety of technical names, such as fundamental law, higher law, jus cogens, or peremptory norms. In a dynamic sense, a bill of rights in action manifests the following features:

Prescription: the bill of rights seeks to protect the most intensely demanded values of human dignity. The fundamental freedoms and rights of the individual are so widely shared, intensely demanded, and highly cherished that they are given special protection by formal prescriptions.

Invocation: special provision is made to enable individuals who allege that their human rights have been violated to challenge putative deprivations and to secure remedies before authoritative decision makers. Provision is made for specialized invocation by representatives of the community.

Application: provision is made for applying intensely demanded individual rights prescriptions to all decision makers and community members, whether official or nonofficial. Officials at all levels of government are required to observe and promote these rights. Prescriptions designed to protect human rights are buttressed by specialized institutions of application.

Termination: such intensely demanded prescriptions can be changed only with extraordinary difficulty or in the same way in which they were created. Special difficulties are placed in the way of formally amending or terminating intensely demanded prescriptions about human rights. Commonly, such prescriptions can be changed only in the ways that they are created.

We turn first to *prescription* — the projection of authoritative community policies. Prescriptions about human rights range from the most deliberate form (agreement) to what can be the least deliberate form (customary development), with the United Nations increasingly playing a paramount role.

The common rising demands of all peoples for all basic values — respect, power, enlightenment, well-being, wealth, skill, affection, and rectitude — have received authoritative expression in a host of human rights prescriptions, from the U.N. Charter to the Universal Declaration of Human Rights, the two international covenants on human rights, and a host of ancillary instruments, both global and regional.

The deliberate efforts to create an international bill of human rights began even before the formal establishment of the United Nations. Although the delegates were not ready to include an international bill of human rights in the U.N. Charter itself, the charter, as finally adopted, did contain several important human rights provisions.

When the Commission on Human Rights was created in February 1946, atop its agenda was "an international bill of rights." It was soon decided that the contemplated international bill of human rights would consist of a declaration, a convention (covenant), and "measures of implementation." The first part of this international bill — the Universal Declaration of Human Rights — was adopted unanimously on December 10, 1948, by the General Assembly as a resolution. Ideological divisions after its adoption led to the General Assembly's decision in 1952 to create two covenants — one on civil and political rights and the other on economic, social, and cultural rights — each containing its own "measures of implementation." The two international covenants, plus the first optional protocol to the Covenant on Civil and Political Rights, were adopted in 1966 and became operative in 1976. Thus, in familiar form, the International Bill of Human Rights, as contemplated at the founding of the United Nations, has been projected.

More than the familiar form, this developing International Bill of Human Rights has been greatly strengthened in substance by various ancillary instruments dealing with particular categories of participants (women, refugees, stateless persons, aliens, youths, children, the elderly, mentally retarded persons, and so on) or with particular values or subjects (genocide, apartheid, discrimination, racial discrimination, sex-based discrimination, slavery, forced labor, war crimes, crimes against humanity, torture, nationality, political participation, employment, education, environment, marriage, and so on), by decisions and recommendations of international governmental organizations (especially by U.N. organs and entities), and by customary developments in the transnational arena. Signifying a new era, the United Nations has projected in no uncertain terms a new commitment toward world order, seeking to secure not only a minimum order (in the sense of minimizing unauthorized coercion) but also a maximum order (in the sense of the greater production and wider distribution of all values). The U.N. Charter contains multiple provisions — notably Articles 1(3), 55, and 56 — that suggest that the protection of human rights is a coequal, even indistinguishable, goal in relation to the maintenance of peace and security. Article 1(3) specifies a primary purpose of the United Nations: "To achieve international co-operation in solving international problems of an economic, social, cultural, or humanitarian character, and in promoting and encouraging respect for human rights and for fundamental freedoms for all without distinction as to race, sex, language, or religion." Article 55 states:

> With a view to the creation of conditions of stability and well-being which are necessary for peaceful and friendly relations among nations based on respect for the principle of equal rights and self-determination of peoples, the United Nations shall promote:
> a. higher standards of living, full employment, and conditions of economic and social progress and development;
> b. solutions of international economic, social, health, and related problems; and international cultural and educational co-operation; and
> c. universal respect for, and observance of, human rights and fundamental freedoms for all without distinction as to race, sex, language, or religion.

"All Members pledge themselves," under Article 56, "to take joint and separate action in co-operation with the Organization for the achievement of the purposes set forth in Article 55."

In spite of lingering dissent, the human rights provisions of the charter appear to be accepted (at least since the 1970s) as law in the sense of imposing definite legal obligations on member states and others. This position was authoritatively confirmed by the International Court of Justice in the advisory opinion concerning Namibia of 1971.[6]

The general human rights prescriptions of the U.N. Charter were given somewhat more detailed specification in the Universal Declaration of Human Rights, which celebrated its anniversary in 1998. This declaration has acquired the attributes of authority in two ways. First, it is widely accepted as an authoritative identification and specification of the content of the human rights provisions of the U.N. Charter. Second, its frequent invocation and application by officials, at all levels of government and in many communities around the world, have conferred on its content those expectations characteristic of customary law. (See chapter 22.)

The two international covenants on human rights and the optional protocols to the Covenant on Civil and Political Rights are naturally binding for all states (and their nationals) that have ratified or acceded to them. In addition, like the Universal Declaration, they constitute not only authoritative interpretations of the charter provisions on human rights but also vital components in the flow of communication that creates and shapes the expectations comprising customary international law. By further specifying the content of internationally protected human rights and providing structures and procedures (albeit with inadequacies) to remedy deprivations, they help stabilize authoritative expectations about the defense and fulfillment of human rights. In the same vein, a growing body of more particular conventions dealing with certain types of deprivers or deprivations has also fostered the enrichment and growth of the core content of the human rights prescriptions projected in the U.N. Charter.

Together these important human rights instruments extend to all basic values widely cherished:

Respect:
right to recognition as a person before the law
right to individual dignity and worth
freedom from slavery or servitude
freedom from forced labor
freedom from discrimination on such invidious grounds as race, sex religion,
    language, opinion, and birth status
right to equal protection of the law
right to privacy
right to personal honor and reputation

Power:
right of self-determination
right of participation in the political process
right to an authoritative government based on the will of the people
right to vote
right to hold office, elective and appointive
right to nationality
freedom from deprivation of nationality
right to change nationality
freedom of movement and residence
right to leave any country
right to return to one's own country
right to seek asylum from persecution
right of access to appropriate tribunals for remedies and to effective remedies
right to a fair and public hearing by an impartial tribunal
protection of minorities

Enlightenment:
freedom of opinion and expression
freedom of peaceful assembly and association
right to education
right to take part in cultural life
right to enjoy the benefits of science and technology

Well-being:
right to life
freedom from genocide
right to liberty and security of person
freedom from arbitrary arrest, detention, or exile
freedom from imprisonment for inability to fulfill a contractual obligation
freedom from torture
freedom from cruel, inhuman, or degrading treatment or punishment
right to a high standard of physical and mental health

Wealth:
right to own property
right to share public resources
freedom from arbitrary deprivation of property
right to work
right to free choice of employment
right to just and favorable conditions of work
right to equal pay for equal work
right to an adequate standard of living
right to social security for unemployment, disability, old age, and so on
right to special protection and assistance

Skill:
right to form and to join trade unions
right to vocational education and skill training
right to protection of intellectual property

Affection:
right to marry and to found a family
freedom of association
right to special protection of motherhood and childhood
parental rights regarding children's education

Rectitude:
freedom of thought, conscience, and religion
right to presumption of innocence
freedom from ex post facto law

Some commentators have observed the remarkable development of contemporary human rights in terms of first generation rights (civil and political
rights), second generation rights (economic, social, and cultural rights), and
third generation rights ("solidarity" or group rights). The solidarity rights,
with their emphasis on the aggregate, are said to include the right to self-
determination, the right to enjoy other group processes or institutions, the right
to development, the right to participate in and benefit from "the common
heritage of mankind," the right to peace, the right to a healthy environment, and
the right to humanitarian disaster relief.[7] Human rights are also at stake with
respect to international crimes.

In any event, the authoritativeness of the charter provisions on human rights,
and of the specification of these rights in the universal declaration and related
instruments, has received tremendous fortification by the practice of international governmental organizations, especially the organs of the United Nations,
and by regional and related domestic efforts. The successful model of the
European Convention of Human Rights is widely admired and is beginning to
be emulated. Within the framework of the Organization of American States, the
commitment to a regional bill of rights is enunciated in the OAS Charter, the
American Declaration of the Rights and Duties of Man, and the American
Convention on Human Rights adopted in 1969. The Organization of African
Unity, in fulfilling its aspirations for a bill of rights for Africa, adopted in 1981
the African Charter on Human and Peoples' Rights, also known as the Banjul
Charter on Human and Peoples' Rights. (Note the inclusion of "Peoples" in the
title.)

Another important body of practice contributing to the establishment and
maintenance of a global bill of rights is the customary international law of the
responsibility of states concerning the treatment of aliens. This vital inheritance
continues to serve common interest. In fact, the customary international law of
state responsibility, in constant interaction with and as an integral part of the
contemporary human rights movement, has contributed mightily to the sum
total of the human rights protection helping to lift the level of transnational
protection of nationals as well as of aliens.

The upshot of this comprehensive and continuing prescription, ranging in
modality from the most deliberate to the least deliberate, would appear to be
that the core content of the various communications has been prescribed as a
global bill of human rights. This bill is in both form and policy content much
like the bills of rights created and maintained in some national communities. Its
core content expresses the intensely demanded values of human beings about
the world. Some call it a global bill of human rights, some talk in terms of jus
cogens, some speak of customary law. The point is that there are crystallized ex-

pectations for the defense and fulfillment of human rights that are widely shared
and articulated, even though the degree of deprivation and fulfillment differs
from community to community, the degree of achievement varies widely, and
institutional practices diverge.

Turning to *invocation,* the central question is: When human rights deprivations occur, can victims or others bring complaints to appropriate transnational
(as well as domestic) decision makers for remedies?

The provision by global constitutive process for the invocation of human
rights prescriptions is progressing in directions appropriate to a genuine bill of
rights. The most notable improvement is in the increasing opportunity accorded
to the individual to challenge in appropriate transnational structures of authority the lawfulness of deprivations imposed on him or her. The change in authoritative interpretation permitting individuals and private groups to petition the
United Nations Human Rights Commission regarding certain gross violations
of human rights now seems fairly established. The right of individual petition is
provided in the optional protocol to the International Covenant on Civil and
Political Rights and in the International Convention on the Elimination of All
Forms of Racial Discrimination, the Convention on the Protection of All Persons from Being Subjected to Torture and Other Cruel, Inhuman or Degrading
Treatment or Punishment, and the Convention on the Rights of Migrant Workers. The continuing importance of individual petition is amply demonstrated by
cumulative experience under the European Convention on Human Rights. Indeed, the great bulk of the complaints brought before the European Commission on Human Rights originates from either individuals or private groups.

A further improvement in invocation comes from expansion of the historic
modality of state complaint. Because of the realities of effective power (especially the enormous discrepancy between the power of the state and that of
the individual), proposals continue to be made for more effective invocation
through representatives of the general community. It is often too formidable a
task for the deprived individual successfully to confront, even before an authoritative decision maker, the depriving state. Demands for the improvement of
international constitutive process prevailed, over the opposition of many states,
when the Vienna Declaration (1993) proposed that the General Assembly establish a United Nations High Commissioner for Human Rights. The High Commissioner's mandate is to advance cooperation, comprehensive approaches, and
the participation of all actors in accounting for the protection of human rights at
international, national, and local levels.

The *application* of prescriptions in particular instances is, of course, crucial
to human rights. This and the enjoyment of rights are the outcomes sought in all
human rights policies. As important as it is to challenge unlawful deprivations,

it is equally urgent to secure applications that both put basic community policies into controlling practice and mobilize a continuing consensus, in support
of prescription, toward the greater future protection and fulfillment of human
rights. Human rights committees, such as the Committee on the Rights of the
Child (established under the Convention on the Rights of the Child), have
worked to fight human rights abuses worldwide.

The contemporary transnational prescription for the protection of human
rights would appear to project the same broad compass in applicability characteristic of the bills of rights in some national communities. These prescriptions
apply to the United Nations and its organs and other international governmental
organizations, to nation-states and all their officials, and to all the nongovernmental groups and individuals active in world social process.

The U.N. Charter is commonly expected to be the most fundamental law of
the global community binding all participants. For member states this is explicitly stipulated in Article 103, the charter's supremacy clause: "In the event
of a conflict between the obligations of the Members of the United Nations
under the present Charter and their obligations under any other international
agreement, their obligations under the present Charter shall prevail." Member
states and their global audience were not to understand by these words that the
members were creating an organization or agencies competent to transgress the
obligations, regarding security and human rights, that they themselves were
assuming. In light of the charter as a whole and the broader flow of community
expectation it appears incontrovertible that any exercises of authority by the
organization or its subsidiary organs must, if they are to be lawful, accord with
the basic human rights prescriptions of the charter, as supplemented by the
Universal Declaration of Human Rights and other legally relevant instruments.

With regard to nation-states and their officials, these human rights prescriptions apply to all state acts, whether unilateral acts or bilateral or multilateral
agreements. The applicability of the human rights prescriptions to the unilateral
acts of particular states is inherent in the nature of international law as supreme over national law and the law on which legitimate sovereignty is based.
The doctrine of the supremacy of international law has been affirmed and
reaffirmed. This doctrine makes contemporary international law for the protection of human rights paramount over all incompatible state practice. It is well
established, for example, that a state cannot evade its international responsibility arising from injuries to aliens by invoking its internal decision processes, constitutive or otherwise.

It seems axiomatic that what states may not lawfully do by their unilateral
acts in contravention of human rights prescriptions they may not lawfully do in
concert or combination through agreement, whether bilateral or multilateral.

The contemporary human rights prescriptions apply to all activities of nation-states and their officials. This has been clearly fortified not only by Article 103 of the charter but also by the emerging doctrine of jus cogens and the increasing recognition of the lack of claimed immunities for violations and the reach of international law.

The newly emphasized notion of jus cogens had its origin in various national legal systems, as expressed in such technical terms as *public policy* and *public order*. In the modern law of nations the concept of a jus cogens, so fundamental that it cannot be changed by agreement, begins with the great founders of the system. The more recent developments in the formulation of the doctrine are traceable to the International Law Commission in its work on the law of treaties.

The consensus favoring some doctrine of jus cogens gained authoritative expression in the Vienna Convention on the Law of Treaties of 1969, which for the first time offered some identification in empirical terms of what prescriptions might be jus cogens. The Vienna Convention, in dealing with "treaties conflicting with a peremptory norm of general international law (jus cogens)," stipulates in Article 53: "A treaty is void if, at the time of its conclusion, it conflicts with a peremptory norm of general international law. For the purposes of the present Convention, a peremptory norm of general international law is a norm accepted and recognized by the international community of States as a whole as a norm from which no derogation is permitted and which can be modified only by a subsequent norm of general international law having the same character." Article 64 of the convention adds: "If a new peremptory norm of general international law emerges, any existing treaty which is in conflict with that norm becomes void and terminates."

It should not be surprising that the great bulk of the contemporary human rights prescriptions, so insistently demanded by so many peoples around the world, and projecting (along with peace and security) the basic purposes for which the contemporary global constitutive process is maintained, should be widely regarded today as among the principles clearly identifiable as jus cogens. Thus, particular states, whether or not members of the United Nations, will not be protected today by global constitutive process in the making (with or without reservations) and performance of agreements, any more than in the performance of unilateral acts, that contravene the basic policies of contemporary human rights prescriptions.

The contemporary human rights prescriptions would appear to apply equally to individuals and private groups — that is, to all nongovernmental actors — and to states and international governmental organizations and their officials. Indeed, most are documented in terms of the right of persons and not in terms of participation in or protection from the state. They are, in the words of the International Court of Justice, *obligatio erga omnes* (owing by and to all humankind). This applicability to individuals and private groups is achieved sometimes through the international prescriptions being made part of the internal law of particular states either directly or indirectly and sometimes through a more direct subjection of individuals and groups to the international prescriptions. Whether the human rights prescriptions are expressed through customary expectation or multilateral agreement or both, states have no real difficulty in making such prescriptions internal law through their constitutive processes.

The appropriate specialized institutions at the international level to ensure the application of the human rights prescriptions are still being established. The bulk of the application of such prescriptions occurs in the foreign-office-to-foreign-office diplomacy of nation-states. Whatever transnational redress most private parties can secure for deprivations of their rights has to do with this traditional remedy, although the domestic arena has been and is the primary arena for effective invocation, application, and enjoyment of human rights. There are, however, some initiatives toward more inclusive and more effective institutions and procedures. The United Nations Human Rights Commission, as assisted by the Sub-Commission on Prevention of Discrimination and Protection of Minorities, has removed its self-imposed shackles in order to deal with complaints not only from states but also from private groups and individuals. In spite of its somewhat cautious attitude, the commission apparently constitutes a worldwide forum with authority, both existing and potential, in general community expectation to apply the basic prescriptions to systematic, gross deprivations of human rights wherever they may occur. The Human Rights Committee, established under the International Covenant on Civil and Political Rights and its optional protocol, is charged with applying the important policies of the covenant to a significant segment of the world's population. The Committee on the Elimination of Racial Discrimination, established under the International Convention on the Elimination of All Forms of Racial Discrimination, has dealt with many issues involving racial discrimination and is quickly becoming a major institution to combat racial discrimination in all its manifestations.

On the regional level, an excellent model for the application of human rights prescriptions is, as is well known, the system establishing the European Convention of Human Rights. The application of the European convention is effected by a complex of specialized institutions, consisting of the European Commission on Human Rights, the European Court on Human Rights, and the Committee of Ministers of the Council of Europe. Within the framework of the Organization of American States, the Inter-American Commission on Human Rights, with its expanding authority, and the Inter-American Court of Human Rights are making serious efforts toward application.

In addition to transnational institutions (global and regional) established to secure compliance with the high standards set forth in the global bill of human rights, transnational prescriptions of human rights are increasingly invoked and applied in domestic courts. Recently, prosecutors in Spain invoked universal jurisdiction to initiate criminal actions under Spanish law against former Argentinian military officers, based on the disappearances, detentions, and torture of Spanish nationals during Argentina's "dirty war" against dissidents in the 1970s. In the famous decision of *Filartiga v. Peña-Irala,* the United States Court of Appeals for the Second Circuit in 1980 applied international human rights law to establish that freedom from torture is protected under customary international law, which forms a part of the supreme law of the land in the United States.[8] Therefore, the alleged act of torture committed in Paraguay by a local police chief, Pena-Irala, against a Paraguayan national became an actionable tort before U.S. courts under the Alien Torts Claim Act. The victim's family, living in the United States, brought the lawsuit against Pena-Irala when he was held in custody pending deportation for illegal overstay in the United States.

In addition, some European countries, invoking international human rights law instruments that prohibit capital punishment, have refused extradition of their nationals to the United States and other countries in death penalty cases.[9]

We turn finally to *termination,* which means ending an existing prescription. Since the human rights prescriptions are so widely and intensely demanded and so highly cherished, modification or termination of such prescriptions has been made extremely difficult.

The difficulties that the global constitutive process presents to terminating or modifying contemporary human rights prescriptions appear comparable to those presented by some national constitutive processes to changing basic, most intensely demanded policies. Under prevailing customary international law these prescriptions can be changed only by modalities in prescription comparable to those in which they were created. For the human rights prescriptions properly regarded as jus cogens, which, as indicated above, include the bulk of such prescriptions, this consequence is made explicit by Article 53 of the Vienna Convention on the Law of Treaties. This article, in its somewhat tautological definition, describes a "peremptory norm of general international law" as one that permits "no derogation" and "can be modified only by a subsequent norm of general international law having the same character."

As has been observed, the contemporary human rights prescriptions have been created through a comprehensive, complex process of continuing communication that embraces both the deliberate and formal modalities of multilateral agreement and parliamentary procedures and the less deliberate and mostly informal modalities of customary behavior and expectation. The cumulative and mutually reinforcing effect of these modalities of communication establishes the core content of the human rights prescriptions as authoritative and controlling within the expectations of most of humankind. Termination or modification of these expectations must require a process of communication no less comprehensive and complex, employing the same modalities. The special difficulties that the global constitutive process places in the way of employing each of these modalities for purposes of change may be noted.

Insofar as the human rights prescriptions are grounded in the U.N. Charter, any formal change in these prescriptions must conform to the procedures established to change the charter. Because of the obvious difficulty associated with the built-in veto in the amending procedure contained in Article 108 of the charter, formal amendment of the charter has been extremely modest, reflecting only the numerical changes in the composition and voting procedures of key organs as a consequence of the vast expansion of U.N. membership. Any proposal to terminate or drastically alter the human rights prescriptions would not be immune from this difficulty.

When the human rights prescriptions are incorporated in other multilateral agreements, any proposals for change must encounter the characteristic difficulties in changing agreements between many parties. The two pillars — the International Covenant on Civil and Political Rights (and its optional protocols) and the International Covenant on Economic, Social, and Cultural Rights — contain no provision for denunciation; the commitments undertaken under the covenants are so fundamental and intensely demanded that they are not expected to be modified, certainly not by unilateral action. Even in human rights conventions containing provisions for denunciation, such provisions are so hedged that they cannot easily be made effective.

Insofar as the human rights prescriptions are based on the uniformities that create customary law, any termination or modification of their content requires the development of new customary expectation and behavior. The difficulty in this mode of terminating the human rights prescriptions is obvious in the requirement of the subjectivities of "rightness" or "oughtness" that must attend the behavior from which customary expectations are inferred. Given the intensities with which the basic content of the human rights prescriptions is presently demanded by the peoples of the world, it is difficult to foresee a context in which opposite content could be demanded with the requisite subjectivities of "rightness" to transform uniformities in behavior, in contravention of the contemporary prescriptions, into acceptable bases for inferring an opposite international law. This is in no way intended to suggest that the existing human rights prescriptions cannot be changed, refined, and improved. What is being suggested is that, so long as the peoples of the world continue to exhibit the same widespread and high intensities in demand for the basic human rights expressed in the existing prescriptions, any changes in the fundamental content of such prescriptions must encounter enormous difficulties and be effected through the same modalities by which the prescriptions were created.

CONJUNCTION OF HUMAN RIGHTS AND STATE RESPONSIBILITY

What does this all mean? What is the significance of the emerging global bill of human rights brought about by the contemporary human rights movement? Has it superseded the customary protection under the responsibility of states for the treatment of aliens? Such questions are often asked.

The new epoch in the international protection of human rights ushered in by the United Nations has, paradoxically, been attended by unnecessary confusion about the continued protection of aliens. The rapid multiplication of newly independent states (arising from the emancipation of colonial peoples and, in recent years, the break-up of existing states), differing conceptions about authority and self-determination in various social contexts, and the ideological rifts about the world have brought intense challenges to many customary norms, including those concerning the responsibility of states. The principle of the minimum international standard for the protection of aliens has been attacked especially severely.

The objections to such a universal standard, voiced by Latin American states as well as newly independent states, stress that these rules were fashioned without their participation and that the minimum standard reflects and perpetuates the imbalance of power between the industrialized world and themselves. They further claim that the customary law of responsibility of states for aliens in general should not be considered an authoritative, universal norm of international law. The minimum standard constitutes an infringement on state sovereignty by requiring states, without their consent, to provide special protection to the alien's person and property. It is contended that this practice, whereby a state affords such protection to aliens but not its own nationals, destroys transnational interaction by institutionalizing disparate treatment between aliens and nationals.

This line of argument ignores the role of the international standard in maintaining a world economy and society, underestimates the interests of any particular state in achieving such an outcome, minimizes the importance of the international protection of the human rights of a state's own nationals, undercuts the

vast flow across states' lines of prescriptive communication about the protection of both nationals and aliens, and aggrandizes the technical concepts of
sovereignty and of territorial jurisdiction.

In the context of such confusion it is understandable that the International
Law Commission has made little headway in its protracted effort to clarify and
codify the law of state responsibility. The first special rapporteur of the commission, Francisco V. García-Amador, essayed a noble "synthesis" of the newer
emerging law of human rights and the older law designed to protect aliens in
proposing both that the newer human rights prescriptions be employed to give
more precise content to the inherited minimum international standard for aliens
and that the newer remedies being established for the protection of human
rights generally be made to supersede certain aspects of the hallowed state
interposition on behalf of its injured nationals. His basic proposal was for
equality of nationals and aliens, with both a minimum and a maximum in
internationally recognized "fundamental human rights."[10]

This imaginative proposal by García-Amador has failed to obtain wide support. Whereas some have thought his proposal goes too far, some have thought
it might weaken an important traditional remedy to protect aliens before any
effective new remedy is established in replacement. (Subsequently, as the International Law Commission scrapped García-Amador's efforts and shifted its
focus away from state responsibility for injuries to aliens to state responsibility
in general, the task of codifying international law governing the treatment of
aliens fell to the Sub-Commission on Prevention of Discrimination and Protection of Minorities in 1972, with Baroness Elles of Great Britain as its driving
force. The effort culminated in the adoption of the Declaration on the Human
Rights of Individuals Who Are Not Nationals of the Country in Which They
Live by the General Assembly in December 1985.)[11]

The newly emerged contemporary human rights prescriptions, including
both the U.N. Charter and ancillary expressions, would appear to have importantly increased the transnational protection that the world constitutive process
affords aliens. Although nowhere in the charter or other nondiscrimination
prescriptions is alienage specifically included as such among the impermissible
grounds of differentiation, clearly in the future differentiation of treatment
because of alienage will be much more strictly confined, and unlawful discrimination, regarding many values, may be much more readily found. Moreover,
Article 2 of the Universal Declaration contains the interrelated prohibition of
discrimination per se on the basis of national origin, a prohibition mirrored in
other human rights instruments.

Although the U.N. Charter enumerates only four grounds of impermissible
differentiation — race, sex, language, and religion — these are intended to be

illustrative and not exhaustive. The more detailed formulation in the Universal Declaration of Human Rights makes this abundantly clear. The standard formula employed by the universal declaration is: "Everyone has the right to. . . ." Negatively, the formula is: "No one shall be. . . ." "Everyone" certainly refers to all human beings, national and alien alike. Only in Article 21 does the declaration reserve a specified right exclusively to nationals:

1. Everyone has the right to take part in the government of country, directly or through freely chosen representatives.
2. Everyone has the right of equal access to public service.

This provision reflects only the long-shared community expectation that differentiation on the basis of alienage is permissible in regard to participation in the making of local community decisions — namely, voting and holding office. The concern in the declaration that human rights be protected for every human being, regardless of nationality, is further manifested in the latter half of Article 2: "Furthermore, no distinction shall be made on the basis of the political, jurisdictional or international status of the country or territory to which a person belongs, whether it be independent, trust, non-self-governing or under any other limitation of sovereignty."

The same concern for the protection of all human beings, based on the same prescriptive formulas, is equally evident in both international covenants on civil and political rights and on economic, social, and cultural rights. Even human rights conventions with a more restrictive focus are, again, formulated generally in terms of each human being.

Similarly, the two regional human rights conventions — European and American — are cast in broad language designed to protect aliens as well as nationals. The European convention, in Article 1, provides: "The High Contracting Parties shall secure to everyone within their jurisdiction the rights and freedoms defined in Section I of this Convention." Thus, the European Commission on Human Rights has over the years received innumerable individual petitions ("applications") brought by nonnationals resident in the member states of the Council of Europe. Contrary to the traditional practice, nationality is not prerequisite to the protection of individuals. Significantly, the American convention contains, in its preamble, the unique proclamation that "the essential rights of man are not derived from one's being a national of a certain state, but are based upon attributes of the human personality." The convention proceeds to specify in Article 1:

1. The States Parties to this Convention undertake to respect the rights and freedoms recognized herein and to ensure to all persons subject to their

jurisdiction the free and full exercise of those rights and freedoms, without any discrimination for reasons of race, color, sex, language, religion, political or other opinion, national or social origin, economic status, birth, or any other social condition.

2. For the purposes of this Convention, "person" means every human being.

In short, the principal thrust of the contemporary human rights movement is to accord nationals the same protection formerly accorded only to aliens while at the same time raising the standard of protection for all human beings, nationals as well as aliens, far beyond the minimum international standard developed under earlier customary law. When the new human rights prescriptions are considered in mass, they extend to all the basic human dignity values the peoples of the world today demand, and the more detailed standards specified with regard to each of these values exhibit all the precision that rational application either permits or requires. This makes the continuing debate about the doctrines of the minimum international standard and equality of treatment highly artificial, because an international standard is now authoritatively prescribed for all human beings. It does not follow, however, that these new developments in substantive prescription about human rights have rendered obsolete the protection of individuals through the traditional procedures developed by the customary law of the responsibility of states for injuries to aliens.

The notion, popularized by Vattel, that an injury to an alien is an injury also to the state of nationality served to justify the protection of the interests both of the state and of an important category of individuals in a later epoch when the nation-state was often regarded as "the exclusive and sole subject" of international law. Even when more catholic conceptions of the subjects of international law prevail and individuals are being given more direct access to authoritative arenas for their self-protection, however, the historic remedy of state claims to protect the individual would not appear to have ceased to serve common interest. Rather, the transnational channels of protection through a state, together with the newly developed procedures under the contemporary human rights program of claim by individuals, would appear to achieve a cumulative beneficient impact, each reinforcing the other, in the defense and fulfillment of individual human rights. Individuals have recently gained, for remedy of deprivations, either direct or derivative access to transnational arenas of authoritative decision, both global and regional. Notable among them are the United Nations Commission on Human Rights, Human Rights Committee, the Committee on the Elimination of Racial Discrimination, the European Commission on Human Rights, the Committee Against Torture, and the Inter-American Commission on Human Rights. Yet the prospect of further direct access by individuals to authoritative transnational arenas, though encouraging, remains far from adequate. As long as states remain the most important and effective participants in transnational processes of decision, espousal of claims by states for deprivations suffered by individuals would appear indispensable to full protection. Remedy through claim by a protecting state and through individual petition need not be mutually incompatible (they are not mutually exclusive); they can be made to reinforce each other for the better defense and fulfillment of the human rights of the individual. And traditional remedies at the domestic level, of course, must continue to be nurtured and enhanced.

13

Vertical Allocation of Authority

Authority, conceived as the expectations of community members about who will decide what and how, has always been an important base of power. As Lord Acton and others have long observed, authority in this sense builds on itself and constitutes a most effective base of power for any decision maker. A conception of authority, with its concomitant role in decision making, is apparent, in various equivalent forms, in the notions of customary law prevalent in primitive societies, ancient China, India, classical Greece, ancient Rome, Western Europe, and the Americas. This conception represents the insistent historic demands made by many peoples through the centuries and up to the contemporary democratic polities that authority rightfully come from the whole people. It is reflected, further, in Article 21(3) of the Universal Declaration of Human Rights and also finds expression in the interrelated principle of self-determination. The importance of such a conception in international law is easily demonstrable.

In the world arena, allocation of authority takes two basic forms: the vertical allocation of authority between the general community and particular states, and the horizontal allocation of authority between and among states. We deal with the former here and the latter in the next chapter.

In the vertical allocation of authority between the general community and particular states, the most conspicuous development is the continuing expansion of the concept of "international concern," along with the concomitant erosion of the concept of "domestic jurisdiction." As transnational interaction accelerates and the interdependencies of peoples everywhere are better perceived, the authority of the organized community has grown steadily.

The dichotomy between matters of international concern and those of domestic jurisdiction inheres in the very concept of international law, even of a world rationally organized on a geographic basis. It signifies the necessity of a continuing allocation and balancing of competence between the central, general community and its component territorial communities, states, or regions, in ways best designed to serve the common interest. The technical terms *international concern* and *domestic jurisdiction* and their equivalents represent two polar concepts, like the blades of scissors, designed to maintain a proper balance between inclusive and exclusive competence. Neither is absolute. Hence, by *international concern* is meant that certain matters, including events occurring within the territorial boundaries of particular states, are relatively important to a general, transnational community so that such a community can make and apply law to such matters in defense of the common interests of peoples affected by those matters. An important function of international law is to permit external decision makers to intercede in matters that would otherwise be regarded as essentially internal to a particular state.

In contrast, *domestic jurisdiction* refers to certain matters that are regarded as of predominant importance only to a particular state. Ever since the rise of the modern state system, built on the notion of sovereign equality of all states, particular states have enjoyed, and continued to insist on, a large domain of exclusive competence. This insistent demand has been made and protected under such technical concepts as equality of states, sovereignty, independence, and nonintervention. The cumulative effect of these concepts is to insulate internal elites from external regulation.

Sovereignty, as made popular by Jean Bodin in the sixteenth century with the emergence of the modern state system, referred to the alleged supreme authority and power wielded by the absolute monarch. Whereas the concept of sovereignty in Bodin's sense was somewhat fitting in an era of absolute monarchs, it is not at all apt in describing the authority enjoyed by the individual nation-state in the contemporary epoch of popular sovereignty (authority in the people) and growing interdependences. The persisting assertion and use of sovereignty, with its sixteenth-century absolutist connotation, thus appear out of place in today's world of interdependence. Indeed, sovereignty was never so absolute as to prevent community intervention and sanctions.

The use of the technical term *domestic jurisdiction* to protect the exclusive competence of internal elites is relatively recent in origin. It made its first formal appearance in the Covenant of the League of Nations. Article 15(8) of the covenant stated: "If the dispute between the parties is claimed by one of them, and is found by the Council, to arise out of a matter which by international law is solely within the domestic jurisdiction of that party the Council shall so report, and shall make no recommendation as to its settlement." The Charter of the United Nations has adopted this formula with slight modification. Article 2(7) of the charter reads: "Nothing contained in the present Charter shall authorize the United Nations to intervene in matters which are essentially within the domestic jurisdiction of any state or shall require the Members to submit such matters to settlement under the present Charter; but this principle shall not prejudice the application of enforcement measures under Chapter VII." Consequently the label *domestic jurisdiction* has largely superseded its many historic equivalents for claiming exclusive competence.

Although some commentators have read great significance into the difference in wording — the substitution of "essentially" for "solely" and the omission of specific reference to "international law" in the new formulation — the real significance of Article 2(7) can be meaningfully ascertained only by reference to its application.

Time and again competing claimants have invoked the legislative history of Article 2(7). Yet the records of the San Francisco Conference offer no conclusive answer. The framers of the charter neither saw fit to deprive the United Nations of the authoritative competence essential to the effective performance of its tasks, or curtail that competence, nor wanted the organization to pry into matters generally regarded to be within the exclusive domain of individual states. The line to draw between what is essentially of domestic jurisdiction or of international concern is far from obvious.

Concepts in international law are definite to the extent that they are uniformly understood in content and procedure. Expectations about content are necessarily vague, since the contingent circumstances to which they refer are alluded to in general terms. Hence the importance of procedure — of who is authorized to act and how to apply the content to concrete situations.

Whenever a dispute comes to the notice of the United Nations, Article 2(7) necessarily receives initial attention, save in certain clear-cut cases. Claims and counterclaims concerning U.N. authority are generally juxtaposed. No one state has a monopoly on invoking the plea of domestic jurisdiction. It has been claimed by many states large and small, new and old, authoritarian and nonauthoritarian.

Though it may appear simple to ascertain the immediate objective sought by competing claimants who repudiate or accept U.N. authority in a particular dispute, it is by no means easy to detect and demonstrate the real policy considerations that underlie their claims. Even the attitudes of a single state are far from consistent. Its position is more often than not dictated by the degree of involvement and interest perceived in a particular dispute, and it often appears to fluctuate independent of the level of crisis at a given time.

In particular controversies, the critical question confronting decision makers, representing the larger community of humankind, is how best to relate options in allocating inclusive and exclusive competence to the more fundamental policies of the larger community. Fortunately, the intellectual task involved in making a rational choice among options in the allocation of those competences was clearly recognized as requiring careful, contextual scrutiny. This view found authoritative expression from the Permanent Court of International Justice in the *Tunis-Morocco* case of 1923.[1] In that case, the issue was whether the dispute between France and Great Britain over the applicability to British subjects of certain French nationality decrees, proclaimed in 1921 in Tunis and the French zone of Morocco (both under French protection), fell within the domain of Article 15(8) and thus lay outside the competence of the League Council. In rejecting the French claim, the court held that in principle questions of nationality are within a state's "reserved domain" but that certain treaties concerning Tunis and Morocco to which France and Great Britain were respectively parties made the instant dispute over the nationality decrees an international dispute. The court added that the question of treaty obligation "does not, according to international law, fall solely within the domestic jurisdiction of a single state." The court further proclaimed, in words that have since become well worn: "The question whether a certain matter is or is not solely within the domestic jurisdiction of a State is an essentially relative question; it depends upon the development of international relations."[2] Determining whether a matter is of "international concern" or essentially within "domestic jurisdiction" thus depends not only on facts but on changing facts in light of the context of world conditions and relevant legal policies; this permits a continuing readjustment of inclusive and exclusive competences as conditions might require.

The trend in authoritative decision within the United Nations toward expansion of international concern can be seen by the scope of subjects handled by various U.N. organs. In spite of the familiar, understandable invocations of the plea of domestic jurisdiction in resisting inclusive authority, especially at the early years of the organization, the United Nations has exercised its authority to deal with a wide range of matters extending to every value sector of human and community life. The long and comprehensive list includes matters of peace and security (including peace-keeping operations, matters of disarmament, and arms control); matters of decolonization and self-determination (including trust territories, non-self-governing territories, and others); territorial disputes; humanitarian emergencies; questions concerning the form of government of a state; international cooperation in economic, social, and cultural fields; human rights matters; codification and development of international law; and so on. The list can be greatly multiplied by reference to the ongoing activities carried out by various U.N. specialized agencies and other international governmental organizations.

The trend toward inclusive authority through expansion of international concern has been further facilitated by clarifying the meaning of "intervention" contained in Article 2(7) of the charter. The following definition offered by Hersch Lauterpacht has gained wide acceptance: "Intervention is a technical term of, on the whole, unequivocal connotation. It signifies dictatorial interference in the sense of action amounting to a denial of the independence of the State. It implies a demand which, if not complied with, involves a threat of or recourse to compulsion, though not necessarily physical compulsion, in some form."[3] Thus conceived, it would appear that a vast difference exists between the unilateral interference by one state in the internal affairs of another state and the general community's inclusive making and application of law to protect the common interest of all (and, thus, the affairs of all). One is prohibited by law; the other is in defense of law. The Security Council continues to give broad scope to expanding the definition of "threat to" and "breaches of the international peace," authorizing increasingly multifunctional actions in intrastate conflicts, such as missions to Somalia and to Kuridish regions in Iraq.[4]

The expansion of international concern in U.N. practice is manifested in all decision functions. In terms of the intelligence function (that is, the gathering, processing, and dissemination of information), Article 2(7) is no bar to inscription in the agenda of, and debate on, any issue having an "undeniable international impact, even if there is no consensus over the degree to which international law does or should regulate the matter."[5] The United Nations is fully competent "to talk about a situation, to discuss it, to debate, to persuade, to negotiate,"[6] without doing violence to the mandate of Article 2(7). In terms of the promoting function (advocacy and recommendations), the organs and agencies of the United Nations, as amply shown in countless resolutions, have not been deterred from making recommendations on subject matters claimed to be beyond their competence. With regard to the prescribing function (that is, the projection and communication of authoritative policies), no limit has been easily identifiable; it encompasses practically every aspect of human life, every value sector. The Security Council is becoming so active in enforcing collective security that some commentators have suggested the possibility that the World Court may soon have to "judicially review" the legality of certain Security Council resolutions.[7] But it appears that there has been a "diminishing willingness to insulate internationally important activity from international legal control by deference to the dogma of domestic jurisdiction"[8] or the equally circular notion of "intervention" into the affairs of a state versus the affairs of the community.

The exercise of the invoking function (that is, the provisional characterization of concrete circumstances in terms of authoritative prescriptions) has found little impediment in Article 2(7); this is most vividly illustrated by the remedies of state complaint and individual petition against human rights violations and by the statements of states to monitor, even in political arenas, human rights compliance by other states, as this is no longer a matter of domestic jurisdiction. In terms of the applying function (that is, authoritative characterizations of particular events in terms of prescriptions), the U.N. organs have overruled the plea of domestic jurisdiction in numerous cases relating to threats to peace and security, to self-determination, to human rights, and to numerous other situations. As to the terminating function (the ending of prescription and other arrangements) and the appraising function (the evaluation of decision process), it is generally assumed that the general community has the same broad inclusive competence, free of domestic jurisdiction barriers, that it has in relation to the intelligence and prescribing functions.

Note that it is the general community, the global constitutive process, that ultimately determines what matters are within international concern and what within domestic jurisdiction. As the dynamics of interdependence accelerate and peoples' perceptions of their interdependence deepen and become more realistic, the established processes of authoritative decision can be expected to encounter less difficulty in bringing matters having transnational ramifications within the compass of inclusive competence. Events occurring inside the boundaries of one state with appreciable effects on others have always been subject to claim, decision, and review on the international plane. Individual states rarely succeed, even by invoking the plea of domestic jurisdiction, in precluding effective accommodations in keeping with inclusive interest when transnational impacts are clearly generated. Domestic jurisdiction means little more than a concession by the general community to particular states of a primary, though not exclusive, competence over matters arising within the boundaries and predominantly affecting the internal public order of such states. When particular events engender significant inclusive impacts, the general community can be expected to internationalize jurisdiction and to authorize appropriate inclusive decision and action.

The overwhelming trend toward expansion of the scope of "international concern" notwithstanding, nation-states are prone to invoke, and often abuse, the plea of "domestic jurisdiction" in order to insulate abusive conduct from international scrutiny. China's unceasing threat toward Taiwan in the name of domestic jurisdiction exemplifies such an abuse. The PRC's threat to use missiles and other types of force against Taiwan constitutes a lawless act in violation of the U.N. Charter, but the PRC has sought to justify it by claiming that Taiwan is "part of China" and "an internal affair of China."

In light of the discussions in this chapter and in chapter 2 above, it would appear that Taiwan's present and future status are not internal affairs of China but are matters of international concern. To elaborate:

1. As stated in chapter 2, Taiwan is a sovereign, independent state, not part of China. For more than fifty years since its founding in 1949, the PRC has not exerted "effective control" over Taiwan for a single day.
2. Controversies over Taiwan's sovereignty and international legal status involve an interpretation of international agreements (such as the San Francisco Peace Treaty with Japan) and hence fall within the scope of international concern.
3. The PRC's acts of military threat and state terrorism against Taiwan endanger peace and security in the Asian-Pacific region and in the world and constitute "threats and breaches of the peace" in violation of the U.N. Charter.
4. Taiwan's past, present, and future involve the principle of self-determination under international law.
5. Taiwan's present and future status will affect the fundamental human rights of its 22 million inhabitants and hence fall within the scope of international concern.

14

Horizontal Allocation of Authority

The horizontal allocation of competence between states remains vital in the contemporary state-centered world, where most authority over particular events is still exercised at the national level. In the preceding chapter, we dealt with the vertical allocation of authority — the allocation between the general community and the territorial communities. Here we are concerned with horizontal allocation — allocation of authority among different territorial communities regarded as equal.

The central concern of this chapter differs from the claims for comprehensive, continuing control over territory, resources, and people as described in chapters 8 through 12. The concern here is with a state's assertion of competence to make and apply law to particular events, persons, and property. The emphasis is on "particular events" rather than "comprehensive and continuing control." This, in the conventional usage, is the question of jurisdiction. *Jurisdiction* as a term of art has been given a wide range of references.

Some have used the term so broadly as to embrace all the subjects covered in chapters 8 through 12 and in this chapter. Others take an extremely restrictive view, confining it to what is called "judicial jurisdiction," or "jurisdiction to adjudicate." For those who adhere strictly to the artificial distinction between "public" and "private" international law (popularly known as conflict of laws in the United States), they tend to refer to cases in which states are parties as public international law and to cases in which individuals and private associations are parties as private international law.

In an interdependent world in which transnational interaction has grown enormously and in which nonstate and state actors are in constant interplay under changing, complex conditions, generating value outcomes of varying magnitudes across state boundaries, it is highly artificial to delineate between public and private international law. As Judge (then Professor) Philip C. Jessup pointed out, "transnational law" would be more fitting in description and more in tune with the realities of contemporary international life.

The factual situations that would give rise to claims to prescribe and apply law to particular events range over every value and phase of interaction of a particular value process, as witness these examples:

- A U.S. soldier on a training exercise in Japan fatally shoots a Japanese woman in the back with a grenade launcher.
- Three U.S. G.I.s stationed in Okinawa kidnap and rape a Japanese schoolgirl and are then tried and sentenced by a Japanese court.
- Colombian nationals produce cocaine in Colombia and smuggle it into the United States.
- A Mexican national is abducted to the United States to be tried for the kidnap and murder of a U.S. Drug Enforcement Administration special agent and the Mexican pilot working with the agent.
- Fighting their own "war on drugs," Mexican police detain and kill U.S. citizens in Mexico allegedly involved in the marijuana trade. Some claim the murders are part of a cover-up to hide Mexican police involvement in the drug trade.
- The U.S. Coast Guard boards an American-owned vessel twelve miles from land in the Bahamas, finding half a ton of marijuana and arresting the crew, including Jamaican and Bahamian nationals.
- A U.S. citizen residing in Paris fails to reply to subpoenas served on him in Paris that require him to be a witness on behalf of the United States in a criminal trial.
- Gas leaks at a pesticide plant of a multinational chemical corporation, head-quartered in the United States, causing thousands of deaths and injuries in Bhopal, India.
- Two Shiite Moslem gunmen commandeer Trans World Airline Flight 847, with 153 aboard (104 of them American), forcing it to fly from Athens to Beirut, to Algiers, and back to Beirut. The hijackers, members of the Party of God, are later joined by a dozen members of AMAL, a more moderate Shiite group, while negotiations for the release of hostages are in progress. All the hostages are freed in stages, but one American marine is killed.
- A Pakistani terrorist, wanted for the deaths of two CIA agents, is extradited and flown from Pakistan to the U.S. on an American military plane with no formal hearing in his home country.
- Four Palestinian terrorists hijack the Italian cruise ship *Achille Lauro,* with eighty passengers and crew, on the high seas as it approaches Port Said,

Egypt. After killing an American passenger, the hijackers surrender to the Egyptian government in return for a promise of safe passage. Four U.S. fighter planes intercept an Egyptian aircraft carrying the hijackers to freedom and force it to land at the NATO airbase at Comiso, Sicily. The Italian authorities take custody of hijackers but allow the person believed to be the mastermind of the hijacking to leave Rome for Belgrade aboard a Yugoslavian airline (later, however, trying and convicting him in absentia).

- A Georgian diplomat is tried and convicted in the United States, despite claiming diplomatic immunity, for a drunk-driving incident that resulted in the death of a young girl. The Georgian government agrees to withdraw his diplomatic immunity so that he may be tried by a U.S. court.
- Holocaust survivors and their families, now U.S. citizens, claim millions of dollars in gold and assets that Swiss banks allegedly seized and hid in collaboration with the Nazis during World War II.
- The British government refuses to extradite a German national wanted for homicide in the United States, claiming that waiting on death row in the U.S. will be "cruel and unusual punishment" under international human rights law.
- Pan Am Flight 103 explodes over Lockerbie, Scotland, allegedly the result of actions of Libyan terrorists. Libya refuses to extradite the suspects for trial in Scotland.
- The U.S. lures a Lebanese citizen to a yacht in international waters where he is then arrested and brought to the United States to stand trial for hijacking and destroying a Royal Jordanian plane in Beirut in which three U.S. nationals were on board (all three of whom survived).
- The U.S. Congress passes a law enabling courts here to seize the assets of non-U.S. companies that buy Cuban properties expropriated from owners who now live in the United States, punishing such companies for activities they have conducted completely outside of U.S. territory.
- Former dictator Augusto Pinochet faces extradition from England to Spain to stand trial on charges of human rights abuses during his seventeen-year rule in Chile. The charges brought against him are some of the most serious allegations of crime ever to come before English courts.
- United States courts in Florida decide to return Elián Gonzalez, the child who was found in the waters after his mother and stepfather died while trying to escape Cuba, to his father in communist Cuba, even though his Miami relatives objected.
- Egyptian Air Flight 990 crashes into the Atlantic Ocean off the Massachusetts coast on October 31, 1999, killing all 217 people aboard. No information as to the cause of the crash has been discovered, although speculation as to terrorist activity is being considered.

- An Indian airplane is hijacked for eight days on Christmas Eve, 1999. Many are blaming Pakistani terrorists, but Pakistan rejects India's accusations concerning the hijacking. India launches a plan to place armed commandos ("sky marshalls") aboard flights on a random basis.

Which state or states have authority to make and apply law to such events? What are the limits on laws that may be chosen for application? When more than one state asserts competence to make and apply law to a particular event or to prosecute the same person, how should competing claims for jurisdiction be resolved? What factors are to be taken account?

From a transnational perspective, *jurisdiction* as used here is confined neither to criminal or civil jurisdiction nor to judicial jurisdiction. Jurisdiction (horizontal allocation of authority) is concerned here with the competence of a state to make and apply law to particular events, which may or may not occur within the borders of a state and which may or may not involve nationals of the state. It extends to all activities having to do with making and applying law and involves not only the judicial branch of government but the legislative and executive branches (including the latter's administrative agencies). In this sense, it certainly encompasses what have been characterized, by the American Law Institute in its work of revision on "Restatement of the Law, the Foreign Relations Law of the United States," as the three key components of jurisdiction: jurisdiction to prescribe, jurisdiction to adjudicate, and jurisdiction to enforce.[1]

We speak in terms of the state's competence to make law and to apply law to particular events. The competence to apply law includes the competence to adjudicate and the competence to enforce law. Although it is convenient to approach the field in terms of competence to prescribe, to adjudicate, and to enforce because of the familiar tripartite system of government — the legislative, the judicial, and the executive — this distinction is more formal or structural than functional. It is closely tied to the traditional notion of the separation of powers under such a tripartite form of government. From a functional perspective, the twofold distinction between the competence to prescribe and the competence to apply suffices.

In an inherited, horizontal legal order, this authority of states is, initially, allocated under certain reciprocally honored principles of jurisdiction — namely, the principle of territoriality, the principle of nationality, the principle of impact territoriality (also known as the protective principle), the principle of passive personality (also known as the victim theory), and the principle of universality. The passive personality principle is highly controversial.

The principle of territoriality empowers states to prescribe and to apply law to all events occurring within their boundaries, regardless of whether such events involve nationals or nonnationals. The nationality principle authorizes states to make and apply law to their own nationals, wherever they may be. Under the principle of impact territoriality, a state may take measures against direct attack on its security and against activities having substantial impact on its other important values, though the events occur outside its territory. The principle of passive personality authorizes states to make and apply law to people who injure their nationals, wherever the events may occur. The principle of universality, rooted in the perception that certain events (such as those involving piracy, slave trading, war crimes, and genocide) are great threats to common interests of all humanity, authorizes any state having effective control over the offenders to apply certain inclusive civil or criminal prescriptions on behalf of the international community. Together these principles confer on any state the competence to make and apply law regarding all events having significant effect on it.

The competences over particular events achieved by states under most of these primary principles of jurisdiction are complemented by certain secondary allocations of competence under doctrines such as "act of state" and "sovereign immunity." In a world social process in which people and goods constantly move across state lines, the primary principles of jurisdiction can not achieve their appropriate ordering purpose if states do not in substantial measure honor one another's exercises of authority. Hence, states that have effective control over persons and resources are often required, under the doctrine of the act of state, to forgo the exercise of their own authority in deference to the prior legislative, executive, and judicial acts completed within another state. Or they may be required to do so because of immunities accorded heads of state, diplomats, public ships, public corporations, and state agencies, under the doctrine of sovereign immunity.

The five principles of jurisdiction relate to both the competence to make law for particular events and the competence to apply law. In case of competence to apply law in the restrictive sense of "judicial jurisdiction," it further requires considerations of fairness and convenience by taking into account such factors as the presence of persons and assets, domicile of the parties, the place of business, and intent or foreseeability and consent (express or implied) of the parties to adjudication.

International law accords nation-states broad grants of competence in making and applying law to particular events through the five familiar principles of jurisdiction.

The Principle of Territoriality

Under the principle of territoriality, states are authorized to make law and apply law to all events occurring within their borders, regardless of whether such events involve nationals or nonnationals. It reflects the overriding importance of territoriality in the present-day state system. Under this principle the authority of the state extends to the limits of its territory. This territorial domain of the state, as described in chapters 8, 9, and 10, includes not only land masses but also internal waters, territorial waters, and the airspace above its territorial lands and waters. Within this domain the state exerts comprehensive and continuing authority.

The state's competence to make law to regulate actors and activities within its territorial domain and to apply law to events, persons, and property within its borders are both manifestations of such authority.

The Principle of Nationality

Under the principle of nationality, a state is empowered to make law with respect to its nationals, wherever they may be, and to apply such law within its territory, outside the territory of other states, or in another state with permission. A state can thus exercise jurisdiction over the conduct of its nationals in foreign states and outside the jurisdiction of any state. This follows from a state's claim to control its own people as a base of power.

Examples of application of the nationality principle are the exercise of jurisdiction over United States nationals violating trademark laws overseas (*Steele v. Bulova Watch Co., Inc.,* 1952),[2] the taxing of income derived from foreign property by a foreign-domiciled U.S. citizen (*Cook v. Tait,* 1924),[3] and the regulation of U.S. military service personnel (*United States v. Calley,* 1973).[4] The War Crimes Act of 1996 has extended U.S. jurisdiction to cover "grave breaches" of the Geneva Conventions where the perpetrator or victim was a U.S. national. It fails to apply universal jurisdiction.

The issues of nationality relate not only to natural persons (human beings), as discussed in chapter 11, but also to juristic persons, including corporations, ships, aircraft, and spacecraft. Many treaty provisions define *nationals* to include corporations for various purposes, and many contain provisions ascribing a national character to corporations and other associations, based on the place of their incorporation or that of their principal office of business.

The competence of nation-states to ascribe national character to vessels has long been recognized, although such competence is most often related to the fiction of territoriality. This policy has historically made enormous contributions to the maintenance of the public order of the oceans.

The nationality of aircraft, as provided by the Chicago Convention of 1944, is governed by the state of registration. The Tokyo Convention on Offenses Committed on Board Aircraft of 1963 stipulates that the state of registration has exclusive competence to make and apply law to offenses and acts committed on board. The general practice is to sustain freedom in conferring national status by registration.

The Outer Space Treaty of 1967 refrains from employing the concept of nationality in relation to objects launched into outer space. Under Article VIII of the treaty, the state of registration "shall retain jurisdiction and control over such object, and over any personnel thereof, while in outer space or on a celestial body." The launching state is required to maintain a registration of space objects under the Convention on Registration of Objects Launched into Outer Space of 1974.

The Principle of Impact Territoriality

The principle of impact territoriality, once called the protective principle, authorizes a state to take measures against direct attack on its security or against activities that have substantial impacts on its important value processes, even though the activities occurred outside its territorial limits. The principle of impact territoriality is sometimes strictly distinguished from the protective principle. The former allows for jurisdiction, for example, when there is an intent to produce effects (or such is foreseeable), and the events to be controlled are not within state territory but their detrimental effects do occur there, whereas the latter seeks to prevent value deprivations within the state before they occur. It is not necessary to draw too fine a line, since the potential events encompassed often constitute a continuum.

In an interdependent world, acts committed partly or wholly outside the territory of a state not infrequently generate effects within the state's territory. Under a strict application of the territorial principle, such acts would not fall within the jurisdiction of the affected state. Thus has developed the doctrine of impact territoriality, whereby a state may exercise jurisdiction over such extraterritorial acts when there is an intent to produce effects (or such is forseeable) and their adverse effects, actual or potential, are felt within the state's territory. Examples would be extraterritorial acts of drug smugglers, of those involved in stock fraud, and of people fraudulently fabricating, selling, or obtaining visas to enter a state.

This principle has been slowly accepted by U.S. courts, due to the generally accepted requirement that some nexus be demonstrated between the extraterritorial acts and actual, intended, or potential in-state effects. As early as 1804, however, the U.S. Supreme Court recognized the applicability of the principle by a foreign state in *Church v. Hubbart,*[5] which involved a suit by the owner of a ship seized by the Portuguese off the coast of Brazil against its insurers. The court found that the law of nations allowed Portugal to seize the vessel beyond the limits of its territorial domain in order to "secure itself from injury."[6]

The efforts by the United States to prescribe and apply its antitrust law on the basis of impact territoriality has been especially controversial, causing friction with other countries.[7] Such attempts at extraterritorial application by a state of its economic regulatory laws are regarded as especially intrusive and intolerable when the challenged conduct was lawful where it took place.

In an interdependent world, states, by their exercises of competence to make and apply law to particular activities, will have substantial impacts on the internal value processes of other states. The only relevant question is whether a state can reasonably exercise its competence with respect to extraterritorial events and how appropriate accommodation can be reached in the common interest.

The Principle of Passive Personality

The principle of passive personality allows a state to exercise jurisdiction over a party based on the effects of that party's conduct on the state's nationals. Recent attempts on the part of the United States to secure and prosecute perpetrators of acts of international terrorism, such as in the Lockerbie, World Trade Center, and *Achille Lauro* incidents, are based in part on this principle, although they rest on universal jurisdiction by treaty. Champions of the Helms-Burton Act have argued the principle of passive personality as well, although with less success. This is partly because many of those affected were not U.S. citizens at the time of the nationalizations, and because the targets of the legislation are private firms rather than the Cuban government itself, the source of the injury.[8]

Perhaps the most notable assertion of the passive personality principle was in the dictum in the case of the S.S. *Lotus,* argued before the Permanent Court of International Justice in 1927.[9] The central issue was whether Turkey had the competence to apply its criminal laws to the conduct of a French officer whose faulty navigation caused a collision on the high seas between his vessel and a Turkish vessel, resulting in the sinking of the Turkish vessel and the death of a number of Turkish nationals. Although the majority decision was based largely on the principle of impact territoriality and expressly refused to decide the issue whether passive personality was acceptable, several judges expressed willingness to accept Turkish justifications in terms of the principle of passive personality.

Some commentators consider this principle redundant, reasoning that the principle of universality, aided by the doctrines of state responsibility, is sufficient to cover the situations in which it has been applied. For example, in the *Eichmann* case (1961),[10] which involved the chief organizer of Hitler's "final solution," the District Court of Jerusalem upheld Israeli jurisdiction on the universality principle but further justified its jurisdiction on the ground that Jews were the principal victims of the defendant's war crimes.

The Principle of Universality

Under the principle of universality, a state is authorized to punish certain offenses that pose threats to the common interests of humankind wherever the offenses may occur and whoever may be the perpetrators or victims. Community prescriptions identifying customary international crimes are regarded as so vital to the world community that any state which apprehends or secures effective control over an offender is deemed authorized to apply such prescriptions. Any state that possesses an accused violator of specified prescriptions is authorized to try and, if appropriate, to punish an offender without the need to consider links of territoriality with the offense or of nationality with the offender or the victim. The trend in recent practice, for example, is to invoke universality in jurisdictional claims relating to individual terrorist activities.[11]

The number of offenses subject to universal jurisdiction has historically been relatively few, notably war crimes, piracy, breaches of neutrality, attacks on diplomatic personnel, slave trading, and a few others.

Piracy has long been considered "an offense against the law of nations." In the absence (until now) of an international criminal court, criminal and civil sanctions for piracy have been left to the state that seized the offender and private suits with domestic fora. Building on the Convention on the High Seas of 1958, the Law of the Sea Convention of 1982 deals with piracy in Articles 101 through 107. "Piracy," as defined by Article 101, "consists of any of the following acts":

(a) any illegal acts of violence or detention, or any act of depredation, committed for private ends by the crew or the passengers of a private ship or a private aircraft, and directed:
  (i) on the high seas, against another ship or aircraft, or against persons or property on board such ship or aircraft;
  (ii) against a ship, aircraft, persons or property in a place outside the jurisdiction of any State;
(b) any act of voluntary participation in the operation of a ship or of an aircraft with knowledge of facts making it a pirate ship or aircraft;
(c) any act of inciting or of intentionally facilitating an act described subparagraph (a) or (b).

In recent decades, thanks to a keen sense of human dignity and solidarity under global conditions of intimate interdependence, the list of offenses covered by universal jurisdiction has expanded considerably to include genocide, apartheid, and hijacking of aircraft. According to the Rome Statute of the

International Criminal Court, the International Criminal Court will have jurisdiction over (1) the crime of genocide, (2) crimes against humanity, (3) war crimes, and (4) the crime of aggression.[12]

The concept of war crimes was expanded and genocide became a subject of universal jurisdiction after World War II. The principles of the Nuremberg Charter and Judgment, punishing crimes against peace, war crimes, and crimes against humanity, received unanimous approval by the U.N. General Assembly in 1946. "Crimes against peace" include the "planning, preparation, initiation or waging of a war of aggression, or a war in violation of international treaties, agreements or assurances."[13] "War crimes" involve "violations of the laws or customs of war."[14] "Crimes against Humanity" include "murder, extermination, enslavement, deportation, and other inhumane acts committed against any civilian population, before or during the war; or persecutions on political, racial or religious grounds."[15]

The Charter of the Nuremberg Tribunal sought to introduce "crimes against peace" and "crimes against humanity" into the same commonly abhorred categorization as war crimes but fell short of total success. Indeed, the failure of the International Military Tribunal at Nuremberg to accept jurisdiction over "crimes against humanity" *in times of peace* precipitated the formulation and acceptance of the Genocide Convention, designed to apply international law directly to offending individuals and groups.

To mobilize the conscience of humanity in the wake of the Nazi atrocities and the war crimes trials, in 1948 the General Assembly adopted the Convention on the Prevention and Punishment of the Crime of Genocide, imposing international proscriptions against the intentional destruction, in whole or in part, of racial, ethnic, national, and religious groups. The convention forbids not only acts of "genocide" but also conspiracy, incitement and attempt to commit genocide, and "complicity in genocide." All persons, "whether they are constitutionally responsible rulers, public officials or private individuals," who commit genocide or any of the other prohibited acts are subject to punishment. The contracting states are obligated to "enact, in accordance with their respective Constitutions, the necessary legislation to give effect" to the convention and to provide "effective penalties." Trial is expressly appropriate in "a competent tribunal of the State in the territory of which the act was committed" or "such international penal tribunal as may have jurisdiction with respect to those Contracting Parties which shall have accepted its jurisdiction." The convention has been widely adhered to, although universal jurisdiction to punish genocide has been established as a matter of customary law. International Tribunals for ex-Yugoslavia and Rwanda, established under the Security Council's Chapter VII authority, are now in full operation to try individuals for war crimes, genocide, and crimes against humanity. The newly established International Criminal Court is to have jurisdiction over these crimes as well.

The Genocide Convention has also served as a model for the prohibition of other activities regarded as serious threats to the common interest. This is exemplified by the International Convention on the Suppression and Punishment of the Crime of Apartheid (Apartheid Convention) adopted by the General Assembly in 1973. Building on the Genocide Convention, the Apartheid Convention makes apartheid a "crime against humanity" subject to universal jurisdiction. Article 5 spells out universal jurisdiction in these words: "Persons charged with the acts [of apartheid] of the present Convention may be tried by a competent tribunal of any State Party to the Convention which may acquire jurisdiction over the person of the accused or by an international penal tribunal having jurisdiction with respect to those States Parties which shall have accepted its jurisdiction."

More recently, on December 9, 1985, the General Assembly unanimously adopted a landmark resolution condemning as criminal "all acts, methods and practices of terrorism wherever and by whomever committed."[16] Terrorism, as an international crime, presumably is subject to universal jurisdiction. In addition, the International Law Commission is still engaged in its protracted efforts to formulate a Draft Code of Crimes Against the Peace and Security of Mankind. What crimes will be covered, and whether the code will have any significant relation to International Criminal Court, is not yet clear.

In August 1992, the United States urged the creation of a war-crimes tribunal to try those indicted on the basis of evidence collected by the Balkans War Crimes Commission of war crimes and crimes against humanity in the former Yugoslavia. A list of Serbian and Croatian military figures was published, and the names and details of the alleged crimes supplied to the U.N. War Crimes Commission to determine whether prosecution was warranted. The alleged crimes against humanity included murders of men, women, and children, mass executions and rapes, torture, and forced expulsion of civilians from their villages, most carried out under the banner of "ethnic cleansing." In 1993, the Security Council adopted a resolution (15–0) establishing an eleven-judge court for the trial of the accused individuals.

It is sometimes debated whether the community prescriptions being applied partake of the "true nature" of national or of international law. If the fundamental policies in the protection of common interest incorporated within the prescriptions are applied, the issue of labeling would appear a matter of Tweedledum and Tweedledee. Indeed, universality has always operated as a domestic competence to impose or allow criminal or civil sanctions with respect to what is proscribed under international law.

The need to apply such inclusive community prescriptions by domestic courts was recognized in the United States in the Judiciary Act of 1789, which granted federal district courts original jurisdiction over cases arising from a tort committed "in violation of the law of nations."[17] The famous decision of *Filartiga v. Pena-Irala,*[18] rendered in 1980 by the U.S. Court of Appeals for the Second Circuit, inspired keen interest in this area. In *Filartiga,* Judge Irving R. Kaufman applied international human rights law in finding that freedom from torture is protected under customary international law, which forms a part of the law of the land in the United States. The alleged act of torture committed in Paraguay by a local police chief against a Paraguay national thus became an actionable tort before U.S. courts under the Alien Torts Claim Act. The dead victim's family were able to bring suit against Pena-Irala, held in custody pending deportation for illegally overstaying his visa in the United States. Similarly, prosecutors in Spain, claiming universal jurisdiction, recently brought actions under Spanish criminal law against former Argentinian military officials. The charges are based on the detention, torture, and disappearance of Spanish nationals and their families during Argentina's "dirty war" in the 1970s. This line of actions was dramatized by Pinochet's case in November, 1998, when the Law Lords of the House of Lords, Britain's highest court, ruled that General Augusto Pinochet, the former Chilean dictator, did not have sovereign immunity from arrest under British law and that such crimes as hostage-taking and torture could not be considered part of public functions of a head of state. In sum, cases such as these show the universal principle in action.

Though the *Filartiga* precedent initially received less than uniform support, its continuing impact has been enormous, especially in bridging the traditional gap between international human rights activists and domestic civil liberties practitioners. It has contributed to a growing awareness of the dynamic interplay between transnational and national processes of decision in the defense and fulfillment of human rights and has stimulated continuing efforts in the United States to use domestic courts to defend and enforce international human rights.

Sovereign Immunity

That a nation-state generally cannot be sued without its consent has long been established under both international law and the law of most states. This immunity from suit, commonly known as sovereign immunity, finds its historical roots in the eighteenth century. In a famous decision, *The Schooner Exchange v. M'Fadden* (1812),[19] in which plaintiffs were denied a hearing for the recovery of their ship, seized on the high seas and condemned without due process by France, Chief Justice John Marshall declared, in words that have since lost some validity:

This full and absolute territorial jurisdiction being alike the attribute of every sovereign, and being incapable of conferring extraterritorial power, would not seem to contemplate foreign sovereigns nor their sovereign rights as its objects. One sovereign being in no respect amenable to another; and being bound by obligations of the highest character not to degrade the dignity of his nation, by placing himself or its sovereign rights within the jurisdiction of another, can be supposed to enter a foreign territory only under an express license, or in the confidence that the immunities belonging to his independent sovereign station, though not expressly stipulated, are reserved by implication, and will be extended to him.

This perfect equality and absolute independence of sovereigns, and this common interest impelling them to mutual intercourse, and an interchange of good offices with each other, have given rise to a class of cases in which every sovereign is understood to waive the exercise of part of that complete exclusive territorial jurisdiction, which has been stated to be the attribute of every nation.[20]

This is often thought to reflect an absolute theory of sovereign immunity, but the U.S. Supreme Court recognized that U.S. territorial jurisdiction was absolved and that foreign immunity was basically a matter of discretion. Ten years later, dictum in *The Santissima Trinidad* recognized an exception to immunity for acts in violation of international law. When nation-states confined themselves essentially to traditional functions of states, the absolute theory was widely accepted.

After World War I, with the establishment of communist and socialist regimes, the pattern of international commerce began to change radically, and nation-states increased their participation in the process. This trend accelerated greatly after World War II. No longer are commercial activities the monopoly of the private sector. More and more states embark on the path of state trading, though they differ in the degree of state participation in the process.

When sovereign immunity was made applicable to disputes arising from business transactions involving states, nonstate trading parties suffered. This upset the stability of expectations so essential to an effective global economy and to other transnational interactions. Although sovereign immunity continues to play a useful role in interstate transactions, a shift with respect to commercial transactions — that is, from the so-called absolute theory to the restrictive theory of sovereign immunity — has been visible.

Unlike the absolute theory, which would treat all governmental activities as "governmental," "public," and "sovereign," the restrictive theory extends sovereign immunity only to truly governmental activities. Hence the distinction between public acts (*jure imperii*) and private acts (*jure gestiones*). This is designed to secure the stability of expectations necessary to promote the free flow of goods and services across national boundaries and the wide shaping and sharing of values.

In the United States, the restrictive theory was enunciated in the famous Tate Letter of 1952,[21] which espoused the idea that immunity from suit be granted only to jure imperii. In practice, the State Department thereafter assumed an important responsibility in deciding whether a particular dispute fell within the sphere of jure imperii. When a foreign state thus became a defendant in U.S. courts, it generally turned to the State Department for help, for an indication of immunity, in its plea of defense. The State Department instituted an informal hearing procedure permitting litigants to argue the issue before its legal adviser, who would decide whether the defendant was sovereign and whether immunity should be granted. The department's nonreviewable determination for or against immunity shaped the response of the courts, which generally followed department suggestions almost to the point of subserviency. In the absence of application to the State Department, the courts felt free to apply their own standards — usually those embodied in the Tate Letter.

What began as a prudent attempt to minimize potential friction and foster good relations with other states gradually became an onerous burden that ill served the best interests of the United States and those of private parties dealing with foreign governments. Hence the enactment of the Foreign Sovereign Immunities Act (FSIA) of 1976.[22] The FSIA relieves the State Department of the burden of deciding pleas of sovereign immunity and shifts this responsibility to the judicial branch. It enunciates the general principle of sovereign immunity but excludes commercial activities, acts jure gestiones, of a foreign state from the purview of immunity. What is meant by commercial activity is to be determined by reference not to the purpose but to "the nature of the course of conduct or particular transaction or act."[23] This is not an easy task.

In other countries, comparable prescription exists. The United Kingdom, for instance, enacted the State Immunity Act of 1978,[24] incorporating essentially the provisions contained in the European Convention on State Immunity of 1972. The general support for a relatively sovereign immunity reflects a common interest of nation-states in bestowing reciprocal immunity from suit so as to facilitate harmonious interstate relations.

The problem of diplomatic immunity raises different policy considerations from those of sovereign immunity and will be dealt with in the next chapter.

The Act of State Doctrine

The doctrine of act of state is closely linked to and supplements that of sovereign immunity. When a controversy involves private parties and the foreign state is not a direct defendant, the act of state doctrine is frequently invoked.

The act of state doctrine requires that the courts of one state honor, rather than sit in judgment on, the lawfulness of the public acts of another state taken and completed within their jurisdiction and in accord with relevant substantive international law. These state acts include acts of different branches of government — legislative, executive, and judicial.

Like the policy of reciprocal honoring of sovereign immunity, the doctrine of act of state is designed both to secure friendly relations among nation-states through minimizing interference in legitimate acts of others and to achieve the stability of expectations essential to the optimum production and distribution of goods, services, and other values in the world economy and other transnational interactions.

In the United States, the controversy concerning the act of state generated by *Banco Nacional de Cuba v. Sabbatino* (1964)[25] has continued to reverberate. In this case, involving a confiscation of sugar by the Cuban government, the U.S. Supreme Court held that "the Judicial Branch will not examine the validity of a taking of property within its own territory by a foreign sovereign government [subject to certain possible limitations]."[26] This decision was built on a famous passage contained in *Underhill v. Hernandez* (1897): "Every sovereign State is bound to respect the independence of every other sovereign State, and the courts of one country will not sit in judgment on the acts of the government of another done within its own territory. Redress of grievances by reason of such acts must be obtained through the means open to be availed of by sovereign powers as between themselves."[27]

In the view of the court in *Sabbatino,* the act of state doctrine is mandated neither by international law nor by the U.S. Constitution but does have "constitutional underpinnings,"[28] meaning presumably separation of powers considerations.

Though the lawfulness of the Cuban expropriation measure was under severe attack, the court was not swayed. Deeming the content of customary international law governing expropriation uncertain and unclear, Justice John M. Harlan, speaking for the majority, defended the applicability of the act of state doctrine. In his words:

> [R]ather than laying down or reaffirming an inflexible and all-encompassing rule in this case, we decide only that the Judicial Branch will not examine the validity of a taking of property within its own territory by a foreign sovereign government, extant and recognized by this country at the time of suit, in the absence of a treaty or other unambiguous agreement regarding controlling legal principles, even if the complaint alleges that the taking violates customary international law.[29]

The property involved in this case was taken by the government of a recognized state within its own territory, and the legal challenge to the act of taking was grounded in claims concerning customary international law rather than a specific international agreement, but the Court was unpersuaded that the content of custom was clear.

The critical response to the *Sabbatino* decision was immediate and overwhelming, leading Congress to pass the Second Hickenlooper Amendment to the Foreign Assistance Act of 1963.[30] The amendment declared that no court shall decline to adjudicate a case on the merits dealing with any claim of title traced through a foreign expropriation measure that violated international law. The amendment was expressly made inapplicable in cases where the expropriation is lawful under international law or where the president determines that the act of state doctrine should be applied. The presumption relied on by the *Sabbatino* court, that foreign acts of state should not be questioned by the courts absent an indication from the executive branch, was thus reversed.

In subsequent decisions, the Supreme Court has sought to contain the harm caused by the *Sabbatino* decision but has not seen fit to overrule it. In *First National City Bank v. Banco Nacional de Cuba* (1972),[31] for example, the National Bank of Cuba brought suit to recover deposits and excess of collateral held by Citibank of New York. Having sold the property of the Cuban bank to pay off a loan, with the proceeds of the sale exceeding the outstanding balance on the loan, Citibank sought to set off this balance against its claims stemming from nationalization of Citibank's branches in Cuba. The issue was whether the act of state doctrine prevented Citibank from litigating its counterclaim on the merits. The Supreme Court said no. A majority of the court held that the act of state doctrine was no bar to a counterclaim.

The court did not give an opinion. Three justices (William Rehnquist, Warren Burger, and Byron White) reached the result by recognizing what is known as the Bernstein exception to the act of state doctrine. They recognized the position taken by the State Department that "the act of state doctrine should not be applied to bar consideration of a defendant's counterclaim or set-off against the Government of Cuba in this or like cases." Justice William Douglas invoked the *Republic of China* case,[32] rather than the doctrine of act of state, to support the setoff. Justice Lewis Powell, who had joined the court after *Sabbatino*, concurred in the judgement because he doubted the soundness of the *Sabbatino* decision. The four dissenting justices (William Brennan, Potter Stewart, Thurgood Marshall, and Harry Blackmun) rejected the Bernstein exception, mandating the court to follow direction by the executive branch, and considered *Sabbatino* applicable.

In another case, *Alfred Dunhill of London, Inc. v. Republic of Cuba* (1976),[33] U.S. importers of Cuban cigars made payment to interveners appointed by the

Cuban government following the nationalization by the Cuban government of the assets of cigar manufacturers. Payment was made not only for postnationalization shipments but, mistakenly, also for prenationalization shipments. When the importers demanded the return of the monies mistakenly paid, the Cuban interveners refused and invoked the defense of an act of state in the ensuing litigation. The Supreme Court rejected the act of state claim on the ground that the interveners possessed no sovereign authority. Four justices took the position that repudiation by a foreign government of a commercial debt does not constitute an act of state, and a fifth justice maintained that a mere statement by counsel in court was not an act of state.

In its work on revising the restatement on foreign relations law of the United States, the American Law Institute has tendered this formulation: "In the absence of a treaty or other unambiguous agreement regarding controlling legal principles, courts in the United States will generally refrain from examining the validity of a taking by a foreign state of property within its own territory, or from sitting in judgment on other acts of a governmental character done by a foreign state within its own territory and applicable there."[34] Some feared this formulation to be resurrection of *Sabbatino,* but recently the Helms-Burton Act specifically prohibited any U.S. court's use of the act of state doctrine to decline making a determination on the merits in any action brought under the law against a foreign company who "traffics" in confiscated Cuban property.

Some view the *Sabbatino* doctrine as requiring the honoring of acts of state even when such acts are contrary to international law, but others disagree. The genuine doctrine is built on a strong policy in common interest. The genuine doctrine of act of state, very different from *Sabbatino,* has a clear place in international law. This doctrine is a functional equivalent of the U.S. Constitution's Full Faith and Credit Clause in the world arena.[35] In a global arena in which people, goods, and services move across state lines constantly and rapidly, it would be inimical to both minimum order and optimum order if prior prescriptions and applications of one state were subject to perpetual challenge by others. All participants have a common interest in ensuring that the necessary stability of expectations be maintained by affording reciprocal deference to official acts of other states, provided those acts conform with international law. The emphasis is on lawful acts. Unlawful acts — acts that fail to conform to international law — are beyond the authority of the state and do not, and should not, enjoy such respect, for a nation-state cannot be expected to be an accessory to an act of lawlessness. In their dual role, both as claimants and decision makers, state officials are expected to defend, not subvert, international law. And national courts should be encouraged to play a more active part in applying and developing international law under a decentralized international legal system where transnational judicial tribunals, lacking compulsory jurisdiction, have played only a modest role.

In short, the genuine act of state must be distinguished from a spurious one. The act of state doctrine, as a protector of genuine acts of state, has an important part to play in international law, but it must not be subverted into a device to compel domestic (national) courts to enforce lawless acts of foreign states.

Toward a Test of Reasonableness

In an interdependent and decentralized world where everything affects everything else and the assertions of sovereign equality remain strong, states are apt to stretch their jurisdictional arms as far as they can. The broad grants of competence to prescribe and apply law in terms of the five principles often lead to overlapping and conflicting claims, subjecting the same events to many competences. Hence the existence of frequent clashes arising from assertions of competing, concurrent jurisdiction — on the same or different bases — over the same events. Finding ways to resolve such controversies so as to serve the common interest is crucial in a decentralized, horizontal legal order.

Although no hierarchy has been set among the four distinctive principles of jurisdiction other than universality, the principle of territoriality has been widely applied simply because the state system is the cornerstone of our contemporary international legal order. Similarly, the principle of nationality has gained wide acceptance. When it comes to the principle of impact territoriality or the principle of passive personality, the matter grows more tangled. The discussion of extraterritorial application of a state's law is interlocked with these principles. For instance, when the United States seeks to extend its competence to reach events abroad having adverse antitrust impact, other states may simply invoke the principle of territoriality or that of nationality in response. What then? The United States should not press its competence to make and apply law to events occurring within the borders of some other states without considering possible effects on others. For some, the crucial test is whether a particular exercise of competence, as ascertained by reference to the degree of value impact on the claimant state and other communities, and other relevant factors involved in a particular context, is reasonable. Others note that these tests are insufficiently concerned with individual and community interests in effective remedies for value deprivation. The overall test of reasonableness seems to have gained growing support both in theory and in practice.

At the secondary level, although the act of state and sovereign immunity should be kept distinct both in theory and in practice, there is a tendency to blur the distinction. Each in its own way may achieve the outcome of deference to legitimate acts of foreign states that are not violative of international law: sovereign immunity, by refusing to entertain a lawsuit against a foreign state, and act of state, by honoring substantively the public acts completed within its territory by a foreign state. But the policy for the restrictive theory of sovereign immunity may be subverted by virtue of applying a so-called absolute act of state doctrine that fails to distinguish properly "genuine" from "spurious" acts of state.

The operation of these doctrines of secondary competence may result in immunizing state officials from responsibility for deprivational acts and thus compound and exacerbate the original wrong. These principles, designed primarily to protect the interests of state elites in controlling people and resources as bases of power, obviously must be tempered by considerations of the rights of private parties and overall interests of the community reflected in international legal standards.

PART SIX

STRATEGIES

The strategies employed in global constitutive process can be conveniently examined by reference to the basic instruments of policy: diplomatic, ideological, economic, and military. These instruments, or strategies, involve the management of two critical components: communications (symbols) and resources. The diplomatic instrument refers to communications from elite to elite, and the ideological instrument involves communications directed to general audiences. The economic instrument relates to the management of goods and services, whereas the military instrument involves resources specialized to violence. All may be employed either singly or in varying combinations.

15

The Diplomatic Instrument

The diplomatic instrument is concerned with certain communications between elites of nation-states. The most common policy instrument, it is the one by which other measures are often transmitted. Elite-centered and from foreign office to foreign office, diplomatic communication can be carried out either by signs (verbal and written) or by deeds, openly or secretly.

The diplomatic instrument is ordinarily employed for constructive purposes in the framework of order. In the course of diplomatic communication, a nation-state transmits its position on a controversy to another nation-state and receives the other's response. Its directness of communication, its relatively noncoercive nature, and its subtlety and flexibility have enabled it to resolve differences between nation-states through the continuous process of adjustment and accommodation. Although nation-states may intensify their differences through various measures, they can also settle differences by extensive use of the diplomatic instrument, provided all participants are willing to negotiate. As modern means of transportation and communication have greatly diminished the importance of distance and boundaries, communications from official elites to elites will continue to loom large in interstate relations.

The diplomatic instrument is indispensable to effectuating international agreements between nation-states and peaceful accommodation of conflicts. The making of international agreements is so paramount that the next chapter is devoted to this subject.

Establishment of diplomatic relations between the recognizing state and the recognized state generally follows "recognition" (see chapter 2). But it is not necessarily so. Recognition and the establishment of diplomatic relations, though linked, are distinct steps. Even before recognition, nation-states may need to communicate with one another, to negotiate outstanding issues, and thus find ways to communicate with one another without being deterred by lack of a formal ritual of recognition or of formal diplomatic relations. In the 1950s and 1960s, for example, the United States withheld recognition from the People's Republic of China, but both countries did send their diplomatic representatives to engage in bilateral negotiations on a range of issues.

DIPLOMATIC AND CONSULAR PRIVILEGES AND IMMUNITIES

Once diplomatic relations are established, with official elite-to-elite communications, especially exchange of diplomatic missions, it is in the common interest that such relations be kept harmonious and effective. Essential to maintaining such effective and harmonious diplomatic relations is the reciprocal bestowal of diplomatic and consular privileges and immunities.

Although the granting of diplomatic privileges and immunities was theorized in terms of extraterritoriality (viewing the premises of a diplomatic mission as an extension of the territory of the sending state) or governmental representation in the past, the dominant view today is that of functional necessity. For diplomats to perform effectively in the host country, it is vital that they enjoy protection from interference so that they may operate within an environment of security and confidentiality.

In an interactive world of reciprocity, almost every state plays the dual role — both as a sending state and a receiving state of diplomatic missions. Just as a state wishes to have its own diplomats, embassies, and diplomatic communications protected, so it must reciprocate, in hosting the diplomatic missions of other countries, by providing such protection. The interests of the sending state and those of the receiving state require proper accommodation.

The shared perception of such common interest has long been manifested. In fact, international law for the protection of diplomats and legations is one of the oldest areas of customary law, perhaps as old as diplomacy itself, having its roots in the relations of the city-states of ancient Greece. As Grotius stated in 1625, "Now there are two rights of ambassadors which we see are everywhere referred to the law of nations: The first is that they be admitted; the second, that they be free from violence."[1]

In our time, the centuries-old customary law in this area has found concrete codification in the Vienna Convention on Diplomatic Relations of 1961 and the Vienna Convention on Consular Relations of 1963. (In the United States, the Diplomatic Relations Act was enacted in 1978 to give effect to these conventions.)[2]

The Vienna Convention on Diplomatic Relations protects the performance of the diplomatic function by forbidding local interference and by requiring positive protection by the receiving state. Special protection, phrased in terms of "inviolability," is extended to personnel, premises, and communications. Diplomatic immunities and privileges are accorded the diplomatic staff (people having diplomatic rank), the administrative and technical staff (such as administrative officers, secretary-typists, mail and file clerks), the service staff (for example, chauffeurs, butlers, gardeners, cooks, and maids), and the members of a diplomatic agent's family (including private servants). Diplomatic immunities include immunity from ordinary criminal, civil, and administrative jurisdiction of the receiving state. Diplomatic missions enjoy exemption from local taxes and customs duties. Diplomatic agents and their families are exempt from social security provisions, all taxes, personal services, military obligations, customs duties, and baggage inspection. Individual immunities and privileges run from the moment of entry into the receiving state, are good while in transit through third states, and cease on departure from the receiving state or on lapse of a reasonable period for departure.

The convention protects the premises of a diplomatic mission from external interference. Article 22 states:

1. The premises of the mission shall be inviolable. The agents of the receiving State may not enter them, except with the consent of the head of the mission.
2. The receiving State is under a special duty to take all appropriate steps to protect the premises of the mission against any intrusion or damage and to prevent any disturbance of the peace of the mission or impairment of its dignity.
3. The premises of the mission, their furnishings and other property thereon and the means of transport of the mission shall be immune from search, requisition, attachment or execution.

This inviolability extends to the private residence of a diplomatic agent, including his or her papers, correspondence, and property.

The inviolability of communications covers official correspondence, diplomatic papers and archives, diplomatic bags, and diplomatic couriers and messages in code or cipher.

The institution of the consul is traceable to medieval Italy. Though the consular function was historically concerned with commercial and trade matters, the line between commercial and diplomatic activity is becoming ever more difficult to draw. Just as diplomatic negotiation and trade promotion go hand in hand, diplomatic and consular services tend to merge in practice. The major consular functions, as noted in the Vienna Convention on Consular Relations of 1963, are promotion of commerce, supervision of shipping, protection of nationals, and representational functions. Like diplomatic functions, consular functions require immunity from local jurisdiction. Thus the Vienna Convention on Consular Relations incorporates most of the protections and assistance embodied in the Convention on Diplomatic Relations. There is a basic difference. In theory, consuls are not diplomatic agents. Hence they enjoy immunity from local jurisdiction only in respect of acts performed in the exercise of consular functions, and not in respect of private acts, unless otherwise provided by bilateral agreement.

The degree of compliance is high in this area because the perception of common interest is widely shared, as policed by reciprocity and retaliation. Gross violations do occur, however. Vivid in memory is, of course, the Iranian hostage case.

On November 4, 1979, several hundred militant Iranian students stormed the U.S. embassy in Tehran, seizing as hostages ninety diplomatic personnel present on the premises, including sixty-six Americans. The Iranian students demanded that the United States extradite the former shah of Iran, Muhammad Reza Pahlavi, who, having been overthrown in a revolution late in 1978, was then in the United States for medical treatment. Though the Iranian government had not expressly called for the embassy takeover, it soon became apparent that it backed the militants.

On November 9 the United States asked the U.N. Security Council to take measures to effectuate the release of the hostages, and on the same day both the president of the Security Council and the president of the General Assembly made declarations appealing to Ayatollah Ruhollah Khomeini, the head of Iran's government, to release them. In defiance, Khomeini publicly threatened on November 18 to try some of the embassy personnel as spies.

In response, President Jimmy Carter froze all Iranian assets in American banks, cut off oil imports from Iran, severed diplomatic relations with Iran, and called for the collective deportation of Iranian students illegally in the United States.

Meanwhile, the United States continued its efforts to appeal to the world community to take steps against Iran. On November 29, 1979, the United States filed an application and a request for interim measures of protection in proceeding against Iran. The United States requested the International Court of Justice both to adjudge and declare that Iran had violated its legal obligations under both customary and treaty law by failing to ensure the inviolability of diplomatic and consular officials and premises, and to order Iran to ensure the release and safe departure of the hostages, to pay reparations to the United States, and to prosecute those responsible for the illegal seizure of the embassy and the hostages.

Although Iran neither argued before the court nor submitted formal written arguments (except two letters), the court proceeded to render, on December 15, 1979, a unanimous interim order granting provisional measures in favor of the United States,[3] and on May 24, 1980, its final judgment against Iran.[4] The court based its jurisdiction on the fact that both the United States and Iran were parties to the Vienna Convention on Diplomatic Relations (1961) and the Vienna Convention on Consular Relations (1963) and to the optional protocols thereto affording the court compulsory jurisdiction in "disputes arising out of the interpretation or application of each convention."

In issuing interim measures of protection, the court emphasized:

> [T]here is no more fundamental prerequisite for the conduct of relations between States than the inviolability of diplomatic envoys and embassies, so that throughout history nations of all creeds and cultures have observed reciprocal obligations for that purpose; and . . . the obligations thus assumed, notably those for assuring the personal safety of diplomats and their freedom from prosecution, are essential, unqualified, and inherent in their representative character and their diplomatic function. . . .
>
> [T]he institution of diplomacy, with its concomitant privileges and immunities, has withstood the test of centuries and proved to be an instrument essential for effective co-operation in the international community, and for enabling States, irrespective of their differing constitutional and social systems, to achieve mutual understanding and to resolve their differences by peaceful means.[5]

In its final judgment, the court, after dismissing "the alleged criminal activities of the United States in Iran," concluded that "Iran, by committing successive and continuing breaches of the obligations laid upon it by the Vienna Conventions of 1961 and 1963 on Diplomatic and Consular Relations, the Treaty of Amity, Economic Relations, and Consular Rights of 1955, and the applicable rules of general international law, has incurred responsibility towards the United States. As to the consequences of this finding, it clearly entails an obligation on the part of the Iranian State to make reparation."[6] By unanimous vote, the court ordered the immediate release of the diplomatic and consular staff and other nationals of the United States and the restoration of the embassy to U.S. control (including the premises, property, archives, and documents) and enjoined Iran from subjecting the hostages to Iranian judicial proceedings in any form.

General Augusto Pinochet Ugarte was arrested in London on October 16, 1998. The Spanish judge presented Britain with an extradition warrant to bring Pinochet to trial in Spain for human rights abuses. Although the High Court did accept that he had a prima facie case to answer, it also accepted the main defense presented by Pinochet's lawyers that since he was Chile's head of state at the time of the crimes, international law granted him sovereign immunity from prosecution. Furthermore, since the Chilean government protested the arrest, refusing to exercise its power to waive Pinochet's immunity, the High Court ruled that it had no legal right to begin extradition proceedings against him. The crimes allegedly committed by General Pinochet, however, are crimes that cannot be considered as normal acts of a head of state. Thus, on October 8, 1999, a British magistrate cleared the way for General Pinochet's extradition to Spain. Nonetheless, appeals are likely to keep Pinochet in London for quite some time.

In less dramatic fashion, the world community is increasingly witnessing abuses of such immunities and privileges. In 1984 a British policewoman was murdered by shots fired from the Libyan embassy during a protest demonstration outside the embassy (the Libyan People's Bureau, as Libya called it) in London. The embassy was not stormed, and after diplomatic relations were broken by the United Kingdom, the gunman, a Libyan national, was given safe passage out of the country, on account of diplomatic immunity, and his diplomatic bags (which certainly contained the weapons) were not seized. In 1983 two women were raped in New York City allegedly by the son of a Ghanaian attaché. The man was arrested, then released and sent back to Ghana. In 1982 a bouncer was shot at a bar in Washington, D.C. Charged with shooting was the eighteen-year-old son of a Brazilian diplomat. But the youth was allowed to leave the United States without detention or prosecution — again, on account of diplomatic immunity. In addition, certain diplomatic missions are known to have used diplomatic bags to import firearms calculated to intimidate and harass the dissident elements of their expatriate community in the host country. The problem of abuse has become more serious today partly because of a vast increase of diplomatic missions and personnel, thanks to a rapid growth of new states with less diplomatic experience. Such abuses have generated outcry by local residents and prompted calls for change, as witnessed by the uproar over diplomatic parking "privileges" in New York City.

The outcry of local residents, demanding an end to such abuses, is understandable. But the problem it reflects cannot be fixed quickly. Remedies to deal with violations in this area depend in large measure on sanctions of reciprocity and retaliation. The right of *agréation* and the power to demand recall, though not fully effective, are important safeguards against abuse in a decentralized system.

DIPLOMATIC ASYLUM

The degree of immunity, inviolability, and protection accorded the diplomatic premises of accredited states makes those premises a potential refuge for local fugitives wanted by their governments. Should diplomatic premises be used as an instrument to defend human rights at the risk of endangering the normal diplomatic function? In other words, how does international law deal with claims for diplomatic asylum?

Unlike territorial asylum, which, as discussed in chapter 11, occurs within the granting state's territory, diplomatic asylum is granted by the granting state in its embassies or legations. Diplomatic asylum is thus extraterritorial in nature and meets more objection.

International law does not recognize a state's competence to grant diplomatic asylum. In the Asylum case (1950) brought before the International Court of Justice by Colombia against Peru, Colombia, having granted asylum to a Peruvian national (Haya de la Torre) at its embassy in Lima, requested that the Peruvian government guarantee his safe passage from Peru.[7] Peru refused to offer such a guarantee and challenged the legal effect of the Colombian grant of asylum. The court rejected Colombia's claim that a custom existed for granting diplomatic asylum. Given "so much uncertainty and contradiction" and "so much fluctuation and discrepancy" in state practice and views, the court was unable to find "any constant and uniform usage, accepted as law" regarding diplomatic asylum.[8] Thus the court held that there is no general right to grant diplomatic asylum and that it can be granted, on a temporary basis, only in cases where the individual seeking asylum is in imminent danger or where a treaty or local custom recognizes it.

The Vienna Convention on Diplomatic Relations deliberately does not include any provision on diplomatic asylum. Presumably, the reference to "special agreements" in its Article 41 would allow recognition of such right by virtue of a specific agreement.

The practice of diplomatic asylum is fragmented and uneven. It is a challenging task to determine how to secure the common interest by using diplomatic premises to shelter fugitives from political persecution and augment human rights protection in ways that would not unduly interfere with the diplomatic function of interelite communication.

Another aspect of diplomacy is its constructive function to protect nationals vis-à-vis external entities. This refers to the customary remedy of diplomatic protection, discussed in chapter 12. In recent times, as the transnational impact of human rights deprivations has been more realistically perceived, states have been somewhat willing to use the diplomatic instrument to protect not only their own nationals but also nonnationals. The diplomatic instrument readily lends itself to inquiries about alleged violations, to expressions of general and particular concern, to suggestions about the termination of certain practices, to recommendations of measures of amelioration, and to subtle messages of possible consequences of continuing practices of deprivation. This is the essence of what is called "quiet diplomacy," which should not be allowed to degenerate into a diplomacy of timidity and inaction. For instance, in securing "people power" in the Philippines in February 1986 and in achieving "the political miracle" in South Korea in the summer of 1987, the U.S. diplomatic role was by no means trivial.

COERCIVE USE OF THE DIPLOMATIC INSTRUMENT

Although the diplomatic instrument is normally used for constructive purposes, it may occasionally be used for coercive purposes, especially measures designed to block a target state's access to the transnational arenas of formal authority. Charges of unlawfulness tend to arise in connection with what is regarded as premature recognition or deliberate nonrecognition, as mentioned in chapter 2.

An additional charge often relates to severance of diplomatic relations. This type of coercion includes withdrawing or requiring the target state to withdraw heads of diplomatic missions, trade agencies, and consular officials. The severance of diplomatic relations may be partial or complete. It may be carried out gradually by first withdrawing heads of diplomatic missions only. It may be taken as an expression of disapproval of a target state's conduct or as a deliberate means of coercion. At times it serves as a preliminary warning to a target state of more drastic coercion. Often it is used as a form of sanction against a prior, unlawful act.

DIPLOMATIC SANCTIONS

In an interactive world of decentralization, because the attitudes and concomitant behavior of other participants bear critically on the establishment or stabilization of any situation, the organized community of nations has increasingly resorted to a collective policy of nonrecognition as a sanctioning measure against situations considered to violate fundamental international policy. This policy had its origin in the Stimson doctrine, which called for nonrecognition of any situation, treaty, or agreement brought about unlawfully, in response to the Japanese invasion and occupation of Manchuria in 1931. The League of Nations soon reinforced this policy, in dealing with any situation, treaty, or agreement brought about by means contrary to its covenant or to the Pact of Paris of 1928 (the Kellogg-Briand Pact, which denounced war as an instrument of national policy).

Within the framework of the United Nations, the policy of nonrecognition played a prominent role in dealing with the Southern Rhodesian and Namibian situations. When the Ian Smith regime declared unilateral independence of Southern Rhodesia in November 1965, the Security Council characterized the Smith regime as illegal and called on all member states not to recognize it.

In the case of Namibia the United Nations called on member states to adopt a policy of nonrecognition toward the continued illegal occupation of the territory by apartheid South Africa after the U.N. decision to terminate the mandate in 1966. In its famous Namibia opinion of 1971, the International Court of Justice expressed an array of views by individual judges on the question of how third states should behave regarding South Africa's continued illegal presence in Namibia.[9]

Namibia, known as South West Africa until renamed in 1968 by the General Assembly, is the only one of seven African territories once under the mandate system of the League of Nations that was not placed under the trusteeship system of the United Nations after World War II. Over the years South Africa, purporting to act as mandatory, intensified its control over the territory in defiance of the resolutions of U.N. bodies and decisions of the International Court of Justice.

In 1950, in *Advisory Opinion on International Status of South-West Africa,* the International Court of Justice declared that South Africa, lacking unilateral "competence to modify the international status of the territory," remained subject to, despite the demise of the league, the terms and obligations prescribed in the covenant and the mandate, and that the supervisory function of the league was to be assumed by the United Nations.[10] This opinion laid the legal framework for subsequent U.N. action regarding Namibia.

After the 1950 opinion, South Africa continued its course of defiance, refusing to submit its administration of the territory to U.N. supervision. Hence, in 1966, the General Assembly adopted Resolution 2145, terminating the mandate of South Africa over South West Africa (Namibia) and assuming direct responsibility for the territory until its independence.[11] The Security Council reiterated this resolution in 1969 and 1970, declaring that "the continued presence of the South African authorities in Namibia is illegal and that consequently all acts taken by the Government of South Africa on behalf of or concerning Namibia after the termination of the Mandate are illegal and invalid."[12]

Confronted with the continued defiance of the South African government, the Security Council turned to the International Court of Justice for an advisory opinion on the following question: "What are the legal consequences for States of the continued presence of South Africa in Namibia, notwithstanding Security Council resolution 276 (1970)?"[13] The court held that "the continued presence of South Africa in Namibia being illegal, South Africa is under obligation to withdraw its administration from Namibia immediately and thus put an end to its occupation of the Territory"[14] and that "States Members of the United Nations are under obligation to recognize the illegality of South Africa's presence in Namibia and the invalidity of its acts on behalf of or concerning Namibia, and to refrain from any acts and in particular any dealings with the Government of South Africa implying recognition of the legality of, or lending support or assistance to, such presence and administration."[15]

In accord with the duty of nonrecognition imposed by Security Council Resolution 276 (1970), U.N. member states are obliged, among other things, "to abstain from sending diplomatic or special missions to South Africa including in their jurisdiction the Territory of Namibia, to abstain from sending consular agents to Namibia, and to withdraw any such agents already there."[16] The court emphasized that "no State which enters into relations with South Africa concerning Namibia may expect United Nations or its members to recognize the validity of such relationship, or of the consequences thereof."[17] The court also added that "it is incumbent upon States which are not Members of the United Nation to give assistance, . . . in the action which has been taken by the United Nations with regard to Namibia."[18]

The U.N. Charter and numerous General Assembly resolutions, several International Court of Justice opinions, and a host of international human rights treaties provided the basis for a new international legal norm of racial equality. This new legal norm in turn inspired the response of the international community, in support of Namibia and in the form of diplomatic sanctions. The force of diplomatic sanctions played a great role in dismantling apartheid in South Africa and allowing Namibia to proclaim its independence. Today, Namibia finds itself again before the ICJ, this time as a full-fledged state and first-time litigant in a boundary dispute.[19] The success of both Namibia and South Africa in finding self-determination and independence illustrates the potential impact of diplomatic sanctions in a world where the force of international law is respected by all parties.

16

International Agreements

The international agreement, in all its many manifestations, represents the most deliberate form of prescription, in which governments cooperate with one another in explicitly formulating and undertaking commitments. International agreements perform a critical lawmaking function in the contemporary world. The making of international agreements is an important strategy by which nation-states choose to commit themselves to particular policies. The shared commitment results from the process of persuasion in search of the common interest of the participants.

In a world community lacking centralized legislative institutions, international agreements offer a convenient avenue through which to project shared expectations in future policy. The making of an international agreement, as a most deliberate form of prescription, is somewhat comparable to the act of legislation in national arenas. It is through agreement-making that states project their policies into all areas of the international legal system. The amazing growth of the network of international agreements testifies vividly that the mechanism of agreement-making is crucial in the pursuit of world public order. With the ever-increasing volume and tempo of transnational interaction, the number of international agreements has increased remarkably. Since the establishment of the United Nations, more than 25,000 international agreements (with varying designations) have been registered or filed and recorded with that organization. Agreement-making will undoubtedly accelerate as transnational interaction increases.

International agreement instead of *treaty* is chosen as a generic term of reference here. A variety of labels have been used to designate international agreements, including *act, agreement, articles of agreement, charter, concordat, convention, covenant, declaration, exchange of notes, modus vivendi, pact, protocol, statute,* and *treaty.* Though the labels are not legally significant, some may be used more frequently to design agreements on a particular subject or those of an especially solemn nature. (For instance, *convention* has been used most frequently in connection with specific categories of human rights, and *treaty* is the common designation for agreements of friendship, commerce, and navigation.) The lack of uniform terminology is due partly to the survival of diplomatic traditions and partly to a reluctance on the part of nation-states to standardize treaty usage.

Under Article 2 of the U.S. Constitution, the term *treaty* refers specifically to an international agreement made by the president with the advice and consent of the Senate by a two-thirds vote. Other international agreements, not concluded in accordance with the procedure of Article 2, are generally known as *executive agreements.* Executive agreements represent a unique American practice. Unlike a treaty, an executive agreement does not require Senate approval. Technically speaking, executive agreements can be further divided into three types: (1) congressional-executive agreements, which are concluded with prior authorization or subsequent approval by the Congress; (2) treaty-executive agreements, which are authorized by treaty; and (3) sole executive agreements or presidential agreements, which are concluded under the authority of the president acting as the chief executive and spokesperson of the United States in dealing with other countries. In terms of external effect, executive agreements are functional equivalents of treaties. The commitments assumed under executive agreements must be performed in good faith. In terms of internal effect, there are nuances of difference. Perhaps the most well known and controversial executive agreement is the Yalta Agreement, concluded by President Franklin D. Roosevelt on February 11, 1945.

International agreements exhibit significant differences in terms of number of participants sharing commitment, the subject and content of policies projected, and the expectations concerning the degree of permanence engendered. Building on the functional categories developed by Lord McNair in 1930,[1] international agreements can be grouped as follows:

1. *Constitutive* (organic) agreements, which establish basic feature of the comprehensive process of authoritative decision, such as the Charter of the United Nations.
2. *Lawmaking* (legislative) agreements, which prescribe particular policies concerning particular events or values, such as the Vienna Convention on Diplomatic Relations and the International Convention on the Elimination of All Forms of Racial Discrimination.
3. *Contractual* agreements, which create shared expectations of commitment

between two or more states for policies of differing scope and importance and generate expectations of general community prescription, such as trade agreements of all kinds.

4. *Dispositive* agreements in the nature of conveyances, which involve exchange in relatively consummated transactions, with minimal projection of future policy, such as treaties of lease or cession and boundary treaties.

It is sometimes debated what agreements between nation-states are lawmaking and what are not. But this quest is futile, since all agreements between nation-states project policies into the future. The number of participants affected by such projections is a matter not for dogmatic assertion about the nature of agreement but for empirical, rational inquiry in light of all the values at stake. Making, performing, and terminating international agreements involves more than just words on paper. An international agreement is a process of communication through which shared policies toward the future are formulated and reformulated.

The process of agreement, like the prescribing process generally, can realistically be understood only by reference to the participants and their perspectives, situations of interaction, base values, modalities in communicating commitment, outcomes in shared expectations, and effects on value processes. The relevant participants are state officials and the other parties with whom they interact. Their demands, identifications, and expectations are shaped largely by nuances in culture, class, interest, personality, and crisis. The general objective of parties in making an international agreement is to project a community policy toward a future distribution of values. The more detailed objectives of the parties may relate to any value (security, power, respect, enlightenment, well-being, wealth, skill, affection, and rectitude) or to any feature of a value process (participation, situations, base values, strategies, and outcomes). The range of values sought to be secured by international agreements may be illustrated by reference to some of the more important types of international agreement made by states: treaties of alliance and mutual defense (security, power); conventions for the protection of human rights (respect); agreements relating to communications and cultural exchange (enlightenment); agreements concerning narcotic control and environmental protection (well-being); treaties of friendship, commerce, and navigation (wealth); agreements for the transfer of technology and the exchange of technical personnel (skill); agreements for facilitating family reunion (affection); and treaties guaranteeing freedom of religion (rectitude).

The situations in which international agreements are negotiated and performed vary in features relevant to the communication of demands and expectations about commitment. Such differences relate to temporal and geographical features, degree of institutionalization, and intensities in exposure to crisis. All values potentially serve as base values in processes of negotiation, and the relative positions of the parties in control over particular base values significantly affect both the degree and content of their commitment. The sequence of negotiations and other activities by which the parties mediate their subjectivities to achieve outcomes in shared commitment may be direct and explicit or indirect and implicit, expressed in both words and deeds. International agreements differ in many ways: the number of parties sharing commitment, the scope and content of policies projected, and the expectations of permanence or impermanence attending commitment.

In the most comprehensive and dynamic sense, the process of agreement can be divided further into a complex of component subprocesses: the making of a commitment, the performance or nonperformance of commitments, and the modification or termination of commitment. An exposition of the law of international agreements would require examination of each of these subprocesses by reference to the familiar institutional categories of participants, perspectives, situations, base values, strategies, and outcomes. Here only some of the more important features of each subprocess can be highlighted.

BASIC COMMUNITY POLICIES

Three fundamental policies pervade the field of the law of treaties. First, the policy of freedom of choice, which encourages and fosters persuasion and voluntary cooperation in transnational interaction. Treaty commitments must be freely expressed and voluntarily assumed. Second, sanctity of treaty commitments, as expressed in the Latin maxim *pacta sunt servanda*. Once treaty commitments are voluntarily assumed, they must be carried out in good faith. Once shared expectations are created, the stability of expectations must be honored and maintained. Without this policy, the basic stability of transnational interaction cannot be secured. Indeed, when the fundamental policy of pacta sunt servanda is flouted the very foundation of international law will crumble. Third, the policy of recognizing the necessity of change. International agreements do not operate in a vacuum. They do not exist merely as pieces of paper. The working expectations must be sustained through time. As social process is in perpetual flux, so is the context of conditions. In the realm of treaty law, as in other areas, room must be made to allow such change to accommodate the changing demands and expectations of the parties in the light of changing conditions.

To strike a proper balance between stability of expectations and the necessity of change is a delicate, yet vital, task. These policies are substantially reflected in the development of the law of international agreements.

TRENDS IN DECISION AND CONDITIONING FACTORS

The development of treaty law long depended largely on customary law. A milestone in the development and codification concerning international agreements is the Vienna Convention on the Law of Treaties concluded in 1969. Known as "the treaty of treaties," the Vienna Convention represents an extremely useful formulation of contemporary treaty law. It came into effect on January 27, 1980, on ratification by the requisite thirty-five states. Even before its entry into force, the convention had been widely recognized as "the authoritative guide to current treaty law and practice."[2] It sets forth community prescriptions governing the various phases and aspects in the processes of commitment, performance, and termination (modification). It has struck a remarkable balance between demands for stability and demands for change. The principle of pacta sunt servanda and the impartial procedures for settlement of disputes are matched by the doctrines of jus cogens and *rebus sic stantibus*.

The traditional literature concerning international agreements is generally concerned only with agreements to which nation-states are parties. This follows from the traditional doctrine that only states are subjects of international law. As nonstate participants (notably international governmental organizations and, to a lesser degree, private associations and individuals) become increasingly important in the world arena, a comprehensive study on the law of treaties should extend from agreements between or among states to agreements involving all these nonstate participants as well. For present purposes, the usage adopted in Article 2(1)(a) of the Vienna Convention is followed: " 'Treaty' means an international agreement concluded between states in written form and governed by international law, whether embodied in a single instrument or in two or more related instruments and whatever its particular designation." The trends in decision and development are highlighted by reference to three subprocesses of agreement.

The Process of Commitment

This is the process by which contracting parties obtain rights and assume obligations. It involves not one act but various steps toward reaching shared commitment. Among the issues of primary concern are, first, whether the contracting parties have made any commitment, and, if so, what is its substantive content.

The process of commitment is complex; officials of all participating states perform a number of distinct yet related functions:

1. Formulating national policies to govern the conduct of negotiations with other states: A nation-state begins by formulating national policies as guidelines for negotiations with other states;
2. Conducting negotiations with the representatives of other nation-states: After the decision to commence negotiations with others, the first step is to appoint representatives, with appropriate powers and credentials, to conduct negotiations with the representatives of other nation-states;
3. Approving an agreement for internal application;
4. Approving an agreement to signify the external commitment of the state; and
5. Communicating the external commitment of the state to other states, through final utterance of the agreement and a complex of other events.

Competence

Within individual nation-states, the constitutional allocation of competence to perform these functions varies widely but also exhibits, with exceptions, a remarkably similar pattern.

In relation to the process of commitment, the Vienna Convention begins by affirming, in Article 6, that "[e]very state possesses capacity to conclude treaties." Assuming the capacity of a nation-state to conclude an international agreement, the question immediately arises as to who is authorized to represent a state to conduct negotiations and other acts leading to the conclusion of an agreement. Such authority is generally determined by a formal document known as "full powers," which designates a person or persons to represent the state to negotiate and conclude an agreement. The representative of a state is generally expected to produce appropriate full powers unless, as stated in Article 7(1), "it appears from the practice of the States concerned or from other circumstances that their intention was to consider that person as representing the State for such purposes and to dispense with full powers."

The concept of full powers historically assumed much greater significance than it does today. During the era of absolute monarchy, an international agreement was regarded as an expression of the sovereign's will, and the full powers was designed to clothe the personal agent of the sovereign with authority to bind his principal, provided that he acted within his authority. Hence, the authority of the sovereign representative was, as a rule, defined with precision in advance of the negotiation so as to minimize subsequent refusal to ratify on the ground that the agent acted in excess of his authority.

Since the demise of this era, the importance attached to full powers has greatly diminished. As a measure of democratic control over foreign policy gradually took hold, in the wake of the American and French revolutions, "ratification" became discretionary in state practice, even if the representative who had negotiated the agreement had acted entirely within the limits of the authority embodied in the full powers. The ever-increasing ease of communications, as accentuated by the development of telecommunications and other technologies, has made it possible to ensure that negotiators do not exceed the limits of their authority.

In addition, nation-states have shown a tendency to conclude agreements in simplified form, such as by exchanging notes or letters, thereby dispensing with full powers. Such an informal approach is necessitated by the increasing complexity and frequency of transnational interaction, calling for a growing network of treaty arrangements to deal with all kinds of subjects and to cope with manifold complex relationships accentuated by the proliferation of new states.

Adoption and Authentication of the Text

Negotiations will result in the adoption of the text. For a bilateral agreement this will naturally require unanimity. The unanimity rule will also apply to a multilateral agreement with limited participation (for example, a treaty between riparian states concerning the development of a river basin). For a multilateral agreement, designed for and opened to wide participation, and generally concluded through an international conference, the unanimity rule obviously will not be practicable. Hence, the Vienna Convention, in Article 9(2), prescribes that "the adoption of text of a treaty at an international conference takes place by the vote of two-thirds of the States present and voting unless by the same majority they shall decide to apply a different rule." This is commonly effected through a final act, which also serves to authenticate the text of the treaty.

Consent to Be Bound

"The consent of a State to be bound by a treaty," as stipulated in Article 11 of the Vienna Convention, "may be expressed by signature, exchange of instruments constituting a treaty, ratification, acceptance, approval or accession, or by any other means if so agreed." It admits of considerable flexibility in the modality of expressing consent, giving particular deference to the choice of the contracting parties.

Ratification, however, remains the most common form. Where required, ratification is the final and formal act by which a state becomes bound by an international agreement. It is an unequivocal expression of consent to be bound; it signifies the external commitment of the ratifying state. Because of the vast proliferation of international agreements in the contemporary world, the cumbersome process of ratification is applied to more solemn types of agreement. Ratification is not retroactive in effect. Even after an agreement is signed by a state's delegate, the signatory is in theory under no legal obligation to ratify it. In practice, however, good faith is expected. Contracting parties may also agree to apply a treaty provisionally pending ratification.

The ratification procedure is maintained for several reasons. Additional time after signing affords a state the chance to scrutinize closely the provisions of a complicated agreement. This is especially so for nations that are relatively inexperienced in making international agreements. Occasionally an agreement requires changes in the domestic law of a state before becoming operative, and ratification allows for an interim period of preparation. In some states, the treaty-making power is vested in a body that can neither directly negotiate nor delegate its power to the actual negotiators. In democratic polities, ratification affords the opportunity of public exposure and approval through consultation with elected legislative representatives.

Reservation
A state interested in establishing a treaty relationship will naturally seek to shape the terms of the agreement to its advantage in the process of negotiation. If it fails to fully convince its negotiating partner or partners but still wishes to be a party to the agreement, it may resort to the device of reservation as a safeguard.

A reservation, as defined by Article 2 of the Vienna Convention, is "a unilateral statement, however phrased or named, made by a State, when signing, ratifying, acceding to, accepting or approving a treaty, whereby it purports to exclude or to vary the legal effect of certain provisions of the treaty in their application to that State." For bilateral agreements, a reservation constitutes in effect a counteroffer by the reserving state, to be accepted or rejected by the other state. If rejected, there will be no agreement; if accepted, there is an agreement on the terms of the counteroffer.

In the case of multilateral agreements, reservations tendered by one or more parties present more complex and troublesome problems. Though in principle reservations should not be valid without the consent of all parties to an international agreement, this principle is not adhered to in practice. The use of reservations is so common and objections to them so infrequent that a requirement of consent of all parties is far too cumbersome to work adequately. Two alternate methods of determining the status of a state's reservations in the face of objections by other ratifying states have been available in international law.

The Pan-American formula is to allow the agreement to operate in its original form between the states that accept it without reservation and to operate between the reserving state and any other states willing to accept the reservations made. Under this scheme, objecting states will likely have no treaty relationship with reserving states but a third state may establish treaty relations with both. This system operates to augment the number of participants to multilateral agreements but tends to fragment large multilateral agreements into a number of small bilateral treaty regimes.

The International Court of Justice, in the famous case *Reservation to the Genocide Convention,*[3] employed a different test, permitting reservations to be effective on all parties (objecting or not), provided the reservations are "compatible with the object and purpose" of the agreements.[4] Articles 19–23 of the Vienna Convention reflect the compatibility test. The major difficulty with this test is that, in the absence of compulsory third-party decision making, the determination of what is compatible is left to the subjective autointerpretation of the individual states. The danger of potential misinterpretation is obvious.

The potentially catastrophic difficulties involved with reservations in theory rarely occur in practice. The element of surprise is minimized through careful draftsmanship in expressing genuinely shared commitments. Also, as an anticipatory measure, most formal agreements contain specific reservation clauses to stipulate guidelines for dealing with particular reservations and to specify provisions not susceptible to reservations.

Registration

Upon the ratification (or its equivalent) of an international agreement, the written documents that evidence consent to be bound are deposited or exchanged. In the case of multilateral agreements, the ratifications are placed in the care of a depositary. The depositary may be the foreign office of one or more states or an international organization such as the United Nations. International agreements ordinarily contain a provision as to how deposit will be handled. According to Article 77 of the Vienna Convention, the functions of a depositary generally include custody of the text of the agreement, custody of all documents relevant to its ratification, providing information as to the time of its effective operation, and registering the treaty.

Registration of international agreements is provided by the U.N. Charter. Article 102(1) of the charter requires that "[e]very treaty and every international agreement entered into by any Member of the United Nations after the present Charter comes into force shall as soon as possible be registered with the Secretariat and published by it." The central purpose is to discourage secret diplomacy and to make public the texts of international agreements so as to elicit public concern. The act of registration in no way implies that a determination has been made by the United Nations as to the nature or validity of the documents. Failure to comply with Article 102(1) will not affect the validity of an agreement, though it may not be invoked before any organ of the United

Nations, including the International Court of Justice. This question was drama-tized in the recent past in connection with the military operations in Grenada conducted by the United States and certain Caribbean nations in October 1984. The military operations were in part justified by reference to the terms of the collective security treaty among these Caribbean nations — the Treaty Estab-lishing the Organization of Eastern Caribbean States, concluded on June 18, 1981 — as a collective self-defense measure authorized by the treaty. But that treaty had not been registered with the United Nations.

Lack of Genuine Commitment (Grounds for Invalidity)
Central to the process of commitment is concern over whether genuine commit-ments are shared by the contracting parties. Defects in the original commitment may bear on the genuineness of such commitments and preclude the parties from being bound by the agreement. Such defects may thus give rise to claims to invalidate the agreement.

Such defects include violation of internal law, error, fraud, representative's corruption, coercion of a state or its representative, conflict with a peremptory norm of general international law (jus cogens), and conclusion of "unequal treaties."

Although it is sometimes asserted that national constitutional limitations determine the validity of a treaty on the international plane, it has long been established that a state is bound regardless of internal limitations (constitutional or otherwise) if consent has been given by a properly authorized agent under international law. This is an aspect of the supremacy of international law. Thus, the Vienna Convention, in Article 46(1), stipulates that "[a] State may not invoke the fact that its consent to be bound by a treaty has been expressed in violation of a provision of its internal law regarding competence to conclude treaties as invalidating its consent unless that violation was manifest and con-cerned a rule of its internal law of fundamental importance." A violation is deemed "manifest," as stated in Article 46(2), "if it would be objectively evident to any State conducting itself in the manner in accordance with normal practice and in good faith." Article 47 deals with the separate but related issue of consent granted by a state's representative in violation of an executive or administrative restriction on his authority. Such a violation may not be put forth as a ground for invalidity "unless the restriction was notified to the other negotiating States prior to [the representative's] expressing such consent."

The related issue of error and fraud as grounds for invalidity, though some-times treated as one and the same, is distinct and is treated as such by the Vienna Convention in Articles 48 and 49. Article 48, dealing with error, places several restrictions on invoking error as a ground for invalidity. The error must relate to a fact or situation assumed by the invoking party to exist when the treaty was concluded, and this supposed fact or situation must have been an "essential basis" of the state's "consent to be bound by the treaty." Furthermore, the error will not be deemed sufficient if the state "contributed by its own conduct to the error or if the circumstances were such as to put that State on notice of a possible error."

For the purposes of Article 48 no distinction is made between unilateral or mutual mistake, as is the case under some domestic legal systems. Purely textual mistakes, agreed to be such by all parties, are handled under a separate article.

"Fraudulent misrepresentation of a material fact inducing an essential error" is also covered by Article 48. Attempts were made to deal with other forms of fraud in a separate article. Due to the difficulty in reconciling the various domestic concepts of "fraud," however, the Vienna Convention left its precise formulation in the treaty context to be worked out in practice. The effect of Article 49 is not to make a treaty void *ab initio* but only "voidable at the option of the injured party."

Although it was argued that a state representative's corruption in negotiating a treaty would be adequately covered by a general provision regarding fraud as a basis for invalidity, the Vienna Convention, following International Law Commission's report, incorporated a separate article to deal with such a situation. Article 50 allows the state whose representative was corrupted by other negotiating parties to claim corruption as the basis for the treaty's invalidity. "Corruption," as it is used in the article, includes "only acts calculated to exercise a substantial influence on the disposition of the representative to conclude the treaty."

On the matter of coercion, the Vienna Convention adopted two articles: Article 51 deals with the coercion of a representative in his personal capacity, and Article 52 deals with coercion by the threat or use of force against a state itself. Article 51 includes threats of violence, both physical and psychological, and moral pressure regarding the representative's private acts of indiscretion, a disclosure of which might be devastating. "A treaty is void," according to Article 52, "if its conclusion has been cured by the threat or use of force in violation of the principles of international law embodied in the Charter of the United Nations." Although a condemnation of "economic or political pressure" appears in the conference's final act, the suggestion that such conduct be prohibited within Article 52 was rejected, in part as being too vague.

The notion of peremptory norms (jus cogens) was incorporated in the Vienna Convention, though not without controversy. In the treaty context, it means that there are certain agreements into which states may not enter in the interest of maintaining world public order. It limits the freedom of states to make agreements, comparable to limits on the freedom of contract that exist in virtually all national legal systems. Article 53 of the convention defines "a peremptory norm of general international law" in terms of "a norm accepted and recognized by the international community of states as a whole as a norm from which no derogation is permitted and which can be modified only by a subsequent norm of general international law having the same character." It requires general, rather than universal, acceptance by the members of the world community. The specific norms of international law that fall within this category of jus cogens were not spelled out in the Vienna Convention due to a lack of consensus. Further, it was thought better to leave such specification to the developing patterns of state practice and decisions of international tribunals. Nevertheless, some of the intensely demanded prescriptions, such as those relating to the principle of non-use of force, the principle of self-determination, and the core content of international human rights are widely regarded as within the domain of contemporary jus cogens. If an international agreement conflicts with a peremptory norm at the time of its conclusion, it is void. Under Article 64, furthermore, when a new peremptory norm emerges, any existing agreement which conflicts with that norm becomes void and terminates.

Claims for invalidation based on the concept of "unequal treaties" are highly controversial. The concept itself is ill-defined, and its utility is seriously questioned. For those who espouse this concept, a treaty is said to be unequal when it contravenes the basic principle of sovereign equality of states, as measured by the relative bases of power of the contracting parties, the objects of the treaty, the degree of coercion involved in the strategies employed, and the outcomes of treaty performance. First espoused by Communist states, the concept of unequal treaties has been echoed by newly independent states. Western jurists generally reject the concept as vague and elusive. The Vienna Convention did not incorporate this concept, though such elements as coercion are treated elsewhere in the convention.

The Process of Performance

The process of performance involves implementation of the agreed-upon commitment. From the fundamental principle of good faith, through the task of interpretation, to actual performance by the contracting parties and effects on third parties, a paramount concern is that performance approximate as closely as possible the shared commitment.

Pacta Sunt Servanda

Central to the entire operation of the law of treaties is the doctrine of pacta sunt servanda, the sanctity of treaties. This doctrine has roots in Greco-Roman-

Christian tradition and in other religious and cultural traditions. The Vienna Convention, in Article 26, phrases it in these words: "Every treaty in force is binding upon the parties to it and must be performed by them in good faith." Pacta sunt servanda is indispensable to the common interest in establishing and maintaining the stability of expectations for all parties concerned. Stable international relations depend on the ability of states to put faith in one another's expressed intent to fulfill treaty commitments.

In dealing with the doctrine of pacta sunt servanda the Vienna Convention was faced with the task of defining its limits. The doctrine is deemed jus cogens, since it admits of such exceptions as *clausula rebus sic stantibus,* the doctrine of fundamental change in circumstances. A link has further been suggested between Article 2(2) of the United Nations Charter and pacta sunt servanda. The choice of words, "treaty in force," in Article 26, is understood to refer only to "valid treaty" — one based on "the consent of the parties and having a lawful purpose."

The Task of Interpretation

Once an international agreement comes into effect, the question of interpretation occurs sooner or later. Indeed, the bulk of the cases coming before the International Court of Justice and its predecessor have involved disputed interpretations of international agreements. In view of the relevant features involved in the processes of agreement, claim, and decision, some interpretation obviously is always necessary in applying agreements to particular circumstances. Since the words used in an agreement rarely have exact and entirely unambiguous meanings, and since all possible contexts that may arise under it cannot be fully foreseen and explicitly provided for by the parties in the process of reaching the agreement, the necessity of interpretation occurs.

Two polar positions are taken. One extreme holds that the text of an international agreement speaks for itself, and the task of interpretation is simply to give it a "plain and ordinary" meaning. The opposite extreme maintains that the task of interpretation is so enormously complicated as to render it an exercise in futility.

The reality would appear to fall between these two extremes. The words of an international agreement cannot be regarded as timeless absolutes. They have meaning only in the light of all the relevant contexts in which they are employed. It is hardly possible to impose a literal, plain, or natural meaning on any legal language, particularly on that of a constitutive document such as the U.N. Charter, whose admittedly broad language is designed to meet the changing conditions of an undefined future. But the posture of impossibility and futility is highly destructive, in that it is an attempt to escape the realities of complex international relations. To accept it will result in the failure to mobilize all available intellectual skills toward problem solving. The end result would likely be stagnation or anarchy.

Efforts toward treaty interpretation have thus traditionally taken the form of formulating particular canons of construction or principles of interpretation. Notable among these are the principle of plain and ordinary meaning, the principle of effectiveness, the principle of major purposes, and the principle of restrictive interpretation. These canons of construction, presented without a coherent, contextual framework, tend to contradict or overlap one another in application.

True to their policy-oriented approach, McDougal and Lasswell, in collaboration with James C. Miller, offer a contextual alternative in *The Interpretation of Agreements and World Public Order: Principles of Content and Procedure,*[5] building on the insights of contemporary communication theories. The goals of interpretation, as they postulate them, are threefold: (1) ascertaining the genuinely shared expectations of the particular parties to an agreement; (2) supplementing such shared expectations by reference to community policies when gaps, contradictions, or ambiguities exist in the parties' communication; and (3) integrating or policing, in the sense of the appraisal and possible rejection of the parties' expectations, however explicit or implicit they may be, so as to ensure their conformity with fundamental community policies.[6] To further these goals, they recommend the systematic employment of a comprehensive set of principles of content and procedure, grounded in the full contextuality of the processes of agreement, claim, and decision.

The interpreter of an international agreement should thus consider all relevant signs and deeds taking place at any time before, during, or after the agreement is concluded. The interpreter should consider the whole process of agreement and its context of conditions, the process of claim and decision, and possible impact on expectations of the current decision process. It is essential to inquire: Who, says What, to Whom, for what Objectives, How, under what Conditions, and with what Effects. The interpreter should not allow any detail to dominate his or her judgment before all has been considered. Above all, he or she should give preference both to interpretations that have been considered in the context of factors affecting the processes of agreement and claim and all the community policies at stake and to interpretations that "harmonize most fully with public order prescriptions" and "will probably do most to influence future agreements toward harmony with public order goals."[7] A considerable degree of contextuality is reflected in the guidelines for interpretation in the Vienna Convention on the Law of Treaties. The two key provisions are Articles 31 and 32. Article 31, setting forth the "general rule of interpretation," provides:

1. A treaty shall be interpreted in good faith in accordance with the ordinary meaning to be given to the terms of the treaty in their context and in the light of its object and purpose.
2. The context for the purpose of the interpretation of a treaty shall comprise, in addition to the text, including its preamble and annexes:
   (a) any agreement relating to the treaty which was made between the parties in connection with the conclusion of the treaty;
   (b) any instrument which was made by one or more parties in connection with the conclusion of the treaty and accepted by other parties as an instrument related to the treaty.
3. There shall be taken into account, together with the context:
   (a) any subsequent agreement between the parties regarding interpretation of the treaty or the application of its provisions;
   (b) any subsequent practice in the application of the treaty which establishes the agreement of the parties regarding its interpretation;
   (c) any relevant rules of international law applicable in the relations between the parties.
4. A special meaning shall be given to a term if it is established that the parties so intended.

Article 32, dealing with "supplementary means of interpretation," stipulates that

Recourse may be had to supplementary means of interpretation, including the preparatory work of the treaty and the circumstances of its conclusion, in order to confirm the meaning resulting from the application of article 31, or to determine the meaning when the interpretation according to article 31:
(a) leaves the meaning ambiguous or obscure; or
(b) leads to a result which is manifestly absurd or unreasonable.

Another provision, Article 33, is concerned with "interpretation of treaties authenticated in two or more languages."

The formulation of the Vienna Convention, as embodied in Articles 31, 32, and 33, has raised the question whether it represents a textualist or a contextual approach. It is neither; it represents an eclectic approach, combining the essential elements of both. Fidelity to the text of the treaty, to be sure, is the starting point, but the convention avoids the trap of a rigid, simplistic version of "plain and ordinary" meaning. The ordinary meaning will be given to the terms of the treaty "in their context and in the light of its object and purpose." The principle of major purposes (effectiveness) is thus incorporated. So is the principle of contextuality. Though the relevant contextual factors specified here are not as comprehensive and open-ended as those urged by McDougal and Lasswell, they do embrace the preamble, annexes, and related instruments made by the contracting parties, the whole flow of subsequent agreements and practice, "any relevant rules of international law applicable," and "the preparatory work of the treaty and the circumstances of its conclusion" as well as other supplementary means. Such a framework of interpretation, when appropriately employed, could contribute significantly to the necessary task of treaty interpretation.

Interparty Application

The concern here relates to the geographical and temporal aspects of treaty performance.

Depending on the subject of an international agreement, the territorial scope of its applicability may or may not be expressly stated. Sometimes the territorial applicability need not be delimited, as in treaties of extradition, under which the territorial scope is deemed the entire territory over which a state exerts formal authority and control. In other treaties, a territorial scope less than that of the state's entire territory may be specified. The Vienna Convention, in Article 29, stipulates that "[u]nless a different intention appears from the treaty or is otherwise established, a treaty is binding upon each party in respect of its entire territory." Special difficulties may arise when federal-state clauses are involved.

An international agreement operates prospectively rather actively, unless the agreement itself indicates otherwise. This is inscribed in Article 28 of the Vienna Convention, which also allows for proof of a retroactive effect based on circumstances outside of the parties' intent as that appears in the agreement.

International law requires that negotiating states to an agreement do nothing to frustrate the objectives of the agreement already negotiated but not yet ratified. This "provisional application" was included in Article 25 of the Vienna Convention, which also allows a state to terminate the provisional applicability of the treaty as to itself by notifying negotiating states of its intention not to become a party.

Questions may arise concerning which agreement's provisions apply when two successive agreements deal with the same subject or in some other way interrelate or conflict. The Vienna Convention covers this issue in Article 30, under which an agreement may specify that it is subject to the provisions of an earlier or later agreement. When the parties to a previous agreement are all parties to a latter one, the provisions of the former are applicable insofar as they are compatible with those of the latter in the absence of express arrangements to the contrary. When all the parties to an earlier agreement are not parties to a latter agreement, as between states that are parties to both, the provisions of the earlier apply to the extent they are compatible with the latter; and, as between a state-party to both agreements and a party to only one, the provisions of the agreement in common apply.

Effects on Third Parties

That international agreements apply only to the contracting parties is expressed in the maxim *pacta tertiis nec nocent nec prosunt,* meaning that agreements neither impose obligations nor confer rights on third parties. This reflects the policy of volition in treaty commitments in independent states. A controversial issue has been whether this principle allows for exceptions under international law. According to Article 35 of the Vienna Convention, two conditions must be met in order for a nonparty to be bound by a treaty provision: (1) the parties to the treaty must have intended it, and (2) the nonparty must agree to be so bound. Its acceptance of the obligation must be express and in writing.

Even more controversial than the means by which obligations may be imposed on third-party states, is the question of when rights so conferred on third states become "perfect and enforceable" by them. There are two different views. One holds that a third state may so benefit only if it assents to a conferring of the rights, expressly or implicitly. Another maintains that what is determinative is not assent by the third state but the intent of the contracting parties to confer the right. Article 36 of the Vienna Convention took a middle course, requiring the third state's assent and simultaneously presuming such assent in the absence of contrary expression. A failure to exercise the rights thus conferred may be considered evidence of nonassent.

A major exception to the prescription that obligations may not be placed on third states without their consent exists in the U.N. Charter. According to Article 2(6) of the charter, states not members of the United Nations are required to act in accordance with the charter principles to the extent necessary to ensure the "maintenance of international peace and security." Even though the Vienna Convention made no reference to this provision, the U.N. Charter has become the fundamental and supreme law of the world community, endowed with unique, overall responsibilities to maintain world public order.

The Process of Change and Termination

An international agreement involves the shared expectations of the contracting parties. From the process of commitment to the process of performance, such shared expectations may change for various reasons, especially a fundamental change in circumstances. Such a change may affect the common interest in varying degrees.

In a decentralized world, lacking appropriate centralized institutions with compulsory authority to monitor and respond to the flow of facts and demands for change, heavy reliance continues to be placed on individual states to deal with claims relating to change in treaty relationships. How demands for change are to be accommodated with the stability of expectations is a delicate, yet extremely important, task.

In response to different kinds of change demanded, the Vienna Convention has adopted a number of distinct yet related terms: amendment, modification, withdrawal, denunciation, suspension, and termination. Whereas *amendment* means revision of the commitment of all original parties, *modification* involves revision of the commitment between certain of the parties only. A *withdrawal* is effected by a party's declaration that it is no longer a party to a multilateral treaty, and in a *denunciation,* a party simply declares that it regards a multilateral treaty as terminated. Whereas *suspension* involves the postponement of performance for a definite or indefinite time till the particular conditions alleged to have been changed are restored to normalcy, *termination* entails putting an end to a commitment.

Amendment and Modification

Amendment and modification, though related, involve distinct aspects and extents of applicability. Amendment of a treaty changes its provisions, affecting all the parties to the treaty. Modification of a treaty, in contrast, involves an inter se agreement entered by particular parties to a treaty, designed to vary some of the treaty provisions as between or among themselves only.

A treaty may of course be amended by the unanimous consent of all the parties concerned. For a bilateral treaty, this presents little problem. For a multilateral treaty, however, the unanimity requirement would mean frustration of any demand for change. Hence many multilateral treaties set forth specific conditions for amendment.

For example, the U.N. Charter, in Article 108, adopts the two-thirds rule instead of the unanimity rule: "Amendments to the present shall come into force for all Members of the United Nations when they have been adopted by a vote of two thirds of the members of the Assembly and ratified in accordance with their respective constitutional processes by two thirds of the Members of the United Nations, including all the permanent members of the Security Council." Note, however, the formidable requirement of unanimity of the five permanent members of the Security Council.

The Vienna Convention contains a catchall provision in Article 40 to deal with amending problems for multilateral treaties that lack provisions for amendment.

Modification, under Article 41 of the convention, may be effected by two or more parties to a particular treaty when the treaty expressly allows it. In the absence of such an explicit authorization, modification is permissible only if it has not been prohibited by the treaty, does not affect the rights or obligations of the other parties, and is not inimical to "the effective execution of the object and purpose of the treaty as a whole."

Withdrawal, Denunciation, Suspension, and Termination
The means of bringing a treaty to a temporary or permanent end include withdrawal, denunciation, suspension, and termination. Such occurrences may be provided for in the treaty itself, for example, after a specified period has passed, on the occurrence of a certain event, or on the fulfillment of certain conditions. Such occurrences may also result from the consent of all the contracting parties.

In the absence of explicit treaty provision or of mutual consent, does an implied right of denunciation or withdrawal exist? While one school of thought denies such an implied right, another affirms its existence under customary international law. Article 56 of the Vienna Convention cautiously incorporates the latter view, requiring that at least a year's advance notice be given. In determining whether such a right is implied in a treaty, the intent of the parties is crucial; absent a clear intent, the nature of the treaty itself must be considered. For example, it would not be correct to imply a right of denunciation for a peace treaty, but the same cannot be said of a treaty of alliance. In addition, as will be elaborated in chapter 25, it would be inappropriate to infer a right of denunciation regarding human rights conventions.

Suspending or terminating the operation of a treaty may be accomplished either in accordance with the terms of the treaty or by the unanimous consent of the parties. The Vienna Convention, in Article 58, enables parties to a multilateral treaty to suspend the operation of some or all of its provisions as between themselves alone, much in the manner of modification. Termination or suspension may also result by implication when the same contracting parties conclude a new treaty, as prescribed in Article 59.

The most troublesome area in the process of change relates to termination or suspension in the absence of mutual consent. This raises the issues of breach of a treaty (nonperformance of treaty obligations), a fundamental change in circumstances, and impossibility of performance.

A breach of a treaty generates certain legal consequences: A breach not only constitutes an internationally wrongful act that gives rise to state responsibility but also makes it lawful for certain unilateral responses that would otherwise be impermissible. Among such unilateral responses is the option for the aggrieved party to suspend or terminate the treaty. But the breach that gives rise to such an option must meet certain standards of materiality and cannot be trivial. The Vienna Convention distinguishes a material breach from all other breaches.

Article 60(3) defines "a material breach of a treaty" in terms of either "a repudiation of the treaty not sanctioned by the present Convention" or "the violation of a provision essential to the accomplishment of the object or purpose of the treaty." To ascertain what constitutes a material breach is not an easy task, as was exemplified by the U.S.-USSR exchange of charges of noncompliance with the Treaty on the Limitation of Anti-Ballistic Missile Systems of 1972, popularly known as the ABM treaty. It would require not a mechanism of automation but a contextual scrutiny by reference to relevant features involved in the processes of commitment and performance.

When a material breach occurs in a bilateral treaty, the aggrieved party has the option of "terminating the treaty or suspending its operation in whole or in part." When a material breach occurs in a multilateral treaty, action may be taken by individual states or by all parties in concert. If the former method is employed, the party may repudiate its obligations under the treaty only as to the breaching party and must not jeopardize the interests of other, nonbreaching parties.

Customary international law allows a party to a treaty unilaterally to repudiate its obligations under the treaty when there is a fundamental change in circumstances. This is the controversial doctrine of *rebus sic stantibus,* involving a basic incongruence between the original expectations of the parties and the changed conditions. It dramatizes the tension between the policy for stability of expectations and the policy for responsive change. The Vienna Convention, in Article 62, affirms this customary doctrine but places rigorous restrictions on invoking it as "a ground for terminating or withdrawing from the treaty." The changed circumstance involved must be "fundamental," one that relates to circumstances "existing at the time of the conclusion of a treaty" and "was not foreseen by the parties." In addition, "the existence of those circumstances" must have "constituted an essential basis of the consent of the parties to be bound by the treaty," the "effect of the change" must be "radically to transform the extent of obligations still to be performed under the treaty," and the change must not be "the result of a breach by the party invoking it either of an obligation under the treaty or of any other international obligation owed to any other party to the treaty." Article 62 further stipulates that the doctrine of changed circumstances is inapplicable to boundary treaties. Incidentally, the grounds that enable a state party to withdraw from a treaty or terminate it can be invoked for the purpose of suspension.

Rebus sic stantibus is to be distinguished from a closely related doctrine of "supervening impossibility of performance." The former applies to circumstances that existed when a treaty came into force, whereas the latter comes into play as a result of the temporary or permanent "disappearance or destruction of an object indispensable for the execution of the treaty" (Article 61). Examples of the latter would include situations in which the submergence of an island or the drying-up of a river makes it impossible to perform the treaty. Article 61 of the Vienna Convention makes impossibility of performance a ground for termination or suspension (in the case of temporary impossibility). The article is expressly limited to loss of an "object" necessary for performance, and such situations as the severance of diplomatic relations may not be invoked as a case of impossibility of performance. (Article 63, separately, deals with the consequences of severing diplomatic relations.)

A party invoking any of the foregoing grounds for "terminating a treaty, withdrawing from it, or suspending its operation" is required under Articles 65–67 to give notice of its claim and reasons to the other parties and to comply with other procedural requirements set forth in these provisions. The outcome of withdrawal, termination, or suspension will not be automatic but is contingent on compliance with the procedural requirements.

Finally, note that a treaty is deemed terminated as the result of the emergence, after the entry into force of the treaty, of a new and contradictory peremptory norm (jus cogens) of international law. Such a situation will have no retroactive effect.

17

The Ideological Instrument

The ideological instrument, unlike the elite-to-elite communication of the diplomatic instrument, is directly communicated to a wide audience. Concerned with reaching a wide audience, it possesses tremendous potential to mobilize world public opinion to protect the common interest of all humankind. It involves the mobilization both of enlightenment and of transnational identifications and loyalties as bases of power.

CONSTRUCTIVE USE

The potential to manage world public opinion in the enhanced protection of common interests, though yet to be realized, has begun to find expression, as vividly dramatized by the growing movement toward nuclear freeze and effective arms control.

The potential to communicate instantaneously around the globe to mass audiences beyond elite groups promises both to generate increased participation in the global constitutive process and to affect many policy functions, especially promoting, prescribing, and applying. The ideological instrument is particularly important to international governmental organizations in performing their functions. Because of limited resources, international governmental organizations have tended to stress the use of symbols to publicize and focus world attention on matters of common concern and to enlighten and stimulate members of the public as vanguards in protection. It is the ideological instrument, stressing contemporary communication technology and skills, that enables these organizations to use bases of power that would otherwise be unavailable to them. As the late Secretary-General of the United Nations U Thant put it, "a purposeful and universal programme of public information is, in fact, a programme of implementation — an essential counterpart of the substantive activities of the Organization."[1]

The major weapon the United Nations relied on to combat apartheid in South Africa, for example, was sustained use of the ideological instrument. A protracted world war of publicity was waged to enlighten public opinion on the evils of apartheid and to overcome the vehement resistance of the South African government. The achievements in consciousness-raising against apartheid cannot be overemphasized. The use of publicity has been extended from the antiapartheid crusade to other human rights matters. With its global constituency, the United Nations has employed a strategy of selective attention through publicity by commemorating a particular day, year, or decade in reference to a particular matter of vital shared concern or a particular category of people, for instance, Human Rights Day (December 10 of each year, in commemoration of the adoption of the Universal Declaration of Human Rights); International Day for the Elimination of Racial Discrimination (March 21 of each year, the anniversary of the Sharpeville incident in South Africa); International Year of the Child (1979); the United Nations Decade for Women: Equality, Development, and Peace (1975–85); the United Nations Decade of the World's Indigenous People (1994–2003); the United Nations Decade for Human Rights Education (1995–2004); and the United Nations Decade for the Eradication of Poverty (1997–2006).

Private groups and individuals are able through the availability of the ideological instrument to mobilize a wide range of effective participants in both the private and public sectors to awaken, educate, engage, and even enrage public opinion. In the race to win the hearts and minds of the world's population, private groups and individuals are formidable, despite limited resources and imposed governmental regulations. The nongovernmental sector can offer more inclusive identifications to humanity and is less inhibited by such parochial notions as sovereignty and domestic jurisdiction. It is freer to tell the truth as it is. With appropriate skill, the ideological instrument can be mobilized to reach a worldwide audience and to build a global constituency in support of both minimum public order and optimum public order.

Rhetoric is far from cheap. Increased rhetoric in articulation and support of the common interest can help to generate, cultivate, sustain, and fortify the expectations of the peoples around the globe in the direction of a world public order of human dignity.

COERCIVE USE

Although the ideological instrument is commonly identified with its constructive use for enlightenment, it may also be put to coercive use. This is nothing new; it has been used sporadically on a small scale since time immemorial. It was not recognized as an influential instrument and largely ignored, however, until about the time of the French Revolution. World War I was the first total war in human history, not only because of its mobilization of industrial and human resources but also in the systematic use of the ideological instrument, so-called propaganda warfare. People came to realize that total war could be won only by attacking people's minds as well as their bodies, and the ideological instrument was resorted to on a larger scale.

All the techniques of the ideological instrument used in World I were repeated in World War II, but their effectiveness was greatly enhanced with the aid of vaster and more efficient governmental machinery and the spectacular development of radio broadcasting.

Since World War II, the use of the ideological instrument has been greatly amplified and systematically organized. The Cold War era was one of great tension. With little or no apparent restraint, charges of coercive use of the ideological instrument were made almost daily, becoming routine. Even after the end of the Cold War, the ideological instrument continues to be used as a means of coercion, employed singly or in combination with the military, economic, or diplomatic instruments — take, for example, the use of terrorist tactics engaged in by governments or others as part of an effort "to send a message."

Certain types of coercive use of the ideological instrument have caused particular concern, including (1) communications designed to deprive respect (libelous communications against heads of state or other governmental officials and race-mongering propaganda); (2) communications likely to cause significant deprivations of power (such as those calculated to foment civil strife, popularly known as subversive propaganda); and (3) communications calculated to incite major coercion (war-mongering propaganda, incitement of war). Charges are generally matched by countercharges.

A significant example is the Radio Martì incident. When the United States inaugurated its official Radio Martì broadcast to Cuba on May 20, 1985, the Cuban government immediately condemned the new broadcasting service as "an aggressive act" against Cuba and an insult against Cuba in usurping the name of a Cuban independence hero, Jose Martì. Cuba responded sharply by taking retaliatory measures, including suspending implementation of a major immigration agreement with the United States, which contemplated the return to Cuba of 2,746 "undesirable" Cubans languishing in U.S. prisons and mental health facilities and the release of 3,000 political prisoners by Cuba, and the admission of up to 20,000 Cuban immigrants to the United States annually; and imposing a ban on visits to Cuba by Cubans living in the United States.[2] It remains yet to be seen what impact the newly inaugurated Radio Free Asia, directed at China, will have on international relations. (A more recent case involves Elian Gonzalez, whose mother and stepfather died as a result of the shipwreck of their refugee boat. Today, Elian's case is one of an international custody battle. The U.S. courts are keeping him in the United States to determine if going back to his father in communist Cuba would harm him. The Cuban government is outraged at the Miami court ruling that gave temporary custody to Elian's uncle. Furthermore, many in Cuba consider the judge's decision to be illegal and arbitrary, claiming that the unknown uncle had the boy kidnapped.)

The central issue raised is: To what extent does international law regulate the use of the ideological instrument? In other words, when is the use of the ideological instrument impermissible? How to draw the line between impermissible propaganda as a means of coercion and permissible use of the ideological instrument as a means of persuasion?

BASIC COMMUNITY POLICY

At the heart of these issues is the paramount policy that would promote the free flow of information across state lines to foster enlightenment, to facilitate transnational interaction by persuasion. The complementary policy is to ensure that activities designed to secure enlightenment through the free flow of information would not unduly disrupt minimum public order and destroy other states' values, especially security, power, and respect.

Simply put, the basic community policy is to encourage enlightenment and persuasion and to discourage regimentation and coercion. But the line between permissible and impermissible use of the ideological instrument is extremely delicate to draw.

TRENDS IN DECISION

The world community long tolerated any use of ideological strategy (propaganda) at a time when major use of coercion and violence was permitted in interstate relations. With the rise of radio and its massive use and impact, as dramatized during World War I, transnational propaganda through radio became a topic of concern and regulation.

The problem of radio broadcasting first came before the League of Nations in 1926, and in 1936 the Convention Concerning the Use of Broadcasting in the Cause of Peace was enacted. The contracting states undertook, under Article 1 of the convention, to prohibit radio broadcasting within their territories of any transmission calculated to disturb international understanding or to "incite the population of any territory to acts incompatible with the internal order or the security" of a contracting party. It may be noted that this proscription covers precisely the activities in which the major contending powers in the Cold War engaged after the end of World War II. The convention further forbade the use of false or distorted statements or news and required the contracting state to provide correct information and news over their broadcasting stations. The convention, still in force today, is regarded as applicable to television broadcast.

The Nuremberg trials represented an important development in this area. A major charge of the indictment that led to the trials was that the defendants had committed "crimes against peace" by "the planning, preparation, initiation and waging of wars of aggression."[3] Preparation included psychological and educational dimensions. The indictment referred specifically to the participation or promotion of the "educational" and "psychological preparations of war" — acts calculated to reshape the German educational system and cultural activities and to disseminate the Nazi ideology to secure citizens' support of an overall aggressive plan.[4]

In the United Nations' efforts to define aggression through the International Law Commission and the Special Committee on the Question of Defining Aggression, suggestions were made that "ideological aggression," in the sense of war propaganda, subversive propaganda against another state, or incitement of civil strife by propaganda, be included in the concept of aggression.[5] Though the proposals were rejected as vague and unworkable, they reflected contemporary apprehension about the coercive use of the ideological instrument. Article 20 of the International Covenant on Civil and Political Rights, moreover, prohibits any "propaganda for war" and any "advocacy of national, racial or religious hatred that constitutes incitement to discrimination, hostility or violence."

In this connection, the International Convention on the Elimination of All Forms of Racial Discrimination (1965) has given rise to a comparable controversy concerning race-mongering propaganda. Article 4 of the convention condemns "all propaganda and all organizations" preaching the "superiority" of one race and promoting "racial hatred and discrimination" and seeks the elimination of "all incitement to, or acts of," racial discrimination. Toward this end, the article mandates state parties to "declare an offence punishable by law all dissemination of ideas based on racial superiority or hatred, incitement to racial discrimination, as well as all acts of violence or incitement to such acts against any race or group of persons of another color or ethnic origin, and also the provision of any assistance to racist activities, including the financing thereof," and, further, to "declare illegal and prohibit organizations, and also organized and all other propaganda activities, which promote and incite racial discrimination, and

[to] recognize participation in such organizations or activities as an offence punishable by law." Although Article 4 also states that "due regard" be given to "the principles embodied in the Universal Declaration of Human Rights and the rights expressly set forth in article 5 of this Convention" — ostensibly with special reference to the rights of "freedom of opinion and expression" and "freedom of peaceful assembly and association" — it has not allayed a shared sense of anxiety about its far-reaching ramifications. In the United States, for example, this article is widely regarded as incompatible with the First Amendment freedom of expression and association protected by the Constitution.

THE DRIVE TOWARD A NEW WORLD INFORMATION AND COMMUNICATION ORDER

For centuries proponents of freedom of information and proponents of rigid state control have struggled to control the ideological instrument. Recently this struggle has been accentuated on a global scale by the intense demands for and debates concerning a new world information and communication order.

Human history has been accelerated by communication technology. From sole reliance on oral communication to the invention of writing and printing, from movable type to a penny press, from the visual dimension of camera and film through the audio dimension of radio and telephone to the complete audiovisual mass communication symbolized by television and new computer networks, humankind is entering a new epoch of information-rich civilization.

Modern technology has enabled almost instantaneous transmission of messages around the globe; it has overcome the natural barriers of time and space. Recent developments, such as broadcasting satellites, computers, data processing, and teleinformatics, have had a revolutionary impact on the concept of communication and on the breadth of the flow of information. The rapid development and merger of computer and telecommunications technology have led to what has come to be known as the "information society": a society in which information is a predominant factor in economic, social, political, and other important sectors of life. The size and pace of information flow are staggering. The contributions, both existing and potential, that modern communications can make to enhance people's perceptions of the intimate interdependencies of humanity and the world community are enormous. Modern communications have the tremendous potential to bind the peoples of the world and make a global village a reality. The Internet has afforded many people access to information that they normally would not have. For example, many NGOs advocating the rights of indigenous peoples have helped to bring greater awareness to the international community of the claims of these peoples throughout the world, in particular, their claims for self-determination.

Although electronic communications and information technologies have created and promised tremendous benefits, they also raise increasingly complex questions. Advances in communications and information technologies and services open up new frontiers: the outer space, terrestrial, and undersea communications, with the practical global linkage of information flows and the potential for extraterrestrial communications.

As modern technologies overcome the barriers of time and space in communication, the problem of the flow of information across national boundaries grows more pressing. More barriers to the free flow of information (both transnationally and internally) are erected by an increasing number of countries. A wide range of governmental measures based on varying degrees of formal or effective power are employed to interfere with the flow of information, operating directly on the content of communication itself, on the reporters of information, or through imposition of undue economic burdens.

Such unilateral national measures of restrictions are increasingly justified in terms of national sovereignty, national security, national interest, cultural heritage, internal order, development need, privacy interest, and so on.

The trend toward assertions of greater national controls over the transfrontier flow of information occurs at a time when nation-states, both developed and developing, are becoming more sensitive and manifesting divergent perspectives about the nature and role of communication and information in the global process of decision and in the nation-building processes. The imbalances in the transnational flow of information (one-way rather than two-way flow) and the great disparities in the distributions of communication technologies and resources are keenly perceived and felt. Moreover, information can be threatening to power elites seeking to maintain their value position in less-than-democratic countries. Hence, in addition to unilateral national measures, some developing nations continue after a first failed attempt in the 1980s to unite in demanding the establishment of a "new world information and communication order."

Although the precise demands made in the name of the new world information order remained somewhat elusive and uncertain, the thrust of these was propagated with intensity. Notable among this constellation have been demands for:

Freedom from distorted communications
Freedom from external domination and monopoly of the media of
    communication
Effective participation in the transnational process of communication
An aggregate, balanced flow of information

Access to communication technology and resources

Special assistance in acquiring and developing communication capacities to overcome handicaps

National control of the flow of information

Responsible journalism

Freedom to initiate and constitute institutions specialized in the gathering processing, and dissemination of information at all community levels.

The demand for a new world information and communication order was obviously inspired by, and patterned after, that for a new international economic order. Considerable economic, social, and political changes in the world, however, including a transformation in the attitude of Western journalists, indicate that the latest round of demands advocated by remnants (mostly military leaders) of the Group of Seventy-Seven will enjoy still less support than in the 1980s.

In a fundamental sense, demand for a new world information and communication order involves more than just information and communication and entails an attempt to modify significantly the functioning of the global constitutive process of authoritative decision and to achieve reallocation of power, wealth, skill, and other values. The demand for a new world information order has injected a new dimension in the evaluation of the right to information. The predominant demand for the new order has shifted the traditional concern for individual freedom in the gathering, processing, and dissemination of information to the concern of particular states or official elites about the overall flow and content of information across national boundaries. Claims are made in the name not of the individual but of the nation-state as a participant in the global process of communication and decision.

Easing the flow of information across community boundaries in ways to promote the common interest must be a paramount concern of a genuine new world information order. How can communication between people and groups be freed from the fetters that inhibit rational decisions in relation to value processes?

The fundamental policy in defense of the freedom to acquire, use, and communicate information and knowledge has been eloquently projected in both the Universal Declaration of Human Rights and the International Covenant on Civil and Political Rights and in other documents. The Universal Declaration, today widely accepted as part of customary international law, and the covenant are two key components of the emerging global bill of human rights.

The Universal Declaration, in Article 19, provides that "[e]veryone has the right to freedom of opinion and expression; this right includes freedom to hold opinions without interference and to seek, receive and impart information and ideas through any media and regardless of frontiers." This generic right to transnational and domestic freedom of expression is necessarily broad; its formulation is as profound as it is simple. It includes freedom to seek, receive, and impart information and ideas through any media regardless of frontiers. This freedom of information, as prescribed, encompasses all activities relating to the gathering, processing, and dissemination of information. It embraces not only the passive reception of information but also the active role in seeking and disseminating information — it protects activities relevant to the communicator-communicatee relationship. Its concern extends to the process as well as the content of communication. It protects communication activities through any media and extends to both internal and transnational communications. In its broadest reach, the freedom is indeed a functional equivalent of the "right to communicate," as reflected in recent proposals.

Similarly, the International Covenant on Civil and Political Rights, in Article 19(1) and (2), stipulates:

1. Everyone shall have the right to hold opinions without interference.
2. Everyone shall have the right to freedom of expression; this right shall include freedom to seek, receive and impart information and ideas of all kinds, regardless of frontiers, either orally, in writing or in print, in the form of art, or through any other media of his choice.

The addition of "either orally, in writing or in print, in the form of art, or through any other media of his choice" is meant to be all-inclusive, making more explicit what is meant by "through any media" in the Universal Declaration. The third paragraph of Article 19 adds:

The exercise of the rights provided for in paragraph 2 of this Article carries with it special duties and responsibilities. It may therefore be subject to certain restrictions, but these shall only be such as are provided by law and are necessary:
(a) For respect of the rights and reputations of others;
(b) For the protection of national security or of public order (ordre public), or of public health or morals.

In relation to the Universal Declaration, a comparable general limitation clause is found in Article 29(2):

In the exercise of his rights and freedoms, everyone shall be subject only to such limitations as are determined by law solely for the purpose of securing due recognition and respect for the rights and freedoms of others and of meeting the just requirements of morality, public order and the general welfare in a democratic society.

These provisions reflect clear recognition that a person's freedoms and rights must be accommodated with the comparable rights and freedoms of others and with the aggregate common interest. The built-in safeguards also suggest that states may not impair the individual's right to full participation in the enlightenment process merely on a pretext or to stay in power, especially in view of the requirement of a "democratic society." Application of these prescriptions to concrete cases requires, naturally, a disciplined, contextual scrutiny. Comparable provisions can also be found in European and American regional human rights conventions.

Whereas the projection of the fundamental freedom of information, both globally and regionally, has received widespread early support, U.N. efforts to prescribe more detailed content to this fundamental freedom and related measures of implementation have encountered tremendous difficulty.

The General Assembly, at its first session in 1946, characterized freedom of information as "a fundamental human right" and "the touchstone of all the freedoms to which the United Nations is consecrated."[6] Subsequently, the United Nations organs concerned have experienced considerable difficulty in formulating a more detailed content to freedom of information and related measures of implementation. Although the Convention on the International Right of Correction of 1952 entered into force in 1962, the General Assembly has continued to postpone consideration of its agenda item on "Draft Convention on Freedom of Information" from year to year.

The United Nations' failure to give substance to what was once proclaimed "a fundamental human right" and the "touchstone" of all the other rights reflects vividly the changing dynamics of global politics within the United Nations as a result of the massive influx of the newly independent states, the new patterns of bloc politics and voting coalition, and the divergent perspectives representing different cultures, communities, and systems. For many years now the issue of freedom of information has been put on the back burner in the agenda of the General Assembly.

To fill this vacuum, the United Nations Educational, Scientific, and Cultural Organization (UNESCO) has emerged in recent years as the focal organization of action in the field of transnational information and communication. The constitution of UNESCO, in Article 1, mandates the organization to "collaborate in the work of advancing the mutual knowledge and understanding of peoples, through all means of mass communication and to that end recommend such international agreements as may be necessary to promote the free flow of ideas by word and image." As the specialized agency responsible for promoting the free flow of ideas and knowledge through the use of the mass media, UNESCO has undertaken a wide range of activities in the field of communication.

Over the years UNESCO has sought to meet the challenge of the vastly increased volume of international communication and flow of information and to develop the means and structures to gather, process, and disseminate information and knowledge in all countries. Its approach has moved progressively toward the concept that a truly free flow of information must be balanced as well as free.

From emphasizing technical assistance to foster communication infrastructures in the developing world in the 1950s and 1960s, UNESCO has shifted its focus to the content of news and the role of the media in society since 1970. Among its notable recent achievements are the adoption of the Mass Media Declaration of 1978 (Declaration on Fundamental Principles Concerning the Contribution of the Mass Media to Strengthening Peace and International Understanding, the Promotion of Human Rights and to Countering Racialism, Apartheid and Incitement to War),[7] the work of the International Commission for the Study of Communication Problems (the MacBride Commission), and the establishment of a formal International Program for the Development of Communication (IPDC). Thanks to these efforts, the complex problems involved in communication and information have been seriously studied from a comprehensive global context. A lengthy international agenda has been projected for years to come.

Included in this agenda are two matters, of special concern to the International Telecommunication Union (ITU), that are worthy of notice. The first is the global allocation of the radio spectrum. Radio frequencies have historically been allocated on a first-come-first-served basis through the World Administrative Radio Conference (WARC) under the ITU sponsorship. This policy naturally favors the developed nations that already possess substantial communications capacities: it is estimated that at present some 10 percent of the world's population controls 90 percent of the spectrum. This patent disparity and inequity, together with the growing demands for telecommunications services, has made the use of the radio spectrum a highly complex issue — how this limited resource can be equitably shared among different communities and different users in ways that would maximize the potential uses of the spectrum and minimize interference. The developing nations demand that the first-come-first-served policy be replaced by a priori planning so that an adequate number of frequencies and orbital slots will be available to them when they achieve advanced communications technologies. But the developed nations generally maintain that improvements in technology will ease expanded use of the spectrum when the developing nations need it and that the policy of a priori allocation could stifle technological developments.

The second is the use of satellites for direct television broadcasting. Direct broadcast satellites (DBS) have been in use since 1963, when the first trans-Atlantic color television pictures were sent via satellite. Although many benefits can be gained from direct broadcast satellites, particularly in education, many countries fear that their nascent telecommunications industries would be obliterated by these transmissions. And many countries, developed and developing, fear that even greater cultural homogenization would result, with concomitant loss of national identity. Others fear loss of control over political content. The problem related to DBS can be reduced to two issues: whether the state undertaking such broadcasting is required to obtain the prior consent of the receiving states, and whether the receiving state may exercise any control over the signals being transmitted.

In any event, recent endeavors revolving around the intense demands for a new world information and communication order have led to many strong reaffirmations of the crucial importance of the freedom of information in the world community today. But they have also generated continuing controversies, including the proper role of UNESCO. States in which the free press prevails, in particular, have tended to view this demand with skepticism and reservation; for some, a new world information and communication order is nothing but a code word for state elite control of the press. (Indeed, charges of "politicization" and mismanagement culminated in the formal withdrawal of the United States from UNESCO, effective as of January 1, 1985. The United Kingdom and Singapore took similar steps, but the U.K. has since announced plans to rejoin the organization.) More recently, UNESCO has actively opposed suggestions by developing nations that it help sponsor a "world seminar" addressing their by-now familiar demands.

Amid the continuing debate about the shape of order to come in the field of world information and communication, the fundamental community policy of protecting the freedom of information — the freedom to acquire, use, and communicate information and knowledge — must be sustained and fortified. The increasing concern for the interests of particular states must not be at the expense of the classic concern for individual freedom. The individual should remain the cornerstone concern of any communication system.

The way to foster a more efficient and equitable world order of information and communication is not to erode, dilute, or hamper this fundamental policy. The key, rather, is positive facilitation by making pertinent technology, knowledge, and resources available to all and by increasing the capacity for communication at every community level. More channels of communication, more voices, not stifling the existing channels and voices, is the answer.

Genuine freedom and enlightenment for all human beings will be possible only when necessary conditions are created and maintained to enable them to be effective, active, equal participants in the communication processes at different community levels and in different social settings. Individuals need not be the mere passive recipients of messages dictated by the top elite but must be able to think and speak for themselves. In the most profound sense, this is the essence of a free and balanced flow of information, an interactive, horizontal pattern of communication. A new order must move toward making the individual a communicating being who can think, choose, and express: think freely, with adequate access to the total stock of human knowledge and information; choose freely and intelligently; and express opinions and ideas freely. This is the essence of the emerging right of communication, with all its emphases on participation and access at every community level.

Wisely applied in a spirit of cooperation for the common interest, the new technologies can generate an unprecedented abundance of communication channels, more diversified message flows, and greater citizen participation in a pluralistic world of interdependence. Concerted community efforts at positive facilitation, within a framework fostering the free and balanced flow of information, would contribute mightily to the aggregate enlightenment and ultimately toward a world community of human dignity. A genuine new world information and communication order, if established, should be a new order of human dignity in which persuasion prevails over coercion and the wide shaping and sharing of enlightenment and all other values are secured. It should be a world order that contributes to the maintenance of minimum public order, in the sense of minimization of unauthorized coercion, and to the achievement of optimum public order, in the sense of the widest possible shaping and sharing of all values.

18

The Economic Instrument

The economic instrument involves activities and facilities to manage a flow of capital, goods, and services across state lines. Its employment affects not only all phases of wealth processes — production, conservation, distribution, and consumption — but also value processes. The economic instrument can be used by the general community of states, through a growing network of international governmental organizations, and by individual states to promote aggregate interests. Positively, it can facilitate fulfillment of wealth and other values, and negatively, it can serve as a sanctioning measure against violations of international law. Given the enormous importance of wealth (control of and access to capital, goods, and services) as a base for all other values, the economic instrument is obviously important for multiple purposes.

The positive use of the economic instrument by the general community has greatly expanded, thanks to a global network of organizations consisting of the United Nations, its subsidiary organs, and many specialized agencies. This expanding network of agencies has employed the economic instrument to foster development in its manifold dimensions and to maximize the production and distribution of all important values. The basic goal, as projected in the preamble of the U.N. Charter, is to "promote social progress and better standards of life in larger freedom" and to "employ international machinery for the promotion of the economic and social advancement of all peoples." This growing network encompasses the Economic and Social Council (including its four regional economic commissions and a number of functional commissions), the United Nations Conference on Trade and Development (UNCTAD), the United Nations Development Program (UNDP), the World Bank Group (the International Bank for Reconstruction and Development, the International Finance Corporation, and the International Development Association), the International Monetary

Fund (IMF), and the World Trade Organization (WTO), formerly known as the General Agreement on Trade and Tariffs (GATT). Together they deal with international investment, monetary policy, humanpower, health, education, food and agriculture, and transportation and communication of all kinds.

ECONOMIC COERCION

Although the economic instrument is commonly used for productive and constructive purposes, it can also be manipulated as a means of coercion. A host of measures ranging from boycott and trade embargo to freezing of assets and withholding of economic aid can generate coercive effect in varying circumstances.

The Arab boycott of pro-Israeli enterprises and the oil embargo of 1973–74 in particular dramatized the impact of economic coercion and generated a continuing debate about the lawfulness of economic coercion under contemporary international law. Most recently the debate has continued over embargoes against Iraq and Cuba, and the impact of such sanctions on ordinary citizens in those countries as opposed to elites.

When military force was a permissible form of value change, economic coercion naturally did not receive serious attention. Today, with the U.N. Charter ban of the threat or use of force and the ostensibly disruptive impact of economic coercion under an interdependent world economy, the lawfulness of economic coercion has become a matter of continuing debate. The debate has centered on the interpretation of Article 2(4) of the charter, which stipulates: "All Members shall refrain in their international relations from the threat or use of force against the territorial integrity or political independence of any state, or in any other manner inconsistent with the Purposes of the United Nations." What does "force" mean? Does it refer only to military force? Or does it include nonmilitary coercion (economic, ideological, and diplomatic) as well?

One view takes the position that since coercion generated by economic and other nonmilitary measures may conceivably be more coercive and produce equally or more devastating outcomes than that generated by military force, economic coercion is included in the proscription of Article 2(4). The coercive effect created in a particular context and the consequences of such coercion, not the modality of instrument employed, are said to be determinative.[1] Further, the word "force" in Article 2(4) is not limited by the word "armed," which framers of the charter used in Article 51. The opposing view, which appears to prevail, maintains that the Article 2(4) ban does not extend to economic coercion. Its conclusion is based largely on argument concerning the ordinary meaning attached to the word *force* and the intent of the framers of the charter.[2]

In the real world, though any instrument can be used singly, it is most often used in various combinations with other instruments of policy. A particular use of a nonmilitary instrument can conceivably be highly coercive under rare circumstances; yet when the military instrument becomes involved, the question of lawfulness of a particular coercion tends to become more serious. To what extent does Article 2(4) forbid the threat or use of military force? What three categories are mentioned? This question, controversial as it is, continues to receive a priority consideration in the international law literature (see chapter 19).

ECONOMIC SANCTIONS

Just as economic coercion can be used to coerce, it can also be used as a means of sanction in response to a prior violation of international law. Economic sanctions may be undertaken unilaterally or collectively and by any effective participants in the world social process. A unilateral undertaking of economic sanctions is more apt to raise the question of its lawfulness, quite apart from its effectiveness.

Unilateral or collective, using the economic instrument as a measure of sanction against violations of international law brings formidable difficulties. The difficulties are accentuated in cases of sanctions taken unilaterally.

Employed as a means of sanction, the economic instrument may isolate the violator state from the flow of outside resources and services, upset its economic influence in third states, and impair its efficient use of internal resources. The most notable economic measures designed to sanction the violator state are commodity and financial controls. Commodity controls seek to regulate or cut off the trade relations of both the sanctioners and third states with the violator state. They may involve imposing an embargo on direct exports from the sanctioners to the violator state and on direct imports by the sanctioners from the violator and preventing re-exportation or transshipment from third states of goods from the sanctioners to the violator state or vice versa. An embargo on exports, total or selective, is designed to weaken the violator state by denying its access to strategic and other critical supplies; and an embargo on imports (boycott) is calculated to deprive the violator state of the foreign exchange needed to finance its purchases from abroad. Embargoes may be enforced and supplemented by ancillary controls on communications and transportation (land, sea, and air) lines and facilities and by such other measures as blacklisting.

Financial controls may involve halting the flow of capital to the violator state by such measures as the denial or withholding of grants (aid), loans investments, and credits, and the suspension of payments. Other measures include blocking or freezing assets of the violator state and its nationals. Like the import embargo (boycott), the measures of financial control are designed to minimize the purchasing power abroad of the violator.

The effectiveness of economic sanctioning strategies depends on many variables relevant to a particular context. Among the important factors affecting such effectiveness are the vulnerability of the violator state to economic sanctions, the costs of such sanctions, capabilities for bearing costs, the extent of coordination, and time factors. The relative vulnerability of the violator state to the impact of economic sanction is affected by the degree of its industrial development and of its dependence on foreign trade. A highly industrialized state that relies heavily on foreign trade for markets or energy and other raw materials, or both, may be particularly vulnerable to embargoes. A state with a larger agrarian sector may not be significantly affected by an embargo on food or raw materials (food especially is likely to affect the masses first and foremost), but its capabilities to maintain internal order by coercion may be greatly weakened by being denied access to arms and strategic materials. Conversely, an arms embargo may be ineffective against a highly industrialized state. The violator state, moreover, may be able to offset the adverse effect of economic sanctions through its network of established or potential trading partners and through a host of remedial measures including stockpiling, substituting, and rationing commodities and reallocating resources.

Note that economic measures of sanction are not without cost to the sanctioning states that employ them. The damage done to the violator state may in measure be matched by a corresponding loss spilled over into the economies of the sanctioning states. The costs may thus become prohibitive to the sanctioning states, unless the burden is widely shared and sanctions are collectively applied. Similarly, the efficacy of economic sanctions imposed for a protracted period against states capable of economic endurance tends to diminish as time passes. Sanctioning states gradually tend to defect unless economic sanctions are well coordinated and effectively applied in conjunction with other strategies.

The upshot is that, because of the continuing domination of the world's wealth by individual nation-states, the general community cannot expect to employ the economic instrument effectively as a sanction against violations of international law without the cooperation of many nation-states. Since any use of the economic instrument is so closely interlocked with the welfare of particular states, it appears extremely difficult to persuade states to undertake and coordinate economic sanctions to defend the common interest. During the tenure of the League of Nations, for example, collective economic sanctions against Italy for its invasion of Ethiopia were less than successful.

Under the regime of the United Nations, the experiences of economic sanctions against Southern Rhodesia and against South Africa are illuminating. In response to the unilateral declaration of independence of Southern Rhodesia by the minority regime of Ian Smith on November 11, 1965, the Security Council, acting under Chapter VII of the U.N. Charter, took the unprecedented action of imposing mandatory, though selective, sanctions against Southern Rhodesia under Resolution 232 of December 16, 1966. The Security Council, in urging "all States to do their utmost to break off economic relations with Southern Rhodesia," mandated that all U.N. members impose import and export embargoes against Southern Rhodesia and refuse financial or other economic aid to the Smith regime.[3] Although the record of compliance was for the most part dismal, the collective sanctions were in part responsible for the ultimate solution leading toward majority rule in the new state of Zimbabwe.

In the case of South Africa's policies and practices of apartheid and its "illegal occupation" of Namibia, both the General Assembly and the Security Council passed numerous resolutions urging U.N. members to undertake, among other things, embargoes on arms and other goods (both export and import) and measures of financial control. A point of particular emphasis was to "dissuade the main trading partners of South Africa and economic and financial interests from collaborating with the Government of South Africa and companies registered in South Africa."[4] For many years, collective action against apartheid remained far from effective. As Reisman sharply observed: "In a world of fragmented and selfish loyalties . . . [o]ne of the sad ironies of the struggle for freedom in Africa has been that a number of African states, vociferous in their condemnation of racism, have slipped under the economic dam which they themselves erected against white minority regimes in southern Africa."[5]

In July 1985 the South African government, faced with heightening racial violence and tension, declared a state of emergency in thirty-six cities and towns, empowering police to impose curfews, make arrests without warrants, and detain people indefinitely. The world community was aroused to renewed action by such illegal acts. The Security Council in July 1985 urged member states to adopt sanctioning measures against the Republic of South Africa, including suspension of all new investment in South Africa; prohibition of the importation or sale of Krugerrands; restrictions on sports relations; suspension of guaranteed export loans; prohibition of all new contracts in the nuclear field; and a ban on all sales of computer equipment that could be used by the South African army and police.[6]

States with economic ties to South Africa responded, individually and collectively. The European Parliament urged that the European Community sever all economic, financial, cultural, and military ties with South Africa. The member states of the European Community agreed on such measures as a ban on arms trade, a sports boycott, an end to all oil exports, and cessation of exports of sensitive equipment destined for the police and armed forces of South Africa.[7] The Canadian government took a firm stand, undertaking such measures as fortifying the voluntary "Code of Conduct Concerning the Employment Practices of Canadian Companies Operating in South Africa"; abrogating the Canada–South Africa double taxation agreements; banning exports of such sensitive equipment as computers for use by the police and the armed forces; placing an embargo on the importation of arms from South Africa; discontinuing the program designed to assist Canadian exporters with market development in South Africa; placing an embargo on both cargo and passenger air flights to or from South Africa; and recommending a voluntary refusal to buy Krugerrands, a voluntary ban on loans to the government of South Africa and all its agencies, and a voluntary ban on the sale of the crude oil and refined petroleum products to South Africa.[8]

Within the United States, the subject of economic sanctions against South Africa became a topic of serious concern not only for the public sector — federal, state, and local governments — but also for the private sector. Consciousness-raising — most notably through arrests courted by peaceful demonstrations in front of the South African Embassy in Washington (a forbidden zone) by celebrities and noncelebrities alike — was accompanied by specific measures. Under mounting congressional and popular pressures, President Reagan preempted imminent legislation on economic sanctions by issuing an executive order of limited economic sanctions on September 9, 1985.[9] The order banned all computer exports to agencies involved in enforcing apartheid and to security forces, exports of nuclear goods and technology to South Africa, loans to the South African government, and imports of arms from South Africa. The ineffectiveness of these executive measures led Congress to impose, overriding a presidential veto, tougher economic sanctions on South Africa in October 1986. The congressional act prohibited new American investments in South African businesses, banned the importation of such products as steel, coal, uranium, and textiles from South Africa, and canceled South African airlines' landing rights in the United States.[10]

The issue of divestment of stock in corporations doing business in South Africa became a cause célèbre around university campuses and for pension funds. Closely related in this regard was the effort to secure wide adherence to the Sullivan principles, designed to promote racial quality in employment practices for U.S. firms operating in South Africa toward the ending of apartheid. The Sullivan principles, as initially formulated in 1977 and subsequently amplified, are as follows:

(1) Non-segregation of the races in all eating, comfort and work facilities;
(2) Equal and fair employment practices for all employees;
(3) Equal pay for all employees doing equal or comparable work for the same period of time;
(4) Initiation of and development of training programs that will prepare, in substantial numbers, Blacks and other nonwhites for supervisory, administrative, clerical and technical jobs;
(5) Increasing the number of Blacks and other nonwhites in management and supervisory positions; and
(6) Improving the quality of employees' lives outside the work environment in such areas as housing, transportation, school, recreation and health facilities.[11]

Throughout 1985, protest raged and pressures — internal as well as external, private as well as public — mounted as the antiapartheid momentum grew. When American and other foreign banks curbed their lending to South Africa by refusing to extend deadlines for the repayment of debts, the impact was swift and dramatic. Effects included the sharp plunging of South Africa's currency, the temporary closing of the stock and currency markets in South Africa, and a four-month moratorium imposed by the Botha government on repayments of principal on South Africa's debt.

The gathering momentum was slowed when the South African government imposed sweeping news curbs to seal South Africa's black townships from outside scrutiny. Vivid television images of protest and violent suppression that had previously galvanized American opposition to the apartheid regime of South Africa were removed.

Frustrated by the slow pace of reform toward dismantling the apartheid system, Reverend Sullivan, after a decade of crusading with the Sullivan principles as a weapon to end apartheid, adopted a new position in June 1987. He called on all U.S. corporations to withdraw from South Africa within nine months and to end all commercial ties with South Africa. In addition, he urged the United States to impose a total trade embargo on South Africa and to sever diplomatic relations with South Africa. The United Nations stepped up its international campaign, which eventually extended across the globe, increasingly isolating South Africa. The U.N. persisted with embargoes and boycotts of arms, oil, sports, and cultural events, attracting support from virtually every nation, including South Africa's main trading partners. The process was undeniably slow but eventually led to the downfall of apartheid and the democratic election of Nelson Mandela as president of the Republic of South Africa in April 1994.

Thus, the general difficulties with mobilizing effective economic sanctions do not mean that the economic instrument is under all circumstances ineffective as a sanctioning measure against violations of international law. Given a wide range of potential sanctioners and the intricate division of labor in the contemporary world, skillful management can exploit selective vulnerabilities. For instance, in the field of human rights, the U.S. Congress has made it the policy of the United States to refuse "security assistance" (both military and economic) to "any country the government of which engages in a consistent pattern of gross violations of internationally recognized human rights."[12] Although a blanket application of this policy may not produce desired results in the short run, its long-term beneficial effect on the protection of human rights cannot be doubted. Comparable observations could be made in regard to attempts by multilateral lending agencies, such as the World Bank, to withhold international loans from states that grossly violate human rights. The freezing of Iranian assets in the United States in response to the illegal seizure of American diplomats during the Iranian hostage crisis was instrumental in achieving a final settlement.

Other attempts at economic sanctions, as initiated by the United States, include the following:

1. In response to the Soviet invasion of Afghanistan, the United States, in January 1980, imposed an embargo on wheat exports ("the grain embargo"), fishing privileges, and export of high-technology equipment to the Soviet Union. A boycott of the 1980 Summer Olympics in Moscow by the United States and other countries soon followed. Four years later, the Soviet Union and most of its allies retaliated by boycotting the 1984 Summer Olympics in Los Angeles.

2. In May 1985 the United States imposed an embargo on U.S.-Nicaragua trade to punish the Sandinista government for its "aggressive activities" in Central America and for its threat to U.S. national security. Nicaraguan aircraft and ships were also banned from the United States.

3. The United States in January 1986 imposed a ban on importation of Libyan oil and froze all Libyan government assets in the United States and in American bank branches overseas in response to Libya's purported role in support of international terrorism. In 1996, Congress passed the Iran-Libya Sanctions Act, allowing Washington to impose sanctions on foreign companies doing business with Libya.

4. In March 1988, the United States suspended scheduled U.S. payments to Panama and froze the flow of funds to Panamanian banks to hasten the passing of the "illegitimate" regime of Gen. Manuel Antonio Noriega, amid

the mounting crisis precipitated by the grand jury indictments in Miami of Noriega for his involvement in narcotic trafficking and by his usurpation of power in Panama. The sanctioning measures largely backfired.

5. In 1996, the Helms-Burton Act codified many existing sanctions against Cuba and added new, innovative sanctions against foreign companies doing business with Cuba. Under Title III, foreign companies who "traffic" in property confiscated by the Cuban government from U.S. nationals (who may have been Cuban nationals at the time of the confiscation) are liable for damages of up to three times the value of the property, and may have their assets on U.S. soil seized.

In these instances, U.S. appeals to its allies for support elicited lukewarm response or mere lip service for many reasons. Those allied countries obviously have their own perceptions of the situations involved and their own calculations of potential gains and losses. The mutual defense responsibilities of alliance members are not always perceived to extend automatically to the peacetime trade of commercial goods. In addition, there has been real concern as to how far certain states can jointly apply trade sanctions under international law when their proposal to do so has failed in the United Nations. Furthermore, it often raises a range of complex jurisdictional issues. In response to the Helms-Burton Act mentioned above, for instance, some European countries have challenged the U.S. assertion that it may extend its jurisdiction over foreign companies beyond its own borders and "pass laws on a global scale."[13]

THE DRIVE TOWARD A NEW INTERNATIONAL ECONOMIC ORDER

Although direct control over resources and the management of wealth processes are still largely within the exclusive competence of nation-states, the organized general community is acquiring an increasing experience in promoting economic development and in managing credit and monetary policies. The increasing realization on the part of the elites of nation-states that their own prosperity depends on the prosperity of all communities, especially those less developed, has injected a critical dimension in the global program of development.

The widening gap between the developed and the developing nations in an interdependent world has caused the general community to pay special attention to the developing areas. Economic strategies to enhance the development of less developed communities include programs to pool and make available technological and managerial skills and provision for a continuing and expanded flow of international capital into developing communities. Other important components include environmentally sustainable development, the achievement of high and stable levels of employment, the integration of production potential into the global economy, the avoidance of widespread depressions, the coordination of the increasing number of national and transnational agencies concerned with economic assistance and financing programs, and, in the decade since the collapse of communism, privatization and commitment to a market ideology.

Frustrated by the slow pace of development and the persistence of glaring gaps, the third world countries have continued to demand the establishment of a "new international economic order." Their demands first found formal expression in the Declaration and Programme of Action on the Establishment of a New International Economic Order (General Assembly Resolution 3201) and in the Charter of Economic Rights and Duties of States (General Assembly Resolution 3281), both adopted by the General Assembly in 1974.[14] These resolutions were adopted during a period marked by a series of crises that threatened the stability of the world economy. The international monetary system instituted in 1944, popularly known as the Bretton-Woods system, had collapsed in 1971. The global energy crisis of skyrocketing oil prices, as precipitated by OPEC in the wake of the outbreak of hostilities in the Middle East in October 1973, captured headlines day after day. Other signs of instability included rising prices of other commodities and manufactured goods; shortages of food; depletion of reserves; trade imbalances; growing burdens of debt; and spiraling inflation.

It is highly significant that the famed Agenda for Peace issued by Boutros Boutros-Ghali in 1992 was followed by a twin Agenda for Development in 1994.[15] The Agenda for Development proclaims economic development to be a "fundamental human right" and "the most secure basis for peace," affirms the Bretton-Woods institutions as an integral source of policy advice and assistance, and calls for increased long-term international cooperation in economic matters. Together these resolutions have all addressed a wide range of different yet interrelated economic matters, including production and prices of raw materials and primary commodities; international trade; international monetary and financial matters; sharing of resources; foreign aid; transfer of technology; private foreign investment; regulation of transnational corporations; participation in the global decision-making process affecting wealth; and North-South or East-West economic relations. Among other things, they have called for nonreciprocal, preferential access to the markets of developed countries for manufactured goods of developing countries; equality between developed and developing nations in decision making within multilateral monetary institutions concerning financial and monetary matters instead of the present weighted voting based on the amount of each state's subscribed capital; allowing formation of interstate "producer associations" and price fixing; the indexation of the

export prices of third world goods according to the cost of exported manufactured goods and capital from the developed nations; the right of developing
countries to financial assistance for industrialization from developed countries;
special measures to alleviate the burden of external debt contracted by developing countries on hard terms; and the formulation of an international code of
conduct for transnational corporations to facilitate the transfer of technologies.

In the decade following the end of the Cold War, representatives of organizations from the Group of Seventy-Seven and former Eastern bloc nations have
pledged to move toward development policies that emphasize "individual initiative." The new approach is conciliatory, reflecting Western approaches to
development and turning away from socialist doctrines. Although there are no
longer the radical appeals for redistribution of the world's wealth as made in the
1970s, leaders from developing states continue to call for more aid from developed states.

With the end of the Cold War, there has been an increased rivalry between the
southern hemisphere and Eastern Europe. At the 1992 Earth Summit in Rio, it
became clear that the developing countries, for the first time, have in environ-
mentalism new leverage to get much-needed funds. Those countries are demanding increasing aid and transfer of technology in exchange for compliance
with the tougher environmental measures necessary to the new "sustainable
development."

Wealth deprivation, commonly known as expropriation or nationalization —
the taking by a state of foreign property located within its territory — is a very
controversial area. Article 2(2)(c) of the Charter of Economic Rights and Duties
of States (Assembly Resolution 3281) declares that each state has the right to

> nationalize, expropriate or transfer ownership of foreign property, in which case
> appropriate compensation should be paid by the State adopting such measures,
> taking into account its relevant laws and regulations and all circumstances that the
> State considers pertinent. In any case where the question of compensation gives
> rise to a controversy, it shall be settled under the domestic law of the nationalizing
> State and by its tribunals, unless it is freely and mutually agreed by all States
> concerned that other peaceful means be sought on the basis of the sovereign
> equality of States and in accordance with the principle of free choice of means.

This is a radical departure from the customary international law in the field,
under which a taking of foreign property is lawful, provided three conditions
are met: (1) the taking is for a public purpose; (2) it is not discriminatory; and
(3) prompt, adequate, and just compensation is made.

The subject of expropriation has been one of the most controversial areas in
contemporary international law. Beginning with the nationalization measures

taken by the Soviet and Mexican revolutionary governments following World War I, differences of opinion developed over what constitutes a lawful taking under international law. The debate intensified with the rapid multiplication of newly independent states after World War II. Although the "nondiscrimination" and "public purpose" criteria are generally accepted, controversy has raged over the issue of compensation.

Most of the old Communist states contended, at least in theory, that no compensation was required, in keeping with the general Soviet rejection of the binding nature of customary international law. In practice, however, Communist states did not act on this theory; in the years following World War II, at least seventy-two relevant agreements entered into with Communist states never repudiated the compensation requirement.

Capital-exporting states have generally followed the customary law mentioned above and have insisted that a taking of property be accompanied by compensation. They may differ about what precisely the standard of compensation entails — "prompt, adequate, and just" compensation or simply "just" or "appropriate" compensation. Just compensation ordinarily refers to fair market value.

Conversely, capital-importing states have increasingly asserted that whether compensation is granted and how much, if any, depends on the circumstances. The backbone of this contention is the assertion that all states exercise "permanent sovereignty" over their natural resources. The relevant factors are said to include the entire historical relations between the foreign enterprise and the host state; the ability of the taking state to pay compensation; the degree of unjust enrichment, if any, on the part of the taking state; the extent of prior exploitation by the foreign enterprise; and the extent of undue advantage enjoyed by the foreign property owner before expropriation.[16]

The formulation of Article 2(2)(c), as noted above, expresses largely the demand of the capital-importing countries and ostensibly seeks to substitute the standard of "appropriate" compensation for that of "prompt, adequate, and just" compensation. More fundamentally, it represents an attempt to remove the matter entirely from the realm of international law and to place it within the domain of national law. It is obviously unacceptable to the capital-exporting states, and it might in the long run be self-defeating for the capital-importing states. It is at odds with the prevailing state practice and in clear contradiction to General Assembly Resolution 1803, "Permanent Sovereignty over Natural Resources," adopted in 1962. This resolution, in paragraph 4, declares:

> Nationalization, expropriation or requisitioning shall be based on grounds or reasons of public utility, security or the national interest which are recognized as

overriding purely individual or private interests, both domestic and foreign. In such cases the owner shall be paid appropriate compensation, in accordance with the rules in force in the State taking such measures in the exercise of its sovereignty and in accordance with international law. In any case where the question of compensation gives rise to a controversy, the national jurisdiction of the State taking such measures shall be exhausted. However, upon agreement by sovereign States and other parties concerned, settlement of the dispute should be made through arbitration or international adjudication.[17]

The authoritative effect of the above-mentioned resolutions, particularly the Charter of Economic Rights and Duties of States and the Resolution on Permanent Sovereignty over Natural Resources — as law, "law in the making," or pious aspirations — remains a subject of continuing controversy. This point will be further discussed in chapter 22 on the prescribing (lawmaking) function.

Controversy notwithstanding, continuing adoption of these resolutions, though changing somewhat, represents what is called a "normative strategy" on the part of the third world countries. The fact of their adoption serves to illustrate and underscore the essence of how international law is made and remade — search for the common interest amid competing claims and claimants, in response to the changing demands and expectations of participants under ever-changing conditions. The expectations of the members of the world community do not remain static but are in constant flux. Although any claim of wholesale repudiation of customary international law cannot be taken seriously, demands to modify particular international norms in light of changing demands, expectations, and conditions cannot be lightly dismissed.

The new international economic order called for would have represented a conspicuous power shift to the third world. Although it failed to get the gains demanded in the 1970s, efforts have continued, although emphasis has shifted away from socialism. The new order continues seeking to generate basic changes in world economic relations and especially to remedy past deprivations and injustices through a new world trade pattern and economic arrangements favorable to the developing nations. There are still far-reaching implications involved that would engender the reshaping not only of world economic relations but, ultimately, the entire global constitutive process of authoritative decision. These demands for a new international economic order, at best, represent demands to better employ the economic instrument to facilitate greater fulfillment worldwide of wealth and other values, especially for the vast and increasing segment of the world's population that remain deprived and underfulfilled; at worst, they are said to be demands for aggrandizement of local elites at the expense of multitudes. In any event, the legitimate aspirations of the peoples in the developing world can be ignored only at the peril of the common interest.

The capital-importing countries cannot go it alone in meeting their long agenda of development. They need the cooperation of the capital-exporting countries. Numbers in voting strength are no substitute for effective control of wealth, resources, skills, and technology. The inflow of outside capital cannot be expected without adequate assurance of safety, return, and clean growth. The painstaking and persevering effort to identify and secure the common interest is the key to such cooperation between the developed and developing nations. Law, after all, is a continuing process of clarifying and securing the common interest of interacting participants under changing conditions.

The positive use of the economic instrument could facilitate an integrated solution to the global problems of sustainable development, enhancing aggregate production and fulfillment of wealth and other values. The expansion of this constructive role, built on rich experience, could greatly augment the potential of the economic instrument to promote a desired world public order of human dignity, provided the imperative of common interest is taken seriously and given effective expression.

19

The Military Instrument

The military instrument, involving implements of destruction, is commonly associated with coercion and the destruction of values. But, constructively employed for collective security, either by the organized general community or by individual states, this instrument is vital to the maintenance of minimum world public order. And minimum public order is indispensable to achieve the optimum shaping and sharing of all values.

The employment of violence and other intense coercion against human beings is inimical to human dignity. A general community aspiring toward human dignity values must seek to minimize the employment of such violence and coercion as an instrument of change in the shaping and sharing of values. Violence and coercion in authoritative sanctioning measures can only be used as a last resort.

The employment of the military instrument for the purpose of maintaining minimum public order (peace and security) has not been very effective. This remains a critical problem in the contemporary international legal system. Individual nation-states continue to control the implements of military strategy. Efforts to transfer to the general community the sole privilege of permissible employment of force have not been successful. The original plan to establish a permanent U.N. military force to maintain world order was stillborn.

BASIC COMMUNITY POLICY OF PEACEFUL CHANGE

International law governing the use of the military instrument by nation-states has undergone profound changes since the establishment of the U.N. Charter. Although the charter avoids the difficulties created by the term *war*, by no means has it removed the controversy about the permissibility of the exercise of certain coercions.

Before the conditional prohibition of major coercion, as established by the Covenant of the League of Nations, international law did not prohibit resort to war, conceived as the most intense and comprehensive form of violence. In the nineteenth century, there was understandably less of a common interest in restraining violence, because the effects of an instance of violence were less than they would be today. Private coercion and violence were then accepted as permissible not only for self-help and self-vindication of rights but also for effecting changes in the distribution of values among nation-states.

Despite the permissibility of major coercion, certain concepts about the responsibility of states governed minor coercion. A few prescriptions purported to regulate noncomprehensive and less intense uses of coercion, the so-called measures short of war. The permissible application of minor coercion was restricted to cases in which a previous unlawful act, or a failure to carry out international obligations, was imputable to the state against which coercion was applied. Conceptually, it may be likened to "a municipal enactment that punished petty thieving while condoning armed robbery."[1] This apparent paradox illustrates the manner in which international law has developed over the centuries in a world of sovereign states. The resort to major coercion was difficult to control because nation-states in modern times employed major coercion not for trivial reasons but only when a conviction of some vital interests to be served seemed to provide justification, at least in their own eyes. If the interest involved was not sufficiently great to justify, internally or externally, a resort to major coercion, it was a degree of magnitude susceptible to legal regulation.

As shown by past practices, measures short of war were generally taken only by a stronger state against weaker ones. A nation-state, in resorting to those measures, frequently invoked such concepts as intervention and reprisal to communicate its allegedly limited objectives to nonparticipants, thus hoping to allay their fears and prevent their possible involvement prompted by balance of power considerations. The initiating state could at any time characterize its operations as war and thus escape the application of the above-mentioned prescriptions. In fact, the methods employed in the instances of measures short of war were more often than not indistinguishable from those used in undertakings to which the label "war" was attached. In sum, it reflected the general nineteenth-century policy of international law, which sought to localize coercion by giving community approval to a quick settlement of disputes through superior strength.

There is a certain unreality in attempting to formulate prescriptions regarding the exercise of minor coercion while admitting that a state might resort to major coercion without breaching the law. The Covenant of the League of Nations represented the first significant break with traditional doctrine. "Resort to war" was made unlawful under certain circumstances, and an attempt was made to distinguish permissible from impermissible resort to coercion (Articles 12–16). But the continued availability of various labels to justify the use of coercion became the focus of considerable concern. "Resort to war," as proscribed in the covenant, gave rise to confused contention with respect to the continuing legality of force and violence if participants used some labels other than "war," such as "reprisal" or "intervention" or other "measures short of war."

The General Treaty for the Renunciation of War of 1928, also known as the Pact of Paris or the Kellogg-Briand Pact, sought to close these gaps. Condemning "recourse to war for the solution of international controversies," the Pact of Paris denounced "war as an instrument of national policy" and sought to resolve "all disputes or conflicts, of whatever nature or whatever origin they may be" exclusively by "pacific means" (Articles 1 and 2). But by keeping the term *war,* the pact failed to eliminate the continued debate with regard to the permissibility of armed force that participants might verbally designate a "measure short of war."

The establishment of the U.N. Charter has fundamentally changed the traditional community prescriptions about the exercises of coercion between nation-states. Discarding the confused term "war," the charter has prohibited the deliberate use of coercion in terms of "threat or use of force," "threat to the peace," "breach of the peace," and "act of aggression" (Articles 2[4] and 39–51). These references, taken as a whole, cover not only war, understood as comprehensive and highly intensive use of the military instrument, but also those applications of force or threats of force of a lesser intensity and magnitude that in the past had been labeled short of war.

Article 2(4), which is the cornerstone of the charter system, states: "All Members shall refrain in their international relations from the threat or use of force against the territorial integrity or political independence of any state, or in any other manner inconsistent with the Purposes of the United Nations." This provision is not explicit with respect to whether the nature of "force" to be prohibited was limited to military force. It was generally thought that it was not intended to cover coercive measures of an economic, ideological, or political nature, but there is a split of opinion on the issue.

Although the charter avoids the difficulties created by the legalistic invocation of the term "war," the fundamental distinction it provides between permissible and impermissible coercion has by no means eliminated the controversy with regard to the permissibility of the exercises of certain coercion. The issue whether the use of military force for purposes other than self-defense and community police action is still permissible under Article 2 of the charter has continued to arouse debate among decision makers and international lawyers.

SELF-DEFENSE

That self-defense, individual or collective, in case of an armed attack, remains permissible is beyond doubt. The fundamental community policies in defense of minimum public order, as projected in customary international law and in the U.N. Charter, are complementary. In a world arena in which authoritative and effective power remains largely unorganized and decentralized, various lesser communities can hardly be expected to achieve even minimum security, much less optimal fulfillment of all values, if they are denied appropriate capabilities and measures of response. The authoritative prescriptions of customary international law and the U.N. Charter thus make a rational distinction between impermissible coercion (acts of aggression, threats to the peace, breach of the peace, intervention, and so on) and permissible coercion (self-defense, collective self-defense, police action, and so on).

Central to the maintenance of minimum world order is to distinguish impermissible coercion from permissible coercion. The general proscription of the threat or use of force in the U.N. Charter is accompanied by preservation of the inherent right of self-defense. Article 51 of the Charter states clearly:

> Nothing in the present Charter shall impair the inherent right of individual or collective self-defense if an armed attack occurs against a Member of the United Nations, until the Security Council has taken measures necessary to maintain international peace and security. Measures taken by Members in the exercise of this right of self-defense shall be immediately reported to the Security Council and shall not in any way affect the authority and responsibility of the Security Council under the present Charter to take at any time such action as it deems necessary in order to maintain or restore international peace and security.

What is meant by aggression? What is self-defense? Through special committees and other bodies, the United Nations was engaged in formulating a definition of aggression for more than two decades. The protracted effort did result in the General Assembly's adoption in December 1974 of the Definition of Aggression, containing eight articles, as drafted by the Special Committee on the Question of Defining Aggression.[2] "Aggression" is defined in Article 1 as "the use of armed force by a State against the sovereignty, territorial integrity or political independence of another State, or in any other manner inconsistent with the Charter of the United Nations." This is practically a restatement of Article 2(4) of the U.N. Charter, except it is limited explicitly to "armed force." Indeed, Article 6 of the definition makes it clear that "[n]othing in this Definition shall be construed as in any way enlarging or diminishing the scope of the Charter, including its provisions concerning cases in which the use of force is lawful." Article 2 of the definition makes the first use of armed force by a state as prima facie evidence of an act of aggression, and Article 3 enumerates certain acts as acts of aggression, such as invading or attacking the territory of another state, bombarding the territory of another state, and blockading the ports or coasts of another state. (Defining aggression remains a problem even today. Yet the term made its way into the Draft Declaration for an International Criminal Court (hereinafter "ICC") and finally into the completed statute for an ICC. The statute, however, acknowledges in Article 5, section 2 that the international community has not yet resolved the issue of what a clear definition of *aggression* should be and that no provision in the statute has yet been established for it.)

Such definitional exercise is hardly adequate to deal with the dynamics of military coercion. In a decentralized world arena where nation-states constantly make initial and important decisions, response must be prompt in an exigent situation of major coercion. The employment of military coercion is a process, producing coercion of varying degrees of intensity and magnitude. A contextual framework of analysis, such as the one recommended by McDougal and Feliciano, which offers operational indices in distinguishing impermissible from permissible coercion, would appear to offer a more useful way of dealing with the troublesome question of aggression and self-defense.[3] According to this contextual framework, many features in the developing process of coercion must be taken into account in distinguishing impermissible from permissible coercion. In the process of transnational coercion, participants pursue various objectives by applying to one another coercion of varying degrees of intensity, by all available instruments of policy, under all the constantly changing conditions in the world arena. In a developing process of coercion there may be a culminating point that creates reasonable expectations on the part of a target state that an immediate military response is indispensable (that is, necessary) to the protection of its own existence — to safeguard its important bases of power from destruction. Because of the imminent danger of destruction, the common interest in authorizing self-defense in the form of a proportionate military response has long been recognized. Law cannot reasonably ask and expect a target state to wait like a sitting duck to see its own destruction in the face of such danger. Whether reasonable expectations about imminent destruction are created can be ascertained by taking into account every feature of the process of coercion — namely, through use of the familiar social process category of participants, objectives, situation, base values, strategies, and outcomes.

Self-defense involves employing the military instrument against an alleged attacker to protect territorial integrity and political independence. The classic formulation by Secretary of State Daniel Webster, in the *Caroline* incident of 1837 (involving the destruction by a British force of a private American steamer, used in support of the Canadian rebellion, while anchored at the American side of the Niagara River, and the deaths of American citizens), specified the element of necessity for permissible self-defense in terms of being "instant, overwhelming, leaving no choice of means and no moment for deliberation."[4] The test for lawfulness commonly applied is that the target state is permitted to use the military instrument when it reasonably decides, as third-party observers may appraise reasonableness, that the threat to its territorial integrity or political independence is so imminent that it must respond immediately by the military instrument in order to protect itself. This test involves two important elements. First, the attacker must not only possess the subjectivity to attack the territorial integrity or the political independence of the target state but must also engage in operations that are sufficiently consequential to create in the target state reasonable apprehension of imminent destruction. Second, the responding force must be necessary and proportionate in relation to the provocation. Whether the requirements of necessity and proportionality are met must be subject to a disciplined, contextual scrutiny by reference to each feature surrounding the provocative acts and the responding measures. In addition, Article 51 of the U.N. Charter mandates that the provisional measures of response by individual states be subject to the inclusive community review process. Member states of the United Nations must report immediately to the Security Council the self-defense measures they have taken; and the Security Council, of course, is empowered with the authority and responsibility to maintain international peace and security.

A focal point of contention in applying Article 51 of the charter relates to the wording, "an armed attack." Does it mean that self-defense must always wait for an actual armed attack? Or do certain circumstances warrant what is known as "anticipatory" self-defense? The question is not a matter for mere academic exercise but a practical matter of grave concern, one of common interest and human survival in the nuclear age. The U.S. quarantine of Cuba during the missile crisis of October 1962 and Israel's destruction of an Iraqi nuclear reactor in 1981 both raised this vital question.

Two divergent views exist. The first takes a textualist view in stressing that "armed attack" means "only if armed attack," and unless and until there is an actual armed attack or process of attack, the target state cannot respond militarily in self-defense even in the face of "imminent danger." The second view holds that the U.N. Charter is not a suicide pact and that the target state cannot be expected to be a sitting duck awaiting its own destruction in this nuclear age even if a process of attack has not begun. It adds that Article 51 was designed to reaffirm, not to curtail, the customary right of self-defense. Recent state practice would appear to support the latter view, although many disagree.

The Cuban quarantine case provides an apt example. The United States imposed a quarantine (blockade) against Cuba in October 1962 in response to Cuba's importation of offensive nuclear weapons from the Soviet Union. Although the U.S. government justified its quarantine action largely in terms of authorization by the OAS, a form of regional collective self-defense, the international legal community showed keen interest in the issue of anticipatory self-defense involved. Many observers have had little difficulty in finding that the requirements of both necessity and proportionality were met by the U.S. response.

A rigorous contextual analysis at its best, made by Myres S. McDougal in the July 1963 issue of the *American Journal of International Law,* has been especially influential.[5] Appraising the Soviet threat and the American response, respectively, in terms of the salient features (participants, objectives, situation, bases of power, strategies, and outcomes) of the larger context, McDougal concluded that the quarantine measure was lawful. The threat in this instance came not from Cuba but from the Soviet Union, a superpower then as powerful as the United States. The Soviet objective was expansionist rather than conservatory. Russia was moving into an area traditionally regarded as of special importance to the United States, as symbolized for many decades by the Monroe Doctrine. The Soviet Union had never before asserted a military presence of such magnitude in this area. It was moving with offensive weapons that would cut U.S. reaction time from six or seven minutes to some three minutes. The provocative operations and subjectivities of the Soviet Union thus created reasonable apprehension of imminent danger to the territorial integrity and political independence of the United States. The U.S. military response, in concert with that of other members of the OAS, was defensive, seeking only the elimination of nuclear weapons from Cuba. It was made as limited as it could possibly have been under the circumstances. The use of the military instrument to interdict certain types of weapons on the high seas entailed the least possible interference and destruction of the bases of power of other states. The United States immediately reported its undertaking to the Security Council and sought appropriate action from that body. The quarantine, reversible in nature, was a highly measured response, entailing force only to the extent necessary to removal of the provocation. In sum, the U.S. response was a lawful exercise of self-defense in accord with customary expectations about the requirements of necessity and proportionality.

In a complaint brought before the International Court of Justice in 1984, Nicaragua charged the United States with unlawful use of force and intervention in violation of the U.N. Charter, the OAS Charter, and general principles of customary law. The United States justified its position largely in terms of collective self-defense, maintaining that because Nicaragua had carried out armed attacks on El Salvador by providing Salvadoran insurgents with arms, technical support, and military guidance, it was permissible for the United States to take necessary and proportionate measures in and against Nicaragua to help El Salvador repel the attacks. Although the United States did not participate in the proceedings at the stage of the merits, as noted in chapter 7, the court rendered its judgment on the merits on June 27, 1986, rejecting the U.S. claim of collective self-defense and declaring that there is no right to use force in self-defense except in cases of "armed attack" under "customary international law," as distinguished from "multilateral treaty law." Emphasizing that "an armed attack" is the sine qua non for the exercise of collective self-defense, the court concluded that this condition was not met — the flows of arms from Nicaraguan territory to opposition forces in El Salvador for a period through early 1981 did not constitute an armed attack. Such an interpretation is indeed a far cry from the contextual approach discussed above.[6]

SELF-HELP

Although there is a clear consensus on the inherent right of self-defense by recourse to the military instrument, serious debate continues about the permissibility of using the military instrument as a form of self-help for lesser transgressions. Though self-help has a number of equivalent synonyms (retortions, retaliations, reprisals, intervention, minor coercion, measures short of war), *self-help* is perhaps the generic term that is most useful in the present context. Self-help is broader in reference than self-defense; indeed, self-defense is the most dramatic example of self-help. Both self-help and self-defense depend for their legal characterization on the prior fact that somebody else has acted unlawfully. Self-help, even that involving the use of military force, was long regarded as vital in providing some measure of enforceability in the decentralized international system. Allowing the victim state to take enforcement into its own hands, if inclusive procedure of remedy is realistically unavailable, is an essential element in a decentralized legal order.

One view takes the position that self-help, beyond self-defense, is now impermissible. The arguments for this view may be summarized as follows: (1) Article 2(3) and 2(4) of the charter project the fundamental community policies of promoting peaceful change and of minimizing coercion; (2) Article 2(4), read in conjunction with Article 51 and the rest of the provisions contained in Chapter VII of the charter, dealing with "action with respect to threats to the peace, breaches of the peace, and acts of aggression," shows clearly that the U.N. Charter as a whole prohibits the use of military force save for self-defense and collective enforcement action (community police action); (3) the blanket prohibition of the use of force embodied in Article 2(4) suggests that self-help is inconsistent with the purposes of the United Nations and hence impermissible, a point affirmed in part by the International Court of Justice in the *Corfu Channel* case of 1949;[7] (4) highly susceptible to abuse, self-help is an instrument of aggrandizement by the powerful against the weak; and (5) in the nuclear age, when humanity lives under the shadow of nuclear holocaust, forcible self-help could readily escalate beyond management. This view, highly influential in the early years of the United Nations, has come under increasing pressure because of the contemporary realities of state practice in the use of military force.

A contrary view maintains that Article 2(4) is not a blanket prohibition of all uses of military force and expressly prohibits only threats or uses of force directed "against the territorial integrity or political independence of any state, or in any other manner inconsistent with the Purposes of the United Nations." When it seeks neither a territorial change nor a challenge to the political independence of the state concerned, an act of self-help taken in response to a prior unlawful act in order to secure compliance with international law is to help secure "justice," as enunciated in Article 2(3) of the charter, and is not inconsistent with the purposes of the organization, which are generally listed in Article 1 and the preamble to the charter. Hence, Article 2(4) is no necessary bar to an otherwise permissible act of self-help.

Although some evidence suggests that the framers of the charter intended to permit use of force only for self-defense and collective police action, this is far from conclusive. Neither is the pronouncement of the International Court of Justice in the *Corfu Channel* case that force has no place in the contemporary international law.[8] Although the court held that it was unlawful for the United Kingdom to undertake mine-sweeping operations in the channel, it did not impose much of a penalty on the United Kingdom. In fact, the court held that it was lawful for Britain to assert its rights by force in sending its warships through the straits, with guns mounted and ready for action if necessary, in response to the prior unlawful act of Albania.

In interpreting Article 2(4), it is important to consult *travaux preparatoires*, but it is even more important, as shown in chapter 16, to interpret it in the light of the entire context of the U.N. Charter, especially the major purposes of the organization and the subsequent practice. In addition to the words of the charter and preliminary negotiations, the whole subsequent flow of words and interpretation by conduct are relevant to the interpretation of what the law is today.

A critical component of the shared expectations of the framers of the charter was that the United Nations would become the effective global institution of community police action, endowed with adequate formal authority and sufficient effective power and guided by the big-power unanimity in the making of important decisions. Under this shared assumption, the charter included both Article 2(4) and Article 51, contemplating that collective machinery of law enforcement would replace self-help and there would be no need and no place for unilateral use of military force except for the inherent right of self-defense.

Unhappily, as amply shown by the practice and reality of the more than five decades since the founding of the United Nations, this fundamental shared expectation that was to be the keystone of the entire U.N. system, in its pursuit of both minimum and optimum world order, has been ruthlessly shattered. Individual nation-states continue to control the implements of military strategy, and efforts to bestow on the general community the sole privilege of permissible employment of force have been unsuccessful. Although the past decade has seen a renewal of hope for a more active Security Council, the United Nations has been unable, with rare exceptions, to take effective action to deal with conflicts that threaten world peace and security and gross violations of international law. This continues to be due largely to the paralysis of the Security Council that results from the veto power. Many states have resorted to military force in situations short of the requirements of self-defense to protect national interests.

Accordingly, in the absence of effective collective machinery to protect against lawlessness and deprivation, the remedy of self-help cannot be ruled out. The charter's general proscription of the use of force was predicated on the establishment within the United Nations of effective centralized decision and enforcement. So long as this projected condition remains unfulfilled, the general community cannot afford a paralysis that invites lawlessness and deprivation by particular states with impunity. In circumstances in which the organized general community — through an authoritative organ of the United Nations or a relevant regional organization — cannot act or cannot act with adequate dispatch, the self-help of particular states may offer the only alternative to defend the common interest in securing compliance with international law. It would otherwise be tantamount to honor lawlessness to hold that a state can violate international law with impunity, causing deprivation to other states or the international community, with no fear of response. Therefore, insofar as a self-help measure is precipitated by a prior lawless act and deprivation and conforms strictly to the international legal regulations governing the use of force — notably the principles of necessity and proportionality — such a measure constitutes a vindication and functional enforcement of international law.

Although the remedy of self-help may continue to have a place under contemporary international law, one should recognize that, in a decentralized world in which the effective power of state actors is patently discrepant, this remedy is highly susceptible to abuse and misuse. Hence, assertions of necessity and proportionality must be subjected to the most searching community scrutiny lest self-help become an impermissible weapon of the powerful against the weak. Any state engages in self-help at its own peril. The characterization of particular activities as requiring self-help partakes of the nature of a provisional determination in precisely the same way as a claim of self-defense and remains subject to both the contemporaneous appraisal of other states and to any subsequent review the organized community may eventually exercise.

No easy and dogmatic intellectual procedures distinguish genuine from spurious acts of self-help. Serious review requires contextual scrutiny. Lawfulness and unlawfulness must depend on the answers to many questions about each feature of the context, with the significance of any one feature depending on the total configuration. Some of the more important questions about relevant features may be highlighted:

Participants: Who initiates the measure of self-help? Against whom? Is the measure of self-help by or against a legitimate government or by or against segments of a community only? Is the action prompted by a prior unlawful act? If so, what unlawful act?

Perspectives: Is the action taken to secure a remedy or to put an end to a prior or continuing lawless act? Are both manifest and genuine objectives related to securing compliance with international law?

Situation: How intense are expectations of imminent irreparable loss in the absence of the recourse to the military instrument? Are the violations of international norms systematic and of long duration or sporadic and occasional?

Base Values: What are the disparities in relative strength of the responding state and the target state or entity? Do patent discrepancies in strength suggest coercion or overreaction?

Strategies: What instruments of policy could have been used? Have the diplomatic, ideological, and economic instruments been mobilized and employed before the recourse to the military instrument? Have bilateral negotiations, with or without the assistance of a third party, been conducted? Have the parties involved been willing to subject themselves to an impartial fact-finding process? Has recourse to available remedies through organized collective action been exhausted or futile?

Outcomes: With what intensity and destruction has the military instrument been used? What values were conserved and what values were destroyed? Was the use of the military instrument in proportion to the magnitude of actual deprivations or the threats of deprivation? Was the military action ended as soon as its manifest objectives were accomplished?

Note that the condition of necessity cannot be met until a prior lawless act and deprivation have been established and the inability to secure a remedy after having exhausted all available noncoercive means has been demonstrated. Unlike the case of self-defense, a situation calling for self-help rarely entails dangers of imminent destruction of the responding state, but certainly could entail a similar danger for its nationals or those of other states. In principle, the victim state is not authorized to take immediate, unilateral response. Good faith effort to obtain a remedy through exhaustion of all available, noncoercive means is imperative. Furthermore, a strong presumption is that, save in extremely rare circumstances, self-help in the form of military force in response to a prior nonmilitary coercion or action will fail the test of proportionality.

In a better-organized world, humankind might be able to dispense with a doctrine of self-help that permits a state unilaterally to employ even the military instrument where reasonably necessary against another state or entity, in response to a prior unlawful act for which a remedy is unavailable after all noncoercive procedures have been exhausted, including recourse to inclusive community machinery. Until that better organization is more nearly achieved, the task of those who are genuinely committed to human dignity values is, however, to clarify and apply a concept of self-help that will best serve the common interest in achieving at least the conditions of minimum order.

It may be noted that those who take the position of the blanket prohibition of the use of force except for self-defense and for community enforcement action tend to invoke the label of self-defense to justify any use of force that may be more properly characterized as self-help. Different doctrines may be invoked to justify the same recourse to force, and the same label may be used to mean quite different things. For instance, the U.S. bombing of Libya in April 1986, in retaliation for Libya's prior acts of terrorism, has been supported by some as a permissible self-defense and by others as a permissible self-help.

HUMANITARIAN INTERVENTION

Humanitarian intervention can be regarded as a special kind of self-help. Historically, when states have resorted to the military force to protect human rights within other states, their action has been depicted and justified in terms of the doctrine of humanitarian intervention. Reflecting natural law traditions and more secular perceptions of humanitarian responsibilities that transcend community boundaries, this doctrine symbolizes a basic human solidarity to defend the sanctity of human life and dignity. Such protection has traditionally been extended, first, to nationals abroad in order to secure compliance with the minimum standard for the treatment of aliens under customary international law and, second, to non-nationals in order to deter and end atrocious deprivations of human rights by a state against its own nationals or the nationals of third states. Sometimes the label "humanitarian intervention" is used restrictively to refer only to the latter situation. According to this doctrine, where egregious violations of human rights are occurring within a state whose government will not or cannot stop them, the general community, or in exigent circumstances a single state, may enter the territory of the defaulting state to secure an end to the outrage and compliance with minimum international standards of human rights.

The practice of humanitarian intervention gained prominence and acceptance during the nineteenth century and the early twentieth century, especially for the protection of religious minorities. Notable examples include the intervention in 1860–61 by Austria, France, Great Britain, Prussia, and Russia on behalf of the persecuted Christian population in Syria; the intervention in 1866–68 on behalf of the oppressed Christian population in Crete; the intervention in 1903–08 by Austria, France, Great Britain, Italy, and Russia against Turkey for its misrule of Macedonia; and the humanitarian intercession in 1904–16 on behalf of Armenians by the United States and other states against Turkey. With the operation of the United Nations Charter, the general proscription of military force embodied in its Article 2(4) has generated continuing controversy not only about the permissibility of self-help but also about the permissibility of humanitarian intervention under contemporary international law. This controversy has grown especially acute in recent times, with the expansion in the use of peacekeeping forces for humanitarian intervention in places like Somalia and Haiti, or Bosnia and northern Iraq.

As with self-help, again, two diametrically opposing views have been presented. The arguments in support and in rejection of humanitarian intervention follow essentially the lines of arguments and counter arguments concerning self-help.

Since we have concluded that self-help, as disciplined by strict requirements of necessity and proportionality, remains permissible, it is even easier to defend the permissibility of humanitarian intervention, again as policed by rigorous requirements of necessity and proportionality.

This is so because of the paramount policy to protect and promote human rights that pervades the U.N. Charter and a host of related human rights instruments. As expounded in chapter 12, the paramount policy of human rights has been made amply clear in the charter and in the emergence of a global bill of human rights. The protection of human rights is one of the two central purposes of the United Nations. The overriding commitment to protect and fulfill human rights, coequal with the goal to maintain peace and security, finds expression throughout the charter. Under Article 56, all member states commit themselves to "take joint and separate action in co-operation with the Organization" to achieve "universal respect for, and observance of, human rights and fundamental freedoms for all without distinction as to race, sex, language, or religion." This paramount commitment has been fortified by the vast flow of ancillary prescriptions, including the Universal Declaration of Human Rights, the International Covenant on Civil and Political Rights (and its protocols), the International Covenant on Economic, Social, and Cultural Rights, and a multitude of related documents. Given this overriding commitment to human rights, as well as the reality and widespread perception that human rights and peace and security are closely tied, the use of military force to defend human rights may emphatically serve the common interest as an aid to the maintenance of world minimum public order.

Accordingly the use of military force for purposes of genuine humanitarian necessity not only does no violence to the charter but contributes in important ways to several of the paramount goals of the United Nations, including human rights. A genuine act of humanitarian intervention, threatening neither the territorial integrity nor the political independence of the target state, is not inconsistent with the purposes of the United Nations. In conformity with the major purposes and norms of the charter, the remedy of humanitarian intervention not only remains permissible but appears to have been fortified under contemporary international law.

The continued availability in general community expectation of the remedy of humanitarian intervention would appear confirmed by recent practice. In the aftermath of the Cold War the United Nations and some nation-states have intervened forcibly in Liberia (1990), northern Iraq (1991), southern Iraq (1992), Somalia (1992), Rwanda (1994), and Haiti (1993–94). Post–Cold War crises have seen blatant and gruesome disregard for human rights, bringing the international community to intervene increasingly in affairs of nations whose citizens are subject to widespread human rights deprivations. The Bosnia-Herzegovina mission (UNPROFOR, 1992) may not be considered by all to be a true example of humanitarian intervention because the conflict was international in character, and the intervention was authorized by the Security Council.

Although the charter does not expressly recognize the right unilaterally to use military force to protect a people from their own governing (or brokendown) authorities, even in the face of genocide, starvation, disease and violence, it is clear that humanitarian intervention may be an emerging norm in international law, as necessary to both minimum and optimum world order.

Like self-help, the remedy of humanitarian intervention is a weapon for the powerful and is highly susceptible to abuse and misuse. The onerous strings attached to permissible self-help are thus equally applicable in the context of humanitarian intervention. Although the remedy cannot be precluded in a world that lacks centralized, effective enforcement, its use should be subject to vigorous contextual review by the general community for its strict conformity to the requirements of necessity and proportionality.

FROM THE LAW OF WAR TO INTERNATIONAL HUMANITARIAN LAW

The traditional international law made a conceptually rigid distinction between peace and war. Different sets of law were developed and made applicable — the law of peace, the law of war, and the law of neutrality — by reference to the existence or nonexistence of a technical state of "war" or "belligerency." The law of war, for example, deals with the commencement of war, the conduct and methods of war, certain protections for the victims of war, and the termination of war. The general dissatisfaction with this traditional approach has been resounding.

The U.N. Charter, as mentioned, has discarded the use of "war" and instead employed "the threat or use of force" and "threats to the peace, breaches of the peace, and acts of aggression" to designate a wide continuum of coercion. The war-peace dichotomy squares neither with the modern nature of "total" war nor with the contemporary reality of no-war, no-peace conditions. It has thus been suggested that "state of intermediacy" or "a third status intermediate between war and peace" would more aptly characterize the present state of world affairs.[9]

Although the U.N. Charter does away with the technical term "war," the world has not been spared the tragedies and scourges of armed conflicts of various scales — undeclared wars perhaps, but coercion, violence, armed conflicts nevertheless. Like it or not, armed conflicts, internal and transnational, remain a fact of contemporary international life.

Hence, in spite of growing dissatisfaction with the peace-war dichotomy, the traditional law of war regulating the conduct of armed conflict has not altogether lost relevance and vitality. Fundamentally speaking, two complementary policies underlie the traditional laws of war: the policy of military necessity and the policy of humanity. The policy of military necessity permits the exercise of that violence necessary to achieve legitimate belligerent objectives through conduct not otherwise proscribed, as disciplined by the requirements of relevancy and proportionality. The policy of humanity seeks to minimize unnecessary infliction of death, injury, and suffering and other destruction of values even in times of hostility, distinguishing noncombatants from combatants and directing military operations to legitimate military targets. Although it

is at times extremely difficult to strike a proper balance between the two policies, attempts have been especially pronounced in two areas: the prohibition of
certain types of weapons in warfare and the humanization of the conduct of
warfare — humane treatment of combatants as well as noncombatants.

First, the community efforts to proscribe certain types of weapons in warfare:
Beginning with the 1863 Lieber Code, which recognized a prohibition of poison, and the St. Petersburg Declaration of 1868,[10] which prohibited explosive
projectiles and incendiaries under four hundred grams, a series of treaties prohibited the employment of particular weapons in warfare. All arms, projectiles,
or materials of a nature to cause unnecessary death, injury, or suffering were
outlawed. The Geneva Protocol of Gas Warfare of 1925 banned the use of
asphyxiating, poisonous, or other gases and of bacteriological warfare. Efforts
continue to fortify the prohibitions against biological and chemical warfare, as
exemplified by the Convention on the Prohibition of the Development, Production, and Stockpiling of Bacteriological (Biological) and Toxin Weapons and on
Their Destruction of 1972. The advent of the atomic bomb has brought notable
efforts to prohibit the use, manufacture, and testing of nuclear weapons.

A second major effort was made in the humanization of the conduct of armed
conflicts. This corpus of law, both customary and conventional, has received
renewed attention in recent years. Increasingly, this branch of international law
has been approached in terms of "international humanitarian law in armed
conflicts" or even "human rights in times of armed conflict" instead of laws
and regulations of warfare. It is part of the contemporary global human rights
movement, the distinct emphasis of which is on the human rights dimension.
Armed conflicts may be unavoidable, but humanity, not barbarism, must be
made to prevail even amid a hopelessly brutal situation.

At the core of international humanitarian law are the four Geneva Conventions of 1949 and Protocols I and II Additional to these conventions, concluded
in 1977. The Geneva Conventions were built on the Hague Conventions of
1899 and 1907.

The four Geneva Conventions are the Geneva Convention for the Amelioration of the Condition of the Wounded and Sick in Armed Forces in the Field; the
Geneva Convention for the Amelioration of the Condition of the Wounded,
Sick, and Shipwrecked Members of Armed Forces at Sea; the Geneva Convention Relative to the Treatment of Prisoners of War; and the Geneva Convention
Relative to the Protection of Civilian Persons in Time of War. In force since
1950, these conventions have received wide adherence by more than 180 states
and are considered to reflect customary international law.

As their titles clearly indicate, these conventions set forth detailed prescriptions for humane treatment of wounded and disabled members of the armed

forces (on land or at sea), prisoners of war, and civilian populations. They make a fundamental distinction between international armed conflicts (armed conflicts between two or more states or "belligerents" in the case of a traditional civil war) and internal armed conflicts ("armed conflict not of an international character occurring in the territory of one of the High Contracting Parties," or insurgencies that are localized). The bulk of the provisions are directed to international armed conflicts. Only one provision in the 1949 conventions — generally known as common Article 3 (and Protocol II) — prescribes rules for application to internal armed conflicts.

Article 3 requires "each Party to the conflict" (notably the government, the insurgent group) to accord humane treatment to all "persons taking no active part in the hostilities, including members of armed forces who have laid down their arms and those placed *hors de combat* by sickness, wounds, detention, or any other cause" without invidious distinction on such grounds as race, religion, sex, and wealth. The article categorically prohibits certain acts, including "violence to life and person," "taking of hostages," "outrages upon personal dignity," and arbitrary sentencing and execution. It requires that the wounded and sick be "collected and cared for" and grants a special role for the International Committee of the Red Cross in offering "its services to the Parties to the conflict." Common Article 3 is now considered to be customary law and to provide a minimum set of rights and duties even during an international armed conflict.

Protocols I and II, entering into force in 1978, were designed to supplement and reinforce the four Geneva Conventions. Protocol I in general relates to international armed conflicts, and Protocol II relates to internal armed conflicts. The line between the two is becoming increasingly difficult to draw in today's world.

Of foremost concern, as humankind lives under the constant threat of nuclear holocaust, is the question of lawfulness of nuclear weapons under contemporary international law. Some people think it an exercise in futility to attempt to answer this question because "vital national interests" would be involved in any use of nuclear weapons and these weapons do not lend themselves to effective regulation. In the 1980s, however, the growing worldwide demands for effective control of nuclear weapons (no-first-strike pledge, nuclear freeze, nuclear-free zones, and so on) renewed serious interest in this question on the part of the international legal community.

The question can be examined in terms of nuclear weapons possession and use. Community efforts have resulted in modest successes in banning nuclear tests in the atmosphere, space, and water, but it appears that possession of nuclear weapons per se cannot be realistically banned, especially in view of recent tests by India and Pakistan. The post–Cold War era is still a nuclear age, and nuclear weapons continue to reflect the realities of effective world power and to serve as weapons of deterrence and defense. Barring a genuine, comprehensive disarmament, based on effective verification and mutual trust, humankind cannot realistically expect to completely dismantle existing nuclear arsenals. The INF treaty between the United States and the former Soviet Union, which has continued in effect under successor states, has been a promising first step. With developing countries such as India and Pakistan insistent upon becoming nuclear powers, however, there is still a long way to go.

The debate has thus centered on the lawfulness of the use of nuclear weapons. Opinions diverge greatly. One view holds that the use of nuclear weapons is per se unlawful. The opposite view maintains that the use of nuclear weapons is lawful. A third view takes the position that the lawfulness of the use of nuclear weapons depends on the context involved and even the type of nuclear projectile.

In 1996, the International Court of Justice, at the request of the World Health Organization and the General Assembly, handed down an advisory opinion on the legality of the threat or use of nuclear weapons.[11] The decision was essentially a "nondecision," because the court, while concluding that the threat or use of nuclear force is "generally contrary" to international law, was unable to conclude definitively either way; the opinion allows the use of nuclear weapons in "extreme circumstances of self defense."[12] Such an opinion illustrates the limitations of a United Nations still dominated by limitations of the national sovereignty mindset and the shortcomings of the rule-oriented, positivist approach.

To reach a decision, the court first decided that the relevant applicable law was that of the rules of armed conflict, as provided in various international agreements including Article 51 of the U.N. Charter, which provides for the legitimacy of self-defense. The court decided that the requirements of proportionality and necessity did not necessarily exclude nuclear force where a nation's ultimate sovereignty was threatened.

The various international agreements prohibiting poisonous, chemical, and biological weapons were also examined, but because such treaties were concluded without literal reference to nuclear weapons, the court found them inapplicable.

Nor would the ICJ accept the existence of an emerging peremptory norm based on efforts to restrain the nuclear camp. Rather, the court was swayed more by the reasoning of the states that argued that the acceptance of nuclear agreements by non-nuclear states (such as the Treaty on Non-Proliferation of 1968) demonstrated international consent to the policy of deterrence rather than any emerging norm of prohibition. Also, the court agreed with the nuclear weapon states that these partial agreements only confirmed the fact that there exists no total prohibition on the use of these weapons. Trapped by a positivist approach, the court was bound by precedent without regard to the effects of its decision on the values and goals of the law examined.

Despite considering customary law, consisting of the principles of neutrality and humanitarian law applicable in armed conflict (*ius in bello*), the court stated that the use of nuclear weapons was not necessarily at variance with these principles. It was also argued that the numerous General Assembly resolutions proclaiming the illegality of nuclear weapons use should have normative value, even if not binding. The court, however, noted that such resolutions had been adopted with substantial numbers of negative votes and abstentions. Because consent is a key issue in the interpretation of international agreement, United Nations resolutions have the force of law only with overwhelming support of the member states.

The opinion appears to reflect three widely diverging views. The first view holds that use of nuclear weapons would be unlawful because it would be contrary to the twin policies of military necessity and humanity that infuse the entire law of war, customary and conventional. Thus, many dissenters relied on the Martens Clause as a peremptory norm that rules out altogether any threat or use of such weapons; community proscriptions of destructive and lethal weapons would extend by analogy to nuclear weapons. Because the use of nuclear weapons would obliterate the traditional distinction between civilian populations and military targets, their threat or use is illegal.

To buttress their position, supporters of this view have drawn on diverse sources, ranging from customary law, to treaty law, to national judicial decisions (for example, the notable *Shimoda* case decided by the District Court of Tokyo in 1963).[13] They have attached a particular weight to Resolution 1653, Declaration on the Prohibition of the Use of Nuclear and Thermo-Nuclear Weapons, adopted by the General Assembly in 1961.[14] This declaration, in pronouncing the unlawfulness of the use of nuclear weapons, aptly sums up the thrust of the familiar argument:

(a) The use of nuclear and thermo-nuclear weapons is contrary to the spirit, letter and aims of the United Nations and, as such, a direct violation of the Charter of the United Nations;

(b) The use of nuclear and thermo-nuclear weapons would exceed the scope of war and cause indiscriminate suffering and destruction to mankind and civilization and, as such, is contrary to the rule of international law and to the laws of humanity;

(c) The use of nuclear and thermo-nuclear weapons is a war directed not against an enemy or enemies alone but also against mankind in general, since the peoples of the world not involved in such a war will be subjected to all the evils generated by the use of such weapons;

(d) Any State using nuclear and thermo-nuclear weapons is to be considered as violating the Charter of the United Nations, as acting contrary to the laws of humanity and as committing a crime against mankind and civilization.

Those who flatly assert that the use of nuclear weapons is lawful rely more or less on a traditional maxim in international law, attributable to the *S.S. Lotus* decision,[15] that states are permitted to do that which is not expressly prohibited. This second view was held by Judge Schwebel, who stated that prohibition "would be an aggressor's charter."[16] In addition, this camp refuses to view nuclear weapons contextually in terms of their fundamental differences from ordinary weapons, and asserts that analogies drawn from the laws of wars past are inapposite. It would indeed be the height of absurdity to assert that a state is free to risk the destruction of the world on the ground that nowhere is that competence expressly denied, but this was the reasoning put forth. It is clear, however, that the destruction of humankind would deprive the sovereignty of all states of all meaning.

The third view, more contextual in its approach, calls special attention to the realistic role of deterrence played by nuclear strategies in the maintenance of contemporary world public order and to the critical need of approximate conjunction between expectations of authority and control. This appears to be the view relied upon by Judge Fleischauer, who balanced the principles of humanitarian law, neutrality, and self-defense. Although all have equal ranking, self-defense trumps the others. Thus was permission granted in the noted paragraph 2E of the decision to allow the use of nuclear arms in an emergency, and to accept the policy of deterrence. This view eschews a per se rule but stresses a particular context. Some nuclear projectiles, in fact, are "tactical" in nature, posing minimum risk outside legitimate military targets.

The dissenters, including Judge Weermantry and Judge Shahabuddeen, pointed out some contemporary developments that should be brought to bear on legal thought. Article 2 [4] of the U.N. Charter has significantly restricted the right of nation states to resort to force. The world has become interdependent, with a movement away from state sovereignty and toward a universal international community. And because nuclear weapons have the potential to destroy civilization, the law of war must be reoriented to face the new reality. The rules must be examined not in a vacuum, but contextually, in view of the purpose and relevance to the shaping and sharing of values.

PART SEVEN

OUTCOMES

The outcomes of the comprehensive world constitutive process of authoritative decision are the various decisions taken when making and applying law to manifold problems. These decisions may be conveniently classified into seven functions: intelligence (information), promotion, prescription, invocation, application, termination, and appraisal. The effectiveness and the economy with which these functions are performed directly affect the quality of protection afforded by international law. Thanks to continuous improvement of every feature of the constitutive process, the performance of each function has improved. The relevant decisions appear to be becoming more comprehensive in embracing all necessary policy functions; more inclusive in the extension of participants and interactions affecting common interests; more rational in the degree of conformity to the basic public order demands and expectations of the world's peoples; and more integrative by molding the potentially divisive claims of peoples into the perception and fact of common interest.

These decision functions, though distinctive, are closely interrelated. Each contributes to, and is affected by, the performance of every other function.

20

The Intelligence Function

The intelligence (information) function entails gathering, processing, and disseminating information essential to make decisions. Facts must be explored in order to perform each decision function. The intelligence process directly affects this performance. The availability of a continuing flow of dependable, comprehensive, and relevant information is essential to recommend concrete proposals in pursuit of the common interest, to generate rational prescriptions, to initiate timely invocation against a violation of international law, to secure effective application of norms with minimal coercion, to foster a timely end to obsolete prescriptions, and to undertake a critical yet constructive appraisal. In a decentralized, state-centered world in which mobilization of world public opinion plays a crucial role in articulating and defending the common interest, effective and continuing exposure to the facts of compliance or noncompliance of norms is vital to maintain world order.

Most intelligence gathering is traditionally done by the officials of nation-states. This is one of the oldest activities that governments undertake. Some of these activities have been legal and some illegal. Though governmental agencies, such as the CIA and the defunct KGB, are well known for their intelligence task, other officials and governmental agencies do gather, process, and disseminate information in the broadest sense.

The role of diplomatic officials merits some consideration. An important task of diplomats is to gather intelligence of all kinds to facilitate diplomatic and other strategies of influence. Most information is gathered from public sources, but information gathered by covert agents often supplements it. States generally maintain secrecy regarding matters of a vital or sensitive nature, and secrecy breeds curiosity, suspicion, and anxiety. Thus, great efforts are often made to penetrate the veil of secrecy, including breaking communication codes, wiretapping telephones, and planting electronic devices in diplomatic missions. The diplomatic missions themselves may employ electronic surveillance devices to intercept telephone, radio, and other communications in the host country. Are such activities compatible with the policy of affording diplomatic privileges and immunities? In spite of a tendency toward routinization and mutual tolerance, excesses and abuses in this area on occasion do exacerbate difficulties in interstate relations. In 1893, for example, the French government was compelled to recall virtually the entire staff of its legation at Copenhagen because of the abortive French attempt to secure, through an intermediary, information concerning Anglo-Russian relations. Contrast this with the following modern incident: In September 1985 the United Kingdom ordered the ouster of twenty-five Soviet officials after a Soviet defector, the chief of the British branch of the KGB, identified them as spies. The Soviet Union retaliated by ordering the expulsion of twenty-five Britons, including diplomats, embassy staff members, journalists, and business people. The expulsion of six more Russians by the United Kingdom was further matched by the Soviet ouster of six more Britons.

States have long used the guise of domestic jurisdiction (noninterference in internal affairs) to insulate events within their borders from outside scrutiny. The press blackout imposed in the autumn of 1985 on the national and international news media by the Botha government of South Africa illustrates how power elites seek to frustrate the intelligence function. To minimize the effects of information gathering by antiapartheid governments, organizations, and individuals, media coverage of violence, military rule in certain nonwhite districts, and even funeral processions was outlawed.

International governmental organizations are increasingly engaged in gathering information, making studies, and dispatching fact-finding missions, in spite of state reluctance to cooperate. Similarly, the role of private associations in such activities has grown, operating both within states and beyond their borders.

In recent times demands have increased for better information about the conduct of states and world conditions. Many voices are being raised in international organizations and private associations, and the geographic range of demands is extending to remote areas of the globe. People are agitating for fuller information about the conditions that affect security, development, the environment, human rights, and so on. Many intelligence activities perforce must go beyond the boundaries of any state. The process of disseminating information is made easier by a global network of mass communications. Consequently, there has been an immense flow of information about the shaping and sharing of values around the globe and about the conditions under which security, development, human rights, and so on can be secured.

International governmental organizations increasingly play a vital role in information gathering, processing, and dissemination through the bureaucratic structures. Specific authority is conferred on various U.N. structures and other international governmental entities. The General Assembly is empowered to initiate studies to promote international cooperation in the economic, social, cultural, educational, and health fields and to foster better protection and fulfillment of human rights. The Economic and Social Council is authorized to make or initiate studies and reports concerning international economic, social, cultural, educational, health, and related matters. The council is further authorized to take proper steps to obtain regular reports from the specialized agencies and to request member states and the specialized agencies to provide information pertaining to matters that fall within its competence.

In performance, informational activities vary and include seminars of all kinds, fellowship programs, advisory services of experts, special studies, exchanges of information and documentation, technical assistance, press and information services, the reporting system, fact-finding missions, and on-the-spot observation and investigation. The U.N. Secretariat provides formally within its cellular bureaucracy for the gathering, processing, and dissemination of information about various problems.

A continuing flow of information reaches the U.N. Secretariat from a variety of sources, including speeches made in the general debate of the General Assembly and in other U.N. bodies, written reports from other international governmental organizations, oral and written communications between U.N. officials and national delegates, information centers, field missions, and observations and findings of visiting missions, and a host of U.N. committees, studies, and researches. The Economic and Social Council and its network of regional economic commissions, UNCTAD, WTO, and UNDP collect, process, and spread information regarding transnational wealth processes. The World Bank group and the International Monetary Fund are particularly concerned with data about the fluctuations of national economies and transnational monetary trends. UNESCO engages in informational activities relating to trends in enlightenment and skills. The concern of the International Labor Organization (ILO) extends to sectors of wealth, skill, and well-being. The World Health Organization gathers and disseminates information about health and safety conditions around the globe, and the Food and Agriculture Organization assembles and spreads information concerning the world's food resources and supplies. The United Nations Environment Programme (UNEP) collects and spreads information about the world environment. The United Nations High Commissioner for Refugees (UNHCR) is an important center for gathering and disseminating information about the plight of the world's refugees. This comprehensive flow of information, as further supplemented and fortified by various regional organizations, extends to every value sector.

International governmental organizations rely heavily on the cooperation of nation-states in performing the intelligence function. Since states remain the primary gatherers and disseminators of information, the world constitutive process must rely extensively on government reports in many matters. The League of Nations instituted the government reporting system in relation to mandated territories and the international regime of minority protection. Under the United Nations system, governmental reports on trust territories and non-self-governing territories are required by its charter. The Economic and Social Council, under Article 64(1) of the charter, may arrange with U.N. member states to "obtain reports on the steps taken to give effect to its own recommendations and to recommendations on matters falling within its competence made by the General Assembly."

In human rights, the reporting system has become an important channel to obtain information about conditions of human rights in various communities. This system is established under the U.N. Commission on Human Rights and in most of the transnational human rights instruments, especially the two international covenants on human rights and the International Convention on the Elimination of All Forms of Racial Discrimination. The creation of the post of high commissioner indicates recognition of this system's increasing importance to the global monitoring of human rights violations. Though many states may be delinquent in filing required reports or self-serving in their submitted reports, this system has become an important institutional feature by which to obtain pertinent information, especially when it is coupled with the opportunity to examine, in situ or in open session, the country concerned. Even self-serving reports can affect a domestic legal process, making an impact on attitudes and behavior.

An important method of obtaining dependable information is on-the-spot investigations in the form of fact-finding commissions. This practice antedates the emergence of contemporary international organization and has long been employed by nation-states, both bilaterally and multilaterally. It gained wide acceptance especially at the Hague Convention of 1899. International governmental organizations have since adopted this technique and used it in a wide range of contexts. The General Assembly has established commissions of inquiry and directed them into the field to collect information relating to various questions. The International Labor organization uses this technique in the form of its Committee of Experts. The committee solicits information from local employer and worker organizations and receives the formal national reports submitted to the ILO. This fact-finding method has proved highly effective.

Nation-states are notorious in their resistance to on-the-spot investigations of human rights or other matters, in the name of "sovereignty" or "domestic jurisdiction." In United Nations history, the General Assembly's dispatch of a human rights mission in 1963 to investigate the oppression of Buddhists in South Vietnam was a notable exception, thanks to a unique combination of factors. In such other areas as southern and central Africa, the Israeli-occupied territories, and Iraq, efforts at on-the-spot-investigations have been frustrated.

The tendency of nation-states toward insulation has been remedied somewhat by the increasing role played by nonstate actors in the world arena. Channels of information are open to many other actors — not only international governmental organizations but also pressure groups and private associations.

The growing role of pressure groups and private associations in the world constitutive process has made them an indispensable source of information about economic development, the environment, human rights, and so on. Because these nongovernmental organizations (NGOs) tend to focus attention on the particular value process in which they specialize, they often possess a wealth of information in their areas. An increasing number of NGOs have sought and attained consultative status in relation to the Economic and Social Council of the United Nations and from this position disseminate to the world at large information about the value sectors of their concern. Other NGOs, national and transnational, assemble and spread information through unofficial communication channels that eventually reach both transnational and national decision makers. These organizations, representing every value sector, afford a vital dimension in the intelligence function, supplying and disseminating information that is often otherwise unavailable. Although these organizations are diverse and may present conflicting information, the aggregate flow of information generated and disseminated by them likely ensures the sifting of fact from falsehood or fantasy. The very diversity of NGOs may also aid in policing special interests in light of the common interest of a more inclusive community.

The recent proliferation of international governmental organizations and the expanded participation of political parties, pressure groups, and private associations in the constitutive process have enormously increased facilities to gather, process, and disseminate globally the information essential to rational decision. The developing technology of observation and communication through various instruments promises to augment this potential, especially with cooperation on a scale larger than ever before.

Diplomats continue to play their traditional role in gathering information, but new techniques of information gathering, especially electronic surveillance against and from foreign legations, raise new problems. In addition to electronic developments, other modern intelligence-gathering "devices," such as chemical tracers, or "spy dust," are of more questionable legality. In 1985, before the Soviet Union fell, the United States claimed that the KGB was using a potentially harmful invisible chemical agent, applied indirectly to embassy personnel and other Americans in the Soviet Union to track their movements and contacts, presumably by spreading it on doorknobs and steering wheels they would be likely to touch. The Soviet government denied these allegations, but such accusations regarding covert intelligence-gathering often pass between nation-states engaged in "high-tech" intelligence methods.[1]

Another sensitive area relates to the lawfulness of collecting information about coastal states by electronic means from the high seas. The seizure of the USS *Pueblo* by North Korea on January 23, 1968, created considerable controversy about such electronic reconnaissance from the high seas. There was some disagreement on the questions of fact. The North Korean government accused the ship of the deliberate intrusion into their territorial sea (twelve miles as they and most states so claimed), but the United States denied this allegation. The North Korean government did not claim the authority to seize a ship engaged in intelligence missions on the high seas but asserted that the ship had deliberately intruded into its territorial waters and was engaged in non-innocent passage. It would appear that international law in principle does not ban electronic reconnaissance from the high seas (or, it may be noted, from outer space) and that the coastal state cannot interfere with foreign warships or aircraft engaged in such electronic reconnaissance unless they enter territorial waters.

Outer space provides a vast new arena for various activities involving the collection of important information, as exemplified by the use of reconnaissance satellites for strategic purposes, commercial espionage, and remote sensing of information about vital resources on the earth.

The Outer Space Treaty, in Article 4, provides that the moon and other celestial bodies be used "exclusively for peaceful purposes." Article 4, however, does not contain the same blanket mandate with regard to spacecraft in earth orbit — it provides instead that nuclear weapons and other weapons of mass destruction shall not be placed in orbit around the earth. The difference in formulation is significant, having to do especially with the permissibility of using spacecraft in earth orbit for reconnaissance. More generally, Article 3 requires that activities be conducted "in the interest of maintaining international peace and security," but such a requirement does not prohibit reconnaissance serving peace and security in the common interest (that is, "in the interests of all countries" as with the meaning of Article 1). In the course of negotiating the

Outer Space Treaty, the former Soviet Union, as a "closed society," contended that the use of satellites for reconnaissance purposes was unlawful and should be banned by the treaty. The United States emphatically disagreed. The use of reconnaissance satellites would prove critical in verifying compliance with disarmament agreements. This was in keeping with President Eisenhower's call during the Cold War for "open skies," on the belief that only by candidly revealing to each other the state of their military establishments could the Soviet Union and the United States ensure peace. Eisenhower called for each nation to engage in continual overflights of the other so that any attempts at large-scale attack would be impossible to conceal. Intelligence-gathering activities were thus seen as vital to maintain peace in a divided world, especially in the absence of open societies. The open skies policy was thought to be a way of bringing intelligence gathering out in the open, to prevent some of the problems and dangers associated with covert efforts.

In regard to remote sensing of the earth's resources, developing nations increasingly demand that their resources not be examined or analyzed without their prior consent and that they be able to gain access to, and exercise some control over, the data collected by remote sensing satellites. In the contemporary information society, information, of course, is an important base not only for enlightenment but also for wealth, power, and other values. The legal issues stemming from remote sensing involve conflicting facts. Although the earth's resources are without doubt subject to the sovereignty of the state in which they are located, this does not preclude activities outside the state's territorial domain that have no immediate instate impact. Problems will arise when an attempt is made to use the information in the sensed state. It has been argued that there is no need to control space sensing because control of the resources remains in the state's hands. This ignores the role of information in the marketplace. The state's supreme authority could be abridged by such a use of information gathered by remote sensing, and so controls of some kind have been called for.

In spite of the great potentials of science-based technology, it remains difficult to obtain a continuing flow of dependable and comprehensive information relevant to rational decision making for security, development, human rights, and other matters. Even where information has been gathered and processed, access to that information is much more than a question of referral to appropriate sources. Required also is the ability to comprehend and use the knowledge gained. For example, when information vital to global or individual national environmental management is only or most readily obtainable within a particular country or region, political or other barriers may interfere with its transfer. The United States and the former Soviet Union recognized that the exchange of environmental information could transcend political differences, and were able to come to a bilateral Agreement on Cooperation in the Field of Environmental Protection.

In the post–Cold War world, it is hoped that new threats to global security, such as ozone depletion and global warming, can be better met through the use of American spy satellite photographs from the 1960s. The declassification of these photos in 1995 marked the beginning of a new spirit of cooperation and the decline of Cold-War-era secrecy, and the photographs will hold great meaning for scientists, scholars, and environmentalists studying environmental change.

It is a commonplace that the nation-state remains unwilling to subject itself to effective external scrutiny. A greater difficulty is the effective processing and use of available information. Considerable interstate controversy still surrounds the subject of prior consultation concerning proposed activities. Such information is vital to project the impact on the environment or resources of bordering states. The duty to provide official and public knowledge of technical data relating to probable environmental consequences of proposed activities and the overall obligation of information and prior consultation have been accepted in General Assembly Resolution 3129, but the content and means of such notification have to be agreed on and institutionalized.

Our data-rich civilization has no dearth of facts but, rather, suffers from an information explosion. Information is out there waiting to be tapped. It is critical that it be collected, processed, and disseminated to meet effectively and in a timely manner the ongoing, and often pressing, needs of rational decision making. A notable shortcoming is the lack of a comprehensive conception of the goals and ramifications in gathering, processing, and disseminating information. Another is the absence of a centralized clearinghouse procedure capable of absorbing and consolidating the many fragmented items of information into a coherent, contextual, and comprehensive whole. Only with such a comprehensive frame of reference can intelligence efforts yield significant, cumulative impact on the making of timely and rational decisions.

21

The Promoting Function

The promoting function refers to the advocacy of policy alternatives, including taking initiatives to attain the enactment of prescriptions and mobilizing opinion toward particular policies. It adds the intensity of demand to expectation. Three sequences are often involved: the exploration of facts; the formulation of demands; and the propagation of demands by mobilizing people and resources to secure necessary commitments. In this function, effective power brings its influence distinctively to bear on authoritative community policy.

Of primary importance is the promotion of common rather than special interests. An integrated policy should be encouraged through channels of promotion open to all participants engaged in effective means of persuasion.

The promoting function has historically been performed by all groups and individuals holding or participating in processes of effective power. These promoters are sometimes governmental officials but are often active members of political parties, pressure groups, and private associations. A principal function of political parties is to organize and promote explicit programs. Pressure groups are concerned with both general and particular policy purposes. Private associations, dedicated to values other than power, seek to shape and share their specialized values. These groups and individuals operate through a variety of organizational techniques and a range of mass communication media. Promotional messages are directed not only to official and effective elites but also to general audiences. Promoters create and maintain an ever-expanding network of organizations and contacts about the world. Besides small-group bargaining, they engender a massive flow of propaganda and agitation. Their ongoing activities are crucial in managing and mobilizing world public opinion and in transforming policy alternatives into authoritative prescription and application.

The increasing democratization of participation in world processes of effective power, the availability and openness of the new structures of authority, and the modern means of communication have brought a new comprehensiveness and intensity to the active advocacy of competing policy alternatives before authoritative decision makers. The essence of promotional strategies is effective and provocative communication. As such, promotion often involves elements of intense demands, verging at times on coercion, characterized by the agitations of elite groups in order to provoke the formulation of authoritative prescriptions. Coercive strategies, however, have no place in the promotional process of a public order of human dignity.

The nation-state, with its dominant control of effective power, traditionally played a leading role in transnational promotional activities. For such activities nation-state officials do not require any particular authorization; indeed, much of the framework of international law is their charter.

The importance attached to the promotional role of international governmental organizations testifies to the imperative need for transnational cooperation. The General Assembly, for example, is authorized by the United Nations Charter to recommend international cooperation in the economic, social, cultural, educational, and health fields and to help protect and fulfill human rights. A similar mandate is extended to the Economic and Social Council. The General Assembly, the Economic and Social Council, and specialized agencies have made innumerable recommendations concerning multiple values and problems. Many of the recommendations have further matured into either multilateral treaties or customary international law.

Increasingly evident, as discussed in chapter 4, is the prominent role played by nongovernmental organizations (pressure groups and private associations) in fostering the achievement of both minimum and optimum world order. Many nongovernmental organizations have acquired consultative status with the Economic and Social Council and with other international governmental organizations (such as ILO, UNESCO, WHO, FAO, and ITU). Depending on their recognized status, such organizations may be permitted to be present at the council's deliberations or even suggest items for inclusion in the provisional agenda. Many U.N. recommendations and decisions in various fields have resulted, directly or indirectly, from the initiatives and efforts of nongovernmental organizations and associations.

To pool their resources and coordinate their activities, to minimize duplication and maximize the use of resources, and to extend their reach and influence, NGOs have increasingly formed larger umbrella organizations. Notable examples include the Union of International Associations, the Conference of Non-Governmental Organizations, the International Coalition for Development Action, the International Confederation for Disarmament and Peace, the International Council of Scientific Unions, the Non-Governmental Organization Committee on Human Rights, the Non-Governmental Organizations Forum to the Advancement of Women, and the International Baby Food Action Network.

A strategy employed with increasing frequency and effectiveness by NGOs in promotional activities is to organize parallel forums to complement and support international conferences convened by the United Nations or other international governmental organizations. Notable among these special conferences are the Conference on the Human Environment (Stockholm, 1972); Habitat: United Nations Conference on Human Settlements (Vancouver, 1976); the World Conference of the U.N. Decade for Women (Copenhagen, 1980); the World Conference to Review and Appraise the Achievements of the Decade for Women (Nairobi, 1985); the United Nations Conference on Environment and Development (Rio de Janeiro, 1992); the World Conference on Human Rights (Vienna, 1993); and the Beijing Women's Conference (1995). Through such parallel activities, NGOs are able to channel world attention to matters of global concern and to enhance their collective influence on governmental decision making processes. For example, while the Seventh Special Session of the General Assembly on Development and International Cooperation was in session in September 1975, the NGO Forum on the World Economic Order was simultaneously held at U.N. headquarters in New York to both support and parallel the official proceedings, with 500 representatives from 165 organizations in attendance. By 1995, the Beijing Conference attracted so many NGOs that the parallel forum was the largest gathering of NGOs in the United Nations' history: approximately 35,000 people from more than one hundred countries attended the forum, in contrast with the 8,000 people who attended the NGO forum at Copenhagen in 1985.[1]

Nongovernmental organizations and associations have been extremely active in such fields as human rights, advancement and equality for women, environmental protection, economic development, peace, and disarmament.

In human rights, many NGOs have taken an extremely active role in specialized seminars, established and maintained close contacts with governmental delegates, and occasionally supplied the initiative to prepare draft conventions. At the United Nations conference in San Francisco of 1945, the campaign waged by a number of NGOs was instrumental in the ultimate incorporation of the comprehensive human rights provisions in the charter. Since the creation of the Commission on Human Rights, nongovernmental organizations have actively promoted the formulation and enactment of an International Bill of Human Rights (including the Universal Declaration of Human Rights and the two covenants) and various other human rights instruments designed to protect particular categories of people or dealing with particular subjects. In the early years when the commission was preoccupied with formulating human rights standards and norms, for example, the International League for Human Rights spent an enormous amount of time and resources on extensive research and reporting for the Economic and Social Council, the commission, and its Sub-commission on Prevention of Discrimination and Protection of Minorities. The adoption in 1966 of the Optional Protocol to the International Covenant on Civil and Political Rights, affording the remedy of individual petitions for the rights protected in the covenant, was largely due to the intense and sustained effort of NGOs. The campaign to abolish torture, waged by Amnesty International and joined by the International Commission of Jurists and others, led the General Assembly to adopt the Declaration Against Torture in 1975 and the Convention Against Tortu   and Other Cruel, Inhuman or Degrading Treatment or Punishment in 1984.

Nongovernmental organizations have been no less active in the drive toward equality of the sexes and the advancement of the status of women. They have taken various initiatives and have greatly affected the agendas of the Commission on the Status of Women, culminating in the adoption of both the Declaration (1967)[2] and the Convention on the Elimination All Forms of Discrimination Against Women (1979) and other special conventions to protect women. From the International Women's Year (1975) to the Beijing Women's Conference (1995), women's groups have accelerated their efforts toward equality, development, and peace and look toward the twenty-first century. The importance of NGOs to the cause of women is such that the General Assembly, in Resolution 40/108, "Implementation of the Nairobi Forward-Looking Strategies for the Advancement of Women," adopted in December 1985, specifically acknowledged the constructive contribution made by NGOs in general and the Non-Governmental Organizations Forum to the Advancement of Women in particular and invited their continued participation in implementing the strategies formulated at the Nairobi Conference.[3] Ten years later, the Chinese Organizing Committee for the Beijing Conference slyly moved the location of the NGO Forum to a remote site thirty-five miles away, indicating the considerable impact these groups are now recognized as having on the promotion of human rights.

Nongovernmental organizations have been vital in the global effort toward environmental protection. The Stockholm Conference on the Environment in 1972 heralded a new era of humankind's concern for global environment when the conference secretary-general, Maurice Strong, reached out to multitudes of nongovernmental organizations, including those not in formal consultative status with the United Nations. As a result, more than 550 NGOs attended the

Stockholm Conference, and draft proposals written by one prominent NGO were considered and adopted.

In 1972 the United Nations established a new agency, the United Nations Environment Program (UNEP), providing a built-in structural relationship between environmental NGOs and the U.N. The wide participation on the part of nongovernmental organizations has contributed mightily to the continuing vigor of the global environmental movement. One of the largest United Nations conferences in history was the 1992 Earth Summit at Rio (UNCED), the first global gathering of heads of state on environment and development. The Earth Summit drew some 9,000 NGOs as well as delegates from 175 nations and representatives from numerous IGOs and U.N. agencies. In 1997, for the first time ever, NGOs addressed a special session of the General Assembly on implementation of "Agenda 21," the program of action adopted at Rio.

In the efforts to protect the earth's remaining whales that led to the commercial whaling ban of 1986 by the International Whaling Commission, nongovernmental organizations played a vital role by lobbying governments and organizing boycotts of fish and other products from whaling countries. These environmental groups continue to oppose efforts by some countries to ease the ban for "scientific" purposes.

Development issues in the north-south context have attracted increasing attention and interest from NGOs. This is exemplified by the wide participation in the NGO Forum on the World Economic Order, as described above, and at the Earth Summit, where "sustainable development" emerged as the dominant theme. The formation of the International Coalition for Development Action represents an important attempt by many national NGOs to extend their collective influence in the development area, while the Overseas Development Council, created in 1969, has raised consciousness about north-south issues and global interdependence in the developed countries, especially the United States. The World Trade Organization, established as successor to the GATT, has provided for consultative relations with nongovernmental organizations, in the interest of promoting environmentally responsible free trade. Article V (2) of the WTO Charter reads as follows: "The General Council may make appropriate arrangements for consultation and cooperation with nongovernmental organizations concerned with matters related to those of the World Trade Organization." Nongovernmental organizations will be invaluable in reconciling the conflicting demands for trade, environment, and green growth.[4]

In the related area of food and hunger, the role of NGOs is no less important, as exemplified by their extensive involvement in the committee and other inner workings of the U.N.-sponsored World Food Conference held in Rome in 1974.

Some NGOs, such as Church World Service and the World Conference on Religion and Peace, were even made members of drafting committees at the conference. Oxfam, based in Great Britain, has been involved in rendering humanitarian assistance and in a wide range of other activities. Although its initial efforts focused on postwar European relief, over time the organization has expanded its scope from short-term to long-term solutions to the hunger problems in Africa. Believing that helping the third world countries to develop and improve living conditions is essential for world peace, Oxfam has established contact at the grass-roots level as well as the governmental level and fostered a spirit of partnership and brotherhood. It has an extensive network of field specialists who guide and train local people in agricultural and medical areas.

To promote peace and disarmament, numerous peace research institutions around the globe have engaged in research and made recommendations to their national governments and to relevant transnational entities. Nuclear issues have attracted an array of NGOs to the field, including the Campaign for Nuclear Disarmament, the European Nuclear Disarmament Movement, the International Confederation for Disarmament and Peace, the NGO Disarmament Committee, International Physicians for Prevention of Nuclear War (IPPNW), the Pugwash Movement, the Union of Concerned Scientists, the World Council of Churches, and the National Conference of Bishops. International Physicians for Prevention of Nuclear War was the recipient of the Nobel Peace Prize for 1985, for its dedicated work toward combating the nuclear threat by disseminating reliable information and by heightening humankind's awareness of the catastrophes of nuclear warfare. With a membership of 200,000 physicians in 1997, IPPNW has been able to transcend ideological and cultural barriers and has greatly facilitated effective communications among the world's physicians. The 1997 Nobel Peace Prize was bestowed on the International Campaign to Ban Landmines and on its coordinator, an American woman who organized at the grass-roots level to promote a network of community coalitions that has achieved change on a global level. An international treaty outlawing landmines has been drafted and approved by nearly one hundred governments and will go into effect upon ratification.

The promise of the promoting function resides in the ease with which private groups and individuals who entertain strong demands for values today can organize proper groups to take the initiative, to agitate, and to propose alternatives. A crucial task is to find and forge sufficiently inclusive symbols to attract, manage, and mobilize world public opinion in pursuit of the common interest. In an interdependent, dynamically changing world, effective power groups are increasingly mobile and changing. More than ever it is possible to assemble the resources and to organize the activities necessary to change peoples' perceptions of common interest.

The less promising aspect of promotion is that promotional activities are still too often carried forward from parochial and fragmented, rather than inclusive, perspectives. A frequent limitation on adequate performance of the promoting function comes from the all too common domination of public channels of communication by agents (official or unofficial) of special interests. Once having degenerated into propaganda for special interests, promotional activities all too often have been perceived in terms of interbloc warfare — East against West in the past, today North against South, and so on — keeping effective elites in effective power. Problems arise, for example, when ideological polemics (such as "unilateral nuclear freeze") become a substitute for serious negotiation toward effective reduction and control of strategic and conventional armaments, or when global warming measures are opposed in the name of development and free trade. "Nonnegotiable" polemics and strategies are anything but genuine expressions of common interests.

22

The Prescribing (Lawmaking) Function

A central yet difficult task confronting international lawyers and scholars is to explain how international law is made. Scholars and practitioners seasoned in domestic legal contexts often find their knowledge and experience inadequate for the complexities of international affairs and sometimes simply come away frustrated with the notion that there is no international law. But of course international law exists — as we have seen, numerous effective international norms make possible stable, ongoing interactions across national borders in a world of ever-increasing interdependence and transnational exchange. An understanding of how international law is made and, perhaps, of how to participate in making it, is tremendously important. In any community, national or transnational, how law is made greatly affects the shaping and sharing of all values.

Inquiry about prescription (the lawmaking function) has commonly gone forward in terms of quests for "bases of obligation" or the "binding nature" of law, or of efforts to identify mysterious "sources" of international law. These sources are located variously in transempirical absolutes, in national group expectations, in the express consent of the sovereign state, or in the expectations of elites. Many ambiguities are further involved in using the term *sources* with these shifting references.

These inherited confusions have their roots in Article 38 of the Statute of the International Court of Justice, which provides:

1. The Court, whose function is to decide in accordance with international law such disputes as are submitted to it, shall apply:
   a. international conventions, whether general or particular, establishing rules expressly recognized by the contesting states;
   b. international custom, as evidence of a general practice accepted as law;

    c. the general principles of law recognized by civilized nations;

    d. subject to the provisions of Article 59, judicial decisions and the teachings of the most highly qualified publicists of the various nations, as subsidiary means for the determination of rules of law.

2. This provision shall not prejudice the power of the Court to decide a case *ex aequo et bono,* if the parties agree thereto.

Much of the continuing debate has centered on the comprehensiveness and priorities of these itemized "sources" and "evidences," the "formal" or "material" nature of these sources, the precise wording and meaning of each item, and the potential significance of each item in concrete application.

What has been strikingly absent is the ability to grasp the very nature of the prescribing function, the process by which international legal norms are made. From a general community perspective, the items in Article 38 are merely components of the ongoing flow of communication and collaboration; their significance is to indicate broader community expectations, as generated and reflected in a dynamic process of communication and practice. Only when the prescribing function is explicitly related to the ongoing, larger processes of communication and decision can the dynamics inherent in lawmaking be realistically and fully brought to the fore.

Thus conceived, prescription refers to the projection of an authoritative policy about the shaping and sharing of values. It results from a process of communication that proceeds on three levels: the designation of the content of a policy (factual contingencies, a norm about the future); the creation of expectations about the authority of the policy so designated; and the creation of expectations that this policy will be put into controlling practice (the potential sanction). In the world community, as in its lesser component communities, processes of communication by which prescriptions are shaped range from the most deliberate form of expression — formal agreement — through many gradations to the least deliberate form-the vast flow of expectations derived from uniformities in decision and behavior.

When prescriptive processes are most deliberate, formal, and organized, four sequential phases can be observed: initiation of the process; exploration of relevant facts and potential policies; formulation of policy to be projected as authoritative for the community; and communication of the prescriptive content and expectations about authority and control to the target audience. Even when a prescribing process is highly informal and unorganized, some rough approximation to, or functional equivalence of, these sequential phases may be observed.

The diversity and abundance of the processes of communication by which legal norms are made in the contemporary world are staggering. The peoples of the world communicate to one another expectations about policy, authority, and control through reciprocal claims and mutual tolerances in all interactions as well as through state or intergovernmental entities. The participants (communicators and communicatees) in relevant processes of communication exhibit a wide range of specialization to the prescribing function, from the most to the least specialized. Included are not only the officials of states and intergovernmental organizations but also the representatives of political parties, pressure groups, and private associations and the individual human being qua individual and others with all his or her manifold identifications. The perspectives of participants, from the most to the least deliberate, display demands, identifications, and expectations with varying degrees of compatibility or incompatibility with common interests and fundamental general community policies.

The situations of communicative interaction are both official and unofficial, direct and indirect, organized and unorganized. The organized situations include the familiar arenas (that is, diplomatic, parliamentary-diplomatic, parliamentary, adjudicative, and executive), and all situations may be described in terms of geographic reach, temporal features, degrees of institutionalization, and expectations of crisis. Many base values (including authority and effective control) are brought to bear on particular interactions by the participants. The strategies participants employ to manage their base values manifest varying degrees of explicitness and implicitness in relation to prescription and a wide continuum of persuasion and coercion. They encompass the modalities suggested in Article 38 of the Statute of the ICJ, the whole complex of procedures used in different arenas, and all the strategies characteristic of the value processes.

The culmination of this communication, as expressed in a continuing flow of words or other signs and of behavior, ranges widely both in facts about shared perspectives regarding policy, authority, and control and in the evidences of such perspectives in the form of explicit formulations and unarticulated assumptions. The dynamic outcome in shared expectation, in whatever degree it approaches prescription and however it may be evidenced, is a function of the total configuration of variables that affect and produce it in ongoing social processes. In sum, the prescribing process encompasses all the historic modes of international lawmaking — including explicit formulations in agreements and official declarations and implicit communications through uniformities in behavior.

The most deliberate form of prescription, by which governments cooperate with one another in their interaction, is the international agreement in all its manifestations and labels. Because of its overriding importance, an entire chapter—chapter 16—has been devoted to this subject. The Vienna Convention on the Law of Treaties, in Article 2(1)(a), defines *treaty* as "an international agreement concluded between States in written form and governed by international law, whether embodied in a single instrument or in two or more related instruments and whatever its particular designation." In the absence of centralized legislative institutions in the world, international agreements offer the closest approach to the considered and deliberate prescription of future policies, which is characteristic of legislative institutions in national arenas. The occasional debate about what agreements between nation-states are "lawmaking" and what are not is more futile than rewarding. It would appear that all agreements between nation-states project policies into the future, and the number of participants thus affected is a matter for empirical inquiry in light of all the values at stake rather than dogmatic conclusion based on implicit assumptions about the natures of law or agreement.

The process of agreement, as described in chapter 16, can be realistically understood only by reference to the participants, their perspectives (demands, expectations, and identifications), situations of interaction, base values, modalities in expression of commitment, outcomes in shared expectations, and effects on different value processes. In projecting shared commitments and community policies through international agreements, state officials and other participants, operating under changing situations, undertake negotiations and other activities by using available base values. Agreements between states differ in various ways: the number of parties sharing commitment, the scope and content of policies projected, and the expectations of permanence or impermanence attending commitment.

In cumulative impact, agreements between states play a crucial role the development of customary international law. Because state officials in the world arena function both as claimants and as decision makers, agreements may not only express the demands or claims of certain states against the general community but also establish the expectation of uniformities in behavior, which adds up to lawfulness. That many uniform agreements have been made, and tolerated without protest, over time is often adduced as strong evidence of customary law.

The least deliberate form of prescription—customary law—builds on expectations about policies, authority, and control, as generated by official and unofficial attitudes and cooperation. The perspectives of peoples, especially of decision makers, may so crystallize that certain past uniformities in behavior are expected to continue in the future. Restatement Third of Foreign Relations Law of the United States, in section 102(2), states, "Customary international law results from a general and consistent practice of states followed by them from a sense of legal obligation."[1] As noted, the focus on "states" is unrealistic, but the identification of two primary components of customary law is appropriate.

The technical requirements for establishing a customary international law are commonly said to be two: a "material" element in certain past uniformities in behavior and a "psychological" element, or *opinio juris*, certain subjectivities of legal "oughtness" attending the uniformities in behavior (for example, an expectation that something is legally appropriate or required). In the North Sea Continental Shelf case (1969),[2] which pitted the Federal Republic of Germany against Denmark and the Netherlands concerning norms applicable to delimit the continental shelf in dispute, the ICJ pointed out that "an indispensable requirement" to "the formation of a new rule of customary international law" is that "State practice, including that of States whose interests are specially affected, should have been both extensive and virtually uniform . . . and should moreover have occurred in such a way as to show a general recognition that a rule of law or legal obligation is involved."[3] The court elaborated further:

> Not only must the acts concerned amount to a settled practice, but they must also be such, or be carried out in such a way, as to be evidence of a belief that this practice is rendered obligatory by the existence of a rule of law requiring it. The need for such a belief, i.e., the existence of a subjective element, is implicit in the very notion of the *opinio juris sive necessitatis*. The States concerned must therefore feel that they are conforming to what amounts to a legal obligation. The frequency, or even habitual character of the acts is not in itself enough. There are many international acts, e.g., in the field of ceremonial and protocol, which are performed almost invariably, but which are motivated only by considerations of courtesy, convenience or tradition, and not by any sense of legal duty.[4]

The application of both material and psychological requirements is, however, highly flexible. Uniformity is no more realistically required than unanimity.

The relevant patterns in behavior extend not only to the acts and utterances of transnational and national officials located at many positions in structures of authority but also to those of private individuals and representatives of nongovernmental organizations. Such acts diverge both in frequency of repetition and in duration of recurrence. The subjectivities of oughtness required for such patterns of behavior may relate to various systems of norms, including prior authority, natural law, reason, morality, or religion. The critical subjectivities are those of expectation of future uniformities in decision, regardless of the norms of justification; this is borne out by the practice of honoring law-creating consequences even of subjectivities initially asserted in contravention of prior authority. The evidence that decision makers may consult in order to ascertain past behavior and subjectivities ranges from such familiar items as international agreements, resolutions of international governmental organizations, public utterances by international and national officials, diplomatic correspondence and instructions, national court decisions, legislative measures, and the writings of publicists to "every written document, every record of act or spoken word which presents an authentic picture of the practice of states in their international dealings."[5]

Confusion often develops regarding the degree of uniformity required to establish customary international law. In the Asylum case (1950), involving Colombia's claim for unilateral competence to grant diplomatic asylum against Peru, the International Court of Justice first emphasized "a constant and uniform usage practiced by the States" as essential to customary international law.[6] The court rejected the Colombian claim by declaring:

> The facts brought to the knowledge of the Court disclose so much uncertainty and contradiction, so much fluctuation and discrepancy in the exercise of diplomatic asylum and in the official views expressed on various occasions, there has been so much inconsistency in the rapid succession of conventions on asylum, ratified by some States and rejected by others, and the practice has been so much influenced by considerations of political expediency in the various cases, that it is not possible to discern in all this any constant and uniform usage, accepted as law, with regard to the alleged rule of unilateral and definitive qualification of the offence.[7]

The requisite patterns in past behavior and subjectivities are *generality,* not universality. Article 38(1)(b) of the ICJ Statute thus speaks of "international custom" in terms of a "general" rather than universal "practice." The express consent of every nation-state is not a prerequisite to the authority of a particular customary law. Whereas a keystone of the Westphalian concept of international law is the notion of consent, the function of customary international law is precisely to vitiate the requirement of specific consent as the basis of international obligation. The honoring of somewhat diffuse expectations generated by cooperative reciprocal behavior permits "sovereign" states — new as well as old — to be subject to international law without specific consent. Thanks to such a process of accommodation, nation-states can, without undue affront to their inflated notions of sovereignty, take account of their conditions of interdependence and reciprocity and cooperate in the pursuit of common goals and policies without explicit agreement. A customary prescription thus need not be unanimous; it need only be "applied by the overwhelming majority of states which hitherto had an opportunity to apply it."[8] Normally, this overwhelming majority would include all the major powers and the states especially affected by a particular customary prescription. No customary international law in outer space is conceivable, for example, without the participation of a major space power.

Another element relates to the length of time required to form customary international prescription. The time requirement is a function both of general community expectations and of circumstances in context. In establishing certain decision makers with competence to prescribe future policies, the world community attempts to secure prescription in accordance with contemporary expectations. The temporal requirement is calculated to make certain that these expectations are accurately ascertained. Understandably, the central concern of contemporary demands and expectations is to distribute values toward the future rather than the past. "Time-honored practice is not a necessary element in customary International Law,"[9] though it serves importantly as evidence, which may be otherwise provided, of contemporary expectations and demonstrates the stability of relevant patterns of expectation. In certain contexts the requisite degree of certainty about contemporary expectations has been ascertained by reference to past behavior and subjectivities of relatively short duration.

In any event, the significance of the traditional requirements of a flow of patterns in behavior and subjectivity through time can be understood only in their larger context. These historic emphases refer only to certain features of the broader process of communication by which customary expectations about policy, authority, and control are created. The full exposition of how customary expectations are created requires a thorough exploration of every feature of the process of communication involved. The relevant features include communicators and communicatees (both officials and nonofficials) and the range of participation; participants' perceptions about the content of their communication and its relation to existing law; the geographical, temporal, institutional, and crisis factors of the situation; the knowledge, skill, and other resources possessed by participants; strategies in generating the flow of words and the flow of behavior; the degree of uniformity in words and behavior; and shared expectations about policy, authority, and control. These patterns can also be viewed in terms of intensity of demand or commitment as well as degree of sharing.

The most striking recent development in the prescribing function relates to the growing role of international governmental organizations. Contrary to the lingering myth that such organizations enjoy little direct prescriptive competence, they play an increasingly important role as forums for the flow of explicit communications and acts of collaboration that create peoples' expectations about authoritative community policy. This is especially true of the United Nations and its affiliated agencies.

The General Assembly, in particular, has adopted many resolutions that deal with major problems in international law. The legal effect of these resolutions is debated among specialists. The availability of the General Assembly, coupled with the wide acceptance of the requirements of customary law, seems to point to a new modality of lawmaking. When resolutions enjoy the overwhelming support of the member states, *including* all the major powers, they would appear to have the force of law whether they are characterized as "instantaneous customary law," as "quasi legislation," or as something else. The crucial point is that there emerges a new institutional mode by which the peoples of the world can clearly communicate expectations of authority and control in relation to all problems and value processes. The traditional time requirement associated with the creation of customary law ensures that such expectations are widely shared and thus exist. With this new institutional modality of lawmaking, the time requirement recedes to a minimum.

This is not to suggest that all General Assembly resolutions are law. Some bear little resemblance to genuine expressions of what law is in terms of shared expectations. Whether a resolution of the General Assembly genuinely expresses community expectations about authority and control depends on every feature of the process of communication involved. One needs to know who voted for it or against it and how many participated in the flow of communication. One needs to know the content of the policy and its relation to the overriding goals of the community. One must know how deliberately the resolution was considered and how long and in what mode it was communicated. One needs to know how well decision makers were aware of past decisions and their bearing on the resolution adopted. One needs to know not only isolated communications but the total flow of communications both within and outside the United Nations. One must examine outcomes in communication: How clear was the policy specified, and what are shared expectations of authority and control?

Much controversy has been generated, as discussed in chapter 18 regarding the authoritative effect of both General Assembly resolutions on permanent sovereignty over natural resources and on the establishment of a new international economic order. The issue of expropriation has aroused particularly intense debate. The debate centers on the relative authority of General Assembly Resolution 1803 (paragraph 4), Permanent Sovereignty over Natural Resources (1962),[10] vis-à-vis Article 2(2)(c) of Resolution 3281, the Charter of Economic Rights and Duties of States (1974) and Resolution 3171 (paragraph 3) (1973).[11] Although Resolution 1803 emphasizes the payment of "appropriate compensation" in accordance with "international law" and settlement of the dispute "through arbitration or international adjudication," Article 2(2)(c) of the charter leaves it to the expropriating state to determine "appropriate compensation" by "taking into account its relevant laws and regulations and all circumstances" it "considers pertinent" and to settle any dispute, unless otherwise agreed on by all states concerned, under its "domestic law" and "by its tribunals." Paragraph 3 of Resolution 3171, similar to Article 2(2)(c), states that "the application of the principle of nationalization carried out by States, as an expression of their sovereignty in order to safeguard their natural resources, implies that each State is entitled to determine the amount of possible compensation and the mode of payment, and that any disputes which might arise should be settled in accordance with the national legislation of each State carrying out such measures." Resolution 1803 (paragraph 4) abides by international law, yet both Article 2(2)(c) of Resolution 3281 and Resolution 3171 (paragraph 3) rely on domestic law. Obviously the two positions are incompatible. Which one, then, is authoritative?

This issue was spotlighted in the arbitral award of *Texaco Overseas Petroleum et al. v. Libyan Arab Republic* (1977),[12] which involved claims against Libya for its nationalization of all of the rights, interests, and property of two international oil companies in Libya. The two oil companies relied heavily on Resolution 1803, but Libya strongly invoked, among others, Article 2(2)(c) of the charter (Resolution 3281) and Resolution 3171. The sole arbitrator, René-Jean Dupuy (appointed by the president of the ICJ), rejected Libya's claim that "any dispute relating to nationalization or its consequences should be decided in conformity with the provisions of the municipal law of the nationalizing State and only in its courts,"[13] and delivered an award on the merits in favor of the companies. (Though Libya refused to take part in the arbitral proceedings, it set forth its position in a memorandum to the president of the court.)

Dupuy discussed the legal effect of U.N. General Assembly resolutions in general and that of the above-mentioned resolutions in particular. He noted that the "legal value" of U.N. resolutions "differs considerably depending on the type of resolution and the conditions attached to its adoption and its provisions."[14] Hence, in "appraising the legal validity of the above-mentioned Resolutions," he resorted to "the criteria usually taken into consideration, i.e., the examination of voting conditions and the analysis of the provisions concerned."[15]

Noting that Resolution 1803 was "passed by the General Assembly by 87 votes to 2, with 12 abstentions," he stressed that the majority voting for this text included "many States of the Third World" and "several Western developed countries with market economies, including the most important one, the United States."[16] He pointed out, however, that the conditions under which Resolutions 3171 and 3281 were adopted were "notably different." The "specific paragraph concerning nationalization, disregarding the role of international law," as contained in Resolution 3171, "not only was not consented to by the most important Western countries, but caused a number of the developing countries to abstain."[17] Similarly, "paragraph 2(c) of Article 2 of the Charter, which limits consideration of the characteristics of compensation to the State and does not refer to international law, was voted by 104 to 16, with 6 abstentions, all the industrialized countries with market economies having abstained or having voted against it."[18]

Thus, "only Resolution 1803" was "supported by a majority of Member States representing all of the various groups." In contrast, the other resolutions mentioned above were "supported by a majority of States but not by any of the developed countries with market economies which carry on the largest part" of international trade. "On the basis of the circumstances of adoption mentioned above and by expressing an *opinio juris communis,*" he concluded that Resolution 1803 "seems to this Tribunal to reflect the state of customary law existing in this field." He further stated that "the absence of any connection between the procedure of compensation and international law and the subjection of this procedure solely to municipal law cannot be regarded by this Tribunal except as a *de lege ferenda* formulation, which even appears *contra legem* in the eyes of many developed countries." This position is "further reinforced by an examination of the general practice of relations between States with respect to investment."[19]

The evolution of the Universal Declaration of Human Rights as "quasi legislation" and custom offers another instructive example. When the Universal Declaration was adopted unanimously in December 1948 by the General Assembly, the original shared expectation was that it represented only "a common standard of achievement" without direct legal authority and enforceability. But the authoritative nature of the Universal Declaration has grown in the five decades since then. It has been affirmed and reaffirmed by numerous resolutions of U.N. entities and related agencies, invoked and reinvoked by various participants, and incorporated into many international agreements and national constitutions; it has also found increasing expression in judicial decisions, both transnational and national. Today, the Universal Declaration is widely acclaimed as a Magna Carta of humankind, to be observed by all the participants in the world arena. The authoritative effect of the Universal Declaration is recognized in a number of ways: as the authoritative identification and clarification of human rights guaranteed under the U.N. Charter, as part of customary international law, as a vital component of jus cogens, and/or as an indispensable component of the developing global bill of human rights.[20]

A comparable evolution occurred with the Helsinki Accords (officially, the Final Act of the Conference on Security and Co-operation in Europe, now

called the Organization for Security and Cooperation in Europe), an important
instrument that once delimited East-West relations and contained the famous
"basket three,"concerned with human rights and humanitarian affairs. It was
said to be a "nonbinding treaty."[21] But, given the frequency with which it was
invoked and applied by officials and nonofficials alike, and the machinery
established for periodic review, it was not surprising that the nonbinding treaty
in due course generated and crystallized ample expectations in support of its
authority.

The modalities of prescription do not mutually exclude; depending on context, one mode may be more economic and effective than another. The crucial
point is not so much the modality of communication as the degree to which the
policies projected become a part of the working expectations of the effective
participants in the world community. Human expectations, or the demands and
identifications with which they interlock, are not static. It cannot be taken for
granted that the words of treaties or other written documents reflect community
expectations without appropriate verification. As viewpoints are in flux, so is
today's structure of expectation open to inevitable change, as new conditions
arise and new suggestions are put forth.

International law has historically been made by articulated multilateral agreement and by unarticulated, habitual, cooperative behavior, from which expectations about authority and control are derived. United Nations practices have not
only boosted these traditional modes of lawmaking but added a new dimension
that more closely approximates parliamentary enactment. The activities of the
General Assembly, through its committees and other subsidiary entities, have
greatly rationalized prescription by multilateral agreement. The opportunities it
provides for the representatives of many communities to articulate their conceptions of law and to incorporate them in formal resolutions have substantially
eased the historic burden of identifying customary law and clarifying its content. This latter modality of General Assembly resolution, greatly foreshorten-
ing the requisite time to establish customary law and affording an economical
mode to articulate consensus about common interest, increasingly bears the
hallmarks of parliamentary enactment.

Thanks to the potentials of global communications and the availability of
different modalities of lawmaking, the global prescribing process exhibits inclusivity, rationality, and effectiveness. An appropriate inclusivity is greatly
fostered by the informal components in transnational prescribing process that
permit expectations about policies, authority, and control to be created by cooperative behavior of both official and unofficial participants. Such processes
represent a preferred policy of democracy and representativeness because they
entail a constant accommodation of the interests and behavior of all participants

affected by the prescriptions being created. Both groups and individuals may participate. The General Assembly and other structures of authority communicate to the worldwide audience, articulating and reflecting the expectations of the peoples of the world.

In spite of encouraging developments, difficulties remain. The world arena lacks a well-organized, centralized lawmaking institution; hence the continuing reliance on three modalities of lawmaking. Under the deliberate mode of prescription, states are not bound by a particular international agreement, as an agreement, unless they give express consent. Over time an agreement may become customary law. For example, the 1982 Law of the Sea Convention was a goldmine of controversy over which parts represented customary law and which parts new formulations, until differences were resolved and the treaty implemented in 1994.

The parliamentary mode of prescription (lawmaking) is not necessarily democratic. It may be democratic in the sense that states are nominally equal (one state, one vote) but not in the sense that individuals participate democratically. The crude, cumbersome procedures in the General Assembly mean that prescription may be manipulated to serve special interests rather than common interests.

Although the least deliberate mode of prescription affords greater participation by groups and individuals, the process is extremely slow and fragmentary. In the absence of a centralized body empowered to prescribe and proclaim, whether and when a particular customary law has emerged is always controversial. Given the realities of the world's effective power process, neither the United Nations procedure nor multilateral agreements can effectively bind nation-states large and small.

23

The Invoking Function

The invoking function refers to the provisional characterization of events in terms of community prescriptions. This function is a prelude to the applying function and sets an application in motion. An invocation ordinarily includes initiation, exploration of facts and potential policies, provisional characterization of the selected facts by reference to authoritative policies, and stimulation of applicative arenas. Like other claims to authority, an invocation involves assertions about facts, relevant policies (prescriptions), and appropriate remedies. People who invoke make allegations about what has happened, what policies have been violated, and what future action might remedy the wrong. Invocation thus serves as a bridge from prescription to application. A provisional characterization of events as deviations from prescribed norms, whether it sets the applying function into motion, may of itself entail significant value consequences.

The participants in invocation before transnational arenas include states, international governmental organizations, nongovernmental organizations and groups, and individuals. The objectives of invocation extend from obtaining the benefits of an informal appreciation of events to setting in motion a formal application by authoritative decision makers. Invocation may occur in situations laden with crises. In situations of a lesser degree of institutionalization, invocation is generally open to all effective participants; in arenas of a higher degree of institutionalization, access is available only through formal channels and may be highly restricted. The international process has both features, especially since individuals are often effectively locked out of formal decisional arenas but can help to shape attitudes and behavior.

The base values of invokers may vary greatly in relative strengths, abilities, skills, and resources. Invokers may employ strategies in the forum of private communications (letters, telegrams, and so on), the media, mass communication (editorial, reporting, letter writing, computer networking, picketing or demonstrating on camera, and so on), or highly formal procedures. Outcomes may involve changing public opinion, arousing the attention of selective elites, or initiating the process of application.

Broad access to and participation in invocation are indispensable to a global constitutive process designed to secure both minimum world order and optimum world order, especially human rights. Maintenance of minimum world order depends on timely invocation in response to breach of peace and other gross violations of international law. Respect for and confidence in processes of authoritative decision depend greatly on the ability of individuals and private groups to challenge unlawful deprivations. An effective public order of human dignity requires that representative organs of the general community be enabled to stimulate decision when imminent threats to public order or human dignity occur when injured parties are unable to do so. A trend toward broader participation in the invoking function is evident, although current access to invocation is far from optimum. Individuals are increasingly accorded the competence to invoke processes of transnational decision to defend their rights.

Nation-states are historically the most important formal invokers in the world arena, responding to matters ranging from breaches of peace to violations of human rights, yet individuals and groups have always played at least informal roles. States request emergency meetings of the Security Council or the General Assembly to deal with serious threats to peace and security, global or regional. But complaints by states extend to a wide range of other matters.

In the area of human rights, state officials have traditionally played a vital role in invoking the customary international law of state responsibility to protect their nationals abroad. In addition, an important modality of invocation — the state-to-state complaint — has been institutionalized for the global and regional human rights programs.

The remedy of diplomatic protection of nationals, as discussed in chapter 12, is based on a nationality test but is otherwise discretionary. A state generally does not invoke transnational decision to protect non-nationals. Even with regard to its own nationals who have suffered deprivations imposed by other governments, a state may choose not to espouse claims because of either special policy considerations or ambiguous conceptions of nationality.

The state-to-state complaint system under the contemporary human rights movement is becoming increasingly important. A host of international human rights treaties, notably the International Covenant on Civil and Political Rights, the International Convention on the Elimination of All Forms of Racial Discrimination, the Constitution of the International Labor Organization, the

UNESCO Protocol Instituting a Conciliation and Good Offices Commission in Relation to the Convention Against Discrimination in Education, the European Convention on Human Rights, and the American Convention on Human Rights, explicitly authorize a state party to invoke transnational prescription against defaulting parties. Though the Convention of the International Labor Organization, the UNESCO Protocol, and the European Convention make the state-to-state complaint procedure mandatory, the Covenant on Civil and Political Rights and the American Convention make it optional. The usefulness of the state-to-state complaint procedure has been questioned because of its potentially harmful effects on friendly relations between states, its possible abuse from political motivation, and its likely infrequent use. But the experiences under the European Convention on Human Rights and under the ILO appear to support its value. In the words of Lady Gaitskell, "The infrequency of complaints demonstrated the responsible attitude taken towards the procedure and its value; the procedure's very existence was a deterrent, serving to encourage a Government to remedy more quickly any abuse of human rights within its territory."[1]

In spite of its utility, state elites are undeniably reluctant to resort to the formal state-to-state complaint procedure to accuse other governments of human rights violations, lest they themselves become targets of complaints. The dynamics of reciprocity and retaliation in a decentralized world here operate to the detriment of world public order. Hence, invocation by individuals and private groups in human rights matters is imperative. Unless individuals and nongovernmental groups can invoke transnational authority for remedy on their own behalf or on behalf of other victims, the elaborate human rights prescriptions may become nothing more than illusory aspirations.

The increasing access of individuals and private groups to transnational arenas of decision, as described in chapter 7, is most notable in the area of human rights. Individuals and private groups are accorded access to the United Nations Commission on Human Rights, the Committee Against Torture, the Committee on the Elimination of Racial Discrimination, the European Commission of Human Rights, and the Inter-American Commission on Human Rights. The optional protocol to the International Covenant on Civil and Political Rights allows petitions to the Human Rights Committee by individuals but not by private groups. The procedures for individual petition are, however, far from simple, open, and effective. Contemporary prescriptions create extraordinary obstacles to the effective exercise of the right of individual petitions, as illustrated by the procedures within the United Nations and the cumulative experience under the European Convention on Human Rights.

The facts of effective power suggest that petitions by individuals are not at present the most effective form of remedy for human rights deprivations. The discrepancy in effective power between an individual petitioner and a respondent state is simply too great. It appears crucial that, in addition to state-to-state complaints and individual petitions, some form of invocation, representative of the general community and backed by its strength, be made available. A promising alternative has at last appeared with the long-awaited creation of a United Nations High Commissioner for Human Rights. The high commissioner is an international ombudsperson charged with the responsibility of invocation on behalf of victims and the general community. The high commissioner, with a broad mandate, is able, for example, to deploy human rights officers to troubled areas to investigate suspected rights violations and prevent future ones.

The role of the representatives of the general community extends not only to human rights matters but to all aspects of international law. The role of the secretary-general of the United Nations is particularly noteworthy. The secretary-general is empowered to call attention to crises that threaten world peace and security and to call for an emergency meeting of the Security Council or of the General Assembly. The effective role of this office could be greatly enhanced through strong leadership by calling world attention to matters of enormous importance affecting humankind.

The foregoing emphasizes invocation in the context of formal decision arenas. To grasp the dynamics of the invoking function, however, one must take into account the flow of informal invocations that occur in a less institutionalized fashion. Specific and responsible allegations of violations of international legal norms, though falling short of mobilizing formal application by authoritative decision makers, could in the aggregate produce significant effects in ending lawless acts or in securing greater compliance with established international standards. World public opinion is the court of last resort for informal invocations, which can be undertaken day in and day out by nongovernmental groups, the media of mass communication, and concerned individuals. Publicity mobilizes support, support leads to action, and action alleviates abuses.

In the field of human rights, for example, exposing the dark side of governmental behavior is widely believed to be an effective and economical weapon. Many nongovernmental organizations undertake the important task of "monitoring," in the sense of reporting general conditions of human rights in many communities and in bringing to public attention instances of violations. Such informal invocations (sometimes accompanied by mass protests, rallies, letter-writing campaigns, publicity campaigns, and other tactics) often produce constructive results, for example, concessions by the government concerned in order to placate both external condemnation and internal opposition. The pointed finger of shame, especially when directed by a reputable organization known for its impartiality and independence, has often resulted in the stay of executions, commutation of death sentences, release of prisoners, discontinuation of torture, amelioration of prison conditions, permission for emigration, withholding of mass expulsion, or general improvement of human rights conditions.

In the field of environmental protection, the incident of the *Rainbow Warrior* in New Zealand in 1985 illustrates such informal invocation. The environmentalist pressure group Greenpeace, in its concern for environmental safety regarding oceanic nuclear weapons testing, threatened to interrupt French nuclear tests in the Pacific Ocean by sailing its schooner into the test zone. French governmental intelligence officers, provoked by the group's frequent anti-French press statements expressing its intention to sail despite France's repeated warnings against such activity, turned to violence. They planted explosive charges on the Greenpeace vessel, the *Rainbow Warrior,* which flew a British flag, and detonated the explosives while the ship sat in the harbor of Auckland, New Zealand, killing a crew member and destroying the schooner. The French government first denied responsibility but soon confessed, thanks to a vigilant world press and world public opinion. The sequence of events, though tragic, did bring a strong opposition to the nuclear testing to world attention and exerted significant restraint on the French government. It not only led to successful mediation of the dispute between New Zealand and France by former U.N. Secretary-General Javier Pérez de Cuéllar, but also culminated in an unprecedented international damages case arbitrated by agreement between a sovereign state and a nongovernmental organization (ordering France to pay more than eight million dollars in damages to Greenpeace).

24

The Applying Function

The applying function refers to a relatively final characterization of events by decision makers in terms of community prescription and the management of sanctioning measures to secure enforcement. In conventional usage, many imprecise terms are employed to describe constituent parts of, and varying approximations to, application. These labels include investigation, fact-finding, on-the-scene observation, reporting, commissions of inquiry, negotiation, good offices, mediation, conciliation, arbitration, and adjudication. Viewed comprehensively, application may embrace the following sequential features: exploration of potentially relevant facts, including the precipitating events and their larger context; exploration of potentially relevant policies; identification of significant facts; determination of the authoritative policies applicable; making of the decision, including the projection of future relations between the parties; enforcement; and review.

The application of prescriptions is the culmination of all other functions. Other functions are in some way designed to assist in securing rational, uniform, effective, and constructive applications. Unless such outcomes are obtained, the other functions are largely hortatory. As important as it is to challenge unlawful violations, it is equally urgent to secure applications that put basic community policies into controlling practice and mobilize a continuing consensus in support of both minimum world order and optimum world order.

Most applications of international law continue to be made by national officials in an ongoing process of unilateral determinations and reciprocal responses. This process goes forward from foreign office to foreign office, in internal and external arenas. Many applications are made by national courts, and some even by legislative bodies. National officials play important roles in application in all transnational arenas, often in concert with the officials of international governmental organizations. Such applications take place in normal diplomatic activities and occasional conferences, or in the more formal parliamentary, adjudicative, and executive structures existing on the global scale. Even nonofficials may partake in a range of equivalent activities. What appears to be private may in effect be a functional application of transnational prescriptions.

The chief objective in application is to put prescriptions into controlling practice. The demand for an application is thus a demand to perform the sequence of activities that constitute an application, including exploring and characterizing facts and exploring and choosing policies. The exploration of policies characteristically entails three interrelated subgoals: interpretation of prescriptions to achieve the closest approximation to the communications made; supplementation by filling gaps and removing ambiguities; and integration, in the sense of policing and accommodating prescriptions in terms of priorities in community policies.

The transnational structures of authority involved in application include all five types of arenas mentioned above. Diplomatic interaction is the scene of the bulk of official applications at the international level. Adjudicative arenas, including judicial and arbitral tribunals (both transnational and domestic), are noted for their specialization in application. Even parliamentary bodies, such as the General Assembly and the Security Council, cannot escape the task of characterizing particular instances in terms of prescriptions. The transnational arenas of application are increasingly open and are moving slowly toward some degree of compulsoriness. The base values (authority and effective control) at the disposal of various appliers differ immensely. A burgeoning body of transnational prescriptions is increasingly available to appliers in all arenas. Whereas the effective power of national officials depends on the overall power of their states and perceptions of common interest, that of international officials remains extremely modest. Strategies of application vary according to arena and to activity. The strategies of initiation and exploration in an adjudicative arena are markedly different from those in a diplomatic or an executive arena.

In the pre-enforcement phase, agencies undertake various activities to explore and characterize relevant facts and policies. The outcomes of application, as expressed in a continuing flow of characterizations of instances in terms of community prescriptions, affect all patterns of value allocation and future behavior.

Where deviations from decision persist, community intervention is needed to enforce the determined allocation of values or projection of future policy. Enforcement may rely on inducement as well as coercion. Sanctioning measures may be tailored to the goals of prevention, deterrence, restoration, rehabilitation, reconstruction, and correction. In a dynamic process of interaction and decision under ever-changing conditions, no decision is final. Each application is an experiment toward realization of projected goals that is tested through time and changing context by the responses of those affected and of the general community.

Ongoing review becomes necessary at different levels and through different modalities.

EXPLORATION OF FACTS

In a decentralized legal system where autointerpretation prevails, where state officials function as both claimants and judges, where no centralized structure has sufficient authority to compel recalcitrant parties to appear before it, ascertaining the facts of a dispute becomes the first indispensable step in application.

When a dispute arises, claimants commonly have different versions as to what occurred. In the tragic incident of Korean Air Lines flight 007 of September 1983 (involving a Soviet SU-15 fighter's shooting down of a South Korean Boeing 747 jetliner that strayed into Soviet airspace and the death of all 269 people aboard), for example, the contending sides differed fundamentally on crucial facts (whether, for example, the civil aircraft was involved in some sort of spy mission). When relevant facts are perceived differently, legal arguments diverge. Without a decision maker to determine authoritatively what the relevant facts are, the disputants could simply go on arguing over alleged violations. Impartial fact-finding is obviously crucial. If relevant facts could be ascertained through an impartial, third-party process, it would contribute significantly to settling a dispute.

Because exploring and ascertaining facts is integral to the dispute-settling process, it merits special attention. Much international effort toward application has been directed to achieve just that. The devices of investigation, fact-finding, on-the-scene observation, reporting, and commissions of inquiry all cater to this purpose. The underlying assumption is that once relevant facts are established by an impartial third party, dispute settlement can move from there.

RECOURSE TO DIRECT NEGOTIATIONS

The emphasis on "pacific" settlement of disputes through bilateral negotiations between "equal," "sovereign" states is understandable. Even in an interdependent world where the absolute supremacy inherent in the concept of sovereignty would appear archaic and absurd, nation-states do not hesitate to play up such rhetoric when it serves their purposes. This overriding concern of international law is neither to punish states nor to embarrass them but to secure compliance with international legal norms. When compliance can be secured through peaceful, noncoercive procedures, it enhances the effectiveness of international law under the principle of economy with minimal insult or embarrassment to states.

In the contemporary world of decentralization, as sustained by shared perception of common interest and reciprocity, participants are expected to act on their own to settle differences in a noncoercive manner with minimal involvement of inclusive authority. The most common procedure to settle differences and secure compliance is through diplomatic negotiations between contending states. Since most negotiations are conducted without drawing public attention, the achievement of ordinary diplomatic channels may always not be duly recognized. Numerous international agreements concerning the pacific settlement of disputes confine their application to disputes that cannot be solved by diplomacy. Recognizing the importance of diplomatic negotiations as a form of application, the Permanent Court of International Justice declared that "before a dispute can be made the subject of an action at law, its subject matter should have been clearly defined by means of diplomatic negotiations."[1]

Direct bilateral negotiations can be successful between contending parties. But such negotiations may often become deadlocked; hence the utility of such noncoercive devices as good offices, mediation, and conciliation. These devices inject into the application process a disinterested third party agreeable to both disputants, with varying degrees of authorized involvement, to facilitate peaceful settlement even for participants who have become too estranged to negotiate. The third party assists, not replaces, bilateral negotiations. The technical distinctions traditionally made regarding good offices, mediation, and conciliation reflect the degree of authorized involvement for the third party and do not affect the essence of bilateral negotiations. The ultimate settlement is contingent on the consent of the disputing parties.

These procedures have a long history in dispute settlement. Under the Hague Convention of 1899 for the Pacific Settlement of International Disputes, the signatory states, in consideration of the desirability of attempting pacific settlement, pledged to make such efforts and acknowledged the right of third parties to offer assistance in arriving at peaceful solutions. With the establishment of the League of Nations, permanent agencies were created to perform functions of good offices, mediation, and conciliation. These procedures are incorporated in the Charter of the United Nations. Commentators have sought to make technical distinctions among the procedures of good offices, mediation, and conciliation. But in practice these terms have been used with considerable flexibility. The tasks can be performed by a single third party but can also be done collectively. Their usefulness is limited in the sense that they cannot be successful, or even be initiated, without the cooperation of the disputants. But if such procedures do work toward composing differences and helping to secure compliance with international legal norms, so much the better.

THIRD-PARTY DECISION MAKING

Arbitration and judicial settlement, as discussed in chapter 7, are typical modes of third-party decision making. The U.N. Charter explicitly includes both among the means of peaceful settlement of disputes. In arbitration and judicial settlement (through the International Court of Justice and other judicial tribunals), characterized by adverse proceedings with contending parties, the thrust of the emphasis differs from that prevailing in the previous phase of pacific settlement — with the third party playing the role the claimants want it to play.

During the nineteenth and the early part of the twentieth centuries, arbitration was frequently used to settle international disputes. In order to facilitate and encourage its use, nation-states entered into bilateral and multilateral agreements for arbitration. In spite of the establishment of the permanent Court of Arbitration in 1899, the procedure of arbitration is essentially ad hoc.

Widespread recognition of serious deficiencies in arbitral procedure led to the eventual establishment of the Permanent Court of International Justice, which was replaced by the International Court of Justice, one of the principal organs of the United Nations. As discussed in chapter 7, however, because of a lack of compulsory jurisdiction — and in cases of acceptance of compulsory jurisdiction (by less than a third of the members of the U.N.), they are so highly qualified as to be more symbolic than substantial — the usefulness of judicial settlement by the court has not been maximized as contemplated. The U.S. withdrawal, in October 1985, of its previous acceptance of compulsory jurisdiction in reaction to the court's assumption of jurisdiction in the case of *Nicaragua v. United States* was an especially severe blow,[2] although the United States (as most states) is bound by several treaties recognizing special acceptance of the court's competence to interpret and apply such treaties. Special acceptance seems to be the preferred mode at present.

The chamber procedure the ICJ used in the *Gulf of Maine* case (1984)[3] has somewhat encouraged more use of this economical and effective procedure. In this case Canada and the United States invoked Article 27 of the ICJ Statute, which provides for use of a Special Chamber by agreement of the parties. A five-person panel was selected by consent of the parties to decide the disputed fisheries jurisdiction in the Gulf of Maine. Both agreed to submit drafts of their proposed methods for drawing the baselines and settling the dispute, which would determine each state's territorial waters and continental shelf rights. But by virtue of Article 27 both parties also agreed to abide by the decision of the panel without reservation. The Special Chamber, after accepting proposals from each party, independently determined the new line. The compulsory third-party decision making mechanism of the Law of the Sea Convention has been another encouraging step toward the peaceful and lawful settlement of international disputes since it was implemented in 1994. Such dispute settlement processes are based on consent of the parties, and their involvement and participation in the decision process affords a greater chance of compliance.

Judicial adjudication has developed at the regional level — notably, the Court of European Communities, the European Court of Human Rights, and the Inter-American Court of Human Rights. The development of new forums to settle disputes peacefully increases the accessibility of various parties to effective arenas, thereby fostering greater compliance with community goals.

RECOURSE TO INTERNATIONAL GOVERNMENTAL ORGANIZATIONS (ESPECIALLY THE UNITED NATIONS)

When contending parties fail to settle disputes through either direct negotiations or third-party decision making, what can they do? Can they turn to international governmental organizations — most notably the United Nations — for help?

The United Nations is not designed to be a centralized agency for general law enforcement at the global level, though it is endowed with enormous responsibility to maintain international peace and security. The U.N. Charter encourages the settlement of disputes through noncoercive procedures outside the organization, expressing the policy of economy and effectiveness. The charter proclaims the basic principle of settling disputes by peaceful means in Articles 1(1) and 2(3). The charter's framers contemplated that most disputes should be settled by noncoercive methods and that settlement by organs of the United Nations should be resorted to only when other procedures fail. Article 33 thus obliges the member states to solve a dispute "by negotiation, enquiry, mediation, conciliation, arbitration, judicial settlement, resort to regional agencies or arrangements or other peaceful means of their own choice." In practice, member states tend to bring disputes before the Security Council without exhausting these peaceful means.

Although the United Nations is less than a general law enforcement agency, it is entrusted with the tremendous responsibility to maintain minimum world order. This has been especially the case in the past few years. As a whole, the charter is much more concerned with disputes that are likely to disrupt minimum order. Thus the application of Chapter VI of the charter is expressly limited to disputes "the continuance of which is likely to endanger the maintenance of international peace." Violations of international law embrace a range of situations; a violation may or may not constitute a breach of such magnitude. Unless requested otherwise by the contenders, the Security Council or the General Assembly is empowered to recommend either procedures of peaceful settlement or terms of settlement only if a preliminary investigation indicates that the "dispute or situation is likely to endanger the maintenance of international peace and security" (Article 34). The noncoercive procedures of settlement set forth in the charter have been carefully designed to permit a gradual approach to each dispute — the competence of the United Nations is contingent on the seriousness of the dispute and the degree of danger to minimum world order. The United Nations would normally step in only when a dispute is likely to disrupt minimum public order. Even then the United Nations is confined to recommending only procedures or terms of settlement.

In addition to the framework for peaceful settlement of disputes, the United Nations is authorized to take enforcement measures. The Security Council is empowered, under Article 39 of the charter, to determine the existence not only of "an act of aggression" or "breach of the peace" but also "a threat to the peace" and to take proper enforcement measures. Any violation falling short of threatening the peace will be outside the scope of the Security Council's competence. The concept of what constitutes such a threat has been increasingly broadened in the recent past, however, with the Security Council becoming a much more active decision making body since the end of the Cold War.

How effective has the United Nations been in performing its sanctioning functions? The veto power of the permanent members of the Security Council has made it extremely difficult, if not impossible, to enforce effectively the measures provided by Chapter VII of the charter, even against a clearly identified challenge to minimum world order. This has continued to be true after the Cold War, as witnessed by failure in Bosnia and difficulty in maintaining support from all the superpowers for sanctions against Iraq. In a bold peacetime experiment, the Security Council has undertaken multilateral efforts to destroy Iraq's warmaking capabilities through sanctions and on-site inspections. The Security Council has much at stake here. These sanctions, begun in 1990, could see the Security Council functioning in the way envisioned by the United Nations founders; their failure, however, could mean an erosion of council authority at a time when there is much hope invested in the new multilateralism in world security. The General Assembly's formal authority in peace-keeping, as described in chapter 3, has been greatly enlarged thanks to the Uniting for Peace Resolution and the Agenda for Peace, but it continues to be handicapped.

The United Nations continues, despite some success in the Gulf War, to face limitations in performing the applying function to deal with a range of acts of lawlessness, especially in the very area that constitutes one of the organization's major goals.

RECOURSE TO UNILATERAL MEASURES OF SELF-HELP

The U.N. Charter represents the general efforts of the organized community of nations to substitute effective collective measures for unilateral measures of nation-state self-help, which are highly susceptible to abuse. Yet the existing structures of authority and procedure provided by the charter are not sufficiently comprehensive and effective to enable the United Nations to function as a centralized organ for securing compliance with international law across the board. When states that are victims of all sorts of lawless acts cannot, despite their genuine efforts, secure justice or peace through either noncoercive methods or international governmental organizations, will they be permitted to resort to unilateral coercive measures in response to prior unlawful acts?

In the past, resort to unilateral coercive measures was a recognized means of enforcement. Enforceability of international law depended in large measure on such patterns of unorganized and uninstitutionalized remedies. Measures thus taken by states were generally labeled self-help, reprisal, retaliation, or other measures short of war. *Self-help* would appear to be a generic term appropriate for the present purpose. Forcible self-help was regarded as permissible when it was reasonably necessary and taken in response to a prior unlawful act, including failure to carry out international obligations, when such act was imputable to the state against which the self-help measure was directed.

The U.N. Charter, with its general proscription of the threat or use of force as contained in Article 2(4), has generated a continuing controversy about the permissibility of self-help involving the use of armed force. As elaborated in chapter 19, we have reluctantly concluded that absent effective machinery for collective law enforcement under the present world conditions, self-help, even involving military force, remains permissible as a measure of last resort, subject to the rigorous requirements of necessity and proportionality. The necessity for self-help will occur only when all good faith efforts in exhausting all available noncoercive means in response to a prior act of lawlessness have proved futile. The requirement of proportionality must be appraised by reference to all factors relevant in a particular context, considering especially the nature of the precipitating act of lawlessness and the harm it has caused, and the modality (military or nonmilitary) of the responding measure and the deprivation it may cause.

Self-help measures that are nonmilitary in nature can be permissible, provided the conditions of necessity and proportionality are met.

TOWARD EFFECTIVE MANAGEMENT OF SANCTIONING MEASURES
TO OPTIMIZE SANCTIONING GOALS

The enforceability of international law is a long-standing question. To this day
skeptics harbor the notion that international law is not law at all, because it
lacks "enforceability" or has only "marginal enforceability." Such a view
approaches the question of enforcement in terms of a centralized system of
command and community coercion and fails to grasp the dynamics inherent in a
decentralized legal system. It often confuses sanctions, moreover, with use of
military instruments without reference to the real world impact of economic,
diplomatic, and ideologic modalities.

Although it is sometimes suggested that *enforcement* and *sanction* be kept
separate, they are often used interchangeably. For the present purpose, we
adhere to the popular usage, but with a comprehensive dynamic orientation.

In grappling with the question of enforceability, one must project a comprehensive set of sanctioning goals and mobilize all participants and available
means of sanction, both coercive and noncoercive, taken from both short-term
and long-term perspectives. The specific sanctioning goals are prevention, deterrence, restoration, rehabilitation, reconstruction, and correction.

Prevention aims both to develop in decision makers strong preferences to
conform to international legal norms and to minimize the probabilities of violations and deprivations. It is a long-term goal, projected into the indefinite
future. Prevention embraces a range of measures and activities designed to
minimize violations and the probability of undesirable outcomes. The Canadian
government, for example, has enacted the Waters Pollution Prevention Act, "a
model attempt by one state to provide comprehensive environmental policing
for its designated area of coverage."[4] The act prohibits and prescribes penalties
for the deposit of "waste" in Arctic waters or on the islands or mainland under
conditions that such waste may enter Arctic waters. Other nations have made
differing arrangements in accordance with what they understand as the nature
and scope of their pollution responsibility for their own waters and in regard to
inclusive resources.

Deterrence, unlike prevention, is concerned with a potential violation that
has emerged and been clearly posed. Deterrence is not a new goal in the field of
sanction. Because of the "balance of terror" (or MAD, mutual assured destruction) brought about by the development of Cold War nuclear strategies, the term
has gained not only a specific emphasis but a distinctive connotation. It is

usually this connotation that commentators refer to when they speak of the "strategy of deterrence" nowadays. Deterrence, for the present purposes, is not to be understood in this distinctive sense but is more general in reference. It is designed to deter impending impermissible acts.

Once a violation takes place, the goal of restoration comes into play. Restoration aims at compelling the violator state to terminate its impermissible act.

Rehabilitation is concerned with immediate reparation of the values deprived or compensation for injury sustained and the facilitation of quick resumption of peaceful and normal interactions between the contenders. Violations of international obligations are generally assumed to result in the "duty to make reparation," one of the cardinal principles in the realm of state responsibility. Further, as Article 8 of the Universal Declaration of Human Rights makes clear, every human being has the right to an effective remedy for violations of his or her human rights.

The goal of reconstruction is to avoid the recurrence of impermissible acts by bringing about structural changes in the value processes of the violator state and to create and maintain conditions conducive to peaceful, normal interaction. Thus conceived, reconstruction may merge into prevention. Whereas prevention operates within existing structures and processes, reconstruction is concerned with long-term efforts to cause structural changes favorable to peaceful interactions among states. Furthermore, whereas prevention addresses all territorial communities, efforts for reconstruction are primarily directed to the identified violator state.

The goal of correction is directed to persons held responsible for conduct offensive to the conscience and decency of humanity, with a view toward changing their dispositions. The mobilization of the international community to sanction and inspect Iraq until its chemical, nuclear, and biological warfare capacities are completely eliminated, as well as the extraction of war reparations from Iraq for victims of Iraqi aggression, are a striking contemporary illustration of these sanctioning goals at work under international law.

Each goal is distinct, yet all are related. The relative prominence of each is a function of context. After the context is analyzed, the arsenal of sanctioning measures must be tailored to these goals.

This is not an ideal model of centralized sanction and enforcement in a highly organized legal system. But it is a more realistic approach in an essentially decentralized legal system — an approach that would inspire some confidence that much more can be done rather than generate the paralysis that results from a sense of futility.

25

The Terminating Function

The terminating function involves removing the authority of prescriptions, and of arrangements or processes effected under prescriptions, when prescriptions and arrangements cease to conform to demanded goals of world public order. Ending a prescription is itself a prescription, with the distinction that it is directed toward changing a prior prescription. Termination communicates that a prior prescription or arrangement is no longer authoritative. Conceived comprehensively, termination entails a sequence of activities, including initiating the function; investigating the facts about alleged obsolescence of a prescription or an arrangement; exploring community policy relevant to the end of such prescription or arrangement; canceling the prior prescription or arrangement; and ameliorating the loss caused by such termination.

When performed in an effective and timely fashion, the terminating function fosters expectations that change can be made in ways compatible with basic community goals and that a balance can be struck between stability and change. A public order that cherishes human dignity will continue to alter outmoded prescriptions to conform them to newly clarified goals of human dignity, while deferring to existing arrangements and the expectations created by such arrangements. It will further seek to minimize all losses and costs likely to result from necessary change and to lessen potentially disruptive impact through contextual scrutiny of relevant facts and policies. A hallmark of a functioning public order is sensitivity to the claims and expectations grounded in the manifold events of the past, present, and future.

The participants in the terminating function, as in the other functions, are those active in the effective power process, including officials of nation-states, officials of international governmental organizations, representatives of private associations and groups, and individuals. This function is maintained for two basic demands: to keep the prescriptions of the world community compatible with the goals of world public order, both minimum and optimum, and to strike a balance between necessary stability and dynamic change. The demand for change caused by the exigencies of radically different conditions is tempered by the demand to minimize potential deprivations attendant upon the obsolescence and more formal change of prescriptions. It is further disciplined by realistic expectations about the dynamics of intensifying interaction in an interdependent world.

Decisions about change occur in all structures of authority, both transnational and national, and even in the habitual interactions of nonofficial processes. The base values at the disposal of all participants embrace authority and all the value assets of effective power. "Authority" is found in a complex of prescriptions (both written and unwritten) about the termination of agreements, in specified requirements for customary change (*desuetudo*), and in specific provisions for collective procedures. A significant base of effective power is the conspicuous mobilization of opinion and effort for change. (Witness, for example, the domino effect of reform throughout Eastern Europe and Russia, or the dramatic demonstration of "people power" in the Philippines and, comparably, in South Korea.) The strategies of termination vary by type of prescription: multilateral agreements are ended by new agreements, by unilateral denunciation because of changed conditions, and by obsolescence or preemption through customary development; customary prescriptions are terminable either by appropriately comprehensive agreements or by the development of new customs; finally, termination may occur through collective procedures maintained by the organized community within the framework of the United Nations. Its outcomes, as discussed in chapter 16, involve degrees of change, including amendment, modification, suspension, withdrawal, and termination of the prescription.

Perhaps the most dramatic recent example of the termination function occurred on December 8, 1991, when the leaders of Byelorussia, the Russian Federation, and Ukraine signed an agreement in Minsk to found a commonwealth of independent states, effectively proclaiming the end of the USSR. The Minsk Agreement begins as follows:

Preamble
We, the Republic of Belarus, the Russian Federation and the Republic of Ukraine, as founder states of the Union of Soviet Socialist Republics (USSR), which signed the 1922 Union Treaty, further described as the high contracting parties, conclude that the USSR has ceased to exist as a subject of international law and a geopolitical reality.[1]

The U.N. Charter anticipates the necessity of change by stipulating the amending process. Article 108 of the charter reads: "Amendments to the present Charter shall come into force for all Members of the United Nations when they have been adopted by a vote of two-thirds of the members of the General Assembly and ratified in accordance with their respective constitutional processes by two-thirds of the Members of the United Nations, including all the permanent members of the Security Council." Article 109 contemplates a general conference to review the charter for the purpose of charter revision but embodies the same amending requirement as Article 108: "Any alteration of the present Charter recommended by a two-thirds vote of the conference shall take effect when ratified in accordance with their respective constitutional processes by two-thirds of the Members of the United Nations including all permanent members of the Security Council." Evidently, the two-thirds requirement is compounded by the requisite unanimity of the five permanent members of the Security Council. Owing to this built-in veto in the amending procedure, change of charter provisions through formal amendment has been rare, although the United Nations has undergone profound constitutive development since its establishment, largely as a result of patterns of expectation and behavior outside any formal amending process. The only formal changes thus far relate to enlarging the membership of the Security Council and the Economic and Social Council and to corresponding changes in the requisite voting to make decisions, in light of the vast increase in the total U.N. membership.

The existing human rights prescriptions erect considerable barriers for termination, because they express, as discussed in chapter 12, the basic, most widely shared and intensely demanded policies for which the global constitutive process is maintained. Some human rights conventions do not contain withdrawal provisions; others do. Some do not contain denunciation provisions; others do. Most provisions became customary in the 1990s, and some have even become jus cogens, or peremptory norms. The two most important treaties — the International Covenant on Civil and Political Rights (and its optional protocols) and the International Covenant on Economic, Social, and Cultural Rights — contain no provision for denunciation, nor does the Universal Declaration contemplate such a result. This ostensible omission is highly significant: it signifies that the human rights obligations stipulated in the covenants are not expected to be unilaterally disregarded. They are *obligatio erga omnes*. Article 56 of the Vienna Convention on the Law of Treaties is instructive:

1. A treaty which contains no provision regarding its termination and which does not provide for denunciation or withdrawal is not subject to denunciation or withdrawal unless:
   a. it is established that the parties intended to admit the possibility of denunciation or withdrawal; or

    b. a right of denunciation or withdrawal may be implied by the nature of the treaty.

2. A party shall give not less than twelve months' notice of its intention to denounce or withdraw from a treaty under paragraph 1.

Given the authoritative policy in support of the intense demand for global protection of human rights, and given the absence of explicit provision for denunciation, it would appear that the commitments incorporated in the two covenants were intended neither to admit the possibility of denunciation or withdrawal nor to imply a right of denunciation or withdrawal.

Furthermore, even provisions for denunciation contained in certain human rights conventions cannot easily be made effective. The denunciation clauses typically embody certain temporal constraints: barring an exercise of denunciation within a specified period (such as five or ten years), or barring the operative effect of a formal denunciation pending the lapse of a specified period (normally twelve months). Thus, an act of denunciation does not, immediately on notification, relieve the denouncing party of the obligations embodied in the denounced treaty, and the denouncing party may still be held accountable under the treaty obligations during the interim.

Above all, an act of denunciation does not exempt the denouncing party from obligations, which may parallel or reproduce those in the denounced convention, prevailing under general customary international law. The Vienna Convention on the Law of Treaties, in Article 43, states unequivocally: "The invalidity, termination or denunciation of a treaty, the withdrawal of a party from it, or the suspension of its operation, as a result of the application of the present Convention or of the provisions of the treaty, shall not in any way impair the duty of any State to fulfill any obligation embodied in the treaty to which it would be subject under international law independently of the treaty."

The content of all treaties, including the U.N. Charter, naturally can be changed, as even national constitutions are changed, through the development of new customary law. This, however, is a complex process of communication involving a range of participants in continuous interaction. To ascertain whether the communications in past uniformities of behavior, with their attendant subjectivities about lawfulness, have crystallized into the expectations about content, authority, and control that constitute a new customary law requires a comprehensive inquiry. The relevant questions are: Who are the primary communicators and communicatees; what demands and expectations have been communicated; what patterns of general expectation are extant; what is the complex matrix of interaction in terms of spatial, temporal, institutional, and crisis features; what inferences can be drawn from the relative bases of power of the participants; what signs and behavior have been employed as strategies of communication; and what is the culminating mediation of expectations about future policy, authority, and control?

The same U.N. machinery used to expedite the prescribing function can also be used to expedite the terminating function. The making of a new custom — and hence a termination through customary development — can be expedited by contemporary collective procedures. The United Nations, particularly the General Assembly, furnishes a unique, and an exceptionally convenient, forum in which most of the world's peoples can be represented to articulate demands. The tempo of communication can be accelerated through institutional arrangements; the certainty of peoples' expectations about policy, content, authority, and control can be established without lengthy time lapses. Just as custom can now be created "instantaneously" through this new modality, so change and termination of prescription, if sufficiently demanded by the world's peoples, can now be rapidly achieved.

Nevertheless, in this era of perpetual change a vexing problem remains: the tension and uncertainty likely to be generated when an established norm is severely challenged and an emerging alternative has crystallized into a new authoritative norm. The controversy concerning the changing standard of compensation in the case of expropriation (nationalization) offers a prime example (see chapters 18 and 22).

The question of the width of territorial sea offers another excellent example. Before 1982 an array of claims (ranging from three to two hundred miles) had jeopardized the customary rule of three-mile territorial sea and created tremendous confusion regarding the permissible width of territorial sea. The three-mile rule, as originated in the cannonshot rule of the eighteenth century, became widely accepted in the nineteenth century. During the twentieth century, although the major maritime powers insisted on the three-mile rule, states increasingly departed from this norm, especially the new states that proliferated in the era of the United Nations. The insistence by the major powers on a narrow belt of territorial sea (and hence a wide domain allowing high seas freedom) clashed with the growing demands of the lesser powers to protect security and fishery interests. Failures to agree on the width of territorial sea by both the First and the Second United Nations Conferences on the Law of the Sea in 1958 and 1960 further aggravated the situation. By the early 1980s, of the 137 independent coastal states, only a minority of 24 still adhered to the three-mile rule, while an overwhelming majority of 79 states claimed twelve miles, with the rest claiming either six miles or more than twelve miles and up to two hundred miles. The Law of the Sea Convention, adopted in 1982, settled this long-standing controversy by allowing coastal states to claim territorial sea not in excess of twelve nautical miles.

In the *Fisheries Jurisdiction* case between the United Kingdom and Iceland (1974),[2] which involved Britain's challenge of Iceland's unilateral competence to extend its fisheries zones from twelve to fifty miles, the International Court of Justice confronted conflicting claims about customary law governing a coastal state's fisheries rights. The ICJ declared that since 1960 there had developed a customary norm that permitted coastal states to claim exclusive fishery zones of twelve miles, including the territorial sea, but not zones of fifty miles. It stated that the coastal state enjoyed a preferential right of fishing in adjacent areas of sea beyond the twelve-mile limit, insofar as the coastal state, like Iceland, depended economically on local fisheries, but that it could not exclude other states from fishing in such areas, especially if they had traditionally fished there and economically depended on fishing there. In a joint separate opinion, Judges Isaac Forster, Cesar Bengzon, Eduardo Jiménez de Aréchaga, Nagendra Singh, and José Maria Ruda noted specially that:

If the law relating to fisheries constituted a subject on which there were clear indications of what precisely is the rule of international law in existence, it may then have been possible to disregard altogether the legal significance of certain proposals, declarations or statements which advocate changes or improvements in a system of law which is considered to be unjust or inadequate. But this is not the situation. There is at the moment great uncertainty as to the existing customary law on account of the conflicting and discordant practice of States. Once the uncertainty of such a practice is admitted, the impact of the aforesaid official pronouncements, declarations and proposals most undoubtedly have an unsettling effect on the crystallization of a still evolving customary law on the subject.[3]

26

The Appraising Function

The appraising function involves evaluating the decision process in terms of policy objectives of the larger community and identifying the participants responsible for past successes and failures. It is concerned with the adequacy of past decision in achieving postulated goals and widely shared and intensely felt expectations. It relies on the intelligence and promoting functions to determine how well the process of decision is functioning and how it can be improved. The sequence of activities involved in appraisal includes gathering the necessary information about the decision process and its outcomes; evaluating the economy, effectiveness, and consequences of decision; and disseminating findings and recommendations to relevant audiences.

To evaluate the constitutive process in terms of desired public order, appraisal must be both comprehensive and appropriately selective. Operating effectively, the appraising function will ascertain the successes and failures of demanded values, probe for the factors in all phases of the decision functions that affect successes and failures, and ascribe responsibility for such successes and failures as a strategy for improvement. Appraisal seeks to bring relevant intellectual skills (identifying and clarifying goals, surveying trends, analyzing conditions, projecting developments, and inventing alternatives) to bear on every feature of both constitutive process and public order. To ensure necessary independence and impartiality, appraisers must be insulated from immediate threats or inducements and self-appraisals scrutinized by other appraisers. Though intermittent appraisals may mobilize needed occasional attention and support, most sustained and creative effects are likely to transpire when the appraising function is continuously performed within stable structures capable of relating each detail to the set of community goals and the spectrum of conditions.

Generally speaking, participation in the appraising function is highly democratic. All participants in all structures and processes of authority, national and transnational, are to a degree always engaged in self-appraisal and appraisals of others, reviewing and assessing authoritative decision in terms of its content, economy, effectiveness, and consequences. Other participants interested in the quality of public order, including political parties, pressure groups, private associations, and individuals, are also constantly involved in appraisal, through political platforms, demands of pressure groups, private views, and so on. Intellectuals both within and outside the academic community play a special role in performing the difficult tasks of appraisal.

The basic objective of the appraising function is to secure a continuing reform of the decision process in the light of changing demands and expectations under ever-changing conditions. Although structures of authority may sometimes be specialized to the appraising function, appraisal is generally incidental to structures specialized for other functions. The task of formal appraisal tends to be more widely dispersed than concentrated, and more episodic than continuous. The structures are yet to be established to make systematic appraisal an important, continuing feature of the process of decision.

Most of the base values employed to gather, process, and disseminate information bear directly on appraisal. Capacities for appraisal have expanded greatly, thanks to the proliferation of information about world social process, the acquisition of new knowledge and skills to evaluate public order effects, the development of expertise in many fields to analyze the past and the present and forecast the future, and the growth of interdisciplinary cooperation. Most of the strategies employed for intelligence and promotion are equally useful for the appraising function. The culminations of appraisal are a continuing flow of information and assessment and the ascertainment of responsibility regarding features of the decision process and its outcomes and effects.

The appraising function through institutional effort is amply reflected in provisions of the U.N. Charter, including Articles 15, 17, 24(3), 62(1), 64, 87, 88, and 98. The General Assembly is authorized under Article 15 to receive and consider annual and special reports from the Security Council and other U.N. organs. In dealing with budgetary matters under Article 17, the General Assembly is inevitably involved in evaluating past successes and failures as a guide for priorities and allocations. The bulk of the annual report of the Economic and Social Council deals comprehensively with economic, social, cultural, and humanitarian matters. The reporting has been greatly eased by the provision of Article 64:

1. The Economic and Social Council may take appropriate steps to obtain regular reports from the specialized agencies. It may make arrangements

with the Members of the United Nations and the specialized agencies to obtain reports on the steps taken to give effect to its own recommendations and to recommend matters falling within its competence made by the General Assembly.

2. It may communicate its observations on these reports to the General Assembly.

The secretary-general of the United Nations occupies a unique position. The role of the office, extant and potential, in appraisal is worth special notice. The secretary-general is required by Article 98 to submit an annual report to the General Assembly on the work of the organization. When taken seriously and performed effectively, the secretary-general's annual report can provide not only essential information about the work of the United Nations but also an important occasion to appraise the state of the world community in all major fields and sectors. Given a unique vantage point and a continuing and comprehensive authority, as assisted by a substantial corps of international civil servants in the Secretariat, the secretary-general can contribute immensely through the annual report. It can highlight (without being polemic or strident) past successes and failures in matters of peace and security and in economic, social, cultural, human rights, and other fields and focus world attention on matters that deserve top priority or require continuing follow-up efforts, thereby eliciting the timely collaboration of all parties concerned (governmental and nongovernmental sectors alike) to enhance both minimum and optimum world order.

Appraisal can take many forms. The reporting system developed in the field of human rights has proven highly useful. Under this system, as instituted by the Economic and Social Council, U.N. member states, specialized agencies, and certain nongovernmental organizations submit periodic reports to the Commission on Human Rights. Though the reports submitted by governments tend to be perfunctory and self-serving, their quality and importance can be greatly enhanced if the commission and the council take their tasks of appraisal seriously rather than serve merely as transmitters of superficial information.

The contemporary human rights conventions generally establish a reporting system designed to afford a continuing channel of appraisal. The list includes the International Covenant on Civil and Political Rights; the International Covenant on Economic, Social, and Cultural Rights; the International Convention on the Elimination of All Forms of Racial Discrimination; the Convention on the Political Rights of Women; the Convention Relating to the Status of Refugees; the European Convention on Human Rights; the European Social Charter; and the American Convention on Human Rights. Appraisal has not yet reached its potential.

The International Labor Organization provides the most successful example of sustained institutional appraisal through the reporting system. The ILO Constitution requires a member to submit an annual report to the International Labor Office, specifying the measures it has taken to give effect to the provisions of conventions to which it is a party. The report must conform, both in form and in substance, to the prescribed regulations of the governing body. Such reports, essential for application of ILO Conventions, add to realistic appraisal. To aid the applying and appraising functions, the director general must submit a summary of the governments' reports to each session of the International Labor Conference, and the member governments must transmit, in keeping with the unique, tripartite character of the ILO, copies of their annual reports to the representative organizations of employers and workers. These annual reports are closely examined by a committee of experts composed of independent persons of the highest standing, whose findings are reviewed by the Conference Committee on the Application of Conventions and Recommendations. The committee of experts takes its essential function of "criticism" seriously and draws up a report after a thorough examination. The Conference Committee executes its appraising task by reference to the summary of reports submitted by the director general, the report of the committee of experts, and the additional information provided by governments. At the Conference Committee, governmental representatives can add desired observations or clarify any obscurities to which the committee of experts has drawn attention. Because the Conference Committee is tripartite in composition (representing governments, employers, and workers), nongovernmental interests are well represented in the appraising process. This unique character has proved to be a major asset of the long-standing reporting system of ILO.

In addition to the continuing channels of established structures and procedures, formal appraisal can be performed through occasional international conferences devoted to a particular subject. Notable examples include the International Conference on Human Rights, the United Nations Conference on Environment and Development, the Beijing Women's Conference, the International Conference on Population and Development, and the World Food Conference. Conferences of this kind usually involve such multiple purposes as exchanging information and knowledge, making new proposals, and mobilizing support for action. A key purpose is appraisal. For instance, the International Conference on Human Rights, convened in Tehran in 1968, aspired, among other things, to evaluate "the effectiveness of methods and techniques employed in the field of human rights at the international regional levels."[1] Unfortunately, its achievements in this regard were less than impressive, but the efforts to build on the principles of the United Nations Charter and the Universal Declaration on Human Rights are continuing, as could be seen at the World Conference on Human Rights held in Vienna in 1993. The World Conference of the International Women's Year, convened in Mexico City in 1975, was fairly successful in appraising the process of decision for the advancement of women; the conference also adopted plans of action for the years to come, calling for efforts at all community levels (global, regional, and national) and in all sectors (governmental and nongovernmental). Ten years later, in July 1985, the United Nations Decade for Women Conference was held in Nairobi to praise the Decade for Women. In spite of divergent assessments and political wrangling, the conference ended on a note of unity and a shared sense of purpose and formulated "Forward-Looking Strategies" for advancement of women toward the year 2000 and beyond.[2] In 1995 the Fourth United Nations Conference on Women was held in Beijing, demanding the eradication of discrimination against and violence toward women, reaffirming the right to equal education and freedom of association and speech, and appraising achievements toward goals proclaimed at Nairobi. And, despite efforts by the Chinese authorities to discourage activism, the conference was able to issue a Declaration and Platform for Action providing a blueprint for every country regarding ways to enable the participation of women in society as full citizens.

The persistent financial and other crises confronting the United Nations have kindled a sense of urgent need to make a comprehensive appraisal of the functioning of the organization itself. Even though the U.N. Charter, in Article 109, contemplates a general conference of member states to review the charter in due course, such a conference did not materialize for a long time. The Report of the Joint Inspection Unit on Personnel Problems in the United Nations, known as the Bertrand Report, submitted to the United Nations in 1971,[3] showed devastatingly the absence of any effective appraising function for most of the U.N.'s political and technical programs. When the United Nations commemorated its fortieth anniversary in a somber mood amid the gathering storms, the General Assembly established a group of high-level intergovernmental experts to undertake a comprehensive review of the efficiency of U.N. administrative and financial functions.[4] The group of eighteen lost no time in carrying out its task and submitted a report to the General Assembly in time for consideration at the forty-first assembly session, commencing in September 1986.[5] The report, dealing with the intergovernmental machinery of the U.N. and its subsidiary organs, the structure of the Secretariat, the personnel policy of the organization, activities related to coordination, monitoring, evaluation, and inspection, and the planning and budget procedure, contained numerous recommendations. It noted that as the U.N. agenda had grown, so had the intergovernmental machinery to sustain it. Agendas and work had become duplicated, particularly in the economic and social fields, and efficiency had suffered.[6]

Perceiving the report as a beginning of a long, continuing process of reform rather than an end, the General Assembly in December 1986 accepted for implementation the recommendations of the group of eighteen and adopted a set of principles to guide the U.N. planning, programming, and budgeting process.[7] Pursuant to one of the recommendations the Economic and Social Council in February 1987 established a special commission to evaluate U.N. functions and structure in the economic and social fields.[8] The task of effective appraisal was long overdue and the agenda lengthy, but the challenging task was begun.

By 1995, an independent working group on the future of the United Nations convened at the request of Secretary-General Boutros Boutros-Ghali was able to issue a report titled "The United Nations in Its Second Half-Century." The report appraised the changing role of the United Nations at a time of sweeping transformation in the world's political, social, and economic order, in communications, and in the environment. The report divided its appraisal and recommendations into four areas: security, the economic sphere, the social fabric, and the United Nations leadership.

Goals were set for the next fifty years in all these areas. Chief among the report's recommendations for "refitting" the good vessel was a major restructuring of the U.N. machinery to create three interrelated councils: an Economic Council and a Social Council, each to function in the same way as the Security Council. ECOSOC would be dissolved. In addition, recommendations were made for the expansion of Security Council membership; a more streamlined General Assembly with a smaller agenda; reorganization of the Secretariat to oversee the restructuring of the U.N. central core into the three-council arrangement; and new options and sources of funding not dependent on internal spending cuts.

In addition, An Agenda for Peace and An Agenda for Development, both issued in 1995 by Boutros Boutros-Ghali, appraised the United Nations achievements and made recommendations for the use of policies such as "preventive diplomacy" and "sustainable development" to meet the challenges posed by changing times.

It may be hoped that the reinvigorated world organization, fortified by renewed commitment and support from its members, can continue to perform its appraising function with all seriousness and turn the present crises into opportunities for the twenty-first century.

On the national level, nation-states are constantly involved, in form or another, in the appraising function regarding events occurring within their borders, for internal or transnational consumption. It is equally urgent that the processes of appraisal in light of the paramount goals of securing minimum and optimum world order be pressed forward simultaneously at national and local levels. The appraising function is also open to nongovernmental participants. Requiring no institutional or representative authority, nongovernmental organizations and individuals play an important role in appraisal, beyond the more familiar roles of intelligence and promotion. For example, they can assess the content and efficiency of authoritative decision and quality of public order and provisionally ascribe responsibility. Mass communication media play a vital role in appraisal, with varying degrees of deliberateness. The intellectual community contributes both individually and collectively to appraisal. The importance attached to scholarly appraisal is most vividly demonstrated in Article 38 of the Statute of International Court of Justice, which includes "the teachings of the most highly qualified publicists of the various nations" as a "subsidiary means for the determination of rules of law" for the court. Ultimately, of course, the aggregate of individuals provide the final review or appraisal through an interacting process of shaping attitudes and behavior. A multiplicity of appraisers (governmental and nongovernmental) democratizes and adds rich diversity to the process of appraisal and serves certain policing functions in the common interest.

The appraising function, viewed as a whole, however, seems sporadic, fragmentary, and unorganized. A more centralized, systematic structure, with adequate authority and effective bases of power, is needed. Though organized appraisal is ultimately reviewable by all participants, an organized process can usefully guide, stimulate, and effectuate both minimum and optimum order. Given the tremendous potentials of modern technology, a proper balance between systematic and sporadic, centralized and decentralized, and organized and unorganized appraisal would vastly upgrade the quality of performance of the function, thereby contributing to the efficiency of all other functions and indeed of the global constitutive process of authoritative decision.

PART EIGHT

EFFECTS

27

Responsibility of States

Nation-states are expected to bear the consequences of their actions or inaction; they may be held responsible for what they do or fail to do. In playing their roles, in interacting with other actors, to pursue their objectives, through institutions, by using resources and employing strategies to perform decision functions, nation-states create complex relations with one another. Their activities in the aggregate generate important value consequences, some intended, some not. But, on the whole, they are held accountable for their actions or inaction, especially when foreseeable damage is involved. This is the area of concern known as responsibility of states, or international responsibility.

In the vast literature this subject is traditionally discussed in terms of responsibility of states for injuries to aliens, with all the related doctrines of minimum international standard versus standard of national treatment, denial of justice, diplomatic protection, and so on. State responsibility in this restrictive sense, constituting the core of customary law in this area in the past, has been substantially dealt with in chapter 12. For present purposes, a larger focus is needed.

Viewed comprehensively, the question of state responsibility relates to every aspect of state activity. It brings all aspects of international law together. It is indeed a vast, complex area in which divergent views and approaches have vigorously contended.

State accountability can occur in many ways: a breach or nonperformance of treaty obligations; violations of international legal norms; failure to maintain internal order; unintentional acts that foreseeably create harmful effects on others. Just a quick list of examples:

- About 500 Iranian militants seized the U.S. embassy in Tehran, taking 90 hostages (including 66 Americans).
- A Soviet military aircraft shot down a South Korean civilian aircraft that

strayed off course into and was leaving Soviet airspace, killing all 269 people aboard.

- Canada fired on and seized a Spanish fishing vessel outside the twelve-mile limit, claiming that the vessel was using undersized nets to capture immature fish in violation of international law.
- After repeated denials, the French government admitted that its agents sank an antinuclear protest ship belonging to Greenpeace, an international environmental group, in New Zealand.
- The United States accused Libya of aiding terrorists who carried out airport attacks in Rome and Vienna.
- In December 1987, Pan Am Flight 103 exploded over Lockerbie, Scotland, allegedly the result of actions by Libyan terrorists, whom Libya subsequently refused to hand over for trial.
- The United States supplied the contras in Nicaragua with military supplies and a manual depicting illegal tactics.
- In July 1988, the U.S. cruiser *Vincennes* shot down an Iranian civilian airbus with 290 people on board after it did not respond to repeated warnings on civilian and military radio channels.
- A state expropriated property owned by foreign corporations without adequately compensating them.
- Iraq, state party to a cease-fire, refused to allow U.N. inspectors to continue monitoring its compliance with disarmament commitments.
- Israeli agents, using forged Canadian passports, attempted to poison a Hamas leader on Jordanian territory.
- Although it was a party to the ANZUS Treaty of Mutual Security of 1951, New Zealand refused to allow port visits by U.S. ships capable of carrying nuclear weapons.
- Acid rain originating in the United States has caused damage to plant and animal life and to aquatic ecosystems in Canada.
- The nuclear-powered Cosmos 954 naval surveillance satellite, launched by the Soviet Union in September 1977, crashed to earth in January 1978, leaving debris on Canadian territory that necessitated a costly joint U.S.-Canadian cleanup operation.
- On April 26, 1986, the Chernobyl nuclear power station, about seventy miles north of Kiev, exploded and burned, spewing radioactive particles into the atmosphere, causing deaths and injuries by the hundreds and forcing the evacuation of some 100,000 people from the surrounding area. It took two weeks to bring the ensuing fire under control. Because the Soviets withheld information about the accident, most of the world did not learn of it until April 28, forty-eight hours later, when Sweden detected abnormally high radiation

levels in Scandinavia. The disaster spread radioactive fallout across much of Europe, contaminating farm vegetables and the forage of cows and sheep.

- During the Gulf War, retreating Iraqi forces bombed oil wells and production facilities in Kuwait, causing widespread atmospheric and ecological damage.
- The military action taken in Kosovo has created an array of problems. For example, it has resulted in air and water pollution due to all the chemicals used by NATO forces during the war. Children are suffering from both short- and long-term exposure to psycho-traumatic experiences. Not only have many children lost their lives because of this war, but those who have survived have also lost big parts of their lives due to the destruction of the country's economical potential and their limited access to education. Finally, even cultural monuments of great historical value have suffered as a result of the war.

A proper focus would thus require locating the question of state responsibility in the context of a state's dealings with other actors, not only in terms of protection and treatment of aliens (which remains, of course, a vital aspect of this field) but in other areas of international law.

In the necessarily brief treatment of this vast and complex field, we are especially concerned with a range of questions involving "who does what to whom, how, under what circumstances, with what outcomes and effects, and what responses." More specifically: What action or inaction will trigger international responsibility for states? An internationally wrongful act? What is an internationally wrongful act? A breach of treaty obligations? A violation of international legal norms, customary or conventional? Failure to act? Is deprivation (actual and potential) required? What type of damage and harm? Are states held responsible for all acts of their state officials, or only when such acts occur under the authority or color of authority of the state? In other words, what acts are regarded as attributable, or imputable, to states and what acts are not? How about the acts of private parties and individuals? Acts of private armies? What standard of conduct is expected and required of states? Is negligence always required, or is the strict (no-fault) standard applicable? What procedures must victim states follow to seek a remedy, and what remedies are available?

BASIC COMMUNITY POLICY

The paramount objective sought through the law of state responsibility is the minimization of all unauthorized coercions and deprivations. More specifically, as developed in chapter 24, this overriding goal can be described in terms of six subgoals: (1) prevention of violation of international legal norms, both customary and conventional, and of deprivations; (2) deterrence of impending violations or deprivations; (3) restoration of conditions altered by violations; (4) rehabilitation of resulting deprivations through reparation or compensation; (5) reconstruction of overall conditions in ways that would minimize future incidences of violations and deprivations; and (6) corrections directed at individual human actors, who are the ultimate driving force behind state actions.

Each goal is distinct yet closely related to the others. The relative weight of each is a function of the context involved.

TRENDS IN DECISION AND CONDITIONING FACTORS

International law of state responsibility has historically been an outgrowth of customary law, centering on the subject of treating aliens and protecting nationals abroad and extending to other areas of international law. The development of customary law in this area — especially by Latin American countries and by the Soviet Union after the Bolshevik Revolution — has not gone unchallenged in the past.

The emancipation of peoples from the shackles of colonialism and the proliferation of new states after the establishment of the United Nations have had tremendous impacts on the development of contemporary international law. One area of contention has been the responsibility of states. Many newly independent nations assert that the customary law of state responsibility is a relic of colonialism and imperialism, a product of past Western domination, in the formulation of which they had played no part. Some would like to choose what customary prescriptions apply to them — which of course cannot be tolerated if minimum world public order is to be maintained.

The clarion call has been to codify international law of state responsibility, a call that came shortly after the International Law Commission began its work in the codification and progressive development of international law. Codification — providing workable guidelines in service of the common interest — in this complex area is no mean task, as the members of the International Law Commission have learned in abundance. Progress has been painfully slow, and the commission has had considerable difficulty in deciding what its focus should be — whether comprehensive or narrow. At its inception in 1949, the commission identified "the law of state responsibility" as a topic suitable for codification. In its early phase, when García-Amador was the special rapporteur (1955–61), it focused on the responsibility of states for injuries to aliens. Altogether García-Amador submitted six reports to the commission. Unfortunately, the commission was unable to devote its attention to these reports, which contained some very innovative ideas and proposals.

Instead, in 1963 the commission scrapped its old efforts and charted a new course in its work on state responsibility. As Roberto Ago became the new special rapporteur, the commission shifted to a more comprehensive focus: dropping the subject of state responsibility for injuries to aliens and undertaking the subject of international responsibility of states in general, dealing with "general rules" and "general aspects." After Ago submitted many reports, the commission in 1980 at last completed the first reading of part 1 of the draft articles on state responsibility, which deals with the origin of international responsibility and contains thirty-five articles.[1] Part 1 contains chapters titled "General Principles," "The 'Act of the State' Under International Law," "The Breach of an International Obligation," and "Implication of a State in the Internationally Wrongful Act of Another State." The commission has since proceeded to work on part 2 of state responsibility, dealing with the content, forms, and degrees of international responsibility, including the problems of reparation and punitive consequences of an internationally wrongful act of a state. Current draft article 19 would permit the finding that a state is criminally liable for certain occurrences, although this article is presently opposed by the United States and France.

In spite of the slow progress in the work of the International Law Commission and the divergent views that continue to exist in this vast complex area, some general and tentative observations, including the contours and highlights of the Draft Articles, may be made.

What Act or Omission: An Internationally Wrongful Act

State responsibility on the international plane is the consequence of a state's violation of its substantive legal obligations — namely, acts or omissions regarding treaty and customary law obligations. Thus, Draft Article 1 states: "Every internationally wrongful act of a State entails the international responsibility of that State."[2]

Under this formulation, an internationally wrongful act of a state consists of two elements:

1. An action or omission is attributable to the state: this raises the question of state action in international law, traditionally discussed in terms of "attributability" or "imputability."
2. The action or omission involved constitutes a violation of an international obligation, customary or conventional.

A fundamental change of perspective is reflected in this new formulation, moving from the traditional damage-oriented approach to an obligation-centered approach. A violation of an international obligation, not the occurrence of damage, triggers international responsibility for a state. Even without damage, the mere fact that an international obligation has been violated will result in international responsibility.

This fundamental shift in perspective leads to the crucial question: At what moment is international responsibility triggered? The moment of violation, not that when actual damage occurred, is determinative. Situations may exist in which a violation of an obligation cannot be determined without verifying the existence of damage. An example in point is transfrontier pollution insofar as the pollution-causing activity is not subject to any specific conduct-related norms of international law. In such a situation, damage is an unavoidable criterion for ascertaining conduct that violates international law. When action or failure to act is attributable to a state and internationally wrongful, then the question of possible remedies arises. This is reflected in Articles 20–26 of the draft articles.

By Whom: The Concept of State Action—Imputability or Attributability

International responsibility arises only when an act or omission is imputable to the state. A state is responsible for any breach of its international obligations through action or inaction by state organs, agencies and governmental officials, employees, and agents. This extends not only to conduct within the scope of governmental authority but also to conduct under color of such authority. The concept is broad: it matters little which branch of government — executive, legislative, judicial, or other — is involved. Similarly, governmental officials and employees, regardless of their position in governmental hierarchy, are within the reach of this broad concept of state action.

For state officials in the field of external affairs, such as heads of state, foreign ministers, and diplomats, their acts are easily imputable to the state because of their authority to represent the state according to its internal law. For governmental officials in the area of internal affairs, the determination of what is imputable may seem to pose a greater problem. But a basic community policy is that every state is expected to maintain its internal decision-making processes in such a way as to fulfill international obligations. An excuse based on internal law is no defense. This is the essence of the supremacy of international law over national law.

When governmental officials act within the limits of their authority under internal law, their acts naturally are attributable to the state. A particularly controversial issue is whether unauthorized acts or acts deemed to be *ultra vires* under international law may give rise to state responsibility.

In ascertaining the attributability of actions to the state the respective domains of international and domestic law are generally distinguished. Although reference is commonly made to national law to determine if an individual is competent to act on behalf of the state, the question of whether an outcome is attributable to the state is governed exclusively by international law. State responsibility is imputed only if an injury is inflicted in a wrongful manner under international law; a state may not plead principles of its domestic law in defense of an international claim.

Therefore, although the putative wrong may result from an ultra vires act, the official and the state will not be immune from legal consequences. It is sufficient that the act was taken pursuant to general or apparent authority — as in the use of measures appropriate to the actor's official character, which is distinguished from some personal independent act.

Even when the breach of an international norm is attributable to a state so as to make it internationally responsible, certain conditions, as stipulated in Articles 29–35, may justify the state's act or omission, thereby "precluding wrongfulness." These "circumstances precluding wrongfulness" are consent, countermeasures in respect of an internationally wrongful act, *force majeure* and fortuitous event, distress, state of necessity, and self-defense. Some of these justifications, such as assumption of risk and contributory negligence, are familiar from basic municipal law. Others involve the various forms of self-defense, individual or collective.

Force majeure in the sense of an "irresistible force" or "unforeseen external event" beyond a state's control may also justify a state's breach of an international obligation.[3] This defense would seem to be analogous to the impossibility of performance doctrine of treaty law.

"Necessity" as a justification for a state's breach of an international norm is highly restricted. Under Draft Article 33, it may not be invoked when the norm breached arises out of "general international law," when a treaty breached expressly excludes necessity as a defense, or when "the State in question has contributed to the occurrence of the state of necessity."[4] In the situation of war, however, military necessity may be invoked to justify certain actions (such as seizure of alien ships within a state's jurisdiction) but not others (such as violations of the requirements of the Geneva Conventions not expressly limited by the principle of necessity).

Standard of Conduct

The customary standard of state responsibility is based on the fault principle. A state is held responsible for an act performed with some degree of guilty knowledge or negligence that causes a proscribed result. The subjectivity underlying a particular conduct is significant. If, for example, a state expropriates a foreign investor's property for the purpose of political reprisal or other retaliation, such taking is deemed "arbitrary" and hence impermissible. But if a government takes private property pursuant to a genuine public purpose (for example, land reform or industrial nationalization) in a nondiscriminatory manner, such a taking is presumed lawful, provided just compensation is made.

Whether a state is at fault can also be presumed. A state is presumed responsible, for example, when injury results from a state's failure to exercise effective control over its territory or to maintain an effective system of justice. A most instructive example of the relation between a state's exercise of sovereign control and the imputation of culpable knowledge, and thus international responsibility, is the *Corfu Channel* case (1949).[5] In that case, the International Court of Justice held Albania liable for damage incurred by British ships passing through Albanian territorial waters in which mines had been placed. Because Albania had exclusive control over these waters (and Britain the right to unobstructed passage), Albania was obligated to warn Britain of dangers known or reasonably foreseeable to Albania; its failure to do so — a reasonable inference was that it was wrongfully negligent — resulted in the imposition of international responsibility. Significantly, it was immaterial that a specific agent of Albania was not shown to be directly culpable: "Strictly, every breach of duty on the part of a state must arise by reason of the act or omission of one or more of the organs of the state, and since in many contexts the principle of objective responsibility applies, the emphasis is on causal connexion and the 'conduct appropriate' to a given situation."[6]

The adequacy of the fault principle in connection with activities that generate transnational pollution and damage the global environment has been increasingly questioned in recent years. The central issue is whether fault is required in order to find liability or whether the mere fact of transnational pollution-caused damage is sufficient.

At present, the fault principle remains the applicable general international standard. Neither case law nor practice recognizes the imposition of strict liability for occurrences of transnational pollution. As discussed in chapter 10, however, a trend toward the no-fault principle may be the making. This is most evident in the area of so-called ultrahazardous activities (such as nuclear energy generation or spacecraft launching). Under the Convention on International Liability for Damage Caused by Space Objects (1972), for example, the launching state assumes absolute liability for damage caused by its space object on the surface of the earth. And the no-fault principle is incorporated in the Convention on the Liability of Operators of Nuclear Ships (1962).

It is crucial to determine when an activity is hazardous. Without such determination, any transnational damage due, for example, to pollution from a particular activity would not give rise to absolute or strict liability. The extent of damage, however, if sufficient, could itself serve as evidence that the activity is ultrahazardous.

A further controversy relates to whether a state may be held strictly liable for transnational pollution damage resulting from private ultrahazardous activity. The better view is that in such a situation the control of the state may be presumed, and thus the state should be liable. As the state is presumed to benefit from the hazardous activity, so it should be held accountable for any associated transnational costs. It may even be that in a given case fault is provable.

With the growing expansion of ultrahazardous activities on an interdependent planet, it is increasingly urged that the concept of "responsibility" be kept distinct from that of "liability." Whereas responsibility is attached to an internationally wrongful act for violating an international obligation, liability may result from lawful activities that damage others. For the former, state responsibility is predicated on a violation of an international obligation rather than on damage; for the latter, damage is the basis of liability. In its work on state responsibility, the International Law Commission has maintained this distinction: state "responsibility" for internationally wrongful acts and international "liability" for the injurious consequences of activities that are lawful, activities that are not prohibited per se by international law but that have deleterious consequences.

Procedure for Remedy

State responsibility may sometimes be characterized as "direct" or "vicarious." When a state imposes deprivation on another state, its wrongful act results in "direct" responsibility. The aggrieved state can thus make an international claim for remedy against the offending state without first submitting itself to the domestic legal procedure of the offending state. Where an alien suffers deprivation, the host state does not automatically become "responsible." International law, however, may require, given the nature of the deprivation, that the host state take some action to punish the wrongdoer and provide an appropriate remedy through its domestic courts or other agencies for the injured alien. Indeed, failure to do so would constitute a breach of the state's international obligations and result in its international responsibility. The responsibility of the state stems not from the wrong originally committed against the injured alien but from the state's failure to provide reasonable access to its courts and to afford an effective remedy for this wrong.

In regard to state responsibility arising from injuries to aliens, customary law has developed what is known as the doctrine of exhaustion of local remedies. Under this doctrine, before a protecting state may espouse, on behalf of its nationals, an international claim against another state for alleged injuries to its nationals, the injured party must first exhaust all remedies available under the domestic law of the defendant state. This includes the full use of all the state's procedural devices, such as the use of witnesses and the procuring of depositions and documentation.

An alien, in entering the host country, is presumed to submit voluntarily to the legal order there. Civil claims against him or her "follow the person" into the host territory. In addition, the doctrine of exhaustion of local remedies expresses the policy of effectiveness and economy, seeking to foster localization of dispute settlement and minimize international friction. Local remedies must be exhausted before a claim can be internationalized.

A key issue concerning the duty to exhaust "local judicial remedies" is the extent to which the private party must go in order to satisfy that duty. The test has been that of reasonableness. Reasonableness, as third-party decision makers may determine, can be ascertained by reference to judicial jurisdiction, the degree of independence of the judicial system concerned, available compensation, and temporal factors.

Will the courts of the host state hear the claim on its merits? Or would the local courts dismiss it on such grounds as political question? When will continued efforts at local remedies become patently futile? If the case has already been heard at the trial level and the state's appellate courts may only address questions of law, a question of fact may remain in issue. If so, further attempts at redress may be futile. Similarly, if, due to political pressure and interference, the courts of the state are apparently in no position to perform their function independently and impartially, there may be no need to pursue local remedies. That a remedy exists on paper does not necessarily mean the presence of effective remedies, as international tribunals have often acknowledged. As a matter of practical wisdom, the costs of proceeding further on the local level are often balanced against the chances of eventual "satisfaction." Finally, a remedy that is not forthcoming within a reasonable time may be no remedy at all. Justice unduly delayed will be justice denied.

In the famous *Interhandel* case of 1959,[7] the Swiss company Interhandel had sought in vain, through litigation in American courts for more than a decade, the release of assets seized by the United States during World War II. The government of Switzerland, in extending diplomatic protection to its national company, urged the International Court of Justice to make an exception to the rule of exhaustion of local remedies in light of the protracted legal proceedings involved. The court, however, declared the case inadmissible for failure to exhaust local remedies and expressed confidence in the judicial system of the United States, especially its Supreme Court, to treat the matter in conformity with international law.

Types of Remedy Available

The commission of an internationally wrongful act gives rise to state responsibility and commonly results in the duty to make some form of reparations. The purposes of reparations are not only to restore conditions altered by violations and to rehabilitate resulting deprivations but also to prevent and deter future incidences of violation. "[R]eparations must," in the words of the Permanent Court of International Justice in the *Chorzow Factory* (Indemnity) case (1928), "as far as possible, wipe out all the consequences of the illegal act and reestablish the situation which would, in all probability, have existed, if that act had not been committed."[8] Broadly conceived, this may take the form of restitution, compensation, punishment of responsible individuals, official apology, or other forms of satisfaction. The form of reparation in a particular case would depend largely on the injuries and damages involved and the demands of the injured state or other claimant.

Restitution, the preferred form of reparations, is essentially a return to the status quo ante and entails the performance of an obligation, revocation of an unlawful act, return of property wrongfully removed, or abstention from further wrongful conduct. Restitution includes two forms, legal restitution and restitution in kind. The former occurs when a tribunal refuses to recognize, or declares invalid, an act of the offending party. Restitution in kind, which is exceptional, is often not the most appropriate method of reparation; in many situations it is preferable to have a remedy that accommodates the internal authority of governments while redressing the injured party.

Indemnity or money payment should be made if restitution in kind is impossible. Generally, this should compensate for all damages that result from the unlawful act. Costs, interest, and even attorney fees are typically awarded by arbitral and domestic tribunals. In some instances even punitive or aggravated damages have been awarded to states and private litigants. In the case of Iraq, the Cooperation Commission, established in 1991 to administer and provide compensation to victims of Iraqi aggression in the Gulf War, is processing more than 2.6 million claims valued at more than $160 billion.

Finally, satisfaction is appropriate for nonwealth deprivations and takes the form of regrets, apologies, punishment of guilty officials, measures to prevent recurrence, or formal acknowledgment or judicial declaration regarding the wrong. The "year of the spy" (1985) in the United States reached its climax when a civilian counterintelligence analyst for the U.S. Navy was charged with selling military secrets to the Israelis for large amounts of money. It sent tremors through official Washington, causing shock or disbelief among Israel's friends and supporters. It raised, among other things, the question of the degree of ministerial responsibility for Israel's purported espionage operation in the United States, its staunchest ally. Was this an act of the government of Israel, or was it merely the work of a "loose cannon" in the Israeli intelligence apparatus? Who was to be held responsible? Under growing U.S. pressures and after some stutters of embarrassment, the Israeli government apologized for its espionage in the United States to the extent that it did take place. And the United States quickly welcomed Israel's apology and closed the book.

On July 3, 1988, the U.S. cruiser *Vincennes* shot down an Iranian civilian airbus (Iran Air Flight 655) en route to Dubai from Bandar Abbas with 290 people on board for having failed to respond to seven warnings on civilian and military radio channels. The United States shortly expressed "regret," though not an "apology," for the tragic incident and promised to pay compensation directly to the victims' families out of humanitarian concern and compassion, pending an authoritative determination of responsibility. The case was withdrawn from the ICJ when both countries were able to reach an agreement settling all claims.

During NATO's campaign to force the Yugoslav army out of Kosovo, U.S. warplanes, on May 7, 1999, inadvertently bombed China's embassy in Belgrade, killing three Chinese journalists and injuring more than twenty others. Despite President Clinton's apologies, the Chinese government rejected the official U.S. explanation that the embassy had been accidentally targeted, and mobs of angry demonstrators attacked and damaged the U.S. embassy in Beijing. On July 30, 1999, the two countries reached a partial settlement, and the United States agreed to pay China $4.5 million as compensation for the victims. In December 1999 the two countries reached a further agreement: the United States would pay $28 million for the destruction of the Chinese embassy in Yugoslavia, and China would provide $2.87 million to cover damages to the U.S. embassy and consulates in China caused by the angry demonstrators.

28

Succession of States

A nation-state is like a living organism, having a life cycle of its own — from birth, through growth and maturity, to demise. Just as change is a fact of life for a human being, so it is for a nation-state. Changes for a territorial community are manifested in various ways, relating to each of the important features of its community process. Changes may occur in patterns of participation, involving both effective elites and established officials. They may involve perspectives, as manifested in fundamental constitutional policies and in ideological orientation. Changes may relate to the aggregate situation of interaction, especially changes in structures of government. They may occur in the aggregate bases of power, in terms of control over territory, resources, and people. Changes may be manifested in the strategies employed, in terms of relative emphasis on persuasion and coercion and management of differing instruments of policy. Finally, changes may relate to outcomes in the performance of various decision functions, especially prescriptions and applications.

These changes occur in differing degrees and combinations. Some are relatively insignificant, leaving a territorial community virtually as it was before. Some may be so fundamental as to give birth to a new territorial community. In response to such changes, territorial communities have made certain distinctive claims, traditionally under the labels of "state" and "governmental" succession.

Central to the distinction between state and governmental succession is whether a change fundamentally affects the legal identity and continuity of a territorial community as a nation-state. When changes involve only the government itself — notably changes in leadership (effective elites or established officials), basic constitutional policy, internal or external policies, or structures of government — the question of governmental succession arises, entailing no effect on the legal identity and continuity of the state it represents. This involves

no change in territorial domain. When changes involve continuity or disconti-
nuity in authoritative and effective control over territory, people, and resources,
the question of the legal identity and continuity of statehood is seriously implicated, giving rise to the question of state succession.

Sometimes such a distinction is far from easy to draw. After the Bolshevik
Revolution of 1917, for example, the new government claimed itself to be not
only a new government but also a new state, and hence not responsible for the
international obligations assumed by the previous regime. Other states rejected
such claims, holding the USSR responsible for those obligations. After the
dissolution of the USSR in 1991, the Russian Federation, existing as a successor state to the former Soviet Union, voluntarily assumed legal responsibility for all treaty and international obligations of its predecessor. At any
rate, the traditional distinction between changes in state and changes in government, with its inordinate emphasis on the territorial factor, has been increasingly attacked.

The present focus, nevertheless, is the question of state succession. This
question historically arose in the transfer of territory from one nation to another
through cession, annexation of colonial territories, federation, or dissolution of
a federation. Since the establishment of the United Nations, thanks to the
process of decolonization, a predominant phenomenon has been the emergence
of new states via the independence of colonial territories and peoples. As
decolonization runs its course, problems of succession arise in other contexts,
including secession, the dismemberment of existing states, and the formation of
unions of states.

Among the important questions raised are: To what extent does a successor
state acquire the treaty rights and obligations of its predecessor? Does the
successor inherit its predecessor's membership in international governmental
organizations? Do the inhabitants of the transferred territory become nationals
of the successor? To what extent does the predecessor's state property pass to
the successor? What state is to be held liable for public debts of the predecessor? Where do the state archives of the predecessor go?

BASIC COMMUNITY POLICY

Two theoretical constructs for state succession have historically contended:
universal succession and outright nonsuccession.

Universal succession, posited by Grotius, was the earliest theory and lin-
gered until the twentieth century. This view, derived from an analogy to the
Roman law of testamentary succession, held that all rights and obligations of

the predecessor state passed to the successor state automatically on the former's extinction, since its legal personality continued on. Certain absolute natural rights, once established, were deemed to attach to the state, as defined by its territorial domain, and were inherited even though rulers may subsequently have changed. Arrangements undertaken by the sovereign in a public capacity, including debts, treaties, and contracts, descended to the successor state. The universal succession theory was a general response to the frequent political and boundary changes caused by wars and other upheavals in Europe during the eighteenth and nineteenth centuries.

The nonsuccession theory gained support in the late nineteenth century. Moving to the polar opposite of universal succession, negative theorists maintained that all rights and obligations of the predecessor state were to lapse on succession. Law was conceived of as an expression of "sovereign will"; the substitution of a sovereign necessarily implicated a change in will and a change in the legal order. In treaty matters, as will be described below, the negative theory did allow certain exceptions to the rule.

Neither of these polar views — universal succession and automatic nonsuccession — can be expected to secure the common interest in accommodating the need for stability and the demand for change in the contemporary world. The complementary policies sought by the larger community here, as in the field of international agreements, are that of maintaining a reasonable stability of expectations of people and that of fostering peaceful change, responsive to changing demands, expectations, and conditions. To strike a proper balance between the two is no mean task; it requires a contextual scrutiny of all relevant factors by reference especially to the overriding goals of minimum and optimum order.

TRENDS IN DECISION AND CONDITIONING FACTORS

During the colonial era, the law of state succession largely mirrored the progress of empires: rise, struggle, and fall. The law of state succession was just another branch of law that reflected the permissibility of the use of force to acquire territory through conquest and other coercion.

In the contemporary era of decolonization and self-determination, state succession has been linked most closely to the birth of independent states newly freed from colonial bondage. New problems have developed that cannot be adequately dealt with by customary law. This has proved even more true with the post–Cold War creation of new states in the former Soviet Empire. Current practice is as diverse as it is confusing. The need to clarify the common interests involved and formulate workable guidelines has been evident.

In recognition of this need, the International Law Commission has undertaken the task, culminating in the conclusion of the Vienna Convention on Succession of States in Respect of Treaties of 1978 (hereafter the Treaty Succession Convention) and the Vienna Convention on Succession of States in Respect of State Property, Archives, and Debts of 1983 (hereafter the Other Succession Convention).

The Treaty Succession Convention is patterned after the Vienna Convention on the Law of Treaties, and seeks to maintain continuity with it. The International Law Commission, in designing the Treaty Succession Convention, deemed it important to incorporate language paralleling the earlier convention. The Treaty Succession Convention applies only to the effects of a succession occurring "in conformity with international law." Hence, its prescriptions will not apply to transfers of territory through the use of force or in violation of the principle of self-determination, as in the case of South African Bantustans. The convention applies prospectively only, but states may on their own declaration have the convention apply in respect of their own succession occurring before the effective date of the convention, provided that other state parties to a treaty in question consent.

The Other Succession Convention deals with state succession in respect only to the categories listed — state property, archives, and debts — and is inapplicable to other subjects. Like the Treaty Succession Convention, the Other Succession Convention applies only to the effects of succession that occur lawfully in accordance with the principles of the United Nations Charter. Its application is prospective, extending only to the effects of succession that occur after the convention enters into force. Successor states may, however, declare that the convention shall apply to the effects of their own succession occurring before that time, in relation to another party to the convention, which by declaration accepts such retroactive application. It would thus appear that, in terms of time and space, the scope of application for the two succession conventions is limited.

In the following sections, major aspects of state succession are highlighted in light of recent state practice as well as the new succession conventions.

International Agreements

The two major theories of state succession — universal and outright nonsuccession — have been particularly relevant to treaty matters.

According to the theory of universal succession, a successor state inherits the rights and obligations of its predecessor. This was the controlling theory until the later part of the nineteenth century, an age in which relatively few treaties were extant. As the number of international agreements multiplied, the inadvisability of the universal succession theory became increasingly apparent.

The negative theory of state succession evolved in the late nineteenth century and was highly influential in the early part of the twentieth century. It relied heavily on the contract principle that obligations contemplating personal performance are erased by the death of a party to the contract, owing to impossibility of performance. This theory also relied on the distinction between succession of government and succession of state: only in the latter are treaty obligations erased. This distinction has contributed significantly to the intellectual confusion in this area of law.

An important exception allowed by the negative school to its general theory of noncontinuation of treaties concerns "dispositive" or "impersonal" treaties. This class of treaties consists of those which determine boundaries or establish servitudes and easements or other related rights of a permanent character (for instance, transit, navigation, and demilitarization).

The negative theory, furthermore, distinguishes total from partial succession: total succession involves extinction of the predecessor state, whereas partial succession involves only the cession of a portion of a state's territory, not the legal personality of the ceding state. In regard to total succession, the "clean slate" doctrine makes all treaty rights and obligations lapse automatically. In the case of partial succession, the "moving treaty frontiers" doctrine prevails: the predecessor's treaties cease to apply to the lost territory, but the successor state's treaties become applicable.

In recent decades, writers have espoused three major theories of state succession. Two represent reformulations of the traditional theories, and the third is an eclectic approach that incorporates elements of both.

The universalists point to the need for stability in international relations and the chaos that would result if every change of "sovereignty" became a pretext to repudiate treaty obligations. For support they rely heavily on the general practice of newly independent states.

The neonegativists, in contrast, assert that the issue of state succession is essentially a matter of policy rather than law. Under this theory, the entire issue of succession to treaties is itself viewed as a matter of treaty law rather than succession law. A treaty cannot be assumed to apply automatically to a successor state unless the intentions of the parties were that it would so apply, and even then the doctrine of rebus sic stantibus might well prevail.

The eclectic theory, which seeks a proper balance, has taken two forms. One approach relies on the special status of dispositive treaties, and state practice concerning them, and by analogy attempts to identify other types of treaties that should also be accorded automatic survival. These include, notably, extradition treaties and lawmaking, or legislative, treaties. The latter group refers to treaties that codify customary international law or prescribe new standards for various activities having transnational effect. The other approach, termed the Nyerere doctrine, involves a voluntary provisional period of application by a successor state of all the predecessor's treaties in force.

The modern practice of successor states as to treaties has been less than consistent. The traditional distinction between dispositive and personal treaties lingers: dispositive treaties are inheritable and personal treaties are not. Dispositive treaties have in general been considered to survive succession, under both state practice and international judicial decisions. The trend concerning multilateral conventions has also been toward continuity.

The main trouble area has been that of "personal treaties" between states. Whatever consistency is exhibited in this area depends largely on the specific type of state succession involved. In cases of annexations, cessions, and secessions, the treaties of the predecessor state have generally lapsed and those of the successor have taken over. In cases of succession involving union or federation, treaties have generally lapsed when they result in constitutional problems or inconsistent obligations.

Newly independent states — the predominant form of successor states in the post–World War II era — have employed diverse and inconsistent practices. These new states, plagued by bitter experiences of colonial rule, kindled by a new sense of pride, nationalism, and adventure, handicapped by relative inexperience and ignorance, and disciplined by the hard realities of a complex, interactive world, have been extremely assertive on the question of succession to the treaties of their predecessor states. Moving away from the general pattern developed in the era of European colonization, the new states have followed five paths:

1. *Total rejection:* This follows the negativist position by rejecting totally prior treaties under the doctrine of clean slate. A new state thus commences its national life unfettered by the treaties that had applied to its territories before independence. Notable examples are Israel, Algeria, and Upper Volta (Burkina Faso).
2. *Devolution agreements:* By virtue of a devolution agreement, a new state explicitly agrees to assume the rights and obligations of the treaties that the prior administering power had concluded for, and applied to, the territory of the new state. A British innovation, this device was used extensively in terminating all types of British dependencies. France and the Netherlands followed this practice to a lesser extent.
3. *Temporary application:* This in essence is the Nyerere doctrine, allowing preindependence treaties to continue for an interim period pending review. When Tanganyika attained independence, President Julius Nyerere refused

to conclude a devolution agreement with the United Kingdom. Instead, he declared that, for a period of two years, all of the predecessor's treaties affecting Tanganyika would provisionally continue in force. During this period, Tanganyika would review each treaty individually, with a view to reaching an accord with the interested parties on continuing or modifying such treaties in a mutually agreeable manner. If Tanganyika took no action before the interim expired, preindependence treaties would lapse automatically. This formula has been followed by such states as Botswana, Burundi, Kenya, Lesotho, Malawi, and Swaziland.

4. *Selective acceptance:* Under this approach, a new state simply picks and chooses, unilaterally declaring which of the predecessor's treaties it will honor and which it will disregard. Examples include the Congo (Brazzaville) and the Republic of the Congo (Leopoldville). (Earlier examples include the Soviet Union and the People's Republic of China; the independent former Soviet republics have not followed this approach.)

5. *Deferment of decision:* Some new states have found it more convenient not to take an immediate stand on the question of succession to treaties. They adopt a noncommittal posture by deferring a decision and prefer to deal with particular problems as they arise. A notable example is Madagascar (formerly Malagasy Republic).

Unlike "newly independent" states, the "separating" state's international legal identity is said to remain relatively constant. The separating seccessor state is obligated to maintain the international obligations of the predecessor state. The dissolution of the union of the United Kingdom of Sweden and Norway in 1905 illustrates state practice in cases of separation.

In the case of the former USSR, it has been suggested that its division into fifteen separate entities after the breakup makes these new republics "separating" states. Although the Russian Federation has voluntarily agreed to assume the obligations of the former Soviet Union, however, it has been pointed out that because the former republics may not satisfy the traditional understanding of the "dependent territory test" used to determine the status of new states, the new republics need not assume these former obligations. Under the "dependent territory test," former states that were not dependent upon a predecessor state for international relations are deemed to have consented to preexisting international agreements. In the case of the former Soviet republics, however, many may in fact have been essentially colonial states; and many of the agreements to which they are party may not have been consensual. Thus, conventional international law's static and rigid distinction between separate and newly independent states fails to address "hybrid" situations such as that of the former USSR.

It would appear, from the foregoing, that contemporary state practice is characterized by diversity and considerable freedom of choice.

The Treaty Succession Convention (the Vienna Convention on Succession of States in Respect of Treaties) was greatly influenced by the newly independent states' actions concerning their predecessor states' treaties. While reiterating "the principles of free consent, good faith and *pacta sunt servanda*," the convention also underscores the basic principles of international law embodied in the U.N. Charter, including self-determination, sovereign equality and independence of all states, noninterference in the domestic affairs of other states, nonuse of force, and protection of human rights. The outcome was considered more the development, rather than the codification, of law in this area.

The Treaty Succession Convention painstakingly sought to accommodate the complementary policies of stability and change (flexibility), giving partial expression to both major traditional theories on state succession. The policy differentiation is made contingent on the factual context of succession. Generally speaking, in the case of succession due to unification or separation of states, the policy is to continue the predecessor's treaties; in the context of newly independent states, the policy of clean slate prevails. Article 16 states: "A newly independent State is not bound to maintain in force, or to become a party to, any treaty by reason only of the fact that at the date of the succession of States the treaty was in force in respect of the territory to which the succession of States relates."

Much language in the convention can be traced to the Vienna Convention on the Law of Treaties, and, to the extent possible, the International Law Commission attempted to be consistent as to both conventions. Several situations are expressly excluded from the scope of the convention. They include state succession in violation of international law, successions in respect of international organizations, questions regarding treaties resulting from hostilities, and questions relating to military occupations.

A significant departure from previous law is found in Articles 11 and 12, which leave the continuity of dispositive treaties open to question. A succession of states "as such" is said not to affect such treaties, but there is no positive requirement that they be continued by successor states. This seems to be in keeping with the fact that the convention imposes no requirement that treaties continue in operation with regard to newly independent states.

An interesting and highly controversial provision of the convention appears in Article 7, dealing with the temporal application of the convention. Article 7(1) declares that, "except as may be otherwise agreed" between a successor state and a party to the convention, "the Convention applies only in respect of a succession of States which has occurred after the entry into force of the Convention." The problem with an absolute bar to retroactive application would have been that newly independent states would be precluded from taking advantage of the convention, since they could not become parties until after their succession. This problem was overcome in Article 7, paragraphs 2 and 3, whereby newly independent states are enabled to apply the convention retroactively to their own successions, once they agree to be bound by it, through declarations to this effect. Only those state parties accepting the successor state's declaration are bound as to the convention's applicability to the successor state's succession. The successor state is also able to apply the convention provisionally to its own succession before the convention's entry into force.

Membership in International Governmental Organizations

A matter of related concern to newly independent states is their admission to membership in international governmental organizations, such as the United Nations, the International Labor Organization, the International Monetary Fund, or, as in the case of some Eastern European countries, membership in the European Union and NATO. The central issue is whether such organizations will readily extend admission opportunities to new states, or whether they will be extended membership by virtue of a predecessor's membership. Joining an organization as a new member or as a successor to the membership of an existing state can be of considerable significance. As a successor to an existing membership, for example, a state is expected to assume the burden of indebtedness for expenses and so on incurred by its predecessor or to inherit the benefits of standing credit.

The issue of state succession to membership in an international governmental organization is governed by the constitution and specific membership rules of each organization.

The United Nations addressed the issue of succession to membership when it considered Pakistan's membership on gaining independence by splitting from India in 1947. Pakistan claimed that it should be treated as an original member of the United Nations by virtue of India's membership in the organization. The Legal Committee of the United Nations Secretariat disagreed, concluding that Pakistan was a new state and as such must apply for admission as a new member. India, however, was said to have retained its legal identity and its membership as well. The committee declared that a state does not "cease to be a Member simply because its Constitution or frontier has been subjected to changes, and that the extinction of the State as a legal personality recognized in the international legal order must be shown before its rights and obligations can be considered thereby to have ceased to exist."[1] In 1992 the General Assembly addressed the dissolution of the former Socialist Federal Republic of Yugoslavia by voting overwhelmingly to expel the Serb-dominated government of the new Yugoslavia from its seat in the United Nations.[2] It was the first such expulsion in history.

The Treaty Succession Convention, in Article 4, stipulates its applicability to treaties establishing international governmental organizations but "without prejudice to the rules concerning acquisition of membership and without prejudice to any other relevant rules of the organization."

Nationality

Two distinct views on the effect of succession on the nationality of inhabitants of the predecessor state have been voiced. The dominant view holds that nationality changes automatically to that of the successor state, because it is not only the sovereign authority but also the duty of the successor state to confer nationality to a population localized on the territory concerned. The other view maintains that nationality is essentially a matter of domestic jurisdiction and hence that it is up to the national law of the successor state to decide.

State practice generally reflects the dominant view. When one state cedes a territory to another, the ceding state is traditionally deemed competent to transfer the allegiance of the inhabitants, and the successor state is required to confer its nationality on these inhabitants. This occasionally is tempered by considerations of self-determination and human rights. A plebiscite may be held to determine whether the territorial transfer accords with the wishes of a majority of the inhabitants. More frequently, individual inhabitants of the ceded territory are offered, through specific stipulation, an option on nationality, including the retention of the original nationality (where the predecessor state continues to exist).

International law, in deference to human rights, requires that in order for the successor state to confer its nationality on the inhabitants of the predecessor territory there be a genuine link between those persons and the territory. States are thus not regarded as competent to impose nationality on individuals who are not physically present within a territory at the time of its transfer. The nationality of the successor state can be conferred on nationals of the predecessor state only if they submit voluntarily to its jurisdiction, by virtue of an explicit declaration or voluntary return to their land of origin. This position was underscored in *United States ex rel. Schwarzkoph v. Uhl, District Director of Immigration* (1943),[3] where the court held that an Austrian national who had been resident in the United States when Germany annexed Austria had not acquired German nationality.

State Property

According to the Other Succession Convention (Vienna Convention on Succession of States in Respect of State Property, Archives, and Debts), state property owned by the predecessor state shall pass, without compensation, to the successor state, unless otherwise agreed between the states concerned. "State property" includes all property that at the time of a succession of states belongs to the predecessor state according to its law. When such property passes to a successor state under the convention's terms, all rights of the predecessor in the property are extinguished.

A succession of states has no effect, in and of itself, on the property of third states located in the predecessor state and identified as the third state's by the predecessor's internal law. The predecessor state is obliged to prevent damage or destruction to property that will pass to a successor.

The convention, in Articles 14–18, sets forth detailed provisions for the succession of state property according to the specific category of state succession involved. There are five distinct categories:

1. *Transfer of part of the territory of a state:* When one state transfers part of its territory to another state, the passing of state property is settled by agreement. If no such agreement is reached, all immovable state property in the transferred territory goes to the successor, and all movable state property in that territory, connected with the predecessor's activities in that territory, also passes to the successor.

2. *A newly independent state:* When a successor state is a "newly independent state," all movable state property within its territory that belonged to the predecessor and was either originally the property of the territory in question or was used by the predecessor in connection with its activities there passes to the successor state. Other movable property "to the creation of which the dependent territory has contributed" also passes in proportion to that contribution. All immovable state property in the territory passes to the successor state.

3. *Uniting of states:* In a uniting of states, all state property of the predecessors passes to the successor state.

4. *Separation of part or parts of the territory of a state:* "When part or parts of the territory of a State separate from that State and form a successor State," unless otherwise agreed, the following state property of the predecessor state passes to the successor state: immovable state property within the territory; movable state property connected with the predecessor's activities in the territory; and equitable proportions of other movable state property located in the territory.

5. *Dissolution of states:* When a state dissolves into two or more successor states, unless those states agree otherwise, immovable property of the predecessor goes to the successor territory in which it is situated; immovable property of the predecessor located outside its territory passes to the successor states "in equitable proportions"; movable property of the predecessor state connected with its activities in a successor's territory goes to the successor state concerned; and other movable property passes to the successor states in equitable proportions.

In sum, these guidelines clearly take into account the nature, situs, and functions of property involved and the principle of equity. Throughout the basic distinction is made between immovable and movable property. Immovable property of the predecessor state located within the successor state passes to the successor state. Movable property of the predecessor state connected with its activities in the successor state's territory passes to the successor state. Otherwise, the overriding concern is to effect equitable distribution.

State Debts

State debt, as defined in Article 33 of the Other Succession Convention, refers to "any financial obligation of a predecessor State arising in conformity with international law towards another State, an international organization or any other subject of international law." Debts to private persons are not covered. The modality by which state succession occurs becomes especially important in regard to state debts, as in the case of state property. If the successor state was created by either a transfer or separation of part or parts of the predecessor's territory, the predecessor's state debts are extinguished on succession and pass to the successor state. The obligation passes in equitable proportion to the accompanying property rights and interest received by the successor. Such a passing of state debt does not in itself affect the rights and obligations of creditors.

In the case of newly independent states, no state debt passes unless the predecessor and the new state reach an agreement otherwise. To buttress this point, the International Law commission, in its report for the Thirty-third Session, invoked a prominent precedent: the United States did not succeed to any debt of Great Britain. Agreements with the predecessor state, Article 38(2) admonishes, "shall not infringe the principle of the permanent sovereignty of every people over its wealth and natural resources."

In all other forms of state succession, state debt passes in an equitable proportion unless the relevant states agree otherwise.

State Archives

The Other Succession Convention deals not only with state property and state debts but also with state archives. The initial provisions of the part concerned with state archives more or less mirror comparable provisions dealing with state property.

State archives refers to "documents of whatever date and kind" that "belonged to the predecessor State according to its internal law" and were held by the predecessor state in the exercise of its functions (Article 20). Absent specific agreement, state archives relating to the successor state's territory shall pass to the successor state. All rights of the predecessor in any archives that pass to a successor state are extinguished, and such passing is accomplished without compensation. Again, the succession of states has no effect on archives that, according to the predecessor's internal law, are the property of a third state.

A unique provision, Article 25, refers to the "preservation of the integral character of groups of State archives of the predecessor State." The convention exercises no control over any question relating to such issues. Again, the predecessor state is obliged to preserve state archives that pass to the successor.

The underlying policy consideration is to ensure that each resulting successor state procures all archives that deal with its territory. When archives deal with more than one territory, reproductions are to be made available so that all states interested in the information will have it at their disposal.

One issue dealt with in particular is archives concerning the delimitation of a successor state's territory, which must be furnished by a predecessor. Archives concerning history and cultural heritage are also emphasized. With regard to newly independent states, the separation of part or parts of a state's territory, or the dissolution of a state, the convention stipulates that an agreement concerning archives between the predecessor state and the successor state "shall not infringe the right of the peoples of those States to development, to information about their history, and to their cultural heritage."

PART NINE

PROSPECTS

29

Toward a World Community of Human Dignity

It is sometimes lamented that, whereas most of humankind's problems are global in their reach, the processes of law maintained to cope with these problems are not. This, as amply demonstrated in the preceding chapters, would appear to be a profound misperception.

With ever-growing interdependence, the contemporary world arena does manifest a comprehensive process of authoritative decision. Although it has not yet achieved that high stability in expectations about authority and in degree of control over constituent members characteristic of the internal processes of mature national communities, this process does provide in more than rudimentary form the features essential to the effective making, application, and review of law on a global scale.

In recent decades, this dynamic process of authoritative decision has been expanding and improving itself at an accelerating rate, making itself more adequate to cope with global problems. The development of this ongoing process of authoritative decision wholly parallels, and is an integral part of, the larger development of world social process.

Not surprisingly, the basic features of a global constitutive process have been delineated only within relatively recent times. For millennia the conditions essential to the establishment and maintenance of larger community and decision processes were absent; the peoples of the world lived in isolated groupings with little physical contact, much less cooperative interaction in the pursuit of the common interest. As populations increased and interactions grew more frequent, institutional practices became differentiated and specialized, culminating in decision processes capable of sustaining stable contact and of restoring severed relations. The ancient civilizations of China, India, Greece, and Rome all recognized expectations of authority and control shared between different territorial communities as vital to clarify and protect common interest. Indeed, the Greek concept of a natural law shared by all humankind and the Roman notion of a jus naturale and a jus gentium shared by many peoples have for centuries exerted tremendous influence on the development of what is regarded as contemporary international law. Over many millennia the fragmentary practices in cooperation that began merely as exchanges of intermediaries have developed into a highly complex system of organized decision making, sustained by bilateral and multilateral arrangements. Many predispositions shaped in the primitive, preglobal arrangements of humankind continue to affect the configuration of contemporary decision making.

The universal decision institutions of the contemporary world are commonly regarded as having been shaped largely by the internal and external dynamisms of a Western Europe recovering from the centuries that followed the collapse of the Roman Empire and of feudalism in the West. As Europe's impact on peoples external to it gained momentum and international interactions accelerated and expanded, the world began to be molded into a single system of public order. In the seventeenth century, the relatively unipolar European system based on the supremacy of the pope and Christian unity began to develop into a multipolar state system. The loyalties of individuals shifted significantly from family, church, guild, and community to the nation-state, and the nation-state assumed a new authority to discharge security and other functions. This process of transformation climaxed in 1648, when the Peace of Westphalia ended the Thirty Years' War.

Spawned by the spiritual disunity in Christendom, the Peace of Westphalia marked a fundamental shift in the locus of power—from the church to the secular nation-state. A relatively centralized system of public order was transformed into a highly decentralized system, with many contending centers of power. Under this new system, a continuous balancing of power between changing alliances was crucial to maintain minimum public order and to effect the operation of the system.

The great writers regarded as the founding fathers of contemporary international law (Francisco de Vitoria, Hugo Grotius, Christian Wolff, Emmeric de Vattel, and so on) developed a framework of a law of nations appropriate to this new role. They drew on both the law of nature and custom as sources of substantive policy and conceived a process of decision, guided by practical considerations of reciprocity and retaliation, in which individual states were alternately both claimants and decision makers, thereby ensuring that claims be based on at least a modicum of common interest. Consequently, though the peoples of the world lived under the immediate authority of different territorial communities, they were "united in a larger legal community under the rule of a law higher in kind than the law of those bodies."[1] They enjoyed individual rights and had individual duties relating even to human rights or the "rights of man" or "mankind."

The formal institutional structures within the European-based constitutive process developed somewhat slowly. In the wake of the settlement of Vienna of 1815 and the Congress of Aix-la-Chapelle of 1818, a loose system of consultation among the great powers, known as the Concert of Europe, came into being to maintain a precarious peace under a delicate balancing of power. Although the Concert of Europe fell short of institutionalizing permanent structures of authority, it provided a framework for occasional great-power consultations and conferences, demonstrating that the European states shared a larger community interest. This community, with its developing constitutive process, expanded as European empire-building accelerated; its growth found further impetus in the Hague Conferences of 1899 and 1907, whose participants included non-European as well as European states, small as well as great powers.

With the establishment of the Pan American Union near the end of the nineteenth century, followed by a series of inter-American conferences, the states of the Western hemisphere quickly became a distinctive subgroup within the larger multistate system. In the meantime, various nation-states, responding to the new needs and demands stimulated by the spread of modern science and technology and the new means of transnational communication and transportation, joined to create international governmental organizations specialized to particular values other than power. Both geographic and functional structures of authority gradually grew beyond the confines of the European territorial context to a larger world.

The structures of authority appropriate to a global constitutive process began to emerge only with the advent of the short-lived League of Nations and with its successor, the United Nations. The Covenant of the League of Nations sought to establish a relatively universal and permanent constitutional structure for the larger community of humankind. But the attempt failed; the reasons for the failure and the lessons to be learned have been recounted many times. The successor United Nations, building upon the league's experience, offers a vast and complex network of institutions. This interlocking network contains both highly centralized components to facilitate the making and application of law for multiple and universal purposes and more dispersed components to govern the workings of a host of regional and functional organizations for limited purposes. This immense maze of institutions within the United Nations, reinforced by many other relatively independent intergovernmental organizations, comprises the core structure of representative authority that gives form to the contemporary world constitutive process.

Recent trends in decision and practice suggest modest movement toward greater adequacy in global constitutive process. The end of the Cold War has made way for a new spirit of institutional cooperation and multilateralism. The number of states has increased tremendously, with a rapid expansion from European to non-European states and movement toward universality in participation. The number of democracies has increased. Nonstate participants, including private associations specialized to many values, have multiplied and continue to play important roles (and now with increasing formal recognition). The perspectives of all these participants manifest demand not only for a minimum public order to reduce unauthorized coercion but also for an optimum public order to facilitate the largest production and widest possible sharing of all values. In a world of growing interdependence, there appears a gradual expansion of identifications with the most inclusive community of humankind and deepening perception of common interest. The arenas of decision have moved from loose institutionalization to a high degree of institutionalization; diplomatic and diplomatic-parliamentary arenas have been fortified by parliamentary, adjudicative, and executive arenas; sporadic interactions have been replaced by more permanent structures of authority; finally, the geographic distribution of arenas has been improved, ranging from local and national to regional and global.

Turning to bases of power, the trend has been from exclusive to inclusive authority, with erosion of the concept of domestic jurisdiction and expansion of the domain of international concern, and from exclusive to more inclusive control over other values. In relation to strategies, the customary modalities of creating expectations about authority by cooperation have been supplemented by deliberate lawmaking through explicit agreement, especially by parliamentary procedures. In terms of outcomes, the pristine unity of undifferentiated functions has developed into highly differentiated decision functions (that is, intelligence, promotion, prescription, invocation, application, termination, and appraisal) each of which is distinct yet related.

ACHIEVEMENTS AND FAILURES IN THE PURSUIT OF PUBLIC ORDER GOALS

These trends are encouraging, but how well does the process function? Aside from each feature of the global constitutive process that maintains necessary institutions to perform indispensable functions and the apparent need to improve each feature, the effectiveness of the process must ultimately be judged by the products that flow out of, and are sustained by, it. That is, the effectiveness of the global constitutive process must be appraised not only by each of its operating features but, ultimately, by the flow of public order decisions, representing the aggregate quality of human life, that is achieved.

Public order decisions determine how human rights are protected or deprived; whether the making of community decisions is shared or monopolized; how resources are allocated and developed, and wealth produced and distributed; how information and knowledge are acquired and communicated or denied and impeded; how health, safety, and comfort are fostered or neglected; how acquisition and exercise of skills are promoted or slighted; how family or other intimate personal relations are fostered or neglected; and how norms of responsible conduct are cultivated or ignored.

Public order decisions and the constitutive process constantly interact and reinforce each other. Thus, any meaningful appraisal must raise this fundamental question: To what extent are the overriding public order goals of minimum and optimum order expressed in the ongoing flow of public order decisions that relate to different value processes?

The goals of both minimum and optimum world order, as discussed in chapter 6, have been clearly projected, in varying degrees of generality, to guide the making and application of international law. Minimum order, in the sense of minimizing unauthorized coercion and violence, is commonly expressed in terms of peace and security. Optimum order, in the sense of widest possible shaping and sharing of values, has been expressed in such equivalent terms as human dignity, justice, development, human rights, and quality of life.

The pursuit of minimum world order has been a magnificent obsession of humankind. Unhappily, the global constitutive process has failed to marshal and establish sufficient control over individual nation-states to preclude recourse to unauthorized coercion and violence. Although humankind has managed to avoid a third world war or a nuclear holocaust for the past five decades, the minimum order that exists is extremely precarious. Although it is widely assumed that war has no place under contemporary international law, armed conflicts and coercion of various scales (regional, national, and local) persist in many parts of the world. Witness, for example, the Iraq-Iran war that lasted for eight years, or the savagery of the conflict in ex-Yugoslavia. "Just wars" of the past have been increasingly replaced by wars of religious and ethnic rivalry in our time. Terrorist activities of all sorts, which threaten not only specific targets but the innocent public, have generated a considerable personal sense of "international anarchy."

In the pursuit of an optimum order, the peoples of the world, both elite and rank and file, have invoked, with varying intensity and specificity, various catchwords, including development, modernization, nation-building, quality of life, human rights, ecology, a new international economic order, a new world communication and information order, a humane order, and so on. Whatever their preferences in catchwords and whatever their differences in cultural traditions and institutional practices, the peoples of the world are today increasingly demanding the greater production and wider distribution of all basic values. They demand effective participation in the shaping and sharing of all basic values: respect, power, enlightenment, well-being, wealth, skill, affection, and rectitude. They demand a fundamental freedom of choice to participate in different value processes, equality that minimizes discrimination on grounds irrelevant to personal capabilities and maximizes effective opportunity, and a large domain of personal autonomy (respect). They demand full participation as persons in the processes of both authoritative decision making and effective power sharing (power). They seek freedom to acquire, to use, and to communicate information and knowledge (enlightenment). They seek health, safety, and comfort (well-being). They seek access to goods and services (wealth). They demand the freedom to discover, to mature, and to exercise latent talents (skill). They seek to establish and enjoy congenial personal relationships (affection). They demand freedom to form, express, and maintain norms of responsible conduct (rectitude).

But what are the contemporary realities? To what extent are their rising demands for protection and fulfillment satisfied? A cursory look at daily events around the world shows that deprivations and nonfulfillments continue to characterize the value-institutional processes of vast segments of the world's population. Though the nature, scope, and magnitude of the values at stake may differ from one community to another, the deprivations and nonfulfillments extend to every value sector.

Examples are dramatic. The demand for freedom of choice, for equality and for personal autonomy meets with persistent discrimination on such invidious grounds as race, sex, religion, and political opinion, and the massive invasion of the civic domain of personal autonomy. The demand to share power meets with the persistence of totalitarian regimes, one-party rule and military dictatorships, martial "law," arbitrary arrest, detention, censure, imprisonment, and torture in many police states; restrictions on emigration and immigration; ethnic cleansing and mass and collective expulsion of aliens. The search for enlightenment encounters suppression of political dissent, widespread censorship by official elites, inadequate education for children, and systematic indoctrination as an instrument of policy. The search for well-being is blunted by overpopulation, hunger and starvation, and deprivations of life caused by war, oppression, terrorist activities, ecocide, and genocide. A striving for wealth faces poverty in developed as well as developing nations and the widening gap between rich and poor. The demand for skill development must cope with consequences of skill obsolescence due to technological advances, brain drain, unemployment, and underemployment. Longings for a moral integrity meet with denial of freedom of worship, intolerance and persecution of religious minorities, massacres and warfare involving religious fanatics.

CONDITIONS AFFECTING WORLD PUBLIC ORDER

The conditions that have produced these great disparities between the rising common demands of people for human dignity values and the degree of their achievement are both environmental and predispositional. These sets of factors are in constant interplay.

Among the most important environmental factors are population resources and institutional arrangements and practices.

The explosive growth of the population is one of the most striking trends in human history. The population of the world today is characterized by massive numbers, continued high rates of growth, and uneven distribution, both globally and nationally. Whereas it took at least a million years for human numbers to reach the billion mark, it took only 130 years for the second billion and 30 years for the third billion. According to recent population projections, the world population of 4.8 billion in 1985 will grow to 6.1 billion by the year 2000 and to 8.2 billion by 2025. The problem of numbers is compounded by the concentration of high growth rates in developing countries that are already congested, poor, and possessed of the least capacity and resources to absorb the increased population. More than two-thirds of today's world people inhabit the developing regions, and more than 90 percent of the projected increases in the coming decades is expected in these regions. The implications of the population explosion are not confined to the Malthusian dimension of food supply but extend to the quality of life in every value sector. In the words of Lasswell:

> Uncontrolled population growth is expected to impair the aggregate output of values in every sector of society and to sharpen inequalities of distribution everywhere. An overcrowded world can be expected to swing between extremes of political conflict and massive apathy, and between exaggerated personal hostility and indifference. The control of values such as enlightenment, wealth, skill, and respect will be concentrated in the control of a few. From shortages of food and medicare will rise crises of malnutrition, disease, and defect. As numbers multiply and competition intensifies, human conduct will grow progressively egocentric and socially irresponsible.[2]

Although human numbers annually increase significantly, the amount of natural resources available to sustain the growing population, to eradicate mass poverty, and to improve the quality of human lives remains finite. Indeed, the natural resources of the world appear to be diminishing in quantity and deteriorating in quality, as dramatized by the energy and ecological crises. Resources are unevenly distributed, and discrepancies in the pattern of resource consumption are glaring. The energy crisis in past years and the host of problems it exacerbated (rampant inflation, monetary instability, uncontrolled deficit, mass unemployment) underscore the potential threats of impairment of resources on the enjoyment and fulfillment of all values. Similarly, massive diversion of resources for purposes of military overkill or oppression at a time of global ecological crisis dramatizes vividly the dangerous consequences of the mismanagement of resources. Military expenditures worldwide continue to reach mind-boggling figures, despite the Cold War's end. A steady flow of conventional arms continues to find its way to third-world countries, causing death and destruction, even as certain other countries reduce their military establishments. Yet without stronger efforts and expenditures toward methods for sustainable development, potentially disastrous consequences from global warming and deforestation loom on the horizon.

Confronted with the unprecedented challenges of our planetary ecosystem, the institutions and practices of humankind appear to be inadequate. Geographically, these value institutions and practices are too state-centered. Functionally, they are too tradition-bound to make timely responses and adjustments to the accelerated change, both in pace and dimension, as generated by the universalization of science and technology and the ever-intensifying global interdependence. The problems in the contemporary world are global in nature and scale, yet the basic organizational framework to deal with them continues to rest on the problem-solving capacities of separate and highly unequal states and thus remains essentially partial and fragmentary. The ascendancy of the nation-state has been such that the search for common interest is more often than not distorted by the inordinate emphasis on national "sovereignty."

Closely linked to the inadequacies of the institutional arrangements and practices in meeting the contemporary challenges in the pursuit of human dignity values are basic predispositional factors, which include the more fundamental demands, identifications, and expectations of the peoples of the world. And the aggregate pattern of demands, expectations, and identifications is deeply affected by the maximization postulate. According to this postulate, people act in social process, both consciously and unconsciously, in such a way as to maximize all basic values, and they adopt one course of action rather than another as guided by their expectations about net advantage.

The peoples of the world, whatever their differences in cultural traditions and institutional practices, are intensifying their demands to participate in shaping and sharing all basic values of human dignity. In a world marked by stark contrasts in rights and development, however, many popular demands tend to express special rather than common interests. Unable to clarify and agree on common interests, some peoples tend to be preoccupied with short-term, separate payoffs rather than long-term, aggregate consequences.

Attenuated conceptions of common interest are sustained by, and in turn foster, systems of identification that give primacy to national loyalties rather than to common humanity. The advent of cities broke the earliest syndromes of parochialism, reaching back to the family and the tribe, and facilitated identifications with the public order of civilized states. In recent times the nation-state has become the prime symbol around which collective identifications are formed. With nationalism continuing to run high, nation-states, old and new alike, compete intensely to exact loyalties from individuals, and national identities have gained such primacy as often to inhibit the growth of more inclusive identities, especially those associated with common humanity. This vigorous syndrome of national parochialism has contributed not insignificantly to further fragmenting an already divided world.

Fragmented identifications have been sustained and fortified by persisting and widespread assumptions that, whether we like it or not, many conflicts will be settled by violence and coercion. Living under the perpetual threat of violence, most peoples (both elite and rank and file) are highly insecure, manifesting a pervasive sense of frustration over the inability to eradicate or deal effectively with armed conflicts, terrorism, and other forms of coercion. Too often measures that deprive individuals and groups and deny them fulfillment of basic values are justified and condoned because of chronic obsession with internal and external disorder. Gripped by anxieties and a keen sense of vulnerability, the effective elites are hypersensitive about openly initiating a change in world public order that would appear to subordinate them to other powers. They tend to be preoccupied with calculations of short-term payoffs and their own value positions rather than long-term aggregate gain. The peoples of the world exhibit varying degrees of realism about the conditions under which human dignity values can be fulfilled. They often fail to perceive the fact and the depth of contemporary interdependencies or to take them seriously and thus fail to explore, articulate, and implement common interests.

Indeed, the global interdependencies, in all their manifestations and dimensions, as they affect the aggregate pattern of human life on this planet, are still not sufficiently understood or taken seriously enough. Business as usual and obsolete institutions and practices are allowed to drift. The quality of life of every human now depends on many factors that operate beyond community and national boundaries. The interdependencies of peoples transnationally within a particular value process inexorably form a matrix with the interdependencies of peoples everywhere as between different value processes. In an earth-space arena in which the means of mass destruction threaten all civilization, no people can be secure in the shaping and sharing of values unless all peoples are secure.

PROJECTIONS OF FUTURE WORLD ORDER

Looking toward the future, what developments for world order are likely? What will the new trends be in the twenty-first century? Will there be few changes to life as we know it now? Or will the international community continue to advance and strive in its ultimate search for world peace and cooperation? Will the United States play an even more active role in the international arena? And if so, will that be tolerated? How do we combat terrorists such as Osama bin Laden?

To contemplate the future is to allow the mind to assess possibilities in terms of probable occurrence. The trend, not the instance, is the distinctive emphasis in this projective thinking, concerned as it is with an estimate of the probability that significant features of a social context will stay the same or change in stated direction.

Probable developments cannot be realistically projected in terms of "inevitability" or of simple-minded extrapolation of the past. The continuation of past events depends on the total configuration of the many variables that may or may not support the direction and intensity of the trend. One useful tool is what Harold Lasswell has called "developmental constructs," which range through a broad spectrum of possibilities from the most optimistic to the most pessimistic.[3]

Central to our concern is whether future world order will move toward or away from the values, practices, and institutions of human dignity. To project most comprehensively, two basic constructs might be developed. The optimistic construct envisages a continuing progress toward a world public order of human dignity, which will foster, with minimal organized coercion and control, the wide shaping and sharing of power and other values, based on a more inclusive sense of identification and a deepening perception of the common interest. The pessimistic construct imagines a regressive movement toward a world public order of garrison-prison states that will be characterized by increasing power concentration, governmental regimentation, militarization, and Orwellian manipulation, as sustained by heavy coercion and control.

Which way will future world order move? Signals are somewhat mixed as judged by historic trends. From the trend away from caste societies, through the spread of urban civilization, to increasing interdependence, the tempo of change in human affairs has accelerated, due in no small measure to the universalization of science and science-based technology. Together they have contributed to a deepening shared perception about the common interest of all members of the human race in a common destiny and have inspired an abiding faith in the beneficent potential of science and technology and in the capacity of human intelligence and judgment.

But the drift toward a massive garrison state may be more than episodic; hierarchical barriers in power, wealth, and other value positions may become self-fulfilling and self-perpetuating, as fueled by continued expectations of violence. These expectations, fed by unyielding perceptions of threats and enemies from "across," "below," or "above," will continue to generate high levels of festering anxiety and personal insecurity for elites and nonelites alike. Instead of releasing the enormous potential of science and technology for constructive uses, people more often than not manipulate them so that they serve as instruments of control, oppression, and tyranny. Witness, for example, the growing threats to the individual in the form of physical, psychological, and data surveillance.

The mixed signals notwithstanding, the future clearly is not predestined. The projection of future contingencies may help increase the likelihood that humankind can avoid the undesirable and achieve the desirable. The course of development depends on the constellation of factors, both predispositional and environmental, in the emerging context. It is largely within the power of people to make choices to shape the constellation of factors and to affect future developments in preferred ways. The actions and inactions of each participant will have consequences.

ALTERNATIVES FOR A WORLD ORDER OF HUMAN DIGNITY: A GRAND STRATEGY OF SIMULTANEITY AND TOTAL MOBILIZATION

What alternatives to move toward a world community of human dignity are available? Are the only options a world government or the mindless drifting of the status quo dominated by the "sovereign" nation-states? McDougal has incisively observed:

There is of course no dearth in recommendation, either ancient or modern, about how global constitutive process and public order might be changed for the better. For centuries philosophers, clerics, and kings have proffered plans for perpetual peace, and contemporary proposals for world government, and lesser modifications of the existing anarchy, abound. Some of these proposals envisage grandiose transformations in the structures and processes of authoritative and effective power, others, in contrast, are characterized by concern for small changes about particular problems in incremental, cosmetic gimmickry. The difficulty with the grandiose approach is that its proponents seldom offer the hands and feet necessary to put the vast changes they recommend into reality; the difficulty with the more humble approach is that the proponents of fragmented and anecdotal options offer little other than hands and feet, or isolated features of rule and procedure, without adequate relation to the larger processes of authoritative decision and effective power. Considered comprehensively most of the proposals share a but modest regard for the context of clarifying policies and conditions which affects both rationality and acceptability.[4]

Of the many proposals, the efforts of the World Order Models Project (WOMP), as represented by Richard A. Falk, Saul H. Mendlovitz, and others, are especially noteworthy.[5] The project, initiated in 1968, has sought to promote a just world order by assembling scholars, intellectuals, and activists from various parts of the world to undertake research, publication, education, and other promotional activities. Perceiving the contemporary world as beset by such complex and interrelated problems as war, poverty, social injustice, ecological instability, and alienation, they employ an analytic-ethical scheme of inquiry, organizing around the basic themes of peace, economic well-being, social justice, ecological stability, positive identity, and meaningful participation. The project has helped to transnationalize the world order inquiry, even though its inability to come to grips with the complex problems of transition has opened it to charges of idealism and utopianism. Instead of being preoccupied with the formal authoritative institutions rooted in the state-centric system, it has paid increasing attention to social movements and grass-roots initiatives.

The choice open to humankind in future world order is by no means an either-or option. It is not one of simple dichotomy: either a world controlled solely by sovereign nation-states or a world government supplanting all the existing nation-states. The period of transition will be a continuing process, long and halting.

True, nation-states remain the predominant participants in the contemporary world arena. Yet it is well to remember that the "omnipotent" nation-state is but one of many structures that are created and maintained by human beings to protect and realize their interests. As a shield for individuals against the tyranny and exploitation of feudal lords, the nation-state was widely perceived to be the structure most appropriate for obtaining a more secure and fulfilling life for humankind. When the nation-state fails to serve adequately such common interest, its ongoing role cannot escape scrutiny in light of competing institutions.

Our world is one of pluralism and diversity. It is a global arena in which major powers, intermediate powers, small states, and ministates coexist, along with a multiplicity of nonstate participants operating at different community levels — global, regional, national, and local. States and nonstate participants (groups and individuals) constantly interact under changing conditions. This has been and will be the course in the foreseeable future. The operations of the nation-states are modulated by the functional imperatives of interdependence, interdetermination, and human survival and by functional cooperation across state boundaries.

Even with the problems of imbalances caused by the explosive world population, unevenly distributed, in relation to the uneven distribution of limited resources, the present state of affairs can be improved, given the enormous potential released by advances and universalization of science-based technology in communication and other fields.

The marriage of the computer and the communication technologies has obliterated the barriers of time and space and has increasingly offered the individual greater access to knowledge and information (making its acquisition a matter of private choice in a mass society) and participation in other value processes (such as wealth and power). The information revolution of our time, with the constant interplay of all the information media (aural, verbal, and visual), offers a step toward an abundance of information of universal availability, characterized by both massification and individualization of information. Increasingly, a person can choose to draw his or her private stock of knowledge and information more easily and economically from the total accumulated by humankind. The new electronic storage systems for information, interlinked globally, could provide not only accessibility of knowledge but a renewed sense of the unity of humankind.

To what extent can the potential benefits of the universalizing science and technology be shared by the whole of humankind? Decisions affecting institutional arrangements and practice are crucial. New technologies of communication and development, as in other areas, are inextricably connected with the pattern of human institutions and practice. In the face of the unprecedented challenge facing humankind, can the elites of the world transcend national parochialism and the demand of special interests (for example, monopoly of power in the guise of the public interest, national interest) to act together for the common interest, from short term, mid-term, and long-term perspectives? Will they even be surpassed as increased access and participation obviate some institutional arrangements?

The advance in science-based technology cannot be reversed; it reflects a general tendency toward universalization. There is no escape from technological advance. It is important to seize what science-based technology has offered humankind, not to retreat from it, and to make wise policy choices and necessary institutional adaptations in response to the pressing challenges of global interdependence. And the sooner the better. Demands for new world orders — in economic development, in communication and information, in political development, in global environment, in human rights, and so on — have underlined the dynamic of global interdependencies and deepened the shared sense of interdependence. Can the traditional human institutions and practices centered on individual nation-states be modified to respond to these challenges? The choice is vital. The existing dependency, imbalance, and inequalities manifested in the contemporary global social process should be redressed, through concerted effort, so that viable communities with adequate resources can be maintained, affording optimum opportunities to shape and share values for all human beings, in whatever community (earth-based or in future space settings) they may live.

To enhance the wide shaping and sharing of values, amid the rising debate about the shape of world order to come, it is crucial that the fundamental freedom of choice to participate in all value processes be sustained and fortified. The increasing concern for the interests of particular states must not come at the expense of the classic concern for individual freedom and fulfillment and must make no mistake about the concern of officials who feign to represent the state at the expense of their people.

The way to foster a new and equitable world order is not to erode, dilute, or hamper this fundamental policy for freedom of choice and other human rights. The key, rather, is positive facilitation by making pertinent technology, knowledge, and resources available to all and by increasing the capacity of development and communication at every community level.

Recall that international law is a continuing process of authoritative decision through which the common interests of the members of the human community are clarified and reclarified, fashioned and refashioned. It impacts all members of the global community, elites and nonelites alike.

Confronted with the stark reality of the global effective power process, as punctuated by the tremendous disparities in the effective power of individual nation-states, the elites of the world must be made to realize that they have more to gain by cooperating with one another than by destroying one another. Education for the rank and file is equally important, because the differences in personality, class, interest, culture, and crisis experience are real, but the barriers can be overcome through genuine enlightenment and mutual understanding.

What is required is a grand strategy of simultaneity that would mobilize all participants — groups and individuals — to the common task of human survival and fulfillment.

Human history cannot start from a clean slate (barring, of course, a nuclear holocaust). Humankind must build its future on past legacies and present conditions. Although grand visions and incremental improvement can accompany the perpetual process of transition, the ultimate task is to mobilize and educate all citizens of the world.

Just as control of weapons of mass destruction is too important to leave to politicians alone, so is international law too important to be a monopoly for international lawyers and decision makers. What is crucial is to mobilize all available technology and resources of enlightenment and communication, using every available network, forum, and opportunity, to wage a continuous worldwide citizenship education.

Genuine protection and fulfillment of human dignity values will be possible only when necessary conditions are created and maintained to enable individuals to be effective, active, equal participants in the social processes at different community levels and in different social settings. Most fundamentally, it requires education. The people all over the world must be educated in ways that will enable them to make informed choices and judgments for participation so that they can interact meaningfully with others and participate in the community processes both as communicator and communicatee in ways that serve policy goals.

Individuals need not be the mere passive recipients of messages directed by the top elite; they must be able to think and speak for themselves. A new world order must move toward making the individual person a communicating being who can think, choose, participate, and express — think freely with adequate access to the stock of human knowledge and information; choose freely and intelligently; express opinions and ideas freely; and participate effectively in all other value processes. Citizens of the world must be made to think globally, temporally, contextually, and creatively:

Think globally to meet the challenge of global interdependence and interdetermination. The quest for a world order of human dignity that promotes both minimum and optimum order requires sustained global thinking and collaboration.

Think temporally not only about the present generation but about posterity. Responsible decision making, national as well as transnational, requires that concern be extended to long-term aggregate consequences as well as short-term effects for human survival and solidarity and for the totality of the global environment for this and succeeding generations.

Think contextually to relate decision making to all community levels and all value sectors of social interaction. No people can be secure until all peoples are secure, and no contemporary community can endure and thrive in seclusion and isolation from the rest of the world.

Think creatively in the common interest to mobilize all available intellectual skills toward solving problems in the pursuit of both minimum world order and optimum world order. Just as all human problems are created by human beings, so can they be managed and solved by human beings, no matter how formidable particular problems may be. The quest for the common interest of all humanity toward a world community of human dignity calls for ingenuity, goodwill, vigilant endeavor, and boundless creativity.

A new world order should be a new order of human dignity, in which persuasion prevails over coercion and in which the wide shaping and sharing of all cherished values are secured and fulfilled. It should be a new world order that will maintain minimum order, in the sense of minimizing unauthorized coercion and violence, and achieve optimum order, in the sense of the widest possible shaping and sharing of all values.

Notes

Citations to individual treaties (international agreements) are omitted from the notes unless otherwise specified. Instead, a Table of Treaties is appended below.

CHAPTER 1. INTERNATIONAL LAW IN A POLICY-ORIENTED PERSPECTIVE

1. *See, e.g.,* R. Falk, The Status of Law in International Society 7–40, 642–59 (1970); Dillard, *The Policy-Oriented Approach to Law,* 40 Va. Q. Rev. 626 (1964); Higgins, *Integrations of Authority and Control: Trends in the Literature of International Law and International Relations,* in Toward World Order and Human Dignity: Essays in Honor of Myres S. McDougal 79–94 (W. Reisman & B. Weston eds. 1976); Higgins, *Policy Considerations and the International Judicial Process,* 17 Int'l & Comp. L. Q. 58 (1968); Moore, *Prolegomenon to the Jurisprudence of Myres S. McDougal and Harold Lasswell,* 54 Va. L. Rev. 662 (1968); Morison, Myres S. McDougal and Twentieth-Century Jurisprudence: A Comparative Essay, in Toward World Order and Human Dignity, *supra,* at 3–78; Suzuki, *The New Haven School of International Law: An Invitation to a Policy-Oriented Jurisprudence,* 1 Yale Stud. World Pub. Ord. 1 (1974); Tipson, *The Lasswell-McDougal Enterprise: Toward a World Public Order of Human Dignity,* 14 Va. J. Int'l L. 535 (1974).

2. *See* M. McDougal & Associates, Studies in World Public Order (1960); M. McDougal & F. Feliciano, Law and Minimum World Public Order: The Legal Regulation of International Coercion (1961); M. McDougal & W. Burke, The Public Order of the Oceans: A Contemporary International Law of the Sea (1962); M. McDougal, H. Lasswell, & I. Vlasic, Law and Public Order in Space (1964); M. McDougal, H. Lasswell, & J. Miller, The Interpretation of Agreements and World Public Order: Principles of Content and Procedure (1967); M. McDougal, H. Lasswell, & L. Chen, Human Rights and World Public Order: The Basic Policies of an International Law of Human Dignity (1980); M. McDougal & W. Reisman, International Law Essays: A Supplement to International Law in Contemporary Perspective

(1981). *See also Tributes: Myres S. McDougal,* 108 Yale L.J. 921 (1999) (including a selected bibliography).

3. 57 A.J.I.L. 279 (1963).

4. *See* note 2 *supra.*

CHAPTER 2. NATION-STATES

1. Lissitzyn, Introductory remarks, 1953 Proceedings, Am. Soc'y Int'l L. 80.

2. B. Roling, International Law in an Expanded World 56–67 (1960).

3. 54 Congressional Record 1742 (Jan. 22, 1917).

4. G.A. Res. 1514, 15 U.N. GAOR Supp. (No. 16) at 66, U.N. Doc.A/4684 (1960).

5. G.A. Res. 2625, 25 U.N. GAOR Supp. (No. 28) at 121, U.N. Doc. A/8028 (1970).

6. M. Kaplan & N. Katzenbach, The Political Foundations of International Law 121 (1961).

7. G.A. Res. 2758, 26 U.N. GAOR Supp. (No. 29) at 2, U.N. Doc. A/8429 (1971).

8. United States Policy on Non-recognition of Communist China, Department of State Memorandum to Missions Abroad, 39 Dep't State Bull. 385 (1958).

9. Joint Communiqué on the Establishment of Diplomatic Relations Between the United States and the People's Republic of China, 79 Dep't State Bull. 25–26 (1979).

10. Taiwan Relations Act, 22 U.S.C. §3301 et seq. (1979).

11. Id. §3303(a).

12. Rest. 3rd, Restatement of the Foreign Relations Law of the United States §201, comment f.

13. Testimony of Ralph Johnson, Deputy Assistant Secretary of State for European and Canadian Affairs, Oct. 17, 1991, Vol. 2, No. 3, Foreign Policy Bulletin 39, 42n (Nov.–Dec. 1991).

14. European Community: Declaration on Yugoslavia and on the Guidelines on Recognition of New States (Dec. 16, 1991), *reprinted in* 31 I.L.M. 1485 (1992).

CHAPTER 3. INTERNATIONAL GOVERNMENTAL ORGANIZATIONS

1. *See* Anthony Clark Arend, *The United Nations, Regional Organizations, and Military Operations: The Past and Present,* 7 Duke J. Comp. & Int'l L. 3 (1996).

2. *See The Boston Globe,* July 10, 1997, at A1.

3. 1949 I.C.J. 173 (Advisory Opinion of Apr. 11).

4. *Id.* at 175.

5. *Id.* at 178.

6. *Id.* at 179.

7. *Id.*

8. *Id.*

9. Conditions of Admission of a State to the United Nations (Charter Article 4), 1948 I.C.J. 57 (Advisory Opinion of May 28); Competence of the General Assembly for the Admission of a State to the United Nations, 1950 I.C.J. 1 (Advisory Opinion of Mar. 3).

10. C. Alexandrowicz, The Law-Making Function of the Specialized Agencies of the United Nations 161 (1973).

11. S.C. Res. 827, U.N. SCOR, 48th Sess., 3217th mtg. at 1, U.N. Doc. SC/RES/827, *reprinted in* 32 I.L.M. 1203 (1993) (ex-Yugoslavia); S.C. Res. 955, U.N. SCOR, 49th Sess., 3452th mtg. at 2, U.N. Doc. S/RES/955 (1994), *reprinted in* 33 I.L.M. 1598, 1601 (1994) (Rwanda).

12. Koch, *The United Nations: Is There Life After Forty?* 21 Stan. J. Int'l L. 1 (1985).

13. *Id.*

14. Sean D. Murphy, Humanitarian Intervention: The United Nations in an Evolving World Order 1–3 (1996).

15. *Id.*

16. N.Y. Times, Mar. 8, 1993 at 1–10, col. 1.

17. Uniting for Peace Resolution (Nov. 3, 1950), G.A. Res. 377A(V), 5 U.N. GAOR Supp. (No. 20) at 10, U.N. Doc. A/1775 (1951).

18. Khan & Strong, *Proposals to Reform the U.N., 'Limping' in Its 40th Year,* N.Y. Times, Oct. 8, 1985, at A31, col. 1.

19. San Diego Union-Trib., Aug. 3, 1997, at G1.

20. N.Y. Times, Oct. 22, 1995, at 1–1, col. 5.

21. N.Y. Times, Sept. 10, 1984, at A13, col. 1.

22. The United Nations in Its Second Half-Century: A Report of the Independent Working Group on the Future of the United Nations 3 (1995).

CHAPTER 4. NONGOVERNMENTAL ORGANIZATIONS AND ASSOCIATIONS

1. Yearbook of International Organizations, 1999/2000, app. 3 at 2356–57 (Union of International Associations ed. 36th ed. 1999).

2. *See* Donini, *The Bureaucracy and the Free Spirits: Stagnation and Innovation in the Relationship Between the U.N. and NGOs,* in NGOs, the UN, and Global Governance 67 (Thomas G. Weiss and Leon Gordenker eds. 1996).

3. *See* Cook, *Amnesty International at the United Nations,* in The Conscience of the World: The Influence of Non-Governmental Organizations in the UN System 181 (Peter Willetts ed. 1996).

4. N.Y. Times, Oct. 30, 1996, at A11, col. 1.

5. Goormaghtigh, *How an INGO Contributed to Broadening the Scope and Competence of an IGO,* in Unofficial Diplomats 250, 254 (M. Berman & J. Johnson eds. 1977).

6. Wash. Post, Sept. 8, 1994, at B11.

7. Wash. Post, Jan. 23, 1997, at A17.

8. Richard J. Barnet and John Cavanaugh, Global Dreams: Imperial Corporations and the New World Order (1993).

9. United Nations Association of the United States of America, A Global Agenda: Issues Before the 50th General Assembly of the United Nations 129 (1995–1996).

CHAPTER 5. THE INDIVIDUAL

1. International Military Tribunal (Nuremberg), Judgment and Sentences, Oct. 1, 1946, 41 A.J.I.L. 172, 221 (1947).

CHAPTER 6. MINIMUM ORDER AND OPTIMUM ORDER

1. Doyle, *Liberalism and the End of the Cold War,* in International Relations Theory and the End of the Cold War 85 (Lebow & Risse-Kappen eds. 1995); *see, e.g.,* Gene M. Lyons & Michael Mastanduno eds., Beyond Westphalia? State Sovereignty and International Intervention (1995).

2. Reisman, *International Law After the Cold War,* 84 A.J.I.L. 859 (1990).

3. McDougal & Lasswell, *The Identification and Appraisal of Diverse Systems of Public Order,* 53 Am. J. Int'l L. 1, 3 (1959).

4. *Id.* at 10.

5. *Quoted in* Lipson, *Peaceful Coexistence,* 29 Law & Contemp. Prob. 871, 874 (1964).

6. *See* Reisman, *supra* note 2, at 874.

7. *Id.* at 859.

8. *Id.*

9. Koslowski & Kratochwil, *Understanding Change in International Politics: The Soviet Empire's Demise and the International System,* in Lebow & Risse-Kippen, *supra* note 1.

10. Snyder, *Myths, Modernization, and the Post-Gorbachev World,* in Lebow & Risse-Kappen 109, *supra* note 1.

11. *Id.*

12. Koslowski & Kratochwil, *supra* note 9, at 131.

13. *Id.* at 130–131.

14. *See* Reisman, *supra* note 2, at 863.

15. *Id.* at 864.

16. *Id.* at 865.

17. Lebow, *The Long Peace, the End of the Cold War, and the Failure of Realism,* in Lebow & Risse-Kappen 42, *supra* note 1.

18. Lebow & Risse-Kappen, *Introduction, id.* at 16.

19. Reisman, *supra* note 2, at 865.

CHAPTER 7. ESTABLISHMENT OF AND ACCESS TO ARENAS OF AUTHORITY

1. A. H. Robertson, Human Rights in the World 72–73 (1972).

2. G.A. Res. 2144A, 21 U.N. GAOR Supp. (No. 16) at 46, U.N. Doc. A/6316 (1966) (italics added).

3. E.S.C. Res. 1503, 48 U.N. ESCOR Supp. (No. 1A) at 8, U.N. Doc. E/4832/Add. 1 (1970).

4. Res. 1 (XXIV) of the Sub-Commission on Prevention of Discrimination and Protection of Minorities, August 13, 1971, *Report of the Twenty-Fourth Session of the Sub-Commission on Prevention of Discrimination and Protection of Minorities to the Commission on Human Rights, New York, 2–20 August 1971,* at 50–52, U.N. Doc. E/CN.4/1070 (E/CN.4/Sub.2/323) (1971).

5. E.S.C. Res. 1503, *supra* note 3.

6. Case Concerning United States Diplomatic and Consular Staff in Iran (U.S. v. Iran), 1980 I.C.J. 3 (Judgment of May 24).

7. United Nations, Multilateral Treaties Deposited with the Secretary-General, Status as at 31 December 1984, U.N. Doc. ST/LEG/SER.E/3, a 24 (1985) [hereinafter cited as Multilateral Treaties].

8. *Id.*

9. Military and Paramilitary Activities in and Against Nicaragua (Nicar. v. U.S.), 1984 I.C.J. 392 (Judgment on Jurisdiction and Admissibility).

10. Military and Paramilitary Activities in and Against Nicaragua (Nicar. v. U.S.), 1984 I.C.J. 169 (Order on Provisional Measures of May 10).

11. Judgment, *supra* note 9, at 404.

12. *See, e.g.,* Multilateral Treaties, *supra* note 7, at 25.

13. *Id.* at 24.

14. *Id.* at 25.

15. Judgment of Nov. 26, *supra* note 9, at 419.

16. Statement on the United States Withdrawal from the Proceedings Initiated by Nicaragua in the International Court of Justice, *reprinted in* 24 I.L.M. 246 (1985).

17. *Id.*

18. *Id.* at 248.

19. *Id.* at 247.

20. *See, e.g.,* Case Concerning Oil Platforms (Iran v. U.S.), 1992 I.C.J. 2 (Application of Nov. 2); Questions of Interpretation and Application of the 1971 Montreal Convention Arising from the Aerial Incident at Lockerbie (Libya v. U.S.), 1992 I.C.J. 2 (Application of March 3); Aerial Incident of 3 July 1988 (Iran v. U.S.), 1992 I.C.J. 225 (Order of June 5); Electronica Sicula S.p.A. (ELSI) (U.S. v. Italy), 1989 I.C.J. REP. 15 (July 20). *See generally* Robert Jennings, *The UN at Fifty: The International Court of Justice After Fifty Years,* 89 A.J.I.L. 493 (1995).

21. Jonathan I. Charney, *The Implications of Expanding International Dispute Settlement Systems: The 1982 Convention on the Law of the Sea,* 90 A.J.I.L. 69 (1996).

22. Dinah Shelton, *The Participation of NGOs in International Judicial Proceedings,* 89 A.J.I.L. 611, 614 n.15 (1994).

23. Interpretation of Peace Treaties with Bulgaria, Hungary and Romania, 1950 I.C.J. 221 (Advisory Opinions of Mar. 30 & July 18).

24. United Nations, Office of Public Information, The Work of the International Law Commission 37 (1967).

25. G.A. Res. 1262, 13 U.N. GAOR Supp. (No. 18) at 53, U.N. Doc. A/4090 (1958).

26. *See* Charney, *supra* note 21.

27. For the text of the declaration and related documents, *see* 20 I.L.M. 223 (1981). For discussion of the tribunal and its work *see* Brower, *Current Developments in the Law of Expropriation and Compensation: A Preliminary Survey of Awards of the Iran–United States Claims Tribunal,* 21 Int'l Lawyer 639 (1987); Lowenfeld, *The Iran–United States Claims Tribunal: An Interim Appraisal,* Arb. J., Dec. 1983 at 14; 1984 Proceedings A.S.I.L. 221.

28. S.C. Res. 687 (April 3, 1991), U.N. SCOR, 48th Sess., U.N. Doc. S/INF/47 (1991), *reprinted in* 30 I.L.M. 846 (1991).

CHAPTER 8. CONTROL OVER TERRITORY

1. 1 L. Oppenheim, International Law 576 (H. Lauterpacht ed. 8th ed 1955).

2. R. Jennings, The Acquisition of Territory in International Law 23 (1963).

3. 2 Rep. Int'l Arb. Awards 829 (1948).

4. Award rendered at Rome, Jan 28, 1931, 26 A.J.I.L. 390 (1932).

5. 1933 P.C.I.J. (ser. A/B), No. 53

6. McDougal, Lasswell, Vlasic, & Smith, *The Enjoyment and Acquisition of Resources in Outer Space,* 111 U. Pa. L. Rev. 523 (1963).

7. Steven R. Ratner, *Drawing a Better Line: UTI Possidetis and the Borders of New States,* 90 A.J.I.L. 590 (1996).

8. W. Michael Reisman, *Sovereignty and Human Rights in Contemporary International Law,* 84 A.J.I.L. 866, 873 (1990). *See also,* e.g., Makau wa Mutua, *Why Redraw the Map of Africa? A Moral and Legal Inquiry,* 16 Mich. J. Int'l L. 1113 (1995); Charles William Maynes, *The New Pessimism,* Foreign Pol'y (1995).

9. G.A. Res. 2625, 25 U.N. GAOR Supp. (No. 28) at 121, 123, U.N. Doc A/8028 (1970).

10. S.C. Res. 242 (1967), Resolutions and Decisions of the Security Council, 1967, at 8.

11. Western Sahara, 1975 I.C.J. 12 (Advisory Opinion of Oct. 16).

12. *Id.* at 14.

13. *Id.* at 68.

14. S.C. Res. 502 (1982), Resolutions and Decisions of the Security Council, 1982, at 15.

15. G.A. Res. 37/9, 37 U.N. GAOR Supp. (No. 51) at 18, U.N. Doc. A/37/51 (1982).

CHAPTER 9. CONTROL AND USE OF THE SEA

1. 22 U.N. GAOR C.1 (1516th mtg.) at 1–3, U.N. Doc. A/C.1/PV.1516 (1967).

2. Fisheries Case (U.K. v. Nor.), 1951 I.C.J. 116 (Judgment of Dec. 18).

3. Corfu Channel Case (U.K. v. Alb.), 1949 I.C.J. 4 (Judgment on Merits of Apr. 9).

4. Delimitation of the Maritime Boundary in the Gulf of Maine Area (Can./U.S.), 1984 I.C.J. 246 (Judgment of Oct. 12).

5. Agreement Relating to the Implementation of Part XI of the United Nations Convention on the Law of the Sea of 10 December 1982, *reprinted in* 33 I.L.M. 1309 (1994).

6. Sohn, *International Implications of the 1994 Agreement*, 88 A.J.I.L. 696 (1994).

7. Charney, *The Implications of Expanding International Dispute Settlement Systems: The 1982 Convention on the Law of the Sea*, 90 A.J.I.L. 69 (1996).

8. Proclamation by President Ronald Reagan, Mar. 10, 1983; Proclamation No. 5030, 48 Fed. Reg. 10,605 (1983); Statement by President Reagan, Mar. 10, 1983, para. 7.

CHAPTER 10. CONTROL AND USE OF OTHER RESOURCES

1. International Law Association, Report of the Fifty-Second Conference Held at Helsinki, August 14th to August 20th, 1966, at 477–533 (1966).

2. *Id.* at 484–85 (Article 2).

3. Convention on the Law of the Non-Navigational Uses of International Watercourses, art. 5(2), *reprinted in* 36 I.L.M. 700, 705 (1997).

4. G.A. Res. 1721, 16 U.N. GAOR Supp. (No. 17) at 6, U.N. Doc. A/5026 (1961).

5. Declaration of the First Meeting of Equatorial Countries (1976), *reprinted in* 2 Manual on Space Law 383 (N. Jasentuliyana & R. Lee eds. 1979).

6. Legal Status of Eastern Greenland (Den. v. Nor.), 1933 P.C.IJ. (ser. A/B) No. 53 (Judgment of Apr. 5).

7. U.N. Doc. A/37/P.V. 10 (1982). For a discussion of the General Assembly's relationship with the Madrid Protocol, *see, e.g.,* Francesca Francioni, ed., International Environmental Law for Antarctica (1992); Douglas M. Zang, *Frozen in Time: The Antarctic Mineral Resources Convention,* 76 Cornell L. Rev. (1991).

8. McDougal & Schneider, *The Protection of the Environment and World Public Order: Some Recent Developments,* 45 Miss. L.J. 1085 (1974).

9. Corfu Channel Case (U.K. v. Alb.), 1949 I.C.J. 4 (Judgment of Apr. 9).

10. Trail Smelter Case, 3 Rep. Int'l Arb. Awards 1905 (1949).

11. The Lake Lanoux Case, France, Spain, Arbitrated Decision of Nov. 16, 1957, [1957] Int'l L. Rep. 101; 53 A.J.I.L. 156 (1959).

12. Corfu Channel Case, *supra* note 9, at 22.

13. Declaration of the United Nations Conference on the Human Environment, U.N. Doc. A/CONF. 48/14 (1972); *reprinted in* 1972 Y.B.U.N. 319; 11 I.L.M. 1416 (1972).

14. Rio Declaration on Environment and Development (in Agenda 21) Adopted June 14, 1992, at the United Nations Conference on Environment and Development, Rio de Janeiro, UN Doc. A/CONF. 151/5/Rev. 1, *reprinted in* 31 I.L.M. 874 (1992).

15. A Global Agenda 34 (1995).

CHAPTER 11. CONTROL OF PEOPLE: NATIONALITY AND MOVEMENT

1. 356 U.S. 44 (1958).

2. 387 U.S. 253 (1967).

3. 356 U.S. 86 (1958).

4. *Id.* at 101–102.

5. 372 U.S. 144 (1963).

6. P. Weis, Nationality and Statelessness in International Law 124 (1956).

7. For example, Albania, Nationality Act No. 377 of 16 December 1946, Art. 14, United Nations Legislative Series, Laws Concerning Nationality, U.N. Doc. ST/LEG/SEA. B/4, at 4, 6 (1954); Poland, Nationality Act of 8 January 1951, Art. 12(b), *id.* at 386, 388.

8. Universal Declaration of Human Rights, art. 5; International Covenant on Civil and Political Rights, art. 7.

9. H. Arendt, The Origins of Totalitarianism 297 (1958).

10. Nottebohm Case (Liech. v. Guat.), 1955 I.C.J. 4 (Judgment on Second Phase of Apr. 6).

11. *Id.* at 22.

12. Merge Claim (U.S. v. Italy), 14 Rep. Int'l Arb. Awards 236 (1955).

13. G.A. Res. 2312, 22 U.N. GAOR Supp. (No. 16) at 81, U.N. Doc. A/6716 (1967).

CHAPTER 12. PROTECTION OF PEOPLE: FROM ALIEN RIGHTS TO HUMAN RIGHTS

1. Nottebohm Case (Liech. v. Guat.), 1955 I.C.J. 4 (Apr. 6).

2. Flegenheimer Claim, 25 I.L.R. 91 (Italian–United States Conciliation Commission 1963).

3. Barcelona Traction, Light and Power Co., Ltd. (Belg. v. Spain), 1970 I.C.J. 3 (Judgment on Second Phase of Feb. 5).

4. Nottebohm Case, *supra* note 1, at 6–7.

5. *Id.* at 23.

6. Legal Consequences for States of the Continued Presence of South Africa in Namibia (South West Africa) Notwithstanding Security Council Resolution 276 (1970), 1971 I.C.J. 16 (Advisory Opinion of June 21).

7. *See, e.g.,* Marks, *Emerging Human Rights: A New Generation for the 1980s?* 33 Rutgers L. Rev. 435 (1981).

8. Filartiga v. Pena-Irala, 630 F.2d 876 (2d Cir. 1980).

9. *See, e.g.,* Soering v. United Kingdom, 161 Eur. Ct. H.R. (ser. A) (1989).

10. International Responsibility: Second Report, [1957] 2 Y.B. Int'l L. Comm'n 104, 112–13, U.N. Doc. A/CN.4/106 (1957).

11. G.A. Res. 40/144, 40 U.N. GAOR Supp. (No. 53) at 252, U.N. Doc. A/40/53 (1985).

CHAPTER 13. VERTICAL ALLOCATION OF AUTHORITY

1. Tunis-Morocco Nationality Decrees, 1923 P.C.I.J. (ser. B) No. 4 (Advisory Opinion of Feb. 7).

2. *Id.* at 24.

3. H. Lauterpacht, International Law and Human Rights 167 (1950).

4. S.C. Res. 688, U.N. SCOR, 46th Sess., 2982th mtg. U.N. Doc. S/RES/688 (1991) (Iraq); S.C. Res. 814, U.N. SCOR, 48th Sess., 3188th mtg., U.N. Doc. S/RES/814 (1993) (Somalia).

5. H. Steiner & D. Vagts, Transnational Legal Problems: Materials and Text 324 (2d ed. 1976).

6. United Nations, Repertory of Practice of United Nations Organs, Supplement No. 3, at 109 (1972).

7. *See* Alvarez, *Judging the Security Council,* 90 A.J.I.L. 1 (1996); Reisman, *The Constitutional Crisis in the United Nations,* 87 A.J.I.L. 83 (1993).

8. Falk, *On the Quasi-Legislative Competence of the General Assembly,* 60 A.J.I.L. 782, 785 (1966).

CHAPTER 14. HORIZONTAL ALLOCATION OF AUTHORITY

1. Rest. 3rd, Restatement of the Foreign Relations Law of the United States §401.

2. 344 U.S. 280 (1952).

3. 265 U.S. 47 (1924).

4. United States v. Calley, 46 C.M.R. 1131 (A.C.M.R.), aff'd 22 C.M.A. 534, 48 C.M.R. 19 (1973); petition for writ of habeas corpus granted sub nom. Calley v. Calloway, 382 F. Supp. 650 (M.D. Ga. 1974), rev'd 519 F.2d 184 (5th Cir. 1975), cert. denied 425 U.S. 911 (1976).

5. Church v. Hubbart, 6 U.S. (2 Cranch) 187 (1804).

6. Id. at 234.

7. *See, e.g.* , U.S. v. Nippon Paper Industries Co., No. 96–2001 (1st Cir. March 17, 1997).

8. *See* Lowenfeld, *Agora: The Cuban Liberty and Democratic Solidarity (LIBERTAD) Act,* 90 A.J.I.L. 419 (1996).

9. The S.S. Lotus, 1927 P.C.I.J. (ser. A) No. 10 (Judgment of Sept. 7).

10. The Attorney-General of the Government of Israel v. Eichmann, Criminal Case No. 40/61, District Court of Jerusalem. Judgment of Dec. 11, 1961; *reprinted in* 56 A.J.I.L. 805 (1962).

11. *See, e.g.,* United States v. Yunis, 924 F.2d 1086 (D.C. Cir. 1991).

12. Rome Statute of the International Criminal Court, A/CONF. 183/9 (17 July 1998), especially Articles 5–8.

13. International Military Tribunal (Nuremberg), Judgment and Sentences, Oct. 1, 1946, 41 A.J.I.L. 172, 174 (1947).

14. *Id.*

15. *Id.* at 175.

16. G.A. Res. 40/61, 40 U.N. GAOR Supp. (No. 53) at 301, U.N. Doc. A/40/53 (1985); *reprinted in* 25 I.L.M. 239 (1986) and 80 A.J.I.L. 435 (1986).

17. 28 U.S.C. §1350.

18. 630 F.2d 876 (2d Cir. 1980).

19. 11 U.S. (7 Cranch) 116 (1812).

20. Id. at 136.

21. Letter from Acting Legal Adviser Jack B. Tate to Acting Attorney General Philip B. Perlman, 26 Dep't State Bull. 984 (1952).

22. Foreign Sovereign Immunities Act, 28 U.S.C. §§1330, 1602–11 (1976).

23. *Id.* §1603(d).

24. State Immunity Act 1978, *reprinted in* 17 I.L.M. 1123 (1978).

25. 376 U.S. 398 (1964).

26. *Id.* at 428.

27. 168 U.S. 250, 252 (1897).

28. Banco Nacional de Cuba v. Sabbatino, *supra* note 25, at 423.

29. *Id.* at 428.

30. 22 U.S.C. §2370(e)(2).

31. 406 U.S. 759 (1972).

32. National City Bank of New York v. Republic of China, 348 U.S. 356 (1955).

33. 425 U.S. 682 (1976).

34. Restatement of the Foreign Relations Law of the United States, *supra* note 1, §443(1).

35. U.S. Const. art. IV, §1.

CHAPTER 15. THE DIPLOMATIC INSTRUMENT

1. H. Grotius, Law of War and Peace 440 (F. Kelsey transl. 1925).

2. 22 U.S.C. §254(d) (1978).

3. Case Concerning United States Diplomatic and Consular Staff in Tehran (U.S. v. Iran), 1979 I.C.J. 7 (Provisional Measures Order of Dec. 15).

4. Case Concerning United States Diplomatic and Consular Staff in Iran (U.S. v. Iran), 1980 I.C.J. 3 (Judgment of May 24).

5. U.S. v. Iran, *supra* note 3, at 19.

6. U.S. v. Iran, *supra* note 4, at 41–42.

7. Asylum Case (Colom./Peru), 1950 I.C.J. 266 (Judgment of Nov. 20).

8. *Id.* at 277.

9. Legal Consequences for States of the Continued Presence of South Africa in Namibia (South West Africa) Notwithstanding Security Council Resolution 276 (1970), 1971 I.C.J. 16 (Advisory Opinion of June 21) [hereinafter cited as Advisory Opinion on Namibia].

10. 1950 I.C.J. 128, 143–44 (Advisory Opinion of July 11).

11. G.A. Res. 2145, 21 U.N. GAOR Supp. (No. 16) at 2, U.N. Doc. A/6314 (1966).

12. S.C. Res. 276 (1970), Resolutions and Decisions of the Security Council, 1970, at 1, 25 U.N. SCOR, U.N. Doc. S/INF/25; S.C. Res. 264 (1969), Resolutions and Decisions of the Security Council, 1969, at 1–2, 24 U.N. SCOR, U.N Doc. S/INF/24/Rev. 1.

13. S.C. Res. 284 (1970), Resolutions and Decisions of the Security Council, 1970, at 4, 25 U.N. SCOR, U.N. Doc. S/INF/25.

14. Advisory Opinion on Namibia, *supra* note 9, at 58.

15. *Id.*

16. *Id.* at 55.

17. *Id.* at 56.

18. *Id.*

19. *See* Peter H. F. Bekker, *Recent Developments at the World Court: Botswana and Namibia Bring a New Case,* A.S.I.L. Newsletter, 1996.

CHAPTER 16. INTERNATIONAL AGREEMENTS

1. McNair, *The Functions and Differing Legal Character of Treaties,* 11 Brit. Y.B. Int'l L. 100 (1930). *See* M. McDougal & W. Reisman, International Law in Contemporary Perspective 1119–20 (1981).

2. Kearney & Dalton, *The Treaty of Treaties,* 64 A.J.I.L. 495 (1970).

3. Reservations to the Convention on the Prevention and Punishment of the Crime of Genocide, 1951 I.C.J. 1 (Advisory Opinion of May 28).

4. *Id.* at 29.

5. M. McDougal, H. Lasswell, & J. Miller, The Interpretation of Agreements and World Public Order: Principles of Content and Procedure (1967).

6. *Id.* at 39–45.

7. *Id.* at 47–48.

CHAPTER 17. THE IDEOLOGICAL INSTRUMENT

1. Introduction to the Annual Report of the Secretary-General on the Work of the Organization, 16 June 1965–15 June 1966, 21 U.N. GAOR, Supp. (No. 1A) at 2, U.N. Doc. A/6301 /Add. 1 (1966).

2. N.Y. Times, May 21, 1985, at A12, col. 3.

3. International Military Tribunal (Nuremberg), Judgment and Sentences, Oct. 1, 1946, 41 A.J.I.L. 172, 174 (1947).

4. *Id.* Dept. of State, Trial of War Criminals 25, 39 (1945); Wright, *The Crime of War-Mongering,* 42 A.J.I.L. 128, 129–30 (1948).

5. *See* B. Murty, Propaganda and World Public Order 160–65 (1968).

6. G.A. Res. 59 (I), U.N. Doc. A/64/Add. 1, at 95 (1946).

7. UNESCO Res. 4/9.3/2, 20 UNESCO Gen. Conf. Rec., UNESCO Doc. 20C/Resolution, at 100 (1979).

CHAPTER 18. THE ECONOMIC INSTRUMENT

1. *See* Paust & Blaustein, *The Arab Oil Weapon—A Threat to International Peace,* in Economic Coercion and the New International Economic Order 121–52 (R. Lillich ed. 1976). *The Use of Nonviolent Coercion: A Study in Legality Under Article 2(4) of the Charter of the United Nations,* 122 U. Pa. L. Rev. 983, 997–1011 (1974).

2. *See* Brosche, *The Arab Oil Embargo and United States Pressure Against Chile: Economic and Political Coercion and the Charter of the United Nations,* 7 Case W. Res. J. Int'l L. 3, 16–35 (1974).

3. S.C. Res. 232 (1966), Resolutions and Decisions of the Security Council, 1966, at 7, 21 U.N. SCOR, U.N. Doc. 5/INF/21/Rev. 1 (1966).

4. G.A. Res. 2506, para. 5, 24 U.N GAOR Supp. (No. 30) at 23, U.N. Doc. A/7630 (1969).

5. Reisman, *Polaroid Power: Taxing Business for Human Rights,* 4 Foreign Policy 101, 103–4 (1971).

6. S.C. Res. 569, U.N. Doc. S/RES/569 (1985); *reprinted in* 24 I.L.M. 1483 (1985).

7. European Community News, No. 24/1985 (Aug. 8, 1985) and No. 26/1985 (Sept. 11, 1985); *reprinted in* 24 I.L.M. 1474 (1985).

8. *Reprinted in* 24 I.L.M. 1464 (1985).

9. Exec. Order No. 12532, 50 Fed. Reg. 36861 (1985).

10. Comprehensive Anti-Apartheid Act of 1986, Pub. L. No. 99-440, 100 Stat. 1086 (1986). *See* Paretsky, *The United States Arms Embargo Against South Africa: An Analysis of the Laws, Regulations, and Loopholes,* 12 Yale J. Int'l L. 133 (1987).

11. The Sullivan principles were drafted by Rev. Leon Sullivan, a Baptist minister and member of the General Motors Corporation Board of Directors. As initially formulated, they are reprinted in Editor's Note, *Perspectives,* 15 Law & Pol. Int'l Bus. 445–46 (1983); Fourth Amplification *reprinted in* 24 I.L.M. 1496 (1985).

12. Foreign Assistance Act of 1974, Pub. L. No. 93–559, 88 Stat. 1795 §502(B); Foreign Assistance Act of 1976, Pub. L. No. 94-330, 90 Stat. 771. Salzberg, *Human Rights and U.S. Foreign Policy Under Carter: A Congressional Perspective,* 8 Den. J. Int'l L. & Pol. 525, 526 (1979).

13. N.Y. Times, Sept. 30, 1997, at A12, col. 1.

14. Declaration on the Establishment of a New International Economic Order, G.A. Res. 3201 (S-VI), May 1, 1974, U.N. GAOR, 6 Spec. Sess. Supp. (No. 1) at 3, U.N. Doc. A/9559 (1974); *reprinted in* 13 I.L.M. 715 (1974). Charter of Economic Rights and Duties of States, G.A. Res. 3281, 29 U.N. GAOR Supp. (No. 31) at 50, U.N. Doc. A/9631 1974); *reprinted in* 14 I.L.M. 251 (1975).

15. An Agenda for Development, Report of the Secretary-General of May 6, 1994, U.N. Doc. A/48/935 (1994).

16. *See* Jiménez de Arechaga, *State Responsibility for the Nationalization of Foreign-Owned Property,* 11 N.Y.U. J. Int'l L. & Pol. 179, 185 (1978).

17. G.A. Res. 1803, 17 U.N. GAOR Supp. (No. 17) at 15, U.N. Doc. A/5217 (1962).

CHAPTER 19. THE MILITARY INSTRUMENT

1. M. McDougal & F. Feliciano, Law and Minimum World Public Order 137 (1961).

2. G.A. Res. 3314, 29 U.N. GAOR, Supp. (No. 31) at 142, U.N. Doc. A/9631 (1974).

3. *See* M. McDougal & F. Feliciano, *supra* note 1, at 121–260.

4. Mr. Webster to Mr. Fox, April 24, 1841, in 29 British and Foreign State Papers 1129, 1138 (1840–41).

5. McDougal, *The Soviet-Cuban Quarantine and Self-Defense,* 57 A.J.I.L. 597 (1963).

6. Case Concerning Military and Paramilitary Activities in and Against Nicaragua (Nicar. v. U.S.), 1986 I.C.J. 14 (Judgment on Merits of June 27).

7. Corfu Channel Case, 1949 I.C.J. 4 (Judgment on Merits of Apr. 9).

8. *Id.* at 35.

9. Jessup, *Should International Law Recognize an Intermediate Status Between Peace and War?* 48 A.J.I.L. 98 (1954).

10. Text in Holland, The Laws of War on Land (1908).

11. Legality of the Threat or Use of Nuclear Weapons (Advisory Opinion of July 8, 1996), *reprinted in* 35 I.L.M. 809 (1996). *See also* Michael J. Matheson, *The Opinions of the International Court of Justice on the Threat or Use of Nuclear Weapons,,* 91 A.J.I.L. 417 (1997).

12. Advisory Opinion on the Legality of the Threat or Use of Nuclear Weapons, *supra* note 11 at 830, 831.

13. Shimoda Case, Judgment of Dec. 7, 1963, District Court of Tokyo, *translated into English and reprinted in full in* 8 Jap. Ann. Int'l L. 212 (1964).

14. G.A. Res. 1653, 16 U.N. GAOR Supp. (No. 17) at 4, U.N. Doc. A/5100 (1961).

15. The S.S. Lotus (Fr./Turk.), 1927 P.C.I.J. (ser. A), No. 10.

16. Advisory Opinion on the Legality of the Threat or Use of Nuclear Weapons, *supra* note 11 at 839 (Schwebel, J.).

CHAPTER 20. THE INTELLIGENCE FUNCTION

1. N.Y. Times, Aug. 22, 1985, at A1, col. 6.

CHAPTER 21. THE PROMOTING FUNCTION

1. *See* Valerie Oosterveld, *Reports of ASIL Programs: U.N. Fourth World Conference on Women,* A.S.I.L. Newsletter, Nov. 1995.

2. Declaration on the Elimination of Discrimination Against Women, G.A. Res. 2263, 22 U.N. GAOR Supp. (No. 16) at 35, U.N. Doc. A/6716 (1967).

3. G.A. Res. 40/108, 40 U.N. GAOR Supp. (No. 53) at 223, U.N. Doc. A/40/53 (1985).

4. Reichert, *Resolving the Trade and Environment Conflict: The WTO and NGO Consultative Relations,* 5 Minn. J. Global Trade 219 (1996).

CHAPTER 22. THE PRESCRIBING (LAWMAKING) FUNCTION

1. Rest. 3rd, Restatement of the Foreign Relations Law of the United States §102(2).

2. North Sea Continental Shelf Case (Ger. v. Den. and Neth.), 1969 I.C.J. 3 (Judgment of Feb. 20, 1969).

3. *Id.* at 43.

4. *Id.* at 44.

5. G. Finch, The Sources of International Law 51 (1937) (quoting Walker).

6. Asylum Case (Colom./Peru), 1950 I.C.J. 266, 276 (Judgment of Nov. 20).

7. *Id.* at 277.

8. Kunz, *The Nature of Customary International Law,* 47 A.J.I.L. 662, 666 (1953).

9. A. Ross, A Text-Book of International Law 89 (1947).

10. G.A. Res. 1803, 17 U.N. GAOR Supp. (No. 17) at 15, U.N. Doc. A/5217 (1962).

11. G.A. Res. 3281, 29 U.N. GAOR Supp. (No. 31) at 50, U.N. Doc. A/9631 (1974); G.A. Res. 3171, 28 U.N. GAOR Supp. (No. 30) at 52, U.N. Doc. A/9030 (1973).

12. Texaco Overseas Petroleum Company/California Asiatic Oil Company v. Libyan Arab Republic (Award on the Merits of Jan. 19, 1977), *translated into English and reprinted in* 17 I.L.M. 1 (1978).

13. *Id.* at 31.

14. *Id.* at 29.

15. *Id.* at 28.

16. *Id.*

17. *Id.* at 29.

18. *Id.*

19. *Id.* at 30.

20. *See* M. McDougal, H. Lasswell, & L. Chen, Human Rights and World Public Order 325–30 (1980) and references therein.

21. See Schachter, *The Twilight Existence of Nonbinding International Agreements,* 71 A.J.I.L. 296 (1977). The text of the Final Act is found in 73 Dep't State Bull. 323 (1975) and *reprinted in* 14 I.L.M. 1292 (1975).

CHAPTER 23. THE INVOKING FUNCTION

1. 21 U.N. GAOR C.3 (1415th mtg.) 223, U.N. Doc. A/C.3/SR.1415 (1966).

CHAPTER 24. THE APPLYING FUNCTION

1. Mavrommatis Palestine Concessions Case, P.C.I.J., Ser. A, No. 2, at 15 (1924).

2. U.S. Department of State Letter and Statement Concerning Termination of Acceptance of I.C.J. Compulsory Jurisdiction, *reprinted in* 24 I.L.M. 1742 (1985).

3. Delimitation of the Maritime Boundary in the Gulf of Maine Area (Can./U.S.), 1984 I.C.J. 246 (Judgment of Oct. 12).

4. R.S.C. 1970 (1st Supp.), C. 2 (1970).

CHAPTER 25. THE TERMINATING FUNCTION

1. The Agreement Establishing the Commonwealth of Independent States, 8 December 1991 (The Minsk Agreement), *reprinted in* 31 I.L.M. 138 (1992).

2. Fisheries Jurisdiction (U.K. v. Ice.), 1974 I.C.J. 3 (Judgment of July 25).

3. *Id.* at 48.

CHAPTER 26. THE APPRAISING FUNCTION

1. Final Act of the International Conference on Human Rights, Tehran, Apr. 22–May 13, 1968, U.N. Doc. A/CONF.32/41 (Sales No. E 68 XIV 2); *reprinted in* 63 A.J.I.L. 674 (1969).

2. G.A. Res. 40/108, 40 U.N. GAOR Supp. (No. 53) at 223, U.N. Doc. A/40/53 (1985).

3. Beijing Declaration and Platform for Action, United Nations Fourth World Conference on Women, U.N. Doc. A/CONF. 177/20 (1995), *reprinted in* 35 I.L.M. 401 (1995).

4. Report of Personnel Problems in the United Nations (Maurice Bertrand, Joint Inspection Unit), U.N. Doc. JIU/REP/71/7 (1971).

5. G.A. Res. 40/237, 40 U.N. GAOR Supp. (No. 53) at 60, U.N. Doc. A/40/53 (1985).

6. Report of the Group of High Level Intergovernmental Experts to Review the Efficiency of the Administrative and Financial Functioning of the United Nations, 41 U.N. GAOR Supp. (No. 49), U.N. Doc. A/41/49 (1986).

7. G.A. Res. 41/213, U.N. Doc. 41/RES/213 (19 Dec. 1986).

8. UN Chronicle, Vol. 24, No. 2, May 1987, at 57.

CHAPTER 27. RESPONSIBILITY OF STATES

1. Report of the International Law Commission on the Work of Its Thirty-second Session (5 May–25 July 1980), *reprinted in* [1980] 2 Y.B. Int'l L. Comm'n (Part 2) 1, 26–63, U.N. Doc. Al/CN.4/SER.A/1980/Add. 1 (Part 2).

2. *Id.* at 30.

3. *Id.* at 33 (Draft Article 31).

4. *Id.* at 33.

5. Corfu Channel Case (U.K. v. Alb.), 1949 I.C.J. 4 (Judgment on Merits of Apr. 9).

6. I. Brownlie, Principles of Public International Law 433 (2d ed. 1973).

7. Interhandel Case (Switz. v. U.S.), 1959 I.C.J. 6 (Judgment of Mar. 21).

8. Chorzow Factory Case (Ger. v. Pol.), 1928 P.C.I.J. (ser. A) No. 9, at 31.

CHAPTER 28. SUCCESSION OF STATES

1. U.N. Doc. A/5209, A/CN.4/149.

2. G.A. Res. 47/229, U.N. GAOR, 47th Sess., Supp. No. 49, Vol. 2, U.N. Doc. A/47/49 (1992).

3. 137 F.2d 898 (2d Cir. 1943).

CHAPTER 29. TOWARD A WORLD COMMUNITY OF HUMAN DIGNITY

1. W. Schiffer, The Legal Community of Mankind 46 (1954).

2. Lasswell, *Population Change and Policy Sciences: Proposed Workshops on Reciprocal Impact Analysis,* in Policy Sciences and Population 117, 118 (W. Ilchman et al. eds. 1975).

3. See H. Lasswell, World Politics and Personal Insecurity (1935; 1965); H. Lasswell, A Pre-View of Policy Sciences 67–69 (1971). *See also* Eulau, *H. D. Lasswell's Developmental Analysis,* 11 W. Pol. Q. 229 (1958).

4. McDougal, *International Law and the Future,* 50 Miss. L.J. 259, 330–31 (1979).

5. *See, e.g.,* R. Falk, A Study of Future Worlds (1975); J. Galtung, The True Worlds: A Transnational Perspective (1980); Towards a Just World Order (R. Falk, S. Kim, & S. Mendlovitz eds. 1982).

Suggested Readings

CHAPTER 1. INTERNATIONAL LAW IN A POLICY-ORIENTED PERSPECTIVE

American Law Institute. *Restatement of the Law (Third): The Foreign Relations Law of the United States.* 2 vols. St. Paul, Minn.: American Law Institute, 1987.

American Society of International Law. *International Law in the Twentieth Century.* Edited by Leo Gross. New York: Appleton-Century-Crofts, 1969.

Bos, Maarten, ed. *The Present State of International Law and Other Essays.* Deventer, Netherlands: Kluwer, 1973.

Brierly, J. L. *The Law of Nations.* 6th ed. Edited by Sir Humphrey Waldock. New York and Oxford: Oxford University Press, 1963.

Brownlie, Ian. *Principles of Public International Law.* 5th ed. Oxford: Clarendon Press, 1998.

Buergenthal, Thomas, and Harold G. Maier. *Public International Law in a Nutshell.* St. Paul, Minn.: West Publishing, 1985.

Burley, Anne-Marie Slaughter. "International Law and International Relations Theory: A Dual Agenda." *American Journal of International Law* 87 (1993): 205.

Butler, William E., ed. *International Law in Comparative Perspective.* Alphen aan den Rijn, Netherlands: Sijthoffen Noordhoff, 1980.

Cassese, Antonio. *International Law in a Divided World.* Oxford: Clarendon Press, 1994.

Chen, Lung-chu. "Constitutional Law and International Law in the United States of America." *American Journal of Comparative Law, Supplement* 42 (1994): 453.

D'Amato, Anthony. *International Law: Process and Prospect.* Dobbs Ferry, N.Y.: Transnational Publishers, 1987.

De Visscher, Charles. *Theory and Reality in Public International Law.* Rev. ed. Translated by P. E. Corbett. Princeton: Princeton University Press, 1968.

Falk, Richard A. *The Status of Law in International Society.* Princeton: Princeton University Press, 1970.

Falk, Richard, Friedrich Kratochwil, and Saul H. Mendlovitz, eds. *International Law: A Contemporary Perspective.* Boulder: Westview Press, 1985.

Head, John W. "Supranational Law: How the Move Toward Multilateral Solutions Is Changing the Character of International Law." *Kansas Law Review* 42 (1994): 601.

Henkin, Louis. *How Nations Behave: Law and Foreign Policy.* 2d ed. New York: Columbia University Press, 1979.

Higgins, Rosalyn. *Problems and Process: International Law and How We Use It.* Oxford: Clarendon Press, 1995.

Janis, Mark W. *An Introduction to International Law.* 3d ed. Boston: Little, Brown, 1999.

Jennings, Robert, and Arthur Watts. *Oppenheim's International Law.* Vol. 1. 9th ed. Harlow, Essex, England: Longmans Group, 1992.

Koh, Harold Hongju. "Why Do Nations Obey International Law? Review Essay: The New Sovereignty: Compliance with International Regulatory Agreements by Abram and Antonia Handler Chayes." Yale Law Journal 106 (1997): 2599.

Macdonald, R. St. J., and Douglas M. Johnston, eds. *The Structure and Process of International Law: Essays in Legal Philosophy, Doctrine, and Theory.* Dordrecht: Martinus Nijhoff, 1986.

McDougal, Myres S., and W. Michael Reisman. *International Law Essays: A Supplement to International Law in Contemporary Perspective.* Mineola, N.Y.: Foundation Press, 1981.

———. *International Law in Contemporary Perspective: The Public Order of the World Community.* Mineola, N.Y.: Foundation Press, 1981.

Paust, Jordan J. *International Law as Law of the United States.* Durham, N.C.: Carolina Academic Press, 1996.

Reisman, W. Michael. *Law in Brief Encounters.* New Haven: Yale University Press, 1999.

Reisman, W. Michael, and Andrew R. Willard, eds. *International Incidents: The Law That Counts in World Politics.* Princeton: Princeton University Press, 1988.

Shaw, Malcolm N. *International Law.* 3d ed. Cambridge, England: Grotius, 1995.

CHAPTER 2. NATION-STATES

Agrawala, S. K., T. S. Rama Rao, and J. N. Saxena, eds. *New Horizons of International Law and Developing Countries.* Bombay: N. M. Tripathi, 1983.

Anand, R. P., ed. *Asian States and the Development of Universal International Law.* Delhi: Vikas, 1972.

Buchheit, Lee C. *Secession: The Legitimacy of Self-Determination.* New Haven: Yale University Press, 1978.

Cassese, Antonio. *Self-Determination of Peoples: A Legal Reappraisal.* Cambridge and New York: Cambridge University Press, 1995.

Chen, Lung-chu. "Self-Determination as a Human Right." *Toward World Order and Human Dignity,* ed. W. Michael Reisman and Burns Weston, 198–261. New York: Free Press, 1976.

——. "Taiwan, China, and the United Nations." In *The International Status of Taiwan in the New World Order: Legal and Political Considerations,* edited by Jean-Marie Henckaerts, 189–206. London: Kluwer Law International, 1996.

Chen, Lung-chu, and Harold D. Lasswell. *Formosa, China, and the United Nations: Formosa in the World Community.* New York: St. Martin's Press, 1967.

Crawford, James. *The Creation of States in International Law.* Oxford: Clarendon Press, 1979.

——. *Democracy in International Law.* Cambridge: Cambridge University Press, 1996.

Franck, Thomas M. "The Emerging Right to Democratic Governance." *American Journal of International Law* 86 (1992): 46.

Galloway, L. Thomas. *Recognizing Foreign Governments: The Practice of the United States.* Washington, D.C.: American Enterprise Institute for Public Policy Research, 1978.

Lauterpacht, Hersch. *Recognition in International Law.* Cambridge: Cambridge University Press, 1948.

Lee Teng-hui. "Understanding Taiwan." *Foreign Affairs* (November–December 1999): 9–14.

Movsesian, Mark L. "The Decline of the Nation-State and Its Effect on Constitutional and Economic Law: The Persistent Nation-State and the Foreign Sovereign Immunities Act," *Cordozo Law Review* 18 (1996): 1083.

Richardson, Henry J. III. "Failed States, Self-Determination, and Preventive Diplomacy: Colonialist Nostalgia and Democratic Expectations." *Temple International and Comparative Law* Journal 10 (1996): 1.

Schachter, Oscar. "The Decline of the Nation-State and Its Implications for International Law." *Columbia Journal of Transnational Law* 36 (1997): 7.

Schou, August, and Arne Olav Brundtland, eds. *Small States in International Relations.* Stockholm: Almqvist & Wiksell; New York: John Wiley & Sons, 1971.

Syatauw, J. J. G. *Some Newly Established States and the Development of International Law.* The Hague: Martinus Nijhoff, 1961.

Umozurike, Umozurike Oji. *Self-Determination in International Law.* Hamden, Conn.: Archon Books, 1972.

CHAPTER 3. INTERNATIONAL GOVERNMENTAL ORGANIZATIONS

Alagappa, Muthiah, and Takashi Inoguchi, eds. International Security Management and the United Nations. Tokyo: United Nations University Press, 1999.

Alger, Chadwick F., ed. *The Future of the United Nations System: Potential for the Twenty-first Century.* Tokyo. New York. Paris: United Nations University Press, 1998.

Alvarez, Jose E. "Judging the Security Council." *American Journal of International Law* 90 (1996): 1.

Arend, Anthony Clark. "The United Nations, Regional Organizations, and Military Operations: The Past and Present." *Duke Journal of Comparative and International Law* 7 (1996): 3.

Bailey, Sydney D., and Sam Daws. *The Procedure of the UN Security Council.* 3d ed. Oxford: Clarendon Press, 1998.

Bardow, Doug, and Ian Vasquez, eds. *Perpetuating Poverty: The World Bank, the IMF, and the Developing World.* Washington, D.C.: Cato Institute, 1996.

Bennett, A. LeRoy. *International Organizations: Principles and Issues.* 3d ed. Englewood Cliffs: Prentice-Hall, 1984.

Bowett, D. W. *The Law of International Institutions.* 4th ed. London: Stevens & Sons, 1982.

Childers, Erskine, with Brian Urquhart. *Renewing the United Nations System.* Uppsala, Sweden: Dag Hammarskjold Foundation, 1994.

Claude, Inis L., Jr. *Swords into Plowshares.* 4th ed. New York: Random House, 1971.

Djikeul, Dennis. *The Management of Multilateral Organizations.* The Hague: Kluwer Law International, 1996.

Franck, Thomas. *Nation Against Nation: What Happened to the U.N. Dream and What the U.S. Can Do About It.* New York: Oxford University Press, 1985.

Goodrich, Leland M., Edvard Hambro, and Anne Patricia Simons. *Charter of the United Nations.* 3d rev. ed. New York and London: Columbia University Press, 1969.

Gregg, Robert W. *About Face? The United States and the United Nations.* Boulder, Colo.: Lynne Rienner Publishers, 1993.

Gross, Leo. *Essays on International Law and Organization.* 2 vols. Dobbs Ferry, N.Y.: Transnational; The Hague: Martinus Nijhoff, 1984.

Hajnal, Peter I., ed. *International Information: Documents, Publications, and Electric Information of International Governmental Organizations.* 2d ed. Englewood, Colo.: Libraries Unlimited, 1997.

Higgins, Rosalyn. *The Development of International Law Through the Political Organs of the United Nations.* London: Oxford University Press, 1963.

Jenks, C. Wilfred. *International Immunities.* Dobbs Ferry, N.Y.: Oceana, 1961.

Kirgis, Frederic L. *International Organizations in the Legal Setting: Documents, Comments, and Questions.* St. Paul, Minn.: West, 1977.

Mendlovitz, Saul H., and Burns H. Weston, eds. *Preferred Futures for the United Nations.* Irvington-on-Hudson, N.Y.: Transnational Publishers, 1995.

Michaels, David B. *International Privileges and Immunities.* The Hague: Martinus Nijhoff, 1971.

Roberts, Adam, and Benedict Kingsbury, eds. *United Nations, Divided World. The United Nations' Roles in International Relation.* 2d ed. Oxford: Clarendon Press, 1994.

Schachter, Oscar, and Christopher C. Joyner, eds. *United Nations Legal Order.* 2 vols. New York: Cambridge University Press, 1995.

Sean, Blain. *United Nations General Assembly Resolutions in Our Changing World.* Ardsley on-Hudson, N.Y.: Transnational Publishers, 1991.

United Nations. *The United Nations at Forty: Foundation to Build On.* New York: United Nations, 1985.

United Nations Department of Public Information. *Basic Facts About the United Nations.* New York: United Nations, 1998.

Weiss, Thomas G., David P. Forsythe, and Roger A. Choate. *The United Nations and Changing World Politics.* Boulder, Colo.: Westview Press, 1994.

CHAPTER 4. NONGOVERNMENTAL ORGANIZATIONS AND ASSOCIATIONS

Barnet, Richard J., and John Cavanaugh. *Global Dreams: Imperial Corporations and the New World Order.* New York: Simon and Schuster, 1993.

Barnet, Richard J., and Ronald E. Muller. *Global Reach: The Power of the Multinational Corporations.* New York: Simon and Schuster, 1974.

Berman, Maureen R., and Joseph E. Johnson, eds. *Unofficial Diplomats.* New York: Columbia University Press, 1977.

Charnovitz, Steve. "Two Centuries of Participation: NGOs and International Governance." *Michigan Journal of International Law* 18 (1997): 183.

Chiang, Pei-heng. *Non-Governmental Organizations at the United Nations: Identity, Role, and Function.* New York: Praeger, 1981.

Eaton, Joshua P. "The Nigerian Tragedy, Environmental Regulation of Transnational Corporations and the Human Right to a Healthy Environment." *Boston University International Law Journal* 15 (1997): 261.

Goldman, Ralph M. *Transnational Parties: Organizing the World's Precincts.* Lanham, Md.: University Press of America, 1983.

Keohane, Robert O., and Joseph S. Nye. *Power and Interdependence: World Politics in Transition.* Boston: Little, Brown, 1977.

Lawson, Kay, ed. *Political Parties and Linkage: A Comparative Perspective.* New Haven: Yale University Press, 1980.

Nanda, Ved P., James R. Scarritt, and George W. Shepherd, Jr., eds. *Global Human Rights: Public Policies, Comparative Measures, and NGO Strategies.* Boulder, Colo.: Westview, 1981.

Rubin, Seymour J., and Gary Clude Hufbauer, eds. *Emerging Standards of International Trade and Investment: Multinational Codes and Corporate Conduct.* Totowa, N.J.: Rowman and Allanheld, 1984.

Soroos, Marvin S. *Beyond Sovereignty: The Challenge of Global Policy.* Columbia: University of South Carolina Press, 1986.

Wallace, Cynthia Day. *Legal Control of the Multinational Enterprise.* The Hague: Martinus Nijhoff, 1982.

Weiss, Thomas G., and Leon Gordenker, eds. *NGOs, the UN, and Global Governance.* Boulder, Colo.: Lynne Rienner Publishers, 1996.

White, Lyman Cromwell. *International Non-Governmental Organizations.* New Brunswick, N.J.: Rutgers University Press, 1951.

Willetts, Peter, ed. *The Conscience of the World: The Influence of Non-Governmental Organizations in the UN System.* Washington, D.C.: Brookings Institution, 1996.

CHAPTER 5. THE INDIVIDUAL

Higgins, Rosalyn. "Conceptual Thinking About the Individual in International Law." *New York Law School Law Review* 24 (1978): 11.

Lauterpacht, Hersch. *International Law and Human Rights.* Hamden, Conn.: Archon Books, 1968.

McDougal, Myres S., Harold D. Lasswell, and Lung-chu Chen. *Human Rights and World Public Order: The Basic Policies of an International Law of Human Dignity.* New Haven: Yale University Press, 1980.

Paust, Jordon J. "The Other Side of Right: Private Duties Under Human Rights Law." *Harvard Human Rights Journal* 5 (1992): 51.

CHAPTER 6. MINIMUM ORDER AND OPTIMUM ORDER

Burger, Suzanne, and Ronald Dore, eds. *Convergence or Diversity? National Models of Production and Distribution in a Global Economy.* Working Paper. Cambridge: Massachusetts Institute of Technology Industrial Performance Center, 1994.

Dore, Isaak I. *International Law and the Superpowers: Normative Order in a Divided World.* New Brunswick, N.J.: Rutgers University Press, 1984.

Falk, Richard. *On Humane Governance: Toward a New Global Politics.* University Park: Pennsylvania State University Press, 1995.

Ferencz, Benjamin B. *New Legal Foundations for Global Survival: Security Through the Security Council.* New York: Oceana Publishers, 1994.

Greider, William. *Who Will Tell the People? The Betrayal of American Democracy.* New York: Simon and Schuster, 1992.

Higgins, Rosalyn. *Conflict of Interests: International Law in a Divided World.* Chester Springs, Penn.: Dufour Editions, 1965.

Lebow, Richard Ned, and Thomas Risse-Kappen, eds. *International Relations Theory and the End of the Cold War.* New York: Columbia University Press, 1995.

Lipson, Leon. "Peaceful Coexistence." *Law and Contemporary Problems* 29 (1964): 871.

McDougal, Myres S., and Harold D. Lasswell. "The Identification and Appraisal of Diverse Systems of Public Order." *American Journal of International Law* 53 (1959): 1.

Muzaffer, Chandra. "Human Rights and the New World Order." *American Journal of International Law* 88 (1994): 852.

Ramcharan, B. G. *The International Law and Practice of Early-Warning of Preven-*

tive Diplomacy: The Emerging Global Watch. Dordrecht: Martinus Nijhoff Publishers, 1991.

Reisman, W. Michael. "International Law After the Cold War." *American Journal of International Law* 84 (1990): 859.

Schreuer, Christopher. "The Waning of the Sovereign State: Towards a New Paradigm for International Law?" *European Journal of International Law* 4 (1993): 447.

CHAPTER 7. ESTABLISHMENT OF AND ACCESS TO ARENAS OF AUTHORITY

Anand, Ram P. *International Courts and Contemporary Conflicts.* New York: Asia Publishing House, 1974.

Arend, Anthony Clark, ed. *The United States and the Compulsory Jurisdiction of the International Court of Justice.* Lanham, Md.: University Press of America, 1986.

Charney, Jonathan I. "The Implications of Expanding International Dispute Settlement Systems: The 1982 Convention on the Law of the Sea." *American Journal of International Law* 90 (1996): 69.

Damrosch, Lori Fisler, ed. *The International Court of Justice at a Crossroads.* Dobbs Ferry, N.Y.: Transnational, 1987.

Falk, Richard A. *Reviewing the World Court.* Charlottesville: University Press of Virginia, 1986.

Gross, Leo, ed. *The Future of the International Court of Justice.* 2 vols. Dobbs Ferry, N.Y.: Oceana Publications, 1976.

International Court of Justice. *The International Court of Justice.* 4th ed. The Hague: ICJ, 1996.

Jenks, C. Wilfred. *Prospects of International Adjudication.* Dobbs Ferry, N.Y.: Oceana Publications, 1964.

Jennings, Robert. "The UN at Fifty: The International Court of Justice After Fifty Years." *American Journal of International Law* 89 (1995): 493.

Jonkman, Hans, and Bette E. Shifman. "The Role of the Permanent Court of Arbitration in the United Nations Decade of International Law and the Peaceful Settlement of Disputes, 1990–1999 and Beyond." In Najeeb al-Nauimi and Richard Meese, eds. *Collected Essays: International Legal Issues Arising Under the United Nations Decade of International Law,* edited by Najeeb al-Nauimi and Richard Meese, The Hague: Martinus Nijhoff Publishers, 1995.

Katz, Milton. *The Relevance of International Adjudication.* Cambridge: Harvard University Press, 1968.

Lauterpacht, Elihu. *Aspects of the Administration of International Justice.* Vol. 9, *The Hersch-Lauterpacht Memorial Lecture Series.* Cambridge, England: Grotius Publications, 1991.

Lillich, Richard B., ed. *The Iran-United States Tribunal, 1981–1983.* Sokol Colloquium Series. Charlottesville: University Press of Virginia, 1985.

Lowenfeld, Andreas F. *International Litigation and Arbitration.* St. Paul, Minn.: West Publishing, 1993.

MacDonald, Ronald St. J., Franz Matscher, and Herbert Petzold. *The European System for the Protection of Human Rights.* The Hague: Martinus Nijhoff Publishers, 1993.

Reisman, W. Michael. *Systems of Control in International Adjudication and Arbitration: Breakdown and Repair.* Durham: Duke University Press, 1992.

Reisman, W. Michael, et al. *International Commercial Arbitration: Cases, Materials, and Notes on the Resolution of International Business Disputes.* New York: Foundation Press, 1997.

Rosenne, Shabtai. *The World Court: What It Is and How It Works.* 3d rev. ed. Leiden: A. W. Sijthoff; Dobbs Ferry, N.Y.: Oceana, 1973.

Rosenne, Shabtai, ed. *Documents on the International Court of Justice.* 2d ed. Alphen aan den Rijn, Netherlands: Sijthoffand Noordhoff; Dobbs Ferry, N.Y.: Oceana, 1979.

Schwebel, Stephen M. *International Arbitration: Three Salient Problems.* Cambridge: Grotius, 1987.

Tunkin, Grigorii Ivanovich. *Theory of International Law.* Translated by William Butler. Cambridge: Harvard University Press, 1974.

Wexler, Leila Sadat. "The Proposed Permanent International Criminal Court: An Appraisal." *Cornell International Law Journal* 29 (1996): 665.

CHAPTER 8. CONTROL OVER TERRITORY

Chen, Lung-chu, and W. M. Reisman. "Who Owns Taiwan? A Search for International Title." *Yale Law Journal* 81 (1972): 599.

Hoffman, Fritz L., and Olga Mingo Hoffman. *Sovereignty in Dispute: The Falklands/Malvinas, 1493–1982.* Boulder, Colo.: Westview, 1984.

Jennings, R. Y. *The Acquisition of Territory in International Law.* Manchester: Manchester University Press; Dobbs Ferry, N.Y.: Oceana, 1963.

Makau wa Mutua. "Why Redraw the Map of Africa: A Moral and Legal Inquiry." *Michigan Journal of International Law* 16 (1995): 1113.

Ratner, Steven R. "Drawing a Better Line: UTI Possidetis and the Borders of New States." *American Journal of International Law* 90 (1996): 590.

Sharma, Surya P. *International Boundary Disputes and International Law: A Policy-Oriented Study.* Bombay: N. M. Tripathi, 1976.

Song, Yann-huei. "Managing Potential Conflicts in the South China Sea: Taiwan's Perspective." EAI Occasional Paper No. 14. East Asian Institute, National University of Singapore, Singapore University Press, 1999.

CHAPTER 9. CONTROL AND USE OF THE SEA

Anand, R. P. *Origin and Development of the Law of the Sea.* The Hague: Martinus Nijhoff, 1983.

Annick de Marffy-Mantuano. "The Procedural Framework of the Agreement Implementing the 1982 United Nations Convention on the Law of the Sea." *American Journal of International Law* 89 (1995): 814.

Benvenisti, Eyal. "Collective Action in the Utilization of Shared Freshwater: The Challenges of International Water Resource Law." *American Journal of International Law* 20 (1996): 384.

Charney, Jonathan I. "U.S. Provisional Application of the 1994 Deep Seabed Agreement" (Law of the Sea Forum: The 1994 Agreement on Implementation of the Seabed Provisions of the Convention on the Law of the Sea). *American Journal of International Law* 88 (1994): 705.

Charney, Jonathan I., ed. *The New Nationalism and the Use of Common Spaces: Issues in Marine Pollution and the Exploitation of Antarctica.* Totowa, NJ.: Allanheld, Osmun, 1982.

Churchill, R. R., and A. V. Lowe. *The Law of the Sea.* Manchester: Manchester University Press, 1983.

McDougal, Myres S., and William T. Burke. *The Public Order of the Oceans: A Contemporary International Law of the Sea.* New Haven: Yale University Press, 1962.

Oda, Shigeru. *The Law of the Sea in Our Time.* 2 vols. Leiden: Sijthoff, 1977.

Oxman, Bernard H., et al., eds. *Law of the Sea: U.S. Policy Dilemma.* San Francisco: Institute for Contemporary Studies, 1983.

Payoyo, Peter Bautista, ed. *Ocean Governance: Sustainable Development of the Seas.* Tokyo: United Nations University Press, 1994.

Sohn, Louis B. "The 1994 Agreement on Implementation of the Seabed Provisions of the Convention on the Law of the Sea: International Law Implications of the 1994 Agreement." *American Journal of International Law* 88 (1994): 696.

Sohn, Louis B., and Kristen Gustafson. *The Law of the Sea in Nutshell.* St. Paul, Minn.: West, 1984.

Song, Yann-huei. "Marine Scientific Research and Marine Pollution." *Ocean Development and International Law* 20 (1990): 601.

Song, Yann-huei. "A Pathfinder on the Law of the Sea and Marine Policy." *Ocean Development and International Law* 24 (1993): 205.

Van Dyke, Jon M., Durwood Zaulke, and Grant Hewison, eds. *Freedom for the Seas in the 21st Century: Ocean Governance and Environmental Harmony.* Washington, D.C.: Island Press, 1993.

CHAPTER 10. CONTROL AND USE OF OTHER RESOURCES

Arsanjani, Manoush. *International Regulation of Internal Resources.* Charlottesville: University of Virginia Press, 1981.

Hurrell, Andrew, and Benedict Kingsbury. *The International Politics of the Environment.* Oxford: Oxford University Press, 1992.

Matte, Nicolas Mateesco. *Treatise on Air-Aeronautical Law.* Montreal: ICASL, 1981.

McDougal, Myres S., Harold D. Lasswell, and Ivan A. Vlasic. *Law and Public Order in Space.* New Haven: Yale University Press, 1963.

Myhre, Jeffrey D. *The Antarctic Treaty System: Politics, Law, and Diplomacy.* Boulder, Colo.: Westview, 1986.

Rich, Bruce. *Mortgaging the Earth: Crisis of Development.* Boston: Beacon Press, 1994.

Sands, Phillip, ed. *Greening International Law.* New York: New Press, 1994.

Schachter, Oscar. *Sharing the World's Resources.* New York: Columbia University Press, 1977.

Schneider, Jan. *World Public Order of the Environment: Towards an International Ecological Law and Organization.* Toronto: University of Toronto Press, 1979.

Schoenbaum, Thomas J. "International Trade and Protection of the Environment: The Continuing Search for Reconciliation." *American Journal of International Law* 91 (1997): 268.

Weiss, Edith Brown. "Trade and Environment: Environment and Trade as Partners in Sustainable Development: A Commentary." *American Journal of International Law* 86 (1992): 728.

Weiss, Edith Brown, Daniel B. Magraw, and Paul C. Scasz. *International Environmental Law: Basic Instruments and References.* 1992.

Zhukov, Grennady, and Yuri Kolosov. *International Space Law.* Translated by Boris Belitzky. New York: Praeger, 1984.

CHAPTER 11. CONTROL OF PEOPLE: NATIONALITY AND MOVEMENT

Anaya, S. James. *Indigenous Peoples in International Law.* New York: Oxford University Press, 1996.

Blay, Sam, and Andreas Zimmerman. "Recent Changes in German Refugee Law: A Critical Assessment." *American Journal of International Law* 88 (1994): 361.

Garcia-Mora, Manuel R. *International Law and Asylum as a Human Right.* Washington, D.C.: Public Affairs Press, 1956.

Goodwin-Gill, Guy S. *International Law and the Movement of Persons Between States.* Oxford: Clarendon Press, 1978.

——. *The Refugee in International Law.* Oxford: Clarendon Press, 1983.

Grahl-Madsen, Atle. *The Status of Refugees in International Law.* 2 vols. Leiden: A. W. Sijthoff, 1966, 1972.

——. *Territorial Asylum.* Stockholm: Almqvist and Wiksell International; Dobbs Ferry, N.Y.: Oceana, 1980.

Hathaway, James C. *The Law of Refugee Status.* Toronto: Butterworths Canada, 1991.

Henckaerts, Jean-Marie. *Mass Expulsion in Modern International Law and Practice.* The Hague: Martinus Nijhoff Publisher/Kluwer Law International, 1995.

Nafziger, James A. R. "The General Admission of Aliens Under International Law." *American Journal of International Law* 77 (1983): 804.

Newmark, Robert L. "Non-Refoulement Run Afoul: The Questionable Legality of Extraterritorial Repatriation Programs." *Washington University Law Quarterly* 71 (1993): 833.

Plender, Richard O. *International Migration Law.* Leiden: A. W. Sitjhoff, 1972.

Shearer, I. A. *Extradition in International Law.* Manchester: Manchester University Press; Dobbs Ferry, N.Y.: Oceana, 1971.

Sinha, S. Prakash. *Asylum and International Law.* The Hague: Martinus Nijhoff, 1971.

Sohn, Louis B., and Thomas Buergenthal, eds. *The Movement of Persons Across Borders.* Studies in Transnational Legal Policy, no. 23. Washington, D.C.: American Society of International Law, 1992.

Vasak, Karel, and Sidney Liskofsky, eds. *The Right to Leave and to Return.* New York: American Jewish Committee, 1976.

Weis, P. *Nationality and Statelessness in International Law.* 2d ed. Leiden: A. W. Sijthoff, 1979.

Weissner, Seigfried. "Blessed Be the Ties That Bind: The Nexus Between Nationality and Territory." *Mississippi Law Journal* 56 (1986): 447.

CHAPTER 12. PROTECTION OF PEOPLE: FROM ALIEN RIGHTS TO HUMAN RIGHTS

Alston, Philip, ed. *The Best Interests of the Child: Reconciling Culture and Human Rights.* Oxford: Clarendon Press, 1994.

Davidson, Scott. *The Inter-American Human Rights System.* Aldershot, England, and Brookfield, Vt.: Dartmouth, 1997.

Dawson, Frank G., and Ivan L. Head. *International Law, National Tribunals, and the Rights of Aliens.* Syracuse, N.Y.: Syracuse University Press, 1971.

Garcia-Amador, F. V. *Recent Codification of the Law of State Responsibility for Injuries to Aliens.* Dobbs Ferry, N.Y.: Oceana; Leiden: A. W. Sijthoff, 1974.

Hannum, Hurst. *Guide to International Human Rights Practice.* 2d ed. Philadelphia: University of Pennsylvania Press, 1992.

Henkin, Louis. "U.S. Ratification of Human Rights Conventions: The Ghost of Senator Bricker." *American Journal of International Law* 89 (1995): 341.

Lauterpacht, Hersch. *International Law and Human Rights.* Hamden, Conn.: Archon Books, 1968.

Lillich, Richard B. *The Human Rights of Aliens in Contemporary International Law.* Manchester: Manchester University Press, 1984.

Lillich, Richard B., ed. *International Law of State Responsibility for Injuries to Aliens.* Charlottesville: University Press of Virginia, 1983.

Mayer, Ann Elizabeth. "Universal Versus Islamic Human Rights: A Clash of Cultures or a Clash with a Construction?" *Michigan Journal of International Law* 15 (1994): 307.

McDougal, Myres S., Harold D. Lasswell, and Lung-chu Chen. *Human Rights and World Public Order: The Basic Policies of an International Law of Human Dignity.* New Haven: Yale University Press, 1980.

Meron, Theodor, ed. *Human Rights in International Law: Legal and Policy Issues.* Oxford: Clarendon Press, 1984.

Merrills, J. G. *The Development of International Law by the European Court of Human Rights.* 2d ed. New York: Manchester University Press, 1993.

Ramcharan, B. G., ed. *The Principle of Legality in International Human Rights Institutions.* The Hague: Martinus Nijhoff Publishers, 1997.

Robertson, A. H. *Human Rights in the World.* Manchester: Manchester University Press, 1996.

Roth, Andreas H. *The Minimum Standard of International Law Applied to Aliens.* Leiden: A. W. Sijthoff, 1949.

Ruddick, Elizabeth E. "The Continuing Constraint of Sovereignty: International Law, International Protection, and the Internally Displaced." *Boston University Law Review* 77 (1992): 429.

Sieghart, Paul. *The International Law of Human Rights.* Oxford: Clarendon Press, 1983.

Sinha, S. Prakash. *Asylum and International Law.* The Hague: Martinus Nijhoff, 1971.

Stavropoulou, Maria. "The Right Not to Be Displaced." *American University Journal of International Law and Policy* 9 (1994): 689.

Steiner, Henry, and Philip Alston. *International Human Rights in Context: Law, Politics, Morals, Texts and Materials.* New York: Oxford University Press, 1996.

United Nations Department of Public Information. *The United Nations and Human Rights, 1945–1995.* New York: United Nations, 1995.

Vasak, Karel, ed. *The International Dimensions of Human Rights.* 2 vols. Westport, Conn.: Greenwood Press; Paris: UNESCO, 1982.

CHAPTER 13. VERTICAL ALLOCATION OF AUTHORITY

Franck, Thomas M. "The Powers of Appreciation. Who Is the Ultimate Guardian of UN Legality?" *American Journal of International Law* 86 (1992): 519.

Gassama, Ibrahim J. "Safeguarding the Democratic Entitlement: A Proposal for United Nations Involvement in National Politics." *Cornell International Law Journal* 30 (1997): 287.

Hall, Christopher Keith. "The First Two Sessions of the UN Preparatory Committee on the Establishment of an International Criminal Court." *American Journal of International Law* 91 (1997): 177.

King, Faiza Patel. "Sensible Scrutiny: The Yugoslavia Tribunal and Development of Limits on the Security Council's Powers Under Chapter VII of the Charter." *Emory International Law Review* 10 (1996): 509.

Murphy, Sean D. *Humanitarian Intervention: The United Nations in an Evolving Order.* Philadelphia: University of Pennsylvania Press, 1996.

Rajan, M. S. *The Expanding Jurisdiction of the United Nations.* Bombay: N. M. Tripathi; Dobbs Ferry, N.Y.: Oceana Publications, 1982.

Reisman, W. Michael. "Sovereignty and Human Rights in Contemporary International Law." *American Journal of International Law* 84 (1990): 866.

CHAPTER 14. HORIZONTAL ALLOCATION OF AUTHORITY

Bassiouni, M. Cherif, and Ved P. Nanda, eds. *A Treatise on International Criminal Law*. 2 vols. Springfield, Ill.: Charles C. Thomas, 1973.
Bloomfield, Louis M., and Gerald F. Fitzgerald. *Crimes Against Internationally Protected Persons: Prevention and Punishment*. New York: Praeger, 1975.
Franck, Thomas M., and Gregory M. Fox. *International Law Decisions in National Courts*. Irvington-on-Hudson, N.Y.: Transnational Publishers, 1996.
Gowlland-Dibbas, Vera. "Relationship of the International Court of Justice and the Security Council in Light of Lockerbie." *American Journal of International Law* 88 (1994): 643.
Lowenfeld, Andreas F. "The Cuban Liberty and Democratic Solidarity (Libertad) Act: Congress and Cuba: The Helms-Burton Act." *American Journal of International Law* 90 (1996): 419.
——. *International Litigation and the Quest for Reasonableness: Essays in Private International Law*. Oxford: Oxford University Press, 1996.
Paust, Jordan J. "Extradition and United States Prosecution of the *Achille Lauro* Hostage-Takers: Navigating the Hazards." *Vanderbilt Journal of Transnational Law* 20 (1987): 235.
——. "Suing Karadzic." *Leiden Journal of International Law* 10 (1997): 91.
Randall, Kenneth C. "Universal Jurisdiction Under International Law." *Texas Law Review* 66 (1988): 785.
Schreuer, Christoph. *State Immunity: Some Recent Developments*. Cambridge: Grotius, 1988.

CHAPTER 15. THE DIPLOMATIC INSTRUMENT

Ashman, Chuck, and Pamela Trescott. *Diplomatic Crime*. Toronto: PaperJacks, 1988.
Bundy, McGeorge, William J. Crowe, Jr., and Sidney D. Drell. *Reducing Nuclear Danger: The Road Away from the Brink*. New York: Council on Foreign Relations Press, 1993.
Higgins, Rosalyn. "The Abuse of Diplomatic Privileges and Immunities: Recent United Kingdom Experience." *American Journal of International Law* 79 (1985): 641.
Hufbauer, Gary Clyde, Jeffrey J. Schott, and Kimberly Ann Elliott. *Economic Sanctions Reconsidered*. 2d ed. Washington, D.C.: Institute for International Economics, 1990.
Klotz, Audie. *Norms in International Relations: The Struggle Against Apartheid*. Ithaca, N.Y.: Cornell University Press, 1995.
Lee, Duke. *Consular Law and Practice*. 2d ed. Oxford: Clarendon Press, 1991.

Ramcharan, B. G. *The International Law and Practice of Early-Warning of Preventive Diplomacy: The Emerging Global Watch.* Dordrecht: Martinus Nijhoff Publishers, 1991.

Schrag, Philip G. *Global Action: Nuclear Test Ban Diplomacy at the End of the Cold War.* Boulder, Colo.: Westview Press, 1992.

Sen, B. *A Diplomat's Handbook of International Law and Practice.* The Hague: Martinus Nijhoff, 1979.

Van Ham, Peter. *Managing Non-Proliferation Regimes in the 1990s: Power Politics and New Policies.* London: The Royal Institute of International Affairs/Council on Foreign Relations Press, 1994.

Vicuna, Francisco Orrego. "The Status and Rights of Refugees Under International Law: New Issues in Light of the Honnecker Affair." *University of Miami Inter-American Law Review* 25 (1994): 351.

Wilson, Clifton E. *Diplomatic Privileges and Immunities.* Tucson: University of Arizona Press, 1967.

CHAPTER 16. INTERNATIONAL AGREEMENTS

Bederman, David J. "Revivalist Canons and Treaty Interpretation." *UCLA Law Review* 41 (1994): 953.

Elias, T. O. *The Modern Law of Treaties.* Dobbs Ferry, N.Y.: Oceana Publications; Leiden: A. W. Sijthoff, 1974.

Garvey, Jack I. "Trade Law and Quality of Life in Dispute Resolution Under the NAFTA Side Accords on Labor and the Environment." *American Journal of International Law* 89 (1995): 439.

Gordon, Edward. "The World Court and the Interpretation of Constitutive Treaties." *American Journal of International Law* 59 (1965): 794.

McDougal, Myres S., Harold D. Lasswell, and James C. Miller. *The Interpretation of Agreements and World Public Order: Principles of Content and Procedure.* New Haven: Yale University Press, 1967.

Rogoff, Martin A. "Interpretation of International Agreements by Domestic Courts and the Politics of International Treaty Relations: Reflections on Some Recent Decisions of the U.S. Supreme Court." *American University Journal of International Law & Policy* 1 (1996): 559.

Rosenne, Shabtai. *The Law of Treaties: A Guide to the Legislative History of the Vienna Convention.* Leiden: A. W. Sijthoff; Dobbs Ferry, N.Y.: Oceana Publications, 1970.

Rozakis, Christos L. *The Concept of JUS COGENS in the Law of Treaties.* Amsterdam: North-Holland, 1976.

Sinclair, Sir Ian. *The Vienna Convention on the Law of Treaties.* 2d ed. Manchester: Manchester University Press, 1984.

Steinberg, Richard H. "Trade and Environmental Negotiations in the EU, NAFTA, and WTO: Regional Trajectories of Rule Development." *American Journal of International Law* 91 (1997): 231.

CHAPTER 17. THE IDEOLOGICAL INSTRUMENT

Chen, Lung-chu. "Human Rights and the Free Flow of Information." In *Power and Policy in Quest of Law: Essays in Honor of Eugene Victor Rostow,* edited by Myres S. McDougal and W. Michael Reisman, 247–90. The Hague: Martinus Nijhoff, 1985.

Foster, Francis H. "Information and the Problem of Democracy: The Russian Experience." *American Journal of Comparative Law* 44 (1996): 243.

Hamson, Françoise J. "Incitement and the Media: Responsibility of and for the Media in the Conflicts in the Former Yugoslavia." Papers in the Theory and Practice of Human Rights, no. 3. Essex, England: Human Rights Centre, University of Essex, 1993.

Many Voices, One World: Towards a New, More Just and More Efficient World Information and Communication Order. Report by the International Commission for the Study of Communication Problems. London: Kogan Page; New York: Unipub; Paris: UNESCO, 1980.

Metze, Jamie Frederic. "Rwanda Genocide and the International Law of Radio Jamming." *American Journal of International Law* 91 (1997): 628.

Murty, B. S. *Propaganda and World Public Order: The Legal Regulation of the Ideological Instrument of Coercion.* New Haven: Yale University Press, 1968.

Perritt, Henry H., Jr. "Jurisdiction in Cyberspace." *Villanova. Law Review* 41 (1996): 41.

CHAPTER 18. THE ECONOMIC INSTRUMENT

Childers, Erskine, and Brian Urquhart. *Renewing the United Nations System.* Uppsala, Sweden: Dag Hammarskjald Foundation, 1994.

Doxey, Margaret P. *International Sanctions in Contemporary Perspective.* New York: St. Martin's Press, 1987.

Jackson, John H. *Legal Problems of International Economic Relations.* St. Paul, Minn.: West, 1977.

Lillich, Richard B., ed. *Economic Coercion and the New International Economic Order.* Charlottesville, Va.: Michie, 1976.

Lowenfeld, Andreas F. *International Economic Law.* 5 vols. New York: Matthew Bender, 1973–78.

———. *Trade Control for Political Ends.* 2d ed. New York: Matthew Bender, 1983.

Meagher, Robert F. *An International Redistribution of Wealth and Power: A Study of the Charter of Economic Rights and Duties of States.* New York: Pergamon, 1979.

Nanda, Ved P., George W. Shepherd, Jr., and Eileen McCarthy-Arnolds, eds. *World*

Debt and the Human Condition: Structural Adjustment and the Right to Development. Westport, Conn.: Greenwood Publishing Group, 1993.

Paust, Jordan J., et al., eds. *The Arab Oil Weapon.* Dobbs Ferry, N.Y.: Oceana Publications, 1977.

Schachter, Oscar. "Compensation for Expropriation." *American Journal of International Law* 78 (1984): 121.

Weston, Burns H. "The Charter of Economic Rights and Duties of States and the Deprivation of Foreign-Owned Wealth." *American Journal of International Law* 75 (1981): 437.

CHAPTER 19. THE MILITARY INSTRUMENT

Arms Project of Human Rights Watch/Physicians for Human Rights. *Landmines: A Deadly Legacy.* St. Louis, Mo.: Saint Louis University Law School, 1993.

Blix, Hans. *Aggression, Neutrality and Sovereignty.* Stockholm: Almqvist and Wiksell, 1970.

Bowett, Derek W. *Self-Defence in International Law.* Manchester: Manchester University Press, 1958.

Brownlie, Ian. *International Law and the Use of Force by States.* Oxford: Clarendon Press, 1963.

Caron, David D. "The Legitimacy of the Collective Authority of the Security Council." *American Journal International Law* 87 (1993): 552.

Draper, G. I. A. *The Red Cross Conventions.* London: Stevens, 1958.

Falk, Richard A. *Legal Order in a Violent World.* Princeton: Princeton University Press, 1968.

Falk, Richard A., ed. *The Vietnam War and International Law.* 4 vols. Princeton: Princeton University Press, 1968–76.

Ferencz, Benjamin B. *Defining International Aggression: The Search for World Peace.* 2 vols. Dobbs Ferry, N.Y.: Oceana Publications, 1975.

Gasser, Hans-Peter. "For Better Protection of the Natural Environment in Armed Conflict: A Proposal for Action." *American Journal of International Law* 89 (1995): 637.

Lillich, Richard B., ed. *Humanitarian Intervention and the United Nations.* Charlottesville: University Press of Virginia, 1973.

Maier, Harold G., ed. "Appraisals of the ICJ's Decision: *Nicaragua v. United States* (Merits)." *American Journal of International Law* 81 (1987): 77.

Matheson, Michael J. "The Opinions of the International Court of Justice on the Threat or Use of Nuclear Weapons." *American Journal of International Law* 91 (1997): 417.

McDougal, Myres S., and Florentino P. Feliciano. *Law and Minimum World Public Order.* New Haven: Yale University Press, 1961.

Moore, John Norton. *Law and the Indo-China War.* Princeton: Princeton University Press, 1972.

Moore, John Norton, ed. *Law and the Civil War in the Modern World.* Baltimore: Johns Hopkins University Press, 1974.

Murphy, John F. *The United Nations and the Control of International Violence: A Legal and Political Analysis.* Totowa, N.J.: Allanheld, Osmun, 1982.

Pearson, Graham S. "The Prohibition of Biological Weapons: Current Activities and Future Prospects." *International Review of the Red Cross* 318 (1997): 270.

Reisman, W. Michael, and Christos T. Antoniou, eds. *The Law of War: Basic Documents on the Law of International Armed Conflicts.* New York: Vintage Press, 1994.

Rostow, Eugene V. *Law, Power, and the Pursuit of Peace.* Lincoln: University of Nebraska Press, 1968.

Song, Yann-huei. "China's Missile Tests in the Taiwan Strait: Relevant International Law Questions." *Marine Policy* 23 (1999): 81.

"Special Feature—Restraints on the Unilateral Use of Force: A Colloquy." *Yale Journal of International Law* 10 (1985): 261.

Stone, Julius. *Legal Controls of International Conflict.* London: Stevens, 1954.

Trooboff, Peter D., ed. *Law and Responsibility in Warfare: The Vietnam Experience.* Chapel Hill: University of North Carolina Press, 1975.

Walker, George K. "Anticipatory Collective Self-Defense in the Charter Era: What the Treaties Have Said." *Cornell International Law Journal* 31 (1998): 321.

CHAPTER 20. THE INTELLIGENCE FUNCTION

Bar-Yaacov, Nissim. *The Handling of International Disputes by Means of Inquiry.* New York: Oxford University Press, 1974.

McDougal, Myres S., Harold D. Lasswell, and W. Michael Reisman. "The Intelligence Function and World Public Order." *Temple Law Quarterly* 46 (1973): 365.

Ramcharan, B. G., ed. *International Law and Fact-Finding in the Field of Human Rights.* The Hague: Martinus Nijhoff, 1982.

Shore, William I. *Fact-Finding in the Maintenance of Peace.* Dobbs Ferry, N.Y.: Oceana Publications, 1970.

CHAPTER 21. THE PROMOTING FUNCTION

Alston, Philip. "The United Nations High Commissioner for Human Rights." *American Society of International Law Newsletter,* Sept. 1995.

Gasser, Hans-Peter. "For Better Protection of the Natural Environment in Armed Conflict: A Proposal for Action." *American Journal of International Law* 89 (1995): 637.

Hohman, Harold, ed. *Basic Documents of International Environmental Law.* Vol. 1, *The Important Declarations;* Vols. 2 and 3, *The Important Agreements.* London: Kluwer/Graham & Tratman, 1992.

Larson, Elizabeth L. "Comment: The United Nations Fourth World Conference on Women: Action for Equality, Development, and Peace (Beijing, China, September 1993)." *Emory International Law Review* 10 (1996): 695.

Posner, Michael H. "Reflections on the Vienna Conference." *American Society of International Law Newsletter,* Sept. 1993.

Soroos, Marvin S. *Beyond Sovereignty: The Challenge of Global Policy.* Columbia: University of South Carolina Press, 1986.

Sullivan, Donna J. "Women's Human Rights and the 1993 World Conference on Human Rights." *American Journal of International Law* 88 (1994): 152.

Willetts, Peter, ed. *Pressure Groups in the Global System.* London: Frances Pinter, 1982.

CHAPTER 22. THE PRESCRIBING (LAWMAKING) FUNCTION

Berg, Bradley E. "The 1994 International Law Commission Draft Statute for an International Criminal Court: A Principled Appraisal of Jurisdictional Structure." *Case Western Reserve Journal of International Law* 28 (1996): 221.

Castaneda, Jorge. *Legal Effects of United Nations Resolutions.* Translated by Alba Amoia. New York: Columbia University Press, 1969.

Charney, Jonathan I. "International Agreements and the Development of Customary International Law." *Washington Law Review* 61 (1986): 971.

D'Amato, Anthony. *The Concept of Custom in International Law.* Ithaca: Cornell University Press, 1971.

Falk, Richard. *The Role of Domestic Courts in the International Legal Order.* Syracuse: Syracuse University Press, 1964.

"The International Law Commission's Draft Code of Crimes Against the Peace and Security of Mankind: An Appraisal of the Substantive Provisions." *Criminal Law Forum* 5 (1994): 1.

Lauterpacht, Hersch. *The Development of International Law by the International Court.* London: Stevens and Sons, 1958.

LeBlanc, Lawrence J. *The Convention on the Rights of the Child: United Nations Lawmaking on Human Rights.* Lincoln: University of Nebraska Press, 1995.

McDougal, Myres S., and W. Michael Reisman. "The Prescribing Function in the World Constitutive Process: How International Law Is Made." *Yale Studies of World Public Order* 6 (1980): 249.

McWhinney, Edward. *United Nations Law Making: Cultural and Ideological Relativism and International Law Making for an Era of Transition.* New York and London: Holmes and Meier; Paris: UNESCO, 1984.

Onuf, Nicholas Greenwood, ed. *Law-Making in the Global Community.* Durham: Duke University Press, 1982.

Parry, Clive. *The Sources and Evidences of International Law.* Manchester: Manchester University Press; Dobbs Ferry, N.Y.: Oceana Publications, 1965.

Paust, Jordon J. "The Complex Nature, Sources and Evidences of Customary Human Rights." *Georgia Journal of International and Comparative Law* 25 (1995–96): 147.

Ramcharan, B. G. *The International Law Commission: Its Approach to the Codification and Progressive Development of International Law.* The Hague: Martinus Nijhoff, 1977.

Sinclair, Ian. *The International Law Commission.* Cambridge: Grotius, 1987.

Trade/Development. Vols. 5 and 5(a), *Earth Space Environment.* Irvington-on Hudson, N.Y.: Transnational Publishers, 1994.

United Nations. *Making Better International Law: The International Law Commission at 50.* New York: United Nations, 1998.

CHAPTER 23. THE INVOKING FUNCTION

Anderson, Kym, and Richard Blackhurst, eds. *The Greening of World Trade Issues.* Ann Arbor: University of Michigan Press, 1992.

Carey, John. *UN Protection of Civil and Political Rights.* Syracuse: Syracuse University Press, 1970.

Gassama, Ibrahim J. "The United Nations, NGOs and Apartheid." *Fordham International Law Journal* 19 (1996): 1464.

Guest, Iain. *Behind the Disappearances: Argentina's Dirty War Against Human Rights and the United Nations.* Philadelphia: University of Pennsylvania, 1990.

Huffines, Jeffrey. "United States Ratification of Human Rights Treaties: The Rule of NGOs in United States Ratifications of Human Rights Treaties." *ILSA Journal of Comparative Law* 3 (1992): 641.

Robertson, A. H. *Human Rights in the World.* 2d ed. New York: St. Martin's Press, 1982.

Weston, Burns H. "Human Rights." *Human Rights Quarterly* 6 (1984): 257.

Williamson, Richard L., Jr. "Law and the H-Bomb: Strengthening the Non-Proliferation Regime to Impede Advanced Proliferation." *Cornell International Law Journal* 28 (1995): 71.

CHAPTER 24. THE APPLYING FUNCTION

Barkun, Michael. *Law Without Sanctions: Order in Primitive Societies and the World Community.* New Haven: Yale University Press, 1968.

Berns, Andrew, and Jane Connors. "Enforcing the Human Rights of Women: A Complaints Procedure for the Women's Convention? Draft Optional Protocol to the Convention on the Elimination of All Forms of Discrimination Against Women." *Brooklyn Journal of International Law* 21 (1996): 679.

Bilder, Richard B. "International Dispute Settlement and the Role of International Adjudication." *Emory Journal of International Dispute Resolution* 1 (1987): 131.

Fisher, Roger. *Improving Compliance with International Law.* Charlottesville: University Press of Virginia, 1981.

Nino, Carlos S. "The Duty to Punish Past Abuses of Human Rights Put in Context: The Case of Argentina." *Yale Law Journal* 100 (1991): 2619.

Oellers-Frahm, Karin, and Norbert Wuhler, comps. *Dispute Settlement in Public International Law: Texts and Materials.* Berlin: Springer Verlag, 1984.

Orenlichter, Diane F. "Settling Accounts: The Duty to Prosecute Human Rights Violations of a Prior Regime." *Yale Law Journal* 100 (1991): 2537.

Reisman, W. Michael. *Nullity and Revision: The Review and Enforcement of International Judgments and Awards.* New Haven: Yale University Press, 1971.

Schwebel, Stephen M., ed. *The Effectiveness of International Decisions.* Leiden: A. W. Sijthoff, 1971.

Sohn, Louis B. *Broadening the Role of the United Nations in Preventing, Mitigating or Ending International or Internal Conflicts That Threaten International Peace and Security.* Washington, D.C.: International Rule of Law Center, George Washington University Law School, 1997.

Zalaquett, Jose. "Balancing Ethical Imperatives and Political Constraints: The Dilemma of New Democracies Confronting Past Human Rights Violations." Hastings Law Journal 43 (1992): 1425.

Zoller, Elisabeth. *Peacetime Unilateral Remedies: An Analysis of Countermeasures.* Dobbs Ferry, N.Y.: Transnational, 1984.

CHAPTER 25. THE TERMINATING FUNCTION

Dallin, Alexander, and Gail W. Lapidus, eds. *The Soviet System: From Crisis to Collapse.* Boulder, Colo.: Westview, 1995.

David, Arie E. *The Strategy of Treaty Termination: Lawful Breaches and Retaliations.* New Haven: Yale University Press, 1975.

Mendelbaum, Michael. "Coup de Grace: The End of the Soviet Union." *Foreign Affairs* 71 (1991): 164.

Wachs, Jonathan. "Reviving the 1940 Cuban Constitution: Arguments for Social & Economic Rights in a Post-Castro Government." *American University Journal of International Law and Policy* 10 (1994): 525.

CHAPTER 26. THE APPRAISING FUNCTION

Cohen, Ronald, Goran Hayden, and Winston P. Nagan, eds. *Human Rights and Governance in Africa.* Gainesville: University Press of Florida, 1993.

Lasswell, Harold D. "Toward Continuing Appraisal of the Impact of Law on Society." *Rutgers Law Review* 21 (1967): 645.

Reisman, W. Michael. "The Constitutional Crisis in the United Nations." *American Journal of International Law* 87 (1993): 83.

Report of the Group of High-Level Intergovernmental Experts to Review the Effi-

ciency of the Administrative and Financial Functioning of the United Nations.
United Nations General Assembly, Official Records: Forty-first Session, Supplement no. 49 (A/41/49). 1986.
The United Nations in Its Second Half-Century: Report of an Independent Working Group on the Future of the United Nations. 1996.

CHAPTER 27. RESPONSIBILITY OF STATES

Amerasingh, C. F. *Local Remedies in International Law.* Cambridge: Grotius, 1990.

Arsanjani, Mahnoush H., and W. Michael Reisman. "The Quest for an International Liability Regime for the Protection of Global Commons." In *International Law: Theory and Practice. Essays in Honor of Eric Suy,* edited by Karel Wellens, 469–92. The Hague: Martinus Nijhoff, 1998.

Bales, Jennifer S. "Transnational Responsibility and Recourse for Ozone Depletion." *Boston College International and Comparative Law Review* 19 (1996): 259.

Brownlie, Ian. *System of the Law of Nations: State Responsibility, Part 1.* Oxford: Clarendon Press, 1983.

Haesler, Thomas. *The Exhaustion of Local Remedies: Rule in the Case Law of International Courts and Tribunals.* Leiden: A. W. Sijthoff, 1968.

Handl, G. "Liability as an Obligation Established by a Primary Rule of International Law." *Netherlands Yearbook of International Law* 16 (1985): 49.

———. "State Liability for Accidental Transnational Environmental Damage by Private Persons." *American Journal of International Law* 74 (1980): 525.

Kamminga, Menno T. *Inter-state Accountability for Violations of Human Rights.* Philadelphia: University of Pennsylvania Press, 1992.

Lillich, Richard B., ed. *The United Nations Compensation Commission.* Irvington, N.Y.: Transnational Publishers, 1995.

Lillich, Richard B., and David B. Magraw. *The Iran-United States Claim Tribunal: Its Contribution to the Law of State Responsibility.* Irvington, N.Y.: Transnational Publishers, 1996.

Rosenne, Shabtai. *The International Law Commission's Draft Articles on State Responsibility.* The Hague: Martinus Nijhoff, 1991.

Shelton, Dinah. "Private Violence, Public Wrongs, and the Responsibility of States." *Fordham International Law Journal* 13 (1990): 1.

Turley, Jonathan. " 'When in Rome': Multinational Misconduct and the Presumption Against Extraterritoriality." *Northwestern University Law Review* 84 (1990): 598.

CHAPTER 28. SUCCESSION OF STATES

Beato, Andrew M. "Newly Independent and Separating States' Succession Treaties: Considerations on the Hybrid Dependency of the Republics of the Former Soviet Union." *American University Journal of Law and Policy* 9 (1994): 525.

Chen, Lung-Fong. *State Succession Relating to Unequal Treaties.* Hamden, Conn.: Archon Books, 1974.

Kritz, Neil J., ed. *Transnational Justice: How Emerging Democracies Reckon with Former Regimes.* 3 vols. Washington, D.C.: United States Institute of Peace Press, 1995.

Mullerson, Rein. "New Developments in the Former USSR and Yugoslavia." *Virginia Journal of International Law* 33 (1993): 299.

O'Connell, D. P. *State Succession in Municipal Law and International Law.* 2 vols. Cambridge: Cambridge University Press, 1967.

Tomuschat, Christian, ed. *Modern Law of Self-Determination.* Dordrecht: Martinus Nijhoff Publishers, 1993.

CHAPTER 29. TOWARD A WORLD COMMUNITY OF HUMAN DIGNITY

Bull, Hedley, Benedict Kingsbury, and Adam Roberts, eds. *Hugo Grotius and International Relations.* Oxford: Clarendon Press, 1992.

Clark, Grenville, and Louis Bruno Sohn. *World Peace Through World Law.* 3d ed. Cambridge: Harvard University Press, 1966.

Damrosch, Lori Fisler, Gennady Danilenko, and Rein Mullerson, eds. *Beyond Confrontation: International Law for the Post Cold-War Era.* Boulder, Colo.: Westview Press, 1995.

Donnelly, Jack. *Human Rights in the 1990's: Promise or Peril? International Human Rights.* Boulder, Colo.: Westview Press, 1993.

Falk, Richard. *The End of World Order.* New York: Holmes and Meier, 1983.

——. *Law in an Emerging Global Village: A Post-Westphalian Perspective.* Ardsley, N.Y.: Transnational Publishers, 1998.

——. *Study of Future Worlds.* New York: Free Press, 1980.

Ferencz, Benjamin B. *PlanetHood: The Key to Your Survival and Prosperity.* Coos Bay, Ore.: Vision Books, 1985.

Galtung, Johan. *The True Worlds: A Transnational Perspective.* New York: Free Press, 1981.

Gong, Gerrit W. *The Standard of "Civilization" in International Society.* Oxford: Clarendon Press, 1984.

Grossman, Claudio, and Daniel B. Bradlow. "Are We Being Propelled Toward a People-Centered Transnational Legal Order?" *American University Journal of International Law and Policy* 9 (1993): 1.

Lachs, Manfred. *The Teacher in International Law.* The Hague: Martinus Nijhoff, 1982.

Lasswell, Harold D., and Myres S. McDougal. *Jurisprudence for a Free Society: Studies in Law, Science, and Policy.* 2 vols. New Haven: New Haven Press; Dordrecht: Martinus Nijhoff, 1992.

McDougal, Myres S. "International Law and the Future." *Mississippi Law Journal* 50 (1979): 259.

Nussbaum, Arthur. *A Concise History of the Law of Nations.* New York: Macmillan, 1954.

Seita, Alex Y. "Globalization and the Convergence of Values." *Cornell International Law Journal* 30 (1997): 429.

Stone, Julius. *Visions of World Order: Between State Power and Human Justice.* Baltimore: Johns Hopkins University Press, 1984.

Table of Treaties

The available information concerning the state parties to a particular treaty derives mainly from United Nations, *Multilateral Treaties Deposited with the Secretary-General: Status as of 30 December 1999,* U.N. Doc. ST/LEG/SER. E/6, http://untreaty.un.org/English/sample/EnglishInternetBible/bible.asp and U.S. Department of State, *Treaties in Force: A List of Treaties and Other International Agreements of the United States in Force on January 1, 1999,* Dep't of State Pub. 9434.

The texts of most of these treaties are conveniently reprinted, in part or in full, in B. Carter and P. Trimble, *International Law: Selected Documents, 1999–2000 ed.* (New York: Aspen Law and Business, 1999); L. Henkin, *et al., Basic Documents Supplement to International Law, Cases and Materials,* 3d ed. (St. Paul, Minn.: West, 1993); C. Oliver, *et al., Documentary Supplement to Cases and Materials on The International Legal System,* 4th ed. (Westbury, N.Y.: Foundation, 1995); and B. Weston, R. Falk, and A. D'Amato, *Basic Documents in International Law and World Order,* 2d ed. (St. Paul, Minn.: West, 1990). Pages on which these treaties are mentioned are given in italics.

1899

Convention for the Pacific Settlement of International Disputes, *signed* at The Hague, July 29, 1899, 32 Stat. 1779, T.S. No. 392, 1 Bevans 230 (*entered into force* Sept. 4, 1900). As of Jan. 1, 1999, 88 states were parties to this convention. *P. 360*

1907

Convention Respecting the Laws and Customs of War on Land, The Hague, Oct. 18, 1907, 36 Stat. 2277, T.S. No. 539, 1 Bevans 631. As of Jan. 1, 1999, 43 states were party to this convention. *Pp. 318, 413*

1919

Convention on the Regulation of Aerial Navigation, Paris, 11 L.N.T.S. 174. *P. 150*

1921

Convention on the Regime of Navigable Waterways of International Concern, *adopted* Barcelona Apr. 20, 1921, 7 L.N.T.S. 35 (*entered into force* Oct. 31, 1922). As of Dec. 30, 1999, 43 states were parties to this convention. *P. 148*

1923

Convention and Statute on the International Regime of Maritime Ports, *done* Dec. 9, 1923, 58 L.N.T.S. 285 (*entered into force* July 26, 1926). As of Dec. 30, 1999, 53 states were parties to this convention. *P. 133*

1925

Protocol for the Prohibition of the Use in War of Asphyxiating, Poisonous, or Other Gases, and of Bacteriological Methods of Warfare, June 17, 1925, 26 U.S.T. 571, T.I.A.S. No. 8061, 94 L.N.T.S. 65 (*entered into force* Feb. 8, 1928). As of Jan. 1, 1999, 145 states were parties to this treaty. *P. 318*

1928

General Treaty for the Renunciation of War as an Instrument of National Policy, *adopted* at Paris Aug. 27, 1928, 46 Stat. 2343, 94 L.N.T.S. 57. As of Jan. 1, 1999, 70 states were parties to this treaty. [Kellogg-Briand Pact; Pact of Paris] *Pp. 86, 252, 305*

1930

Convention on Certain Questions Relating to the Conflict of Nationality Laws, *done* Apr. 12, 1930, 179 L.N.T.S. 89 (*entered into force* July 1, 1937). As of Dec. 30, 1999, 21 states were parties to this convention. *Pp. 167, 177, 178*

Protocol Relating to Military Obligations in Certain Cases of Double Nationality, *done* Apr. 12, 1930, 178 L.N.T.S. 227 (*entered into force* May 25, 1937). As of Dec. 30, 1999, 25 states were parties to this protocol. *P. 181*

Protocol Relating to a Certain Case of Statelessness, *done* Apr. 12, 1930, 179 L.N.T.S. 115 (*entered into force* July 1, 1937). As of Dec. 30, 1999, 21 states were parties to this protocol. *P. 177*

1933

Convention on Rights and Duties of States, *done* at Montevideo, Dec. 26, 1933, 49 Stat. 3097, T.S. No. 881, 3 Bevans 145, 165 L.N.T.S. 19 (*entered into force* Dec. 26, 1934). As of Jan. 1, 1999, 16 states were parties to this convention. *P. 25*

   Convention Relating to the International Status of Refugees, *signed* Oct. 28, 1933, 159 L.N.T.S. 199. *P. 185*

1936

Convention Concerning the Use of Broadcasting in the Cause of Peace, *done* Sept. 23, 1936, 186 L.N.T.S. 301, 197 L.N.T.S. 394, 200 L.N.T.S. 557 (*entered into force* Apr. 2, 1938). As of Dec. 30, 1999, 30 states were parties to this convention. *P. 279*

1944

Convention on International Civil Aviation, *done* at Chicago Dec. 7, 1944; 61 Stat. 1180, T.I.A.S. No. 1951, 3 Bevans 944, 15 U.N.T.S. 295 (*entered into force* Apr. 4, 1947). As of Jan. 1, 1999, 88 states were parties to this convention. *P. 150*

   International Air Services Transit Agreement, *signed* at Chicago Dec. 7, 1944, 59 Stat. 1693, 3 Bevans 916, 84 U.N.T.S. 389 (*entered into force* Jan. 30, 1945). As of Jan. 1, 1999, 118 states were parties to this agreement. *Pp. 150, 228*

   International Air Transport Agreement, *opened for signature* at Chicago Dec. 7, 1944, 59 Stat. 1701. (The United States accepted it on Feb. 8, 1945, and withdrew in 1947 due to lack of international interest.) *Pp. 150, 228*

1945

Agreement for the Prosecution and Punishment of the Major War Criminals of the European Axis (the London Charter), *signed* at London, Aug. 8, 1945, 59 Stat. 1544, 3 Bevans 1238, 82 U.N.T.S. 279 (*entered into force* Aug. 8, 1945). As of Jan. 1, 1999, 24 states were parties to this agreement. [The London Charter; the Charter of the International Military Tribunal at Nuremberg] *Pp. 78, 232*

   Charter of the United Nations, *signed* June 26, 1945, 59 Stat. 1031, T.S. 993 (*entered into force* Oct. 24, 1945). As of Dec. 30, 1999, there were 188 member states of the United Nations. *Pp. 32, 51, 53–55, 56, 59, 62, 68, 79, 85–88, 91, 100–101, 107, 111, 121, 122, 123, 175, 197, 200, 201–2, 206, 208–9, 210, 212, 218–19, 220–21, 263–64, 267, 272, 289–91, 293, 305–6, 308–12, 315, 317, 320, 321, 334, 361–64, 368–70, 377–78*

   Statute of the International Court of Justice, 59 Stat. 1055, T.S. 993 (*entered into force* Oct. 24, 1945). As of Dec. 30, 1999, 190 states were parties to the statute. *Pp. 100, 105, 340–42, 344–45, 361, 379*

1946

Convention on the Privileges and Immunities of the United Nations, *adopted* Feb. 13, 1946, G.A. Res. 22A(I), U.N. Doc. A/64 at 25 (1946), 1 U.N.T.S. 15, 90 U.N.T.S. 327 (*entered into force* for each state upon date of its deposit of instrument of accession). As of Dec. 30, 1999, 141 states were parties to this convention. *P. 55*

1947

Treaty of Peace with Italy, *signed* at Paris, Feb. 10, 1947, 61 Stat. 1245, T.I.A.S. No. 1648, 4 Bevans 311, 49 and 50 U.N.T.S. (*entered into force* Sept. 15, 1947.) As of Jan. 1, 1999, 24 states were parties to this treaty. *P. 193*

Treaty of Peace with Romania, *signed* at Paris, Feb. 10, 1947, 61 Stat. 1757, T.I.A.S. No. 1649, 4 Bevans 403, 42 U.N.T.S. 3 (*entered into force* Sept. 15, 1947). As of Jan. 1, 1999, 11 states were parties to this treaty. *P. 109*

General Agreement on Tariffs and Trade, attached to the Final Act of the United Nations Conference on Trade and Employment, *signed* at Geneva Oct. 30, 1947, TIAS No. 1700 (*in force* among the contracting parties by virtue of the protocol of provisional application and the subsequent protocols of accession). As of Jan. 1, 1999, there were 126 contracting parties to the general agreement. [GATT] *P. 290*

1948

Charter of the Organization of American States, *signed* at Bogota Apr. 30, 1948, 2 U.S.T. 2394, T.I.A.S. No. 2361, 119 U.N.T.S. 3 (*entered into force* Dec. 13, 1951). As of Jan. 1, 1999, 35 states were parties to this treaty. *Pp. 204, 309*

Convention on the Prevention and Punishment of the Crime of Genocide, *adopted* Dec. 9, 1948, G.A. Res. 260(III), U.N. Doc. A/810, at 174 (1948), 78 U.N.T.S. 277 (*entered into force* Jan. 12, 1951). As of Dec. 30, 1999, 130 states were parties to this convention. *Pp. 108, 232*

Universal Declaration of Human Rights, *adopted* Dec. 1948, G.A. Res. 217, U.N. Doc. A/810 at 71 (1948). (Technically, this is a resolution adopted by the General Assembly of the United Nations and is not deemed a treaty in the strict sense of the word. However, the Universal Declaration has evolved into a key component of the International Bill of Human Rights, is widely regarded as part of customary international law, and is given repeated references throughout this work.) *Pp. 33, 42, 67, 78, 87, 171–72, 175, 177–78, 182, 185, 199, 200, 202, 206, 213, 216, 277, 281, 283, 284, 349, 366*

1949

Geneva Conventions
Convention for the Amelioration of the Condition of the Wounded and Sick in the Armed Forces in the Field, *dated* at Geneva Aug. 12, 1949, 6 U.S.T. 3114, T.I.A.S.

No. 3362, 75 U.N.T.S. 31 (*entered into force* Oct. 21, 1950). As of Jan. 1, 1999, 166 states were parties to this convention. *Pp. 318–19*

Convention for the Amelioration of the Wounded, Sick, and Shipwrecked Members of Armed Fores at Sea, *dated* at Geneva Aug. 12, 1949, 6 U.S.T. 3217, T.I.A.S. No. 3363, 75 U.N.T.S. 85 (*entered into force* Oct. 21, 1950). As of Jan. 1, 1999, 184 states were parties to this convention. *Pp. 318–19*

Convention Relative to the Treatment of Prisoners of War, *dated* at Geneva Aug. 12, 1949, 6 U.S.T. 3316, T.I.A.S. No. 3364, 75 U.N.T.S. 135 (*entered into force* Oct. 21, 1950). As of Jan. 1, 1999, 184 states were parties to this convention. *Pp. 318–19*

Convention Relative to the Protection of Civilian Persons in Time of War, *dated* at Geneva Aug. 12, 1949, 6 U.S.T. 3516, T.I.A.S. No. 3365, 75 U.N.T.S. 287 (*entered into force* Oct. 21, 1950). As of Jan. 1, 1999, 184 states were parties to this convention. *Pp. 318–19*

1950

European Convention for the Protection of Human Rights and Fundamental Freedoms (European Convention on Human Rights), *adopted* at Rome Nov. 4, 1950, 213 U.N.T.S. 221, European T.S. No. 5 (*entered into force* Sept. 3, 1953). As of Dec. 30, 1999, 21 states were parties to this convention. [European Convention on Human Rights] *Pp. 101, 103, 111, 205, 208, 213, 285, 354, 375*

1951

Convention Relating to the Status of Refugees, *adopted* July 28, 1951, G.A. Res. 429, 5 U.N. GAOR Supp. (No. 20) at 48, U.N. Doc. A/1775 (1950), 189 U.N.T.S. 137 (*entered into force* Apr. 22, 1954). As of Dec. 30, 1999, 134 states were parties to this convention. *Pp. 70, 108, 178–79, 184–85, 375*

1952

Convention on the International Right of Correction, *adopted* Dec. 16, 1952, G.A. Res. 630, U.N. GOAR Supp. (No. 20) at 22, U.N. Doc. A/2361, *opened for signature* Mar. 31, 1953, 435 U.N.T.S. 191 (*entered into force* Aug. 24, 1962). As of Dec. 30, 1999, 14 states were parties to this convention. *P. 285*

1953

Convention on the Political Rights of Women, *opened for signature* Mar. 31, 1953, G.A. Res. 640, 7 U.N. GAOR Supp. (No. 20) at 27, U.N. Doc. A/2361(1953), 193 U.N.T.S. 135 (*entered into force* July 7, 1954). As of Dec. 30, 1999, 114 states were parties to this convention. *P. 108*

1954

Convention Relating to the Status of Stateless Persons, *done* Sept. 28, 1954, G.A. Res. 526A, 17 ESCOR Supp. (No. 1) at 12, ESC Doc. E/2596 (1954), 360 U.N.T.S. 117 (*entered into force* June 6, 1969). As of Dec. 30, 1999, 49 states had ratified this convention. *Pp. 178–79*

1956

Supplementary Convention on the Abolition of Slavery, the Slave Trade, and Institutions and Practices Similar to Slavery, *adopted* Sept. 7, 1956, 266 U.N.T.S. 3 (*entered into force* Apr. 30, 1957). As of Dec. 30, 1999, 118 states were parties to this treaty. *P. 108*

1957

Convention on the Nationality of Married Women, *opened for signature and ratification* Jan. 29, 1957, G.A. Res. 1040, 11 U.N. GAOR Supp. (No. 17) at 18, U.N. Doc. A/3572 (1957), 309 U.N.T.S. 65 (*entered into force* Aug. 11, 1958). As of Dec. 30, 1999, 69 states were parties to this convention. *Pp. 169, 178*

1958

Convention on Fishing and Conservation of the Living Resources of the High Seas, *done* Apr. 29, 1958, G.A. Res. 1105, 11 U.N. GAOR Supp. (No. 17) at 54, U.N. Doc. A/3572 (1958), 559 U.N.T.S. 285 (*entered into force* Mar. 20, 1966). As of Dec. 30, 1999, 36 states were parties to this convention. *Pp. 110, 131, 137*

Convention on the Continental Shelf, *done* Apr. 29, 1958, G.A. Res. 1105, 11 U.N. GAOR Supp. (No. 17) at 54, U.N. Doc. A/3572 (1957), 499 U.N.T.S. 311 (*entered into force* June 10, 1964). As of Dec. 30, 1999, 37 states were parties to this convention. *Pp. 110, 131, 138*

Convention on the High Seas, *done* Apr. 29, 1958, G.A. Res. 1105, 11 U.N. GAOR Supp. (No. 17) at 54, U.N. Doc. A/3572 (1957), 450 U.N.T.S. 11 (*entered into force* Sept. 30, 1962). As of Dec. 30, 1999, 62 states were parties to this convention. *Pp. 110, 131, 140, 231*

Convention on the Territorial Sea and Contiguous Zone, *done* Apr. 29, 1958, G.A. Res. 1105, 11 U.N. GAOR Supp. (No. 17) at 54, U.N. Doc. A/3572 (1957), 516 U.N.T.S. 205 (*entered into force* Sept. 10, 1964). As of Dec. 30, 1999, 51 states were parties to this convention. *Pp. 110, 131, 134, 158*

Optional Protocol of Signature Concerning the Compulsory Settlement of Disputes, *adopted* and *opened for signature* Apr. 29, 1958, 450 U.N.T.S. 169 (*entered into force* Sept. 30, 1962). As of Dec. 30, 1999, 45 states had ratified this treaty. *P. 110*

1959

Antarctic Treaty, *signed* at Washington Dec. 1, 1959, 12 U.S.T. 794, T.I.A.S. No. 4780, 402 U.N.T.S. 71 (*entered into force* June 23, 1961). As of Jan. 1, 1999, 44 states were parties to this treaty — 27 were consultative parties and 17 were nonconsultative parties. *Pp. 88, 158–60*

1961

Vienna Convention on Diplomatic Relations, *done* Apr. 18, 1961, 23 U.S.T. 3227, T.I.A.S. No. 7502, 500 U.N.T.S. 95 (*entered into force* Apr. 24, 1964). As of Dec. 30, 1999, 179 states were parties to this treaty. *Pp. 111, 246–49, 250–52*

Optional Protocol to the Vienna Convention on Diplomatic Relations Concerning the Compulsory Settlement of Disputes, *done* Apr. 18, 1961, 500 U.N.T.S. 241 (*entered into force* Apr. 24, 1964). As of Dec. 30, 1999, 62 states were parties to this treaty. *P. 111*

Convention on the Reduction of Statelessness, *concluded* Aug. 30, 1961, G.A. Res. 896, 9 U.N. GAOR Supp. (No. 21) at 49, U.N. Doc. A/2890 (1954), 989 U.N.T.S. 175 (*entered into force* Dec. 13, 1975). As of Dec. 30, 1999, 21 states were parties to this treaty. *Pp. 108, 177–79*

1962

Convention on the Liability of Operators of Nuclear Ships, *signed* at Brussels May 25, 1962, *reprinted in* 57 Am. J. Int'l L. 268 (1963). *P. 390*

Protocol Instituting a Conciliation and Good Offices Commission to be responsible for seeking a settlement of any disputes which may arise between States Parties to the Convention against Discrimination in Education, *adopted* Dec. 10, 1962, *reprinted in* United Nations, Human Rights — A Compilation of International Instruments 95–103, U.N. Doc. ST/HR/1/Rev.3 (1988) (*entered into force* Oct. 24, 1968). *P. 354*

1963

Vienna Convention on Consular Relations, *done* Apr. 24, 1963, 21 U.S.T. 77, T.I.A.S. No. 6820, 596 U.N.T.S. 261 (*entered into force* Mar. 19, 1967). As of Dec. 30, 1999, 163 states were parties to this treaty. *Pp. 111, 246–47, 249*

Optional Protocol to the Convention on Consular Relations Concerning the Compulsory Settlement of Disputes, *done* at Vienna Apr. 24, 1963, 21 U.S.T. 325, T.I.A.S. No. 6820, 596 U.N.T.S. 487 (*entered into force* Mar. 19, 1967). As of Jan. 1, 1999, 53 states were parties to this treaty. *P. 111*

European Convention on Reduction of Cases of Multiple Nationality and Military Obligations in Cases of Multiple Nationality, European, T.S. No. 43 (1963). *P. 181*

Convention on Offenses and Certain Other Acts Committed on Board Aircraft, *done* at Tokyo Sept. 14, 1963, 20 U.S.T. 2941, T.I.A.S. No. 6768, 704 U.N.T.S. 219 (*entered into force* Dec. 4, 1969). As of Jan. 1, 1999, 168 states were parties to this convention. *P. 228*

Treaty Banning Nuclear Weapon Tests in the Atmosphere, in Outer Space, and under Water, 14 U.S.T. 1313, T.I.A.S. No. 5433, 480 U.N.T.S. 43 (*entered into force* Oct. 10, 1963). As of Jan. 1, 1999, 125 states were parties to this treaty. *P. 319*

1965

International Convention on the Elimination of All Forms of Racial Discrimination, *adopted* Dec. 21, 1965, G.A. Res. 2106, 20 U.N. GAOR Supp. (No. 14) at 47, U.N. Doc. A/6014 (1965), *opened for signature* Mar. 7, 1966, 660 U.N.T.S. 195 (*entered into force* Jan. 4, 1969). As of Dec. 30, 1999, 155 states were parties to this treaty. *Pp. 101, 103, 111, 205, 208, 280–81, 328, 353, 375*

1966

International Covenant on Civil and Political Rights, *adopted* Dec. 16, 1966, G.A. Res. 2200A, 21 U.N. GAOR Supp. (No. 16) at 53, U.N. Doc. A/6316 (1966), *opened for signature* Dec. 19, 1966, 999 U.N.T.S. 171 (*entered into force* Mar. 23, 1976). As of Dec. 30, 1999, 144 states were parties to this covenant. *Pp. 32, 57, 79, 103, 177, 185, 189–90, 201, 208, 210, 280, 284, 316, 353–54, 369, 375*

Optional Protocol to the International Covenant on Civil and Political Rights, *adopted* Dec. 16, 1966, G.A. Res. 2200A, 21 U.N. GAOR Supp. (No. 16) at 49, U.N. Doc. A/6316 (1966), *opened for signature* Dec. 19, 1966, 999 U.N.T.S. 171 (*entered into force* Mar. 23, 1976). As of Dec. 30, 1999, 95 states were parties to this treaty. *Pp. 79, 87, 101, 103, 200–201, 205, 208, 210, 336, 354, 369*

International Covenant on Economic, Social, and Cultural Rights, *adopted* Dec. 16, 1966, G.A. Res. 2200A, 21 U.N. GAOR Supp. (No. 16) at 49, U.N. Doc. A/6316 (1966), *opened for signature* Dec. 19, 1966, 993 U.N.T.S. 3 (*entered into force* Jan. 3, 1976). As of Dec. 30, 1999, 142 states were parties to this covenant. *Pp. 32, 79, 87, 175, 200, 210, 316, 369, 375*

1967

Protocol Relating to the Status of Refugees, *done* Jan. 31, 1967, G.A. Res. 2198, 21 U.N. GAOR Supp. (No. 16) at 48, U.N. Doc. A/6316 (1966), 606 U.N.T.S. 267 (*entered into force* Oct. 4, 1967). As of Dec. 30, 1999, 134 states were parties to this treaty. *Pp. 71, 185*

Treaty on Principles Governing the Activities of States in the Exploration and Use of Outer Space, Including the Moon and Other Celestial Bodies, *done* at Washington, London, and Moscow Jan. 27, 1967, 18 U.S.T. 2410, T.I.A.S. No. 6347, 610 U.N.T.S.

205 (*entered into force* Oct. 10, 1967). As of Jan. 1, 1999, 101 states were parties to this treaty. [Outer Space Treaty] *Pp. 88, 121, 153–54, 229, 330*

1968

Treaty on the Non-Proliferation of Nuclear Weapons, *done* at Washington, London, and Moscow July 1, 1968; 21 U.S.T. 483, T.I.A.S. No. 6839, 729 U.N.T.S. 161 (*entered into force* Mar. 5, 1970). As of Jan. 1, 1999, 189 states were parties to this treaty. *P. 88*

Agreement on the Rescue of Astronauts, the Return of Astronauts, and the Return of Objects Launched into Outer Space, *done* Apr. 22, 1968, 19 U.S.T. 7570, T.I.A.S. No. 6599, 672 U.N.T.S. 119 (*entered into force* Dec. 3, 1968). As of Jan. 1, 1999, 92 states were parties to this treaty. *P. 153*

1969

Vienna Convention on the Law of Treaties, *adopted* May 22, 1969, *opened for signature* May 23, 1969, U.N. Doc. A/CONF. 39/29 (1969) (*entered into force* Jan. 27, 1980). As of Dec. 30, 1999, 90 states were parties to this treaty. *Pp. 111, 207, 209, 259–75, 369–70*

American Convention on Human Rights, *signed* Nov. 22, 1969, O.A.S.T.S. No. 36 at 1, O.A.S. Off. Rec. OEA/Ser. L/V/II.23 doc. rev. 2 (*entered into force* July 18, 1978). As of Mar. 1, 1988, 20 states were parties to this convention. *Pp. 112, 172, 177, 204, 213, 285, 354, 375*

OAU Convention Governing the Specific Aspects of Refugee Problems in Africa, *concluded at* Addis Ababa Sept. 10, 1969, 1001 U.N.T.S. 45 (*entered into force* June 20, 1974), *reprinted in* U.N.H.C.R., Collection of International Instruments Concerning Refugees 193–200 (2d ed. 1979). *P. 186*

1970

Convention for the Suppression of Unlawful Seizure of Aircraft, *done* at The Hague Dec. 16, 1970, *opened for additional signatures* Jan. 1, 1971, 22 U.S.T. 1641, T.I.A.S. No. 7192 (*entered into force* Oct. 14, 1971). As of Jan. 1, 1999, 167 states were parties to this convention. *P. 189*

1971

Convention for the Suppression of Unlawful Acts against the Safety of Civil Aviation, *done* at Montreal Sept. 23, 1971, 24 U.S.T. 564, T.I.A.S. No. 7570 (*entered into force* Jan. 26, 1973). As of Jan. 1, 1999, 166 states were parties to this convention. *P. 189*

1972

Convention on the International Liability for Damage Caused by Space Objects, *done* at Washington, London, and Moscow Mar. 29, 1972, 24 U.S.T. 2389, T.I.A.S. No. 7762 (*entered into force* Sept. 1, 1972). As of Jan. 1, 1999, 87 states were parties to this convention. *Pp. 153, 390*

Convention on the Prohibition of the Development, Production, and Stockpiling of Bacteriological (Biological) and Toxic Weapons and on Their Destruction, Apr. 10, 1972, 26 U.S.T. 585, T.I.A.S. No. 8062. As of Jan. 1, 1999, 141 states were parties to this convention. *P. 318*

European Convention on State Immunity, *done* at Basel May 16, 1972, *reprinted in* 11 Int'l Legal Materials 470 (1972) (*entered into force* June 11, 1976). *P. 236*

Treaty on the Limitation of Anti-Ballistic Missile Systems, *signed* at Moscow May 26, 1972, 23 UST 3435, TIAS No. 7503 (*entered into force* Oct. 3, 1972). [ABM Treaty] *P. 274*

1973

International Convention on the Punishment of the Crime of *Apartheid, adopted* Nov. 30, 1973, 1015 U.N.T.S. 244 (*entered into force* July 18, 1976). As of Dec. 30, 1999, 101 states were parties to this treaty. *P. 233*

Convention on the Prevention and Punishment of Crimes against Internationally Protected Persons, Including Diplomatic Agents, *adopted* Dec. 14, 1973, 1035 U.N.T.S. 167 (*entered into force* Feb. 20, 1977). As of Dec. 30, 1999, 71 states were parties to this treaty. *P. 189*

1974

Convention on Registration of Objects Launched into Outer Space, *adopted* Nov. 12, 1974, G.A. Res. 3235, 29 U.N. GAOR Supp. (No. 31) at 16, U.N. Doc. A/9631 (1973), and *opened for signature* Jan. 14, 1975, 1023 U.N.T.S. 15, 28 U.S.T. 695, T.I.A.S. No. 8480 (*entered into force* Sept. 15, 1976). As of Jan. 1, 1999, 50 states and the European Space Agency were parties to this convention. *Pp. 153, 229*

1975

Final Act of the Conference on Security and Co-operation in Europe, *adopted* Aug. 1, 1975, 73 State Dept. Bull. 323 (Sept. 1975), *reprinted in* 14 Int'l Legal Materials 1292 (1975). The Act was signed by 35 Heads of State or Government. *Pp. 49, 349–50*

1977

Protocol Additional to the Geneva Conventions of 12 August 1949, and Relating to the Protection of Victims of International Armed Conflicts (Protocol I), *adopted*

June 8, 1977, *reprinted in* 16 Int'l Legal Materials 1391 (1977) (*entered into force* Dec. 7, 1978). *Pp. 72, 318–19*

Protocol Additional to the Geneva Conventions of 12 August 1949, and Relating to the Protection of Victims of Non-International Armed Conflicts (Protocol II), *adopted* June 8, 1977, *reprinted in* 16 Int'l Legal Materials 1442 (1977) (*entered into force* Dec. 7, 1978), *Pp. 72, 318–19*

1978

Vienna Convention on Succession of States in Respect of Treaties, *concluded* Aug. 23, 1978, U.N. Doc. A/CONF. 80/31, (*not yet in force* as of Dec. 31, 1987). As of Dec. 30, 1999, 17 states had ratified or acceded to this treaty. *Pp. 398, 403*

1979

Agreement Governing the Activities of States on the Moon and Other Celestial Bodies, *adopted* Dec. 5, 1979, G.A. Res. 34/68, 34 U.N. GAOR Supp. (No. 46) at 77, U.N. Doc. A/34/46 (1979) (*entered into force* July 11, 1984). As of Dec. 30, 1999, 9 states were parties to this agreement. [Moon Treaty] *Pp. 88, 153–54*

Convention on the Elimination of All Forms of Discrimination against Women, *adopted* Dec. 18, 1979, U.N. Doc. A/RES/34/180 (*entered into force* Sept. 3, 1981). As of Dec. 30, 1999, 165 states were parties to this convention. *Pp. 336, 375*

International Convention against the Taking of Hostages, *adopted* Dec. 17, 1979, G.A. Res. 34/146, 34 U.N. GAOR Supp. (No. 46) at 245, U.N. Doc. A/34/46 (1979), *opened for signature* Dec. 18, 1979 (*entered into force* June 3, 1983). As of Dec. 30, 1999, 85 states were parties to this treaty. *P. 189*

1981

Treaty Establishing the Organization of Eastern Caribbean States, *done* June 18, 1981, *reprinted in* 20 Int'l Legal Materials 1166 (1981). *P. 264*

African Charter on Human and People's Rights, *adopted* June 1981 in Nairobi, OAU Doc. CAB/LEG/67/3/Rev.5 (1981), *reprinted in* 21 Int'l Legal Materials 59 (1982) (*entered into force* Oct. 21, 1986). As of Apr. 16, 1987, 33 states were parties to the charter. [Banjul Charter on Human and People's Rights] *P. 204*

1982

United Nations Convention on the Law of the Sea, *concluded* at Montego Bay Dec. 10, 1982, U.N. Doc. A/CONF. 62/122 and Corr. 1 to 11 (1982) (*not yet in force* as of Dec. 31, 1987); *reproduced in* United Nations, The Law of the Sea, U.N. Pub. Sales No. E. 83, V.5 (1983). As of Dec. 30, 1999, 132 states were parties to this convention. *Pp. 29, 88, 112–13, 132–45, 162–63, 351, 371–72*

1983

Vienna Convention on Succession of States in Respect of State Property, Archives, and Debts, *adopted* Apr. 7, 1983, U.N. Doc. A/CONF.117/14 (*not yet in force*), *reprinted in* 22 Int'l Legal Materials 306 (1983). As of Dec. 30, 1999, 5 states were parties to this convention.

1984

Convention against Torture and Other Cruel, Inhuman or Degrading Treatment or Punishment, *adopted* Dec. 10, 1984, U.N. Doc. A/RES/39/46 (*entered into force* June 26, 1987). As of Dec. 30, 1999, 118 states were parties to this convention. *P. 336*

1987

Treaty between the United States of America and the Union of Soviet Socialist Republics on the Elimination of Their Intermediate-Range and Shorter-Range Missiles, *signed* Dec. 8, 1987, Dep't State Bull., Feb. 1988, at 22–30 (*entered into force* June 1, 1988). [INF Treaty] *Pp. 92, 320*

1988

Bilateral Agreement between the Republic of Afghanistan and the Islamic Republic of Pakistan on the Principles of Mutual Relations, in particular on Non-Interference and Non-Intervention, *done* at Geneva, Apr. 14, 1988, *reprinted in* Dep't State Bull., June 1988, at 56–60 (*entered into force* May 15, 1988). [Afghanistan Agreement] *P. 61*

1989

Convention on the Rights of the Child, *adopted* Nov. 20, 1989, U.N. Doc. A/RES/ 44/25 (1989) (*entered into force* Sept. 2, 1990), *reprinted in* 28 Int'l Legal Materials 1448 (1989). As of Dec. 30, 1999, 191 states were parties to this convention. *Pp. 71, 206*

1991

Protocol on Environmental Protection to the Antarctic Treaty, *adopted* Oct. 4, 1991, *reprinted in* 30 Int'l Legal Materials 1455 (1991). As of Dec. 30, 1999, 37 states were parties to the Protocol. *P. 159*

1992

United Nations Framework Convention on Climate Change, *adopted* May 9, 1992, U.N. Doc. A/AC. 237/18 (*entered into force* Mar. 21, 1994). As of Dec. 30, 1999, 181 states were parties to this convention. *P. 162*

1994

Agreement Relating to the Implementation of Part XI of the United Nations Convention on the Law of the Sea of 10 December 1982, *adopted* July 28, 1994, U.N. Doc. A/RES/48/263 (1994) (*entered into force* July 28, 1996). As of Nov. 30, 1998, 93 states were parties to the Agreement. *Pp. 142–45*

1997

Convention on the Law of the Non-navigational Uses of International Watercourses, *adopted* May 21, 1997, U.N. Doc. A /RES/51/229 (1997), *opened for signature* until May 21, 2000. *P. 149*

1998

Rome Statute of the International Criminal Court, *adopted* July 17, 1998, U.N. Doc. A/CONF. 183/9, *opened for signature* until Dec. 31, 2000. *Pp. 231–33, 307*

Index

Lung-chu Chen is a professor of law at New York Law School and a research affiliate in Law at Yale Law School. He received his LL.B. with the first place honor from Taiwan University, his LL.M. from Northwestern University, and his J.S.D. from Yale University. He is chairman of the Lung-chu Chen New Century Foundation, which is dedicated to the advancement of human dignity values for Taiwan as well as for the world community. He serves on the Board of Editors of *American Journal of Comparative Law,* and is a board member of the Policy Sciences Center and of the Resource Center of the United Nations. He is a Governing Council member and a former vice president of International League for Human Rights. Formerly he was chairman of the Section on International Law of the Association of American Law Schools, a member of the Executive Council of the American Society of International Law, and president of the North American Taiwanese Professors' Association. His publications include *An Introduction to Contemporary International Law, Human Rights and World Public Order* (co-author), and *Formosa, China, and the United Nations* (co-author). In addition, he has written or edited a number of books in Chinese.